Indian Treaties in the
United States

Indian Treaties in the United States

AN ENCYCLOPEDIA AND DOCUMENTS COLLECTION

Donald L. Fixico, Editor

BLOOMSBURY ACADEMIC
NEW YORK • LONDON • OXFORD • NEW DELHI • SYDNEY

BLOOMSBURY ACADEMIC
Bloomsbury Publishing Inc
1385 Broadway, New York, NY 10018, USA
50 Bedford Square, London, WC1B 3DP, UK
29 Earlsfort Terrace, Dublin 2, Ireland

BLOOMSBURY, BLOOMSBURY ACADEMIC and the Diana logo
are trademarks of Bloomsbury Publishing Plc

First published in the United States of America by ABC-CLIO 2018
Paperback edition published by Bloomsbury Academic 2024

Copyright © Bloomsbury Publishing Inc, 2024

For legal purposes the Acknowledgments on p. xiii constitute
an extension of this copyright page.

Cover design by Silverander Communications
Cover photos: Sitting Bull holding peace pipe. Originally photographed and published by Palmquist and Jurgens, St. Paul, Minnesota. (LC-USZC4-7960/Library of Congress Prints a Photographs Division); Leather texture. (THEPALMER/iStockphoto); Die for the Thomas Jefferson version of the Indian Peace Medal by John Reich, 1801. (Wehwalt/Wikipedia)

All rights reserved. No part of this publication may be reproduced or
transmitted in any form or by any means, electronic or mechanical,
including photocopying, recording, or any information storage or retrieval
system, without prior permission in writing from the publishers.

Bloomsbury Publishing Inc does not have any control over, or responsibility for,
any third-party websites referred to or in this book. All internet addresses given
in this book were correct at the time of going to press. The author and publisher
regret any inconvenience caused if addresses have changed or sites have
ceased to exist, but can accept no responsibility for any such changes.

Library of Congress Cataloging-in-Publication Data
Names: Fixico, Donald Lee, 1951-editor.
Title: Indian treaties in the United States: an encyclopedia and documents collection /
Donald L. Fixico, editor.
Description: Santa Barbara, California: ABC-CLIO, 2018. |
Includes bibliographical references and index.
Identifiers: LCCN 2017053742 (print) | LCCN 2018004099 (ebook) |
ISBN 9781440860485 (eBook) | ISBN 9781440860478 (alk. paper)
Subjects: LCSH: Indians of North America—Treaties. | Indians of North America—
Treaties—Encyclopedias. | Indians of North America—Legal status, laws, etc. |
Indians of North America—Government relations.
Classification: LCC KIE19 (ebook) |
LCC KIE19.I53 2018 (print) | DDC 342.7308/720261—dc23
LC record available at https://lccn.loc.gov/2017053742

ISBN: HB: 978-1-4408-6047-8
PB: 979-8-7651-1493-3
ePDF: 978-1-4408-6048-5
eBook: 979-8-2161-0212-0

To find out more about our authors and books visit www.bloomsbury.com
and sign up for our newsletters.

Contents

Preface, ix

Acknowledgments, xiii

Introduction, xv

PART I: REFERENCE ESSAYS, 1

Indian Treaty Making: A Native View, 3

    Box: Reserved Rights Doctrine, 5

Indian Treaties as International Agreements, 21

    Box: Domestic Dependent Nation, 36

Canadian Indian Treaties, 53

    Box: Doctrine of Discovery, 54

    Box: Guardianship/Wardship, 63

Colonial and Early Treaties, 1775–1829, 81

    Box: Annuities, 97

    Box: State-Recognized Tribes, 103

Indian Removal and Land Cessions, 1830–1849, 107

    Box: Native American Sovereignty, 116

Reservations and Confederate and Unratified Treaties, 1850–1871, 127

    Box: Trust Land, 134

    Box: Plenary Power, 151

PART II: DOCUMENTS, 155

Colonial and Early Treaties, 1775–1829, 157

    Treaty of Fort Pitt (1778), 157

        Box: Treaty Site—Fort Pitt, Pennsylvania, 158

    Treaty of Hopewell (1785), 162

    Treaty with the Six Nations (1794), 168

    Treaty of Greenville (1795), 174

        Box: Treaty Site—Greenville, Ohio, 176

    Treaty with the Great and Little Osage (1825), 187

    Treaty of Prairie du Chien (1825), 190

Treaties during Indian Removal, 1830–1849, 201

    Treaty of Dancing Rabbit Creek (1830), 201

    Treaty of Cusseta (1832), 218

    Treaty of Payne's Landing (1832), 224

    Treaty of Pontotoc Creek (1832), 227

    Treaty of Chicago (1833), 238

    Treaty of New Echota (1835), 265

        Box: Treaty Site—New Echota, Georgia, 267

    Treaty with the Chippewa (1837), 283

    Treaty of La Pointe (1842), 290

Confederate, Reconstruction, and Unratified Treaties, 1850–1871, 297

    Treaty of Fort Laramie (1851), 297

        Box: Treaty Site—Fort Laramie, Wyoming, 299

    Treaty with the Chippewa (1854), 304

    Menominee Treaty (1856), 314

    Reconstruction Treaties with the Cherokee, Choctaw, Chickasaw, Creeks, and Seminole (1866), 317

Medicine Lodge Treaty (1867), 328

Treaty of Fort Bridger (1868), 339

Treaty of Fort Laramie (1868), 346

Treaty with the Navajo (1868), 364

Appendix A: Treaties by Tribe, 375

Appendix B: Canadian First Nations Treaties, 395

Index, 399

About the Editor, 421

Preface

American Indians hold a unique status in having signed the most treaties of any Indigenous people in the world. After negotiating more than 400 treaties with American officials, a total of 374 were ratified by the U.S. Senate. After an act in 1871 stopped treaty making with the Indian nations, the U.S. government made an additional 97 agreements with American Indian tribes from 1870 to 1904. Together, there are 471 American Indian treaties and agreements.

There is an important question raised about why the United States has negotiated such an enormous number of Indian treaties and agreements. In the early formation of the U.S. government following the American Revolution in 1776, the new government had an exhausted volunteer army with almost no resources to protect its people. Most American Indian nations were stronger than the new union of 13 states. George Washington, John Hancock, and other founding fathers wanted the Indian nations to recognize the sovereignty of the new United States. England and France, who had previous treaties with Indians, continued to court trade relations with the Indian nations, so they still posed as threats to the United States. For the new United States, establishing peace and friendship with American Indians was essential for survival in the late 1700s.

One of the reasons for this book is to explain both what an Indian treaty is and more importantly what it means. These are two basic questions are for those who are unfamiliar with U.S.-Indian relations, which has a long history dating back to the first treaty with the Delawares in 1778, also referred to as the Fort Pitt Treaty. This treaty set an important precedent for the U.S. government in dealing with Indian nations, whose histories dated back hundreds of years. For example, in the first treaty the Delawares recognized the new sovereign status of the United States that had won its independence from Great Britain. Most importantly, the Delaware treaty established a mutual responsibility for both nations to recognize the rights of the other and to act as allies when needed. In other words, the United States needed the military strength of the Delawares—a powerful military force at the time—against the continued threat of Great Britain, which led to the War of 1812.

Treaties and agreements are contracts where at least two sides agree to carry out the agreed-upon responsibilities as written in the provisions of the contract. Based on international law, a treaty is an agreement between two sovereigns, or a person or nation with the right to rule itself. This relationship is known as a "trust" by both sides and it is a legally binding contract for each side to carry out the provisions of the treaty. An important point about Indian treaties is that there are at least two cultural perspectives to each one. The first one is the Anglo-American perspective with the understanding of treaties as formal written documents that are legally binding. The second point is that of indigenous people who had a different view of treaties since they did not have a written language and the emphasis of treaty making was based on the spoken word in the treaty negotiations or treaty councils. All of this was confirmed by a handshake of trust and sealed with a ceremony by smoking a peace pipe, and the giving of peace medals by American officials to Indian leaders as well as other gifts. This difference of cultures as well as language differences has led to misunderstandings of Indian treaties and the breaking of many of them.

Until the 1820s, the treaties benefited the United States more than the Indian nations as new states joined the union. As the United States grew in political power, its expanding population moved westward and settled on lands of Indian nations. The Indian nations defended their homelands, leading to wars and removal of more than three dozen tribes from the east to west of the Mississippi River to an area called Indian Territory. In the following decades, western Indian nations were removed to concentrated areas due to settlers, miners, and railroads.

The nature of U.S.-Indian relations changed as the United States became a stronger nation during the mid-1800s based on military and economic development. In the process, the nature of treaties favored the expanding United States at the expense of more than 300 tribal nations at the time.

Why are Indian treaties important would be a useful question for understanding the treaties. The treaties legally protect American Indians and their nations as the U.S. government is the trustee to ensure that the legal rights of American Indians are upheld. Because not all Indians were American citizens until an act by Congress in 1924, Indian treaties profoundly influenced the history of U.S.-Indian relations. In fact, studying Indian treaties is foundational to understanding the collective history of 567 Indian nations and understanding federal-Indian law of 250 important laws affecting Indians and numerous court cases.

To make this volume most useful, it has been divided into two parts. Part I consists of three categories of long and short essays. The long essays focus on the nature of Indian treaties according to chronology and legal meanings of treaties. The shorter essays are common topics found in Indian treaties and sites of significant treaties. Part II consists of nearly two dozen significant treaties with summary essays pertaining to each treaty. The names of tribes in the treaties are used and their own names for themselves have been added such as Navajos (Dinés), Delawares (Lenápes), Winnebagos (Ho-Chunks), Chastas (Shastas), and Chippewas (Ojibwes or Anishinaabes).

While the majority of Indian treaties were negotiated during the 1800s, they are still viable today. American Indians have certain legal rights such as water rights, hunting and fishing rights, land rights, religious rights, and other rights contained in treaties and agreements. More than a thousand court cases have been decided according to U.S.-Indian treaties, and American Indians have dual rights as members of their tribes and as citizens under the U.S. Constitution.

Donald L. Fixico
Arizona State University

Acknowledgments

This book would not have happened without the extensive work of Marian Perales, editorial manager of Race and Ethnicity and American History at ABC-CLIO. Her suggestions, input, and assembling of the treaties and essays make this volume most useful. I am also grateful for the Marketing Department for creating the cover of the book and promoting it. I am appreciative of Nicole Azze, production editor, and Allison Nadeau, media editor, at ABC-CLIO for their assistance in making this a better volume. I appreciate the help and guidance from Gordon Matchado, senior project manager. At Arizona State University, I am grateful for the support from the ASU Foundation, which sponsors my distinguished professorship of History, and for being a leading university that supports scholarship in American Indian history. I am appreciative of Bridget Groat, my research assistant, who helped in the last stage of this project. I am especially thankful to my fiancée, Michelle Martin, for her encouragement and the support from my son Keytha, who has grown up in a house full of books and now appreciates Indian treaties. I want to acknowledge my four tribes—the Shawnees, Sac and Fox, Seminoles, and Muscogee Creeks—who have signed 72 treaties with the United States, were removed to Indian Territory, and rebuilt their nations. Finally, I would like to dedicate this book to my former graduate students and current graduate students.

Introduction

Peace and friendship is the most commonly used phrase in the language of Indian treaties. The intent of the United States as a young country was to persuade Indian communities to deal only with the United States. Many things were unsettled following the American Revolution, and the tribes found themselves in the middle of it. In the early years of U.S.-Indian relations, the tribes also had common interest with the British, the French, and the Dutch.

Indian agents and other government officials in the United States negotiated more than 400 treaties and agreements with American Indians; treaty talks occurred for more than 100 years. Interestingly, Indian and white leaders met at various sites that often had been the meeting places for previous trading and council meetings. Negotiating in Native languages and English through interpreters was difficult, although some Native people spoke some of the white man's tongue. Beginning in 1778 with the Delawares, when the United States negotiated its first successful treaty with an Indian tribe, a historic precedent was set, one that has made Native Americans a unique minority in their own country. For the record, Indian tribes in what is now the United States also made treaties with the British, the French, the Confederate States during the Civil War, and with other Indian tribes.

In Canada, the federal government negotiated 70 treaties with the First Nations peoples, starting in 1871 and ending in the 20th century. These consist of 13 numbered treaties plus the 4 Robinson and Williams treaties. Early Peace and Friendship treaties included 6 agreements, 25 treaties are categorized as Upper Canada, and there are 14 Douglas Treaties, plus 9 agreements called Modern Treaties.

The mid-19th century represented the zenith of treaty making; during the next 20 years, the practice sharply declined. A rider attached to a congressional appropriations act in 1871 ended the Indian treaty-making business in the United States, although agreements were negotiated until 1917. The Act of 1871 did not end the recognition of Indian treaties, however; it merely halted the treaty-making process.

U.S.-Indian treaties often included more than one tribe, and some tribes signed many treaties. There are 374 ratified treaties and 97 agreements. The first treaty was concluded in 1778; the last one, during the late 19th century. The shortest treaty is with the Kickapoos in 1820. The treaty is 16 lines long, with 8 Kickapoo leaders and 6 American officials who signed, involving $2,000 to be paid for Kickapoo removal. The longest treaty is the Treaty with the New York Indians of 1838 at Buffalo Creek in New York; that treaty is 15 pages long. The Potwatomis signed the most treaties of any tribe, a total of 26. The biggest gathering was the council held at Medicine Lodge, Kansas, during October 1867, at which 500 soldiers met with more than 15,000 Plains Indians gathered from the Cheyennes, Arapahos, Apaches, Kiowas, and Comanches. The largest number of treaties were signed in 1825 and 1836, 20 each year; 19 treaties were signed in 1855, 18 in 1865, and 17 in 1832.

In regard to categories, 229 treaties involve ceded lands; 205 are about payments and annuities; 202 include the phrase *peace and friendship*; 115 are about boundaries; 99 address reservations; 70 include civilization and agriculture; 59 are about roads and free passages; 52 address the sovereignty or the authority of the United States or tribes; 49 include allotment and guaranteed lands; 47 contain gifts, goods, or presents, 38 contain provisions on education; 34 contain provisions on hunting, fishing, and gathering rights; 28 authorize forts and military posts; 25 include trade; 12 address railroads; several include agents for the tribes; and a few treaties deal with one or more of the following: stolen horses, returning prisoners, slavery, returning criminals, intruders, scalping, alcohol, missions, and mail routes.

Treaties between Indian tribes and the United States are binding agreements. For Native peoples, each step of the negotiation was important, not just the resulting words on a piece of paper. Indian agents, military officials, and officials of the Indian Office met with Native leaders to begin negotiations, which usually began with a council held at a previously agreed-upon site. To Native people, the chosen site was important, and the talk itself was just as significant as the resulting treaty or agreement. The site itself, such as the one near Medicine Lodge in southwestern Kansas and Prairie du Chien in western Wisconsin, set the tone of the council. Medicine Lodge has made a lasting impression and is reenacted every five years.

The first meeting, or council, between Indian and white leaders likely made or broke the tone of the talks. The council was a fundamental concept among the Indian nations, and tribal protocols varied from tribe to tribe. Unsure of how to approach the various tribes, federal officials depended upon local whites, guides, and traders to introduce them to the tribes in their areas. Familiar with the ways of the Indian tribe, these individuals advised officials how to approach Native leaders.

In learning the protocol for dealing with tribes, federal officials experienced difficulty in meeting with more than one tribe at the same time. They made the mistake of trying to get enemy tribes to meet at the same council. Even tribes who met only sometimes, such as the Plains Indians, who gathered annually during the summer to hold the Sun Dance, had a mutual understanding of the importance of the arrival at camp, as exemplified by the Medicine Lodge Council in 1867. Dressed in their finest ceremonial garb, a tribe also sometimes wanted to be the last to arrive so that other tribal groups would acknowledge that an important group had arrived.

Protocol is involved in any type of summit, council, or important discussion involving conflicting interests, especially if there are deep differences between cultures. In the general situation of treaty talks, white officials learned a lot about the importance of kinship relations in forming an agreement, especially if it resulted in an alliance between the two sides. Early treaties—those concluded before the mid-19th century—were often peace treaties, for the United States wanted tribes to acknowledge their relationship with the new nation and abrogate relations with the British and the French. Bringing about peace following a battle or other conflict created balance between two opposites, and this tranquil state of existence fostered mutual respect between the two parties and a need for ceremonial acknowledgement. Thus, smoking the pipe was germane to solidifying the new relationship of nonconflict.

The language barrier between the two sides required the exercise of great skills in diplomacy to be exercised. During the height of contact between Indians and whites in the 17th and 18th centuries, more than 250 indigenous languages were spoken. The role of interpreters, both Indian and white, became crucial to treaty negotiations. The varying protocols among tribes for holding councils compelled American officials to learn about tribal leaders before talks of a serious nature began. Cultural differences added to language barriers as problems arose, often intensifying the clashing views of Indians and whites over land. One perceived land and what it meant economically, and the other understood the earth philosophically and celebrated it with ceremonies. The same commodity became homeland for both sides, and ensuing treaties named who owned the land. A new culture of treaty making emerged from the older Indian way of holding council and talking.

Gift giving played a crucial role in the early contact and negotiations between Indian and white leaders. Federal officials typically brought gifts of inexpensive items such as mirrors, metalwork, and beads to get the Indians into a peaceful frame of mind that would lead to the discussion of bigger issues, such as land cessions. As mentioned, at least 47 treaties contained provisions for giving gifts and presents. Officials understood the importance of generosity and sharing among Native peoples and used this against them, hence the "Great White Father" in Washington held a position of respect and generosity.

The cultural difference between Indians and whites proved to be enormous. In addition to the language barriers, both sides operated from different mind-sets; each held different ideas about what was important for the negotiations and what the negotiations meant. Native leaders and federal officials had a challenging situation to overcome before they could begin successful discussions. It is said that on one occasion Osceola, the noted leader of the Seminoles in Florida, disagreeing with tribal leaders who signed the Treaty of Fort Gibson in 1833, stabbed his knife through the piece of paper on the table. This was his angry response to all treaties, letting others know that his mind was set on going to war.

"Touching the pen" became a common occurrence during Indian treaty making. Native leaders were unable to write their names because they did not know the English language, and therefore white officials asked Native leaders to "make their mark"—which was of little importance to American Indians, who believed that the spoken word was superior to any words on a piece of paper, which might be blown away by the wind or destroyed; the spoken word would always be remembered. Several treaty councils witnessed impressive oratory articulated by tribal leaders. This was not the white way. The majority of Indian treaties verify the marks made by the tribal leaders. In other situations, the leaders refused to hold the white man's writing instrument, and the federal officials asked the Native leaders to touch the pen after the names were written by the official in charge.

The most important concern for Native peoples in treaty negotiations was their sovereignty. Sovereignty is an important issue of concern resulting from the U.S.-Indian and Canada-First Nations agreements. The signing of a treaty creates binding responsibilities between both sides and includes the respectful recognition of each for the other. Theoretically, the relationship between the two sides is one of a sovereign forming an agreement with another sovereign—that is, government-to-government in a lateral relationship of similar status. The status is based on the faith of each party to the treaty that is held by the two sovereigns.

Trust is a meaningful legal responsibility between two nations and their people, and treaties established this reciprocal relationship. Both sides of a treaty agreement must abide by the provisions and must continue to fulfill the responsibilities outlined in the document. That trust responsibility continues into this century, in the hands of the assistant secretary of the Department of the Interior, who supervises the Bureau of Indian Affairs for all tribes in the United States.

Treaties were a systematic procedure for dealing with Indian tribes. By examining the history of these agreements, some assessment can be made about them in stages or phases. For example, treaty negotiations, talks, or councils were the first step in this system of agreements. During these important gatherings, significant Indian individuals were recognized and acknowledged so the representatives of the United States would know who they were dealing with. In some cases, such as the Prairie du Chien meeting, "making chiefs" occurred; this happened more than once when government officials persuaded certain individuals to sign for their tribes as leaders. The federal government operated on the political philosophy that a head of state represented a nation, thus an Indian nation must have one significant leader or chief. This was not the case with many tribes, such as the Muscogee Creeks, the Ojibwes, and others, who had leaders for each town or village and settlements scattered over a vast region of the country.

Discussion of the treaty's provisions was another critical phase of Indian treaty making. Both sides met with an agenda of needs, according to their thinking, and they lobbied to obtain agreement from the other side. Some acute Native leaders saw that education was an important part of the future of their people and wanted educational assistance in the form of teachers. Common provisions included goods and annuities over a number of years and perhaps blacksmiths. Most of all, large sums of money were paid to the tribes for their lands.

The next phase consisted of the results of treaties—some of which caused important changes, such as the exchange of enormous tracts of land for perpetual gifts, or changes in fishing or hunting rights on ceded lands. The treaties led to a new era in Indian-white relations and actually marked the decline of the strength of Indian nations. This decline became evident as tribes such as the Potawatomis, Delawares, Chippewas, and others signed several treaties with the United States. After 1800, the federal government almost always had the leverage in treaty talks.

Strategies of treaty making involved several motives, all of which resulted in the decline of the Indian nations. These strategies involved introducing the idea of one nation, one leader; setting boundaries; manipulating leadership; making chiefs; courting treaty signers; and giving gifts to influence tribes and their leaders. Such actions almost always were directed toward Indian men, not toward women (although, in many tribes, women held the authority to select their leaders).

Peace was the main objective in the early U.S. treaties until about 1850. The federal government found it much easier to make peace with the Indian nations than to fight them, which proved costly, especially as great effort was needed just to find them. The United States signed 374 treaties but fought more than 1,600 wars, battles, and skirmishes against Indian tribes. The Navajo Treaty of 1849 and the Fort Laramie Treaty of 1851 were negotiated with peaceful objectives in mind rather than more land cessions. The Fort Laramie agreement involved multiple groups of the northern plains, Sioux, Gros Ventres, Mandans, Arikaras, Assiniboines, Blackfeet, Crows, Cheyennes, and Arapahos. Boundaries were set to keep them apart, with additional provisions for roads and military posts included as part of the treaty.

The establishment of boundaries for tribes was another goal for government officials as they treated with Indian leaders. Many tribes hunted over vast territories; government officials were able to contain tribes within certain areas, and they reminded leaders of the boundaries established in the agreements. Officials introduced Native peoples to the idea of land ownership and individual ownership. In 1858, the Sisseton and Wahpeton Sioux signed a treaty in Washington, D.C. agreeing to new reservation boundaries. This led to the surveying of the tribal land for division into individual 80-acre allotments. In this way, tribal lands were reduced in size.

At times, the United States undermined and manipulated leadership to get the lands it wanted. The importance of kinship played a vital role in treaty making between Indians and the United States. Federal officials learned of the importance of kinship and symbolic bonds in tribal communities and used this knowledge to develop a tribal dependence on the "Great White Father" in Washington. When the leaders of tribes refused to negotiate, federal officials sought out other Indians who were more easily persuaded to sign treaty documents.

Land acquisition was the principal reason for treaties and was pursued to such an extreme extent that, by the end of the 19th century, American Indians held less than 2 percent of the total land that they had once possessed. The unleashed consuming white settler became an uncontrollable force with respect to Indian lands. Such was the settlers' greed that federal officials were forced to deal with tribes, which resulted in many Indian removal treaties or war. A domino effect occurred as eastern tribes moved onto lands of interior groups, who moved onto lands of western tribes, and so forth.

Expansion of the United States was another goal of government officials. During the Civil War, federal officials negotiated, and the government ratified, 18 treaties that called for expanding the territory held by the Union. During the three years between March 1862 and March 1865, federal officials concluded treaties with the Kansa, Ottawa, Chippewa, Nez Percé, Shoshone, Ute, Klamath, Modoc, Omaha, Winnebago, and Ponca Nations. These agreements included land cessions and further diminished the territories of the tribes. Indian lands were further reduced by the systematic creation of "permanent" reservations.

Control of tribal movements was the final strategy and result of the treaties. With treaties in place and with military power greater than that of the tribes, the United States could enforce control over the weakened Indian nations. Once the leaders were undermined and control exerted over them, superintendents controlled the Indians and conditions on the almost 200 reservations throughout Indian country. At this date, the Bureau of Indian Affairs works with tribal governments on 326 reservations, covering 511,000 square miles in 33 states.

Land was the central issue of U.S.-Indian treaties. As more settlers arrived from England and other countries, the need for more Indian land placed considerable pressure on the Indian tribes. A domino effect began to occur as eastern seaboard tribes of the Atlantic coast retreated inland, thereby encroaching on the hunting domains and farming areas of tribes nearby to the west. The expansion of white settlement across the Appalachian Mountains caused the newly formed United States to treat with the inland tribes. British agents and traders worked among the Indian nations to gain their allegiance and convince them to reject the proposed talks of federal officials.

At the same time, other European interests in the form of French, Scots, and Irish traders proved successful in obtaining acceptance among tribes. These trading activities made it more difficult for the United States as more Americans pushed into the Ohio valley and the back country of the Southeast.

The most obvious kind of treaty called for tribes to surrender their lands. In less than 30 years, from 1801 to 1829, federal officials made 31 treaties with the

Chickasaw, Choctaw, Muscogee Creek, Cherokee, and Florida tribes. These cession treaties extinguished Indian title to all of the area east of the Mississippi River from the Ohio River to the Gulf of Mexico.

Officially, treaties had to be ratified by the U.S. Congress and signed by the president of the United States. Congressional ratification was most active during the 1800s, as federal officials met with Native leaders at an increasing rate. Treaty making fell into a pattern: more and more treaties were negotiated with eastern tribes, who were thus forced to keep moving westward; the Delawares, for example, were forced to remove at least nine times.

Unratified treaties were agreements not confirmed by the U.S. Congress. Naturally, many agreements were submitted to Congress; most submissions were ratified, and some had their provisions amended. It is estimated that between 47 and 87 treaties were unratified. Most Native leaders did not understand the ratification process and believed that all the agreements they made were official. The treaties had tremendous impact on American Indians and their rights in the 20th century. During the Reign of Terror in the early 1920s, the Osages had large amounts of oil under their land and possessed headrights to the oil that other people desired. Coal on the Navajo Reservation led to the largest open pit mining operation in the world. The Menominees were the first tribe of 109 cases of termination of trust status with tribes, communities, and bands with the United States starting in 1961. Based on their treaties, the Florida Seminoles legally introduced Indian bingo in 1979 that led to the Indian gaming industry. In Wisconsin, the Ojibwes fought for their fishing rights in the 1980s. In 2016, the Standing Rock Sioux and Cheyenne River Sioux used their Fort Laramie Treaties to try to protect their rights against the North Dakota Access Pipeline. In the 21st century, American Indians and the First Nations of Canada fully realize the significance of their tribal sovereignty and that their legal rights are protected in the treaties. Government-Indian relations are complex, and this volume is intended as an introduction for anyone interested in Indian treaties with the United States and the First Nations of Canada.

Donald L. Fixico
Arizona State University

Part I: Reference Essays

Indian Treaty Making: A Native View

Like other peoples, American Indians have always been concerned with preserving their cultural autonomy, retaining their land, and maintaining political sovereignty. One way tribes have preserved their legal rights is by entering into treaties and agreements with other sovereigns. Approximately 370 Indian treaties were ratified by the United States (Deloria and DeMallie 1999, 181). A number of other treaties that resulted from negotiations between the United States and Indian tribes were never ratified by the U.S. Senate and remain unenforceable.

Indian tribes entered into treaties with other sovereigns for different reasons and with varying results. Treaties created military and political alliances, authorized trade, defined political and jurisdictional boundaries, divided natural resources, established and maintained peace, ensured community survival, and at times provided for the final dissolution of tribal governments.

As a matter of tribal law and policy, a treaty is a binding agreement between two or more nations. Treaties are legal agreements that Indians expected to be binding (Wilkinson and Volkman 1975, 612). Although not every tribe negotiated treaties with the United States, the political consequences of treaty making and the legal principles that flow from court cases involving treaty interpretation continue to define the legal status of tribal governments within the United States today (Monette 1994, 617–618). Even the tribes that never entered into treaties with the United States benefit from the resulting legal framework of Indian nations as sovereigns. Today, there are more than 565 federally recognized tribes within the United States, including Alaska Native villages. Treaties were the foundation of federal recognition of Indian tribes as sovereigns (Porter 2004, 1601).

Although treaties were common among the tribes in the southeastern United States, the Woodlands (eastern United States), the Great Plains, and the Northwest, many tribes in other regions did not routinely negotiate treaties with the United States. For example, few ratified treaties will be found between the United States and tribes in California or between the United States and the Pueblos of the Southwest (Brann 2003, 754–755). The United States did not enter into treaties with any of the Alaska Native sovereigns (Case and Voluck 1978, 16–17).

Muscogee Creek traditionalist Chitto Harjo (Crazy Snake) protested against the United States for breaking treaties after his people moved to Indian Territory. In 1887, the Dawes Act allotted individual lands to the Creeks, thus reducing the Creek reservation, and Harjo protested by leading the Crazy Snake Rebellion in 1909. (Library of Congress)

Treaties are legally binding agreements between sovereigns; they are also called *compacts*, *covenants*, *conventions*, and *memoranda of understanding*. Regardless of the nomenclature, these treaties have been a critical part of the American Indian past and are of continuing importance to tribal governments today. In fact, tribal governments continue to negotiate treaties and agreements with various sovereigns, particularly state and local entities (Deloria and Laurence 1994, 381).

U.S. federal policy ended treaty making with tribes in 1871. In March of that year, Congress placed a rider on an appropriations bill that ended the practice of Indian treaties in the United States (25 U.S.C. § 71). Prior to that date, the executive branch would negotiate treaties with the tribes, and the Senate would either ratify the treaty or not. Some treaties involved monetary payments to tribes, for which Congress needed to appropriate funds. The House of Representatives objected to this process because they were being asked to fund items included in treaties despite the fact that the House had played no role in treaty negotiations. Although the legislation of 1871 prohibited the federal government from negotiating further treaties with Indian tribes, the law on the books differs from what actually happened.

Tribes continued as sovereigns, with territorial control over lands and natural resources. The federal government continued to have a government-to-government relationship with tribes, and political negotiations continued, although not by means of formal treaties as they had before.

As a practical matter, the United States continued to negotiate formal agreements with tribal governments well into the 1910s; however, rather than being submitted to the Senate for ratification, these new agreements were presented to Congress and adopted or rejected by both the Senate and the House of Representatives. In this form, the post-1871 agreements with tribes took the form of congressional enactments rather than ratified treaties. The most common examples of these agreements are the tribally specific enactments to implement allotment on particular reservations. After lengthy negotiations with tribal governments, federal agents prepared formal allotment agreements with the consent of tribal officials. These agreements were formally presented to Congress and adopted as legislation instead of ratified as treaties. The federal-tribal diplomatic process, followed by tribal consent and federal approval, was essentially the same as the treaty-making process prior to 1871.

Reserved Rights Doctrine

Reserved rights are the "bundle of rights" that is rooted in the inherent or original sovereignty of Indian nations. They are property rights that Indian nations retained and did not give or grant to the United States during the negotiation of a treaty or other formal agreement. When Indian nations negotiated and signed treaties with the U.S. government during the 18th and 19th centuries, they often retained certain lands as reservations and reserved the right to harvest natural resources on lands they sold or ceded to the United States. In doing so, Native communities reserved property rights they did not explicitly relinquish to the United States. Such rights are not, as some critics have claimed, "special rights" or rights "granted" to Indian nations by the United States.

The first legal definition of the reserved rights doctrine was articulated by the U.S. Supreme Court in a 1905 decision, *United States v. Winans*. The case before the Court was whether or not the Yakama Nation's treaty right to fish in "usual and accustomed places" was being interfered with by fish wheels placed on the Columbia River by non-Natives. In a decision favoring the Yakamas, the Court enunciated the reserved rights doctrine. It ruled that non-Indian settlement and landscape change would limit, not eliminate, the Yakama's fishing rights. The Court concluded that the fishing rights could not be taken, because "the treaty was not a grant of rights to the Indians, but a grant of rights from them, a reservation of those not granted. And the form of the instrument and its language was adapted to that purpose." This formulation of the reserved rights doctrine recognizes that Indian nations reserved specific inherent or aboriginal property rights and political powers at the same time they granted specific rights to the United States. The United States was not giving or granting rights or powers to tribes.

Analogies can be drawn between Indian treaty-based reserved rights and power and those of the rights and powers that state governments reserved with the Tenth Amendment to the U.S. Constitution. The Tenth Amendment is a reserved powers clause that protects the sovereignty and powers of state governments. It says that the states reserved all those powers that they did not delegate or give to the federal government by the Constitution. In drawing a direct comparison between Indian and state reserved rights, these scholars demonstrate not only that reserved treaty rights are an inherent aspect of tribal sovereignty—that they have a preconstitutional basis—but also that, because they are similar to states' reserved rights, there is a legal, if not a moral, basis for the defense of the Indian reserved rights doctrine.

Conflicting interpretations of the reserved rights doctrine have been at the center of legal disputes between state governments and Indian nations over the continuing existence of off-reservation hunting, fishing, and gathering treaty rights. In both the Pacific Northwest and the Great Lakes regions, the reserved rights doctrine has been a key aspect in judicial interpretations of treaty negotiations, the texts of treaties, and historical and contemporary Indian and non-Indian understandings of the meaning of treaties. Anti-Indian treaty rights groups have attacked court decisions employing the reserved rights doctrine as examples of the courts "granting" special rights to Indian tribes.

The reserved rights doctrine has also been important in defining water rights on Indian reservations in the western United States. In *Winters v. United States*, the Supreme Court ruled that there was an implicit or "implied" reservation of water rights when Indian reservations were created. According to the Court, even though a treaty or agreement creating a reservation did not explicitly mention or reserve water rights for the tribe, there was an implied reservation of enough water to meet the tribe's needs. Otherwise, the reservation would have little economic (i.e., agricultural) value. As a result of this application of the implied reserved rights doctrine, upstream irrigators and water users cannot legally deprive a downstream tribe of sufficient water to meet their needs.

Steven E. Silvern

Further Reading

Deloria, Vine, Jr. *Behind the Trail of Broken Treaties: An Indian Declaration of Independence*. Austin: University of Texas Press, 1994.

Prucha, F. P. *Documents of U.S. Indian Policy*. Lincoln: University of Nebraska Press, 1990.

Wilkins, David E., and K. Tsianina Lomawaima. *Uneven Ground: American Indian Sovereignty and Federal Law*. Norman: University of Oklahoma Press, 2001.

Modern tribal governments continue to enter into agreements with other tribes and with state and local governments. Tribal and state governments frequently negotiated cross-deputization agreements between each other as two sovereigns. These agreements address the jurisdictional ambiguities of law enforcement in Indian country and typically involve shared law enforcement authority in otherwise disputed areas. The agreements permit tribal police officers to make arrests on lands that would otherwise be under the jurisdiction of the state, and vice versa. In some areas of the country, where state and tribal jurisdiction depends on the ownership of neighboring parcels of land, these ongoing agreements are necessary to public safety and effective policing (Pommersheim 1995, 161).

Tribes and states also enter into revenue-sharing agreements as a means of resolving conflicts of taxation jurisdiction (Fletcher 2004, 5–7). These agreements are typically referred to as *compacts*. Where tax jurisdiction is ambiguous or where collection of tax revenues proves burdensome, tribes and states have negotiations compacts in lieu of federal court litigation. One sovereign agrees not to pursue tax claims in court, whereas the other sovereign agrees to share tax revenues with the first sovereign. In some compacts, the sovereigns agree how the funds are to be spent in a mutually beneficial manner both for citizens of the state and for citizens of the tribe.

Treaty Making Past and Present

For more than 500 years, tribes have entered into treaties with the United States and with other international governments. Tribes entered into various treaties with Great Britain, Spain, and other European sovereigns prior to the American Revolution (Deloria and DeMallie 1999, 103).

For centuries prior to European contact, tribes negotiated agreements with other tribes akin to the treaties they would later negotiate with European countries and ultimately with the United States. By the time Europeans arrived, tribes were already skilled in negotiating treaties and agreements for a variety of purposes. Tribes had formed military alliances and political confederations for centuries.

Tribes also had elaborate trade routes that required access to vast territories, including lands owned or controlled by other tribes. Tribes reached agreements that recognized boundaries between tribal lands and passage between those territories. All these negotiations predated European contact and influence. In fact, much of the Indian treaty-making process was passed from the tribes to their European counterparts, who freely adopted Indian treaty-making procedures and diplomatic decorum in the negotiations that followed.

For instance, Indian treaty negotiations often involved long ceremonial meetings, during which past transgressions were set aside, friendships renewed, and gifts exchanged between the parties as a sign of goodwill (Deloria and DeMallie 1999, 685). These formalities and ceremonial gestures preceded any discussion of new parameters or terms of agreement. In this regard, American Indians influenced the manner in which future negotiations would take place, and federal negotiators embraced many of these concepts.

The influence of European and subsequent U.S. treaty-making traditions also altered the way Indian tribes negotiated. There was a shift away from reliance on oral agreements toward a focus on written documents. Prior to European contact, the treaty negotiations of tribes were committed to memory, with the entire discussion constituting the binding agreement of the parties. The non-Indians' insistence on memorializing agreements in writing altered the treaty-making process and, over time, changed the way tribes entered into the negotiating process. The result was a shift in focus: today, many Indian people might know the words of the treaty document but not the context in which the negotiations arose.

Indians and non-Indians alike initially approached the early treaty negotiations with little or no knowledge of each other's traditions or beliefs. The language barrier

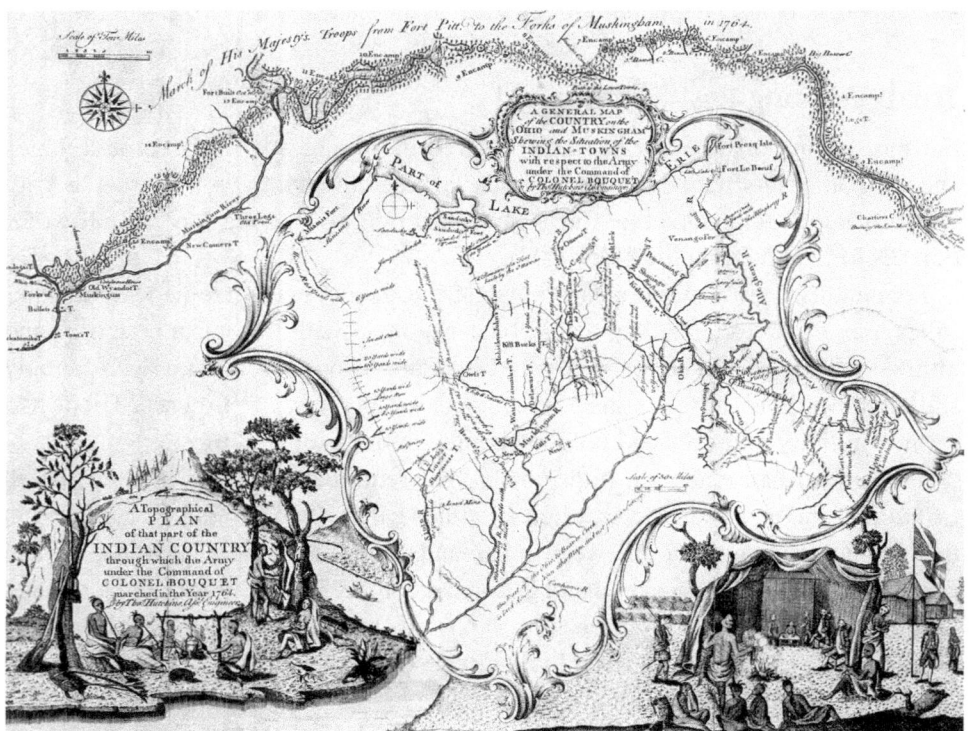

The first U.S.-Indian ratified agreement, called the Fort Pitt Treaty, in 1778 with the Delawares, led to other treaties for the Ohio region and set a precedent for 374 U.S.-Indian ratified treaties. (Library of Congress)

routinely would have made fluid communications nearly impossible, yet agreements were made. In coming together, each side influenced the treaty process of the other sovereign, and a unique system of negotiations emerged that included elements of both the Indian and the European traditions.

The first treaty between America and an Indian tribe was completed during the Revolutionary War, the Treaty of Fort Pitt (Treaty with the Delaware) in 1778. The Delawares (Lenápes) made a formal alliance with the American revolutionaries, and the tribe permitted colonial troops free movement across their territory. In exchange, the Americans agreed to build a fort inside the Delaware Nation to protect the community when soldiers were elsewhere engaged. Beyond its historical significance, this treaty was important because it established that tribes were sovereign entities with the power of diplomacy. It also established, in a legal context, that tribes were property owners with full dominion over territory, including the right to exclude others from their territory. The Delawares were in a position of strength when negotiating with the colonies.

The relative strength of the Delawares diminished over time, and the tribe later found itself in a much weaker diplomatic position. Yet, whether in strength or in weakness, the Delawares continued to negotiate treaties with other sovereigns to accomplish their goals.

In 1867, the Delawares entered into a treaty with the Cherokee Nation that arguably led to a political dissolution of the Delawares (Treaty between the Cherokee and Delaware—April 8, 1867). The Delawares negotiated citizenship rights within the Cherokee Nation to preserve legally protected status for the Delaware people and to ensure a friendly place to settle.

The Delaware story is important because it demonstrates how a sovereign can enter into treaties for various purposes at various times. Sometime tribes are in a position of strength, and sometimes tribes face political or physical annihilation. In each circumstance, the sovereign made a contextual decision and chose to negotiate a treaty to protect its interests or to mitigate a situation. Just as there was no uniform Delaware approach to treaty making over time, there is no uniform Native perspective on treaty making.

In 1867, the Cherokees and the Delawares were both in politically weak positions relative to the United States. In fact, both tribes were pressured to enter into the intertribal treaty by the United States, and the treaty was executed by both tribes, not in Delaware or Cherokee Territory but in Washington, D.C., in the presence of, and for the benefit of, federal officials.

The Delawares were being removed by the United States from their territory and relocated inside Indian Territory. Most of the Indian Territory lands had been accounted for, and the federal government needed land to implement the Delaware relocation. In a treaty with the United States, the Cherokee Nation agreed to accept the Delawares along with the Shawnees. The Cherokees agreed both to the relocations and to the inclusion of the Shawnee and Delaware people as citizens of the Cherokee Nation as a result of a post-Civil War treaty with the United States. The Cherokee Nation, like the Osages, the Muscogee Creeks, the Seminoles, and other Indian nations, entered into treaties of alliance with the Confederate States in 1861. When the Civil War was over, the United States reestablished ties with the Cherokee Nation, but the Cherokee Nation agreed to several concessions, including the settlement of other tribes on Cherokee lands. These post-Civil War treaties were among the last official treaties between Indian nations and the United States. The post-Civil War treaty with the Cherokees is unique because it precipitates additional treaties between tribes on the request of the United States. Rather than using force to require the Cherokee Nation to accept the relocation of other Indian tribes, the United States acknowledged that the tribes would work out the terms of relocation and new citizenship in an intertribal treaty. This illustrates how, even toward the end of formal treaty making with the United States, tribes were viewed as sovereigns who negotiated with each other and with the United States as a means of diplomacy.

The United States officially ended treaty making between the federal government and tribal governments in 1871 (25 U.S.C. § 71). The United States continued to make formal agreements, although they were not considered treaties, with tribes well into the 20th century. One of the most common subjects of these agreements was the allotment of tribal lands.

In the late 1800s and early 1900s, the federal government pushed for Indian lands to be allotted. Rather than holding land in a contiguous land base with a property law system governed by tribal law, the United States pressured tribes to divide their lands and allow individual Indians to own lands without the control or oversight of the tribes. The U.S. Congress passed the General Allotment Act as a statement of federal policy; however, the federal allotment policy was not self-executing (Royster 1995, 7–15).

Allotment of reservation lands was generally implemented only after elaborate negotiations and treaty making with the affected tribes. Some tribes were successful in avoiding the allotment of their lands altogether. The majority of tribes were pressured to allot their lands, and the details were outlined in tribal agreements with the United States.

In fact, more than 20 agreements between the United States and tribal governments were made in the years 1876–1895. The United States did not stop making treaties; it simply relabeled the process and extended ratification rights to both houses of Congress rather than to the Senate alone.

During this period, the tribes did not have the same political and military strength they once had had. By this time, tribes had typically been relocated to reservations or to diminished land bases. Even though very few tribes were militarily conquered by the United States, in previous treaties many tribes had agreed to become protectorates of the United States and had thereby abandoned any effort to maintain their own troops.

The Dawes Allotment Act in 1887 reduced the size of Indian reservations by distributing 160 acres on the average to individual Indians, to civilize them into farmers or to raise livestock, thus creating a surplus of 90 million acres made available to homesteaders and railroad companies. (Library of Congress)

With no military threat and with increased economic dependency of tribes on the federal government, the United States continued to gain political power over the tribes. With increased political power, the United States began to interfere with matters that had previously been internal to the tribe, including how the tribes governed themselves. Increased federal involvement in internal tribal matters quickly led to an effort by the federal government to change the land tenure systems inside Indian country.

As such, the allotment agreements were heavily coerced by the federal government, and the tribes were powerless to demand many concessions. The tribes felt that, if they did not participate in the agreements, the federal government would unilaterally act to allot their lands. The tribes were faced with two options: either to allow Congress to pass a law permitting allotment of tribal lands without tribal consent or input, or to enter into negotiations with the federal government for the allotment of tribal lands on terms more agreeable to the tribes. Those tribes that entered into negotiations with the federal government for the allotment of tribal lands did so under duress. Although the tribes vehemently opposed allotment, they negotiated allotment to avoid being completely voiceless in the process. Tribal input in the allotment process was better than no negotiation at all (Leeds 2005, 64–66).

The federal perspective in negotiating the allotment agreements was that allotment would end tribalism and prepare Indian people for ultimate citizenship in the United States. This would make Indian people members of a national minority and end the notion of tribal sovereignty. Therefore, many of the allotment agreements included provisions that dissolved tribal governments and provided for U.S. citizenship.

The Atoka Agreement of the Choctaw and Chickasaw Nations in 1897 in Indian Territory is a prime example. The agreement divided tribal lands into individual allotments and provided for the ultimate dissolution of the tribal government as a condition precedent to the extension of U.S. citizenship to tribal members.

Several shifts in federal policy occurred after allotment. Since the 1960s, there has been a consistent trend away from the termination of tribal existence toward a policy of respecting tribal self-determination. Tribal governments have rebounded and have resumed the exercise of their inherent sovereign powers, including the right to negotiate treaties and agreements with other sovereigns. Indian treaty making continues throughout Indian country today. Many tribes continue to make agreements with state and local municipalities and with other tribes.

Historically, the Cherokee Nation has completed 22 treaties since 1721, first with Great Britain and then with the United States. The contemporary Cherokee Nation continues to make treaties and currently maintains more than 20 ongoing agreements with state, county, and city law enforcement agencies. Most of the agreements were negotiated in the 1990s, and additional negotiations for new agreements are pending.

The Navajo (Diné) Nation and the State of Arizona have negotiated agreements to control the distribution of tax revenues between the two sovereigns and to cooperate in the delivery of youth and family protective services. The Navajo Nation is geographically located within three states, and each of the sovereign states has engaged in negotiations with Navajo Nation officials.

Tribes in the Puget Sound and Great Lakes areas have recently negotiated intertribal agreements that ensure equitable rights to fish and wildlife harvests. Tribes throughout the country are currently engaged in intertribal cooperatives to restore buffalo herds, manage water resources, and clarify jurisdiction.

A foundational principle of federal Indian law has been the role of the federal government in Indian affairs, to the exclusion of the states. Early cases and federal statutes preclude states from negotiating treaties with tribal governments. However, when formal federal treaty making came to an end, states and local governments increased their willingness to negotiate with tribes, realizing that treaties and agreements are mutually beneficial.

In at least three areas, the federal government has authorized states to enter into agreements with tribes: (1) law enforcement, (2) the care and custody of Indian children, and (3) gaming. Tribes that engage in casino-style gaming routinely negotiate with the states compacts that dictate revenue sharing, maintenance of roads, and other governmental infrastructure. These agreements routinely lead to shared law enforcement responsibilities and clarify jurisdiction of tribal and state courts.

Tribes do not need authorization from the federal government to negotiate agreements with other sovereigns. The right to negotiate and make treaties is an important component of inherent sovereign powers, and tribes will continue to exercise this power into the future. Indian treaties are hardly relics of the past. The ability to negotiate and reach valid legal agreements with other sovereigns is a critical and active component of modern tribal sovereignty.

The Diversity of Tribal Perspectives

The Native perspective of treaty making is diverse. More than 565 federally recognized tribal governments have entered into several hundred treaties, both ratified and unratified, with the United States. Many other treaties have been negotiated with tribes, states, and foreign countries. The sheer number of negotiations and resulting treaties suggests there is no single Native approach to treaty making. From

Following the Battle of Fallen Timbers in 1794, Miami leader Little Turtle negotiated with General Anthony Wayne. Commander William Henry Harrison attended the peace talks, and Captain William Wells interpreted provisions for the Treaty of Greenville in 1795 that opened the Ohio region to U.S. expansion. (Chicago History Museum/Getty Images)

tribe to tribe, the customs, laws, languages, and philosophies greatly differ. It follows that the concepts of treaty making and diplomacy are distinctive as well.

Many differing factors lead to negotiations, depending on the tribes involved. Many tribes never entered into treaties with the United States. Other tribes entered into multiple treaties with multiple sovereigns. The Cherokee Nation, for example, has negotiated treaties with Great Britain, the United States, and the Confederacy, and with several Indian tribes, most notably the Shawnees and the Delawares. The Choctaw Nation entered into treaties with Spain prior to entering into multiple treaties with the United States. The Kashaya Pomo tribe in California entered into a treaty with Russia in 1817. Other tribes have entered into treaties with Mexico and Canada (Deloria and DeMallie 1999, 106–108).

Tribes sometimes negotiated treaties that were never ratified either by the United States or by their tribal citizens. The U.S. Senate failed to ratify 18 Indian treaties after the tribes had agreed to all the provisions (Prucha 1994, 244). But in other circumstances, negotiations ended so that tribal leaders could return home to get the proper assent from their tribal constituents.

Tribes approached the treaty-making process in vastly different ways, according to the political, social, and cultural contexts. Tribal peoples, like their counterparts throughout the world, make political and diplomatic decisions for innumerable reasons. The viewpoints and motivations of the Indian leaders who negotiated and signed treaties are equally diverse. Like sovereigns the world over, tribes have leaders who fall into different camps. Some leaders are true statesmen who represent their people in difficult situations and make the tough decisions based on what they sincerely believe to be in the best interest of their constituents, with or without popular support. Other leaders succumb to greed and allow personal gain to influence their decisions, even to the detriment of the people they represent. Indian country has had a host of leaders in both camps.

The Indian treaty-making process involved leaders who made sincere assessments of the difficulties faced by their nations and made decisions to enter into treaties even though the will of the people did not wish to enter into treaties. Other leaders entered into treaties that directly benefited them personally. In the Treaty of Dancing Rabbit Creek of 1830 (Treaty with the Choctaw), Chief Greenwood LeFlore of the Choctaws consented to have the Choctaw people removed from their ancestral lands and relocated to Indian Territory. Nonetheless, he was permitted to remain in Mississippi and to maintain ownership of his lands (Foreman 1934, 26). Other tribal leaders received favorable land allocations and monetary payments in exchange for signing treaties that bound their nations to opposite fates.

From the perspective of the United States, treaty making is a power of the executive branch of government subject to Senate ratification. Federal agents were sometimes sent out into Indian country to negotiate treaties. At other times, tribal representatives went to Washington, D.C., or other destinations outside their home territories to negotiate.

From the tribal perspective, the authority of individuals or groups within the tribe to participate in negotiations varied. In several instances, the individuals recognized by the federal government as having the power to sign treaties were not the individuals who had the right to speak on behalf of the tribes. As a result, many tribal communities have not recognized certain treaties that the United States has ratified and implemented. The federal government has sometimes declared individual Indians chiefs for the purpose of obtaining signatures, regardless of whether the individuals were recognized by the tribes as the official leaders. The United States continued this practice well into the 1960s by appointing tribal leaders for purposes of securing signatures on leases and other legal documents. In these instances, the federally appointed "chiefs" were not popularly elected by the tribal communities.

Some tribes had treaty councils or treaty delegations that were clearly sanctioned by the tribal people as spokespersons. The Chickasaw Nation, in the 1890s, issued official notarized certificates from the tribal government to individuals who were official delegates to Washington (Viola 1995, 81). These individuals had the right to negotiate on behalf of the people and the ability to enter into treaties and bind the people they represented. But unlike their federal counterparts, many of those who had the apparent authority to negotiate treaties were limited in terms of the subject matter they could concede and were limited in their powers.

Some tribes had elaborate property law schemes of their own and would freely engage in land cessions and land trades. Contrary to some historical accounts, it was not a foreign concept to some tribes to purchase or exchange lands. Many of the tribes in Indian Territory in the late 1800s maintained elaborate property journals as a matter of official tribal government records. These journals are similar to the current county land records in which are recorded deeds and various types of land transactions, such as leases, easements, and land sales transactions. In these tribes, individual citizens could own the surface of the land and were free to alienate those lands to other tribal citizens. The underlying estate, however, was owned by the tribe to preserve the contiguous land base and protect territorial sovereignty from outside encroachment.

Other tribes viewed land as a sacred object that could not be traded, sold, or otherwise negotiated. On this philosophy, the Lakota people have refused to accept money judgments due to them from federal court decisions in which they prevailed on staking claims. They view return of the land as the only solution. Tribes that embraced this philosophy historically would not have conveyed their lands to the United States through treaties. For such tribes, the authority of the tribal leaders would have been limited to other subject areas in diplomacy. Those tribal leaders might have possessed delegated authority from their people to speak and negotiate with other sovereigns in matters of trade, war and peace, and political relationships, but they likely would have lacked the authority to convey real property.

Other tribes did not believe that a small group of people had the authority to represent the full body politic of the tribe and instead required the approval of general councils before decisions could be made. For instance, some treaties had provisions that affirmatively required subsequent amendments to the treaty to be submitted to a popular vote of the tribal people. A single delegate would not have had the authority to bind the tribe to treaty amendments (Treaty with the Kiowa and Comanche of 1867; *Lone Wolf v. Hitchcock*, 187 U.S. 553 1903). Still other tribes were required to consult particular groups of community constituents, such as elders or women, before a final decision or deal could be completed (Berger 2004, 105).

The Treaty as a Negotiation Process

In the early days of treaty making with Europeans and then with the Americans, the process of treaty negotiation was of more importance to the tribes than the legal document that followed. The tribal representatives tended to place more importance on the discussions between the negotiators, the context that brought the parties together, the fellowship and interaction between the people involved, and the oral representations and positive assurances made by the parties (Sullivan 2004, 684–686).

Following the negotiations, the federal representatives would typically create a written document that constituted the agreement of the parties. Given the fact that few tribal representatives spoke English—the written language used in most Indian treaties—it was the spirit of the negotiations that were important to tribal communities, not the piece of paper that followed. Tribal leaders who could not read or write English routinely placed their marks in the form of an X on the treaty document to register assent to the terms of the document, despite the fact that they were relying on oral promises rather than on an independent review of the treaty text. Promises and affirmations that were made during the negotiations were as binding, from the Native perspective, as the document that followed.

Therefore, tribes that later sought compliance with oral promises of negotiations were disenchanted with the non-Indians' strict reliance on the words of the final, written version of the treaty. From the Native perspective, the spirit of the treaty should prevail over the treaty document itself. The spirit of the treaty was the crux of the promises made in good-faith negotiations and not the technical interpretation of words on paper.

The federal courts, when first reviewing the treaties in legal proceedings, tended to agree that the negotiations and historical context were important in addition to the treaty text. The federal courts adopted a set of interpretive rules, to be applied in treaty cases, that give accord to the Native perspective of treaty making. These interpretive rules, known as the canons of Indian treaty construction, have been the basis for tribal legal victories for treaty enforcement. The canons require that Indian treaties and agreements be liberally construed in favor of the Indians. The canons require that the treaty be interpreted not literally but as the tribe would have understood the treaty at the time the agreement was made. In essence, the federal courts that have applied the canons of Indian treaty construction give life to the spirit of the treaty rather than relying solely on a strict interpretation of the text (Wilkinson and Volkman 1975, 623–634).

Although the federal courts began developing these canons in the 1830s with the legal opinions of Justice Marshall, the canons have been applied recently to take into account the Native perspective and the negotiations themselves. In a U.S. Supreme Court case, *Minnesota v. Mille Lacs Band of Chippewa Indians*, various treaties with the Chippewas (Ojibwes) were interpreted to preserve the right of certain tribes to hunt, fish, and gather in lands that were otherwise ceded to the United States. Relying on the canons, the Court concluded that the tribal rights survived despite the fact that, in the treaty, the Chippewas agreed to "fully and entirely relinquish and convey to the United States, any and all right, title, and interest, of whatsoever nature the same may be, which they may now have in, and to any other lands in the Territory of Minnesota or elsewhere" (*Minnesota v. Mille Lacs Band of Chippewa Indians*, 526 U.S. 172 1999).

Strictly interpreted, the treaty language could be viewed as a full cession of all rights to the land. The Court, however, went beyond the written words in the treaty and considered the larger context, giving weight to the tribe's perspective. The tribe would not have understood, at that time, that they were giving up their right to hunt and fish. The case involved several treaties with Chippewa Indians in the Great Lakes region: the Treaty with the Chippewa—October 4, 1842; the Treaty with the Chippewa—August 2, 1847; and the Treaty with the Chippewa—September 30, 1854.

The Force and Effect of Treaties

Many of the guarantees in Indian treaties are promises that were intended in perpetuity. They are typically not limited by time. The Treaty with the Choctaw, 1830, contains language typical of the time period to indicate that the treaty was final and that no further territorial incursions would occur: "The Government and people of the United States are hereby obliged to secure to the said Choctaw Nation of Red People the jurisdiction and government of all the persons and property that may be within their limits west, so that no Territory or State shall ever have a right to pass laws for the government of the Choctaw Nation of Red People and their descendants; and that no part of the land granted them shall ever be embraced in any Territory or State" (Ibid. at Article 4).

Despite the permanent language in the treaties that suggests the treaties will live on forever, the United States has failed to comply with most treaties, at least in part. History tells us that the United States always breaks treaties but that Indians believed that a treaty was sacred and could not be broken. This story is far too simplistic. Context and circumstances change for tribes just as they change for sovereigns the world over. And, although the federal government's history of unilaterally breaking treaties is well documented, changing tribal circumstances and reversals of tribal diplomatic decisions should also be noted. Tribes, too, have abrogated treaties unilaterally.

As previously noted, some tribes entered into treaties with competing factions in order to secure a favorable stance with the victor of a foreign war. During the American Revolution, tribes entered into treaties of alliance with both Great Britain and the colonies. Allegiances change, and treaties are renegotiated. During the American Civil War, tribes with long histories of relations with the federal government entered into treaties with the Confederacy.

Conclusion

The treaty-making process between the United States and Indian tribes has evolved over the centuries and continues today in various forms. The most important legacy of Indian treaties is the legal framework they created. American Indian tribes are governments that have negotiated with other sovereigns in an array of political contexts. Modern tribal governments are the outgrowth of indigenous nations with centuries of experience in diplomacy both internationally and domestically.

Stacy Leeds

Further Reading

Berger, Bethany R. 2004. "Indian Policy and the Imagined Indian Woman." *Kansas Journal of Law and Public Policy* 14, 103.

Brann, Amy C. 2003. "Comment, Karuk Tribe of California v. United States: The Courts Need a History Lesson." *New England Law Review* 37, 743.

Case, David S., and David A. Voluck. 1978. *Alaska Natives and American Law*. Fairbanks: University of Alaska Press.

Clark, Blue. 1999. *Lone Wolf v. Hitchcock: Treaty Rights and Indian Law at the End of the Nineteenth Century*. Lincoln: University of Nebraska Press.

Debo, Angie. 1970. *A History of the Indians of the United States*. Norman: University of Oklahoma Press.

Deloria, P. S., and Robert Laurence. 1994. "Negotiating Tribal-State Full Faith and Credit Agreements: The Topology of the Negotiation and the Merits of the Question." *Georgia Law Review* 28, 365.

Deloria, Vine, Jr., and Raymond J. DeMallie. 1999. *Documents of American Indian Diplomacy: Treaties, Agreements, and Conventions, 1775–1979*, vol. 1. Norman: University of Oklahoma Press.

Fletcher, Matthew L. M. 2004. "The Power to Tax, the Power to Destroy, and the Michigan Tribal-State Tax Agreements." *University of Detroit Mercy Law Review* 82, 1.

Foreman, Grant. 1934. *The Five Civilized Tribes: Cherokee, Chickasaw, Creek, Seminole*. Norman: University of Oklahoma Press.

Kappler, Charles J., ed. 1975. *Indian Treaties 1778–1883*. New York: Interland Press.

Leeds, Stacy. 2005. "By Eminent Domain or Some Other Name: A Tribal Perspective on Taking Land." *Tulsa Law Review* 41, 51.

Monette, Richard A. 1994. "A New Federalism for Indian Tribes: The Relationship between the United States and Tribes in Light of Our Federalism and Republican Democracy." *University of Toledo Law Review* 25, 617.

Pommersheim, Frank. 1995. *Braid of Feathers: American Indian Law and Contemporary Tribal Life*. Berkeley: University of California Press.

Porter, Robert. 2004. "The Inapplicability of American Law to Indian Nations." *Iowa Law Review* 89, 1595.

Prucha, Francis Paul. 1994. *American Indian Treaties: The History of a Political Anomaly*. Berkeley: University of California Press.

Richter, Daniel K., and James H. Merrell, eds. 2003. *Beyond the Covenant Chain: The Iroquois and Their Neighbors in Indian North America 1600–1800*. University Park: Pennsylvania State University Press.

Royster, Judith V. 1995. "The Legacy of Allotment." *Arizona State Law Journal* 27, 1.

Sullivan, Julie E. 2004. "Legal Analysis of the Treaty Violations That Resulted in the Nez Perce War of 1877." *Idaho Law Review* 40, 657.

Viola, Herman J. 1995. *Diplomats in Buckskin: A History of Indian Delegations in Washington City*. Norman: University of Oklahoma Press.

Wilkinson, Charles, and John M. Volkman. 1975. "Judicial Review of Indian Treaty Abrogation: 'As Long as the Water Flows, or the Grass Grows Upon the Earth—How Long a Time Is That?'" *California Law Review* 63, 601.

Williams, Robert A., Jr. 1996. "'The People of the States Where They Are Found Are Often Their Deadliest Enemies,' The Indian Side of the Story of Indian Rights and Federalism." *Arizona Law Review* 38, 981.

Indian Treaties as International Agreements

Communities of peoples have negotiated agreements with one another for thousands of years. Treaties dating from Babylonian, Assyrian, and Hittite times still exist, written in cuneiform on clay tablets and laying out terms of peace, land exchange, and trade. First applied to the negotiation process rather than to the document, the term *treaty* ultimately came to mean an agreement made by the highest authority, or sovereign, as opposed to sponsions and other agreements made without the full commission of the sovereign (Grotius 1925, 391). The current understanding of treaties, as documents negotiated to establish relations among states and as a primary source of international law, developed as Europe moved from the Middle Ages to the Renaissance.

In the 15th century, the Catholic Church, despite its history of corruption and schisms, retained its preeminent power as the religious and secular European authority. The pope, considered God's representative, possessed the authority to crown and dispose of secular rulers, to settle disputes, to excommunicate individuals from the body of the Church and from everlasting salvation, and to bestow legitimacy on new ideas and fields of knowledge or declare them heretical. Three hundred years later, technological advancements, discoveries of new lands and resources, and the rise of the nation-state had severely undermined the authority of the Catholic Church.

The introduction of multiple masts and sails and construction of the caravel (a small, three-masted ship) allowed European rulers to expand their trade and commerce and to sail to new parts of the world, where they found lands of untold resources, sizes, and possibilities. Johannes Gutenberg's invention of movable type around 1450 opened education and knowledge to those beyond the Church. The adoption of gunpowder from China between 1500 and 1600 created a military revolution, allowing European rulers the means to solidify and expand their control over their lands in continental Europe and in the newfound territories.

All these technological improvements assisted the Portuguese and the Spanish in their rediscovery of Africa and the Western Hemisphere. In 1420,

The idea of Indian peace treaties dating back to the 16th century with European nations is similar under international law to the Egyptian-Hittite peace treaty (Treaty of Kadesh) made in about 1259 BC. (tunart/iStock/Getty Images Plus)

under the direction of Prince Henry the Navigator, the Portuguese reached the Madeira Islands and ushered in the European age of exploration. Seven years later, Portuguese explorers had reached the Azores; in 1456, the Cape Verde Islands.

Four years before Bartolomeu Dias sailed around the southernmost tip of Africa in 1488, King John of Portugal had declined to support Christopher Columbus's proposal to sail eastward. Acquiring the support of Queen Isabella of Spain, Columbus rediscovered the Western Hemisphere in 1492. To avoid conflict with Portugal, Queen Isabella requested that Pope Alexander VI divide these newly discovered oceans and lands between the two nations. In 1494, Pope Alexander VI, following negotiations between King John II and Queen Isabella, issued the Treaty of Tordesillas of 1494, dividing the earth by drawing a demarcation line 370 leagues west of the Cape Verde Islands.

As the wealth from these new lands swelled the Spanish and Portuguese coffers, the French and English explorers, disputing the pope's authority to divide the earth, sent their own explorers to claim new lands. Papal authority came under decided political attack in 1576 when the French jurist and natural law philosopher Jean Bodin published *Six Books of the Commonwealth*. Contained within these essays was the new philosophical concept of sovereignty. Sovereignty, Bodin argued, was the existence of a unified authority in a political community. As the sovereign, the French king held absolute and perpetual power within the French state (Bodin 1576). The monarch derived this total authority to govern from God, not from the pope. As sovereign, the king possessed the authority to make laws binding on its subjects, to declare war and peace, to establish state offices, and to act as the final court of redress.

As the political, economic, and military powers of the developing European nation-states grew and the pope's authority declined, monarchs recognized the need to regulate their interactions through the development of binding international legal principles and documents, which bore an assortment of names, including *treaty*, *agreement*, *act*, *statute*, and *covenant*, among many others. By 1739, Jean Barbeyrac had listed 60 subjects of treaties. A reference in the 1427 British Rolls of Parliament is the first known European use of the term *treaty* (Meyers 1957, 579). Approximately a quarter century later, the printing of papal bulls in 1461 is recorded as the first publication of an international document. The first collection of treaties was published in 1643, five years before the negotiation of the Treaty of Westphalia, identified by many scholars as the first modern treaty leading to the development of modern international relations (Liverani 1980, 50).

International law at this time had no prescribed procedure or format for treaty making. As long as the appropriate sovereign authority had approved the negotiations and provisions, the agreement constituted a treaty, whether written or oral. In 1758, Emmerich de Vattel, a Swiss jurist, published the *Law of Nations*, considered the first textbook on international law. In the *Law of Nations*, Vattel defined a treaty as "a compact entered into by sovereigns for the welfare of the State either in perpetuity or for a considerable length of time" (Vattel 1916, 160). The highest state authority could only enter into treaties (Ibid., 160). In Sections 220–221, Vattel emphasized the principle that became a fundamental rule of international law, *pacta sunt servanda*, that treaties are "sacred" and must be kept. States that violate "the faith of treaties"—a faith that is sacred—violates the law of nations. Treaties, the European theorists agreed, created international norms that are binding and inviolable.

Treaty Negotiation between European Powers and Indian Nations

The Spanish monarchs, who were highly religious as well as legalistic, held innumerable discussions and councils to determine the proper treatment of these newly

The arrival of Christopher Columbus in the New World led to European nations initially competing for trade with Indians. Spain, France, England, and the Netherlands negotiated treaties with Indian leaders. Some were oral agreements. The Dutch made several treaties, Spain and France made more than a dozen, the British colonies negotiated more than 70 treaties, and the Russians made at least one Indian treaty. (Library of Congress)

discovered inhabitants and their lands. Laws were published and revised, and conquests stopped for various periods as the most highly regarded intellectuals of the Spanish realm debated any number of issues. Were these Natives a natural part or a new branch of animals or humanity? Did their nature as heathens allow the Spanish to enslave them, to take their lands, to make war and conquer them, and to forcibly convert them to Christianity?

Spanish laws and policies toward the Native inhabitants and their lands initially allowed the unspeakable annihilation of Native communities and confiscation of their lands and resources. Theologians such as Bartolomé de Las Casas, Francisco Suárez, and Francisco de Vitoria (the latter two known as among the first proponents of international law) vociferously argued against Spanish policies in the Western Hemisphere, raising questions and putting forth principles relating to just war, the proper means of obtaining title to inhabited lands, statehood, and the just treatment of peoples. Often referred to as the father of human rights, Vitoria argued that the proper mode for relating to the Native inhabitants was through negotiations and treaties. Only if the Native inhabitants refused to conclude treaties establishing a relationship with Spain could the Spanish legally and morally go to war. Slowly but eventually, Spanish laws in theory (but not always in practice) reflected the ideas and principles espoused by these thinkers.

As explorers and settlers traveled to the Western Hemisphere, increasing the competition among the European powers, rulers directed their representatives to negotiate with the Indian nations for access to land, resources, and trade and to form military alliances. As suggested by Vitoria, the negotiation of treaties proved the most effective procedure for accomplishing these objectives. The total number of treaties concluded by Spain and the other European nations with the Indian nations is unknown. Many early treaties were oral, their existence known only through descriptions written at the time of the councils and the subsequent agreements. Over time, European representatives, needing to prove the existence of these agreements to their competitors, formalized the agreements in written form. Many of these documents have disappeared or remain hidden in state and personal archives and personal collections throughout the world.

As discussed next, European states in general regarded the treaties concluded with the Indian powers as equal to and as legally binding as the treaties they concluded with one another. Vattel also addressed this issue in *Law of Nations*, stating that "faith of treaties has no relation to the difference of religion, and cannot in any manner depend upon it." As for treaties concluded with infidels, Vattel, citing Grotius, states that only natural laws and not spiritual law were to govern the "Rule of treaties of Nations" (Ibid., 162). Grotius, too, had earlier referred to this issue, pointing out that treaties made between equal sovereigns and those made between unequal sovereigns differed in subject matter, not validity. Treaties between equal sovereigns generally dealt with the return of captives, the restoration of property, commerce arrangements, and mutual assistance. Treaties between strong and weak heads of states, in which an impairment of sovereignty resulted, discussed indemnities, withdrawal from territory, and the surrender of fortresses.

Treaty making, no matter the time or culture, involves a negotiation process followed by a symbolic acceptance of the agreed-upon terms. As did most societies, the Indian nations of North, Central, and South America possessed their own traditional forms of negotiating agreements, resolving disputes, and ending wars. Vine Deloria, Jr. and Raymond J. DeMallie, in their important two-volume work, *Documents of American Indian Diplomacy: Treaties, Agreements, and Conventions, 1775–1979*, describe two of these procedures. The Indian nations in the Great Lakes area solidified their agreements with the exchange of wampum and gifts. Other Indian nations employed special and sacred ceremonies that, once performed, signified the end of hostilities and the restoration of mutual peace. Among the Sioux people, the sacred pipe ceremony restored peace among enemies. Deloria and

DeMallie (1999) also provide a general overview of Indian treaty-making procedures. No matter the tribe's particular negotiation procedure or the ultimate symbol of acceptance, the tribal parties, like the Western world, regarded the negotiations and ensuing agreements as binding.

Although the Native and the Western worlds both regarded their negotiated agreements as legitimate and valid, Deloria and DeMallie (1999) point out a subtle but important distinction between the two cultures in their understanding, approach, and ultimate responsibility to these agreements. Among Native communities, agreements—especially those ending a state of conflict—represented a sacred commitment by each side to alter their relationship with one another. The agreement to establish peace was a decision to actively create "a distinct state of being." It was not, as understood in Western society, simply an agreement to desist from certain practices that caused conflict. From a cultural perspective, Indian nations understood treaties and agreements as sacred. The words, whether spoken or written, were living representations of each party's commitment to the other.

The Western approach to treaty making was of a different and far more practical magnitude. Although, as Vattel emphasized, states were bound by natural law to honor their treaty commitments—otherwise they were of little benefit—the treaty process was an efficient procedure and treaties a practical vehicle for obtaining one's objectives through give-and-take. Although they supposedly remained legally binding, the treaty procedure and document, once concluded, had fulfilled their purpose.

This differing cultural understanding of agreements further affected the two cultures' choices of negotiation procedures. Given the sanctity and totality with which many tribal peoples imbued their decisions, the agreement had to be thoroughly considered and supported. In many tribes, those given the authority to negotiate did not possess the power to ratify. Depending upon the particular tribal arrangement, decisions may have required the support of clan leaders, the approval of related bands, or full tribal consensus. This decision-making process often proved lengthy and infuriating to the Europeans and (especially later) to the Americans, who preferred to settle issues quickly and smoothly.

The Dutch negotiated one of the first known treaties in North America, with the Iroquois in 1613 (Van Loon 1968, 22–26). D'Arcy McNickle discusses an important treaty concluded between the Mohawks and Dutch in 1643 that may have played a role in the Mohawks' annihilation of the Huron Nation in 1645. France concluded many treaties with tribes, including a treaty of friendship with the Onondagas on June 2, 1622, two with the Six Nations in 1633 and 1635, and two with the Huron Nation in 1641 and 1645 (McNickle 1973, 130). The total number of pre-Revolutionary War treaties concluded by England and the colonies with the Indian nations is unknown. Benjamin Franklin published 13 treaties concluded by the Pennsylvania colony with various tribes from 1738 to 1762 (Boyd 1938). Later,

Indian Treaties as International Agreements | 27

Dutch governor Willem Kieft discusses a peace treaty with several American Indian tribes at Fort Amsterdam in 1645, ending seven years of hostilities called the Kieft War. (Library of Congress)

on Canada's behalf, Great Britain concluded 11 treaties with Indian nations living within Canadian boundaries. It is interesting to note that Canada did not receive the authority to negotiate treaties as a sovereign entity until the passage of the Statute of Westminster in 1931. Another 54 treaties concluded between the English colonies and the eastern tribes from 1677 to 1768 appear in a 1917 collection by H. DePuy (DePuy 1917). Deloria and DeMallie include information on another five treaties that England concluded with various non-Iroquoian tribes, such as the Chippewas, the Potawatomis, the Ottawas, and others, between 1777 and 1798.

The treaty of 1752 between Governor Peregrine Thomas Hopson and the Micmac Indians serves as an example of the many treaties concluded during the pre-Revolutionary War period. The treaty comprised eight articles, the first of which renewed former treaties. The second article established an alliance between the parties, and the third and fourth articles detailed the signatories' agreements on trade and hunting and fishing practices. The fifth and sixth articles stipulated the payment agreed to by the English, to the tribe in return for their negotiations. In the seventh article, the tribes agreed to assist shipwrecked mariners, and the final article provided a procedure for resolving disputes (DePuy 1917, 30).

Two years later, in October 1754 in Philadelphia, the Massachusetts, Connecticut, and Pennsylvania colonies negotiated one of their most important treaties with the Six Nations (McNickle 1973, 137). In a treaty of military alliance, the Six Nations agreed to align themselves with the English in their war against France—an alliance that may have saved England's claim to the eastern half of the United States (Ibid., 132). A final example is a multilateral treaty negotiated in 1758 among the Pennsylvania and the New Jersey colonies and the Six Nations, the Delaware, the Minisink, and other Indian tribes to settle a land dispute between New Jersey and the Minisink Indians and to cede formerly purchased lands back to the Six Nations (DePuy 1917, 44).

Spain, as mentioned earlier, concluded a number of treaties with Indian nations throughout the Western Hemisphere. Within the area that became the United States, DeMallie and Deloria list two groups of Spanish treaties negotiated with the Indian nations. The first list includes treaties reached between Spain and the southeastern Creek, Seminole, Chickasaw, Choctaw, and Cherokee Nations between 1784 and 1802. The second group covers treaties negotiated between Spain and the Comanches, the Navajos (Dinés), and the Apaches from 1786 to 1819 (Deloria and DeMallie 1999, 106–107).

The Spanish treaties with the southeastern Indian nations are particularly interesting for their insight into the Europeans' view of Indian treaties. Following British cession to Spain of its claims to Florida, the Muscogee Creek chief, Alexander McGillivray, wrote to the Spanish governor, asking that Spain accept the Creek Nation as a protectorate: If in the event of war Britain has been compelled to withdraw its protection from us, she has no right to transfer us with their former possessions to any power whatever contrary to our inclination and interest. We certainly as a free Nation have a right to choose our protector (Caughey 1938, 64–65).

Spain agreed, and in the treaty signed at Pensacola on June 1, 1784, the Creeks promised to "maintain an inviolable peace and fidelity toward Spain" and agreed to the formation of a mutual defense alliance (*American State Papers*, 279). This treaty was the first of several that Spain concluded with tribes in western Florida for military alliances and for small land cessions for the construction of Spanish forts and trading stations (Holmes 1969, 140–154).

Although the Creeks promised in the Pensacola treaty to obey the "sovereign orders" of the province's commandant, the Spanish clearly did not consider the Creeks to be stripped of the external sovereignty. In 1786, the Muscogee Creek Nation, without consulting their Spanish allies, waged war on Georgia for refusing to stop settlers from moving onto the Creek lands. The Creeks reminded their protector that the Pensacola treaty provided for a mutual alliance, and Spain contributed arms and ammunitions to the Creek's war.

Six years later, changes in the political and commercial climate persuaded the Creek Nation to sign the Treaty of New York with the newly formed United States on August 14, 1791. Though displeased, the Spanish governor conceded that he was powerless to alter the situation, as the Creeks were an independent nation and could treat with whom they pleased. In the treaty, the United States agreed to pay the Creeks for lands taken by Georgia citizens. In return, the Creeks offered friendship and accepted protection from the United States over Creek lands located with the American sphere of influence. The Creeks refused, despite U.S. objections, to relinquish Spanish protection over those Creek lands within the Spanish sphere. The Creeks also rebuffed the American offer to establish trade relations with the United States, preferring to maintain the services of the English. Article 2 of the treaty further illustrates the Creeks' decision to maintain their external independence. In this article, the Creeks agreed not to negotiate with any individual, state, or citizen of a state. They did not, however, agree to refrain from treating with other foreign nations. Two years after the Treaty of New York, the Creeks, along with the Alibamon, Choctaw, Chickasaw, and Talapuche Nations, signed another treaty with Spain to protect their boundaries against American encroachment and to provide the tribes with certain necessities. In Article 19, the tribes agreed to maintain an offensive and defensive alliance among the Chickasaw, Creek, Choctaw, Talapuche, Alibamon, and Cherokee Nations.

Mexico's independence from Spain did not end the use of treaty making as a vehicle for settling disputes among the various tribes and between the provincial and national governments, especially along the southern border areas. Annual reports of the commissioner of Indian affairs in 1872 and 1874 refer to Mexico's efforts to secure its borders by negotiating agreements with the Apaches. DeMallie and Deloria list more than 20 treaties, an estimated one-third of the treaties Mexico negotiated from 1821 to 1850, with Indian nations currently found within the U.S. boundaries. Even Russia, which settled only briefly in the continental United States, signed a treaty in 1817 with the Pomo Indians, located north of present-day San Francisco.

Early American Treaties with the Indian Nations

As the outbreak of war appeared imminent, England and the new revolutionary government engaged in a flurry of negotiations with the Indian nations, each seeking military allies or, at minimum, Indian neutrality in the war. Not surprisingly, the new American government, operating under the Articles of Confederation, adopted the English procedure of negotiating with the Indian nations through treaties. This tradition, in fact, directly affected the colonies' agreement over the treaty-making power in Article IX of the Articles of Confederation. Fearful that the new Congress would negotiate unfavorable treaties concerning land cessions, southern representatives to the Constitutional Convention insisted that all treaties required the support of nine states for approval.

The new government concluded its first treaty in 1778, with the Delaware Nation. Differing little in subject and tone from treaties later concluded with European nations, the United States promised peace and friendship with the Delaware Nation, established trade between the two nations, and instituted a procedure for punishing transgressors. Of particular interest was Article 6, which guaranteed that, if the Delawares, in concert with other tribes, wished to form a state within the Union, the Delawares would be appointed leaders of the congressional delegation. Of further importance was the treaty's forthright response to British charges that the United States planned to seize Indian lands illegally and violate its promises to honor prior treaties: "Whereas, the enemies of the United States have endeavored by every artifice in their power, to possess the Indians . . . with an opinion, that it is the design of the States to extirpate the Indians and take possession of their country; to obviate such false suggestions, the United States do engage or guarantee to the aforesaid nation of Delawares, and their heirs, all their territorial rights, in the most fullest and most ample manner, as it hath been bounded by former treaties" (*Article Six*, 1975, 4).

The success of the United States in negotiating with the Delawares was significant, for most eastern tribes, having found their dealings with the colonists less than honorable, aligned with the British. The Americans did succeed in obtaining the support of the Oneida and the Tuscarora Nations—an alliance that effectively split the Iroquois Confederacy and at least reduced, if not ensured, the time frame to American victory.

By the late 1780s, Congress had recognized the failure of the Articles of Confederation as a governing document. In 1789, the states ratified the Constitution, establishing a stronger central government with control over a federal system. Article II, Section 2, clause 2 granted to the president "the Power, by and with the Advice and Consent of the Senate, to make Treaties, provided two thirds of the Senators present concur." On May 25, 1789, President George Washington directed Secretary of War Henry Knox to deliver two treaties to the Senate for its first action of advice and consent. President of the Senate John Adams received in Knox's package two treaties that the Continental Congress had negotiated with Indian nations at Fort Harmar. On June 12, the Senate selected a three-member committee to consider these treaties. On September 8, the *Senate Executive Journals* noted that the Senate had adopted a resolution advising the president "to execute and enjoin an observance of" one of the two treaties, the treaty with the Wyandots and other Indian nations.

After receiving the Senate's approval, President Washington sent another communication to the Senate, asking the Senate to clarify whether Indian treaties required Senate approval: "The treaties with certain Indian Nations, which were laid before you with my message of the 25th of May last, suggested two questions to my mind, viz: 1st, Whether those treaties were to be considered as perfected, and, consequently as obligatory, without being ratified. If not, then 2ndly, whether both, or either, and which of them, ought to be ratified?" (Ralston 1920, 15).

The Senate assigned the question to another three-member committee. The following day, the committee reported its conclusion that Indian treaties did not require

Senate approval. The full Senate rejected the recommendation and responded to Washington that the Constitution required Senate ratification of all treaties negotiated with Indians. For the next three years, representatives and government officials remained at odds over the Constitution's intent regarding the extent and form of the Senate's advice prior and during the negotiation process. To Washington's dismay, during the first few years the senators took it upon themselves to play an integral role in the negotiation process. In 1794, the Senate issued its first refusal to consent to a treaty transmitted from the executive branch. This "first" also involved an Indian treaty—a treaty that the executive branch had concluded with the Illinois and Wabash nations without advance Senate involvement. It is unclear whether the Senate's refusal to consent to the treaty arose from their objections to the treaty's terms or from their lack of prior involvement.

The United States adopted similar procedures whether negotiating with European powers or the Indian nations. International law requires that a valid treaty must be negotiated on the authority of the highest sovereign. Every nation has developed its own diplomatic procedures and documentation to ensure the negotiation authority of other parties. In 1786, Congress authorized the War Department to manage Indian relations. The executive branch continued this procedure under the new Constitution, placing the Indian Office (the precursor of the Bureau of Indian Affairs) under the authority of the War Department. From 1824 until the creation of the Department of the Interior in 1849, the Department of War regulated Congress's relationship with the Indian nations. Once the president or Congress requested the negotiation of a treaty and Congress appropriated the necessary funds, the secretary of war issued a document or commission to the negotiators outlining the government's objectives for the treaty. Whether the government's interest lay in land cessions, trade, alliances, or other matters, these documents provided general instructions concerning the promises made and the funding allowed.

Over time, the treaties concluded by the United States with the Indian nations became increasingly formal and legalistic, using the style and form and covering the subject matter common to all treaties of the time. Indian treaties, written in the same lofty language, were divided into preamble, body, and salutation. The treaty concluded between the United States and the Creek Nation in 1790 at New York opens with the following preamble:

> The parties being desirous of establishing permanent peace and friendship between the United States and the said Creek Nation, and the citizens and members thereof, and to remove the causes of war by ascertaining their limits, and making other necessary, just and friendly arrangements: the President of the United States, Secretary for the Department of War, whom he hath constituted with full powers for these purposes, by and with the advice and consent of the Senate of the United States and the Creek Nation, by the undersigned

kings, chiefs and warriors, representing the said nation, have agreed to the following articles: . . .

The salutation reads, "In witness of all and whole Creek nation, the parties have hereunto set their hands and seals, in the City of New York, with the United States, this seventh day of August, one thousand seven hundred and ninety," after which each participant affixed his signature.

In keeping with Grotius's (1925) discussion of international treaties, Indian treaties dealt with the fixing of boundaries (Treaty of January 21, 1785; Treaty of November 28, 1785; Treaty of August 19, 1825), the promise of mutual assistance (Treaty of January 9, 1789; Treaty of July 22, 1814), the exchange of prisoners and hostages (Treaty of October 22, 1784; Treaty of January 21, 1785; Treaty of November 28, 1785), and the establishment of garrisons and forts (Treaty of June 16, 1802; Treaty of November 10, 1808). Also included as subjects of negotiations, were provisions on passports (Treaty of July 2, 1791; Treaty of August 7, 1790), extradition (Treaty of July 2, 1791; Treaty of March 12, 1858; Treaty of June 19, 1859), white immigration onto Indian lands (Treaty of May 24, 1835; Treaty of March 6, 1861), and the right to declare war and conclude treaties with third powers (Treaty of August 24, 1835; Treaty of May 26, 1837).

The new government's decision to entrust the State Department to maintain copies of Indian treaties among their files of other international agreements further illustrates that the United States regarded Indian treaties as international agreements. Listed first in State Department records is a treaty in 1722 between the Six Nations and New York and Pennsylvania. In 1837, the State Department commissioned Samuel D. Langtree and John Louis O'Sullivan to publish the Indian treaties concluded between 1789 and 1813.

Further evidence exists that, in addition to using international treaty standards of procedure, form, and tone in negotiating Indian treaties, the United States regarded Indian treaties as having an international impact on its domestic and foreign policy decisions. As noted earlier, Indian treaties determined the structure of treaty making under the Articles of Confederation. Indian treaties constituted the first set of treaties delivered to the Senate and rejected by the Senate under the new Constitution. The precedent for obtaining Indian lands through treaties ultimately allayed concerns that President Thomas Jefferson had overstepped his executive authority in concluding a treaty with France for the Louisiana Purchase in 1803. The necessity to subject Indian treaties to the same international legal standards as all treaties also affected U.S. foreign policy decisions. In 1795, England expressed concern to the United States that an American treaty signed that year with several Indian nations had abrogated part of the Jay Treaty of 1794 negotiated between England and the United States the previous year.

The Treaty of Peace ending the American war of independence had left several outstanding issues. Until France's declaration of war on England in 1792, another war appeared imminent between England and the United States. Now anxious to neutralize American involvement in this war, England agreed to sign the Treaty of Amity, Commerce, and Navigation, referred to as the Jay Treaty, with the United States in November 1794. This treaty resolved several key conflicts between the two nations by creating a joint commission to settle boundary disputes, reestablishing American trade with the West Indies, providing for British withdrawal from forts in the Old Northwest, and reaffirming the rights of Indian nations vis-à-vis the new American boundary.

The Indian nations had fought alongside the British in the war as their equals and were incensed at their exclusion from the Treaty of Peace negotiations. Joseph Brant, sachem (the Iroquois called their leaders *sachems*) of the Mohawks, in particular voiced his opposition to the treaty, pointing out that King George had given his personal guarantee that the British would protect the Mohawks' aboriginal lands in New York State and Canada. Anxious to reduce their allies' concerns, in Article 3 of the Jay Treaty the British negotiated an agreement that the Indian nations could freely travel and trade goods across the new border.

The following year, the U.S. government concluded a treaty with several Indian nations, including, among others, the Wyandots, the Miamis, the Delawares, the Shawnees, and the Chippewas. During this period, the relations that traders established with the Indian nations often determined and symbolized the tribes' relationship with Americans.

Given that the United States possessed no jurisdiction over Indian lands, the U.S. government had no control over traders admitted onto Indian lands. In an effort to control traders and commerce with Indian nations, the government included, as a point of negotiation with tribes, an article that requested tribes to admit only those traders who had obtained the proper license from the U.S. government. Upon hearing of this treaty stipulation, Great Britain expressed concern that this provision violated Article 3 of the Jay Treaty. The following year, the United States agreed to negotiate an explanatory note, a document recognized under international law as having the status of a binding treaty, reaffirming the stipulations of the Jay Treaty by stating that the treaty concluded with the tribes at Greenville, August 3, 1795, "can not be understood to derogate in any manner from the rights of free intercourse and commerce, secured by the third article" (*Respecting the Liberty* 1974).

The U.S. recognition of the international legitimacy of the treaties concluded between the Indian nations and other European powers is further illustrated in Article 6 of the 1803 treaty concluded between the United States and France for the Louisiana Cession: "The United States promise to secure Such Treaties and articles as may have been agreed between Spain and the tribes and nations of Indians until by mutual consent of the United States and the said tribes or nations other Suitable articles Shall have been agreed upon" (Treaty with France 1803).

Mohawk leader Joseph Brant, also known as Thayendanegea, led Iroquois warriors to support the British in the American Revolution. Brant also played a role in the Northwest Indian victories against the United States in the early 1790s to stop settlers from advancing into the Ohio region. (National Archives)

The Treaty of Peace of 1776, the Jay Treaty of 1794, and the Explanatory Note of 1796 did not end the competition and suspicion between the United States and England. By 1812, war had again broken out between the two powers, and again both sides sought the alliances of the Indian nations. The great Shawnee chief Tecumseh clearly foresaw the danger that the United States posed to Indian people and worked tirelessly to create a confederacy of tribes from Canada to Florida to fight with the British. A brigadier general in the British army, Tecumseh expressed disgust upon hearing of Britain's capitulation to the Americans two years later.

At the peace negotiations concluding the war, England sought recognition from the United States of an independent Indian buffer state. In a treatise written before the negotiations, Nathaniel Atcheson laid out nine points on which Great Britain should negotiate the treaty, emphasizing that the Indian nations were "independent both of us and of the Americans" and that their independence should be secured. Three of the nine points dealt with the status and security of the Indian nations: a new boundary line for the Indian Territory; that the Americans not be allowed to erect forts, military posts, or other public property in Indian Territory; and that Great Britain guarantee the boundaries of the Indian state (Atcheson 1814).

For months, negotiations stalled over the Americans' refusal to recognize an Indian buffer state. The British finally relented upon the agreement of the United States in Article 9 to restore tribal rights to the 1811 status quo. After ratification of the Treaty of Ghent, ending the War of 1812, both the United States and England negotiated new treaties with their former Indian enemies during the war, restoring recognition of tribal rights to their prewar status. The War of 1812 ended the Indian nations' ability to serve as a master player in the international intrigues of the East. With the East in firm control, the United States turned its attention to the Mexico Gulf and Florida region, where General Andrew Jackson fought against the English, the Spanish, and their military allies, the Muscogee Creek Confederacy, for final control of the region.

From the British, the United States had inherited the right to talk with and secure lands from the Indian nations of the Old Northwest. Over the next several decades, U.S. forces solidified their control of this area by negotiating with the tribes in groups, pairs, and individually. By the late 1820s, the public clamor, especially from the southern states, to move all eastern tribes to lands west of the Mississippi had become an important political platform for presidential hopeful Andrew Jackson. A few of the southern states, such as Georgia, had passed state laws assuming jurisdictional control over tribally held lands. Now president, Jackson introduced legislation in Congress giving the tribes the choice to move west or stay in the South and submit to the state laws. The tribes and their supporters loudly protested passage of this removal bill, pointing out that the United States possessed no jurisdiction over the Indian nations and that such legislation violated previous treaties and laws recognizing Indian sovereignty and title to their lands.

Well known among European powers as an American leader with little integrity in warfare and even less honor in upholding promises, Jackson had no use for the niceties of law, whether domestic or international. Jackson's philosophy was based entirely on necessity; whatever was necessary to expand the glory of the American republic was just. Congress passed the removal bill by a mere five votes.

The Cherokee Nation responded to the bill's passage by filing an injunction before the U.S. Supreme Court as a foreign nation. As a foreign state, the tribe's attorney, former U.S. attorney general William Wirt, argued that the State of Georgia possessed no authority to execute "certain laws [that] . . . go directly to annihilate the Cherokees as a political society and to seize for the use of Georgia the lands of the nation which have been assured to them by the United States in solemn treaties" (*Cherokee* 1831). The Cherokees, Wirt stated, had been sovereigns from time immemorial, "acknowledging no earthly superior."

The *Cherokee Nation v. Georgia* case proved especially inconvenient for John Marshall. A political opponent of Andrew Jackson, Marshall fully realized that Jackson would ignore any Supreme Court decision that contravened his political agenda (*Cherokee* 1831). For a president to ignore a Supreme Court decision so early in the nation's history would jeopardize the Court's future role in U.S. politics, a role not well articulated by the constitutional authors. Wishing to avoid a confrontation with Jackson, Marshall sought to have the case dismissed. By cleverly employing domestic law to answer questions of international law and manipulating the very meaning of treaties, Marshall ruled that the Cherokees had no standing to bring the case directly to the Supreme Court as a foreign nation. The treaties signed between the Cherokee Nation and the United States, Marshall argued, had placed the Cherokees under the protection of the United States. Through this action, Marshall concluded, the Cherokees had given up their foreign status and had become "domestic, dependent nations."

Domestic Dependent Nation

The phrase *domestic dependent nation* refers to the political and legal relationship of tribes to the federal government and state governments. Essentially, it means that tribes are governments, separate from local, state, and federal governments, with the power to pass laws, create court and penal systems, levy taxes, and engage in other traditional governmental functions. However, because tribes are within the boundary of the United States and dependent on the United States for protection, they no longer exercise complete sovereignty as they did before their first contact with Europeans. Instead, the United States has limited tribal sovereignty in significant ways, including prohibiting tribes from freely selling the land they occupy on reservations and from entering into treaties with foreign nations.

Tribes were first characterized as domestic dependent nations in 1831 by Chief Justice John Marshall in the Supreme Court case *Cherokee Nation v. Georgia*. In *Cherokee Nation*, Marshall determined that tribal nations were not foreign nations under the U.S. Constitution, because tribes were "completely under the sovereignty and dominion of the United States." Marshall reasoned that the relationship between Native Americans and the United States was "unlike that of any other two people in existence," because Indian Territory was geographically located within the boundaries of the United States, the United States had the power to regulate trade between foreign nations and Natives, and the tribes had conceded in various treaties that they were under the protection and management of the United States. Due to these "peculiar and cardinal distinctions," Marshall declared that "Native tribes" were domestic dependent nations and that their legal relationship to the United States was "that of a ward to his guardian."

Although the Supreme Court has found that Native tribes are not foreign nations, the Court has held that tribes do constitute "distinct, independent political communities" within the United States, retaining the original right of sovereignty that they possessed prior to the "discovery" of America by the Europeans (*Worcester v. Georgia* 1832). Tribes have the inherent power to "make their own laws and be ruled by them" (*Williams v. Lee* 1959). In order to effectuate their right to self-governance, tribes have adopted criminal and civil laws, exercised their police and taxing power, established courts and regulatory agencies, set rules for determining membership in the tribe, and negotiated state-tribal cooperative agreements.

The status of tribes as domestic dependent nations has two important consequences. First, because tribes are considered wards of the United States, the federal government has a duty to the tribes, called a trust responsibility, to protect and advance tribal interests. The Bureau of Indian Affairs (BIA), an agency of the Department of Interior, has as its primary purpose the development of federal programs, policies, and regulations that will enable the federal government to fulfill its trust responsibility to tribes.

Second, because tribes possess an inherent, preconstitutional right to self-governance, individual states cannot divest tribes of their sovereignty. Historically, the laws of the various states had no force or effect within the boundaries of a reservation, even if the state law attempted to regulate only the behavior of non-Natives (*Worcester v. Georgia* 1832). However, in modern-day jurisprudence, many state laws do apply to non-Natives who are physically present within the boundaries of a reservation. These include, among others, state tax laws, state hunting and fishing regulations, and state criminal laws, if the crime is committed by a non-Native against another non-Native. Nevertheless, state interference in tribal self-governance is still impermissible.

Kimberly Hausbeck

Further Reading

American Indian Lawyer Training Program, Inc. (AILTP). *Indian Tribes as Sovereign Governments*. Oakland, CA: American Indian Resources Institute (AIRI), 1988.

Conference of Western Attorneys General (CWAG). *American Indian Law Deskbook*, 3rd ed. Boulder: University Press of Colorado, 2004.

Deloria, Vine, Jr., and Clifford M. Lytle. *American Indians, American Justice*. Austin: University of Texas Press, 1983.

Wilkins, David E. *American Indian Sovereignty and the U.S. Supreme Court*. Austin: University of Texas Press, 1997.

In his dissent, Justice Smith Thompson refuted Marshall's analysis that the Cherokees had placed themselves under U.S. protection. By comparing the sixth article of the Treaty of Hopewell with the Cherokees in 1785 with the twenty-seventh article of the U.S. treaty with England in 1794, Thompson argued that both provisions dealt with the extradition of wanted criminals from Cherokee and English territory, respectively. "The necessity for the stipulation in both cases must be, because the process of one government and jurisdiction will not run into that of another; and separate and distinct jurisdiction . . . is what makes governments and nations foreign to each other in their political relations" (*Cherokee* 1831).

The Cherokees refused to give up. The following year, Samuel Worcester, Elizur Butler, and two other missionaries deliberately broke a Georgia law requiring a state license to live on Indian lands. Georgia officials arrested the men, who were sentenced to four years in prison at hard labor. Once again, William Wirt appeared before the Supreme Court to argue the inapplicability of Georgia's laws over Cherokee lands. This time, Wirt based his case on the argument that the Constitution granted "the regulation of intercourse with the Indians" exclusively to the federal government. The government, Wirt argued, exercised this power through treaties and congressional acts. Any attempts by states to alter or void federal law violated the Constitution.

Marshall agreed with the plaintiffs, finding the Georgia laws to be an unconstitutional interference with the treaties concluded between the United States and the Cherokees. To support his ruling, Marshall discussed the proper legal interpretation that should be accorded to Indian treaties. In analyzing the first negotiated treaty of the United States with the Delaware Nation, Marshall found that "[in] its language and in its provisions, [the treaty] is formed, as near as may be, on the model of treaties between the crowned heads of Europe." The treaties concluded by the United States with the Indian tribes in general, as Marshall pointed out, arose from the "same necessity and on the same principle" as those treaties concluded with France (*Cherokee* 1831).

The words *treaty* and *nation* are words of our own language, selected in our diplomatic and legislative proceedings, by ourselves, having each a definite and well-understood meaning. We have applied them to Indians, as we have applied them to the other nations of the earth; they are applied to all in the same sense (*Worcester* 1832).

In *Cherokee Nation*, Marshall had used Indian treaties in part to prove that Indian nations were not foreign states. In *Worcester*, he had applied international legal principles to show how Cherokee treaties proved Cherokee sovereignty and independence. Within two years, Marshall had cleverly manipulated and interpreted the role and status of Indian treaties to serve conflicting purposes—a masterful feat not lost on future generations of American judges.

The *Worcester* victory provided the tribes with no practical protection. Hoping to find a new life free of white interference, many tribes negotiated treaties with the United States to move their people west. The U.S. military forcibly "assisted" those individuals and groups who were too reluctant or too slow. The removal of the eastern tribes slowed the government's hunger for tribal lands only briefly.

Looking for new lands, the United States had attempted on more than one occasion to purchase Texas from Mexico. In 1836, Texas declared her independence from Mexico. During her nine years as an independent republic, Texas concluded 12 treaties with various indigenous tribes, including the indigenous Tonkawas, Comanches, Wichitas, and Apaches, as well as with immigrant bands from the Cherokee, Delaware, and Shawnee Nations, fleeing white encroachment of their aboriginal lands.

Congress annexed Texas in 1845 and a year later added the Oregon Territory. Victory in the Mexican War added the entire Southwest in 1848. The discovery of gold in California (1849) and Colorado (1858) brought waves of settlers across tribal lands in the west. Five years later, the Gadsden Purchase completed the present exterior boundaries of the United States. In 10 short years, the country's population increased by 32 percent and its size by 70 percent. Between 1830 and 1860, eight states and five territories were added to the Union. To open up this newly acquired territory to settlement, the government embarked on a negotiating frenzy with tribes, securing 174 million acres of land in 53 treaties with tribes between 1853 and 1857.

For a period, the Civil War interrupted the western exodus as the North fought to preserve the Union. After declaring its independence from the United States, the Confederacy quickly entered into treaty negotiations with the Indian nations in the important border regions. The politics between the Union and the Confederacy proved especially disastrous among the Indian nations referred to as the Five Civilized Tribes: the Cherokees, the Choctaws, the Chickasaws, the Creeks, and the Seminoles. In each of these tribes, a handful of tribal citizens, primarily the wealthier mixed bloods, had adopted the southern agricultural system, which required slave labor in order to be economically efficient. Casting their lot with the Confederacy, these groups seceded from their own tribal nations and established rebel governments.

To solidify their relationship, especially their military and economic contributions, the Confederacy signed approximately nine treaties with these rebel governments and several western tribes. The Confederate treaties were quite liberal in the Confederacy's recognition of tribal authority, land, and resources. In return, the rebel groups accepted the protection of the Confederacy but retained the authority to make treaties with other Indian nations.

In the meantime, the de jure tribal governments, arguing the principle of *pacta sunt servanda* (agreements must be kept), continued to support and fight for the Union, frequently in battles against their own people. After the war, the United States demanded that the Five Civilized Tribes renegotiate their treaties with the federal government. The resulting treaties, supposedly in retaliation for the tribes' treason, were actually negotiated with the southern tribal representatives, who were far more willing to grant away tribal rights and lands than were those who had fought and died for the Union.

Until the Civil War, treaty negotiations with individual tribes often followed a typical cycle. The earliest treaties dealt with peace, friendship, alliances, and land cessions. As immigrants flooded to new western frontiers that encroached on tribal lands, hostilities multiplied. To avoid costly battles, the American government pressured tribes to cede increasingly large areas of land—cessions containing lands often already sold to settlers by eastern speculators. As America's strength grew and the powers of tribes declined, treaty commissioners demanded changes in traditional negotiation and approval procedures, including prohibiting the participation of Native women and demanding that tribal councils forgo their time-consuming consensus building and provide immediate, on-site decisions. Commissioners were also not above appointing any group of Indians as tribal chiefs and investing them with the authority—that is, coercing them with alcohol—to sign treaties. Although treaties signed under duress, or without the sovereign's authority, are illegal, on only a few occasions did Congress refuse to ratify the Indian treaties placed before them. Living under corrupt agents and with little access to food, many tribes increasingly were forced to sign successive treaties that ceded more of their lands, required their children to attend manual labor schools, and allotted communally held lands to individual owners.

In still other instances, tribes negotiated treaties in good faith with U.S. representatives, only to find later that Congress had refused to ratify them or had altered their provisions without tribal approval. The most egregious example involved more than 20 treaties that the California tribes had negotiated with the federal Treaty Commission in 1851. The gold rush had started, and the government directed the Treaty Commission to treat with the Indians to secure title and access to their lands. Convinced that the remaining lands the tribes had reserved for their use also contain gold, the California representatives prevailed upon their colleagues to leave the treaties unratified. For the next 50 years, the physical location of these documents, now referred to as the "lost treaties," was unknown. Without proof of the areas they had ceded and those they had retained as reservation lands, the tribes (except for those in the northern part of the state) were left dependent upon the government to provide them with a land base.

The End of Treaty Making

Initially responsible for enforcing the treaty established boundaries between Indian and white lands, the military's role changed from defending tribal lands from the encroachment of white settlers to suppressing tribes and often evicting them from their own lands. As the western wars escalated, President Ulysses S. Grant in 1867 appointed the Peace Commission to study the situation. The commission reported that the western hostilities primarily derived from the government's refusal to keep its treaty commitments and from its repeated demands for more tribal land cessions. Other government officials, such as Commissioner of Indian Affairs Ely Parker, a Seneca, pointed to the treaty process as the root of the problem, arguing that Congress should stop making treaties with the tribes and pass legislation to civilize them and open their lands to settlement.

Except for a few remaining Plains and Southwest tribal groups, governmental policies and actions had subdued and weakened most tribes, lending some credence to the argument that tribes no longer possessed the political power to negotiate treaties as equals. Justice Department officials countered vigorously that treaty making remained an effective tool for negotiating with tribes and maintained that ending treaty making without tribal consent was both illegal and dishonorable.

Whether tribes retained the capacity to negotiate treaties was of less concern to most policy makers than was the potential control that outside interests stood to gain from a change in the treaty-making policy. Under the current system, the executive branch took the lead in negotiating treaties, leaving the Senate only with the authority to confirm or refuse the treaty. The House of Representatives, jealous of the Senate's role, was left to appropriate funds for decisions into which they had had little input. Which tribes were contacted, which lands were purchased, and which resources were acquired led to decisions that had immeasurable impact on the representatives' constituents and the economic fortunes of their districts. Once again, Indian tribes became unwitting pawns in a competitive power play among the various branches of government and officials representing competing railroad, mining, livestock, and land speculation interests, among others.

In 1871, the House of Representatives attached the following rider to an appropriations bill: "That hereafter no Indian nation or tribe within the territory of the United States shall be acknowledged or recognized as an independent nation, tribe, or power, with whom the United States may contract by treaty" (16 *Stat.* 566). Senator Eugene Casserly of California eloquently pinpointed the reason for the rider's passage:

> I know what the misfortune of the tribes is. Their misfortune is not that they are red men; not that they are semi-civilized, not that they are a dwindling race, not that they are a weak race. Their misfortune is that they hold great bodies of rich lands, which have aroused the cupidity of powerful corporations and of powerful individuals. . . . I greatly fear that the adoption of this provision to discontinue treaty making is the beginning of the end in respect to Indian lands. It is the first step in a great scheme of spoliation, in which the Indians will be plundered, corporations and individuals enriched, and the American name dishonored in history. (McNickle 1973, 208)

The amendment in 1871 did not end the federal government's negotiations with tribes for lands and other matters. In the place of treaties, the government negotiated agreements, documents that were similar to treaties in content and effect but required the approval of both congressional houses before the president's signature. By the close of the 19th century, the United States had negotiated more than 500 ratified and nonratified treaties with various Indian nations.

The end of treaty making allowed the government new freedom to legislate and establish policies and programs designed to educate and assimilate Indian people into the dominant society. Supportive of the rider and eagerly waiting in the wings to assist the government in their endeavors were the eastern reformers, philanthropists, and churches. In 1874, Congress passed a bill requiring tribal members to perform "useful labor" in return for their annuities, even though annuities represented payments for lands already ceded. The following year, in a prelude to the Dawes Act, individual Indians were encouraged to obtain land under the Homestead Act. In 1879, Congress instituted the rudiments of an Indian educational system with the establishment of the Carlisle Indian School, whose intentions were cogently summarized by the school's director in testimony before Congress: "We accept the watchword, let us by patient effort kill the Indian in him and save the man" (Gates 1885, 131).

As traditional tribal society broke down with the education of the young, the rise in power of the Indian agent, and the teaching of Christianity, the government increasingly supplanted Native practices with the Anglo system. Congress authorized Indian police forces and an Indian court of appeals. In 1885, through the passage of the Major Crimes Act, the federal government assumed jurisdiction of major crimes committed by Indians. Two years later, Congress passed the most assimilative piece of legislation to date, the Land in Severalty Act, or the Dawes Act, as it became known. Far surpassing any previous infringement on tribal life, the Dawes Act provided for the allotment of reservation lands among tribal members, with individuals receiving either 40 acres of farmland or 160 acres of grazing land. Land left after the allotment process was sold to white settlers as surplus. Within less than 20 years, Congress had moved from treating with the tribes as national entities and acknowledging their rights to their land and internal sovereignty to restructuring the tribes' internal affairs and attempting to dissolve their reservations.

Tribes were not consulted about these governmental changes and policies, and many leaders protested and lobbied strongly against their imposition. Eventually, some tribes took their complaints to the Supreme Court, asking the Court to determine on what authority the federal government justified its assumption of such widespread authority over a sovereign people. The question was not easily answered. The U.S. Constitution clearly established the federal government as a government of enumerated powers, meaning that the federal government could exercise only those powers granted by the Constitution. Heretofore, the federal government had regulated its relationships with the Indian nations primarily through the treaty process, which affirmed that each sovereign possessed exclusive authority to make and enforce its own laws in its own land. The treaties negotiated between the U.S. government and the tribes dealt with national issues of trade, land, and military alliances. With few exceptions, tribes had not given the United States the authority to enter their lands or to enforce their laws. When tribes had delegated authority to the United States, it was to improve the lives of their community. For example, Indian governments in Indian Territory had for years protested to the surrounding governments that the latter's failure to control lawlessness had caused the problem to spill into tribal lands. Tribal governments had neither the resources nor the inclination to handle what they perceived as an outside problem. Eventually, tribes gave the United States the authority to enter tribal lands in pursuit of these criminals, a fact that the courts later used to justify U.S. authority over Indian lands. For the federal government to claim individual control over Indian people would require the courts to "domesticize" the previously international legal principles that had regulated the treaty relationship between the United States and the various tribes. But, as John Marshall had illustrated, a little judicial ingenuity, creativity, and manipulations could provide the government with virtually any legal angle necessary.

The first major challenge to the U.S. assumption of authority came in the 1886 *U.S. v. Kagama* decision (*Kagama* 1886). The previous year, Congress had tacked the Major Crimes Act onto an appropriations bill. The legislation provided the federal government with the authority to assume criminal jurisdiction over Indian individuals who had committed one of seven major crimes on Indian lands. Until then, tribes had handled violations of their laws according to their own codes and processes. On what basis could the federal government claim to have this authority? Tribes had not delegated this specific authority to the federal government in any of their treaties.

The government spuriously claimed that Congress's authority to pass the Major Crimes Act fell naturally under its authority to regulate commerce with the tribes. The commerce clause, Justice Samuel F. Miller ruled, was not the source of the government's authority. The government had recognized the tribes as semi-independent, "not as States, not as nations, but as separate people, with power of regulating their internal social relations and thus not brought into the laws of the Union or of the States within whose limits they resided," Miller acknowledged; but Congress had now decided to govern the tribes through federal legislation (*Kagama* 1886, 381–382). The tribes' dependent condition warranted this change in procedure, Miller asserted. Admitting that the actions of the federal government had weakened the tribes, they were, nonetheless, now wards of the nation, and the United States had a responsibility to care for its wards. In a masterful and convoluted reinterpretation of treaty law, Miller reasoned that the source of U.S. authority to care for the tribes derived from the very treaties the tribes had negotiated with the United States. The United States had offered its protection to tribes in their treaties. Legislation such as the Major Crimes Act fulfilled this promise of protection.

To conclude that Indian treaties, which tribes had negotiated as protection against the federal government and unwanted governmental incursions, had now become the ultimate source of the government's authority over tribes, has to be one of the most tortuous reinterpretations of law yet found in American history. Marshall had stressed in *Worcester* that Indian treaties represented the government's acknowledgement and agreement to protect tribal self-government; they did not imply the destruction of the protected. After the *Kagama* decision, the protections that tribes thought they had negotiated to preserve were nonexistent.

In 1903, in the *Lone Wolf v. Hitchcock* decision, the Supreme Court indicated the extent to which the government was prepared to divest tribes of their guaranteed treaty provisions (*Lone Wolf* 1903). Article 12 of the Treaty of Medicine Lodge stipulated that Congress could not dispose of certain reservation lands without the consent of three-fourths of the adult males. Unable to secure the necessary votes, the government took the land and sold it. Lone Wolf, on behalf of himself and other members of the Kiowa, Comanche, and Apache tribes, charged the government with disposing of tribal property in violation of the Treaty of Medicine Lodge and the protections afforded by the Fifth Amendment of the U.S. Constitution.

In an unbelievable decision, the Court reasoned that the tribes had misconstrued their treaty and had overlooked their dependent status and the government's role as their guardian. To hold Congress to the treaty would limit the government's authority to care for and protect the Indians. The Court conceded that previous courts had described tribal land rights as sacred as fee simple, but these cases had involved protecting tribal lands from the states and individuals. The treaties could not constrain the federal government because of the federal government's responsibility to care for its wards. Citing an earlier case, the Court ruled that the federal government was limited only by those "considerations of justice as would control a Christian people in their treatment of an ignorant and dependent race" (*Beecher* 1877). Within less than a hundred years, the U.S. courts had legally manipulated or "domesticized" international legal principles that recognized and protected international independence, sovereignty, and treaties into domestic sources of authority that allowed the federal government unlimited control over Indian people.

Indian Treaties in the 20th Century

The United States closed the 19th century having abrogated treaties, forcibly taken Indian lands and lives, and destroyed tribal cultures through brute force and legal manipulations. Indian communities embarked on the 20th century greatly diminished in numbers, land, and resources and having experienced 100 years of war, diseases, famine, and cultural genocide. Against all odds, they had survived, bringing into the century an understanding of their identities, their nationhood, and the values their ancestors had fought to protect.

Over the next 100 years, the U.S. government continued its unrelenting attempt to convince indigenous peoples to forgo their cultures, wisdom, and communal identities by embracing and disappearing into the American maelstrom. By doing so, Indian people would become materially and socially self-sufficient, as had the millions of immigrants who had accepted American ideals. As had their ancestors before them, Indian people in large measure refused. The general U.S. population and its public officials possessed little comprehension and even less patience for this refusal, imposing assimilationist and terminationist policies on Indian people in various forms without their consent throughout the 20th century.

In the 18th and 19th centuries, the treaty process had managed the relationships of the United States with the Indian nations. In the 20th century, the very existence of Indian treaties provided an unbreachable psychological, legal, symbolic, and historical link between the United States and its indigenous peoples, between the past and the future, and between the legal and truly moral. As the preceding discussion illustrated, Congress and the courts can and have legally reinterpreted, misinterpreted, and ignored Indian treaty rights and histories to meet broader domestic policies and objectives. American constitutional law is replete with Supreme Court decisions, such as *Cherokee Nation v. Georgia*, *U.S. v. Kagama*, and *Lone Wolf v. Hitchcock*, that deftly manipulated the existence, status, and protections afforded by treaties to protect Indian nations and individuals.

As discussed previously, tribes, especially in later years, were often at a considerable disadvantage during the treaty negotiation process. Federal negotiators either purposefully or ignorantly negotiated binding agreements with individuals not authorized to represent the tribe, at times resorting to bribery or to intoxicating pliant tribal members as "chiefs." Because agreements were written in English, tribes were often totally dependent upon the facility and the honor of the individual translator. In some instances, government officials threatened to withhold rations or annuities owed by earlier treaties until the tribe agreed to the provisions of a new treaty. Other tribal leaders found themselves with the choice of agreeing to a treaty or facing the threat of war or starvation. In other instances, tribes had negotiated and upheld their agreements in good faith, only to find years later that the Senate had struck out provisions, added new ones, or refused to ratify the treaty and compensate the tribe for their land cessions. In at least 13 cases, when notified that Congress had altered the treaty, tribes rejected it upon its return for approval.

To assist in adjudicating a particularly complex legal area, the courts frequently develop a series of relevant principles or tests to guide judicial analysis. To compensate for these inequalities in the negotiation process and for the lack of precise language, and to ensure a balanced interpretation of the rights at issue, the Supreme Court has established several principles or canons of construction for use in adjudicating Indian treaty issues. The canons include these principles: that ambiguities in treaties must be resolved in favor of the tribes; that Indian treaties must be interpreted as the Indians would have understood them; that Indian treaties must be construed liberally in favor of the Indians; and that reserved rights must be explicitly extinguished by later treaties or congressional action. The following cases exemplify these standards: *Carpenter v. Shaw*, 280 U.S. 363, 367 (1930); *DeCoteau v. District Court*, 420 U.S. 425, 447 (1975); *Bryan v. Itasca County, Minnesota*, 426 U.S. 373, 392 (1976); *Jones v. Meehan*, 175 U.S. 1, 10 (1899); *U.S. v. Shoshone Tribe*, 304 U.S. 111, 116 (1938); *Choctaw Nation v. Oklahoma*, 397 U.S. 620, 631 (1970); *Tulee v. Washington*, 315 U.S. 681, 684–685 (1942); *Washington v. Washington State Commercial Passenger Fishing Vessel Ass'n*, 443 U.S. 658, 690 (1979); and *County of Oneida v. Oneida Indian Nation*, 470 U.S. 226, 247 (1985). Each tribe, tribal history, and negotiated treaty is unique, the Supreme Court emphasized in the *Minnesota v. Mille Lacs* decision (*Minnesota* 1999). The proper interpretation of a particular treaty requires an in-depth historical investigation of the era in which the tribe negotiated the treaty, including but not limited to an examination of government policy, archival records of congressional debates and treaty negotiations, and tribal oral and written histories.

Not surprisingly, a review of the Court's application of the canons of construction in Indian treaty cases over the last half century or so reveals a rather uneven and judicious use of the canons, depending upon the importance of the issue in question. During the 1970s, a time of stated congressional policy to restore tribal sovereignty and tribal governmental powers, several cases pointed to tribal treaties as proof of inherent tribal powers. In three important cases decided between 1959 and 1973, the Supreme Court ruled in favor of Navajo (Diné) sovereignty based on the protections inherent in their 1868 treaty with the United States.

In the *Williams v. Lee* case in 1959, the Court held that the Navajo treaty of 1868 protected the Navajos' authority to exercise control over internal issues—in this instance, the tribal courts' exclusive jurisdiction over a non-Indian's collection of a debt from an Indian on the reservation (*Williams* 1959). In the *Warren Trading Post v. Arizona Tax Commission* case, the treaty of 1868 also prevented the state of Arizona from collecting state taxes from non-Indians whose businesses lay within reservation boundaries (*Warren* 1965). In the *McClanahan v. Arizona State Tax Commission* case of 1973, noting that Indian sovereignty provided "a backdrop" against which to interpret Indian treaties and federal policies, the Court ruled that Arizona could not collect state taxes from Indians whose "income was derived from reservation sources" (*McClanahan* 1973).

The Supreme Court also invoked the existence and protection of Indian treaties in two of its most resounding victories for tribal sovereignty. In 1974, in *Morton v. Mancari*, the Supreme Court ruled that the Bureau of Indian Affairs policy of providing special preference for Indians did not constitute racial discrimination in violation of the Equal Employment Opportunity Act of 1964 (*Morton* 1974). Federal laws regarding Indians were passed to fulfill the government's unique political relationship with tribes. This relationship, the Court emphasized, was illustrated in part by its "history of treaties" with tribes. Four years later, in *United States v. Wheeler*, the Supreme Court considered whether the U.S. Constitution's bar against double jeopardy precluded a Navajo man's trial in federal court on a charge arising out of the same offense for which the Navajo tribal court had convicted him (*U.S.* 1978). The federal courts were not prohibited from trying the individual, the Court concluded. The Navajos had not given up their "jurisdiction to charge, try, and punish members of the Tribe for violations of tribal law" in either their 1849 or their 1868 treaty with the United States. Therefore, the man had broken the laws of two sovereigns and could be tried by both sovereigns.

The federal court's willingness to employ its canons of construction in Indian treaty cases has proven essential in protecting tribal hunting and fishing rights. Among many tribes, hunting and fishing represented far more than economic subsistence. Hunting and fishing symbolized and taught cultural values and one's responsibilities and orientation to one's surroundings. Over time, outside developments and populations crowded out many tribal peoples, preventing them from pursuing the hunting and fishing rights guaranteed by their ancestors. In the 1960s through the early 1990s, tribal peoples moved to reclaim these treaty rights, first through fish-ins and protests and later through court battles. Non-Indian fishing interests, representing the sport and commercial industries, responded to the tribal actions with harassment, violence, and lobbying efforts.

In general, courts from the Northwest to the Great Lakes have concluded that tribal ancestral leaders intended to preserve tribal fishing and hunting rights for their descendants in the treaties they negotiated with the United States more than a hundred years ago. In the *United States v. Michigan* case of 1979, for example, Judge Joel Fox ruled that Michigan tribes preserved their right to fish in Lake Michigan in their treaties of 1836 and 1855 (*U.S.* 1981). Tribes in Wisconsin and Minnesota won similar lawsuits based on interpretation of historic treaties (*Menominee* 1968; *Minnesota* 1999*)*. In a series of northwest fishing cases involving the Treaty of Medicine Creek of 1854 (Treaty with the Nisqually, Puyallup, etc.), the courts interpreted "The right of taking fish, at all usual and accustomed grounds and stations, is further secured to said Indians in common with all citizens of the Territory" to allow treaty tribes with 50 percent of the allowable salmon catch (*Washington* 1979).

The courts have failed to apply their canons of construction consistently when interpreting Indian treaty provisions. Perhaps not surprisingly, the majority of these cases have occurred when such applications would result in Indian ownership of former lands now needed for economic development and the finding that tribes retained jurisdiction to handle non-Indian criminal activities within tribal lands. For example, in the *Federal Power Commission v. Tuscarora Indian Nation* case of 1960, the Supreme Court, by ignoring its own canons of construction and reinterpreting history, concluded that three treaties negotiated in the 1700s to protect tribal lands conveniently did not include Tuscarora lands. The ruling allowed for the submersion of traditional Tuscarora lands beneath a lucrative energy project. In a strongly worded dissent to the decision, Justice Hugo Black wrote, "I regret that this Court is to be that governmental agency that breaks faith with this dependent people. Great nations, like great men, should keep their word" (*Federal Power Commission* 1960). This ruling was also relevant in the *DeCoteau v. District County Court for the Tenth Judicial District* case (*DeCoteau* 1975).

Two weeks before the Supreme Court handed down the *Wheeler* decision, which emphasized that tribes possessed inherent sovereign powers predating those of the United States, the Supreme Court ruled in the *Oliphant* case that tribes did not possess the authority to exercise criminal jurisdiction over non-Indians (*Oliphant* 1978). The case arose from the Suquamish tribal court's conviction of two men for disturbing the peace during Chief Seattle days. The convictions were invalid, the men argued, as the Suquamish possessed no jurisdiction over non-Indians. In line with previous case law and canons of construction, the Court should have determined whether the Suquamish had forfeited their rights in treaties to handle criminal matters within their own lands, or whether Congress had expressly removed such authority from the tribes. After a selected review of congressional legislation from 1834 to the present, the Court rationalized that Congress had intended to preempt the field. Previously, the Court had operated on the principle that tribes retained their inherent governing rights and rights to resources unless specifically removed or limited through treaties or by Congress. The new rule now read that tribes could not legislate on matters limited by treaties or statutes (old test) or in areas that conflicted with the overriding interest of the United States as the superior sovereign. Exactly what was considered to be in the "interest of the overriding sovereign" the Court did not say, beyond stating that the federal government had a responsibility to protect its (non-Indian) citizens.

The 1981 *Montana v. United States* decision, like the *Lone Wolf* decision in 1903, illustrated the Supreme Court's willingness to mangle previously established Indian law and tests. This case involved the right of the Crow Nation to regulate hunting and fishing rights within their reservation boundaries, in this instance the regulation of non-Indians on nonmember lands. As the Crow Nation's attorney argued, without the right to control all hunting and fishing within reservation boundaries, it was impossible to establish and administer legitimate conservation measures. Furthermore, the Crows had never given up their authority to regulate any aspect of their reservation hunting and fishing rights, and no federal legislation had extinguished their right.

The Crow Nation, the Court ruled, did not possess the right to regulate non-Indians fishing and hunting on non-Indian lands within the reservation boundaries. To support this tenuous claim, the justices relied on their interpretation of the Treaty of Fort Laramie (Treaty with the Sioux, etc.) of 1851, finding that nowhere was it "suggested that Congress intended to grant authority to the Crow Tribe to regulate hunting and fishing by nonmembers on nonmember lands" (*Montana* 1981). The Court could only arrive at such an interpretation by completely ignoring its own tests that required Indian treaties to be interpreted as the tribes would have understood them (few people envisioned in 1851 the problem of whites fishing on Crow land), to contain an express extinguishment of authority, and to resolve any ambiguities in favor of the tribe.

Despite periods of egregious failures and the courts' tendency to interpret Indian treaty rights in line with the national political agenda and climate, the United States has refused to completely abandon the guarantees and promises that it negotiated as a young nation. Even after 200 years of conflictual history, the United States legally regards Indian treaties as the supreme law of the land. As contracts between sovereigns, the supremacy clause of the Constitution governs the legal status of Indian treaties within U.S. law, mandating that Indian treaties possess the same effect and force of federal law and supersede state law. States did not—and still do not—possess the requisite sovereignty to enter into treaty relationships.

Congress and the courts today recognize tribes as domestic dependent nations possessing a government-to-government relationship with the federal government—a status supported by the continuing viability of Indian treaties. The treaties and agreements negotiated by Indian nations with the United States will continue to play a critical role in the recognition of tribal sovereignty and in the protection of Indian lands and resources.

Sharon O'Brien

Further Reading

American State Papers, Foreign Affairs, 1832–1861, vol. 1. Washington, DC: Gales and Seaton.

Article Six, Treaties between the United States and the Several Indian Tribes from 1778 to 1837. 1975. Millwood, NY: Kraus Reprint.

Atcheson, N. 1814. *A Compressed View of the Points to be Discussed in Treating with the United States of America.* London: Rie.

Beecher v. Wetherby, 95 U.S. 517 (1877).

Bodin, J. 1576. *Six Books of the Commonwealth.* Abridged and translated by M. J. Tooley. Oxford, England: Basil Blackwell, 1955.

Boyd, Julian P., ed. 1938. *Indian Treaties Printed by Benjamin Franklin, 1738–1762.* Philadelphia: Historical Society of Pennsylvania.

Caughey, John W. 1938. *McGillivray of the Creeks.* Norman: University of Oklahoma Press.

Cherokee Nation v. Georgia, 30 U.S. 1 (1831).

DeCoteau v. District County Court for the Tenth Judicial District, 420 U.S. 425 (1975).

Deloria, Vine, Jr., and Raymond J. DeMallie, eds. 1999. *Documents of American Indian Diplomacy: Treaties, Agreements, and Conventions, 1775–1979*, vols. 1–2. Norman: University of Oklahoma Press.

DePuy, H. 1917. *A Bibliography of the English Colonial Treaties with the American Indians: Including a Synopsis of Each Treaty.* New York: Lennox Club.

Federal Power Commission v. Tuscarora Indian Nation, 362 U.S. 99, 137–138 (1960).

Gates, Merrill. 1885. "Land and Law as Agents in Educating Indians." *Journal of Social Science*, 113–146, quoted by Captain Henry Pratt.

Grotius, H. 1925. "Livy, Book IV." In *De Jure Belli Ac Pacis Libri Tres* [The Classics of International Law], edited by J. Scott, 391. Oxford: Clarendon Press.

Holmes, Jack. 1969. Spanish Treaties with West Florida Indians, 1784–1802. *Florida Historical Society* 48, 140–154.

"Indian Appropriations Act." March 3, 1871. *U.S. Statutes at Large* 16, 566.

Liverani, Mario. 1980. *International Relations in the Ancient Near East, 1600–1100 BC.* New York: Palgrave Macmillan.

Lone Wolf v. Hitchcock, 187 U.S. 553, 23 S. Ct. 216, 47 L. Ed. 299 (1903).

McClanahan v. Arizona State Tax Commission, 411 U.S. 164 (1973).

McNickle, D'Arcy. 1973. *Native American Tribalism*. London: Oxford University Press.

Menominee Tribe of Indians v. United States, 391 U.S. 404 (1968).

Meyers, D. P. 1957. "The Names and Scopes of Treaties." *American Journal of International Law* 51, 579.

Minnesota v. Mille Lacs Band of Chippewa Indians, 526 U.S. 172 (1999).

Montana v. United States, 450 U.S. 544 (1981).

Morton v. Mancari, 417 U.S. 535 (1974).

Oliphant v. Suquamish Indian Tribe, 435 U.S. 191 (1978).

Prucha, Francis Paul. 1994. *American Indian Treaties: The History of a Political Anomaly*. Berkeley, Los Angeles, and London: University of California Press.

Ralston, Hayden. 1920. *The Senate and Treaties, 1789–1817*. New York: Macmillan.

Respecting the Liberty to Pass and Repass the Borders and to Carry on Trade and Commerce. 1974. Explanatory Article to the 3rd Article of the Treaty of November 19, 1794.

Toscano, M. 1966. *The History of Treaties and International Politics*. Baltimore: Johns Hopkins University Press.

Treaty of October 22, 1784, with the Six Nations, 7 *Stat.* 15.

Treaty of January 21, 1785, with the Wyandots and others, 7 *Stat.* 16.

Treaty of November 28, 1785, 7 *Stat.* 18.

Treaty of January 9, 1789, with Wyandot, 7 *Stat.* 28.

Treaty of August 7, 1790, 7 *Stat.* 35.

Treaty of July 2, 1791, 7 *Stat.* 39.

Treaty of June 16, 1802, 7 *Stat.* 68.

Treaty of November 10, 1808, 7 *Stat.* 107.

Treaty of July 22, 1814, with Wyandot, 7 *Stat.* 118.

Treaty of August 19, 1825, 7 *Stat.* 272.

Treaty of May 24, 1835, 7 *Stat.* 450.

Treaty of August 24, 1835, 7 *Stat.* 47.

Treaty of May 26, 1837, 7 *Stat.* 533.

Treaty of March 12, 1858, 12 *Stat.* 997.

Treaty of June 19, 1859, 12 *Stat.* 1037.

Treaty of March 6, 1861, 12 *Stat.* 1171.

Treaty with France for the Cession of Louisiana, April 30, 1803, 8 *Stat.* 200, TS 86.

U.S. v. Kagama, 118 U.S. 375 (1886).

U.S. v. Michigan, 653 F. 2d 277 (6th Cir. 1981).

U.S. v. Wheeler, 435 U.S. 313 (1978).

Van Loon, L. G. 1968. "Tawagonshi: Beginning of the Treaty Era." *Indian Historian*, 1, no. 3 (Summer 1968), 22–26.

Vattel, E. 1916. *The Law of Nations, the Classics of International Law,* edited by J. Scott, 1–558. Washington, DC: Carnegie Institution of Washington.

Vitoria, Francisco de. 1917. "De Indis and De Jure Belli Reflectiones." In *On the Indians and on the Law of War*, edited by Ernest Nys. Translated by John Pawley Bate, sec. 2, titles 6 and 7, 148–149. New York: Oceana, 1964. Originally published Washington, DC: Carnegie Institution.

Warren Trading Post v. Arizona Tax Commission, 380 U.S. 685 (1965).

Washington v. Washington State Commercial Passenger Fishing Vessel Association, 443 U.S. 658 (1979).

Williams v. Lee, 358 U.S. 217 (1959).

Worcester v. Georgia, 31 U.S. (6 Pet.) 515 (1832).

Canadian Indian Treaties

In what is now called Canada, treaty making has been the primary means of fostering colonization since the 1600s. Although it has been the cornerstone of the largely peaceful Indian settler relationship for the past four centuries, its enduring benefits have been overwhelmingly one sided. Treaty making was the approach preferred by the First Nations as well as the European parties to sort out the essential terms of how colonists and their governments would relate to the original owners of the land throughout most of North America. The history of negotiating treaties, their political and legal significance up to the present day, and the many disputes that continue to arise regarding their meaning create a situation that is, however, markedly different from that found in the United States. Understanding the place of treaties in modern Canada is possible only through a full appreciation of the different types of treaties signed over the years, the history of treaty formation, and the evolving legal importance that treaties have acquired more recently. One must also recognize that Indian perspectives on the function of treaties and the precise rights they contain have differed dramatically from the views held by Canadian governments over the intervening decades, and that considerable conflict, disappointment, anger, and frustration have been the result.

Recent judicial interpretations, along with the entrenchment of the protection of treaty rights in Canada's constitution in 1982 [Section 35(1) of the Constitution Act, 1982, states, "The existing aboriginal and treaty rights of the aboriginal peoples of Canada are hereby recognized and affirmed."], have resurrected the importance of historic Indian treaties as well as the necessity for new treaties to be negotiated with Indian, Inuit, and Métis peoples. The Inuit (still called Eskimos by many in the United States) did not share the precontact treaty-making tradition, nor was their interaction with newcomers regulated in this fashion. The Métis—reflecting the emergence of a new people springing from the merger, then reformulation, of both European and Indian cultures and origins—were often shunted aside during treaty negotiations. Occasionally, the Métis were included within the scope of Crown-Indian treaties as individual beneficiaries or as communities adhering to its terms rather than through separate agreements. Both Inuit and Métis peoples have adopted the treaty model in recent years to develop major land claim settlements and new governance arrangements within Canada.

France was the first significant colonizing presence from Europe; it also sought peaceful trading relationships with the Indian nations and negotiated some treaties to encourage such opportunities. The displacement of the French regime from the Maritimes in 1713 and from Quebec in 1763 by Great Britain meant that the latter's legal system and emphasis on treaties has dominated the experience throughout North America. As both Canada and the United States were established predominantly as British colonies, with the same common-law legal system and the same initial approach to dealing with the Indian nations encountered by European settlers, it is not surprising that both countries today share many common perceptions of treaty relationships. American case law, with its far greater volume and earlier vintage, has had considerable influence on the development of Canadian thinking in this regard. In fact, some of the earliest treaties relating to Indian nations resident in Canada were actually negotiated in the American colonies, particularly in Boston. The border between the two countries also bisects the traditional territory of various Indian nations from coast to coast.

The content of the common law and official government policy of Great Britain in the 1600s were both shaped largely by the emerging international law doctrines first enunciated by Spanish theologians and legal thinkers, especially Francisco de Vitoria, and within the Roman Catholic Church in the mid-16th century. After extensive debate and a period of controversy, international law came to recognize the indigenous peoples of the so-called New World as human beings with souls who were entitled to respect and to protection from physical violence. The developing theory of international law also recognized them as "peoples," who constituted sovereign nations with ownership rights over their territories.

Doctrine of Discovery

The doctrine of discovery was a construct of the Christian European nations devised prior to the onset of treaty making with Native American nations. Two important ideas were contained in the doctrine of discovery. First, Europeans could acquire only land that was *terra nullius* (unoccupied); occupied land could not be sought, for the Native population had held title to the land "since time immemorial." Second, the doctrine of discovery internally regulated European nations upon their discovery of new land.

The first nation to come across land had the immutable right to trade with and acquire title to the land of the Native population. However, during the 15th century, the Bulls of Donation, issued by the Pope on behalf of Spain, were used in the acquisition of discovered land in the name of Christianity, disregarding the doctrine of discovery and the rights of the Native Americans. The primary factor was that Natives were viewed as religiously inferior—described as "infidels," "heathens," "savages," and "inferior" beings. Native Americans were non-Christians, and the European self-belief of religious superiority dictated that, by imposing Christianity upon the Natives, the Natives would become civilized. This view was the primary one until 1537, when the pope issued the *Sublimis Deus*, a declaration of human rights, which was the beginning of recognition of the natural rights of Native peoples.

From the 16th century, the doctrine of discovery underwent reform; as international law theorists legitimized and gave credence to Native peoples' right of title and its inherent nature. Such theorists included Francisco de Vitoria, Bartolomé de las Casas, and Hugo Grotius. From this recognition of Native rights, governments began the treaty process, which legitimized Native American nations as sovereign entities. From the 17th century, the emphasis of the doctrine of discovery had been reformed in that it did not divest the Native population of its rights to land title. This was further manifested through the treaty process used by the Dutch, the Swedish, the British, and the United States in acknowledgment of Native American land title to those lands.

Title to land within the United States was settled in the seminal case of *Johnson v. M'Intosh* (1823). European nations were held to be superior, and it was this that entitled the Europeans to exclusive title and possession. The European merchants, agriculturists, and farmers had the superior right to dispose of the Native "savage" and "hunter." Chief Justice John Marshall held that all of Great Britain's land rights transferred to the United States and that the Native peoples were merely occupants. Marshall revised the doctrine of discovery to mean that occupied land could be acquired as a result of the Native peoples being non-Christian savages who practiced hunting and gathering. Implicit in this notion was that the United States would bestow Christianity upon the Native population to civilize them. The United States had the exclusive right to extinguish Native land title, and Native occupancy could be extinguished at any time. Furthermore, Marshall used the doctrine of discovery and converted it into one of conquest, which could not be questioned if it was the law of the land.

However, in *Worcester v. Georgia* (1832), Marshall's *obiter dictum* (a judge's incidental, nonbinding opinion) changed the basis for discovery that he had used in *Johnson v. M'Intosh* by stating that sovereign Natives could not give up their lands to a country far away. He stated that discovery gave the European powers the sole right to acquire the soil through the right to purchase with the consent of the Native peoples. The doctrine regulated the European nations but did not affect the rights of those already in possession. In *Worcester*, Marshall stated that it was an "extravagant and absurd idea" that small settlements acquired the legitimate right and authority to occupy and claim title to land from coast to coast. *Worcester v. Georgia* notwithstanding, Chief Justice Marshall's earlier definition of the doctrine of discovery as applied in *Johnson v. M'Intosh* is applicable today. It is this doctrine, which was revised in order to promote the development of the United States, that remains the basis of land title and law throughout the current United States of America.

Dewi I. Ball

Further Reading

Deloria, Vine, Jr. *Behind the Trail of Broken Treaties: An Indian Declaration of Independence*. Austin: University of Texas Press, 1996.

Wilkins, David E., and K. Tsianina Lomawaima. *Uneven Ground: American Indian Sovereignty and Federal Law*. Norman: University of Oklahoma Press, 2001.

Williams, Robert A., Jr. *The American Indian in Western Legal Thought: The Discourse of Conquest*. New York: Oxford University Press, 1990.

Even though Europeans did not appreciate it at the time of contact, indigenous states practiced treaty making extensively before they ever encountered people from the other side of the Atlantic Ocean. A wide variety of treaty relationships existed among many of the Indian nations in North America, in some places extending over immense distances. Trading of natural resources and produced goods could occur over thousands of miles. Military alliances also were forged in opposition to common enemies, and military conflict was frequently resolved through the creation of new peace and friendship commitments accompanied by solemn treaty promises. From the perspective of Indian nations, turning to the institution of treaties as the primary peaceful method for dealing with newcomers was logical—the only alternatives were war or complete avoidance of contact, both of which were also pursued at various locales and times. However, the flood of migrants from overseas, coupled with their attractive trade goods, quickly led the Indian nations along the Atlantic coast to conclude that peaceful relations were the preferred choice. Likewise, from the European perspective, treaties were a logical device to regulate future relationships, as that was how Europeans themselves attempted to organize their own internal relationships among competing states.

Treaty making, therefore, worked well as a common vehicle for both sides to pursue the establishment of new relations based upon clear understandings. Each party was able to pursue its separate interests within a shared construct. The pure act of negotiating out of self-interest brought together leading representatives in a context of equal status with the common objective of reaching agreement. Treaties became the best way to cement a relationship inspired by desires for peace and friendship, to encourage trading patterns that were economically beneficial to both sides, and to create potentially powerful military alliances against common enemies, be they other European colonial powers or Indian nations.

It should be understood that control over treaty making on the European side rested exclusively with the empire. That is, the imperial government possessed the sole prerogative to decide when to negotiate new treaties, with whom to seek such relationships, and on what terms. Only the Crown could appoint representatives with a mandate to bind the government. The people on the ground—the colonists—could enter into private contracts of trade, but they had no authority whatsoever as private individuals or as communities to negotiate formal treaties or to acquire land directly from Indian nations.

The individual Indian nation that occupied particular territory was viewed as the rightful owner of that soil in accordance with the terms of its own rules or laws. According to those laws, land was usually held with collective or communal title and could not be individually conveyed or sold. This meant that the "discovering" European nation could not claim exclusive title to the "new" lands but merely the sole right, vis-à-vis other European countries, to enter into treaty relations regarding trade and military alliances or to acquire land for settlement from a willing Indian nation. International law did, however, recognize a principle of conquest such that a victor in war obtained the legal right to seize territory and substitute its sovereignty for that of the defeated nation. Local law would remain in force, however, until the conqueror chose to impose any changes, including a decision to establish new governments.

The Evolution of Treaty Making in Canada

Canada has experienced four distinct eras in which treaties were negotiated: (1) from the earliest days of contact to the American Revolution, (2) from 1790 to independence in 1867, (3) from 1867 to 1930, and (4) the modern era, from 1975 to the present. Each period is considered in turn.

Peace and Friendship Treaties

The primary focal points of treaty relations in the 1600s and 1700s—and of international or intergovernmental relationships in general among Europeans and Indian nations at this time—were on trade, military alliances, and peaceful interaction so as to permit colonies to flourish and to generate maximum economic wealth for the mother countries. Early agreements often involved some small land conveyances by the Indian partners for trading posts, military forts, and modest colonial settlements, while also establishing a pattern of gift giving on the part of the Crown. The offering of presents, which was to become a common element in almost all later treaties, made sense to Europeans as well as to indigenous peoples in the Americas, as each was accustomed to presenting tokens of esteem and recognition on formal occasions. Nevertheless, the clear majority of the gifts presented came from the European emissaries.

The first formal treaty between the British Crown and the Iroquois Confederacy, the Treaty of Albany of September 24, 1664—also known as the Two Row Wampum—typifies a number of these elements. The Iroquois, then consisting of five distinct nations but later increasing to six when the Tuscarora Nation joined the Confederacy in 1722, were a major military force and far more numerous than the British in the region. They had previously been allies of the Dutch, who transferred their interest in New Netherlands (renamed New York) to the British in 1664. The Iroquois were also long-standing adversaries of the Huron Nation, who had previously forged an alliance with the French colony of New France in the St. Lawrence

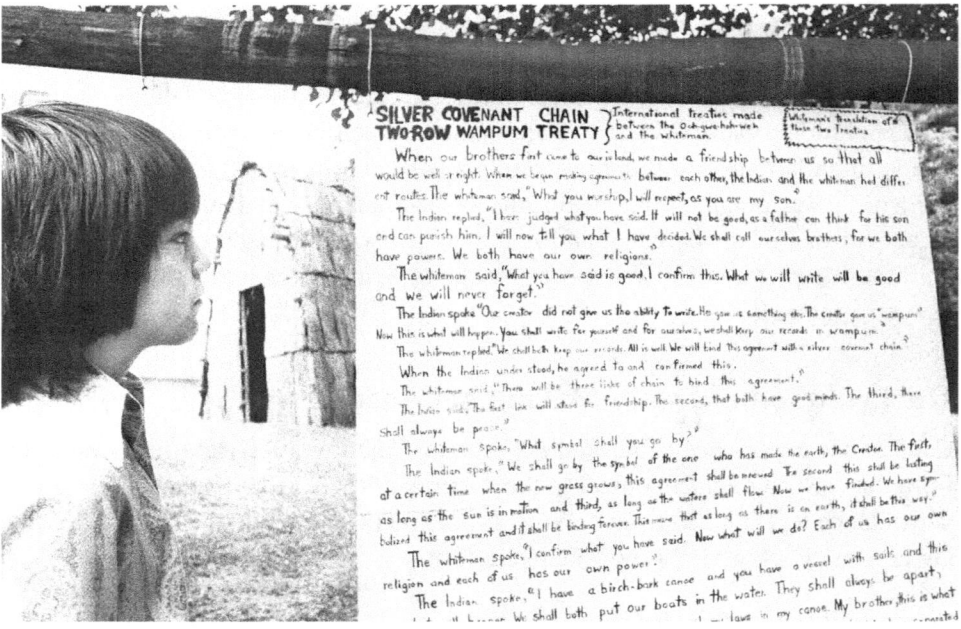

The Two-Row Wampum Treaty or Treaty of Albany in 1613 between the Senecas, Cayugas, Mohawks, Onondagas, and Oneidas of the Iroquois League and the Netherlands was a living agreement between the two sovereign powers to sustain peace and trade relations. This friendship led to the idea of the Covenant Chain in British Colonial-Iroquois relations in the late 1600s based on mutual peace, friendship, and respect. (Don Dutton/Toronto Star via Getty Images)

River valley that included the provision of rifles. Treaty negotiations between the Iroquois Confederacy and the British representatives extended over several days, resulting in separate agreements on September 24 and 25 that consisted of the following key elements:

1. "That the Indian Princes above named and their subjects, shall have all such wares and commodities from the English for the future, as heretofore they had from the Dutch."
2. Each party pledged to capture and punish any fugitive committing any injury or violence to a person under the other's protection so that all due satisfaction would be given to the victim.
3. The English were mandated to "make peace for the Indian Princes, with the Nations down the River."
4. The English promised not to assist the three nations of the Abenaki Confederacy and to provide accommodation to the Iroquois if they should be beaten by those nations. (O'Callaghan 1853–61: 3, 67–68)

The treaty was recorded in English, and an official version on parchment was given to the Iroquois. The treaty was also recorded on a wampum belt, which was delivered to Colonel George Cartwright (on behalf of the Duke of York). The Iroquois method of recording the significance of important events involved the sewing together of beads made from seashells on animal skins in pictorial patterns unique to that particular event. Thus, each party followed its traditional practice of acknowledging the importance of this historic and solemn occasion in a manner that reflected its culture while making mutual assurances to honor in perpetuity the promises made.

Treaty making was rapidly adopted as the preferred strategy of Great Britain, as it expanded Great Britain's colonial and trading empire either through being welcomed by Indian nations into their territory or through acquiring the European claims of its predecessors. A number of treaties were negotiated with the Wabanaki Confederacy (the Mi'kmaq, Maliseet, Penobscot, and Passamaquoddy Nations), in northern New England and the Maritime colonies from 1678 until 1761. These treaties often followed political withdrawals by the Wabanaki's former ally, France. Their purpose, more generally, was the commitment of both partners to peaceful and friendly relations, to exclusivity in trade, to nonmolestation of each other's citizens, to respect for criminal and civil jurisdiction, to the release of prisoners, and to the refusal to aid deserters.

The early success of the treaty mechanism (and the absence of an economically and politically attractive alternative) caused it to be used over and over again to meet immediate needs as well as for longer-term objectives, including the end of any hostilities that may have arisen, so as to restore peace and foster trade. Treaties were negotiated by Britain all along the Atlantic seaboard, from Georgia to Nova Scotia and as far west as the Appalachian Mountain range, from 1664 to the end of the American Revolution.

The emphasis upon England retaining control and the importance of treaty making overall to imperial strategy was later confirmed by the Royal Proclamation issued by King George III on October 7, 1763, after the Seven Years' War between France and Great Britain ended through the Treaty of Versailles. One major objective was to create new colonial governments for the former French colonies (in what later became the provinces of Quebec and Prince Edward Island) as well as for the former Spanish colony of Florida. The Royal Proclamation also sought to confirm the position of Indian nations by declaring that they were to be left unmolested by colonists in their remaining territories inside of the British colonies unless they were willing to sell their lands to properly appointed Crown representatives, who would negotiate the purchase through public meetings resulting in formal treaty arrangements. Outside the colonial borders, largely to the west of the Appalachian Mountains, was expressly confirmed by the king as preserved as Indian country for their continued exclusive use.

American Independence to Canadian Independence

The American Revolution quickly changed everything both for the United States and for Canada. The land demands of colonists had been one of the driving forces underlying the American Revolution; hence the desires of land speculators—including George Washington, military veterans, and others in search of farmland—were able to flourish without the imperial constraints that previously had required the colonies' adherence to treaty promises and had restricted treaty making to the Crown. Although some Indian nations joined with those rebelling and others remained neutral, many tribes had honored their military alliances with the British and were now on the losing side without the continuing protection of the Crown or the existence of prior treaties.

The birth of the new country meant, of course, that all residents needed to decide for themselves where their future lay. Many colonists who had remained loyal to the Crown, the so-called United Empire Loyalists (or UELs), chose to flee the United States and move to what remained of British North America, namely, Canada. They suddenly needed massive quantities of land on which to resettle, a factor that immediately changed the pattern of the prior Indian-Crown relationship on the Canadian side of the border, where colonial settlement had been limited.

The American victory also encouraged a major relocation of many tribes from the eastern coast of the new United States; these Indians moved westward and, in some cases, fled northward into Canada along with the UELs.

Although victorious, the United States was an extremely vulnerable country, its economy in tatters and the solidity of its success in the Revolution uncertain,

The Battle of Lexington in 1775 started the American Revolution and divided the Six Nations of the Iroquois, with Indians fighting on both sides. To the north, the Canadian government made 70 treaties and agreements with the First Nations from 1725 to 1999, starting well before the first U.S.-Indian treaty in 1778 with the Delawares, as treaty-making stopped in 1871 with 374 treaties. (Library of Congress)

with no guarantee against future British invasion. The French Revolution, which occurred only a few years later, provided some political comfort but effectively robbed the United States of its major European ally. Thus, the United States wanted to create peaceful relations with outside powers and to stabilize its domestic situation. To meet these objectives, it wisely sought to inherit the benefits of the treaty relationships possessed by the British within American territory and to form new ones. The United States could not merely succeed to existing British treaties, because they stemmed from the defeated empire; the young country had to form new relationships of its own, which began with the Treaties of Hopewell with the Cherokee, Choctaw, and Chickasaw Nations in 1785 and 1786. Similarly, the United States did not wish publicly to be perceived to be merely following British policies, such that it needed to demonstrate its independence from its former mother country. Therefore, British decrees had to be modified and given new birth as American instruments. The Royal Proclamation of 1763 was transformed by the U.S. Congress into the Non-Intercourse Act, passed on July 22, 1790, although the orientation was largely the same.

A direct effect of the Revolution was an unleashing of pent-up demand for Indian land, thereby weakening the Indian nations that remained within American borders in political terms as well as economic and military ones. A by-product of the necessity for tribes to make peace with their far more populous neighbor was to look to the U.S. judiciary as a potential mechanism for their ongoing protection. Because they could no longer realistically appeal to the British Crown as an ally, and in the face of their declining military and trading importance to the American government, the only available alternative to leaving their traditional territory became the American court system.

This choice also presented serious challenges for Indian nations who saw themselves as fully sovereign. How could they invoke the protection of a foreign court operating in a totally different legal system and in a foreign language? This was not an attractive option by any means, or one that many Indian nations chose, although a few did. What they discovered, not surprisingly, was a judicial system that was itself relatively fragile, a new institution primarily concerned about its own place within the American system of government and the vulnerability of this new country.

Through three key decisions in the 1820s and 1830s, the U.S. Supreme Court, under the leadership of Chief Justice John Marshall, sought to develop a principled legal foundation for what was essentially a political compromise that justified the imposition of U.S. might and law on sovereign, independent countries. The stark options essentially available to the Court were either the continuation of a fully Indian, independent-nation sovereignty theory, or a complete absorption of Indian people into the body politic. The former could threaten American stability, as it would mean that Indian nations would retain the capacity to form treaties with European nations of their choosing—including the British to the north, whom they had defeated on two occasions, the French and Spanish to the south, and potentially others. That possibility, obviously, was not attractive from an American perspective. On the other hand, to deny all Indian sovereignty would contradict the treaty history that existed in North America, as well as the initial post-Revolution efforts of the U.S. government to form peaceful, treaty-based relationships with Indian nations. Such a legal position would also undermine the federal government's own constitutional authority, as the Constitution's division of powers with state governments had not precisely addressed the question of who possessed jurisdiction to engage in lawmaking and other aspects of noncommercial Indian affairs. Denying Indian sovereignty also could have the consequence of making the Indian people subjects or, potentially, citizens with a right to vote. Framed in a different fashion, the latter legal analysis would have meant that the federal government did not have the capacity to regulate the important economic domain of Indian trade, to deal with potential military threats, and to control vital revenue matters. It must be noted that one of the most significant methods of raising revenue before the introduction of the income tax system was the sale of government land. If the federal government controlled the acquisition of land from Indian nations through treaties, then it would acquire the revenue from the resale of those lands to settlers and thereby could direct the growth of populations and the creation of new states.

Therefore, the status of Indian nations and their treaty relationships held grave importance for the U.S. Supreme Court, which was intent on flexing its legal muscles as it strove to confirm its identity as the ultimate arbiter of the U.S. Constitution. Chief Justice John Marshall's response to these opportunities was to develop a hybrid approach—neither full acceptance nor full denial of the competing legal streams. He decided, instead, to construct a legal doctrine that transformed formerly independent Indian sovereignty into a continuing but internal variation through the concept of domestic dependent nationhood. Indian nations were defined as "domestic" in the sense that they were declared to have lost international status or the capacity to form relations with foreign countries. Their governments and their traditional territories were simply stated to be internal to the United States. They were further deemed to be "dependent" in that their authority was rendered subject to some initially undefined power on the part of Congress and the executive branch to infringe upon their autonomy. Marshall also drew upon the imagery that Indian nations, by virtue of being dependent, were somehow like wards in relation to the U.S. government as their protector or guardian.

Guardianship/Wardship

Guardianship/wardship is a theory which holds that tribal nations function under the trust protection of the federal government, Native nations lack political independence, and state governments cannot intrude on tribal affairs It is the responsibility of the federal government to ensure that this trust protection is preserved.

The theory of guardianship/wardship was proposed by Chief Justice John Marshall during two Supreme Court cases, in 1831 and 1832, respectively: *Cherokee Nation v. Georgia* and *Worcester v. Georgia* (1832). The premise of this theory is tribal nations are not sovereign independent entities who can determine their own direction but rather children who must be guided by their parent(s), in this case the federal government. This attitude of ward to a guardian is denoted by the word "paternalism." The federal government would do what was best for Native people according to white norms, which would lead to the taking of Native peoples' hands and leading them down the path toward white civilization and Christianity.

In the *Cherokee Nation v. Georgia* case in 1831, the Cherokee Nation filed for protection from the state of Georgia. The state of Georgia imposed its own state laws and ruled that Cherokee laws were no longer legal. The Cherokees regarded themselves as an independent nation. Chief Justice Marshall declared that tribal nations are "domestic dependent nations" and that the federal government has a responsibility to protect Native people. The Cherokees were declared in a state of pupilage. The following year, in the *Worcester v. Georgia*, the Supreme Court ruled that the state of Georgia did not have the right to interfere with Cherokee affairs. The U.S. government exclusively interacts with tribal nations.

During the rest of the 19th century, federal Indian policies illustrated this paradoxical relationship between the federal government and tribal nations. Thousands of Native people were removed from the eastern part of the United States across the Mississippi River into Indian Territory, now known as the state of Oklahoma. Reservation systems were established to remove and restrict Native interaction with non-Native people. Assimilation tactics were imposed to "white out" Native people. The reservations were divided up into individual allotments to destroy the concept of tribal ownership in favor of individual proprietorship.

In the 20th century, the guardianship/wardship theory would be demonstrated in various back-and-forth federal Indian policies. Assimilation and allotment dictated the relationship between Native people and the federal government in the early part of the 20th century. Native people who still needed guiding were looked over, while those people that assimilated to the larger society were forgotten. Under the Dawes Act (1887) and its amendments, individuals received land allotments and U.S. citizenship, until the Burke Act (1906) put these lands into protective trust status for a period of 25 years. In the early 1920s, federal courts appointed legal guardians over "incompetent" Indians, who did not understand English and lacked experience in handling business affairs in the white capitalist system.

When the Indian Reorganization Act (1934) was passed, the policy of allotment officially ended. Tribal nations were told to return to practicing tribal ways. A decade later, federal Indian policy shifted back toward assimilating Native people into the larger society of the United States. Introduced in 1953 with House Concurrent Resolution 108, the new termination policy extinguished tribal nation status by dissolving their trust status. Tribal nations would no longer exist, according to the federal government. The termination policy proved ineffective and costly in the 1960s. A self-determination policy was introduced in the early 1970s to allow tribal nations to direct their own affairs with some federal government guidance. The self-determination policy is still in effect today; yet, the federal government, through different federal organizations such as the Bureau of Indian Affairs and Public Health Service remains a vital component of Native peoples' lives.

Lloyd L. Lee

Further Reading

American Indian Lawyer Training Program, Inc. *Indian Tribes as Sovereign Governments: A Sourcebook on Federal-Tribal History, Law, and Policy*. Oakland, CA: American Indian Resources Institute (AIRI), 1989.

Deloria, Vine, Jr., and Clifford M. Lytle. *American Indians, American Justice*. Austin: University of Texas Press, 1983.

O'Brien, Sharon. *American Indian Tribal Governments*. Norman: University of Oklahoma Press, 1989.

The source of Marshall's thinking was largely his assessment of the tides of history, in which he drew heavily upon his own research conducted for the preparation of a mammoth biography of George Washington. This was coupled with his desire to draft a compromise that advanced federal interests while simultaneously respecting some recognition of the reality of Indian nations as distinct, self-governing peoples who were the rightful original owners of the soil. His theory indicates that Indian sovereignty remains in existence yet is constrained, such that what remains of the formerly complete sovereignty is the residue that is subject to further intrusions by Congress in the future. This residual sovereignty includes the continuing power to negotiate treaties, but only with the United States, and to surrender territory for sale.

The landmark litigation before the Supreme Court in *Cherokee Nation v. Georgia* (1831) and *Worcester v. Georgia* (1832) did not, in fact, protect the Cherokee Nation; on the orders of President Andrew Jackson, they, among others, were forcibly dispossessed of their territory and marched west of the Mississippi—the infamous Trail of Tears. The Canadian experience during this same time period involved less drama; however, its consequences for many Indian nations were no less dramatic. The pressure for land to accommodate the arriving UELs and allied Indian nations required treaty making to switch emphasis from encouraging trade and peace to obtaining land on a massive scale for settlement and agriculture. Clearing the land in the south for farming meant a drastic reduction in the wildlife population's capacity to support the traditional economy and reduced the importance of the fur trade, causing much of the trapping to relocate north and westward. The new wave of land cession treaties began in the late 1780s in southern Ontario, following the procedures of the Royal Proclamation of 1763 but focusing on acquiring clear legal title to land, in a form of property conveyance in return for a lump-sum payment that consisted of a combination of money and trade goods. Promises were made to reassure the Indian negotiators that they would continue to receive regular presents, would be able to hunt, fish, and trap as before, would be able to harvest wild or grown foods, and would retain some of their traditional lands. Little was said, however, about how the influx of white colonists would drastically reshape the landscape. By 1818, imperial officials were complaining that the cost of treaty payments was becoming too onerous for the local colony to bear; this led to the substitution of a scheme for annual payments (annuities). This effectively meant that an installment payment plan was used, in which Indian nations were compensated for their land out of a small portion of the money that actually came from the resale of Indian land to settlers and speculators, leaving the sizable profits to defray the cost of colonial government.

The next significant development in the nature of treaties in Canada occurred through the negotiation of the Robinson-Huron and Robinson-Superior Treaties, which affected the upper Great Lakes region. Not only did these two treaties operate on a far larger geographic scale (affecting more than twice the territory of all prior land surrender treaties combined), but they also introduced the concept of creating Indian reserves for individual communities out of small portions of the territory surrendered under treaty. These reserves were then set aside, after the extinguishment of aboriginal title, for the exclusive use of individual Indian communities, and the underlying title was claimed by the Crown. The Robinson Treaties effectively set the stage for all of the post-confederation treaties until the modern era.

Treaties from 1867 to 1930

Canada was formally confirmed as a semi-independent country in 1867, with Great Britain retaining ultimate control over all foreign affairs until the Statute of Westminster was passed by the U.K. Parliament in 1931; even then, the parliament's approval was required to amend Canada's constitution until 1982. Canada considerably expanded its territorial base in 1870 by acquiring western and northern lands held by the Crown and those lands owned by the private Hudson's Bay Company under a royal charter issued 200 years earlier. The new national government of Canada immediately launched upon a campaign to negotiate treaties with the Indian nations in the southern portions of these areas to allow agriculture, forestry, and mining on a large scale, while setting the stage for an expected massive influx of new settlers from Europe and the building of a national railway system.

The so-called numbered treaties (numbered from 1 to 11 as they were negotiated from 1871 to 1921, with adhesions to Treaty 9 signed as late as 1930) followed the pattern set by the two Robinson Treaties of 1850. The written form of each treaty (in English only) involved the surrender of vast tracts of traditional territory to the federal Crown by Indian leaders on behalf of their populations. In return, the Indians were promised small parcels of land to be set aside as exclusive Indian reserves for particular communities, annual payments to each member, guarantees of continued hunting and fishing rights, and occasional other benefits (such as schools, farming implements, ammunition, and medical supplies). The indigenous version of the treaty negotiations, the oral promises made during the discussions, and the content of the final agreement are consistently asserted to differ dramatically from the "official" text. Many Indian elders have relayed stories of the negotiations as having focused on sharing the territory with the newcomers rather than surrendering the land absolutely, as Mother Earth could not be "sold." Many others allege that only the surface of the land "to the depth of a plough" was being shared or given but not the subsurface resources, and that the territory was to be left undamaged. Few of the Indian participants could anticipate the large-scale settlements that were to occur in many of the treaty areas or how the influx of farmers and foresters would fundamentally alter the landscape in a way that would virtually destroy the traditional economy in the southern portion of the prairies in only a few years. The thrust of the federal vision was that treaties would open up the region for immigrants and Canadians moving westward, whereas Indian people would disappear or be converted over time into farmers with their own plots of land so as to be assimilated into the general agrarian society. This policy was maintained even in northern areas that were completely ill-suited for agriculture with the technology available at the time. The establishment of the residential school system in the 1880s and its removal of all school-age children, enforced vigorously through pass (permission to leave the reserve) restrictions by police and government officials, coupled with the drastic reduction in wildlife harvesting opportunities and trapping income, left many Indian communities devastated—economically, socially, politically, and spiritually. The Métis Nation was left in an even more destitute situation, as no communal land base was provided for their survival under treaty or otherwise. A federal statutory scheme, started in Manitoba in 1871 to offer individual entitlements to blocks of land or cash (called scrip) to Métis families in lieu of treaty benefits, generated little tangible gain, as most recipients were quickly defrauded by land speculators.

The passage of time led to a significant shift in federal governmental attitudes, as Indian people were thought to face either extinction as a race (in part through the massive death toll from imported diseases) or complete absorption into Canadian society as an underclass of farm workers and domestic laborers. Indian reserves became the means to "smooth the dying pillow" or to serve as a laboratory for social reengineering and assimilation. This perception was far removed from the former view of sovereign Indian nations as military allies and valuable trading partners. Over time, treaties came to be viewed by nonaboriginal citizens as anachronistic documents that had outlived their purpose and were to be neither renewed nor replicated elsewhere. All of this was to change, however, with the decision in 1973 of the Supreme Court of Canada in *Calder v. Attorney General of British Columbia*.

The Modern Treaty Era

The *Calder* case was launched by the Nisga'a Nation of northwestern British Columbia as the latest salvo in their century-long struggle to have their land rights recognized by the Crown. They went to court to assert their rights over their traditional territory through the common law doctrine of aboriginal title and drew heavily upon the Marshall decisions of the U.S. Supreme Court to support their argument. They lost at trial, before the provincial court of appeal and again before the Supreme Court of Canada, ultimately on the procedural basis that they did not have the consent (or "fiat") of the provincial government they were suing at a time when Crown immunity was still absolute. Nevertheless, six of the seven judges who addressed the case on its merits concluded that the doctrine of aboriginal title was still good law in Canada. Both leading judgments relied primarily on American jurisprudence to support their positions. Although these six judges were evenly split on whether or not the aboriginal title of the Nisga'a Nation had been effectively extinguished by general public lands legislation during the colonial era, they all were of the view that the Nisga'a Nation had never surrendered their title by treaty or lost it through conquest.

The judges declared that aboriginal title could only have been extinguished by unilateral Crown action, and they differed on the level of explicitness required to meet the test for extinguishment. Even the leading opinion of Justice Wilfred Judson, which ruled against the Nisga'a Nation continuing to possess aboriginal title, still stated, "the fact is, that when the settlers came, the Indians were there, organized in societies and occupying the land as their forefathers had done for centuries." The fallout of this landmark decision for the federal government was immense, for it compelled both a complete reversal of its previous views and acceptance of the fact that aboriginal title likely still existed in large parts of Canada where no historic treaty had previously been negotiated. The government of Canada issued a major policy pronouncement in August 1973, in which it proposed to negotiate "comprehensive land claims agreements" based on unextinguished aboriginal title in the form of modern treaties. Litigation immediately ensued in the Northwest Territories and Quebec to block major proposed petroleum pipelines and hydroelectric projects. An agreement-in-principle was reached on November 15, 1974, among the Grand Council of the Cree, the Northern Quebec Inuit Association (now called the Makivik Corporation), the federal and provincial governments, Hydro-Quebec, and the James Bay Development Corporation, as the first major land claims agreement in the modern era. The parties concluded the final 455-page agreement the following November; over the next two years, legislation was passed by the National Assembly of Quebec and the Parliament of Canada to give the agreement added legal force.

Major modern land claim settlements have been negotiated between the government of Canada, the relevant provincial or territorial government, and the aboriginal titleholders over the past 30 years, as follows:

The James Bay and Northern Quebec Agreement (1975)
The Northeastern Quebec Agreement (1978)
The Inuvialuit (or Western Arctic) Final Agreement (1984)
The Gwich'in Final Agreement (1991)
The Nunavut Land Claims Agreement (1993)
The Sahtu Dene and Métis Comprehensive

The James Bay and Northern Quebec Agreement of 1975 is one of several Canadian First Naltions treaties and agreements that were made in the late 20th century. President George Manuel of the National Indian brotherhood, Third Vice President Aurilien Gill of the Association of Indians, and Second Vice President Max Louis of the Association of Indians, at at a news conference discussing the agreement. (Bettmann/Getty)

>Land Claim Agreement (1993)
>The Nisga'a Final Agreement (2000)
>Eleven individual Yukon First Nation Final Agreements based on the council for Yukon Indians-Canada-Yukon Umbrella Final Agreement (1993), starting in 1995 and ending with the last one ratified in 2005
>The Tlicho (Dogrib) Land Claims and Self-Government Agreement (2003)
>The Labrador Inuit Land Claims Agreement (2003)

The enabling legislation for the last two agreements on this list was proclaimed law in 2005. These settlements are all modern treaties that confirm exclusive land rights for the Indian, Inuit, and Métis participants of the relevant agreements that exist in Quebec, British Columbia, Yukon, Northwest Territories, Nunavut Territory, and Labrador, totaling more than 600,000 square kilometers (or more than 230,000 square miles). Many of them also include detailed descriptions of self-government jurisdiction. In addition, six large Métis settlements were established by the provincial government of Alberta in the 1930s for the exclusive use of those communities. As a result, almost 7 percent of Canada today is recognized as exclusively in aboriginal hands; however, these territories are not equitably distributed; many aboriginal communities are still without recognized lands.

The ongoing effort to negotiate new treaties in Canada is a long way from a conclusion for many First Nations and Métis peoples, although the process is now completed for the Inuit all across northern Canada. Aboriginal communities in many parts of the country are still struggling for recognition that their traditional territory remains in their exclusive hands. Unresolved aboriginal title claims are in negotiation in southern parts of the Northwest Territories, the Yukon, Labrador, Quebec, the Ottawa valley region of Ontario, and throughout much of British Columbia. Ownership or title and jurisdiction of Canadian portions of the Great Lakes and the offshore waters remain outstanding. One can also anticipate that similar land claims will begin at some stage in the future in other parts of British Columbia and in the rest of Atlantic Canada concerning First Nations as well as the Labrador Métis. Negotiations have finally begun in Nova Scotia concerning the continuing legal and political significance of the treaties of peace and friendship of the early 18th century between the Mi'kmaq Nation and the British Crown in the aftermath of the *Marshall* commercial fishing decisions of 1999. Similar discussions may soon commence in New Brunswick and Prince Edward Island involving the Mi'kmaq and Malecite Nations.

The issue of Métis land rights, in regard to instances of extensive fraud under the 19th century scrip system in the prairies and also based on aboriginal title, has yet to find a sympathetic ear among nonaboriginal governments in Canada (other than the negotiations involving the South Slave Métis Tribal Council, Canada, and the government of the Northwest Territories). The 2003 decision of the Supreme Court of Canada in *Regina v. Powley* may advance the thinking in this regard, although the existence of aboriginal title for the Métis has yet to be brought to court.

Also vigorously pursued by most First Nations is another type of land claim. *Specific claims* relate to unfulfilled treaty promises for the creation of reserves and other breaches of lawful obligations concerning reserve lands and natural resources. Whereas comprehensive land claims are based upon unextinguished aboriginal title, specific claims focus upon the loss of specific reserve lands, federal maladministration of band funds, and failure to fulfill or honor treaty promises in a manner that could be considered to breach Canadian law or equity. More than 600 specific land claims are currently in negotiation, are under review by the federal Departments of Indian and Northern Affairs and Justice, or have been appealed to the Indian Specific Claims Commission. More than 200 other claims have been settled over the past 30 years. A further 300 claims are still in early stages of the assessment process, whereas estimates of 1,000 to 2,000 more claims not yet filed have been suggested.

A further reality is that federal and provincial governments are slowly recognizing that First Nations and Métis communities are not only entitled to govern themselves but should be allowed to resume doing so. Thus, First Nations are confirming their jurisdictions in various parts of the country, with the concurrence of federal, provincial, and territorial governments, through negotiating self-government agreements that can take the form of treaties. Perhaps the best-known, most controversial example in this regard has been the Nisga'a treaty in British Columbia, the validity of which has been unsuccessfully challenged in a number of lawsuits. Eleven self-government agreements are in place in the Yukon (with three more under negotiation), one in the Northwest Territories, and one in Labrador. There are also agreements-in-principle or final agreements on self-government with the Meadow Lake Tribal Council in Saskatchewan, the Sioux Valley First Nation in Manitoba, the United Anishnabeg Council in Ontario, and Deline First Nation in the Northwest Territories as well as a number of sectoral agreements with the Mohawks of Kahnawake.

The Position of Aboriginal Peoples

The 2001 census report on the status of aboriginal peoples indicates that slightly more than 1.3 million people have some aboriginal ancestry, with 976,305 individuals defining themselves as being North American Indian (608,850), Métis (292,310), or Inuit (45,070) (Canada 2003a). The latest data demonstrate that the level of self-identification directly as an aboriginal person grew by 22.2 percent from 1996 to 2001. At least half of this growth stems from personal redefinition, that is, individuals choosing to redefine themselves as to their aboriginal identity. This redefinition can be seen, for example, in the Métis population, as it increased by 43 percent during this short period. The official population of Indian people recognized as such by federal statute (the Indian Act) has also grown at an extremely rapid and varied rate, rising from only 323,782 registered Indians in 1981 to 690,101 twenty years later (Canada 2003b). This growth, however, is inconsistent, as the Indian population grew at an overall annual rate of more than 7 percent from 1986 to 1999 but only 1.9 percent per year from 1991 to 1996 (Guimond 1999).

A number of possible explanations exist for this excessive and varied growth. First, it is clear that higher birth rates and longer life spans have naturally increased the aboriginal population. Nevertheless, natural population growth alone is incapable of explaining levels that far exceed the theoretical maximum of 5.5 percent for natural annual population increase (Guimond 1999). A second possible explanation can be attributed to the changing legal status and definition of the designation *Indian*. The 1985 amendments to the federal Indian Act have caused the percentage change in the registered Indian population growth rate to fluctuate considerably, nearly quadrupling between 1985 and 1986 before returning to pre-amendment levels (Canada 2002). As of December 31, 2001, a total of 112,306 Indians were registered based on the legislative amendments of 1985 and made up 16 percent of the Indian Register (Canada 2002). A third possible explanation may also be attributed to ethnic mobility, a phenomenon whereby the ethnic identity chosen and reported by individuals changes over time (Guimond 1999). This growing aboriginal population is becoming increasingly urbanized, while social problems are still very common, unfortunately, in First Nations communities. The number of status Indian children kept in nonparental care increased by 50 percent during the 1990s. Statistics regarding the state of health among aboriginal peoples are also highly discouraging; however, there are signs of improvement. Since 1975, the life expectancy for an aboriginal male has increased from 59.2 years to 68.9 years in 2000. Similarly, aboriginal women are now expected to live to 76.6 years, whereas in 1975 the life expectancy was only 65.9 years (Canada 2002). Although life expectancy for aboriginal peoples is expected to continue to rise and to draw nearer to that of the general Canadian population, there continues to be a gap between these two groups of approximately 6.3 years (Canada 2002). In comparison to nonaboriginals, the much higher rates of illness, injury, and death among aboriginal peoples serve as a constant reminder of the disparities that exist within Canada. Suicide rates for both male and female registered Indian youth are five and seven times higher, respectively, than the Canadian average; these youth suicide rates represent some of the highest in the world (Guimond 2002). In 1997, the rate of tuberculosis in First Nations was approximately eight times that of the rest of Canada (Canada 2002). Moreover, registered Indians in Canada continue to suffer from far higher rates of diabetes, heart disease, hypertension, arthritis, and violent death.

The rate of incarceration of aboriginal peoples in Canada remains extraordinarily high and disproportionate with respect to the remainder of the nonaboriginal Canadian population. Although Canada already possesses one of the highest incarceration rates among developed countries at 129 per 100,000 Canadians, adult aboriginal people are imprisoned at more than eight times the national rate. High unemployment continues to plague aboriginal communities and ensures that a large segment of the population remains on social assistance. Almost 38 percent of reserve residents (or 148,236 Indian people, on a monthly average) depended upon social assistance payments for survival in 2000–2001 (Canada 2002). Many more relied largely on employment insurance, old age pensions, and payments from the Canada Pension Plan. In this way, the largest source of income for a majority of on-reserve residents came directly from individual federal payments. There were, however, postsecondary education rates of more than 27,000 status Indians per year; 35 percent were over 30 years old, and two-thirds of them were women. It should also be noted that $5 billion from the Department of Indian and Northern Affairs and an additional $2 billion from other federal departments is provided annually; 90 percent of this funding targets only First Nations and Inuit groups. This causes a growing number of complaints and litigation from the Métis and nonstatus Indians, who feel they deserve equivalent attention.

Despite the statistics indicating a growing population, severe societal issues, and highly economically dependent communities, the national land base set aside exclusively as Indian reserves remains at only three million hectares, or approximately 0.3 percent of Canada. This small reserve space provides a thoroughly inadequate natural resource base, creating substantial pressure on most First Nations, who find it increasingly difficult to accommodate their populations and support their economies. Métis peoples face an even more restrictive situation, as fewer than 5 percent have access to the six Métis settlements in Alberta. This dire situation has increased significantly the importance placed, in recent years, on the proper fulfillment of treaty commitments made in historic treaties by the Crown, on settling outstanding land claims, and on negotiating new treaties to reflect current realities and future aspirations. Those aboriginal communities who have successfully concluded modern treaties in recent years face a far brighter future than those without such agreements. It should be appreciated, however, that achieving even a modern treaty is not an end in itself. Ongoing struggles also arise for Inuit, Métis, and First Nations parties in their efforts to seek full implementation of the fundamental commitments made in the new treaties by governments and to ensure that, this time, the relevant government signatories will honor the terms of these solemn promises.

The Modern Legal Status of Treaties

Treaty negotiations have been heavily affected in several critical respects by the jurisprudence that has evolved over the last 20 years. As discussed, the courts have articulated a clear set of principles that must guide all efforts to interpret the proper meaning to be given to historic as well as modern treaties. The Supreme Court has also definitively established the existence of a fiduciary relationship between the Crown and aboriginal peoples, which has received constitutional elevation through Section 35 of the Constitution Act, 1982. Each of these basic tenets is having a profound impact on the way in which both federal and provincial governments must interrelate with Indian, Inuit, and Métis communities.

Legal Interpretation Principles for Treaties

The current chief justice of Canada, Beverley McLachlin, summarized the jurisprudence developed by Canadian courts over the prior three decades in the leading treaty fishing rights case of *Regina v. Marshall (No 1)* in 1999. She listed the following as the proper legal guidelines to be used in interpreting treaty provisions (at paragraph 78 with sources deleted):

1. Aboriginal treaties constitute a unique type of agreement and attract special principles of interpretation.

2. Treaties should be liberally construed and ambiguities or doubtful expressions should be resolved in favour of the aboriginal signatories.

3. The goal of treaty interpretation is to choose from among the various possible interpretations of common intention the one which best reconciles the interests of both parties at the time the treaty was signed.

4. In searching for the common intention of the parties, the integrity and honour of the Crown is presumed.

5. In determining the signatories' respective understanding and intentions, the court must be sensitive to the unique cultural and linguistic differences between the parties.

6. The words of the treaty must be given the sense which they would naturally have held for the parties at the time.

7. A technical or contractual interpretation of treaty wording should be avoided.

8. While construing the language generously, courts cannot alter the terms of the treaty by exceeding what "is possible on the language" or realistic.

9. Treaty rights of aboriginal peoples must not be interpreted in a static or rigid way. They are not frozen at the date of signature. The interpreting court must update treaty rights to provide for their modern exercise. This involves determining what modern practices are reasonably incidental to the core treaty right in its modern context.

It is important to note, however, that these principles may be subject to modification when interpreting a modern treaty, as the circumstances are drastically different. The aboriginal party has received the full benefit of legal counsel and is negotiating highly detailed documents through a lengthy period of time in a language with which they are comfortable. The federal court of appeal has suggested that modern treaties should be viewed quite differently and more akin to other contractual agreements among relatively equal parties. The Quebec Court of Appeal has adopted a somewhat hybrid approach and has suggested that modern treaties should be interpreted according to the intentions of all the parties, rather than automatically assuming that any ambiguities will be resolved in favor of the indigenous signatory. At the same time, the court also noted the fundamental importance of the subject matter in that case—education—to the Cree. The court concluded that a liberal, generous interpretation was warranted for the provisions concerning the participation of the Cree in discussions establishing the annual budget for the Cree school board.

Jurisprudence thus indicates that the Crown and its representatives, in dealing with all historic treaties, must adhere to the general treaty principles elaborated by the courts over the last 42 years since the leading decision of the British Columbia Court of Appeal in *Regina v. White and Bob* in 1964. In the intervening years, these principles have become somewhat modified—but only slightly—in the effort to ascertain the true meaning of the language used in modern treaties and other agreements reached between aboriginal peoples and federal or provincial governments.

The primary focal point for conflicts between First Nations and other governments, resulting in frequent litigation, is the assertion of treaty protected harvesting rights running afoul of general legislation aimed at regulating natural resources on Crown (federal or provincial government-owned) lands. These conflicts became commonplace in the 1950s with the more vigorous enforcement of hunting and fishing laws in rural and northern areas. The amount of litigation escalated considerably in the 1960s with the imposition of more detailed statutory restrictions on impermissible locations for harvesting fish and wildlife, allowed methods and equipment for harvesting, establishment of licensing requirements, identification of precluded and permitted harvesting times, and regulation of the sale of harvested goods. Asserting treaty rights as a ground of defense has been a common strategy in many parts of Canada since the 1970s, and the volume of charges laid for allegedly illegal activity by First Nations members has yet to abate noticeably, even though treaty rights obtained constitutional protection in 1982. It has also become more common of late for Métis and nonrecognized Indian people to be charged with such violations and for them to seek to assert an aboriginal or treaty right to hunt or fish free from such statutory restraints. A major reason for this continuing conflict is that the federal and provincial legislation in this sector has rarely been designed to accommodate the unique legal situation of aboriginal harvesters and treaty rights. As a result, governments have sought to impose a uniform natural resource management regime upon aboriginal peoples, who firmly believe they have an inherent right to maintain their traditional activities free from external regulation. The latter perspective is often further supported, in many parts of the country, by solemn Crown commitments, given in express language in individual treaties, that the Indian parties and their descendants would be free to hunt, fish, and trap forever as they had done for untold number of generations.

In recent years, similar conflicts have extended beyond wildlife to include disputes over aboriginal and treaty rights to log trees on Crown land for personal use, to use in the production of goods, and for sale as raw logs. The Supreme Court of Canada in July 2005 overturned appellate courts in Nova Scotia and New Brunswick that had previously upheld treaty rights to commercial logging (*Regina v. Marshall* and *Regina v. Bernard* respectively). The Supreme Court decided that the specific language in the treaty in question guaranteed only a right to trade goods today that were proven to have been actively traded with the British at the time the treaty was signed in 1760–1761. Because there was some limited trade in wood products at that time but not in raw logs themselves, the defendants did not have the treaty right to harvest trees on Crown land and then sell the logs without provincial government permission in the form of a license. Many other natural resource claims have yet to be pursued on a treaty basis.

Rights have also been asserted through reliance on particular treaty terms for exemption from income tax, for guarantees of financial support for university education, for the provision of free and comprehensive health care, for the availability of adequate housing, and regarding other important governmental initiatives. Efforts have also been made to resist the application of gun control and other laws to First Nations through reliance on treaty commitments. These efforts have met with mixed success. A further recent development in treaty litigation in Canada has been the complaints of First Nations and Inuit peoples, with either modern or historic treaties, that other governments have not consulted with them effectively prior to making decisions that may have a major impact upon their daily lives and territories. This concern has arisen in relation to federal or provincial proposals to launch new policies or programs—or to change existing ones—in allocating natural-resource harvesting rights to companies; in approving planned mines and petroleum developments; and in considering potential environmental impacts of energy projects, the building of new roads, and the like. Similar protests have been launched by First Nations seeking to negotiate new treaty agreements who believe that their position will inevitably be altered for the worse prior to reaching such arrangements if governments authorize large-scale logging, mining, oil drilling, electricity generating, and other such projects on land that is subject to aboriginal title claims. The same strategy has been used to challenge aquaculture operations (fish farms) and other activities in coastal waters, by insisting upon full First Nations' involvement in decision making so as to protect the environment. The Supreme Court of Canada, in the *Haida Nation* case, has confirmed that the federal and provincial governments have a legally enforceable duty to respect the honor of the Crown by consulting meaningfully with aboriginal communities when their unique aboriginal or treaty rights might be negatively impacted. This duty may also require the government to seek to accommodate legitimate aboriginal concerns by altering its proposals or requiring changes from third parties before authorizing the planned activities to proceed if these constitutionally protected rights might be infringed.

Conclusion

Over the past four centuries, Canada has been reasonably successful in forging peaceful relationships within its external borders between the descendants of European settlers (as well as immigrants from the rest of the world) and the original sovereign owners of this land, as succeeded by the First Nations, Inuit, and Métis peoples of today. In many parts of Canada, these relationships have been built upon the foundation of mutually binding commitments in the form of treaties. Canada has been far less successful, however, in ensuring that a common understanding of the fundamental purpose of these treaty compacts, along with a mutual acceptance of the precise meaning of the treaty terms, remained alive among—and were honored by—subsequent generations. Oral histories of the actual treaty negotiations and the words agreed upon are very much a part of the fabric of regular life for many First Nations communities. Most nonaboriginal Canadians, however, have virtually no knowledge whatsoever of the significance of Crown-Indian treaties in their own lives as a critical source of the rights and benefits that they enjoy as members of Canadian society and as the source of much of the prosperity on which the Canadian economy has been built. The ongoing need to negotiate treaties for the first time in some parts of the country, along with the need to revitalize and renew the historic treaty commitments from generations ago, will continue to be a noteworthy aspect of domestic development for quite some years to come. Through devoting greater attention to the import of treaties, whether they result from hands extended in friendship several centuries ago or through the flourish of pens at signing ceremonies yesterday and tomorrow, hopefully Canadians will develop a greater appreciation of their unique opportunity to create a truly modern nation based on profound respect and partnership.

Bradford W. Morse

Further Reading
Court Cases

Calder v. Attorney General of British Columbia, SCR 313 (1973).

Cherokee Nation v. Georgia, 30 U.S. 1 (1831).

Haida Nation v. British Columbia (Minister of Forests), 3 SCR 511 (2004).

Mikisew Cree First Nation v. Canada (Minister of Canadian Heritage), 1 CNLR 78 (2006).

Regina v. Marshall (No. 1), 3 SCR 456 (1999).

Regina v. Marshall (No. 2), 3 SCR 533 (1999).

Regina v. Marshall; Regina v. Bernard, 3 CNLR 214 (2005).

Regina v. Powley, 4 CNLR 321(SCC) (2003).

Regina v. White and Bob, 50 DLR (2d) 193 (B.C.C.A.) (1964).

Thomas Johnson and Graham's Lessee v. William M'Intosh, 21 U.S. 543 (1823).

Worcester v. Georgia, 31 U.S. 515 (1832).

Books and Articles

Alfred, Taiaiake. 1999. *Peace, Power and Righteousness: An Indigenous Manifesto*. Don Mills, ON: Oxford University Press.

Asch, Michael, ed. 1998. *Aboriginal and Treaty Rights in Canada*. Vancouver: University of British Columbia Press.

Bell, Catherine, and Karin Buss. 2000. "The Promise of Marshall on the Prairies: A Framework for Analyzing Unfulfilled Treaty Promises." *Saskatchewan Law Review* 63(2), 667.

Bird, John, Lorraine Land, and Murray MacAdam, eds. 2002. *Nation to Nation: Aboriginal Sovereignty and the Future of Canada*, 2nd ed. Toronto: Iwin.

Borrows, John. 1992. "Negotiating Treaties and Land Claims: The Impact of Diversity within First Nations Property Interests." *Windsor Yearbook of Access to Justice* 12, 179.

Borrows, John. 2005. "Creating an Indigenous Legal Community." *McGill Law Journal* 50, 153.

Brown, George, and Ron Maguire. 1979. *Indian Treaties in Historical Perspective*. Ottawa: Research Branch, Indian and Northern Affairs Canada.

Canada. 2002, March. Department of Indian Affairs and Northern Development, *Basic Departmental Data 2001*. Ottawa: Public Works and Government Services. Available at http://www.ainc-inac.gc.ca/pr/sts/bdd01/bdd01_e.pdf, at 2.

Canada. 2003a, January. *Census: Aboriginal Peoples of Canada: A Semographic Profile*. Ottawa: Minister of Industry. Available at Statistics Canada http:// www12statcan.ca/english/census01/Products /Analytic/companion/abor/contents.cfm?

Canada. 2003b, March. Department of Indian Affairs and Northern Development, *Basic Departmental Data 2002*. Ottawa: Public Works and Government Services. Available at http://www. ainc-inac.go.ca/prsts/bdd02/bidd02_c. pdfat3.

Coates, Ken. 2000. *The Marshall Decision and Native Rights*. Montreal: McGill-Queen's University Press.

Guimond, Eric. 1999. "Ethnic Mobility and the Demographic Growth of Canada's Aboriginal Populations from 1986 to 1996." In *Report on the Demographic Situation in Canada, 1998–1999*. Ottawa: Statistics Canada.

Guimond, Eric. 2002. "Aboriginal Profile 2001." Unpublished. Hull, ON: Indian and Northern Affairs Canada.

Groves, Robert K., and Bradford W. Morse. 2004. "Constituting Aboriginal Collectivities: Avoiding New Peoples 'In Between.'" *Saskatchewan Law Review* 67(1), 257.

Henderson, James [Sakej] Youngblood. 1997. "Interpreting Sui Generis Treaties." *Alberta Law Review* 36(1), 46.

Henderson, James [Sakej] Youngblood. 2000. "Constitutional Powers and Treaty Rights." *Saskatchewan Law Review* 63(2), 719.

Imai, Shin. 1999. *Aboriginal Law Handbook*, 2nd ed. Scarborough, ON: Carswell.

Indian Treaties and Surrenders from 1680–1890. 1905. Ottawa: S. E. Dawson. Reprint, Saskatoon, SK: Fifth House, 1992.

Isaac, Thomas. 2001. *Aboriginal and Treaty Rights in the Maritimes: The Marshall Decision and Beyond*. Saskatoon, SK: Purich.

Mainville, Robert. 2001. *An Overview of Aboriginal and Treaty Rights and Compensation for Their Breach*. Saskatoon, SK: Purich.

Morse, Bradford. 2004. "Aboriginal and Treaty Rights in Canada." In *Canadian Charter of Rights and Freedoms/Charte canadienne des droits et libertés*, 4th ed., edited by Gérald A. Beaudoin and Errol Mendes, 1171–1257. Markham, ON: LexisNexis Butterworths.

O'Callaghan, Edmund Bailey, ed. 1853–1861. *Documents Relative to the Colonial History of the State of New York*. Albany, NY: Weed, Parsons.

Price, Richard, ed. 1979. *The Spirit of the Alberta Indian Treaties*. Montreal: Institute for Research on Public Policy.

Purich, Donald. 1988. *The Métis*. Toronto: James Lorimer and Company.

Royal Commission on Aboriginal Peoples. 1995. *Treaty Making in the Spirit of Co-Existence: An Alternative to Extinguishment*. Ottawa: Canada Communication Group.

Royal Commission on Aboriginal Peoples. 1996. *Report of the Royal Commission on Aboriginal Peoples*. Ottawa: Canada Communication Group.

Slattery, Brian. 2000. "Making Sense of Aboriginal and Treaty Rights." *Canadian Bar Review* 79, 196.

Treaty 7 Elders and Tribal Council with Walter Hildebrandt, Sarah Carter, and Dorothy First Rider. 1996. *The True Spirit and Original Intent of Treaty 7*. Montreal: McGill-Queen's University Press.

Upton, Leslie F. S. 1979. *Micmacs and Colonists: Indian-White Relations in the Maritimes, 1713–1867*. Vancouver: University of British Columbia Press.

Wicken, William C. 2002. *Mi'kmaq Treaties on Trial: History, Land and Donald Marshall Junior*. Toronto: University of Toronto Press.

Williams, Robert A., Jr. 1997. *Linking Arms Together: American Indian Treaty Visions of Law and Peace, 1600–1800*. New York: Oxford University Press.

Colonial and Early Treaties, 1775–1829

For the first 50 years of the republic, the United States, in its relations with the Indian tribes within its borders, focused its diplomatic and political energies on ending wars and establishing peaceful relations, controlling trade, asserting supremacy, extending its criminal and civil jurisdiction, and securing titles to the tribal lands. To achieve these goals, the United States entered into 159 treaties with Indian tribes between 1775 and 1829 (Deloria and DeMallie 1999, 183–190). In doing so, it adopted the precedent established nearly 200 years earlier by European sovereigns—that of negotiating treaties with Native polities. Under the prevailing international law, the land belonged to the sovereign in whose name it was discovered, but the Indian tribes that occupied the land had a perpetual right of use. This right could be extinguished only by abandonment, by a "just war," or by purchase, the last being the most common means.

These legal principles were enunciated by the Spanish jurist Francisco de Vitoria in 1532 and quickly became the law of nations. The treaties negotiated in the half century covered by this essay may be divided into three time periods: the united colonies during the Revolutionary War, the Continental Congress under the Articles of Confederation, and the United States under the Constitution. The last time period began with the United States engaged simultaneously in war and in diplomacy: war in the Northwest Territory, war and diplomacy in the South, and diplomacy in western New York, all resulting in peace treaties and land cessions. The same pattern was followed during the first three decades of the nineteenth century: wage war when necessary, treat with tribes as policy required, and, above all, secure land cessions either as war reparations or sales. The Northwest and the South remained the foci of federal attention, and although western New York ceased to be a concern, it was replaced after 1803 with the lands west of the Mississippi River.

The United Colonies during the Revolutionary War

From the first skirmish at Concord and Lexington in April 1775, Revolutionary War leaders were aware of the threats posed by the Indian tribes within and on the

In 1756, Robert Roger developed wilderness fighting with his Roger's Rangers against Indians in the French-Indian War. Rangers held council with the Ottawa leader, Pontiac, during Pontiac's War in 1763 against the British colonies. (Library of Congress)

borders of the 13 colonies. In writing the Declaration of Independence, the committee of Thomas Jefferson, Benjamin Franklin, John Adams, Robert Livingston, and Roger Sherman made special note of the tribal threats to colonial survival: "He [King George III] has excited domestic insurrections amongst us, and has endeavoured to bring on the inhabitants of our frontiers, the merciless Indian Savages, whose known rule of warfare, is an undistinguished destruction of all ages, sexes and conditions." Although they grossly overstated the situation and expressed it in polemical terms, the Revolutionary War leaders had good reason for concern. At the end of the French and Indian War (1754–1763), a conflict in which most of the Indian tribes bordering the colonies had joined the French, England had established a policy restricting colonial settlement on Indian lands. The restrictions began in 1763, when the Crown issued a proclamation prohibiting settlement west of the Appalachian Mountains. The superintendents for Indian affairs, John Stuart for the southern district and Sir William Johnson for the northern district, negotiated treaties with the various Indian tribes in 1767 and 1768 that established the boundary line envisioned in the Proclamation of 1763. That line ran from a few miles west of Fort Stanwix (in present-day Rome, New York) in the north to the Gulf coast of Florida. There were to be no colonial settlements west of this line. Additionally, the colonies were required to pay a series of taxes to simultaneously recoup the Crown's costs incurred during the French and Indian War and maintain the Crown's continuing protection against Indian attacks—a requirement to which the colonists vehemently and, in some instances, violently objected.

It is not surprising that with few exceptions—most notably the Oneidas and the Tuscaroras, who supported the colonial cause—the Indian tribes west of the property line of 1768 were more sympathetic to the English than to the colonials. Some 20 years before, the English had represented the principal threat to their lands, and consequently an alliance with the French served their collective purpose. Now roles had changed. England appeared ready to protect Indian lands against American incursions.

In this situation, the most the American officials could hope for was that the tribes would remain neutral and perhaps give some quiet support. To accomplish this goal, the Continental Congress entered into seven treaties or agreements with the following tribes (Deloria and DeMallie 1999, 183; *ASP* 1832, 61: 1, 1)

Six Nations, Delawares, and Shawnees (1775)
Senecas, Cayugas, Nanticokes, and Conoys (1776)
Passamaquoddys, Penobscots, and Malecites (1777)
Winnebagos (1778)
Foxes (1778)
Delawares (1778)
Cherokees (1779)

Except for the Delaware and Cherokee treaties, these were informal agreements. Although the treaties in 1775 and 1776 differ in details, they have in common two elements: an explanation or justification of the rebellion against English authority and an appeal for tribal neutrality concerning the conflict between England and the colonies. Witness the speech of John Walker at the Treaty with the Six Nations, Delaware, Shawnee, and Ottawa in October 1775. He pressed the tribes to remain neutral and to recognize that they and the United Colonies had a common destiny.

> *Brothers* we wish to Cultivate so strict a Friendship with you as that your Enemies shou'd be Considered as ours, and our Enemies as yours. . . .
>
> *Brothers* you have no doubt heard of the dispute between us and some of our Fathers evil Counsellors beyond the Great Water, in this dispute your Interest is Involved with ours so far as this, that in Case those People with whom we are Contending shou'd Subdue us, your *Lands* your *Trade* your *Liberty* and all that is dear to you must fall with us, for if they wou'd Destroy our flesh and Spill our Blood which is the same with theirs; what can you who are no way related to or Connected with them Expect? (Deloria and DeMallie 1999, 55)

The treaties with the Winnebagos and the Foxes, negotiated by Colonel George Rogers Clark in August 1778, tied the tribes to an "Alliance and Friendship with the United States of America and [the tribes] Promised to be true and faithful Subjects"

(Ibid. 78, 79). The informality of treaties ended with the Delaware treaty in 1778. The treaty contains seven articles: a mutual forgiveness of all prior offenses; a guarantee of peace, friendship, and mutual assistance in cases of war; free passage of American troops across Delaware Territory to attack English forts; and fair, impartial trials of Delawares and Americans who violated either nation's laws. In addition, the United States agreed to appoint an agent to regulate trade; guaranteed Delaware Territory in perpetuity; and, most interestingly, invited the Delaware Nation "to join the present confederation, and to form a state whereof the Delaware nation shall be the head, and have a representation in Congress" (Kappler 1904, 3; 7 *Stat.* 13). The Cherokee treaty of 1779 contains all the provisions found in the Delaware treaty, with the exception of the statehood offer. Both treaties sought to ally the tribes to the United States in exchange for protections against the two major causes of enmity: dishonesty in trade and incursions on tribal lands.

The Continental Congress under the Articles of Confederation

Although written in 1777, the Articles of Confederation did not become officially operational until 1781. The sticking point was the insistence by the "landless" states—those without claims to western lands—that the "landed" states surrender their claims to the United States. Maryland, in particular, held up acceptance of the articles until Virginia agreed to surrender its claims to the Northwest Territory (the area north of the Ohio River, now the states of Ohio, Indian, Michigan, and Illinois) and what is now Kentucky. Other states with western claims were New York, Massachusetts, Georgia, and North Carolina. Many of the claims overlapped, and all were for lands occupied by a large number of Indian tribes.

Further complicating matters, the Articles of Confederation gave the United States sole control over war and peace but a vague mandate over Indian affairs. According to Article IX, the Continental Congress had the "sole and exclusive right and power of . . . regulating trade and managing all affairs with the Indians, not members of any of the states, provided that the legislative right of any state within its own limits be not infringed or violated." Because a number of states contained sizable areas occupied by Indian tribes, and because these states were anxious to gain title to these lands, Article IX preserved the rights of states to negotiate with the Indian tribes, even at the risk of a general war and in contravention of the interests of the United States. But the states were not the only ones to be concerned about the stability of relations between the United States and the Indian tribes. Congress also faced that concern, which for them had its roots in the Treaty of Paris. Although the Treaty of Paris (September 3, 1783) ended the Revolutionary War and established the Mississippi River as the western boundary of the United States as far south as Florida, it made no provision for ending the wars with the Indian tribes that had joined the English, and therefore it furthered the possibility of unstable relations with those tribes. As a result, it was clear to the Continental Congress that peace treaties with the hostile tribes were a necessity.

The crucial question was: What should be the terms of any peace treaties with the warring tribes?

General George Washington provided an answer in a September 1783 letter written to James Duane, a delegate to the Continental Congress. Washington expressed concern that, in the absence of a quick resolution of hostilities, the Indian lands would "be overrun with Land Jobbers, Speculators, and Monoplisers or even with scatter'd settlers" against the best interest of the United States. Normalizing relations with the tribes was imperative in order to prevent a situation that Washington believed to be "pregnant of disputes both with the Savages, and among ourselves" (Prucha 1994, 1). To this end, Washington felt that the tribes should be informed of the provisions of the Treaty of Paris, should be required to return all prisoners, should agree to a boundary line between the United States and themselves, and should grant to the United States a cession of land. Washington believed that the United States, for its part, should give assurances that it would "*endeavour* to restrain our People from Hunting or Settling" in Indian country as well as prevent dishonesty in trade. Washington concluded his letter by recommending that the lands ceded to the United States be purchased instead of seized by force (Ibid.). "In a word there is nothing to be obtained by an Indian War but the Soil they live on and this can be had by purchase at less expence, and without that bloodshed" (Ibid., 2).

In the winter of 1784, the Continental Congress completed its plans for ending hostilities with the Indian tribes still at war with the United States. To each tribe, the Congress would offer peace and demand a cession of land as reparations for the costs of the war. The latter demand deviated radically from Washington's recommendation to use the long-established practice of purchasing land from Indian tribes or, more precisely, purchasing the Indian tribes' right of use of the land. However, during the 1780s, the United States faced an enormous debt and no means to repay it, as well as a vengeful, restive population intent on settling on the very lands under tribal control. From Congress's point of view, the solution to these two problems was to exact retribution from the hostile Indian tribes via the relinquishment of land.

Between 1784 and 1786, the United States negotiated the following six treaties with hostile tribes:

Treaty at Fort Stanwix with the Seneca, Mohawk, Onondaga, and Cayuga (1784)
Treaty at Fort McIntosh with the Wyandot, Delaware, Chippewa, and Ottawa (1785)
Treaty at Hopewell, South Carolina, with the Cherokee (1785)
Treaty at Hopewell, South Carolina, with the Choctaw (1786)

Treaty at Hopewell, South Carolina, with the Chickasaw (1786)

Treaty at Fort Finney at the mouth of the Great Miami River with the Shawnee (1786)

These treaties have five provisions in common. First, they required the tribes to surrender all prisoners and, in the case of the treaties at Fort Stanwix, Fort McIntosh, and Fort Finney, required the Indian tribes to provide tribal leaders as hostages to assure the prompt prisoner return. The three treaties at Hopewell added the return of property, including slaves. Second, the United States offered the Indian tribes peace and protection, which served to end hostilities and to provide the United States with sole control over the Indian tribes. Third, the United States defined the territorial boundaries of the Indian tribes, reserving land for Indians' sole use and occupancy and taking ownership of the remainder. Fourth, the United States agreed that crimes committed by Americans on the tribal lands would be punished. Fifth, the tribes were to surrender to the United States any Indian who committed crimes against Americans.

A number of treaties contained additional provisions specific to the situations between the United States and particular tribes. In the Fort Stanwix treaty, the United States guaranteed the lands of the Oneidas and Tuscaroras in appreciation of their loyalty to the colonial cause during the Revolutionary War. Similarly, the Fort McIntosh treaty restored tribal rights and property to those Delawares who had remained loyal to the United States. The Hopewell treaties with the Cherokees, Choctaws, and Chickasaws contained guarantees of fair trade. Additionally, the Cherokees were offered the opportunity to send a representative to the Continental Congress. Upon hearing the terms announced by the congressional negotiators at the treaty conferences, the Indian negotiators were nearly unanimous in their opposition. They argued that they had not waged war against the United States without provocation, they had never sued for peace, and they were not empowered to grant the cessions demanded. However, they argued without success. These treaties were not made at arm's length: the terms were dictated by the U.S. commissioners, and the tribes were told to accept them or face annihilation. The words of Richard Butler, who negotiated the treaty with the Shawnees at Fort Finney on behalf of the United States, illustrated the Continental Congress's attitude:

> The destruction of your women and children, or their future happiness, depends on your present choice. Peace or war is in your power; make your choice like men, and judge for yourselves. (Downes 1977, 297)

Once the Indian delegates returned home and their tribal leaders and members heard the terms imposed, the Indian tribes rejected the terms. As the news of the high-handed way the Indian tribes at the treaty conferences had been treated, other

Indian tribes, not party to the treaties but neighbors and allies of those who were, joined in opposition. The result was a loosely formed confederacy of Indian tribes in the Northwest Territory, the area north of the Ohio River to the Mississippi River and including Ohio, Indiana, southern Illinois, Michigan, and a small piece of western Pennsylvania. Although mindful of the rejection and opposition by the tribes, the Continental Congress proceeded to legislate for the area as though its title was clear and peace prevailed. In 1785, it passed "An Ordinance for ascertaining the mode of disposing of lands in the Western Territory," which provided for the survey of the lands between the Ohio River and the Great Lakes and their subsequent division into six-mile-square townships. The land was then to be sold to settlers. In 1787, the Congress passed the Northwest Ordinance, providing for a system of governance for the Northwest Territory. The Continental Congress's intention to survey and sell the land in the Northwest Territory, combined with the increasingly frequent incursions on Indian lands by hunters and squatters, made war inevitable. Within a year of the passage of the Land Ordinance of 1785, the United States began surveying and settling the Northwest Territory. To make the point that the United States considered the land its property and would countenance no interference with its settlement, General George Rogers Clark ordered attacks on Shawnee villages in 1786. Although the attacks resulted in the unremitting hostility of the Shawnees, they had a salutary effect from the American point of view: they served to separate those Indian tribes closer to American territory—Senecas, Delawares, Wyandots, and Chippewas—from those more remote and thus less subject to U.S. intimidation—Shawnees, Miamis, Weas, Piankashaws, Potawatomis, and Kickapoos.

Exacerbating the Continental Congress's problems concerning Indian relations were the actions of some of the states with sizable Indian populations. Georgia held treaties with the Cherokees and the Creeks in 1783 and again with the Creeks in 1785 and 1786. Massachusetts negotiated its claims to what is now the western part of New York State with the Six Nations in 1788. But New York State was by far the most aggressive in securing Indian lands. It negotiated with the Oneidas for a large tract of tribal land in 1785, a year after federal guarantees to that land, and again with the Oneidas in 1788, as well as with the Onondagas in the same year and with the Cayugas the following year. New York went so far as to send individuals to disrupt the federal Treaty of Fort Stanwix (Treaty with the Six Nations) in 1784, although this effort failed to prevent the signing of the treaty. In the final days of the Continental Congress, the United States sought to reaffirm its treaties made between 1784 and 1786 with the hostile tribes by signing two treaties at Fort Harmar in January 1789. The first, with the Wyandots, Delawares, Ottawas, Chippewas, Potawatomis, and Sacs, repeated the terms of the treaties of Fort McIntosh (Treaty with the Wyandot, etc., 1785) and Fort Finney (1786; Kappler 1904), but in a shift of policy, the United States made a payment to the Indian tribes of $6,000 in goods for the land taken (Kappler 1904, 16–18). The second treaty, with the Six Nations of New York, repeated the terms of the Treaty of Fort Stanwix (1784), and it, too, contained a payment in goods for land: $3,000. As the Mohawks under Joseph Brant were not in attendance at the treaty, they were denied any payment. The terms of both treaties were dictated by Arthur St. Clair, governor of the Northwest Territory, who hoped that the treaties would end the warfare. However, most of the tribes in the Northwest Territory had refused to attend; of those who were present, none were represented by their principal chiefs. The treaties were repudiated by the tribes, making war in the Northwest Territory inevitable.

Treaties under the United States Constitution

The United States under the Constitution began functioning in April 1789, beset with a myriad of Indian problems, including an inevitable war with the tribes in the Northwest Territory. However, unlike the Articles of Confederation, the Constitution made the United States supreme in the conduct of Indian affairs. The Congress has the sole power "To regulate Commerce . . . with the Indian Tribes" (Article I, Section 8) and to declare war (Article I, Section 8). It granted to the president the power to make treaties with the advice and consent of the Senate (Article II, Section 2).

The first treaties to reach the president and the Senate were the two negotiated at Fort Harmar. They raised a serious question regarding the handling of Indian treaties. Did Article II, Section 2 of the Constitution apply to treaties between the United States and Indian tribes? Washington proceeded on the assumption that a treaty with an Indian tribe should be treated as any other treaty would under the Constitution. He sent the two treaties, supporting documents, and a report from Secretary Henry Knox to the Senate in May 1789. The following month, the Senate appointed a three-member committee to review the treaty and accompanying materials. The Senate was uncertain of the status of Indian treaties; after much consideration, the Senate advised Washington to carry out the treaty (Prucha 1994, 70–71). This did not satisfy Washington, and he so informed the Senate. He pointed out that treaties made by subordinates were not official until ratified by the sovereign "and I am inclined to think it would be adviseable to observe it in the conduct of our treaties with Indians. . . . It strikes me that this point should be well considered and settled, so that our national proceedings in this respect may become uniform, and be directed by fixed, and stable principles" (as quoted in Prucha 1994, 72). The Senate agreed; Indian treaties were to be treated in the same manner as any other treaty entered into by the United States. Once negotiated, they were submitted to the Senate for its advice and consent, which was given by a two-thirds vote, and then proclaimed by the president.

The Department of War, headed by Secretary Henry Knox, was charged with the implementation of Indian policy. Knox, like Washington, believed it was futile to attempt to take Indian land by force. He advised the president that the best policy was one in which the United States recognized the tribes' rights to the lands they possess and offered to purchase by treaty what they were willing to sell He was certain that the tribes would be willing to sell sections of land at reasonable cost. He explained, "As the settlements of the whites shall approach near to the Indian boundaries established by treaties, the game will be diminished, and the lands being valuable to the Indians only as hunting grounds, they will be willing to sell further tracts for small considerations" (*ASP* 1832–61: 1, 13–14).

But first the nation had to deal with a war in the Northwest Territory, hostilities in the South, and a possible war with tribes of the Six Nations in western New York. To meet these threats, the War Department formulated a threefold approach: First, the United States would wage war on the tribes along the Wabash River, principally the Miamis. Second, the United States would carry on negotiations with the southern Indian tribes, particularly the Cherokees, the Chickasaws, and the Creeks. Third, the president, with the approval of the Senate, would send a commissioner to settle differences with the Six Nations, principally the Senecas, who were angry over the forced land concessions at Fort Stanwix and Fort Harmar.

The United States made two unsuccessful attempts to defeat the Indian tribes north of the Ohio. In the summer of 1790, General Josiah Harmar led an army of 1,453 militia and regulars against the Miamis, and after destroying a number of villages, the army was defeated. The following year, territorial governor Arthur St. Clair assembled an army of 2,770 and marched into Miami country. There he met an army consisting of Miamis, Wyandots, Chippewas, and Kickapoos, led by the Miami chief Little Turtle. The results were disastrous for the United States. Of the 1,400 U.S. troops who participated in the battle, more than 900 were killed or wounded. The rest retreated to the safety of Fort Hamilton (now Cleveland, Ohio) (Mahon 1988, 150; Downes 1977, 317–318). After the battle, General Anthony Wayne replaced St. Clair. Wayne was ordered to raise and train an army to defeat the tribes in the Northwest Territory.

The problems with the Six Nations in New York and the tribes in the South were largely the result of white settlers committing crimes against Indians within tribal territories, dishonest traders who cheated the Indians with shoddy goods and exorbitant prices, and states and citizens who forced or tricked the Indian tribes into selling their lands at paltry rates. To remedy these conditions, Congress in 1790 passed the first of a series of laws known as the Indian Trade and Intercourse Acts. These acts sought to regulate trade by licensing the traders who entered Indian country, making individuals who commit crimes in Indian country subject to state or territorial laws and punishments, and prohibiting the sale of Indian lands to individuals and to states "whether having the right of pre-emption to such lands or not, unless the same shall be made and duly executed at some public treaty, held under the authority of the United States" (1 *Stat.* 137–138). The last provision applied only

The defeat of American commander Josiah Harmar by Northwestern tribes in 1790 led to more war. Finally the United States broke the power of the Indians over the Ohio region in the Battle of Fallen Timbers in 1794, and the Treaty of Greenville in 1795 produced peace until the War of 1812. (U.S. Department of State)

to the original 13 states, which were acknowledged to have retained the preemption right, that is, the right to purchase the Indian lands within their borders; however, the United States determined when that right could be exercised, when Indian title could be extinguished. The Act of 1790 was temporary, set to expire in June 1793, but Congress renewed and strengthened the act in March of that year. (Congress continued to renew and revise the act in three-year increments until 1802, when it was made permanent. Although the act was modified throughout the period, the essential provision prohibiting individuals from purchasing Indian land and the restrictions on states doing the same remained.)

President George Washington affirmed the protection of Indian land guaranteed by the Indian Trade and Intercourse Act to the Seneca sachems Cornplanter, Half-Town, and Great-Tree in December 1790. Responding to a litany of complaints, Washington informed them of the provisions of the act and added, "Here, then, is the security for the remainder of your lands. No State, nor person, can purchase your lands, unless at some public treaty, held under the authority of the United States. The General Government will never consent to your being defrauded, but it will protect you in all your just rights" (*ASP* 1832–61: 1, 142). In addition to the assurances Washington gave to the Six Nations that their lands would be protected, he took the further step of appointing Timothy Pickering, with the consent of the Senate, as Indian commissioner to the New York tribes. Between 1790 and 1794, Pickering held a series of conferences with the Six Nations to keep them neutral and to resolve outstanding differences. While the United States pursued its military efforts in the Northwest and its diplomatic efforts with the Six Nations, it had to contend with frequent border depredations in the South. With its limited resources, the United States could not engage in a war against the Choctaws, Cherokees, Chickasaws, and Creeks, nor could it afford to have these tribes join with the Indian tribes north of the Ohio. In response to the dilemma, Washington chose a diplomatic approach, holding a number of treaty conferences with the southern Indian tribes. In 1790 and 1791, the United States negotiated treaties with the Creeks and Cherokees respectively. The two treaties contained essentially the same provisions: the tribes recognized U.S. protection and "no other sovereign whosoever"; the tribes would return all prisoners; their boundaries would be surveyed and guaranteed by the United States; the tribes were free to punish any citizen or inhabitant of the United States who settled on their land; hunting and entry on tribal land without a passport by citizens or inhabitants of the United States were forbidden; fugitives from justice were to be returned to the United States, and individuals committing crimes on Indian land were to be punished according to the laws of the state or territory where the Indian lands were located; both sides would refrain from retaliation; the tribes would give notice of any threats against the United States; and lastly, so that the Indian tribes "may be led to a greater degree of civilization, and to become herdsmen and cultivators, instead of remaining in a state of hunters," the United States would supply domesticated animals and farm implements. Although these treaties did little to quell the border depredations, their provisions set the tone, format, and language for subsequent treaties.

The year 1794 proved to be a turning point in Indian-United States relations and territorial policy. The previous summer, a U.S. delegation had met with the Ohio tribes to negotiate a settlement but had no success. The tribes insisted that the United States accept the Ohio River as the boundary between the parties, which the U.S. commissioners rejected. Negotiations having failed, Knox directed General Anthony Wayne to begin an offensive to secure the Ohio valley. Wayne waited until the summer of 1794 to begin his campaign, and after building a string of forts on the Maumee and the Great Miami Rivers, he moved to meet the Indian army, which numbered some 2,000. Wayne proceeded deliberately toward the Indian camp at Fallen Timbers, which was protected by an English post, Fort Miami. The tribes had been led to believe by English officials in Canada that the English would support them militarily and that war between the United States and England was imminent. But when Wayne, whose forces outnumbered the Indians, attacked, the English took no action. Although the Battle of Fallen Timbers, on August 20, did not destroy the tribes' ability to fight, the failure of the English to help resulted in dissolution of the Indian fighting force. Wayne went on to destroy Indian villages and crops unopposed. The war in Northwest Territory was over, but the United States had yet to negotiate a settlement of all grievances with the Six Nations of New York, the tribes in the South, and those it had defeated in the Ohio valley. The United States began the process of settling tribal grievances even before the commencement of the offensive in the Northwest. In June 1794, the United States negotiated a treaty with the Cherokees at Philadelphia, Pennsylvania, affirming the boundaries and other provisions of the treaties of 1785 and 1791 and granting the Cherokees annually "goods suitable for their use" worth $5,000 "in lieu of all former sums" (Kappler 1904, 26). Two years later, the United States made a similar treaty with the Creeks; they confirmed the boundary provision of the treaty of 1790 and the boundaries set by the treaties with the Chickasaws, the Cherokees, and the Choctaws (1785–1786). In return, the United States made a onetime payment of $6,000 in goods to the Creeks. The efforts of the federal government to prevent the Six Nations of New York from joining the Ohio tribes had been largely successful. By the fall of 1794, Timothy Pickering was ready to settle their grievances, having met in council with the Indian leaders and heard their complaints during the preceding three years. He called for a treaty council at Canandaigua, New York, which lasted some two months and ended in November. The treaty acknowledged the lands of the Oneidas, the Onondagas, and the Cayugas in New York State to be theirs; nullified the land cession of the Treaty of Fort Stanwix, returning to the Senecas the land taken, except for a four-mile strip along the east bank of the Niagara River from Lake Ontario to Lake Erie; and granted the Six Nations an annuity of $4,500 in perpetuity.

In exchange, the Senecas, Onondagas, Cayugas, and Oneidas surrendered all claims to any other land within the United States. The treaty was signed by Timothy Pickering for the United States and by 59 "sachems and war chiefs" of the Six Nations, including Cornplanter, Red Jacket, Farmer's Brother, the Seneca prophet Handsome Lake, and the Stockbridge chief Hendrick Aupaumut.

Although both sides were aware of Wayne's victory at Fallen Timbers months before, this did not greatly affect the final results. The principal U.S. interest in the treaty was to gain an unconditional surrender of any Six Nations claims to land in the Ohio valley. Pickering justified the return of the Seneca lands in western New York, saying that the United States never had a right to the land because the preemption right belonged to Massachusetts, the lands lay within the boundaries of New York State, and the Senecas would never have agreed to the treaty without the return.

There were other problems concerning tribal land and New York and Massachusetts claims to be resolved, and they presented some knotty legal and political issues. The Indian Trade and Intercourse Acts made provision for the original 13 states and Vermont and Maine, which had been parts of original states, to treat for land with tribes within their boundaries. There were two restrictions on the states: they could only negotiate at a federally held treaty at which a U.S. commissioner was present, and they could only negotiate the price to be paid to the tribe that held the right of use. New York State, under the leadership of Governor George Clinton, aggressively sought the purchase of tribal lands and in 1795 negotiated land sales with the Oneidas, the Cayugas, and the Onondagas, much to the consternation of Secretary of War Timothy Pickering. John Jay succeeded Clinton as governor of New York in 1795, and he chose to comply with the Indian Trade and Intercourse Act, resulting in three federally held treaties. The first of these was a treaty in 1796 with the Seven Nations of Canada: Caughnawagas and St. Regis (Mohawk), Lake of Two Mountains (Nippisings, Iroquois, and Algonquins), St. Francis (Sokoki Abenakis), Becancours (Eastern Abenakis), Oswegatchies (Onondagas, Oneidas, and Cayugas), and Lorettes (Hurons). By this treaty, the Seven Nations surrendered all their claims to land in New York, except for what is now the St. Regis Reservation in upstate New York along the St. Lawrence River, for "the sum of one thousand two hundred and thirty-three pounds six shillings and eight-pence, lawful money" of New York State and an annuity of 213 pounds, 6 shillings, and 8 pence. A year later, under the leadership of Joseph Brant and John Deserontyon, the Mohawks surrendered their tribal claims in New York for $1,600. New York State negotiated treaties under federal auspices with the Oneidas in 1798 and 1802, although the latter treaty was never ratified by the Senate or proclaimed by President Thomas Jefferson. Finally, in 1802, the United States held two treaties with the Senecas. These were unusual in that they were negotiated for the benefit of individuals, in apparent violation of the Indian Trade and Intercourse Acts, which contained an absolute prohibition against individuals purchasing Indian land. The Seneca lands were a unique case. They were the subject of nearly 150 years of dispute over who held the preemption right, Massachusetts or New York. Massachusetts claimed the right from a grant by King James I to the Plymouth Company in 1621 to all the land, from sea to sea, between the 40th and 48th parallels north. New York based its claim to the Seneca lands on a grant from King Charles II to his brother James II, Duke of York. The dispute lingered until 1786, when representatives of the two states met in Hartford, Connecticut, and agreed to a compromise that gave preemption to Massachusetts and jurisdiction to New York. Massachusetts then sold its preemption right to the 6 million acres of Seneca land to private speculators, who in 1788 purchased from the Senecas 2.6 million acres for $5,000 and an annuity of $500 (New York State Assembly Document 51 1889: 16–18).

The owners of the preemption were unable to convince the Senecas to sell any more of their remaining 3.4 million acres until 1797. In that year, Robert Morris, acting as an agent for the owners, met with the Senecas under the authority of a U.S. Indian commissioner and negotiated the Treaty of Big Tree, whereby the Senecas sold some 3.2 million acres for $100,000 in Bank of the United States stock, reserving for themselves approximately 200,000 acres on 9 reservations in western New York State (Ibid., 131–134). In 1802, the Senecas agreed to exchange with owners of the preemption 42 square miles of land of their Cattaraugus Reservation for an equal amount along Cattaraugus Creek. In a separate treaty negotiated at the same convention, the Senecas sold Little Beard's reservation of two square miles for $1,200. These treaties were signed by the most prominent men in the Seneca Nation, including Cornplanter, Farmer's Brother, Red Jacket, and Handsome Lake.

Two additional transactions to which a U.S. Indian commission was present require mention. In 1823, the owners of the preemption right purchased from the Senecas a tract of land for $4,286, and in 1826 the Senecas sold to the same group a second tract of 86,887 acres for $48,260. Neither sale was ratified by the Senate or proclaimed by the president. Returning to the Northwest Territory, the Treaty of Greenville, which ended the war in that region, was signed on August 3, 1795, by General Anthony Wayne and chiefs of the Wyandots, Delawares, Shawnees, Ottawas, Chippewas, Kickapoos, Miamis (including the Piankashaws, Weas, and Eel River bands), Kickapoos, and Kaskaskias. In all, 69 chiefs inscribed their marks on the treaty, including Little Turtle, the great Miami chief, and Blue Jacket, a war leader of the Shawnees. The treaty was similar in form to those that had preceded it: it declared the parties to be at peace; required that prisoners be exchanged and that the United States hold 10 Indian chiefs hostage until the exchange was completed; included a major cession of land north of the Ohio River, plus specific sessions for forts, trading posts, portages, and so forth; and obligated the tribes to warn the United States of any hostile intent by others. In exchange, the United States gave the tribes $20,000 in goods and a perpetual annuity of $9,500 to be divided among them. The tribes were empowered to expel illegal settlers; trade would be opened with the United States, retaliation restrained, and all former treaties voided.

Treaties and National Territorial Expansion, 1800–1829

Four policy goals defined treaty making during the first decades of the 19th century: land acquisition, changing tribes to agrarian-based economies, managing trade, and securing and maintaining peaceful relations. First and foremost was the acquisition of land to satisfy the flood of immigrants and Americans moving westward. This meant the surrender of large sections of tribal land upon which the tribes depended for subsistence. To compensate for the land losses, the United States sought to convince the tribes to give up hunting and adopt European American farming and, by providing funds for schools, to adopt American ways. To supply the tribes with products they could not raise or manufacture, the United States proposed to establish trading posts, sometimes called factories, on the diminished tribal lands. This would have the salutary effect of reducing complaints from tribes about the unfair practices of individual traders and would keep out any foreign influences potentially threatening to the United States. It would, in addition, provide the federal government with information concerning tribal affairs, invaluable for treaty negotiations. Finally, the treaties would establish and confirm peace and commit the tribes to recognize the United States as their sole protector. This was of particular importance because Spain, France, and England possessed land on the nation's borders and, through trade and alliances, had great influence with many of the tribes east of the Mississippi River.

The problem of foreign involvement in what the federal government considered internal national issues became particularly acute in 1802, when President Thomas Jefferson learned of Spain's secret transfer of the Louisiana Territory to Emperor Napoleon Bonaparte of France. However, the threat of a French occupation of New Orleans, and thus control of the Mississippi River, was removed when the United States in 1803 purchased France's preemption right west of the Mississippi River, an area of some 828,000 square miles. That left Spain in control of Florida, and the English along the nation's northern border.

Although President Jefferson was initially concerned that the purchase was unconstitutional, in the end pragmatic factors overcame philosophical ones, and Jefferson embraced the purchase. The United States had nearly doubled its size and brought within its boundaries a then-unknown number of tribes, yet it had not cleared its title to the area it had secured from England in 1783 nor settled its relations with the tribes that occupied these lands. Jefferson recognized that the tribes east of the Mississippi River were growing ever more opposed to selling any of their land, while at the same time the demands for land were increasing exponentially. The dilemma for the national government was how to gain title without provoking another series of Indian wars.

Jefferson made no departure from the Indian policy established during Washington's administration. Congress had enacted the Indian Trade and Intercourse Act in 1790 and had renewed and modified the act in 1793, 1796, and 1799. In the 1796 renewal of the act, Congress established a system of government-owned trading posts "for the purpose of carrying on a liberal trade with the several Indian nations, within the limits of the United States" (1 *Stat.* 452). In 1802, Congress made permanent the provisions of the Indian Trade and Intercourse Acts. The act of 1802 contained a description of the boundary between Indian country and the United States, continued the prohibitions against settlement on Indian land, provided for the punishment of crimes committed in Indian country, required the issuance of passports to enter Indian country and licenses to trade, prohibited the sale of alcohol, and authorized the president "in order to promote civilization among the friendly Indian tribes, and to secure the continuance of their friendship, . . . to cause them to be furnished with useful domestic animals, and implements of husbandry, and with goods and money, as he shall judge proper" (2 *Stat.* 139–146).

Achieving what had emerged as national policy—the acquisition of tribal land without resorting to conquest—depended on convincing the tribes to change their lifestyles; to accomplish this, the tribes would have to abandon hunting and adopt agriculture. "The extensive forests necessary in the hunting life will then become useless," Jefferson wrote to Congress in 1803, "and they will see advantage in exchanging them for means of improving their farms and of increasing their domestic comforts." Jefferson saw that federal government trading posts were an essential part of national policy (Prucha 2000, 21). Thus, trade provisions were incorporated in many of the subsequent treaties.

The South

Between 1801 and 1829, the United States made 39 treaties with the Chickasaws, Choctaws, Creeks, Cherokees, and Florida tribes. These treaties extinguished Indian title to all of the land east of the Mississippi River from the Ohio River to the Gulf of Mexico, except for specific reservations of land for tribal use and occupancy. The first two treaties were with the Chickasaws and the Choctaws in 1801. Collectively, they gave the United States permission to build a road across tribal territory from Tennessee to "Natchez in the Mississippi Territory." These treaties cut a road diagonally from the northeast to the southwest across the tribal territories. In addition, the Choctaw treaty included a provision for the remarking of the boundary lines set by the English before the Revolutionary War and a relinquishment of land east of the Cumberland Mountains (Royce 1881, Pl. LXII).

For their cessions, the Chickasaws received $700 in goods, and the Choctaws received $2,000 in goods (Kappler 1904: 2, 41–43). In 1805, the Cherokees agreed to allow a road to run through their territory to connect Knoxville, Tennessee, with New Orleans. The tribe was paid $1,600 (Ibid., 61). Having gained rights-of-way to the Mississippi River across tribal lands, the United States set out to secure the intervening land. This involved land in four states—Tennessee, Alabama, Georgia, and South Carolina—and in the territory of Mississippi. The western part of Tennessee belonged to the Chickasaw and the Cherokee tribes. The United States title to Chickasaw land was cleared by three treaties in 1805, 1816, and 1818; Cherokee land was purchased in 1805, 1806, and 1819.

The Choctaw land was located in Alabama and Mississippi. By treaties in 1802, 1803, 1805, 1816, and 1820, the Choctaws surrendered their claims in the two states. In 1814, the Creeks sold their land in Alabama. Most of the remaining Creek land was located in Georgia. To clear title to this land, the United States negotiated seven treaties with the Creeks for land in Georgia: 1802, 1805, 1818, two in 1821, 1826, and 1827. The Cherokees also occupied land in Georgia, which they sold in 1804 and 1817. In 1816, they also sold a part of their territory in South Carolina. For their land cessions east of the Mississippi River, the four tribes received the following compensation: the Cherokees, $209,500 and $8,000 in perpetual annuities; the Chickasaws, $449,815; the Choctaws, $282,000 and $9,000 in perpetual annuities; the Creeks, $1,427,000 and $23,000 in perpetual annuities (Kappler 1904, 2). Included in these totals were funds set aside for the construction and operation of schools for tribal children.

Annuities

Annuities were payments of money and/or goods distributed to tribes annually for a specified number of years. Annuities were included in many treaties between tribes and the United States in exchange for land cessions. Many Native Americans came to depend on annuity distributions for survival as hunting grounds and other means of support diminished. The government often used the threat of withholding annuity payments to influence tribal behavior. Annuity payments continued after the government stopped negotiating treaties with Native peoples.

Annuities were included in many treaties, from the treaty of 1778 with the Delawares (Lenápes) through the end of the treaty period in 1871. The government had several reasons for including annuities in treaties. In the *Report of Commissioner of Indian Affairs* for November 1, 1875, Edward P. Smith stated, "The annuity in money or blankets, or bacon and beef, may have a tendency to draw the Indians within the reach of the Government, and prepare them for the beginning of a work of civilization, and also to render them disinclined to take up arms and go upon the war-path. But with any tribe a few years of this treatment is sufficient for the purpose, and after this end has been gained, a continuation of the feeding and clothing, without a reference to further improvement on the part of the Indians, is simply a waste of expenditure."

The distribution of annuities became one of the most important duties of agency personnel and was a complex process. Before distribution each year, the agent took a tribal census to calculate the amount of individual payments. The annuity goods were sent to the superintendent, who was responsible for them until signed payment vouchers were received from the tribe. The distribution was made by the superintendent, agent, and several witnesses to ensure accuracy and legitimacy. The annuity system was faced with numerous problems, including inferior goods, transportation costs, and corruption. Reformers lobbied for the end of annuity payments, claiming that the annuities increased the dependence of Native peoples rather than aided their progress toward self-sufficiency.

Early annuities, in either cash or goods, were paid to the chiefs of a tribe. The chiefs then distributed the payment to the rest of the tribe according to their personal obligations and tribal customs. However, this did not result in the even distribution the government desired. In 1847, the federal government tried to diminish the power and influence of the chiefs by distributing annuity payments directly to heads of families. Goods distributed in annuity payments included beef, flour, sugar, coffee, corn, pork, shoes, clothing, blankets, beads, mirrors, beds, plows, wagons, and other goods deemed necessary to propel Native peoples toward civilization. Individual portions of tribal annuities ranged from a few cents to more than $100. In many instances, cash annuities went directly to traders to pay for goods that had been bought on credit during the year.

The government often threatened to withhold annuity payments to influence the actions of Natives. The Trade and Intercourse Act of 1834 provided for the payment of depredation claims against a tribe from that tribe's annuity. Tribes could also lose their annuity payments if they returned to ceded land, fought with other tribes or white citizens, resisted allotment, or refused to send their children to school.

Tamara Levi

Further Reading

Priest, Loring Benson. *Uncle Sam's Stepchildren: The Reformation of United States Indian Policy, 1865–1887*. Lincoln: University of Nebraska Press, 1975.

Prucha, Francis Paul. *The Great Father: The United States Government and the American Indians,* 2 vols. Lincoln: University of Nebraska Press, 1984.

Washburn, Wilcomb E. *The American Indian and the United States: A Documentary History*. New York: Random House, 1973.

Not all of the money stipulated to be paid by the United States went to the benefit of the tribes. The Choctaws' $50,000 went to cover money owed to traders; $250,000 of the Creek funds were earmarked for a similar purpose. The Cherokees were paid $43,760 to indemnify individual tribal members for damage caused by the U.S. Army and citizens. Payments were made to specific individuals in the tribes, very often chiefs or prominent warriors. George Guess (Sequoyah) received $500 in the Cherokee treaty of 1828 "for the great benefits he has conferred upon the Cherokee people, in the beneficial results which they have are now experiencing from the use of the Alphabet discovered by him" (Kappler 1904: 2, 207). The same treaty allocated $1,000 for the purchase of a printing press. The Choctaw chiefs and warriors received $14,972 for the assistance against the Upper Creeks in the Pensacola campaign during the War of 1812.

On the other side of the coin, because of "an unprovoked, inhuman, and sanguinary war, waged by the hostile Creeks against the United States" (Kappler 1904: 2, 77), the Creeks were forced by the treaty of 1814 to surrender more than 20 million acres in Georgia and Alabama (Prucha 1994, 11). The treaty referred to the Creek War of 1813–1814, fought against the United States by an Upper Towns band of the tribe. It took a combined force of Americans, Cherokees, Choctaws, and Lower Creeks to defeat the Upper Creeks and end the war. No compensation was granted to the Creek tribe in this treaty, even though a part of the tribe had remained loyal to the United States and assisted in the defeat of their fellow tribesmen.

Although the majority of the treaties negotiated with the southern tribes represented the sale of ever-diminishing tribal lands, several made after the Treaty of Ghent in 1814, which ended the War of 1812, provided for the exchange of land east of the Mississippi River for land in the Louisiana Territory. This possibility, a land exchange instead of a sale and reservation, had been foreseen by President Jefferson in 1803 and had been incorporated into law the following year. In 1804, Congress passed legislation establishing a system of governance for the Louisiana Territory. A provision in the act authorized the president "to stipulate with any Indian tribes owning lands on the East side of the Mississippi, and residing thereon, for an exchange of lands the property of the united States, on the West side of the Mississippi, in case the said tribe shall remove and settle thereon" (2 *Stat.* 283).

The Cherokee treaty of 1817 was the first to contain a provision for a land exchange. In exchange for surrendering land in Georgia, those who chose to emigrate were given an equal number of acres in the newly formed territory of Arkansas. The head of each emigrating household was given a rifle and ammunition, a brass kettle or beaver trap, and a blanket for each member of the family. Those who remained east of the Mississippi River and desired to become citizens were to receive 160 acres of tribal land. The annuities due the Cherokee tribe would be divided proportionately between the two groups. A treaty with the Choctaws in 1820 contains similar provisions: land in the Arkansas Territory for their land in Mississippi, equipment for the emigrating families, and citizenship and land for those remaining in the state of Mississippi.

These treaties ran into immediate opposition from settlers in the Arkansas Territory, so much so that they required renegotiation. In 1825, the Choctaws were forced to surrender a large portion of the land they had acquired in Arkansas and to accept a cash payment and an annuity of $6,000 instead. In 1828, the Cherokees found themselves in the same situation. They were forced to exchange their seven million acres in Arkansas for an equal amount of land west of the Mississippi River. The treaty described their title in the following terms:

> Whereas, it being the anxious desire of the Government of the United States to secure to the Cherokee nation of Indians, as well those now living within the limits of the Territory of Arkansas, as those of their friends and brothers who reside in States East of the Mississippi, and who may wish to join their brothers of the West, *a permanent* home, and which shall, under the most solemn guarantee of the United States, be, and remain, theirs forever—a home that shall never, in all future time, be embarrassed by having extended around it the lines, or placed over it the jurisdiction of a Territory or State. (Kappler 1904: 2, 206; emphasis in original)

In addition to the land guaranteed to the tribe, the United States granted the Cherokees "a free and unmolested use of all the Country lying West of the Western boundary" of their reservation, which in 1828 meant all of present Oklahoma.

Florida remained under Spanish control until 1819, when the United States completed its purchase. General Andrew Jackson, one of the principal negotiators of treaties with the southern tribes, had invaded the territory in 1818, precipitating the First Seminole War. Although that action caused a diplomatic flap, it allowed the U.S. negotiator, John Quincy Adams, to pressure Spain to sell its preemption right to the land. In 1823, the United States forced the weakened Florida tribes to sign a treaty whereby they surrendered all the territory, except for a small reservation, for $6,000 worth of "implements of husbandry, and stock of cattle and hogs" and a $5,000 annuity for 20 years (Kappler 1904: 2, 141).

It should not be assumed that these land transactions were accomplished with the full agreement of the tribes involved; quite the contrary. The Cherokee tribe split over the provision for removal in the treaty of 1817. The National Council of the Creek, led by the Upper Creeks, had passed a law in 1811 making it a capital crime to sell land. Their attitudes further hardened following the Creek War 1813–1814, largely because of sales made by the Lower Creeks. Finally, in 1825, when the leader of the Lower Town Creek, William McIntosh, a supporter of removal and active opponent of the Upper Town Creek, signed the treaty of 1825, the Upper Creeks killed him for ceding Creek land.

Nonetheless, by 1829, much of the tribal land of the Cherokees, Chickasaws, Choctaws, Creeks, and Florida tribes had been lost, and many of the tribal members had moved across the Mississippi River. More important, tribal governments had been damaged by factional disputes that, in the cases of the Cherokees and Creeks, had led to a prolonged and at times violent struggle.

The Northwest and Louisiana Territories

The United States followed the same policy objectives and negotiating procedures with the tribes in the Northwest Territory that it had followed with the southern tribes. However, the problems of dealing with the Northwest tribes were much more complicated and convoluted than in the South. In the Northwest, the United States found multiple tribal claims of ownership to the same lands and a continuing and growing resentment against the United States among members of the affected tribes. Tribal feelings were fed by the land forfeited by the tribes at the Treaty of Greenville in 1795 (Treaty with the Wyandot, etc.) and by the waves of settlers who showed little concern for the boundaries between Indian land and that belonging to the United States. To be fair, not all the fault lay with the settlers. Although the United States had gained title to a sizable area in the Northwest Territory, the boundaries of the land cession were not well defined, which led inevitably to disputes. The United States endeavored to remedy this in 1803 by entering into a treaty with nine tribes—Delawares, Shawnees, Potawatomis, Miamis, Eel Rivers, Weas, Kickapoos, Piankashaws, and Kaskaskias—to define the boundary (Kappler 1904: 2, 49), but by then settlements had been established on tribal lands, necessitating new concessions by the tribes.

During the first decade of the 19th century, the United States entered into a series of treaties with individual tribes and groups of tribes covering millions of acres of land in Ohio, Indiana, Michigan, and Illinois. The provisions of these treaties were essentially the same: a land cession in exchange for cash or goods and/or an annuity, generally for a specified number of years. A treaty with the Kaskaskias, "originally called the Kaskaskia, Mitchigamia, Cahokia and Tamaroi," in 1803 proclaimed that, because these tribes "from a variety of unfortunate circumstances . . . are reduced to a very small number," the tribe could no longer use its extensive territory and therefore "do relinquish and cede to the United States all the lands in the Illinois Territory." The tribe reserved but 1,630 acres for its own use. For this sale, the tribe had its annuity increased to $1,000, and because a majority of the tribal members were Catholics, the United States agreed to pay $100 to the Catholic priest for seven years (Kappler 1904: 2, 49–50). In 1809, the United States signed four treaties; the first, with the Delawares, Potawatomis, Miamis, and Eel River Miamis, gave the United States a large cession in Indiana. What was unique about this treaty was that a portion of the promised annuity depended upon individual treaties with two tribes that were not parties to the original treaty, namely the Weas and the Kickapoos. They signed separate treaties agreeing to the terms of the treaty of 1809.

Although the language of these treaties and those in the South suggests that they were the product of arms-length agreements, that the U.S. negotiators were sensitive to the needs and interests of their tribal counterparts, nothing could be farther from the truth. From the first opening session of a treaty council, the pressure brought to bear on the tribal negotiators was unremitting. If the presence of U.S. troops at the treaty council and the veiled threats of the U.S. negotiators did not result in the desired land cessions, often tribal negotiators were bribed. It is no wonder that by 1810 the tribes in the Northwest were preparing for war. As early as 1805, two Shawnee leaders were advocating a return to the ways of their forefathers. Led by Tenskwatawa (the Prophet) and his brother Tecumseh and supported by the English in Canada, some of the tribes in the Northwest had organized to oppose the United States. Tecumseh's movement split the tribes; those who supported Tecumseh in whole or part were mainly the Shawnees at Prophetstown and the Kickapoos, Ottawas, Chippewas, and Piankashaws; those who joined the Americans included the Wyandots, Sanduskys, Senecas, Delawares, Sacs (Sauks), and the main body of the Shawnees. The Miamis, one of the most powerful tribes, remained neutral despite attacks on its villages by the Americans. In addition, the tribes farther west, which included the Sioux, Menominees, Foxes, Iowas, Winnebagos (Ho-Chunks), and Kansas, joined the English. All would face U.S. negotiators at war's end.

The first signs of the impending conflict occurred in 1810 with skirmishes between the two sides. The following year, General William Henry Harrison marched against Prophetstown, Tenskwatawa's village on Tippecanoe Creek. Tenskwatawa's force came out to meet Harrison's, and although the results were inconclusive, the Prophet lost support among his Shawnee followers. In 1812, the English declared war on the United States and openly joined Tecumseh. Hostilities continued, culminating in the Battle of the Thames in Ontario, Canada, on October 5, 1813, where Tecumseh's forces and their English allies were defeated by the U.S. forces, and Tecumseh was killed.

With the death of Tecumseh, Indian resistance in the Northwest collapsed, but there remained the war with England, which continued for another year. The Treaty of Ghent, signed in December 1814, ended the war between the United States and England. By its terms, the United States agreed to make peace with the warring tribes and to restore to them "all the possessions, rights, and privileges" they had possessed in 1811 before the start of hostilities. In 1815, President James Madison appointed commissioners to end hostilities with the tribes in the Northwest and Louisiana Territory. In all, the commissioners negotiated 20 treaties with 22 tribes on both sides of the Mississippi between 1815 and 1817. These treaties, although they varied slightly in detail, generally speaking, contained clauses that established "perpetual peace and friendship" between the parties, recognized past treaties signed by the parties, forgave injuries committed by the parties, and returned any prisoners. The treaties of peace and friendship were but a prelude to an intensive period of land acquisition. The concerns of the United States were threefold: to complete the acquisition of the land in the Northwest, including Wisconsin and the Upper Peninsula of Michigan; to secure title to land along the west side of the Mississippi River; and to establish relations and supremacy over the tribes farther west. To accomplish the first objective, the federal government made 17 treaties between 1818 and 1829 (see Table 1). By these treaties, the United States secured most of the Indian title in the area, with the exception of Wisconsin. The 19 treaties made with the tribes to the west of the Mississippi River secured for the nation control of the Mississippi River, land for settlement, and a place to move the eastern tribes (see Table 2).

Table 1 Treaties of Cession, by State (Northwest)

State	Number of Treaties	Tribes Involved
Ohio	4	Potawatomis, Wyandots, Senecas (Ohios), Delawares, Shawnees, Ottawas, Chippewas, Weas, Miamis
Indiana	11	Potawatomis, Wyandots, Senecas (Ohios), Delawares, Shawnees, Ottawas, Chippewas, Weas, Miamis, Kickapoos
Michigan	9	Potawatomis, Wyandots, Senecas (Ohios), Delawares, Shawnees, Ottawas, Chippewas, Weas, Miamis, Winnebagos
Illinois	9	Sacs, Chippewas, Ottawas, Peorias, Kaskaskias, Potawatomis, Weas, Delawares, Kickapoos, Winnebagos
Wisconsin	5	Sacs, Chippewas, Ottawas, Potawatomis, Winnebagos

Note: Many of these treaties contained cessions of land in more than one state.

Table 2 Treaties of Cession, by State (West of the Mississippi)

State	Number of Treaties	Tribes Involved
Louisiana	1	Quapaws
Arkansas	4	Quapaws, Osages
Indian Territory	3	Quapaws, Osages
Missouri	6	Kickapoos, Sacs, Foxes, Iowas, Osages, Kansas, Shawnees
Kansas	3	Osages, Kansas, Shawnees
Nebraska	6	Kansas
Iowa	1	Sacs, Foxes

Note: Many of these treaties contained cessions of land in more than one state.

While busy with the land acquisitions just described, the United States began its preparation for the next set of treaties in the 1820s. The first step in the process was to secure treaties of friendship. Again, the treaties followed a set form. The tribes acknowledged the supremacy of the United States and its exclusive right to regulate all trade. For its part, the United States undertook to protect the tribes. In the mid-1820s, the United States made treaties with the Poncas, Sioux, Cheyennes, Arikaras, Ministarees, Mandans, Crees, Pawnees, and Omahas. In all, the United States made 53 treaties between 1818 and 1829 with the tribes in Michigan, Ohio, Indiana, Illinois, Wisconsin, and west of the Mississippi River.

State-Recognized Tribes

State-recognized tribes are Native communities acknowledged as legal entities by the state governments in which they reside. The term is used generally to set these groups apart from federally recognized tribes, although communities such as the Poarch Creeks of Alabama and the Cherokees of North Carolina are recognized as both state and federal tribes. In the 1990s, 38 states had some form of relationship with the Native communities within their borders. States with historically significant dealings with Native communities in their jurisdictions include Maine, Connecticut, Massachusetts, New York, Virginia, the Carolinas, Georgia, Alabama, Louisiana, and Texas. State-recognized tribes vary considerably in their community composition, political organization, and racial makeup.

Following the American Revolution, many states assumed trust responsibility for their Native populations. Tribes such as the Mashantucket Pequot of Connecticut came to live on state reserves set apart from non-Native inhabitants.

Unprotected by federal Indian agents and the full force of Indian law, however, many eastern tribes experienced land loss, assimilation pressures, and economic deprivation.

During the 1960s and 1970s, the Coalition of Eastern Native Americans and the Native American Rights Fund helped state-recognized tribes reinvigorate their communities, pursue land claims, and reassert their Native identities. In response, states such as North Carolina and Louisiana established Indian commissions to administer state and federal programs for these tribes. Texas, Alabama, Louisiana, and other states also began to recognize actively non-federal groups such as the Tiguas, Poarch Creeks, and Houmas. States faced criticism for lacking standards when acknowledging tribes; as a result, many states, such as Virginia, developed formal recognition criteria modeled directly on the Bureau of Indian Affairs' Federal Acknowledgment Process.

State recognition provides benefits for groups but is inferior to federal tribal status. After state acknowledgment, groups can qualify for federal Indian programs emanating from the Department of Health and Human Services and the Department of Education, and other general programs of the Departments of Labor, Commerce, and Justice. With a combination of federal grants and aid from the North Carolina Commission of Indian Affairs, the Lumbee Regional Development Association, for example, administers Job Training Partnership Act programs, low-income housing funds, and educational projects for its members.

Under the now-defunct Texas Indian Commission, the Alabama Coushattas and Tiguas ran successful tourist programs on tax-exempt state reservations, using the proceeds to raise the educational and income levels of their members. Louisiana and other states issue identification cards that tribal members can use to validate their identities. State recognition also confers eligibility for certain affirmative action programs. State tribal status, however, essentially does not alter a tribe's relationship within the federal system. State tribes cannot exercise full tribal sovereignty, pursue Indian gaming, or qualify for federal Indian programs of the Bureau of Indian Affairs and Indian Health Service. Members of state tribes are citizens of the states in which they reside and are subject to local civil and criminal laws; state reservations are not "Indian country" within the meaning of constitutional law.

The genetic and community composition of state tribes varies tremendously. Some, like the Jena Choctaws of Louisiana, have a high degree of Native ancestry, whereas others have intermarried with non-Natives and possess significant degrees of African and European ancestry. In terms of population, most are small, such as the MOWA (Mobile-Washington) Choctaws of Alabama; however, the Lumbees of North Carolina have more than 40,000 members, and the

Houmas of Louisiana have more than 17,000, ranking them among the nation's largest Native groups. In political organization, state tribes also vary markedly. While the once-state-recognized Tigua tribe of Texas maintained a formal tribal structure similar to the Pueblos of New Mexico, most tribes are more loosely organized around family, churches, or town governments.

Currently, most state tribes are experiencing renewed pride in their Native heritage. Many are undergoing a significant cultural rebirth, sponsoring cultural programs, powwows, and ethnic exchanges with related Native peoples. Members of state-recognized tribes are also active in modern indigenous concerns, lobbying for the protection of grave sites, pressing for the repatriation of funeral remains, and protesting negative media portrayals of Native Americans. State-recognized groups have been at the center of federal acknowledgment debates as well; the vast majority are currently seeking federal tribal acknowledgment.

Mark Edwin Miller

Further Reading

Clow, Richmond L., and Imre Sutton., eds. *Trusteeship in Change: Toward Tribal Autonomy in Resource Management*. Boulder: University Press of Colorado, 2001.

Hauptman, Laurence M. *Formulating American Indian Policy in New York State, 1970–1986*. Albany: State University Press of New York, 1988.

Miller, Mark Edwin. *Forgotten Tribes: Unrecognized Indians and the Federal Acknowledgment Process*. Lincoln: University of Nebraska Press, 2004.

Taylor, Theodore W. *The States and Their Indian Citizens*. Washington, DC: Department of the Interior, 1972.

Wilkinson, Charles. *Blood Struggle: The Rise of Modern Indian Nations*. New York and London: W.W. Norton, 2005.

Conclusion

In the six decades between the commencement of the American Revolution and the election of Andrew Jackson as president, the United States moved its borders across the continent. The policy of incremental acquisition through purchase established during the Washington administration served the national interest throughout the period. Through the treaty-making process, the nation acquired millions of acres from Indian tribes. Besides the loss of their land, the same treaty process also resulted in the displacement of many of the tribes and the change of their status from recognized, fully independent sovereignties to what Chief Justice John Marshall would describe as "domestic dependent nations."

Jack Campisi

Further Reading

American State Papers, Foreign Affairs, vol. 1. 1832–1861. Washington, DC: Gales and Seaton.

Deloria, Vine, Jr., and Raymond J. DeMallie. 1999. *Documents of American Indian Diplomacy: Treaties, Agreements, and Conventions, 1775–1979*, vol. 1. Norman: University of Oklahoma Press.

Downes, Randolph C. 1977. *Council Fires on the Upper Ohio: A Narrative of Indian Affairs in the Upper Ohio Valley until 1795*. Pittsburgh: University of Pittsburgh Press.

Kappler, Charles J., ed. 1904. *Indian Affairs: Laws and Treaties*, 2 vols. Washington, DC: Government Printing Office.

Mahon, John K. 1988. *Indian-United States Military Situation, 1775–1848*. In *Handbook of North American Indians*, vol. 4, *History of Indian-White Relations*, edited by William C. Sturtevant, 144–162. Washington, DC: Smithsonian Institution.

New York (State) Legislature Assembly. 1889. *Report of Special Committee to Investigate the Indian Problem of the State of New York, Appointed by the Assembly of 1888*. Albany, NY: Troy Press.

Prucha, Francis Paul, ed. 1994. *American Indian Treaties: The History of a Political Anomaly*. Berkeley and Los Angeles: University of California Press.

Prucha, Francis Paul, ed. 2000. *Documents of United States Indian Policy*. Lincoln: University of Nebraska Press.

Royce, C. C. 1881. "Cessions of Land by Indian Tribes to the United States: Illustrated by Those in the State of Indiana." In *First Annual Report of the Bureau of Ethnology to the Secretary of the Smithsonian Institution, 1879–80*, 247–262. Washington, DC: Government Printing Office.

"Treaty of Fort Finney or Treaty with the Shawnee, January 31, 1786." 1904. In *Indian Affairs: Laws and Treaties*, vol. 2, compiled and edited by Charles J. Kappler, 16–18. Washington, DC: Government Printing Office.

Indian Removal and Land Cessions, 1830–1849

The Indian removal policy implemented by the U.S. government in the early 19th century resulted in dozens of land cession treaties with Indian groups east of the Mississippi River. Under the removal policy, treaties were negotiated with numerous eastern tribes, including the Choctaws, the Chickasaws, the Cherokees, the Seminoles, the Muscogee Creeks in the South, and more than 20 tribes in New York, the Great Lakes area, and along the Mississippi River north of the Ohio River. These treaties ceded millions of acres of land to U.S. control and forced the relocation of tens of thousands of Indians to Indian Territory. The causes of the removal policy arose from many sources, including American economic growth, the movement of American settlers west and south, racism toward Indians, and the assertion of states' rights. Although most Americans supported Indian removal for one reason or another, some opposed it as an unjust policy. Indians responded to the call for removal in a variety of ways; some accepted the apparent inevitability of removal and negotiated treaties to their best possible advantage, whereas others refused to accept removal by fighting back legally and physically, staying in their homelands, or moving somewhere other than Indian Territory. The impact of the removal treaties was as dramatic as any other episode in the long history of Indian white relations and continues to shape affairs in Indian country and throughout the United States.

Origins of the Removal Policy

The U.S. government policy that removed Indian groups east of the Mississippi River to Indian Territory in the first half of the 19th century stemmed from many causes, but key officials had suggested the eventuality of Indian removal virtually from the moment the United States became a country. War hero George Washington declared in 1783 that "[the] gradual extension of our settlements will as certainly cause the savage, as the wolf, to retire" (Wallace 1993, 38). Under the new Constitution, which went into effect in 1789, government officials increased the push for Indian removal. In 1789, Secretary of War Henry Knox suggested the inevitability of removal, asserting that "in a short period the idea of an Indian this side of the Mississippi will be found only in the pages of the historian" (Getches, Wilkinson, and Williams 1998, 94). A component of early American Indian policy, which began under President Washington and continued under his successors until President Andrew Jackson, was the "civilization" plan. Under this program, the U.S. government urged Indian peoples to adopt American notions of economy, politics, and gender roles. This meant that Indians should abandon hunting as a source of sustenance for agriculture, especially the production of such cash crops as cotton.

Differing views about the proper use of land divided Indians and European Americans from the earliest days of contact; eastern Indians pointed out that they already grew vast quantities of corn, squash, beans, pumpkins, and sunflowers. Indian men hunted deer and other animals to provide meat protein for their families' diets and to engage in the fur trade, which the U.S. government sought to manipulate. Indian women farmed among the matrilineal eastern tribes, and Indian men tended to view such work as "women's work," contrary to American understandings of gender roles. The U.S. "civilization" policy sought to turn Indian men into farmers and Indian women into spinners and weavers of cotton, thus challenging Indian cultural concepts at a basic level. In addition, and more to the point of land cessions, the U.S. government insisted that Indians who no longer hunted required far less land and thus should sell their excess acreage to the United States to be sold, in turn, to European American settlers. Indians greeted the "civilization" plan with mixed reactions. A minority of elite and well-connected individuals and families in all the eastern Indian groups adapted rather easily to a market-based economy resting on the production of cotton, wheat, and other commodities. These people instituted cultural modifications such as private property, slave ownership, and constitutional government, in accordance with broader American patterns. Nevertheless, Indian groups as a whole remained staunchly resistant to land cessions, thus negating one of the principal desired effects of "civilization" from the American perspective.

Although he did not put Indian removal into action, Thomas Jefferson was the first president to advocate the possibility of removal. In late 1802 and early 1803, Jefferson wrote several letters and issued official messages urging the creation of federally run trading posts, with the intent, among other purposes, of putting Indians into debt. He realized that the fur trade was a dying practice east of the Mississippi River and that Indians would have to pay their debts by land cessions. Jefferson also suggested that any Indian group offering military resistance to the United States would be driven from the East. He further added that Indians "will in time either incorporate with us as citizens of the United States, or remove beyond the Mississippi" (Getches, Wilkinson, and Williams 1998, 95). In July 1803, word reached Jefferson that the purchase of the Louisiana Territory from France was complete, and he and other government officials recognized immediately that the United States now owned a vast area west of the Mississippi River to which Indian people in the East could be banished. The Louisiana Purchase provided the inspiration and the area for pro-removal advocates to remove eastern Indians and to construct a clear-cut dividing line between Americans and Indians.

The War of 1812 furthered the cause of Indian removal in a number of important ways. Unified eastern Indian resistance to the United States became extremely difficult with the defeat of the pan-Indian movement led by Tecumseh and his brother Tenskwatawa, the Prophet, in the Great Lakes area.

Never again would a multi-tribal force arise east of the Mississippi River to counter American expansion. In the South, Indian groups remained divided, and during the War of 1812 the militant Red Stick Creeks failed in their attempt to stem American expansion and American influences on their people. Andrew Jackson, as major general of the Tennessee militia, led the U.S. and Indian forces that defeated the Red Sticks, who had attacked and killed some 400 Americans at Fort Mims, north of Mobile, Alabama. Jackson's forces, aided by Choctaws, Cherokees, and non-Red Stick Creeks, defeated the Red Sticks at the Battle of Horseshoe Bend on the Tallapoosa River in 1814. Jackson, at the subsequent Treaty of Fort Jackson, forced all Creeks to cede about 23 million acres. Jackson then moved his forces south and defended New Orleans from British attack, earning himself national celebrity status.

The United States had found it difficult to enforce its will against Indians as long as another European power, especially Britain, resided in eastern North America and maintained trade with Indians. The War of 1812 essentially eliminated that threat when the United States defeated British forces outside New Orleans and in Canada, thus encouraging American emigration westward, especially into the Old Northwest region of Ohio, Michigan, Wisconsin, Indiana, and Illinois. With the end of the War of 1812, a major economic transformation began, called the Market Revolution by historians, which encouraged Americans of all ranks to seek out profit-making enterprises. That shift from a predominantly subsistence-based lifestyle to one that sought profit by any available means increased pressure on eastern Indians to give up land.

Economic, demographic, and local pressures for Indian removal increased in the early 19th century. Eli Whitney's cotton gin, perfected in 1793, and other new cotton processing machines enabled the efficient processing of short-staple cotton that grew well throughout the interior of the Deep South. As a result, European American settlers relocated to the Mississippi Territory, established in 1798 and encompassing present-day Mississippi and Alabama, to cultivate cotton. These newcomers began demanding access to Choctaw, Chickasaw, Creek, and Cherokee lands in those areas. In Georgia, the calls for Cherokee removal reached new heights when gold was discovered on Cherokee lands in the late 1820s. In the north, the completion of the Erie Canal in 1825 across the state of New York encouraged European American emigration to the west and dramatically increased pressures on Indians from New York to Wisconsin to move westward. Other internal improvements, such as railroads and more canals, encouraged American westward migration, resulting in rapid population growth in the newer western territories. The white population north of the Wabash River in Indiana, for example, exploded from 3,380 in 1830 to 65,897 in 1840. The short-lived Black Hawk War in 1832, in which the Sac and the Fox Indians fought white settlers in Indiana and Wisconsin, further sharpened northern voices against Indians remaining in the East. The cries of settlers in the southern and other western states highlighted another major component of Indian removal, the conflict between states and the federal government over Indian relations and control of land. States demanded control over all lands within their borders, while the federal government insisted that, according to the Constitution, it alone could negotiate with Indians who maintained a treaty relationship with the United States. Settlers and elected officials in the newer western states grew increasingly strident in their denunciation of Indians, and violence sometimes resulted.

No matter how much a particular Indian group became "civilized," Indians encountered uncompromising racism among Americans in the early 19th century. One renowned western politician, Henry Clay of Kentucky, said he did not "countenance inhumanity towards [Indians]," but he did not "think them, as a race, worth preserving," because they were "essentially inferior to the Anglo-Saxon race" (Garrison 2002, 25). Among European Americans, belief in the unique manifest destiny of the United States and in racial explanations for human behavior became firmly entrenched in the early decades of the 19th century. Perhaps more than any other American of the pre-removal generation, Lewis Cass, as governor of the Michigan Territory from 1813 to 1831 and then as secretary of war under Andrew Jackson from 1831 to 1836, formulated the racist moral justification for Indian removal. Conveniently ignoring the horticultural and agricultural reality lived by most eastern Indians, Cass argued that land must be turned over by Indian "hunters" to American agriculturalists, who would make more productive use of it. Only through removal west of the Mississippi, Cass urged, could Indian people acquire the time and space to become "civilized." Cass ridiculed those who "would give to a few naked and wandering savages, a perpetual title to an immense continent," and he insisted that "the Indians shall be made to vanish before civilization, as the snow melts before the sunbeam" (Wallace 1993, 45). Ironically, Indian success under the tenets of "civilization" made them a greater menace to white Americans. The Cherokees, who had formed a constitutional government and aggressively asserted their sovereignty after the War of 1812, had moved far toward economic self-sufficiency by growing and selling cotton, further entrenching their claims to their land. Racial justifications for taking Indian land thus became predominant after 1815, as white Americans greedily sought access to Indian land. Racism surfaced even among Americans who acted in the perceived best interests of Indians. Many American groups, who sought to assist Indians, such as Protestant missionaries, eventually supported Indian removal west of the Mississippi, like Cass, as a method of buying time for Indians to become more acculturated to American customs away from the threats of their American neighbors.

Pro-removal forces in America received a boost in 1828, when one of their own, Andrew Jackson, was elected president. A former congressman, senator, and judge from Tennessee, Jackson had gained fame during the War of 1812 when, as head of the Tennessee militia, he led the fight against the Red Stick Creeks and then with his men he won the Battle of New Orleans. After the War of 1812, Jackson participated in several land cession treaties with the southern Indian groups and urged them to begin migrating west of the Mississippi. By 1820, Jackson's efforts had opened up nearly 50 million acres for American settlement by compelling southern Indians to cede parts of Georgia, Alabama, Tennessee, and Mississippi. In addition, Jackson led an invasion of Spanish Florida in 1818 against the Seminoles and the remaining Red Stick Creek Indians, killing several of their chiefs and two British agents whom Jackson accused of inciting the Indians to attack Americans. Jackson then captured Spanish Pensacola, and after Spain sold Florida to the United States in 1819, Jackson briefly became territorial governor of Florida in 1821.

By 1823, Jackson was running for president of the United States. He won the most votes but did not gain the needed majority of electoral votes in the election of 1824, which resulted in the "corrupt bargain" that brought John Quincy Adams to the presidency. Nevertheless, Jackson's actions in Indian affairs forced the hands of the Monroe (1817–1825) and Adams (1825–1829) administrations to

President Andrew Jackson was a leading advocate of Indian removal while in office from 1829 to 1837, and he supported the Indian Removal Act of 1830. During his tenure as president, the United States made 67 treaties with Indian nations. (Library of Congress)

seek voluntary removal among eastern Indians—a call that select groups of Indians heeded by moving west into Arkansas, Louisiana, and even Texas (part of Spain until Mexican independence in 1821), but that most eastern Indians ignored. In the 1828 election, Jackson and his Democrat Party won easily over Adams, establishing as commander-in-chief of the entire U.S. military the man made famous as an Indian fighter, who possessed a proven record of supporting Indian removal.

State politicians, especially in the South, saw in Jackson a staunch supporter of states' rights, and they responded to his election, even before Jackson was inaugurated as president, by passing laws extending state jurisdiction over Indian lands. Georgia was the first state to do so; on December 20, 1828, it adopted legislation extending state jurisdiction over Cherokee lands in northwest Georgia, although the state delayed enforcement until June 1830 to give Jackson and the federal government time to support their action. Alabama passed a law extending its Indian jurisdiction over Creek Indian lands in January 1829. Mississippi passed a resolution claiming jurisdiction over Choctaw and Chickasaw lands within its borders that was signed into law by the governor on February 4, 1829. Thus, southern states enabled Jackson to mask Indian removal as a solution to the emerging conflict between states' rights and federal jurisdiction and power. In his first State of the Union address in December 1829, Jackson urged eastern Indians to remove west voluntarily or become subject to the laws of the states. After much debate and a close vote in Congress, during which certain Whig politicians—especially the deeply religious Senator Theodore Frelinghuysen of New Jersey—argued against Indian removal on moral grounds, President Jackson signed the Indian Removal Act into law on May 29, 1830.

Jackson defended the Removal Act's passage at the time by emphasizing that this bill "puts an end to the possible danger of collision between the authorities of the General and state Governments, on account of the Indians" (Satz 2002, 44). The act called on the president to negotiate removal treaties with Indian groups and to exchange lands west of the Mississippi River for Indian lands in the east. In his State of the Union speech that December, Jackson applauded the act on humanitarian terms, stating that removal at federal government expense provided Indians with a chance of survival and demonstrated the "humanity and national honor" of the United States in taking action to save "these people" (Wallace 1993, 123). Jackson also insisted that the Removal Act was "so just to the States and so generous to the Indians—the Executive feels it has a right to expect the cooperation of Congress, and of all good and disinterested men" (Satz 2002, 44). Jackson attacked critics of the Removal Act and exposed the ethnocentric and racist essence of the new policy by asking, "What good man would prefer a country covered with forests and ranged by a few thousand savages to our extensive Republic, studded with cities, towns, and prosperous farms, embellished with all the improvements which art can devise or industry execute, occupied by more than 12,000,000 happy people, and filled with all the blessings of liberty, civilization, and religion?" (Satz 2002, 44). Despite Jackson's generous line of reasoning in support of Indian removal, the Indian Removal Act forced Indians to choose between removal and retaining some autonomy, or subjection entirely to the laws of the state wherein they resided. There was no doubt that the states intended to dispossess Indians of their land. The legal mechanism for removal was in place; all that remained were treaties to be negotiated with each tribe establishing the particulars of their deportation.

The Removal Treaties: The South

Treaty with the Choctaw at Dancing Rabbit Creek, 1830

The first American Indians to have the Indian Removal Act forced upon them were the Choctaws of Mississippi. Certain Choctaw leaders, notably Greenwood LeFlore, responded to Mississippi's extension of state laws over Indians in February 1829 by attempting to negotiate a removal treaty on behalf of all Choctaws before the Removal Act had been passed by Congress. The proposed treaty contained generous compensation for the Choctaws, but it did not reflect the will of most Choctaw people. President Jackson forwarded the treaty to the Senate anyway in May 1830, but the Senate, noting significant Choctaw opposition to the LeFlore treaty, decided not to approve it. Jackson then invited Choctaw representatives to meet him at Franklin, Tennessee, to negotiate a new treaty, but they refused and instead suggested a meeting within Choctaw Territory in September 1830. Secretary of War John Eaton and former Indian agent John Coffee, Andrew Jackson's nephew by marriage, represented the United States at the treaty grounds at Dancing Rabbit Creek. Eaton and Coffee, using Jackson's rationalization, warned the approximately 5,000 Choctaws in attendance that they could not prevent the state of Mississippi from taking over their lands and that therefore the Choctaws ought to cooperate in removal and gain terms as favorable as possible from the United States. The Choctaws remained deeply divided over removal; after two weeks, many of them left the treaty grounds having decided not to give up their lands. American agents convinced the remaining Choctaws, including the three leading chiefs LeFlore, Nitakechi, and Mushulatubbee, to sign the treaty on September 27, 1830. Each of these chiefs, along with several other Choctaws with American connections, received personal sections of land in Mississippi as a form of bribery to ease their resistance to removal. These individuals either stayed in Mississippi, as did LeFlore, or sold their sections for profit.

The Treaty of Dancing Rabbit Creek was ratified by the U.S. Senate on February 24, 1831. According to its provisions, the Choctaws ceded all of their land east of the Mississippi River in exchange for land, annuities, and other assistance on land west of the Arkansas Territory that became known as Indian Territory. The

Choctaws were to leave Mississippi within three years. The vast majority migrated west under situations of near starvation; many died along the way. A few hundred moved that first winter after the treaty was signed, and the rest moved in the next few succeeding years. Individual Choctaws could stay in Mississippi on specific allotted sections of land if they so chose, but all communally held land was dissolved. William Ward, the U.S. agent assigned to manage the allotment process, through fraud and incompetence did not register all of the individual claims, however, and many Choctaws who chose to stay did not receive title to their lands and were forced to relocate anyway. As historians have noted, Choctaws who tried to remain in Mississippi became victims of fraud, intimidation, and land speculation. The early 1830s are known as the "flush times" in Mississippi history, for whites squatted on and seized Choctaw lands with no regard for Indian rights or fair play. Yet a couple of thousand Choctaws managed to stay in Mississippi amid discrimination and poverty and are the basis of the Mississippi Choctaws of today.

Treaty with the Creeks, 1832

Muscogee Creek leaders responded to Alabama's extension of jurisdiction over their lands by proposing that they cede lands but retain blocks of private reserves within Alabama under the control of individual families. They took these proposals to Washington, D.C., in March 1832. Secretary of War Lewis Cass disagreed with the size and number of the reserves, but he reached a compromise with the eight Muscogee Creek leaders on March 24. The resulting treaty was not specifically a removal treaty, for even though the Creeks agreed to cede all their lands east of the Mississippi River, they were to receive allotments in Alabama that could be sold or retained under Creek ownership. By April 2, the U.S. Senate had unanimously ratified the treaty.

Although the treaty called on the U.S. government both to assist those Creeks who wished to emigrate west and to guarantee Creek title to allotted lands in Alabama, the federal government refused to assist Creeks in Alabama when whites seized their lands anyway. Land speculators took advantage of the remaining Muscogee Creeks and perpetrated frauds resulting in utter turmoil and loss of the Creeks' homes. The Creeks wandered around Alabama seeking food and shelter, eventually attacking white settlers and seizing crops and livestock in revenge. In 1836, Cass finally intervened, not as guarantor of Creek rights but instead to forcibly remove the remaining Creeks west of the Mississippi. The U.S. military accomplished what diplomacy could not, and by 1837 almost all of the 15,000 or so Muscogee Creeks had emigrated to the West.

Treaties with the Chickasaws, 1830 and 1832

Chickasaw leaders also sought to acquire the best terms possible after the passage of the Indian Removal Act. In the summer of 1830, Chickasaw representatives met with U.S. delegates, including President Jackson, at Franklin, Tennessee, and a treaty was signed on August 31. The Chickasaws agreed to cede their lands east of the Mississippi River in exchange for an equal amount of land in the West, but when a suitable area could not be found, this treaty became void. New negotiations for removal were undertaken in 1832 in Chickasaw Territory at Pontotoc Creek. On October 20, a treaty was signed that ceded Chickasaw lands to the U.S. government; the lands were to be surveyed and sold immediately, and each adult Chickasaw was to receive a temporary allotment, which would also be sold and all monies therefrom placed in a fund to cover the costs of removal. Whites quickly settled on the Chickasaw lands beginning in 1832, despite a provision of the treaty promising that the U.S. government would prevent white intrusion until the Chickasaws had actually left Mississippi. A suitable new homeland in the West was not found until January 1837, when the Chickasaws and Choctaws met at Doaksville, Choctaw Nation, in Indian Territory, and the Choctaws sold the western part of their new territory to the Chickasaws. Although this agreement between the two tribes was not a treaty with the United States, Jackson submitted it to the Senate for approval anyway, which was accomplished in February 1837. Further details about the exact extent of territory and rights granted the Chickasaws were decided in two additional agreements between the two Indian nations in 1854 and 1855.

Treaties with the Seminoles, 1832 and 1833

Florida settlers had long complained about Indian "depredations" committed by the Seminoles, and Georgia, Alabama, and Mississippi plantation owners protested that runaway slaves found refuge among these Florida Indians. Border disputes between Americans and the Seminoles had exploded into full-scale war in 1818, when forces led by Andrew Jackson invaded Florida to punish Seminoles and capture African Americans who lived among them. In 1823, after Spain transferred control of Florida to the United States, the Seminoles signed a treaty with the United States at Fort Moultrie that ceded the bulk of the Florida Peninsula to U.S. control.

Discord between the Seminoles and Americans continued, however, as the Seminoles found living difficult on their reduced acreage. Fulfilling his charge under the new Indian Removal Act, Colonel James Gadsden negotiated a removal treaty with the Seminole Indians at Payne's Landing in northeastern Florida on May 9, 1832. The treaty of 1832 stipulated that removal was conditioned on the Seminoles agreeing to settle in the western territory that the War Department had chosen for them. Under duress, the seven Seminoles who journeyed west to inspect their new land signed a new removal treaty with American agents there at Fort Gibson on March 28, 1833.

The treaty declared that the Seminoles agreed with the location of their new lands, accepted political unification with the Creek Indians, and assented to immediate emigration. Upon their return to Florida, the Seminole agents renounced the

Fort Gibson treaty as coerced, and the Seminoles refused to abide by the stipulations of either treaty. Meanwhile, a Seminole band that lived along the Apalachicola River signed a separate removal treaty with Gadsden in October 1832, and they migrated to Texas in 1834. The confusion over which Seminoles had authority to accept removal for other Seminoles created an impasse that resulted in a bitter, drawn out war between the Seminoles and the United States that began in 1835 and was often referred to as the Second Seminole War. That war did not end until 1842, when all but a fragment of the Seminoles had been killed or forcibly removed; it cost the United States $30–40 million and 1,500 dead soldiers. Pockets of Seminoles and their African American brethren remained in Florida, however, and their descendants are still there.

Treaty with the Cherokees at New Echota, 1835

A few thousand Cherokees had voluntarily moved west after Georgia claimed possession of their lands in December 1828, but the bulk of the Cherokees refused to leave their homeland and instead fought removal through the legal system. In 1830, after the passage of the Indian Removal Act, the Cherokee Nation sued Georgia in the U.S. Supreme Court, asking for an injunction to prevent Georgia's seizure of Cherokee lands. Attorneys for the Cherokees argued that, as an independent nation, the Cherokees could not be subject to state jurisdiction. Chief Justice John Marshall sympathized with the Cherokee position but declined to issue an injunction against Georgia, because Indian nations in the United States were "domestic dependent nations" rather than independent foreign nations; an Indian nation's relationship to the United States therefore "resembles that of a ward to his guardian," thus disqualifying the nation from suing in the Supreme Court. The Cherokees had gained some sympathy for their plight across the United States, and they eagerly pursued another chance to bring the issue of their sovereignty to the Supreme Court.

Native American Sovereignty

Native American sovereignty is a concept defined as the right of Native American tribes to govern independently of the laws and jurisdiction of the federal and state governments. Over the centuries, Native American nations have undergone a transformation from independent sovereign nations to quasi-sovereign nations under the protection of the federal government. The transformation has been developed through federal case law. Additionally, statutes have undermined the sovereignty of Native American nations; such statutes include the Indian Removal Act (1830), the Dawes Act (1887), the Major Crimes Act (1885), and Public Law 280 (1953). Moreover, in 1871, after ratifying nearly 400 treaties,

Congress unilaterally passed legislation formally ending the treaty-making powers of Native American nations.

Native American sovereignty has changed as a result of U.S. Supreme Court decisions. Chief Justice John Marshall in three seminal decisions laid the foundations for the abrogation of Native American sovereignty. In *Johnson v. M'Intosh* (1823), the sovereignty and independence of Native American nations was "diminished." In *Cherokee Nation v. Georgia* (1831), the Supreme Court described Native Americans as "domestic dependent nations" that were under the protection of the U.S. government. Furthermore, Native Americans lost the right to interact in international relations but kept their internal sovereignty. In *Worcester v. Georgia* (1832), the Supreme Court held that the Cherokees possessed self-government, even though it was dependent on the United States. These three cases, known collectively as the Marshall Trilogy, have defined the basic construct of Native American sovereignty, and subsequent cases have limited tribal sovereignty.

The cases that have had a direct effect upon Native American sovereignty include *Oliphant v. Suquamish Indian Tribe* (1978), in which the Court denied that a tribal court has criminal jurisdiction over a non-Native American on a reservation. This was one of the most destructive erosions of tribal sovereignty. In *Nevada v. Hicks* (2001), the Supreme Court ruled that a tribal court lacked jurisdiction and authority to hear a civil lawsuit against state officials. Justice Sandra Day O'Connor took the view that the unanimous decision of the Court undermined the right of tribal authority to make and be governed by its own laws.

However, contemporary sovereignty of tribal governments includes the authority to define their own citizenship and to tax, license, and regulate lands and resources. Criminal and civil laws can be established, to be ruled upon by tribal courts. Tribal government can be developed, structured, and controlled. Additionally, Native American nations have sovereign immunity: inherent sovereignty that predates the U.S. Constitution, general exclusion of state law, and extraconstitutional tribal powers (i.e., the U.S. Constitution does not bind or restrict tribes). A "trust relationship" also exists, based on treaties with the federal government, which protects land, assets, and treaty rights. Additionally, tribal governments are responsible for a plethora of governmental activities, which include education, health, housing, social services, court services, and natural resources. Intertwined here is the authority of tribes to protect and preserve their culture, heritage, language, history, and traditions. To Native Americans, sovereignty is a constantly evolving concept that is defined by the U.S. Supreme Court—the federal government, which continues to have the right to extinguish any aspect of tribal sovereignty—and, more important, by Native

American nations who can directly influence Congress to protect their sovereignty. Many tribes describe themselves as sovereign nations because they assert that the U.S. government has never conquered them. Native American nations are defending their sovereign right to land, water, and hunting rights through treaties and are advancing their claims through the United Nations and in the international arena.

Dewi Ball

Further Reading

Anderson, Terry L. *Sovereign Nations or Reservations? An Economic History of American Indians*. San Francisco: Pacific Research Institute for Public Policy, 1995.

Pommersheim, Frank. *Braid of Feathers: American Indian Law and Contemporary Tribal Life*. Berkeley: University of California Press, 1995.

Wilkins, David E., and K. Tsianina Lomawaima. *Uneven Ground: American Indian Sovereignty and Federal Law*. Norman: University of Oklahoma Press, 2001.

Effective in March 1831, Georgia required any white person living in Cherokee country to have a license issued by the state. Missionaries Samuel Worcester and Elizur Butler ignored this condition, were subsequently arrested by Georgia authorities, and appealed their case to the Supreme Court. In that case, *Worcester v. Georgia* (1832), Marshall declared Georgia's extension of state law over the Cherokees unconstitutional and ordered the release of the missionaries. Georgia refused to abide by the decision, and the executive branch of the federal government had no legal way—short of military intervention—to compel Georgia's compliance had it so desired. The Cherokees won their legal battle, but Georgia's refusal to honor that decision nullified their victory.

After 1832, the Cherokees became less united in their determination to hold onto their lands, and a significant minority, called the Treaty Party, worked to get a removal treaty signed with the U.S. government beginning in 1834. A group of these men signed a removal treaty with Secretary of War John Eaton in Washington, D.C., and Jackson submitted it to the Senate in June 1834. The Senate, however, tabled the treaty, refusing to discuss it. Aware that there existed a group among the Cherokees willing to sign a removal treaty, the Jackson administration sent a representative to the Cherokee Nation in February 1835 to negotiate with them. The "treaty party" was dominated by four related men who aspired to elite status: Major Ridge, his educated son John Ridge, and his two nephews, the brothers Elias Boudinot and Stand Watie.

Opposing them were the majority of Cherokees, united under the leadership of principal chief John Ross. Ridge and his relatives signed a removal treaty on March 14, 1835, but it was rejected by the Cherokee Council and thus nullified. In December 1835, another meeting with U.S. negotiators was held at New Echota; only about 200 Ridge supporters attended. A removal treaty was signed on December 29. The Cherokee Council condemned the treaty, and Ross appealed to the U.S. Senate to reject it, but the Senate approved it by a one-vote margin.

The Treaty Party Cherokees emigrated to Indian Territory immediately, whereas the treaty required the rest of the eastern Cherokees to leave by May 23, 1838. Ross and the more than 15,000 other Cherokees who opposed the treaty appealed repeatedly to have the Treaty of New Echota voided, but they encountered little sympathy in the U.S. government. General Winfield Scott arrived in the Cherokee country in the summer of 1838 to oversee the forced relocation of the Cherokees, which resulted in numerous deaths and the loss of property at the hands of rapacious whites. The split among the Cherokees continued after removal: anti-removal Cherokees killed the two Ridges and Boudinot, and Watie and Ross competed for political power from the late 1830s through the Civil War in the 1860s. Meanwhile, a few hundred Cherokees managed to stay within the mountainous western border of North Carolina, where their descendants live today.

The Removal Treaties: The North

Unlike the large, basically homogenous Indian societies of the South, Indian groups farther north in New York, the Great Lakes, and the Mississippi River valley were smaller, more splintered societies that in many cases had already migrated dramatically from place to place in the years since the American Revolution. Though their particular histories and circumstances differed from the southern Indians, northern Indian groups confronted the same insistent U.S. government and the same rapacious attitude among white Americans. Negotiating from a position of strength, the United States signed treaties with the numerous northern groups to formalize their removal to the West and to clear up conflicting land claims. From 1829 to 1851, the United States signed 86 ratified removal treaties with 26 Indian groups in the North. In many cases, removal for the northern tribes was a continuation of their peripatetic history, though that does not mean that they all accepted removal without resistance or that they did not try to acquire the best possible terms.

Treaties with Ohio Valley Indians, 1831–1832

By 1830, many former Ohio valley Indians had already signed treaties with the state of Ohio requiring them to move north to the Great Lakes or west to the Mississippi River valley. Various bands of these groups had already moved west of the Mississippi River before 1830, and these final removal treaties sought to remove those who remained in the East and to settle any potential eastern land claims. President Jackson appointed Ohioan James B. Gardiner to negotiate removal treaties with remaining Indian groups in Ohio. In August 1831, Gardiner signed treaties with a group of Shawnees and the Ottawas that ceded all their lands in Ohio in exchange for new lands in the western country beyond Missouri. Profits gained from selling the ceded Ohio lands were to be used for infrastructure improvements, such as mills, in the new lands; the remainder of the money was to be invested on behalf of the Indians. The Wyandots in Ohio insisted that they be allowed to inspect and approve of the new western lands before agreeing to removal. When objectionable reports of the western lands came back, they refused to emigrate. Thus, in the removal treaty signed by Gardiner and the Wyandots on January 19, 1832, the Indians agreed to leave Ohio but "may as they think proper, remove to Canada, or to the river Huron in Michigan, where they own a reservation of land, or to any place they may obtain a right or privilege from other Indians to go" (Prucha 1994, 186–187). In October 1832, several former Ohio valley Indian groups, including the Piankashaws, Weas, Peorias, and Kaskaskias in Illinois and the Shawnees, Delawares, Menominees, and Kickapoos, who had left Ohio decades earlier and were living at Cape Girardeau and other points along the upper Mississippi River, met with William Clark at St. Louis and signed treaties for their removal west of Missouri.

Treaties with New York Indians, 1831–1842

The various Iroquois and other Indian groups in New York ceded millions of acres to the United States and other interests in the decades after the American Revolution. In 1831 and 1832, additional Oneida, Stockbridge, and Brotherton Indians migrated to former Menominee lands in Wisconsin as a result of treaties involving the Menominees and the United States. In 1838, residents of western New York, particularly Buffalo, insisted that Indians remaining in the state, especially the Senecas, remove west beyond Missouri. A removal treaty with Senecas and other New York Indians, such as remnant Oneidas, Onondagas, Cayugas, Tuscaroras, St. Regis, Stockbridges, Brothertons, and Munsees, was signed at Buffalo Creek in 1838. Most Wisconsin land reserved to the New York Indians by previous treaties was also ceded for lands west of Missouri. When President Martin Van Buren submitted the treaty to the Senate in April 1838, there erupted significant opposition to the treaty from the Indians and certain missionary groups, who contended that portions of the treaty were fraudulent and that a truly representative body of Indian chiefs did not sign. Nonetheless, the Senate ratified the treaty, based on certain revisions, made in June, that required the Indians to reapprove the treaty. New signatures by more Indian leaders were obtained by September 1838, and the treaty was sent back to the U.S. government for approval. The Senate and President Van Buren passed the new treaty back and forth, neither seeking to be the sole body authorizing the questionable treaty. When the Senate, seeking the president's recommendation, returned the treaty to his desk, Van Buren responded, "That improper means have been employed to obtain the assent of the Seneca chiefs there is every reason to believe, and I have not been able to satisfy myself that I can, consistently with the resolution of the Senate of the 2d of March, 1839 cause the treaty to be carried into effect in respect to the Seneca tribe" (Prucha 1994, 205).

In January 1840, Van Buren again presented the treaty to the Senate, where it was bitterly debated and resulted in several tied votes over the issue of whether or not the Indian signatures had been obtained fraudulently. Eventually, Vice President Richard Johnson broke the tie, and the revised treaty was accepted by simple majority vote in the Senate in March 1840. In spite of its passage, the complicated treaty of 1838 did not result in the movement westward of many New York Indians. A new treaty with the Senecas in May 1842 reestablished their reserves in New York and allowed them to stay there.

Treaties with the Potawatomis, 1832–1836

The Potawatomis negotiated 19 separate treaties with the United States during the removal period. There were numerous Potawatomi villages and bands possessing fragmented areas of land in Michigan, Illinois, Indiana, and Wisconsin, which resulted in the large number of treaties with them. In total, the Potawatomis still claimed more than five million acres until 1832. Three treaties between the Potawatomis along the Tippecanoe River in Indiana and the United States were signed in October 1832. These agreements resulted in land cessions for the Potawatomis, but they also established around 120 reserves of land east of the Mississippi River for individual Potawatomi families. Because these treaties did not specifically require Potawatomi removal to the west, Lewis Cass insisted on a large treaty meeting with the Potawatomis, calling for their removal; the meeting was held in Chicago in September 1833. Catholic Potawatomis were allowed to remain in Michigan because of their conversion to Christianity, although the Potawatomis did agree to transfer most of their eastern land titles for five million acres west of Missouri. Dozens of Americans insisted that they deserved payment from the sale of eastern Potawatomi lands and government annuities to cover supposed costs for services rendered in the form of trade debts, injuries from conflicts such as the Black Hawk War of 1832, severance pay for old Indian agents and merchants, missionary activities, schools, and so on. President Jackson forwarded the Chicago treaty to the Senate in January 1834, despite concerns about the legitimacy of many of the claims.

The Senate approved the treaty that May but changed the area of western land that the Potawatomis were to receive, as Missouri desired the area originally promised to the Indians. The treaty would not be valid until the Potawatomis agreed to the new lands, and the United States did not find any Potawatomis willing to do so until seven representatives signed the revised treaty months later. The Senate ratified the revised treaty on February 11, 1835. Further treaties with individual

Potawatomi landholders between 1834 and 1836 resulted in the cession of nearly all their lands east of the Mississippi River. One Potawatomi group in Indiana consisting of around 850 persons refused to move west; they were seized by the U.S. military and forcibly marched west in 1838, and at least 40 Potawatomis died along the way.

Treaties with the Miamis, 1833–1841

Much of the U.S. effort to extinguish Miami land title east of the Mississippi was enveloped in similar efforts to remove the Potawatomis, as their lands bordered one another. Coming on the heels of the Black Hawk War of 1832, the United States attempted to get the Miami Indians of Indiana to sign removal treaties in 1833. That initial effort failed, but a treaty was signed with them on October 23, 1834, at the Forks of the Wabash. The Miamis ceded most of their remaining lands in Indiana, but individual Miami were allowed to maintain allotments in the state, and the treaty did not explicitly call for Miami removal. President Jackson disapproved of that stipulation and delayed the treaty's hearing by the Senate. His successor, Martin Van Buren, submitted the treaty to the Senate in October 1837, and final approval came in December of that year.

Americans in Indiana opposed the treaty because it allowed Miamis to remain in the state on individual landholdings, so new treaties were negotiated. In 1838, a treaty between the Miamis and the United States assigned individual landholdings in the East. The Miamis insisted that only tribal members could get such grants, that grants should not be given to non-Miamis who had married into the tribe. Six Miami chiefs also traveled to Kansas to examine new lands. In 1840, Miami chiefs negotiated an unofficial treaty with the Indian agent assigned to their area, seeking financial remuneration in return for their removal to the West. This treaty, although not initiated at the federal level, was submitted to the Senate by President Van Buren anyway and approved on May 15, 1841. Removal for most Miamis occurred in 1845–1846, although some Miamis continued to own and live on individual land grants in Indiana.

Treaties with the Winnebagos, Chippewas (Ojibwes), Eastern Sioux, and Menominees, 1829–1851

Treaties with these Indians involved land in Wisconsin and, to a lesser extent, in Michigan and in Minnesota. Henry Dodge, Wisconsin territorial governor and ex officio superintendent of Indian affairs, played the major role in enacting removal treaties among these groups. In 1829 and 1832, the Winnebagos (Ho-Chunks) signed treaties ceding some land in Wisconsin in exchange for a small strip of land west of the Mississippi River between the Sioux to the north and the Sac and Fox to the south. A portion of the Winnebago population moved west, but this land was untenable, for the neighboring Indian groups warred against each other. A small group of Winnebagos who did not have authority to cede lands traveled to Washington, D.C., in 1837 and signed a treaty calling on all Winnebagos to abandon their Wisconsin lands and move west. Some Winnebagos obeyed the treaty stipulations by moving west and eventually settling in Nebraska; other Winnebagos, despite losing title to their lands, stayed in Wisconsin, refusing to abandon their homeland.

In the Pine Tree Treaty of 1837, so named because the United States sought access to timber resources on Chippewa (Ojibwe) land, the Chippewas ceded millions of acres in Wisconsin and Minnesota, but the treaty did not call for their complete removal from the east, and the Chippewas retained usufructuary rights to the ceded lands. In the Copper Treaty of 1842, named for the copper deposits on Chippewa lands, the Chippewas ceded most of northern Wisconsin to the United States while still retaining usufructuary rights; the area experienced a copper mining boom for the rest of the 19th century. In 1850, President Zachary Taylor issued an executive order extinguishing Chippewa usufructuary rights in the ceded lands and ordered their removal to unceded lands in Minnesota. The subsequent forced march of Chippewas west in the winter of 1850–1851 has been termed the "Wisconsin Death March" because more than 400 Chippewas died. Some Chippewas did manage, however, to retain small tracts of land across northern Minnesota, northern Wisconsin, and the Upper Peninsula of Michigan.

The eastern Sioux ceded their lands east of the Mississippi in Wisconsin at a treaty meeting in Washington, D.C., in 1837. Their remaining lands in Minnesota came under increasing pressure from European American settlement, especially after the Minnesota Territory was created in 1849. In 1851, the eastern Sioux ceded most of their land in Minnesota, but land squatting by settlers and foot dragging by the federal government impeded until 1860 the finalizing of payment for those lands and of the actual boundaries of the Sioux reserves remaining in southern Minnesota.

The Menominees ceded portions of their Wisconsin lands in a series of treaties beginning in 1831, the most spectacular being the 1836 treaty that ceded to the United States more than four million timber-rich acres in eastern Wisconsin. The Menominees disagreed sharply, however, over the legality of these cessions, and many Menominees refused to move for decades—or ever. In October 1848, the Menominees signed a removal treaty exchanging their lands in Wisconsin for territory across the Mississippi River in Minnesota, but they refused to leave and finally relocated along the Wolf River in Wisconsin in 1852. The amount of land ceded by Indian people as a result of the removal treaties is staggering. In the South, where the largest areas of eastern land under Indian control existed, the Choctaws ceded more than 10 million acres in Mississippi; the Chickasaws ceded more than 2 million acres in Mississippi and Alabama; the Creeks ceded about 5 million acres in Alabama; and the Cherokees ceded almost 8 million acres in Georgia, Alabama, Tennessee, and North Carolina. Thus land began a craze in the South, as white venture capitalists, land companies, plantation owners, and small farmers all sought quick access to the newly opened lands. The resulting antebellum South, the South in the period between 1830 and 1860, came to be characterized by rapidly expanding cotton production and African American slavery in the areas abandoned by Indians. The creation of the unified, white-dominated, antebellum South would not have been possible without Indian removal, which had ironic consequences for the relationship between the states and the federal government.

Greg O'Brien

Further Reading

Akers, Donna L. 1999. "Removing the Heart of the Choctaw People: Indian Removal from a Choctaw Perspective." *American Indian Culture and Research Journal* 23, 63–76.

Beck, David R.M. 2002. *Siege and Survival: History of the Menominee Indians, 1634–1856*. Lincoln: University of Nebraska Press.

Carson, James Taylor. 1995. "State Rights and Indian Removal in Mississippi, 1817–1835." *Journal of Mississippi History* 57, 25–41.

Clifton, James A. 1987. "Wisconsin Death March: Explaining the Extremes in Old Northwest Indian Removal." *Transactions of the Wisconsin Academy of Sciences, Arts and Letters* 75, 1–39.

DeRosier, Arthur, Jr. 1970. *The Removal of the Choctaw Indians*. Knoxville: University of Tennessee Press.

Edmunds, R. David. 1978. *The Potawatomis: Keepers of the Fire*. Norman: University of Oklahoma Press.

Foreman, Grant. 1932. *Indian Removal: The Emigration of the Five Civilized Tribes of Indians*. Norman: University of Oklahoma Press.

Foreman, Grant. 1946. *The Last Trek of the Indians*. Chicago: University of Chicago Press.

Garrison, Tim Alan. 2002. *The Legal Ideology of Removal: The Southern Judiciary and the Sovereignty of Native American Nations.* Athens: University of Georgia Press.

Getches, David H., Charles F. Wilkinson, and Robert A. Williams, Jr. 1998. *Cases and Materials on Federal Indian Law*. St. Paul, MN: West Group.

Gibson, A.M. 1963. *The Kickapoos: Lords of the Middle Border*. Norman: University of Oklahoma Press.

Green, Michael D. 1982. *The Politics of Indian Removal: Creek Government and Society in Crisis*. Lincoln: University of Nebraska Press.

Horsman, Reginald. 1967. *Expansion and American Indian Policy, 1783–1812*. East Lansing: Michigan State University Press.

Kappler, Charles J. 1904. *Indian Affairs: Laws and Treaties*, vol. 2. Washington, DC: Government Printing Office.

Lancaster, Jane F. 1994. *Removal Aftershock: The Seminoles' Struggles to Survive in the West, 1836–1866*. Knoxville: University of Tennessee Press.

Perdue, Theda, and Michael D. Green, eds. 1995. *The Cherokee Removal: A Brief History with Documents*. Boston: Bedford Books of St. Martin's Press.

Prucha, Francis Paul. 1962. *American Indian Policy in the Formative Years: The Indian Trade and Intercourse Acts, 1790–1834*. Cambridge, MA: Harvard University Press.

Prucha, Francis Paul. 1984. *The Great Father: The United States Government and the American Indians*. Lincoln: University of Nebraska Press.

Prucha, Francis Paul. 1994. *American Indian Treaties: The History of a Political Anomaly*. Berkeley: University of California Press.

Raffert, Stewart. 1996. *The Miami Indians of Indiana: A Persistent People, 1654–1994*. Indianapolis: Indiana Historical Society.

Remini, Robert V. 2002. *Andrew Jackson and His Indian Wars*. New York: Penguin.

Rogin, Michael Paul. 1975. *Fathers and Children: Andrew Jackson and the Subjugation of the American Indian*. New York: Alfred A. Knopf.

Ronda, James P. 2002. "'We Have a Country': Race, Geography, and the Invention of Indian Territory." In *Race and the Early Republic: Racial Consciousness and Nation-Building in the Early Republic*, edited by Michael A. Morrison and James Brewer Stewart, 159–176. Lanham, MD: Rowman and Littlefield.

Royce, Charles C. 1899. *Indian Land Cessions in the United States*. Washington, DC: Government Printing Office.

Satz, Ronald. 2001. *Chippewa Treaty Rights: The Reserved Rights of Wisconsin's Chippewa Indians in Historical Perspective*. Madison: Wisconsin Academy of Sciences, Arts and Letters.

Satz, Ronald. 2002. *American Indian Policy in the Jacksonian Era*. Norman: University of Oklahoma Press.

Sellers, Charles. 1991. *The Market Revolution: Jacksonian America, 1815–1846*. New York: Oxford University Press.

Sheehan, Bernard W. 1973. *Seeds of Extinction: Jeffersonian Philanthropy and the American Indian*. Chapel Hill: University of North Carolina Press.

Sleeper-Smith, Susan. 2001. *Indian Women and French Men: Rethinking Cultural Encounter in the Western Great Lakes*. Amherst: University of Massachusetts Press.

Tanner, Helen Hornbeck, ed. 1987. *Atlas of Great Lakes Indian History*. Norman: University of Oklahoma Press.

Wallace, Anthony F.C. 1993. *The Long, Bitter Trail: Andrew Jackson and the Indians*. New York: Hill and Wang.

Wallace, Anthony F.C. 1999. *Jefferson and the Indians: The Tragic Fate of the First Americans*. Cambridge, MA: Harvard University Press.

Washburn, Wilcomb E. 1973. *The American Indian and the United States: A Documentary History*, vol. 4. New York: Random House.

Young, Mary Elizabeth. 1961. *Redskins, Ruffleshirts and Rednecks: Indian Allotments in Alabama and Mississippi, 1830–1860*. Norman: University of Oklahoma Press.

Reservations and Confederate and Unratified Treaties, 1850–1871

From the point of view of U.S. policy makers, Indian reservations were a necessary aspect of American expansion, nationhood, and state building. The creation of reservations, or reserves, aboriginal homelands, or *areas indigena*, was equally the result of the larger European colonial relationship with indigenous peoples in the Americas, Africa, Asia, and Australia. Whatever they were called, the establishment of these defined, often isolated and greatly compressed indigenous living spaces by means of treaties, agreements, and conventions was a distinct phase in the process of American expansion. Often, reservations were simply the remnants of indigenous homelands. The United States, however, removed a number of Native nations from their homelands to distant territories acquired from other indigenous peoples through treaties.

Between 1850 and 1871, when the federal government officially ended the treaty-making process, more than a hundred Native American treaties were ratified, principally to institute some semblance of order on the American frontiers. Most of these were "peace and friendship" treaties concluded to curtail the warfare between the Native peoples who owned the land and the migratory whites who coveted it for themselves. Essentially, the federal negotiators and the governing bodies of the Native American nations mutually agreed that strict boundaries between whites and Indians must be established and maintained before any kind of peace could be realized. Native negotiators were always seeking peace—or, perhaps, the simple absence of war—so that their peoples could enjoy the permanence of a homeland and the security of physically possessing recognized political boundaries. In short, between 1850 and 1871, the United States entered into the phase of colonialism that rested on the ideas of restricting the movements of indigenous peoples, defining the boundaries between the races, and removing any and all obstacles to the placement of European American colonies in the American West.

Reservations

As it came to be used in the period, the term *reservation* applied to nearly every piece of ground occupied by Native nations having formal treaty relations with the

The massacre of Miniconjou Lakota ghost dancers at Wounded Knee in 1890 led to Miniconjous being placed on the Pine Ridge Reservation in South Dakota in 1891. By the end of the 1800s, the U.S. government had created 200 Indian reservations by treaties, federal laws, and executive orders. (Library of Congress)

United States. Many of these territories were not, strictly speaking, parts of the U.S. public domain that were "reserved for the use of" Native nations. For example, when the Five Civilized Tribes—the Cherokee, Muscogee Creek, Seminole, Choctaw, and Chickasaw Nations—were removed from their traditional homelands in the East, the lands they acquired in the newly established Indian Territory carried titles in fee simple, thus making them relatively well protected from further white encroachment. Many other so-called reservations were in reality greatly diminished homelands that had never become legally a part of the U.S. public domain. Technically, one could argue that Native nations, not the federal government, had by treaty reserved these lands for their own use. Still, as most of the Native nations had concluded some form of diplomatic relations with the United States, the federal government sent agents to the reservations in order to oversee the implementation of treaty provisions and generally to maintain order within their designated areas of responsibility. Agents were also sent as negotiators to the Native nations to acquire more lands.

Until 1849, the agents and the implementation of Indian policies were under the bureaucratic control of the U.S. Department of War. Hence, the developing "reservation system" was viewed as a military operation, and in fact many of the agents for years to come were army personnel. The State Department, arguably the agency that should have maintained diplomatic relations with Native nations, had little to do with Indian affairs except to record the final ratified treaties with the tribes. The reservation system itself became a highly bureaucratic and permanent American institution. After 1849, the Bureau of Indian Affairs, most often referred to as the Indian Office, existed under the Department of the Interior. The "Indian Problem" had essentially boiled down to the impossible administrative predicament of securing more space for non-Indian settlement while at the same time maintaining peace with the Native nations that had to survive on increasingly smaller parcels of land. The Indian Office gained greater discretionary authority over Indian affairs during this period and, by way of administrative fiat, began to emphasize subtle variations in policy. For major Indian policy decisions, Congress, the executive branch, and the Supreme Court set the agenda and formulated the general approach to Indian affairs. The Indian Office implemented, administered, and evaluated the details of policy and within this particular context was often able to direct or redirect the course of Indian-white relations.

From the very outset of European imperialism, numerous individuals advocated the "civilization" and eventual assimilation of Native Americans into the dominant society. President George Washington promoted the notion of "civilizing" Indians in his inaugural address. The idea underpinned the reservation system in one important way. Because the Native nations' land bases were becoming smaller with each new treaty, the Indian Office introduced European American farming methods, livestock production, various home industries such as wool spinning and weaving, and Christianity in the effort to promote "civilization" among the indigenous nations. It was thought that "civilization" and especially its accoutrements—the spinning wheels, livestock, and farm implements—would help Natives survive on what lands they had left. Native peoples, especially on reservations that had been established by treaty, were quickly becoming regarded as "wards" of the U.S. government and, as such, more or less arbitrarily subjected to the caprices of the Indian Office bureaucracy. Ultimately, this system of domestic colonialism deprived Native nations of the ability to experience change on their own terms.

The agents enforced cultural and economic changes on the Native peoples so that they could eke out a meager living on their very much smaller domains. Diminished land bases for Native Americans meant, in turn, the opening of more territory for white settlement. White settlement, it was thought, would further encourage civilization and allegiance to the United States among the Native peoples. In this chain of reasoning, the ultimate aim of the reservation system was to fulfill the goal of American Manifest Destiny in as orderly and relatively nonviolent a fashion as possible.

Surplus Lands

The opening of more land for white settlement between 1850 and 1871 also paved the way for the "take-off" period in American industrial growth. It opened greater acreage not only to farmers and ranchers but also to the logging and mining industries. Railroads were building, and especially after the Civil War, large grants of the American public domain, most often acquired through Native land cessions in treaties, went to subsidize the laying of track. The railroads, in turn, fed off the timber, coal, oil, and steel industries. It is little wonder that many of the treaties signed during the period granted railroad rights-of-way through Indian lands, and in most cases the Indian lands that were acquired by the United States went immediately to subsidize the railroad system without ever having been made a part of the public domain.

Between the years 1850 and 1861, a spate of treaties were concluded to open and secure the lands for the United States on the Pacific coast. Throughout the period, gold seekers were pouring into the newly acquired territory of California. From the beginning of the gold rush in 1849, whites had begun an arbitrary but widespread massacre of indigenous populations. The remnants of the California nations that survived the slaughter either fled into isolation to avoid the heavily armed, remorseless, death-dealing whites or sought sanctuary around the old Spanish missions. By 1850, when California was admitted to the Union, most Native leaders would probably have thought it wise to avoid any and all contact with the whites, no matter their intentions.

California had been ceded to the United States under the Treaty of Guadalupe Hidalgo and the so-claimed title by right of conquest. As a result of the Supreme Court decision in *Johnson v. M'Intosh* (1823), however, the federal government nevertheless recognized that Indians possessed the "right of occupancy" to the land. In consequence, the government sent a three-man commission to California to convince Native Americans to accept the jurisdiction of the federal government and to recognize U.S. sovereignty over California. By January 1852, the commission had negotiated 18 treaties with 139 Native American bands, towns, confederated groups, and tribal subdivisions. The treaties established reservations and provided for the payment of annuities and the services of teachers and blacksmiths, and promised to provide the Native groups with subsistence in the form of livestock. The negotiations went to naught, however; because the Senate could not grasp the intricacies of California Native sociopolitical organization and because the costs of carrying out the provisions of the treaties were becoming very high, it rejected their ratification.

Federal agents were also occupied with negotiating treaties with the tribes of the Oregon and Washington territories. The main thrust of treaty making in the 1850s actually centered on these two potential states of the Union. In 1848, the

United States and Great Britain agreed, after years of dispute, to draw a boundary demarcating the line between the United States and Canada. The U.S. claim to what became the Oregon Territory—the present states of Oregon and Washington—was tenuous. There were several trading posts, both British and American, in the region, but until the 1830s white settlement was relatively insignificant.

After 1831, American immigrants began to pour into the Willamette Valley in Oregon and the Columbia River basin in what is now Washington. The United States had no legal claim to the territory—either by right of discovery or by conquest in a just war—but they had the numbers. Eventually, Great Britain bowed to the land-hungry Americans, and in 1850 Congress passed the Oregon Donation Act, establishing a special commission to negotiate with and extinguish the land titles held by the tribes of the Oregon Territory. This commission, although abolished in February 1851, nevertheless negotiated six treaties with several bands of the Kalapuya and Molala nations. The law abolishing the Donation Act commission transferred its duties to the superintendent of Indian affairs. As a result, the Donation Act commission's treaties were not ratified. Anson Dart, the superintendent, completed at least 13 treaties with tribes in western Oregon on which the Senate took no action. While Dart's treaties with the bands of the Tillamooks, Clatsops, and Chinooks languished in the Senate, the administration and Congress divided

At the Dalles on the Columbia River in Oregon, Indians met to trade. Governor Isaac Stevens negotiated treaties for tribal lands, but provisions protected Indian fishing rights in the local rivers in the Pacific Northwest as decided in the Boldt decision in 1974. (Library of Congress)

the Oregon Territory into the separate territories of Oregon and Washington and gave the power to negotiate with the tribes to the territorial governors.

Unratified Treaties

Many of the settlements negotiated with the Native nations of Oregon and Washington, although still arguably valid and thus operable, nevertheless, have been relegated to status of "unratified" or "invalid" treaties. The numerous agreements with these tribes signed in 1851 are cases in point. Dart's treaties of 1851 with the Clatsop, Tillamook, and Chinook bands ceded the entire Willamette Valley of Oregon to the United States. These treaties were negotiated primarily to transfer legally the already white-occupied valley to the U.S. public domain. Because of the change in policy directing the governors of Washington and Oregon to negotiate agreements with the Native nations located in the territories, the Senate did not ratify the Willamette Valley treaties. In 1906, however, Congress wrote a provision into that year's Indian Appropriation Act authorizing the secretary of the interior to investigate the number of Clatsop, Chinook, and Tillamook peoples, either signatories of the treaties or their descendants, who were affected by the land cession. In 1851, tribal leaders had negotiated monetary settlements to be paid over the course of 10 years. The Native leaders had insisted on the payments because their peoples were in a serious decline as a result of white intrusion and basically did not want the federal government to obtain the land without some kind of exchange or benefit. Because the Senate failed to ratify the treaties, the payments were not forthcoming.

During the first years of the 20th century, the federal government became interested in clarifying both the status of Native peoples under law and the validity of U.S. land claims. On the one hand, the government was attempting to end the reservation system and extract itself from the "Indian business." On the other, there was a growing interest in protecting what was left of tribal lands so that, as individuals, Native people would possess a level of income that would make their gradual assimilation into American society less abrupt, confusing, and painful.

For whatever the reason, Congress prompted a count of the populations of the tribal signatories of the Willamette Valley treaties and in 1913 appropriated $66,000—a sum greater than the original, agreed-upon remuneration—to pay the surviving tribal members for the loss of their lands. This compensatory action proved that even "unratified" treaties could indeed become operable. In the case of the Willamette Valley treaties, both parties—the federal government and the Native nations—mutually agreed to reconstitute the membership of the tribes in order to fulfill the treaties' stipulations. The treaties were thus "ratified" bilaterally because both sides actually complied with the provisions of these specific conventions. The "unratified" treaties with the Chinooks, Tillamooks, and Clatsops did not provide the United States with clear title to the rest of Oregon and Washington. Over the span of only 2 years, 16 treaties were negotiated and eventually ratified with several other nations of the Northwest.

In September 1853, the headmen of the Rogue River peoples signed away a large portion of Oregon Territory, from which they agreed to be removed to another "selected" site at a later date. In the same month, the Umpqua of Cow Creek, also in Oregon, gave up another large tract with the provision that a small section of land be "deemed and considered an Indian reserve until a suitable selection shall be made by the direction of the President of the United States for their permanent residence." In effect, the Umpqua and Rogue River peoples transferred their title to the land to the United States, and a portion was reserved for their temporary use. The very next year, another Umpqua band and the Rogue River leaders were negotiating new treaties. Under the Rogue River treaty of 1854, a portion of the previously reserved land known as the Table Rock reserve was to be put aside as a reservation for the Rogue River people and for other displaced Native bands. The Table Rock land was to be both a reservation and a refuge until the federal government deemed it necessary to remove the people once again. The Rogue River leaders did, however, secure a provision in the new treaty stipulating that, should a future removal take place, the Nation would share individually the $15,000 payment for their lands, as had been secured in the negotiations of the previous year. In the same month, federal agents negotiated a new treaty with the Cave Creek band of the Rogue River people. The new treaty included the Chasta (Shasta) and Scoton tribes and secured a previously unceded stretch of the Rogue River valley and lay along Applegate Creek. The new Umpqua treaty included the confederated Kalapuya peoples' ceded lands along Calapooia Creek and the Illinois River in Oregon. Like the Rogue River agreement, the treaty provided for a residential reserve and cash remuneration to be paid as annuities. The Chastas of Oregon also negotiated a new treaty in 1854 ceding a large tract of land essentially bordering the lands that had formerly belonged to the Rogue River and Umpqua peoples. Moreover, the Chastas were to be removed to the Rogue River's Table Rock Reservation. The Chastas were promised $2,000 annually for the next 15 years for the land; thereafter, their payments would be combined in the Table Rock annuities, of which the Chastas would receive a full share. All the negotiations in Oregon in 1854 contained "civilization" provisions. The Native nations were to receive farm implements, blacksmith services, schoolhouses, medical care, and livestock.

The Umpqua treaty furthered the government's "Indian civilization" policy in another important way. It contained a provision for the allotment of reservation lands at the discretion of the president of the United States. Allotment meant the surveying and division of the Umpqua and Kalapuya reserved lands into 20-, 40-, 60-, and 80-acre lots. The lots would be distributed to single males and to families according to the number of immediate members. A single man would receive 20 acres; a family of 2 would get 40 acres; families with 3 to 5 members would receive

60 acres; and a family of 6 or more could claim 80 acres. Families had to work the land, or their allotments would be redistributed to other tribe members.

The treaty also stipulated that, when Oregon eventually attained statehood, its legislature could not remove any of the federal restrictions placed on the Indian allotments. Here, in one fell swoop, the federal government attempted to encapsulate the intentions of the "civilization" policy. In the first place, it was thought that the individual or private ownership of property would immediately infuse the allottee with the urge to cultivate the land and thus gain an income. In theory, private property would liberate the allottee from tribal customs and dependence on extended family members and would ultimately promote self-reliance. The preemption of state jurisdiction over the allotments was an equally significant step in the attempt to woo Indians away from their identities as members of separate, sovereign nations. An allottee would, presumably, owe his first allegiance to the federal government as the guarantor of the individual's real property.

Every treaty of the period contained an article that not only established peace but also promised perpetual amity between the signatories. The Native nations that negotiated the treaties literally became protectorates of the United States. As such, their sovereignty, especially in a domestic sense, was not eroded in the least. They did, however, enter into a trust relationship with the United States that has been maintained to this day.

Trust Land

Under U.S. law, the Supreme Court, in a series of cases that include *Johnson v. M'Intosh* (1823), and the federal government, in several legislative enactments that include the General Allotment Act and Indian Reorganization Act, recognized that, in accordance with tribal government's "domestic dependent" status, the United States held a trust relationship to Indian tribal governments. As a result of this trust relationship, the United States is the legal title holder of trust assets of tribes and individual Natives, including land. Trust land is real property that may be held in trust for a tribe or an individual. Although the United States holds legal title to the land, a tribe or individual Native holds beneficial title—the use and benefits that derive from the property.

Historically, tribal government ownership of lands set aside as reservations gradually eroded as a result of the federal government's allotment policies of the late 19th and early 20th centuries. An Indian affairs social reform movement, arising first outside and then within the federal government, called for the legislative measures to be implemented to restore and protect Indian lands. Reformers noted that tribal governments' loss of a geographic base resulted in crippling Native poverty throughout the United States. Consequently, in 1934, the U.S. Congress authorized the secretary of the interior to take land in trust for the benefit of Native Americans under the Indian Reorganization Act Today that section is codified as 25 U.S.C. § 465.

By 1999, there were roughly 55 million acres of tribal lands held in trust by the federal government and nearly 11 million acres held in trust for individuals. As a general rule, state and local laws regarding matters such as taxation, zoning, and land use have no application on Native trust lands. Although this is the general rule, P.L. 280 enables certain states (Alaska, California, Minnesota [except Red Lake Reservation], Nebraska, Oregon [except Warm Springs Reservation], and Wisconsin [except Menominee Reservation]) to exercise criminal and civil jurisdiction over tribal lands within their borders. A tribe and a state might enter into a compact or cooperative agreement to clarify the role of courts or law enforcement on trust lands when the relationship is legally uncertain or when authorized or mandated by Congress. For instance, public roads crossing trust lands may legally be considered Indian country, but the practical implications for law enforcement may be unclear.

Because the United States is legal title holder, the federal government is a necessary part in all leases and dispositions of resources including trust land. For example, the secretary of the interior must approve any contract for payment or grant by a tribe for services for the tribe "relative to their lands."

Today, tribes may request the federal government to acquire additional land in trust by purchase or acquisition from surplus federal lands, including former military bases. Tribal governments may acquire land through the approval of the Department of the Interior application and regulatory process pursuant to 25 U.S.C. § 465 and 25 C.F.R. §151 or legislatively conferred trust status. The applicable federal regulations were subsequently modified and now require the Bureau of Indian Affairs to notify "the state and local governments having regulatory jurisdiction over the land to be acquired" and to provide those governments with a 30-day time period "in which to provide written comment as to the acquisition's potential impacts on regulatory jurisdiction."

Placement of newly acquired tribal land into trust has impacts on tribes as well as state and local governments. The land-into-trust process under the regulations is rigorous, requiring the secretary to review several criteria, including tribes' need for the land, the purpose for which the land will be used, the impact on the state and local political subdivisions (especially concerning taxation and any jurisdictional considerations), and compliance with National Environmental Protection Act of 1969.

The status of trust lands has seen the most profound criticism in the context of Indian gaming. All gaming and gaming-related acquisitions must be approved by the assistant secretary, pursuant to the Indian Gaming Regulatory Act of 1988. The practice of placing land into trust for proposed gaming facilities is especially contentious for land outside a tribe's homeland. Such off-reservation trust acquisitions must still be formally approved by the Bureau of Indian Affairs. The tribe must also submit an application and supporting documents to the BIA requesting such approval under 25 U.S.C. § 465 and pursuant to 25 C.F.R. 151.

Litigation challenging the Department of the Interior's trust acquisition authority—on the grounds that 25 U.S.C. 465 is an unconstitutional delegation of legislative power to the Department of Interior because the statute contains no express limits on the secretary's discretion and no judicial review standards—has met with little success. Courts have found that 25 U.S.C. 465 does in fact place limits on the secretary's discretion, and the legislative history identifies goals by which a court may examine the secretary's discretion, including "rehabilitating the Indian's economic life" and "developing the initiative destroyed by . . . oppression and paternalism," and must assure continued "beneficial use by the Indian occupant and his heirs."

Peter D. Lepsch

Further Reading

Clow, Richmond, and Imre Sutton, eds. *Trusteeship in Change: Toward Tribal Autonomy in Resource Management*. Boulder: University Press of Colorado, 2001.

Deloria, Vine, Jr., and David E. Wilkins. *Tribes, Treaties, and Constitutional Tribulations*. Austin: University of Texas Press, 1999.

Pommersheim, Frank. *Braid of Feathers: American Indian Law and Contemporary Tribal Life*. Berkeley: University of California Press, 1995.

Prucha, Francis Paul. *American Indian Treaties: The History of a Political Anomaly*. Berkeley: University of California Press, 1994.

Wilkins, David E., and K. Tsianina Lomawaima. *Uneven Ground: American Indian Sovereignty and Federal Law*. Norman: University of Oklahoma Press, 2001.

Williams, C. Herb, and Walt Neubrech. *Indian Treaties: American Nightmare*. Seattle, WA: Outdoor Empire, 1976.

Williams, Robert A. *Linking Arms Together: American Indian Treaty Visions of Law and Peace, 1600–1800*. New York: Oxford University Press, 1997.

Three ratified treaties negotiated in Oregon Territory were concluded in 1855. In January, the Kalapuya nation entered into another treaty with the United States, one that surrendered more lands along the Columbia River to the Cascade Mountains for a sum of $145,000, to be paid in decreasing amounts over a period of 20 years. The following June, the United States concluded a convention with several bands of Walla Wallas and the Wasco Nation at the Dalles in Oregon. Not only did the treaty of the Dalles cede more territory to the Americans, but it also secured for the Wallas Wallas and Wascos the right to fish in "usual and accustomed stations." This provision essentially said that the Walla Walla and Wasco peoples could take fish even outside the boundaries of their assigned reservations. The treaty in December with the Molala nation extinguished the tribe's "right, title, interest and claim" to the territory bordering the lands surrendered by the Umpqua, Chasta, Scoton, and Rogue River peoples the year before. Except for the Indian reservations, the title to the entire Oregon Territory had shifted to the United States.

The Washington Territory treaties were equally extensive in terms of land surrendered in a relatively short period of time. Between December 1854 and July 1855, the Native nations gave up their "right, title, interest and claim" to the land from the northern border with Canada to Oregon in the south and from the Pacific Ocean in the west to the Great Plains in the east. The lands around Puget Sound and along the Columbia River were especially desirable. The fishing, the timber, the fine harbors, the access to the Pacific Ocean whaling grounds, and the fertile farmlands were much too valuable to the Americans for them to remain in Indian hands. The titles to the vast tracts of land surrounding Puget Sound were transferred to the United States in five treaties concluded between December 1854 and June 1855. The Medicine Creek convention, signed with the Nisqally, Puyallup, Steilacoom, Squaxin S'Homamish, Stehchass, Tapeeksin, Squiaitl, and Sahewamish tribes on December 26, 1854, gave up the southern end of the sound. A month later, the Duwamishs, the Suquamishs, and several other nations agreed to the Point Elliott treaty, which secured the eastern flank of Puget Sound for the United States to a very great depth. In June 1855 came the Point No Point treaty, by which the Clallam, Twana, and Chemakum tribes ceded the lands west of the Point Elliot treaty, thus giving up nearly all of the Olympic Peninsula. The rest of the peninsula was secured in the Neah Bay treaty of June 1855 with the Makahs, and the Quinault River treaty of July 1855 with the Quinault, Queets, Hoh, and Quileute peoples. These treaties contained provisions under which the Native nations pledged eternal friendship with the United States and promised not to harbor anyone suspected of breaking the law. The Point Elliot treaties, for example, stipulated that, should any Indian "violate this pledge" and harm an American citizen in any way, the tribe's annuities would be used to compensate the victims. In essence, the Native nations agreed to become protectorates of the United States and assume liability for the actions of their citizens. Federal agents, however, were given the power to judge whether or not American "depredation" claims against the tribes were "satisfactorily proven." Hence, while the Native nations were asserting the sovereign capacity to enter into protectorate status and take up the responsibility for the actions of their peoples, the Americans were assuming an extensive political jurisdiction over the tribes.

In June 1855, several Native nations and the United States negotiated three treaties at Camp Stevens in the Walla Walla Valley. The Walla Walla, Cayuse, and Umatilla peoples concluded an agreement whereby, in exchange for $100,000, they ceded a large tract of land in Washington and agreed to be moved to a reservation. These confederated nations were to remove to a reservation chosen by the president of the United States, which was to be surveyed for allotment when the president deemed it in the best interests of the Indians to do so. In separate treaties, the Yakimas and Nez Perces agreed to nearly the same stipulations. In July, at Hell Gate in the Bitterroot Valley, the Flathead, Kutenai, and Pend d'Oreille Nations surrendered most of the western half of the territory and agreed to move onto smaller reservations within their former national boundaries. Almost the entire territory of the future state of Washington was in the hands of the United States. Except for a few provisions dealing with reservation boundaries and amounts of money pledged to the tribes, the treaties negotiated in Washington Territory were all very similar in wording and in form. Treaties in the 1850s were becoming more or less standardized. All of the Washington Territory and a few of the Oregon treaties, however, provided that the Native nations would retain the right to fish in their usual and accustomed "stations" or "grounds" and even to set up buildings in these places to cure the catch and house the fishermen during the seasonal fish or whale migrations. The Native negotiators essentially secured the right to fish even outside the boundaries of their reservations. These fishing rights, guaranteed by treaty with the United States, would later become a long, drawn-out battle between the Native nations and the state of Washington. In the end, the treaties superseded state fish and game regulations, thereby conceding a degree of Native sovereignty.

While a number of officials were sedulously seeking to open up the territories of Oregon and Washington, others were equally preoccupied with securing the land routes over which the whites would come in droves to the northwest coast and California. One of the first of these was the Navajo (spelled *Navaho* in the original document) treaty of 1849. Under the Treaty of Guadalupe Hidalgo, the Native nations of the Southwest were specifically placed under the "exclusive jurisdiction and protection" of the United States. The Navajo treaty, one of "peace and friendship," ceded no land and established no reservation but bound the Navajo Nation to the U.S. laws governing the trade and intercourse between Indian and American citizens. For the purposes of enforcing these laws, the Navajo Nation was subjected to a jurisdictional annexation to New Mexico Territory. The annexation meant that the

Navajos were to repatriate American and Mexican captives and return all property taken in raids. The Navajos were also to deliver to the authorities of New Mexico Territory the murderer or murderers, presumably Navajos, of one Micente Garcia.

According to the reasoning at the time, the United States by right of conquest took the territory from Mexico. Presumably, the Spanish had secured legitimate title to the land of the American Southwest either by way of conquest or by right of discovery, according to the established European means of acquiring new lands. Mexico gained the title from Spain when it rebelled and became an independent state. On the other hand, U.S. negotiators nevertheless realized that the Navajo Nation, like the Native peoples of California, had, at minimum, a right of occupancy to their lands. In consequence, federal agents negotiated a "free and safe passage through the territory of the aforesaid Indians" so that white immigrants might traverse northern New Mexico Territory in route to California. The treaty also stipulated that a string of military posts be established "to afford protection to all the people and interests of the contracting parties." The right of occupancy also elicited the agreement that the federal government would "at its earliest convenience, designate, settle and adjust" the boundaries of the Navajo national domain.

"Free-passage" treaties were negotiated with the Apaches in 1852 and with the Comanches, Kiowas, and Apaches (Plains) in 1853. The former treaty was signed at Santa Fe, New Mexico Territory. It established peace and, to enforce the safe passage of whites and maintain order, contained a provision whereby the Apaches agreed to the erection of U.S. military posts in their country. They also approved the stipulation that all cases of aggression by whites against them and their property would be referred to U.S. military authority. It was thought, perhaps, that the assumption of U.S. jurisdiction over all white crimes would end the almost constant state of war between white immigrants and the Apaches. The Comanche-Kiowa-Apache treaty of the next year was signed at Fort Atkinson in the Indian Territory. These Native nations agreed to end warfare, both between themselves and against the United States. They agreed, as did the Apaches in the Santa Fe treaty, to forgo incursions into Mexico and restore captives to both the Mexican government and the United States. The treaty also carried a free-passage clause and bound the Comanches, Kiowas, and Apaches to a provision that called for the laying out of permanent roads through their territories. The Native nations agreed to the erection of military posts and to refer cases of white criminality to military authorities.

The pressing need on the part of the United States to ensure the passage of immigrants to the West Coast led to the demand for the Native nations to surrender more land in what would become the states of Minnesota, Wisconsin, Iowa, Nebraska, and especially Kansas. The list of treaties with the tribes of these areas was remarkably long. Native nations that had been removed from Ohio, Indiana, Illinois, and Michigan and as far away as New York to the "permanent Indian frontier"—a

The Apaches signed three treaties and were included in two more that forced them to remove to reservations in the late 1800s in Arizona and New Mexico. Geronimo was the last noted Apache war leader to surrender in 1886. (Popperfoto/Getty Images)

space that roughly covered what today is southern Nebraska and all of Kansas and Oklahoma—were forced to reduce their landholdings once again to tiny reservations or move south into Indian Territory. These land cessions affected the land bases of the Seneca, Delaware, Miami, Mdewakanton, Wahpakoota, Sisseton, and Wahpeton Sioux, Wyandot, Sac and Fox, Oto and Missouri, Shawnee, Omaha, and Iowa Nations. The Miami, Peoria, Kaskaskia, Kickapoo, Chippewa, Winnebago, and Ottawa Nations also surrendered huge amounts of territory, all with the promise of annuity payments, the protection of the federal government, and, most important, peace. The list of unratified treaties that attempted to reduce Native landholdings to the bare minimum and institute peace all along the American frontier was equally lengthy. Some of these treaties were negotiated with nations that had never before dealt with the Americans. Others were stopgap agreements made to quell violence either immediately or until more comprehensive conventions could be worked out. A number of these treaties could, in fact, contain provisions that might be operable simply because Congress has referred to them in other treaties or in making appropriations to fulfill one or another promise made to Native nations.

The Fort Laramie treaty of 1851, like the Navajo treaty of 1849, stands out in this period because it did not call for a land cession on the part of the Native nations. Basically, it was a peace concord that defined the national boundaries of several indigenous peoples of the northern plains. The Sioux, Gros Ventre, Mandan,

Arikara, Assiniboine, Blackfeet, Crow, Cheyenne, and Arapaho Nations all participated in the negotiations and agreed not only to the stipulated national borders but also to the building of roads and military posts within these boundaries. Ostensibly, the roads were for the free and safe passage of white immigrants on the trail to the West Coast, and the military posts were erected in order to protect both Indians and whites from each other's potential depredations. The federal government, in compensation, was to pay the Native nations $50,000 a year for 50 years "for their maintenance and the improvement of their moral and social customs."

Land Payments

Probably because no land cession was agreed to in the Fort Laramie treaty, Congress did not pass on it without altering one of its most important provisions. Congress essentially decreased the 50 annual payments to 10, with another 5 to be paid at the discretion of the president. This sum of money was hardly enough to aid the nearly 50,000 members of the several Native nations involved in the negotiations; from the point of view of the Native leaders, it was a serious breach of the agreement they had made. The congressional amendment made the treaty's standing hazy at best, even in the eyes of the whites. Charles J. Kappler, in his 1904 compilation of treaties, stated that the Fort Laramie treaty was "never ratified or printed." It was nevertheless valid even in its altered form, and the Native nations, although they voiced concern over the changes made, complied with its provisions. Four years later, however, some of the Native nations involved in the Fort Laramie treaty, as well as some of those engaged in making agreements with federal agents in Washington Territory, were once again at the negotiating table. The Blackfeet Nation (consisting of, and so recognized by the United States, the Piegans, Bloods, and Blackfeet proper); the Gros Ventres from east of the Rocky Mountains; and the Flatheads, Upper Pend d'Oreilles, Kutenais, and Nez Perces from the west side of the range worked out a new and detailed treaty in 1855. In format much like most of the treaties of the period, the Blackfeet agreement was intended to settle territorial boundaries and maintain order along the northern immigrant trail to Washington Territory. Peace and friendship were declared between the United States and the Native nations as well as between each one of the signatory Native peoples. The Native parties to the treaty also agreed to cease hostilities, except in self-defense, with the Crows, Assiniboines, Crees, Snakes (Shoshones), and several Lakota bands. The Blackfeet consented once again to their national boundaries, as had been "recognized and defined by the treaty of Laramie," even though Congress had amended the 1851 convention almost to the point of invalidity.

Perhaps the main point of the Blackfeet treaty was to secure a common hunting ground for the various signatories and to allow whites both to live in and to pass through the large Blackfeet Nation domain. No other tribes were allowed to establish permanent settlements; each Native nation would be allowed to enter the Blackfeet Nation only to use it as a common for the taking of buffalo, and for other purposes only by way of certain designated points of entry. Although the Assiniboine Nation was not party to the treaty, it was specifically mentioned as one of the groups with hunting rights within Blackfeet Territory. The treaty went on to stipulate that all Indians were to stay in their respective lands except when on hunting forays. The treaty allowed for the construction of roads "of every description" and the establishment of telegraph lines and military posts. U.S. citizens were allowed the free navigation of all streams and rivers and the permanent use of land, timber, and other natural resources for the erection of "agencies, missions, schools, farms, shops, mills, stations, and for any other purpose for which they may be required." For the effective opening of the Blackfeet Nation to American colonization, the Blackfeet, Piegans, Bloods, and Gros Ventres were to receive $20,000 annually for a period of 20 years. The president, however, could increase the annuity to $35,000 should circumstance warrant the increase.

The main thrust of treaty making during the 1850s was to acquire more land and thereby gain political efficacy within the territory claimed by the United States as its national domain. Underlying the acquisition of control over Native territories were strategies calculated to smooth over the hostilities aroused when Native Americans were displaced or confined to smaller tracts of land. One such strategy was the introduction to Native peoples of the concept of private property by way of allotment in severalty. For example, in 1858, the Sisseton and Wahpeton Sioux penned a treaty in Washington, D.C., that agreed to new reservation boundaries and to having them surveyed with the intent of dividing the reservation into individually owned, 80-acre plots. The ultimate reason for the acceptance of this new treaty was simply that the U.S. Senate reneged on the Sisseton-Wahpeton agreement of 1851. The Senate unilaterally struck the provision in the treaty of 1851 that set apart a large tract of land for the Sisseton-Wahpeton on the Minnesota River, and instead offered a sum of money "at the rate of ten cents per acre" to the Sisseton-Wahpeton Nation. Other than providing excuses for amending the treaty of 1851, the new convention provided for the same lands to be allotted, which in turn considerably reduced Sisseton-Wahpeton landholdings. Individual tribe members, instead of the Sisseton-Wahpeton Nation, were to hold the land.

Addenda Treaties

The federal government negotiated no fewer than five treaties or addenda to treaties with the Muscogee Creeks, Seminoles, Chickasaws, and Choctaws in the 1850s. These tribes had been forcibly removed from their homelands in the southeastern United States to the Indian Territory (present Oklahoma) in the 1830s. Not all their tribe members, however, had made the trip. A large number of Choctaws remained in Mississippi, and the Chickasaws had not ceded a four-mile-square parcel of land in Tennessee to the United States. The removal of the Seminole Nation from Florida had started a costly war, and even as late as the 1850s, small bands of Mikasuki Seminoles were still living in the Florida backcountry and fighting American soldiers.

In 1852, the Chickasaws entered into negotiations with the federal government, primarily to settle several of the tribe's claims to particular lands. Additionally, the cost of the Chickasaw removal had far exceeded the funds allocated for the purpose. The treaty of 1852 was intended to clear up the cost of removal, to clear the title of Chickasaw lands that had not been ceded east of the Mississippi River, and to address the allegations of corruption that had resulted in the override of Chickasaw removal funds. The Chickasaw Nation agreed to forgo claims to territories in the east for money to be held in trust by the United States, provided that the secretary of the interior audit the Chickasaw account "from time to time." The Chickasaws would have the "privilege" to review the audit and submit objections to it within a reasonable amount of time. The cost to the United States was ultimately quite low. The four mile-square parcel in Tennessee, for example, which had been originally set apart as a reservation under the provisions of the Chickasaw treaty of 1818, was to be purchased at a rate of no more than "one dollar and twenty-five cents per acre."

Two years later, the Chickasaws were back at the negotiating table. When removal took place, the Chickasaws and Choctaws were effectively placed together on one large piece of land that made up most of what would become southern Oklahoma. The Chickasaw and Choctaw leaders more or less agreed to this circumstance, very likely because they recognized that, since they were culturally and linguistically tied, the two nations were once one. By 1854, however, the jurisdictional lines between the two peoples had become unclear. The United States was brought into the dispute over the Chickasaw-Choctaw boundaries, and a new treaty was negotiated. Essentially, the two nations agreed to draw a line between themselves: the Chickasaw jurisdiction was established in the western half of the territory, the Choctaws in the east.

The dispute did not end, and the very next year the Chickasaws and the Choctaws agreed to a redrawing of the boundaries between the two nations and to lease their lands west of longitude 98° to the United States. The two nations separated completely. The Choctaws received a sum of money out of Chickasaw funds and ceded all of the land west of 100° longitude. The nations agreed to the establishment of military forts and roads and to railroad and telegraph rights-of-way.

Similar jurisdictional and national disputes had arisen between the Creeks and the Seminoles. The United States was still attempting to remove the remnants of the Seminole Nation in Florida to the Indian Territory. Those Seminoles who had been forcibly removed were moved, again because of linguistic and cultural ties, onto the lands of the Muscogee Creek Nation. The Creek treaty of 1856 essentially ceded a tract of land to the Seminoles. A sovereign Seminole Nation was thus established in the hope of getting the Seminoles in Florida to cease hostilities and migrate to the Indian Territory. The Seminole Nation West, as it was called, would send a delegation to Florida "to do all in their power to induce their brethren remaining [in Florida] to emigrate and join them in the west." The usual concessions to the railroads, military posts, roads, and telegraph services were also made. The effort to "induce" the Florida Seminoles to remove was not successful. While some Seminoles did, indeed, migrate west after the treaty of 1856, the core of the Mikasuki Seminoles in the east remained in Florida to this day.

By the end of March 1861, the United States had succeeded in securing the title to nearly all of its claimed territory west of the Mississippi River. Save for a very large tract of land recognized as "the Great Sioux Nation" on the northern plains, most of the Indian Territory (present Oklahoma), a very large portion of New Mexico Territory, and smaller reservations dotting the land, the Americans now held all of what would become the continental United States. The Cheyennes and Arapahos had ceded eastern Colorado in February 1861, and on March 6, the united Sauk and Fox and Iowa Nations gave up title to most of Iowa and parts of Nebraska.

Confederate Treaties

All of the great land cessions of the 1850s contributed fuel to the oncoming holocaust of the American Civil War. The opening of the entire West Coast, Iowa, Minnesota, Utah, Colorado, Nebraska, Kansas, and much of New Mexico Territory meant the possibility of bringing in several states into the union. Most of these territories, in accordance with several legal compromises, would not become slave-holding states. Southern politicians, of course, saw the organization of states such as Iowa (1846), Minnesota (1858), Kansas (1861), and Nebraska (1867) as a threat to their continued power in Congress, to their economic systems, and to their sectional culture, all of which were built on chattel slavery.

When the Civil War broke out in April 1861, the newly formed Confederate States actively began to seek Native American allies. The Confederacy was especially interested in the Indian Territory, which could serve as a buffer between Union Kansas and Confederate Texas, and with the mineral-rich New Mexico and Arizona territories. Albert Pike, whose complete title was commissioner of the Confederate States to the Indians west of Arkansas, negotiated 9 treaties with 21 Native nations, at 4 different locations. All of the tribes with which Pike negotiated with were located at the time in the Indian Territory.

The first Confederate treaties were negotiated with the Creeks, Choctaws, and Chickasaws in North Fork Town on the Canadian River in the Creek Nation. The Creek treaty, although concluded on July 10, 1861, nevertheless referred to the

Seminole treaty of August 7 of the same year in order to clarify the exact boundaries and jurisdictions of both nations. A supplementary article was added to the convention to address the claims of the Apalachicola band. Under two previous treaties with the United States, the Apalachicola still had reserves of land in Florida. The Confederacy acknowledged their claims and agreed to pay for the claims and the property the Apalachicolas lost in their removal to the Indian Territory. Remnants of the Apalachicola still living in Florida would be encouraged to move west and reunite with their kinsmen as part of the larger Creek Nation. In the same supplement, the Seminoles were guaranteed payments for their lost property and land in Florida "in consequence of their hurried removal west."

The Choctaws and Chickasaws signed a single treaty with the Confederacy. Concluded on July 12, the treaty was lengthy and detailed. It contained more than 60 articles, many of which focused on clearing up the financial arrangements of land sales and annuities. The Confederate government in Richmond essentially took on the U.S. debt to, and assumed the federal trust responsibility for, the Choctaws and the Chickasaws. Moreover, the Confederacy agreed to pay the Chickasaws close to $700,000 as reimbursement for funds invested by the United States in the state bonds of Maryland, Indiana, Tennessee, Illinois, and Arkansas and in stocks issued by the Richmond and Danville Railroad and the Nashville and Chattanooga Railroad. The Seminole treaty was agreed to in August at the Seminole Council House, and the Confederate Cherokee convention was concluded in October at Park Hill, Cherokee Nation. The Confederacy had thus made binding agreements with all of the so-called Five Civilized Tribes, establishing itself as the protector of the Indian nations. All these treaties offered the Native nations a good deal more than the Union promised. Native soldiers, who were to be equipped by the South, would not have to fight except in defense of their own territory. The Confederacy would assume all of the Union's debts and annuity payments, in addition to a permanent allocation to pay for certain services, such as schools, insane asylums, health care, and orphanages. The Native nations were also given the option of sending delegates to the Confederate House of Representatives. Most important, perhaps, was that the Confederacy pledged its protection from invasion and affirmed each nation's title to its lands in fee simple. The negotiations at Park Hill produced Confederate treaties with the Osage, confederated Seneca and Shawnee, and Quapaw Nations. Like the treaties made with the Five Tribes, these agreements were somewhat formulaic. The treaties guaranteed annuities, the services of teachers, blacksmiths, and landholdings. The Confederacy also agreed to supply the tribes with arms to be used in their self-protection. The same kinds of guarantees were given in treaties to a number of Native groups in the western Indian Territory, including the Comanche, Wichita, Caddo, Waco, Tawakoni, Anadarko, Tonkawa, and western Shawnee and Delaware tribes. Confederate agents obtained an agreement with the Comanches of the Staked Plains to offer a treaty of friendship with the Kiowas, in order to stop completely raids into Texas.

On the surface, the Confederate treaties promised a remarkably peaceful settlement for most of the Native nations living in or near what is now Oklahoma. The Confederate treaties not only established friendship between the nations and the Confederacy but also between all the Native treaty signatories. Each treaty contained an oath of "perpetual peace and brotherhood" with all the Native nations that made treaties with the Confederacy. The Comanches swore not to raid other Native nations; Cherokees and Osages pledged to end long years of animosity; the Wichitas promised to live in peace and forgive those tribes that had threatened them in the past. The Confederacy presumably obtained the safety of its largest state, Texas, and opened the rest of the Southwest for Confederate expansion. The Confederate-initiated peace in the Indian Territory, however, was not to be. Before the ink was dry on the treaties, Creeks and Seminoles loyal to the Union attempted to escape to Kansas, and numerous Cherokees began to doubt the wisdom of allying themselves with the South. Eventually, fighting erupted between loyal and Confederate Indians all over the territory. All-Indian regiments were raised for both the Union and the Confederacy. These military units were even to go into combat outside the territorial limits of the Native nations. The promise that the nations would not have to fight unless in defense of their own country was quickly made moot. Union and Confederate invasions from Kansas, Arkansas, and Texas left the Indian Territory devastated. And the fighting continued there even after the surrender at Appomattox, Virginia.

Predictably, war fever engulfed the western territories and states and led to the inflicting of barbarous cruelties on the Native nations. War broke out in Minnesota between the whites and the Santee Sioux. Instead of attempting to use diplomacy, which perhaps could have averted the Santee war, the whites treated genuine Santee complaints as acts of rebellion, eventually trying and convicting many of the Santee men in a military court. California militiamen stormed into Arizona and New Mexico seeking rebels, only to set off a lengthy war with the Apaches and Navajos. The old scout Kit Carson was enlisted to carry on a frightful roundup of the Navajos, which led to their imprisonment at Fort Sumner in New Mexico. In 1864, the Colorado Volunteers attacked and slaughtered the Cheyennes at Sand Creek, Colorado, not withstanding the fact that the Cheyennes were peacefully living on the lands guaranteed to them in their 1861 treaty with the United States. The horror of the Sand Creek massacre produced a period of general conflict between the Native nations of the Great Plains and the Union.

From a certain perspective, agents of the United States were indeed attempting to ease the tensions with several Native nations during the war and trying to deal with them diplomatically. The federal government negotiated and ratified 18 treaties during the war. Between March 1862 and March 1865, exactly three years, treaties were concluded with the Kansa, Ottawa, Chippewa, Nez Percé, Shoshone, Ute, Klamath, Modoc, Omaha, Winnebago, and Ponca Nations. All these agreements included land cessions and further diminished the territories of the tribes involved. Several established "permanent" reservations or removed the nations to smaller concentrations of landholdings. Despite its focus on winning the Civil War, the United States was nevertheless still very much involved in securing title to new lands in the West.

When the fighting between the whites ended, the United States simply resumed its avowed conquest of the western territories, with a side trip to renegotiate treaties with the nations that had signed on with the Confederacy. The United States extracted a heavy price from the nations that signed Confederate treaties, even though large factions within the tribes had repudiated them and had served in Union regiments. The Osages were forced to cede most of their large reservation and confine themselves to the Indian Territory. For the land cession, they were to receive the proceeds of the sale of their lands in Kansas and Missouri, from which the federal government established a fund to build boarding schools. Portions of Osage land were to be directly handed over in fee simple to several individuals. Certain chiefs and mixed-blood citizens of the Osage Nation were awarded direct payments of Osage funds and grants of land. The Osages put themselves under the protectorship of the United States and agreed to be removed from the ceded lands within a six-month period of time. The federal government also extracted railroad rights-of-way through Osage country. Finally, the Osages submitted to a new kind of treaty provision that stated, "Should the Senate reject or amend any of the above articles, such rejection or amendment shall not affect the other provisions of this treaty." The Senate, in other words, could change the treaty as it liked, whereas the Osages were bound to the agreement no matter what.

Reconstruction Treaties

The Five Civilized Tribes each agreed to reconstruction treaties that not only ceded territory but also gave up land for the resettlement of Native nations from Kansas, Nebraska, and Missouri. The Cherokees, Choctaws, Chickasaws, Muscogee Creeks, and Seminoles agreed to abolish slavery and admit the freed slaves to citizen status within their respective nations. The new treaties gave away railroad rights-of-way but promised the nations that white intruders would be removed from their territorial boundaries. The Cherokee treaty of 1866 was perhaps the most comprehensive of the several "reconstruction" treaties. It first contained a provision declaring the Confederate treaty of 1861 null and void, even though the Cherokees had already repudiated it in 1863. Notwithstanding this repudiation, the United States argued that the previously existing Cherokee treaties were nevertheless insufficient. A portion of the Cherokee Nation was set aside for former slaves and for free blacks who had resided in the Cherokee homeland prior to the Civil War, who individually could take 160-acre plots should they desire to move there within a span of two years. This land, however, was not to be "set apart until it shall be found that the Canadian district is not sufficiently large to allow one hundred and sixty acres to each person desiring to obtain settlement under the provisions of this article." The residents of this reserve-within-a-reserve were enabled to elect their own local officers and judges and to have representation in the Cherokee national government. A U.S. court was to be established in the Indian Territory "nearest to the Cherokee Nation" and was to have jurisdiction over all matters civil and criminal involving whites and blacks. The Cherokee court system retained jurisdiction in Cherokee cases only. The Cherokees were also required to take a census of the nation and to participate in an Indian Territory-wide general council in order to regulate intercourse between the Indian nations and with the "colonies of freemen resident in said Territory." The federal government obtained the agreement from the Cherokees to resettle "civilized" Indians in the Cherokee Nation and admit them as citizens (a Delaware and a Shawnee band eventually were so settled). More Cherokee land was to be ceded for the future resettlement of several "friendly" Native nations. The idea of resettling "friendly" Native nations in the Indian Territory marked the beginning of a new round of Indian removal that would continue well into the 1870s, with the relocation of the Poncas, the Pawnees, and numerous other Native nations that had surrendered their lands in Iowa, Minnesota, Kansas, Texas, Nebraska, the Dakotas, and as far away as New York and Oregon.

The years between 1865 and 1868 produced a very long list of Native American treaties with the United States, some ratified, some simply set aside until more comprehensive agreements could be made. Four unratified but very important treaties that fitted the category of stopgap measures were the covenants that ended the Civil War in the Indian Territory. On June 19, 1865, the principal chief of the Choctaw Nation, Peter Pitchlynn, agreed to cease "acts of hostility" against the United States, and four days later, Confederate Brigadier General Stand Watie, who also had taken the title of principal chief of the Cherokee Nation, agreed to do the same. The Chickasaw Nation capitulated on July 14. In September, Union negotiators arranged what was in effect an armistice between Union forces and Confederate and Union Indians in the Indian Territory. Emissaries from the Cherokee, Creek, Choctaw, Chickasaw, Osage, Seminole, Seneca, Shawnee, Quapaw, and Euchee peoples essentially agreed to accept protectorate status under the United States and end any acts of aggression between themselves. That these treaties were not ratified was very likely due to the fact that these groups were seen as combat units rather than as Native nations. Thus, the treaties were thought to be more akin to the surrenders of the individual Confederate armies under Robert E. Lee, Joseph Johnston, and Edmund Kirby Smith. Military leaders, especially those acting in rebellion against the United States, were not heads of state authorized to conduct formal international relations.

Most of the unratified treaties of 1865, 1866, and 1867 were measures under which Native nations surrendered title to vast territories in the West. This round of treaty making was also an effort on the part of the United States to restore its claim to authority over the relations with Native nations. All the Native nations were doubtless aware of the terrible internecine struggle the Americans had just fought and were probably willing to deal with the winner in order to restore orderly relationships with the whites. These treaties, especially those made with the Paiutes, Shoshones, Crows, several bands of the Apaches, the Arikaras, Mandans, and Hidatsas, the Assiniboines, the Brule and Oglala bands of Lakota, and the Bannocks, were very likely either not even submitted for ratification or had been made by unauthorized military personnel seeking an immediate end to hostilities or by those seeking to earn a measure of fortune or fame for negotiating the surrender of large tracts of Native lands.

Several agreements in the period also went unratified for the same reasons, because they were superseded by subsequent negotiations at the level of formal treaties, or because they were simply nullified by certain events. War was the event that certainly voided most of the agreements and treaties, ratified or not, with several Native nations of the Great Plains and the Southwest. The Apaches were embroiled in a continuous war of attrition for their mineral-rich lands in Arizona and New Mexico territories that ultimately would last until the 1880s. The numerous agreements and ratified treaties made with the individual bands of the Lakota Nation, the Yanktonais, the northern and southern branches of the Cheyenne and Arapaho Nations, the Kiowas, Plains Apaches, and Comanches in 1865 were but interludes of diplomacy in a lengthy conflict that began with the massacre at Sand Creek and engulfed all of the peoples of the Great Plains.

Because of the continuing violence, Congress created the United States Indian Peace Commission on June 20, 1867. The "Great Peace Commission," headed by Commissioner of Indian Affairs Nathaniel G. Taylor and including famous Civil War generals William Tecumseh Sherman and Alfred Terry, negotiated two of the most significant treaties on the Great Plains: the treaties of Medicine Lodge in 1867 and Fort Laramie in 1868. Neither treaty ended the conflict completely. Their very existence, however, ultimately led to the end of formal treaty making altogether. In a very real sense, the Native nations involved in these treaties negotiated from a position of relative strength, something that the United States was not ready to countenance.

The general warfare on the southern plains was a series of strikes and counterstrikes conducted by the United States and the southern branches of the Cheyennes and Arapahos and the Kiowas, Plains Apaches, and Comanches. The Cheyenne Dog Soldiers had carried on an effective hit-and-run campaign against numerous civilian and military targets. The Kiowas and Comanches went on joint raids into Texas and New Mexico and, in the view of American officials, were severely disrupting trade and immigration routes. Although there were a few pitched battles, mostly between small parties of whites and Natives, by and large the war on

Harper's Weekly shows U.S. peace commissioners meeting with Kiowas and Comanches at Medicine Lodge, Kansas, including the Kiowa-Apaches, Cheyennes, and Arapahos in 1867. This was the largest Indian gathering for treaty negotiations of about 15,000 Indians from the five most powerful tribes on the Southern Plains. (Library of Congress)

the Southern Plains between 1865 and 1867 was a costly, confusing, and bitter period of guerrilla warfare. The American press was continually calling for an end to Indian depredations. The army could not find and defeat the tribes in decisive battle, but the continued conflict had begun to wear the Native leaders down. When the Great Peace Commission proposed a meeting that would secure peace at Medicine Lodge Creek in Kansas, many of the Native leaders came with high expectations.

Actually, three treaties were negotiated at Medicine Lodge. The first was with the Kiowas and Comanches. Basically, the price of peace was confinement to a relatively large reservation in southwestern Indian Territory and the withdrawal of opposition to the construction of roads and rail lines into Colorado and New Mexico. Heads of families could select tracts of land not exceeding 320 acres to engage in agricultural pursuits, the boundaries of which would be recorded in the "Kiowa and Comanche land book." The issuance of farming implements, the services of a blacksmith and a physician, and the establishment of reservations schools were promised. Two important provisions in the treaty would eventually become causes for renewed conflicts, one resulting in open warfare and the second in a famous court case.

In Article 11 of the treaty, the Kiowas and Comanches retained the right to hunt the territory south of the Arkansas River "so long as the buffalo may range thereon." With the building of roads and rail lines, immigrant whites, the army, and sportsmen came to these hunting grounds in droves. The great slaughter of the herds had already begun by the time the Native leaders signed the Medicine Lodge agreements. Then, in 1871, a Pennsylvania tannery discovered that bison hides had commercial value. The hides could be used not only for the manufacture of leather goods but also as belting for machinery. Commercial buffalo hunting soon became a leading industry in the West. The Kiowas and Comanches saw the slaughter as a violation of their guaranteed right to hunt, and a war to save the buffalo broke out. It would last until well into the 1870s.

Article 12 of the treaty provided that no further cession of Kiowa-Comanche land could be made without the agreement of three-fourths of the male population of the tribes. When, 30 years later, federal government moved to allot the Kiowa-Comanche Reservation, leaving surplus land to be set aside for white settlement, no three-fourths majority tribal consent was sought or obtained. A lawsuit, launched on behalf of Kiowa chief Lone Wolf, argued that allotment was in violation of Article 12 of the treaty. The Supreme Court, in *Lone Wolf v. Hitchcock*, decided in 1903 that Congress had plenary authority over the tribes and could therefore abrogate unilaterally the provisions of a prior convention.

Plenary Power

The term "plenary power," when used in reference to Indian affairs, describes the supreme authority exercised by the U.S. Congress over all Native matters. Depending on the context in which the term is used, the plenary power of Congress can mean either "exclusive power," "preemptive power," or "absolute and unlimited power." The distinction is important because, although the first two meanings of the term are based clearly on provisions embedded in the U.S. Constitution, the third is not. When it refers to the ability of Congress to regulate Native Americans and tribes to the exclusion of the executive and judicial branches of the federal government, the plenary power of Congress is considered "exclusive." However, when Congress exercises its authority to negate or supersede an action by a state government in the field of Indian affairs, the plenary power of Congress is denoted "preemptive." Alternately, when Congress passes legislation that modifies or eliminates tribal sovereignty, its plenary power is deemed "absolute and unlimited." Thus, the precise meaning of the term *plenary power* shifts subtly according to whether congressional power over Native matters is compared to the power of the other two branches of the federal government, the power of state governments, or the power of tribal governments.

Both the exclusive and the preemptive meanings of congressional plenary power have their origin in constitutional text. The commerce clause—Article I, Section 8, clause 3—of the Constitution confers on Congress "the Power . . . to regulate Commerce with foreign Nations, and among the several States, and with the Indian Tribes." Additionally, the treaty clause—found in Article II, Section 2, clause 2—delegates to Congress the power to approve treaties made with Native American tribes. Finally, the supremacy clause—located in Article VI, clause 2—declares, "This Constitution, and the laws of the United States . . . and all treaties made . . . shall be the supreme law of the land." The U.S. Supreme Court has interpreted these provisions as providing Congress, and only Congress, with complete control over indigenous matters.

In contrast, the "absolute and unlimited" plenary power that Congress exercises in relation to tribal governments does not have a clear constitutional basis. The Supreme Court first announced this doctrine in 1903 in *Lone Wolf v. Hitchcock*, a case involving tribal opposition to the unilateral modification of a Native American treaty by Congress. The Supreme Court reasoned that Congress possessed plenary power over tribal governments because such power had been "exercised by Congress from the beginning, and the power has always been deemed a political one, not subject to be controlled by the judicial department of the government." Scholars critical of the *Lone Wolf* decision have pointed out that the Supreme Court failed to refer to any constitutional provision supporting this congressional power but instead took what was simply congressional practice and declared it constitutionally permissible.

The plenary power of Congress in this context is so broad that the Supreme Court has stated that tribal self-governance "exists only at the sufferance of Congress and is subject to complete defeasance" in *United States v. Wheeler* (1978). Under this rubric, Congress not only has continued to abrogate Native American treaties without tribal consent, but it has terminated the sovereignty of numerous tribes. The only constitutional limitations the Supreme Court has recognized on congressional plenary power over Native nations are those contained in the due process clause and the just compensation clause of the Fifth Amendment. The former clause prevents Congress from discriminating against Native Americans and tribes, whereas the latter clause requires Congress to pay fair compensation for the taking of Native property in *United States v. Sioux Nation of Indians* (1980).

Kimberly Hausbeck

Further Reading

Conference of Western Attorneys General (CWAG). *American Indian Law Deskbook*, 3rd ed. Boulder: University Press of Colorado, 2004.

> Pevar, Stephen L. *The Rights of Indians and Tribes*, 2nd ed. Carbondale: Southern Illinois University Press, 1992.
>
> Pommersheim, Frank. *Braid of Feathers: American Indian Law and Contemporary Tribal Life*. Berkeley: University of California Press, 1995.
>
> Wilkins, David E., and K. Tsianina Lomawaima. *Uneven Ground: American Indian Sovereignty and Federal Law*. Norman: University of Oklahoma Press, 2001.

The second Treaty of Medicine Lodge was effectively an act of union between the Kiowas, Comanches, and Plains Apaches. The Apaches agreed to join the Kiowas and Comanches on the reservation and to abide by the same provisions of their comprehensive convention. The third Treaty of Medicine Lodge enjoined the southern Cheyennes and Arapahos to abide by nearly the same provisions as the Kiowas and Comanches but confined them to an area immediately to the north of the Kiowa-Comanche-Apache Reservations.

War on the northern plains centered on a Lakota-led campaign against the illegally occupied military forts along the Bozeman Trail in Montana. Under the Oglala leader Red Cloud, the alliance consisting of all of the Lakota bands plus the Yanktonais and Santee Sioux and the northern branches of the Cheyenne and Arapaho Nations soundly defeated the U.S. Army and forced its withdrawal from the forts. Like the Native nations of the southern plains, the Lakota and Cheyennes had disrupted the building of the railroad through Nebraska. When the whites began to invade the Powder River country and erect the forts, however, the alliance launched an all-out and decisive campaign. The army's withdrawal prompted the call to diplomacy and the peace conference at Fort Laramie in 1868. Again, three treaties were signed. The first was with the Lakota bands, the Yanktonais, the Santees, and the Arapahos. The Great Peace Commission's treaties were remarkably formulaic, worded nearly the same as those signed at Medicine Lodge except for the detailed boundaries of the new Great Sioux Nation in the Dakotas. The Crow Nation, although an enemy of the Lakota-led alliance, signed the second treaty, which established their present reservation in Montana. The Northern Arapahos and Cheyennes penned a separate treaty in which they agreed to relinquish all land claims outside the southern Cheyenne-Arapaho Reservation in Indian Territory, and lands were set aside for them in the Lakota Reservations. The Cheyenne and Arapaho Nations, in short, were left with little choice except to live either with their southern cousins or with their Lakota allies. Later, the northern Arapahos would be moved to a reservation shared with their former enemies, the Shoshones, and the Cheyennes would be removed to the Indian Territory.

Four more ratified treaties were signed in 1868, with the Ute, Cherokee, Navajo, Shoshone-Bannock, and Nez Percé Nations. In effect, they were the last treaties of their kind. In 1871, the House of Representatives added a proviso to the Indian Appropriations Act that ended the practice of treaty making with Native nations.

Tom Holm

Further Reading

Brown, Dee. 1970. *Bury My Heart at Wounded Knee: An Indian History of the American West*. New York: Holt, Rinehart and Winston.

Cohen, Felix. 1958. *Handbook of Federal Indian Law*. Albuquerque: University of New Mexico Press. Originally published 1942.

Deloria, Vine, Jr., and Raymond J. DeMallie. 1999. *Documents of American Indian Diplomacy, Treaties, Agreements, and Conventions, 1775–1979*, 2 vols. Norman: University of Oklahoma Press.

Deloria, Vine, Jr., and Clifford M. Lytle. 1983. *American Indians, American Justice*. Austin: University of Texas Press.

Jones, Douglas C. 1966. *The Treaty of Medicine Lodge: The Story of the Great Treaty Council as Told by Eyewitnesses*. Norman: University of Oklahoma Press.

Kappler, Charles J., ed. 1904. *Indian Affairs: Laws and Treaties*, vol. 2. Washington, DC: Government Printing Office.

Kickingbird, Kirk, et al. 1980. *Indian Treaties*. Washington, DC: Institute for the Development of Indian Law.

Price, Monroe E., and Robert N. Clinton. 1983. *Law and the American Indian: Readings, Notes and Cases*. Charlottesville, VA: The Michie Company Law Publishers.

Prucha, Francis Paul. 1994. *American Indian Treaties: The History of a Political Anomaly*. Berkeley, Los Angeles, and London: University of California Press.

Part II: Documents

Colonial and Early Treaties, 1775–1829

Treaty of Fort Pitt (1778)

Among the first treaties entered into with a foreign power by the American government was the Treaty of Fort Pitt with the Lenápes, or Delaware Nation, on September 17, 1778. This treaty is significant because it came at a time when the United States had placed an important emphasis upon forging treaty alliances; it was the American government's first ratified treaty with a North American indigenous nation, and many were to follow. The treaty is particularly interesting in light of its language and because the United States, which was at war with England and was operating under its own Articles of Confederation, embraced a strategy that sought either to draw the Delaware Nation into an alliance or to ensure that the Delawares would remain neutral.

The first two articles of the treaty proclaim all offenses to be mutually forgiven and require the contracting parties to assist each other if engaged in a "just and necessary" war with any other nation or nations. Article 3, after announcing that the United States was engaged in a just and necessary war, requested that the Delawares provide their most expert warriors to join the American army against a "common enemy."

Reference to a "common enemy" in Article 2 is interesting because the Delawares were conquered and made a political dependent of the Iroquois, who claimed they could order the Delawares to go to war and to give up land at their discretion. The United States, realizing that the strength of the Iroquois and the Delawares, when combined with British forces, could create disadvantageous conditions, reasoned that a successful alliance with the Delawares could enhance its position in its war for independence. Throughout negotiations, the Delawares were treated by agents of the American government as a people capable of making the politically independent and sound decisions required of such a treaty. The fact that the Delawares had been made a political dependent of the Six Nations, who were still loosely allied with the British, raises the possibility that the common enemy referred to in the treaty was most likely presented to the Delawares as the Iroquois, not the British. Thus, the treaty can be viewed from the perspective of a contract between two distinct cultures allied for the purpose of breaking free from the subjugation of another's rule.

In Articles 4 and 6, it is apparent that the language has been carefully worded to negate any impression that America was exerting dominion over the Delawares. Rather, the treaty favors an image of two distinct nations entering into an activity that acknowledges each other's political competence and character as sovereign entities. For example, Article 4 expresses that the execution of justice over infractions by "citizens" of either party should be adjudicated in accordance with the laws and customs of both contracting parties.

By including an offer to form an "Indian state" replete with congressional representation, the tenor of this treaty can be viewed to adhere to America's espoused philosophy in the division of sovereign powers. On the basis of this offer, the language of the treaty acknowledges the sovereign status of the Delawares and a confidence in the ability of other Native American nations to function as sovereign entities.

S. Neyooxet Greymorning

Further Reading

Morris, Alexander. *The Treaties of Canada with the Indians of Manitoba and the North-West Territories*. Saskatoon, Saskatchewan, Canada: Fifth House, 1991.

Ray, Arthur J., J. R. Miller, and Frank Tough. *Bounty and Benevolence: A History of Saskatchewan Treaties*. Montreal: McGill-Queen's University Press, 2000.

Treaty Site—Fort Pitt, Pennsylvania

The Fort Pitt stronghold played an important role in early American history. Its location at the intersection of three major rivers (the Allegheny, the Monongahela, and the Ohio) was strategically important for anyone wanting to secure the area. During the mid-18th century, England and France jockeyed for position and claims to land in Americas. During the 1750s, the French tried to gain an edge on the English by denying them access to Ohio country. To accomplish this task, the French captured many English settlements in the area now known as western Pennsylvania. One such captured outpost was that founded by the English settler William Trent in the late 1740s at the intersection of those most important three rivers.

The French captured this key outpost in 1754 and immediately began to construct Fort Duquesne. The escalating tension between the French, the English, and the Native Americans peaked in 1756 at the start of the French and Indian War. In the winter of 1758, the English army, led by General John Forbes, was accompanied by George Washington, John Armstrong, and the Swiss officer Colonel Henry Bouquet. Washington commanded 1,900 troops from Virginia, and John Armstrong commanded 2,700 men from Pennsylvania. The troops marched across the Juniata River and over the Allegheny foothills on a course to Fort Duquesne. Washington, sent forward to the fort with 2,500 men, was quite surprised to find only 500 French troops at Fort Duquesne. The French, seeing Washington's forces, burned the fort and ran for cover. On November 25, 1758, the English secured Fort Duquesne and renamed it Fort Pitt in honor of the English statesman William Pitt.

Once the English controlled the strategic area of Fort Pitt, they began construction on a new and improved fort. Construction on the fort officially began on the arrival of General John Stanwix's chief engineer, Captain Harry Gordon. The crew arrived in August, and work began on September 3, 1759. The crew felled trees and dug coal and limestone from the surrounding hills in the area that is now Mount Washington. A sawmill was built upstream from the fort, and lumber was sent downriver to the fort. Due to a lack of necessary lumber resources in the area, General Stanwix ordered the fort to be a dirt one.

Fort Pitt was not only an important geographic location for the French and Indian War, it was the first place where a treaty was signed between the United States and the Delawares (Lenápes). The Treaty of Fort Pitt (1778) was signed on September 17 and was composed of six articles. The first article stated that "all offences or acts of hostilities by one, or either of the contracting parties against the other, be mutually forgiven, and buried in the depth of oblivion, never more to be had in remembrance." This historic document was signed by Andrew Lewis, Thomas Lewis, White Eyes, the Pipe, and John Kill Buck at Fort Pitt.

Arthur Holst

Further Reading

O'Meara, Walter. *Guns at the Forks*. Pittsburgh: University of Pittsburgh Press, 1965.

Prucha, Francis Paul. *American Indian Treaties: The History of a Political Anomaly*. Berkeley: University of California Press, 1994.

Steele, Ian K. *Warpaths: Invasions of North America*. New York and London: Oxford University Press, 1994.

Williams, Robert A., Jr. *The American Indian in Western Legal Thought: The Discourses of Conquest*. New York and Oxford: Oxford University Press, 1990.

Document: Treaty of Fort Pitt

Articles of agreement and confederation, made and entered into by Andrew and Thomas Lewis, Esquires, Commissioners for, and in Behalf of the United States of North-America of the one Part, and Capt. White Eyes, Capt. John Kill Buck, Junior, and Capt. Pipe, Deputies and Chief Men of the Delaware Nation of the other Part.

Article 1

That all offences or acts of hostilities by one, or either of the contracting parties against the other, be mutually forgiven, and buried in the depth of oblivion, never more to be had in remembrance.

Article 2

That a perpetual peace and friendship shall from henceforth take place, and subsist between the contracting parties aforesaid, through all succeeding generations: and if either of the parties are engaged in a just and necessary war with any other nation or nations, that then each shall assist the other in due proportion to their abilities, till their enemies are brought to reasonable terms of accommodation: and that if either of them shall discover any hostile designs forming against the other, they shall give the earliest notice thereof, that timeous measures may be taken to prevent their ill effect.

Article 3

And whereas the United States are engaged in a just and necessary war, in defence and support of life, liberty and independence, against the King of England and his adherents, and as said King is yet possessed of several posts and forts on the lakes and other places, the reduction of which is of great importance to the peace and security of the contracting parties, and as the most practicable way for the troops of the United States to some of the posts and forts is by passing through the country of the Delaware nation, the aforesaid deputies, on behalf of themselves and their nation, do hereby stipulate and agree to give a free passage through their country to the troops aforesaid, and the same to conduct by the nearest and best ways to the posts, forts or towns of the enemies of the United States, affording to said troops such supplies of corn, meat, horses, or whatever may be in their power for the accommodation of such troops, on the commanding officer's, &c. paying, or engageing to pay, the full value of whatever they can supply them with. And the said deputies, on the behalf of their nation, engage to join the troops of the United States aforesaid, with such a number of their best and most expert warriors as they can spare, consistent with their own safety, and act in concert with them; and for the better security of the old men, women and children of the aforesaid nation, whilst their warriors are engaged against the common enemy, it is agreed on the part of the United States, that a fort of sufficient strength and capacity be built at the expense of the said States, with such assistance as it may be in the power of the said Delaware Nation to give, in the most convenient place, and advantageous situation, as shall be agreed on by the commanding officer of the troops aforesaid, with the advice and concurrence of the deputies of the aforesaid Delaware Nation, which fort shall be garrisoned by such a number of the troops of the United States, as the commanding officer can spare for the present, and hereafter by such numbers, as the wise men of the United States in council, shall think most conducive to the common good.

Article 4

For the better security of the peace and friendship now entered into by the contracting parties, against all infractions of the same by the citizens of either party, to the prejudice of the other, neither party shall proceed to the infliction of punishments on the citizens of the other, otherwise than by securing the offender or offenders by imprisonment, or any other competent means, till a fair and impartial trial can be had by judges or juries of both parties, as near as can be to the laws, customs and usages of the contracting parties and natural justice: The mode of such trials to be hereafter fixed by the wise men of the United States in Congress assembled, with the assistance of such deputies of the Delaware nation, as may be appointed to act in concert with them in adjusting this matter to their mutual liking. And it is further agreed between the parties aforesaid, that neither shall entertain or give countenance to the enemies of the other, or protect in their respective states, criminal fugitives, servants or slaves, but the same to apprehend, and secure and deliver to the State or States, to which such enemies, criminals, servants or slaves respectively belong.

Article 5

Whereas the confederation entered into by the Delaware nation and the United States, renders the first dependent on the latter for all the articles of clothing, utensils and implements of war, and it is judged not only reasonable, but indispensably necessary, that the aforesaid Nation be supplied with such articles from time to time, as far as the United States may have it in their power, by a well-regulated trade, under the conduct of an intelligent, candid agent, with an adequate salary, one more influenced by the love of his country, and a constant attention to the duties of his department by promoting the common interest, than the sinister purposes of converting and binding all the duties of his office to his private emolument: Convinced of the necessity of such measures, the Commissioners of the United States, at the earnest solicitation of the deputies aforesaid, have engaged in behalf of the United States, that such a trade shall be afforded said nation, conducted on such principles of mutual interest as the wisdom of the United States in Congress assembled shall think most conducive to adopt for their mutual convenience.

Article 6

Whereas the enemies of the United States have endeavored, by every artifice in their power, to possess the Indians in general with an opinion, that it is the design of the States aforesaid, to extirpate the Indians and take possession of their country: to obviate such false suggestion, the United States do engage to guarantee to the aforesaid nation of Delawares, and their heirs, all their territorial rights in the fullest and most ample manner, as it hath been bounded by former treaties, as long as they the said Delaware nation shall abide by, and hold fast the chain of friendship now entered into. And it is further agreed on between the contracting parties should it for the future be found conducive for the mutual interest of both parties to invite any other tribes who have been friends to the interest of the United States, to join the present confederation, and to form a state whereof the Delaware nation shall be the head, and have a representation in Congress: Provided, nothing contained in this article to be considered as conclusive until it meets with the approbation of Congress. And it is also the intent and meaning of this article, that no protection or countenance shall be afforded to any who are at present our enemies, by which they might escape the punishment they deserve. In witness whereof, the parties have hereunto interchangeably set their hands and seals, at Fort Pitt, September seventeenth, anno Domini one thousand seven hundred and seventy-eight.

Andrew Lewis, [L. S.],
Thomas Lewis, [L. S.],
White Eyes, his x mark, [L. S.],
The Pipe, his x mark, [L. S.],
John Kill Buck, his x mark, [L. S.].
In presence of—Lach'n McIntosh, brigadier-general, commander the Western Department,
Daniel Brodhead, colonel Eighth Pennsylvania Regiment,
W. Crawford, colonel,
John Campbell,
John Stephenson,
John Gibson, colonel Thirteenth Virginia Regiment,
A. Graham, brigade major,
Lach. McIntosh, Jr., major brigade,
Benjamin Mills,
Joseph L. Finley, captain Eighth Pennsylvania Regiment,
John Finley, captain Eighth Pennsylvania Regiment.

Treaty of Hopewell (1785)

The treaty with the Cherokees, made on November 28, 1785, at Hopewell Plantation in South Carolina, better known as the Treaty of Hopewell, was concluded between the Cherokees and the United States. It reflected a generally accepted pattern of treaty making between the United States and American Indian tribes that was commonly practiced throughout the late 1780s. After the American Revolution, the newly constituted federal government decided to use a peaceful treaty process to order its relations with Native Americans rather than subduing them outright through conquest. The 13 articles that constitute the treaty were entered into by four American commissioners and 37 Cherokee "head-men and warriors" on the banks of the Keowee River on November 28, 1785.

Specifically, the Treaty of Hopewell provided for post-hostility prisoner exchange, collective placement of the Cherokees under the protection of the United States, determination of boundaries, prohibition of settlement by U.S. citizens on Indian lands, extradition of non-Indian criminals to the United States and their punishment by the United States, prohibition of retaliation by either side, supremacy of the federal government (over the states) to regulate trade with the Cherokees and special regulation of that trade, notice to the United States by the Cherokees of designs against it which they may discover, allowance of an Indian deputy to Congress, and perpetual peace and friendship.

In legal theory, the inherent sovereignty of the Cherokees to manage internal relations among themselves was preserved and protected from outside interference—either by the federal government or by the governments of the states wherein they resided. American federal jurisdiction was triggered only when the actions and/or rights of U.S. citizens were implicated and in relation to trade.

The Hopewell treaty, like all treaties concluded by Congress as that body existed in its unicameral form under the Articles of Confederation prior to adoption of the Constitution, reflected the broad federal policy of separation that was based upon George Washington's suggestion of 1783:

> As the Country is large enough to contain us all; and as we are disposed to be kind to them and to partake of their Trade, we will . . . draw a veil over what is past and establish a boundary line between them and us beyond which we will endeavor to restrain our People from Hunting or Settling, and within which they shall not come, but for the purposes of Trading, Treating, or other business unexceptionable in its nature.

However, within five years, white settlement had increased dramatically on the lands set aside for the Cherokees in the treaty, despite a proclamation by Congress on September 1, 1788, forbidding such activity and directing those citizens who had settled with their families on Cherokee hunting grounds to depart immediately.

By 1790, under the new American constitutional system of government, President Washington was obliged to ask Congress its pleasure regarding the issue:

> Notwithstanding the [Hopewell] treaty and proclamation upward of 500 families have settled on the Cherokee lands exclusively of those settled between the fork of French Broad and Holstein rivers, mentioned in the said treaty.

[Thus] I shall conceive myself bound to exert the powers entrusted to me by the Constitution in order to carry into faithful execution the treaty of Hopewell, unless it shall be thought proper to attempt to arrange a new boundary with the Cherokees, embracing the settlements, and compensating the Cherokees for the cessions they shall make on the occasion.

Congress directed the president to renegotiate with the Cherokees, resulting in the July 2, 1791, Treaty of Holston, which reiterated the general terms of the Treaty of Hopewell but reduced the breadth of Indian lands. This was followed by a succession of treaties gradually reducing both Cherokee lands and sovereignty until their final removal from the Georgia, Tennessee, and Arkansas area to west of the Mississippi River along the Trail of Tears in 1838.

Michael J. Kelly

Further Reading

Kappler, Charles J., ed. and comp. *Indian Treaties, 1778–1883*. New York: Interland, 1975.

Wardell, Morris L. *A Political History of the Cherokee Nation 1838–1907*. Norman: University of Oklahoma Press, 1938.

Washington, George. "Letter to James Duane (Sept. 7, 1783)." In *Documents of United States Indian Policy*, edited by Francis Paul Prucha, 2nd ed., 1–2. Lincoln: University of Nebraska Press, 1990.

Document: Treaty of Hopewell

Articles concluded at Hopewell, on the Keowee, between Benjamin Hawkins, Andrew Pickens, Joseph Martin, and Lachlan M'Intosh, Commissioners Plenipotentiary of the United States of America, of the one Part, and the Head-Men and Warriors of all the Cherokees of the other.

The Commissioners Plenipotentiary of the United States, in Congress assembled, give peace to all the Cherokees, and receive them into the favor and protection of the United States of America, on the following conditions:

Article 1

The Head-Men and Warriors of all the Cherokees shall restore all the prisoners, citizens of the United States, or subjects of their allies, to their entire liberty: They shall also restore all the Negroes, and all other property taken during the late war from the citizens, to such person, and at such time and place, as the Commissioners shall appoint.

Article 2

The Commissioners of the United States in Congress assembled, shall restore all the prisoners taken from the Indians, during the late war, to the Head-Men and Warriors of the Cherokees, as early as is practicable.

Article 3

The said Indians for themselves and their respective tribes and towns do acknowledge all the Cherokees to be under the protection of the United States of America, and of no other sovereign whosoever.

Article 4

The boundary allotted to the Cherokees for their hunting grounds, between the said Indians and the citizens of the United States, within the limits of the United States of America, is, and shall be the following, viz. Beginning at the mouth of Duck river, on the Tennessee; thence running north-east to the ridge dividing the waters running into Cumberland from those running into the Tennessee; thence eastwardly along the said ridge to a north-east line to be run, which shall strike the river Cumberland forty miles above Nashville; thence along the said line to the river; thence up the said river to the ford where the Kentucky road crosses the river; thence to Campbell's line, near Cumberland gap; thence to the mouth of Claud's creek on Holstein; thence to the Chimney-top mountain; thence to Camp-creek, near the mouth of Big Limestone, on Nolichuckey; thence a southerly course six miles to a mountain; thence south to the North-Carolina line; thence to the South-Carolina Indian boundary, and along the same south-west over the top of the Oconee mountain till it shall strike Tugaloo river; thence a direct line to the top of the Currohee mountain; thence to the head of the south fork of Oconee river.

Article 5

If any citizen of the United States, or other person not being an Indian, shall attempt to settle on any of the lands westward or southward of the said boundary which are hereby allotted to the Indians for their hunting grounds, or having already settled and will not remove from the same within six months after the ratification of this treaty, such person shall forfeit the protection of the United States, and the Indians may punish him or not as they please: Provided nevertheless, That this article shall not extend to the people settled between the fork of French Broad and Holstein rivers, whose particular situation shall be transmitted to the United States in Congress assembled for their decision thereon, which the Indians agree to abide by.

Article 6

If any Indian or Indians, or person residing among them, or who shall take refuge in their nation, shall commit a robbery, or murder, or other capital crime, on any citizen of the United States, or person under their protection, the nation, or the tribe to which such offender or offenders may belong, shall be bound to deliver him or them up to be punished according to the ordinances of the United States; Provided, that the punishment shall not be greater than if the robbery or murder, or other capital crime had been committed by a citizen on a citizen.

Article 7

If any citizen of the United States, or person under their protection, shall commit a robbery or murder, or other capital crime, on any Indian, such offender or offenders shall be punished in the same manner as if the murder or robbery, or other capital crime, had been committed on a citizen of the United States; and the punishment shall be in presence of some of the Cherokees, if any shall attend at the time and place, and that they may have an opportunity so to do, due notice of the time of such intended punishment shall be sent to some one of the tribes.

Article 8

It is understood that the punishment of the innocent under the idea of retaliation, is unjust, and shall not be practiced on either side, except where there is a manifest violation of this treaty; and then it shall be preceded first by a demand of justice, and if refused, then by a declaration of hostilities.

Article 9

For the benefit and comfort of the Indians, and for the prevention of injuries or oppressions on the part of the citizens or Indians, the United States in Congress assembled shall have the sole and exclusive right of regulating the trade with the Indians, and managing all their affairs in such manner as they think proper.

Article 10

Until the pleasure of Congress be known, respecting the ninth article, all traders, citizens of the United States, shall have liberty to go to any of the tribes or towns of the Cherokees to trade with them, and they shall be protected in their persons and property, and kindly treated.

Article 11

The said Indians shall give notice to the citizens of the United States, of any designs which they may know or suspect to be formed in any neighboring tribe, or by any person whosoever, against the peace, trade or interest of the United States.

Article 12

That the Indians may have full confidence in the justice of the United States, respecting their interests, they shall have the right to send a deputy of their choice, whenever they think fit, to Congress.

Article 13

The hatchet shall be forever buried, and the peace given by the United States, and friendship re-established between the said states on the one part, and all the

Cherokees on the other, shall be universal; and the contracting parties shall use their utmost endeavors to maintain the peace given as aforesaid, and friendship re-established.

In witness of all and everything herein determined, between the United States of America and all the Cherokees, we, their underwritten Commissioners, by virtue of our full powers, have signed this definitive treaty, and have caused our seals to be hereunto affixed. Done at Hopewell, on the Keowee, this twenty-eighth of November, in the year of our Lord one thousand seven hundred and eighty-five.

    Benjamin Hawkins, [L. S.]
    And'w Pickens, [L. S.]
    Jos. Martin, [L. S.]
    Lach'n McIntosh Koatohee, or Corn Tassel of Toquo, his x mark, [L. S.]
    Scholauetta, or Hanging Man of Chota, his x mark, [L. S.]
    Tuskegatahu, or Long Fellow of Chistohoe, his x mark, [L. S.]
    Ooskwha, or Abraham of Chilkowa, his x mark, [L. S.]
    Kolakusta, or Prince of Noth, his x mark, [L. S.]
    Newota, or the Gritzs of Chicamaga, his x mark, [L. S.]
    Konatota, or the Rising Fawn of Highwassay, his x mark, [L. S.]
    Tuckasee, or Young Terrapin of Allajoy, his x mark, [L. S.]
    Toostaka, or the Waker of Oostanawa, his x mark, [L. S.]
    Untoola, or Gun Rod of Seteco, his x mark, [L. S.]
    Unsuokanail, Buffalo White Calf New Cussee, his x mark, [L. S.]
    Kostayeak, or Sharp Fellow Wataga, his x mark, [L. S.]
    Chonosta, of Cowe, his x mark, [L. S.]
    Chescoonwho, Bird in Close of Tomotlug, his x mark, [L. S.]
    Tuckasee, or Terrapin of Hightowa, his x mark, [L. S.]
    Chesetoa, or the Rabbit of Tlacoa, his x mark, [L. S.]
    Chesecotetona, or Yellow Bird of the Pine Log, his x mark, [L. S.]
    Sketaloska, Second Man of Tillico, his x mark, [L. S.]
    Chokasatahe, Chickasaw Killer Tasonta, his x mark, [L. S.]
    Onanoota, of Koosoate, his x mark, [L. S.]
    Ookoseta, or Sower Mush of Kooloque, his x mark, [L. S.]
    Umatooetha, the Water Hunter Choikamawga, his x mark, [L. S.]
    Wyuka, of Lookout Mountain, his x mark, [L. S.]
    Tulco, or Tom of Chatuga, his x mark, [L. S.]
    Will, of Akoha, his x mark, [L. S.]
    Necatee, of Sawta, his x mark, [L. S.]
    Amokontakona, Kutcloa, his x mark, [L. S.]
    Kowetatahee, in Frog Town, his x mark, [L. S.]
    Keukuck, Talcoa, his x mark, [L. S.]

Tulatiska, of Chaway, his x mark, [L. S.]
Wooaluka, the Waylayer, Chota, his x mark, [L. S.]
Tatliusta, or Porpoise of Tilassi, his x mark, [L. S.]
John, of Little Tallico, his x mark, [L. S.]
Skeleak, his x mark, [L. S.]
Akonoluchta, the Cabin, his x mark, [L. S.]
Cheanoka, of Kawetakac, his x mark, [L. S.]
Yellow Bird, his x mark, [L. S.]
Witness:
Wm. Blount,
Sam'l Taylor, Major,
John Owen,
Jess. Walton,
Jno. Cowan, capt. comm'd't,
Thos. Gregg,
W. Hazzard,
James Madison,
Arthur Cooley,
Sworn interpreters.

Treaty with the Six Nations (1794)

On November 11, 1794, the United States entered into the Canandaigua, or Pickering, Treaty with the Six Nations of the Iroquois, or Haudenosaunee; these nations include the Senecas, the Cayugas, the Onondagas, the Oneidas, the Mohawks, and the Tuscaroras. This document is esteemed highly by the Haudenosaunee because it promises peace and friendship in perpetuity between the United States and the Iroquois Confederacy as well as clearly acknowledging the sovereignty of the Six Nations. The principal negotiators of the Canandaigua Treaty were Fish Carrier (Cayugas), Clear Sky (Onondagas), Red Jacket (Senecas), Farmer's Brother (Senecas), Little Billy (Senecas), and Cornplanter (Senecas). The United States was represented by Colonel Timothy Pickering and General Israel Chapin, and several Quakers attended to act as mediators at the behest of the Senecas.

This treaty was needed because of ongoing aggression between the colonies, now the United States, and the Six Nations. The Six Nations had initially taken a position of neutrality in the American Revolution, but smaller factions of Iroquois were persuaded to fight with the British against the colonists. The result was enmity toward the Haudenosaunees after the war ended, particularly embodied in George Washington's campaign to burn more than 50 Iroquois villages, for which he earned the name Town Destroyer. At the same time, there was tension between nations farther west and the American settlers, and the relationship between settlers and Natives in the Finger Lakes region was growing strained. If the Six Nations joined the northwestern Confederacy of Indians, the stability of the new American nation would be gravely threatened; thus, Washington was especially anxious to affirm Haudenosaunee friendship.

General Israel Chapin called for a treaty meeting to be held in September 1794 in Canandaigua ("The Chosen Spot") in the heart of Seneca territory, where John Sullivan and Marquis de Denonville had burned numerous villages in recent memory. An estimated 1,600 Haudenosaunees were in attendance. Red Jacket opened negotiations with the following statement: "Brothers, we, the Sachems of the Six Nations will now tell our minds. The business of this treaty is to brighten the Chain of Friendship between us and the fifteen fires. We told you the other day it was but a small piece that was the occasion of the remaining trust in the Chain of Friendship." This allusion to trust refers to the plans to build two four-mile-wide roads between Fort Schlosser and Buffalo Creek and between Cayuga Creek and Buffalo Creek. The two sides were able to reach a settlement in which the first road was built but not the second. The tribes were also able to negotiate for lands that had been ceded in the Treaty of Fort Stanwix and to confirm the rest of their landholdings in the face of impending white expansion. The United States and the tribes affirmed peace and international friendship in the treaty, and both parties signed it on November 11, 1794.

Despite violations of the treaty, including the building of the Kinzua Dam in 1964, which flooded more than 9,000 acres of Seneca land in Pennsylvania and New York, this treaty has never been broken; the Haudenosaunees still receive trade cloth from the U.S. government as agreed in 1794, symbolizing the treaty's continued recognition by the United States. Because this treaty so directly recognizes the sovereignty and right to self-determination of the Six Nations, the tribes have used this treaty on several occasions to advocate for Iroquois rights. Each year, on November 11, delegates from each of the Six Nations and the state (and sometimes federal) government gather to acknowledge the pledge of goodwill set forth in this document.

Penelope M. Kelsey

Further Reading

Jemison, G. Peter, and Anna Schein, eds. *The Canandaigua Treaty, 1794: 200 Years of Treaty Relations between the Iroquois Confederacy and the United States*. Santa Fe, NM: Clear Light, 2000.

McConnell, Michael. *A Country Between: The Upper Ohio Valley and Its Peoples, 1724–1774*. Lincoln: University of Nebraska Press, 1992.

Starkey, Armstrong. *European and Native American Warfare, 1675–1815*. Norman: University of Oklahoma Press, 1998.

Steele, Ian K. *Warpaths: Invasions of North America*. New York and Oxford, UK: Oxford University Press, 1994.

Tebbel, John, and Keith Jennison. *The American Indian Wars*. Edison, NJ: Castle Books, 2003. Originally published 1960 by Harper and Brothers, New York.

Utley, Robert M., and Wilcomb E. Washburn. *Indian Wars*. Boston: Houghton Mifflin, 1977.

Document: Treaty with the Six Nations

A Treaty between the United States of America, and the Tribes of Indians called the Six Nations. The President of the United States having determined to hold a conference with the Six Nations of Indians, for the purpose of removing from their minds all causes of complaint, and establishing a firm and permanent friendship with them; and Timothy Pickering being appointed sole agent for that purpose; and the agent having met and conferred with the Sachems, Chiefs and Warriors of the Six Nations, in a general council: Now, in order to accomplish the good design of this conference, the parties have agreed on the following articles; which, when ratified by the President, with the advice and consent of the Senate of the United States, shall be binding on them and the Six Nations.

Article 1

Peace and friendship are hereby firmly established, and shall be perpetual, between the United States and the Six Nations.

Article 2

The United States acknowledge the lands reserved to the Oneida, Onondaga and Cayuga Nations, in their respective treaties with the state of New-York, and called their reservations, to be their property; and the United States will never claim the same, nor disturb them or either of the Six Nations, nor their Indian friends residing thereon and united with them, in the free use and enjoyment thereof: but the said reservations shall remain theirs, until they choose to sell the same to the people of the United States, who have the right to purchase.

Article 3

The land of the Seneka nation is bounded as follows: Beginning on Lake Ontario, at the north-west corner of the land they sold to Oliver Phelps, the line runs westerly along the lake, as far as O-yong-wong-yeh Creek, at Johnson's Landing-place, about four miles eastward from the fort of Niagara; then southerly up that creek to its main fork, then straight to the main fork of Stedman's creek, which empties into the river Niagara, above fort Schlosser, and then onward, from that fork, continuing the same straight course, to that river; (this line, from the mouth of O-yongwong-yeh

Creek to the river Niagara, above fort Schlosser, being the eastern boundary of a strip of land, extending from the same line to Niagara river, which the Seneka nation ceded to the King of Great Britain, at a treaty held about thirty years ago, with Sir William Johnson;) then the line runs along the river Niagara to Lake Erie; then along Lake Erie to the north-east corner of a triangular piece of land which the United States conveyed to the state of Pennsylvania, as by the President's patent, dated the third day of March, 1792; then due south to the northern boundary of that state; then due east to the south-west corner of the land sold by the Seneka nation to Oliver Phelps; and then north and northerly, along Phelps's line, to the place of beginning on Lake Ontario. Now, the United States acknowledge all the land within the aforementioned boundaries, to be the property of the Seneka nation; and the United States will never claim the same, nor disturb the Seneka nation, nor any of the Six Nations, or of their Indian friends residing thereon and united with them, in the free use and enjoyment thereof: but it shall remain theirs, until they choose to sell the same to the people of the United States, who have the right to purchase.

Article 4

The United States having thus described and acknowledged what lands belong to the Oneidas, Onondagas, Cayugas and Senekas, and engaged never to claim the same, nor to disturb them, or any of the Six Nations, or their Indian friends residing thereon and united with them, in the free use and enjoyment thereof: Now, the Six Nations, and each of them, hereby engage that they will never claim any other lands within the boundaries of the United States; nor ever disturb the people of the United States in the free use and enjoyment thereof.

Article 5

The Seneka nation, all others of the Six Nations concurring, cede to the United States the right of making a wagon road from Fort Schlosser to Lake Erie, as far south as Buffaloe Creek; and the people of the United States shall have the free and undisturbed use of this road, for the purposes of travelling and transportation. And the Six Nations, and each of them, will forever allow to the people of the United States, a free passage through their lands, and the free use of the harbors and rivers adjoining and within their respective tracts of land, for the passing and securing of vessels and boats, and liberty to land their cargoes where necessary for their safety.

Article 6

In consideration of the peace and friendship hereby established, and of the engagements entered into by the Six Nations; and because the United States desire, with humanity and kindness, to contribute to their comfortable support; and to render the peace and friendship hereby established, strong and perpetual; the United States now deliver to the Six Nations, and the Indians of the other nations residing among and united with them, a quantity of goods of the value of ten thousand dollars. And for the same considerations, and with a view to promote the future welfare of the Six Nations, and of their Indian friends aforesaid, the United States will add the sum of three thousand dollars to the one thousand five hundred dollars, heretofore allowed them by an article ratified by the President, on the twenty third day of April, 1792; a making in the whole, four thousand five hundred dollars; which shall be expended yearly forever, in purchasing clothing, domestic animals, implements of husbandry, and other utensils suited to their circumstances, and in compensating useful artificers, who shall reside with or near them, and be employed for their benefit. The immediate application of the whole annual allowance now stipulated, to be made by the superintendent appointed by the President for the affairs of the Six Nations, and their Indian friends aforesaid.

Article 7

Lest the firm peace and friendship now established should be interrupted by the misconduct of individuals, the United States and Six Nations agree, that for injuries done by individuals on either side, no private revenge or retaliation shall take place; but, instead thereof, complaint shall be made by the party injured, to the other: By the Six Nations or any of them, to the President of the United States, or the Superintendent by him appointed: and by the Superintendent, or other person appointed by the President, to the principal chiefs of the Six Nations, or of the nation to which the offender belongs: and such prudent measures shall then be pursued as shall be necessary to preserve our peace and friendship unbroken; until the legislature (or great council) of the United States shall make other equitable provision for the purpose.

NOTE. It is clearly understood by the parties to this treaty, that the annuity stipulated in the sixth article, is to be applied to the benefit of such of the Six Nations and of their Indian friends united with them as aforesaid, as do or shall reside within the boundaries of the United States: For the United States do not interfere with nations, tribes or families, of Indians elsewhere resident.

In witness whereof, the said Timothy Pickering, and the sachems and war chiefs of the said Six Nations, have hereto set their hands and seals.

Done at Konondaigua, in the State of New York, the eleventh day of November, in the year one thousand seven hundred and ninety-four.

Timothy Pickering, [L. S.],
Onoyeahnee, his x mark, [L. S.],
Konneatorteeooh, his x mark, or Handsome Lake, [L. S.],
Tokenhyouhau, his x mark, alias Captain Key, [L. S.],
Oneshauee, his x mark, [L. S.],
Hendrick Aupaumut, [L. S.],

David Neesoonhuk, his x mark, [L. S.],
Kanatsoyh, alias Nicholas Kusik, [L. S.],
Sohhonteoquent, his x mark, [L. S.],
Ooduhtsait, his x mark, [L. S.],
Konoohqung, his x mark, [L. S.],
Tossonggaulolus, his x mark, [L. S.],
John Skenendoa, his x mark, [L. S.],
Oneatorleeooh, his x mark, [L. S.],
Kussauwatau, his x mark, [L. S.],
Eyootenyootauook, his x mark, [L. S.],
Kohnyeaugong, his x mark, alias Jake Stroud, [L. S.],
Shaguiesa, his x mark, [L. S.],
Teeroos, his x mark, alias Captain Prantup, [L. S.],
Sooshaoowau, his x mark, [L. S.],
Henry Young Brant, his x mark, [L. S.],
Sonhyoowauna, his x mark, or Big Sky, [L. S.],
Onaahhah, his x mark, [L. S.],
Hotoshahenh, his x mark, [L. S.],
Kaukondanaiya, his x mark, [L. S.],
Nondiyauka, his x mark, [L. S.],
Kossishtowau, his x mark, [L. S.],
Oojaugenta, his x mark, or Fish Carrier, [L. S.],
Treaty with the Six Nations, 1794 455
Toheonggo, his x mark, [L. S.],
Ootaguasso, his x mark, [L. S.],
Joonondauwaonch, his x mark, [L. S.],
Kiyauhaonh, his x mark, [L. S.],
Ootaujeaugenh, his x mark, or Broken Axe, [L. S.],
Tauhoondos, his x mark, or Open the Way, [L. S.],
Twaukewasha, his x mark, [L. S.],
Sequidongquee, his x mark, alias Little Beard, [L. S.],
Kodjeote, his x mark, or Half Town, [L. S.],
Kenjauaugus, his x mark, or Stinking Fish, [L. S.],
Soonohquaukau, his x mark, [L. S.],
Twenniyana, his x mark, [L. S.],
Jishkaaga, his x mark, or Green Grasshopper, alias Little Billy, [L. S.],
Tuggehshotta, his x mark, [L. S.],
Tehongyagauna, his x mark, [L. S.],
Tehongyoowush, his x mark, [L. S.],
Konneyoowesot, his x mark, [L. S.],

Tioohquottakauna, his x mark, or Woods on Fire, [L. S.],
Taoundaudeesh, his x mark, [L. S.],
Honayawus, his x mark, alias Farmer's Brother, [L. S.],
Soggooyawauthau, his x mark, alias Red Jacket, [L. S.],
Konyootiayoo, his x mark, [L. S.],
Sauhtakaongyees, his x mark, or Two Skies of a length, [L. S.],
Ounnashattakau, his x mark, [L. S.],
Kaungyanehquee, his x mark, [L. S.],
Sooayoowau, his x mark, [L. S.],
Kaujeagaonh, his x mark, or Heap of Dogs, [L. S.],
Soonoohshoowau, his x mark, [L. S.],
Thaoowaunias, his x mark, [L. S.],
Soonongjoowau, his x mark, [L. S.],
Kiantwhauka, his x mark, alias Cornplanter, [L. S.]
Kaunehshonggoo, his x mark, [L. S.].
Witnesses:
Israel Chapin,
William Shepard, jr.,
James Smedley,
John Wickham,
Augustus Porter,
James K. Garnsey,
William Ewing,
Israel Chapin, jr.,
Horatio Jones,
Joseph Smith,
Jasper Parish.
Interpreters.
Henry Abeele.

Treaty of Greenville (1795)

The Treaty of Greenville was a major treaty that established peace between tribal people in the Northeast and the Great Lakes region and Europeans or Americans. Signed on August 3, 1795, with the Wyandottes, Shawnees, Ottawas, Chippewas, Potawatomis, Miamis, Eel Rivers, Weas, Kickapoos, Piankashaws, and Kaskaskias, the Treaty of Greenville ended almost half a century of internecine warfare between Native Americans, the colonial powers, and the new United States.

 Throughout much of the 17th and 18th centuries, the western Iroquois and Ohio tribes had successfully played off the British and French, periodically shifting their allegiance from one side to the other to prevent either colonial power from achieving sufficient power to dominate the Ohio valley and Lake Erie region. Although the British had vanquished the French during the Seven Years' War (1756–1763), tribespeople remained a significant military and political power in the region and during the British attempt to enforce new trade regulations in the conflict's aftermath. Native Americans had risen during Pontiac's Revolt (1763) and had forced British officials to reconsider their Indian policies.

A decade later, when colonial settlers from Virginia attempted to occupy Kentucky, the Shawnees and Mingos rebelled against colonial authority, and, although they had been beaten in Lord Dunsmore's War (1774), they remained a significant factor in any attempts to control the upper Ohio valley. When the Crown and the colonists went to war in the American Revolution, the Ohio tribes sided with the British, renewed their attacks upon Kentucky, and fought the Americans to a standstill. Yet at the Treaty of Paris (1783), which ended the American Revolution (and which was not signed by Native Americans), Britain officially acknowledged American control over the Ohio valley, and the tribes felt betrayed. When the Americans attempted to occupy the region, Miamis, Shawnees, and other tribes opposed their entrance, attacking settlers and inflicting decisive defeats upon two American armies (Harmar's defeat, 1790; St. Clair's defeat, 1791) before suffering a major setback at the Battle of Fallen Timbers (August 1794). In the aftermath of Fallen Timbers, the tribes were forced to sign the Treaty of Greenville, in which they acknowledged federal control over the region and agreed to remain at peace with the Americans.

The Treaty of Greenville was the death knell for Native American political autonomy in the Ohio valley and the Great Lakes region. Although many midwestern Natives would support Tecumseh and his brother's, the Shawnee Prophet, efforts to defend Native American lands and autonomy in the years preceding the War of 1812, the Shawnee brothers' movement was doomed to failure. By 1812, newly settled Americans in the region so outnumbered Native Americans and their reluctant British allies that Tecumseh and his followers had little chance of success. Moreover, significant numbers of indigenous peoples (including many Shawnees) sided with the federal government against the Shawnee war chief. The treaty and its aftermath marked a significant turning point for Native Americans in the Great Lakes region.

R. David Edmunds

Further Reading

Kappler, Charles J. *Indian Affairs: Laws and Treaties*. Mattituck, NY: Amereon House, 1972.

Prucha, Francis Paul. *American Indian Treaties: The History of a Political Anomaly*. Berkeley: University of California Press, 1994.

Richter, Daniel, and James Merrell, eds. *Beyond the Covenant Chain: The Iroquois and Their Neighbors in Indian North America, 1600–1800*. Syracuse, NY: Syracuse University Press, 1987.

Treaty Site—Greenville, Ohio

Greenville, Ohio, is located along Greenville Creek and Mud Creek in western Ohio, about 20 miles west of the city of Piqua. Greenville lends its name to two treaties: the first Greenville Treaty (1795), following the Frontier Wars of the Old Northwest, and the second Greenville Treaty (1814), during the War of 1812 both also known as Treaty with the Wyandotte.

Founded in 1794 by General Anthony Wayne, the original place name of Fort Greene Ville, used as a supply depot, was bestowed by Wayne in honor of his late friend General Nathaniel Greene, a Revolutionary War comrade. Following the American victory in 1795, Wayne ordered all tribes to attend a council and agree to the treaty to put an end to the war and settle "controversies." The U.S. government wished to "restore harmony and friendly intercourse."

On August 3, 1795, an agreement was concluded that established a boundary line between the land belonging to the American Indians and the land belonging to the United States. The Native Americans agreed not to make war on the United States or any of the people on the American or eastern side of the boundary. Though most of this land was in the territory of Ohio and later would become the state of Ohio, some of it extended into what became the territory of Indiana, leaving that area to come into some dispute in the very first decade of the 19th century. The Native inhabitants were to allow whites to freely travel through their country along a chain of posts established in another article of the treaty.

The various Native groups agreed to give up or cede land covering some 16 different areas, including Fort Wayne, Detroit, Michilimackinac, and Chicago. These sites had become or were about to become U.S. military garrisons for the purpose of policing and preventing whites from settling on land nearby. Other exceptions of land included the sites of Fort Knox, near Vincennes on the Wabash River; Fort Massac, on the Ohio; and Clarksville, also on the Ohio. During the years following the first Greenville treaty, the U.S. Army came to be known as the Peace Establishment Army because it was to maintain peace on the frontier and in Indian country and to prevent the intrusion of whites onto land belonging exclusively to Native Americans. Through the agreement, the U.S. government would relinquish land north of the Ohio River and west of the agreed-upon boundary line. This treaty brought about 15 years of uneasy peace—uneasy due to the administration of President Thomas Jefferson in 1801.

In February 1803, President Jefferson commissioned Indiana Territory's governor, William Henry Harrison, to treat for the U.S. government. Harrison was given the power to work out land cession treaties with all tribes in the Old Northwest territory, beginning in April 1803 at Fort Wayne. Jefferson revealed his intentions and interests in a secretive letter that spelled out how the United

States was to encourage the leaders of tribes to run up debts to the U.S. government and then use the land cessions as a way to pay off such debt. In addition, the plan was to eventually move all Native Americans to land west of the Mississippi. At the time, Jefferson was working under the threat of Napoleon's possible reestablishment of the French in the Louisiana Territory. The treaties that followed in 1803, 1805, and particularly in 1809, contributed to increasing tension along the Greenville treaty line and beyond.

As the name of Fort Greene Ville gave way to Greenville, white settlers poured into western Ohio lands. Just before 1804, two Shawnee brothers—Tecumseh, a political leader, and Tenskwatawa, the Prophet—decided to establish a village alongside Greenville that is often referred to as the first Prophetstown. As the brothers spread their political and spiritual gospel, Native Americans as well as whites felt hostilities brewing. As the brothers' influence increased, so did their village; followers flocked to make Greenville their home. Voicing their concerns about the treaties of Harrison's manufacture and seeing the influx of settlers, the brothers felt exposed to their enemies by living so close to the whites. So in 1808, they moved to Indiana Territory, along the Tippecanoe and Wabash Rivers, to establish the second Prophetstown.

As the War of 1812 extended into 1814, the government directed Harrison, now a general, and Lewis Cass, governor of Michigan Territory, to negotiate once again—this time with the tribes that had followed the Shawnee brothers but now were interested in settling in favor of peace. Meeting at Greenville on July 22, 1814, the United States offered peace and asked the tribes to help the United States end the war with Great Britain and the tribes that remained hostile to the United States. In return for the Natives' cooperation and aid, the United States agreed to keep land boundaries as they had been prior to the outbreak of the war. But this treaty was not the end of land boundary protection. With the war ending the following January, this Treaty of Greenville heralded a more pressing and demanding era of land cession treaties.

Sally Colford Bennett

Further Reading

Edmunds, R. David. *The Shawnee Prophet*. Lincoln: University of Nebraska Press, 1983.

Esarey, Logan, ed. *Governors Messages and Letters. Messages and Letters of William Henry Harrison*, 2 vols. Indiana Historical Collections VII and IX. Indianapolis: Indiana Historical Commission, 1922.

Hornbeck, Helen Tanner, ed. *Atlas of Great Lakes Indian History*. Norman: University of Oklahoma Press, 1987.

Sugden, John. *Tecumseh, a Life*. New York: Henry Holt, 1997.

Document: Treaty of Greenville

A treaty of peace between the United States of America and the Tribes of Indians, called the Wyandots, Delawares, Shawanoes, Ottawas, Chipewas, Putawatimes, Miamis, Eel-river, Weea's, Kickapoos, Piankashaws, and Kaskaskias.

To put an end to a destructive war, to settle all controversies, and to restore harmony and a friendly intercourse between the said United States, and Indian tribes; Anthony Wayne, major-general, commanding the army of the United States, and sole commissioner for the good purposes above-mentioned, and the said tribes of Indians, by their Sachems, chiefs, and warriors, met together at Greeneville, the head quarters of the said army, have agreed on the following articles, which, when ratified by the President, with the advice and consent of the Senate of the United States, shall be binding on them and the said Indian tribes.

Article 1

Henceforth all hostilities shall cease; peace is hereby established, and shall be perpetual; and a friendly intercourse shall take place, between the said United States and Indian tribes.

Article 2

All prisoners shall on both sides be restored. The Indians, prisoners to the United States, shall be immediately set at liberty. The people of the United States, still remaining prisoners among the Indians, shall be delivered up in ninety days from the date hereof, to the general or commanding officer at Greeneville, Fort Wayne or Fort Defiance; and ten chiefs of the said tribes shall remain at Greeneville as hostages, until the delivery of the prisoners shall be effected.

Article 3

The general boundary line between the lands of the United States, and the lands of the said Indian tribes, shall begin at the mouth of Cayahoga river, and run thence up the same to the portage between that and the Tuscarawas branch of the Muskingum; thence down that branch to the crossing place above Fort Lawrence; thence westerly to a fork of that branch of the great Miami river running into the Ohio, at or near which fork stood Loromie's store, and where commences the portage between the Miami of the Ohio, and St. Mary's river, which is a branch of the Miami, which runs into Lake Erie; thence a westerly course to Fort Recovery, which stands on a branch of the Wabash; then south-westerly in a direct line to the Ohio, so as to intersect that river opposite the mouth of Kentucke or Cuttawa river. And in consideration of the peace now established; of the goods formerly received from the United States; of those now to be delivered, and of the yearly delivery of goods now stipulated to be made hereafter, and to indemnify the United States for the injuries and expenses they have sustained during the war; the said Indians tribes do hereby cede and relinquish forever, all their claims to the lands lying eastwardly and southwardly of the general boundary line now described; and these lands, or any part of them, shall never hereafter be made a cause or pretence, on the part of the said tribes or any of them, of war or injury to the United States, or any of the people thereof.

And for the same considerations, and as an evidence of the returning friendship of the said Indian tribes, of their confidence in the United States, and desire to provide for their accommodation, and for that convenient intercourse which will be beneficial to both parties, the said Indian tribes do also cede to the United States the following pieces of land; to-wit. (1.) One piece of land six miles square at or near Loromies store before mentioned. (2.) One piece two miles square at the head of the navigable water or landing on the St. Mary's river, near Girty's town. (3.) One piece six miles square at the head of the navigable water of the Au-Glaize river. (4.) One piece six miles square at the confluence of the Au-Glaize and Miami rivers, where Fort Defiance now stands. (5.) One piece six miles square at or near the confluence of the rivers St. Mary's and St. Joseph's, where Fort Wayne now stands, or near it. (6.) One piece two miles square on the Wabash river at the end of the portage from the Miami of the lake, and about eight miles westward from Fort Wayne. (7.) One piece six miles square at the Ouatanon or old Weea towns on the Wabash river. (8.) One piece twelve miles square at the British fort on the Miami of the lake at the foot of the rapids. (9.) One piece six miles square at the mouth of the said river where it empties into the Lake. (10.) One piece six miles square upon Sandusky lake, where a fort formerly stood. (11.) One piece two miles square at the lower rapids of Sandusky river. (12.) The post of Detroit and all the land to the north, the west and the south of it, of which the Indian title has been extinguished by gifts or grants to the French or English governments; and so much more land to be annexed to the district of Detroit as shall be comprehended between the river Rosine on the south, lake St. Clair on the north, and a line, the general course whereof shall be six miles distant from the west end of lake Erie, and Detroit river. (13.) The post of Michillimackinac, and all the land on the island, on which that post stands, and the main land adjacent, of which the Indian title has been extinguished by gifts or grants to the French or English governments; and a piece of land on the main to the north of the island, to measure six miles on lake Huron, or the strait between lakes Huron and Michigan, and to extend three miles back from the water of the lake or strait, and also the island De Bois Blanc, being an extra and voluntary gift of the Chipewa nation. (14.) One piece of land six miles square at the mouth of Chikago river, emptying into the south-west end of Lake Michigan, where a fort formerly stood. (15.) One piece twelve miles square at or near the mouth of the Illinois river, emptying into the Mississippi. (16.) One piece six miles square at the old Piorias fort and village, near the south end of the Illinois lake on said Illinois river: And whenever the United States shall think proper to survey and mark the boundaries of the lands hereby ceded to them, they shall give timely notice thereof to the said tribes of Indians, that they may appoint some of their wise chiefs to attend and see that the lines are run according to the terms of this treaty.

And the said Indian tribes will allow to the people of the United States a free passage by land and by water, as one and the other shall be found convenient, through their country, along the chain of posts herein before mentioned; that is to say, from the commencement of the portage aforesaid at or near Loromie's store, thence along said portage to the St. Mary's, and down the same to Fort Wayne, and then down the Miami to lake Erie: again from the commencement of the portage at or near Loromie's store along the portage from thence to the river Au-Glaize, and down the same to its junction with the Miami at Fort Defiance: again from the commencement of the portage aforesaid, to Sandusky river, and down the same to Sandusky bay and lake Erie, and from Sandusky to the post which shall be taken at or near the foot of the rapids of the Miami of the lake: and from thence to Detroit. Again from the mouth of Chikago, to the commencement of the portage, between that river and the Illinois, and down the Illinois river to the Mississippi, also from Fort Wayne along the portage aforesaid which leads to the Wabash, and then down the Wabash to the Ohio. And the said Indian tribes will also allow to the people of the United States the free use of the harbors and mouths of rivers along the lakes adjoining the Indian lands, for sheltering vessels and boats, and liberty to land their cargoes where necessary for their safety.

Article 4

In consideration of the peace now established and of the cessions and relinquishments of lands made in the preceding article by the said tribes of Indians, and to manifest the liberality of the United States, as the great means of rendering this peace strong and perpetual; the United States relinquish their claims to all other Indian lands northward of the river Ohio, eastward of the Mississippi, and westward and southward of the Great Lakes and the waters uniting them, according to the boundary line agreed on by the United States and the king of Great-Britain, in the treaty of peace made between them in the year 1783. But from this relinquishment by the United States, the following tracts of land, are explicitly excepted. 1st. The tract of one hundred and fifty thousand acres near the rapids of the river Ohio, which has been assigned to General Clark, for the use of himself and his warriors. 2d. The post of St. Vincennes on the river Wabash, and the lands adjacent, of which the Indian title has been extinguished. 3d. The lands at all other places in possession of the French people and other white settlers among them, of which the Indian title has been extinguished as mentioned in the 3d article; and 4th. The post of fort Massac towards the mouth of the Ohio. To which several parcels of land so excepted, the said tribes relinquish all the title and claim which they or any of them may have.

And for the same considerations and with the same views as above mentioned, the United States now deliver to the said Indian tribes a quantity of goods to the value of twenty thousand dollars, the receipt whereof they do hereby acknowledge; and henceforward every year forever the United States will deliver at some convenient place northward of the river Ohio, like useful goods, suited to the circumstances of the Indians, of the value of nine thousand five hundred dollars; reckoning that value at the first cost of the goods in the city or place in the United States, where they shall be procured. The tribes to which those goods are to be annually delivered, and the proportions in which they are to be delivered, are the following.

1st. To the Wyandots, the amount of one thousand dollars. 2d. To the Delawares, the amount of one thousand dollars. 3d. To the Shawanese, the amount of one thousand dollars. 4th. To the Miamis, the amount of one thousand dollars. 5th. To the Ottawas, the amount of one thousand dollars. 6th. To the Chippewas, the amount of one thousand dollars. 7th. To the Putawatimes, the amount of one thousand dollars. 8th. And to the Kickapoo, Weea, Eel-river, Piankashaw and Kaskaskias tribes, the amount of five hundred dollars each.

Provided, That if either of the said tribes shall hereafter at an annual delivery of their share of the goods aforesaid, desire that a part of their annuity should be furnished in domestic animals, implements of husbandry, and other utensils convenient for them, and in compensation to useful artificers who may reside with or near them, and be employed for their benefit, the same shall at the subsequent annual deliveries be furnished accordingly.

Article 5

To prevent any misunderstanding about the Indian lands relinquished by the United States in the fourth article, it is now explicitly declared, that the meaning of that relinquishment is this: The Indian tribes who have a right to those lands, are quietly to enjoy them, hunting, planting, and dwelling thereon so long as they please, without any molestation from the United States; but when those tribes, or any of them, shall be disposed to sell their lands, or any part of them, they are to be sold only to the United States; and until such sale, the United States will protect all the said Indian tribes in the quiet enjoyment of their lands against all citizens of the United States, and against all other white persons who intrude upon the same. And the said Indian tribes again acknowledge themselves to be under the protection of the said United States and no other power whatever.

Article 6

If any citizen of the United States, or any other white person or persons, shall presume to settle upon the lands now relinquished by the United States, such citizen or other person shall be out of the protection of the United States; and the Indian tribe, on whose land the settlement shall be made, may drive off the settler, or punish him in such manner as they shall think fit; and because such settlements made without the consent of the United States, will be injurious to them as well as to the Indians, the United States shall be at liberty to break them up, and remove and punish the settlers as they shall think proper, and so effect that protection of the Indian lands herein before stipulated.

Article 7

The said tribes of Indians, parties to this treaty, shall be at liberty to hunt within the territory and lands which they have now ceded to the United States, without hindrance or molestation, so long as they demean themselves peaceably, and offer no injury to the people of the United States.

Article 8

Trade shall be opened with the said Indian tribes; and they do hereby respectively engage to afford protection to such persons, with their property, as shall be duly licensed to reside among them for the purpose of trade, and to their agents and servants; but no person shall be permitted to reside at any of their towns or hunting camps as a trader, who is not furnished with a license for that purpose, under the hand and seal of the superintendent of the department north-west of the Ohio, or such other person as the President of the United States shall authorize to grant such licenses; to the end, that the said Indians may not be imposed on in their trade. And if any licensed trader shall abuse his privilege by unfair dealing, upon complaint and proof thereof, his license shall be taken from him, and he shall be further punished according to the laws of the United States. And if any person shall intrude himself as a trader, without such license, the said Indians shall take and bring him before the superintendent or his deputy, to be dealth with according to law. And to prevent impositions by forged licenses, the said Indians shall at least once a year give information to the superintendant or his deputies, of the names of the traders residing among them.

Article 9

Lest the firm peace and friendship now established should be interrupted by the misconduct of individuals, the United States, and the said Indian tribes agree, that for injuries done by individuals on either side, no private revenge or retaliation shall take place; but instead thereof, complaint shall be made by the party injured, to the other: By the said Indian tribes, or any of them, to the President of the United States, or the superintendent by him appointed; and by the superintendent or other person appointed by the President, to the principal chiefs of the said Indian tribes, or of the tribe to which the offender belongs; and such prudent measures shall then be pursued as shall be necessary to preserve the said peace and friendship unbroken, until the Legislature (or Great Council) of the United States, shall make other equitable provision in the case, to the satisfaction of both parties. Should any Indian tribes meditate a war against the United States or either of them, and the same shall come to the knowledge of the before-mentioned tribes, or either of them, they do hereby engage to give immediate notice thereof to the general or officer commanding the troops of the United States, at the nearest post. And should any tribe, with hostile intentions against the United States, or either of them, attempt to pass through their country, they will endeavor to prevent the same, and in like manner give information of such attempt, to the general or officer commanding, as soon as possible, that all causes of mistrust and suspicion may be avoided between them and the United States. In like manner the United States shall give notice to the said Indian tribes of any harm that may be meditated against them, or either of them, that shall come to their knowledge; and do all in their power to hinder and prevent the same, that the friendship between them may be uninterrupted.

Article 10

All other treaties heretofore made between the United States and the said Indian tribes, or any of them, since the treaty of 1783, between the United States and Great Britain, that come within the purview of this treaty, shall henceforth cease and become void.

In testimony whereof, the said Anthony Wayne, and the sachems and war chiefs of the beforementioned nations and tribes of Indians, have hereunto set their hands and affixed their seals.

Done at Greenville, in the territory of the United States north west of the river Ohio, on the third day of August, one thousand seven hundred and ninety-five.

Anthony Wayne, [L. S.]
Wyandots:
Tarhe, or Crane, his x mark, [L. S.]
J. Williams, jun. his x mark, [L. S.]
Teyyaghtaw, his x mark, [L. S.]
Haroenyou, or half king's son, his x mark, [L. S.]
Tehaawtorens, his x mark, [L. S.]
Awmeyeeray, his x mark, [L. S.]
Stayetah, his x mark, [L. S.]
Shateyyaronyah, or Leather Lips, his x mark, [L. S.]
Daughshuttayah, his x mark, [L. S.]
Shaawrunthe, his x mark, [L. S.]
Delawares:
Tetabokshke, or Grand Glaize King, his x mark, [L. S.]
Lemantanquis, or Black King, his x mark, [L. S.]

Wabatthoe, his x mark, [L. S.]
Maghpiway, or Red Feather, his x mark, [L. S.]
Kikthawenund, or Anderson, his x mark, [L. S.]
Bukongehelas, his x mark, [L. S.]
Peekeelund, his x mark, [L. S.]
Wellebawkeelund, his x mark, [L. S.]
Peekeetelemund, or Thomas Adams, his x mark, [L. S.]
Kishkopekund, or Captain Buffalo, his x mark, [L. S.]
Amenahehan, or Captain Crow, his x mark, [L. S.]
Queshawksey, or George Washington, his x mark, [L. S.]
Weywinquis, or Billy Siscomb, his x mark, [L. S.]
Moses, his x mark, [L. S.]
Shawanees:
Misquacoonacaw, or Red Pole, his x mark, [L. S.]
Cutthewekasaw, or Black Hoof, his x mark, [L. S.]
Kaysewaesekah, his x mark, [L. S.]
Weythapamattha, his x mark, [L. S.]
Nianymseka, his x mark, [L. S.]
Waytheah, or Long Shanks, his x mark, [L. S.]
Weyapiersenwaw, or Blue Jacket, his x mark, [L. S.]
Nequetaughaw, his x mark, [L. S.]
Hahgooseekaw, or Captain Reed, his x mark, [L. S.]
Ottawas:
Augooshaway, his x mark, [L. S.]
Keenoshameek, his x mark, [L. S.]
La Malice, his x mark, [L. S.]
Machiwetah, his x mark, [L. S.]
Thowonawa, his x mark, [L. S.]
Secaw, his x mark, [L. S.]
Chippewas:
Mashipinashiwish, or Bad Bird, his x mark, [L. S.]
Nahshogashe, (from Lake Superior,) his x mark, [L. S.]
Kathawasung, his x mark, [L. S.]
Masass, his x mark, [L. S.]
Nemekass, or Little Thunder, his x mark, [L. S.]
Peshawkay, or Young Ox, his x mark, [L. S.]
Nanguey, his x mark, [L. S.]
Meenedohgeesogh, his x mark, [L. S.]
Peewanshemenogh, his x mark, [L. S.]
Weymegwas, his x mark, [L. S.]
Gobmaatick, his x mark, [L. S.]

Ottawa:
Chegonickska, (an Ottawa from Sandusky,) his x mark, [L. S.]
Pattawatimas of the river St. Joseph:
Thupenebu, his x mark, [L. S.]
Nawac, (for himself and brother Etsimethe,) his x mark, [L. S.]
Nenanseka, his x mark, [L. S.]
Keesass, or Run, his x mark, [L. S.]
Kabamasaw, (for himself and brother Chisaugan,) his x mark, [L. S.]
Sugganunk, his x mark, [L. S.]
Wapmeme, or White Pigeon, his x mark, [L. S.]
Wacheness, (for himself and brother Pedagoshok,) his x mark, [L. S.]
Wabshicawnaw, his x mark, [L. S.]
La Chasse, his x mark, [L. S.]
Meshegethenogh, (for himself and brother Wawasek,) his x mark, [L. S]
Hingoswash, his x mark, [L. S.]
Anewasaw, his x mark, [L. S.]
Nawbudgh, his x mark, [L. S.]
Missenogomaw, his x mark, [L. S.]
Waweegshe, his x mark, [L. S.]
Thawme, or Le Blanc, his x mark, [L. S.]
Geeque, (for himself and brother Shewinse,) his x mark, [L. S.]
Pattawatimas of Huron:
Okia, his x mark, [L. S.]
Chamung, his x mark, [L. S.]
Segagewan, his x mark, [L. S.]
Nanawme, (for himself and brother A. Gin,) his x mark, [L. S.]
Marchand, his x mark, [L. S.]
Wenameac, his x mark, [L. S.]
Miamis:
Nagohquangogh, or Le Gris, his x mark, [L. S.]
Meshekunnoghquoh, or Little Turtle, his x mark, [L. S.]
Miamis and Eel Rivers:
Peejeewa, or Richard Ville, his x mark, [L. S.]
Cochkepoghtogh, his x mark, [L. S.]
Eel River Tribe:
Shamekunnesa, or Soldier, his x mark, [L. S.]
Miamis:
Wapamangwa, or the White Loon, his x mark, [L. S.]
Weas, for themselves and the Piankeshaws:
Amacunsa, or Little Beaver, his x mark, [L. S.]
Acoolatha, or Little Fox, his x mark, [L. S.]

Francis, his x mark, [L. S.]
Kickapoos and Kaskaskias:
Keeawhah, his x mark, [L. S.]
Nemighka, or Josey Renard, his x mark, [L. S.]
Paikeekanogh, his x mark, [L. S.]
Delawares of Sandusky:
Hawkinpumiska, his x mark, [L. S.]
Peyamawksey, his x mark, [L. S.]
Reyntueco, (of the Six Nations, living at Sandusky,) his x mark, [L. S.]

In presence of (the word "goods" in the sixth line of the third article; the word "before" in the twenty-sixth line of the third article; the words "five hundred" in the tenth line of the fourth article, and the word "Piankeshaw" in the fourteenth line of the fourth article, being first interlined)—

H. De Butts, first aid de camp and secretary to Major General Wayne.
Wm. H. Harrison, aid de camp to Major General Wayne.
T. Lewis, aid de camp to Major General Wayne.
James O'Hara, quartermaster general.
John Mills, major of infantry and adjutant general.
Caleb Swan, P. M. T. U. S.
Geo. Demter, lieutenant artillery.
Vigo.
P. Frs. La Fontaine.
Ant. Lasselle.
H. Lasselle.
Jn. Beau Bien.
David Jones, chaplain U. S. S.
Lewis Beaufait.
R. Lachambre.
Jas. Pepen.
Baties Coutien.
P. Navarre.
Sworn interpreters:
Wm. Wells.
Jacques Lasselle.
M. Morins.
Bt. Sans Crainte.
Christopher Miller.
Robert Wilson.
Abraham Williams, his x mark.
Isaac Zane, his x mark.

Treaty with the Great and Little Osage (1825)

The Treaty of Great and Little Osage signed on August 10, 1825, represented the culmination of a trio of treaties between the U.S. government and the Osage Nation beginning in 1808. These treaties began removing the Osage Nation—comprised of the Great and Little Osage bands—off the lucrative Missouri River and Osage River territory. The goal of the 1825 treaty opened a swath of land for the fledgling Santa Fe Trail.

Prior to 1808, when this series of treaties was signed, the federal government absorbed a large portion of Native lands under the Louisiana Purchase in 1803. As a result of that land cession, many native tribes including the Delawares, Foxes, Potawatomis, and Shawnees began to encroach on the Osage lands in the Missouri River region. As more tribes began encroaching on Osage lands, the first treaty was signed with the Osages ceding 52.5 million acres to the U.S. government in exchange for $1200 and $1500 in merchandise. Despite this treaty, many Osages remained holdouts in their original lands, refusing to move westward to the Kansas Territory. This set the stage for tribal conflicts between them and the west-moving Cherokees.

As a result, a second treaty was signed in 1818 in which the Osages relinquished more land to the federal government. This treaty, in particular, was aimed at alleviating conflicts created by encroaching white settlers, Cherokees, and the Osages. Finally, the last of the trio of treaties was signed in June 1825, which ceded the remaining acreage of the Osage lands and represented a total of more than 95 million acres. In all, the Osages received approximately $166,000 for its tribal lands.

Soon after the signing of the June treaty, the federal government realized that the new Osage reservations lands that included a 50-mile region between Dodge and Fort Scott, Kansas, created new problems between settlers moving through the new reservation lands. As a result, the final treaty was signed on August 10, 1825, at Council Grove, Kansas between Benjamin Reeves, George Sibley, Thomas Mather, and 16 Osage representatives. The treaty stipulated that the Osages would stop raids of travelers, in order to allow that the lands to be cleared for the eventual Santa Fe Trail.

Further Reading

Burns, Louis. *A History of the Osage People*. Tuscaloosa: University of Alabama Press, 2004.

Magoc, Chris, and David Bernsten, eds. *Imperialism and Expansionism in American History: A Social, Political and Cultural Encyclopedia and Document Collection* Santa Barbara, CA: ABC-CLIO, 2015.

Document: Treaty with the Great and Little Osage

WHEREAS the Congress of the United States of America, being anxious to promote a direct commercial and friendly intercourse between the citizens of the

United States and those of the Mexican Republic, and, to afford protection to the same, did, at their last session, pass an act, which was approved the 3d March, 1825, "to authorize the President of the United States to cause a road to be marked out from the Western frontier of Missouri to the confines of New Mexico," and which authorizes the President of the United States to appoint Commissioners to carry said act of Congress into effect, and enjoins on the Commissioners, so to be appointed, that they first obtain the consent of the intervening tribes of Indians, by treaty, to the marking of said road, and to the unmolested use thereof to the citizens of the United States and of the Mexican Republic; and Benjamin H. Reeves, Geo. C. Sibley, and Thomas Mather, Commissioners duly appointed as aforesaid, being duly and fully authorized, have this day met the Chiefs and Head men of the Great and Little Osage Nations, who being all duly authorized to meet and negotiate with the said Commissioners upon the premises, and being specially met for that purpose, by the invitation of said Commissioners, at the place called the Council Grove, on the river Nee-o-zho, one hundred and sixty miles southwest from Fort Osage; have, after due deliberation and consultation, agreed to the following treaty, which is to be considered binding on the said Great and Little Osages, from and after this day:

Article 1

The Chiefs and Head Men of the Great and Little Osages, for themselves and their nations, respectively, do consent and agree that the Commissioners of the United States shall and may survey and mark out a road, in such manner as they may think proper, through any of the territory owned or claimed by the said Great and Little Osage Nations.

Article 2

The Chiefs and Head Men, as aforesaid, do further agree that the road authorized in article 1, shall, when marked, be forever free for the use of the citizens of the United States and of the Mexican Republic, who shall at all times pass and repass thereon, without any hindrance or molestation on the part of the said Great and Little Osages.

Article 3

The Chiefs and Head Men as aforesaid, in consideration of the friendly relations existing between them and the United States, do further promise, for themselves and their people, that they will, on all fit occasions, render such friendly aid and assistance as may be in their power, to any of the citizens of the United States, or of the Mexican Republic, as they may at any time happen to meet or fall in with on the road aforesaid.

Article 4

The Chiefs and Head Men, as aforesaid, do further consent and agree that the road aforesaid shall be considered as extending to a reasonable distance on either side, so that travellers thereon may, at any time, leave the marked tract, for the purpose of finding subsistence and proper camping places.

Article 5

In consideration of the privileges granted by the Chiefs of the Great and Little Osages in the three preceding articles, the said Commissioners on the part of the United States, have agreed to pay to them, the said Chiefs, for themselves and their people, the sum of five hundred dollars; which sum is to be paid them as soon as may be, in money or merchandise, at their option, at such place as they may desire.

Article 6

And the said Chiefs and Head Men, as aforesaid, acknowledge to have received from the Commissioners aforesaid, at the before the signing of this Treaty, articles of merchandise to the value of three hundred dollars; which sum of three hundred dollars, and the payment stipulated to be made to the said Osages in Article 5, shall be considered, and are so considered by said Chiefs, as full and complete compensation for every privilege herein granted by said Chiefs.

In testimony whereof, the said Benjamin H. Reeves, George C. Sibley, and Thomas Mather, commissioners as aforesaid, and the chiefs and head men of the Great and Little Osage tribes of Indians, have hereunto set their hands and seals, at Council Grove, this tenth day of August, in the year of our Lord one thousand eight hundred and twenty-five.

> B. H. Reeves, [L. S.]
> G. C. Sibley, [L. S.]
> Thomas Mather, [L. S.]
> Pa-hu-sha, (white hair,) head chief of the G. O., his x mark, [L. S.]
> Ca-he-ga-wa-tonega, (foolish chief,) head chief of the L. O., his x mark, [L. S.]
> Shin-gawassa, (handsome bird,) chief of the G. O., his x mark, [L. S.]
> Ta-ha-mo-nee, (swift walker,) chief L. O., his x mark, [L. S.]
> Ca-he-ga-wash-im-pee-she, (bad chief,) chief G. O., his x mark, [L. S.]
> Wee-ho-je-ne-fare, (without ears,) chief L. O., his x mark, [L. S.]
> Ca-he-ga-shinga, (little chief,) chief G. O., his x mark, [L. S.]
> Waw-bur-cou, warrior Little Osages, his x mark, [L. S.]
> Maw-sho-hun-ga, warrior Great Osages, his x mark, [L. S.]
> Waw-lo-gah, (Owl,) warrior Little Osages, his x mark, [L. S.]
> Maw-she-to-mo-nee, warrior Great Osages, his x mark, [L. S.]

Che-he-kaw, warrior Little Osages, his x mark, [L. S.]
Ne-ha-wa-she-tun-ga, warrior Great Osages, his x mark, [L. S.]
Ho-no-posse, warrior Little Osages, his x mark, [L. S.]
Waw-kun-chee, warrior Little Osages, his x mark, [L. S.]
Pwa-ne-no-push-re, warrior Little Osages, his x mark, [L. S.]
In the presence of—
Archibald Gamble, secretary,
Jos. C. Brown, surveyor,
W. S. Williams, interpreter,
Stephen Cooper,
Samuel Givens,
Richard Brannan,
Garrison Patrick,
Daniel J. Bahan,
I. R. Walker,
Singleton Vaughn,
Benjamin Jones,
Bradford Barbie,
Hendley Cooper,
John M. Walker,
Joseph Davis,
George West,
Thomas Adams,
James Brotherton.

Treaty of Prairie du Chien (1825)

The actual title of Treaty of Prairie du Chien (1825) is the "Treaty with the Sioux and Chippewa, Sacs and Fox, Menominie, Ioway, Sioux, Winnebago and a portion of the Ottawa, Chippewa, Potawattomie Tribes," also known as the Great Council at Prairie du Chien.

In 1825, federal negotiators invited representatives of nearly a dozen different Indian nations of the Great Lakes to Prairie du Chien in present-day southwestern Wisconsin for what was described as a peace and friendship treaty. More than a thousand Native Americans attended the 16-day gathering. U.S. officials were anxious to end intertribal conflict, especially between the Ojibwes (Anishinabes) and the Dakotas, which was seen as an impediment to white settlement and trade. Indian agents insisted that chiefs and headmen establish boundaries between each tribe. The demarcation of borders paved the way for future land cession treaties.

The fur trade and other activities had created considerable enmity between the tribes in the Great Lakes. Along the Mississippi River, diplomacy between the Dakotas and the Ojibwes had given way to continual attacks and reprisals. In the Fever River valley in present-day southeastern Wisconsin, the Ho-Chunks, Sauks, and Foxes were at odds with more than 10,000 miners who had illegally invaded their territory. The Menominees were nervous about the arrival, several years earlier, of three New York tribes: the Oneidas, the Mohican Nation Stockbridge-Munsee bands, and the Brothertowns, who were trying to buy Menominee land. Representatives of the Great Lakes tribes viewed the council at Prairie du Chien as an opportunity to settle some of these disputes.

At the council, General William Clark and Governor Lewis Cass insisted that the tribes declare their boundaries, an exercise that confused some of the Native leaders. Carimine, the Ho-Chunk chief, expressed the sentiments of many tribal leaders at the gathering. Members of the Anishinabe Confederacy—Ojibwes, Potawatomis, and Odawas (Ottawas)—were also reluctant to declare their borders. Chambly, an Odawa chief, told the gathering, "I never yet heard from my ancestors that any one had an exclusive right to the soil." Eventually, with the exception of the Menominees, who were underrepresented at the conference, most of the tribes declared their territories and negotiated boundaries.

Federal negotiators complained about the "dispersed condition" of tribes like the Ojibwes and the lack of principal chiefs with whom they could bargain. Each Ojibwe band had several clan leaders and headmen who "governed" by consent rather than ruled by authority. The decentralized nature of the tribes represented at the treaty negotiations was evident in the number of signatures on the document. A total of 41 Ojibwes, 26 Sioux, and 29 Sauk and Fox chiefs and headmen signed the treaty.

Although at the time tribal leaders did not understand the implications of declaring boundaries, within a few years they began to realize what it meant. The U.S. government began to approach Indian nations individually and negotiate land cessions.

In 1830, President Andrew Jackson signed the Indian Removal Act, by which government officials began moving tribes located in the eastern portion of the United States to lands west of the Mississippi River. Officials first removed the Sauks and Foxes, then the Ho-Chunks, then the Potawatomis. Removal orders against the Ojibwes and Menominees were signed but never carried out. The "peace and friendship treaty" at Prairie du Chien had laid the groundwork for the disenfranchisement of thousands of indigenous people from their lands in the Great Lakes region.

Patricia A. Loew

Further Reading

Loew, Patty. *Indian Nations of Wisconsin: Histories of Endurance and Renewal.* Madison: Wisconsin Historical Society Press, 2001.

Proclamation. "Treaty with the Sioux and Chippewa, Sacs and Fox, Menominie, Ioway, Sioux, Winnebago, and a portion of the Ottawa, Chippewa, Potawattomie, Tribes (1825)." 7 *Stat* 272 (February 6, 1826).

Document: Treaty of Prairie du Chien

Treaty with the Sioux and Chippewa, Sacs and Fox, Menominie, Ioway, Sioux, Winnebago, and a portion of the Ottawa, Chippewa, and Potawattomie, Tribes.

THE United States of America have seen with much regret, that wars have for many years been carried on between the Sioux and the Chippewas, and more recently between the confederated tribes of Sacs and Foxes, and the Sioux; and also between the Ioways and Sioux; which, if not terminated, may extend to the other tribes, and involve the Indians upon the Missouri, the Mississippi, and the Lakes, in general hostilities. In order, therefore, to promote peace among these tribes, and to establish boundaries among them and the other tribes who live in their vicinity, and thereby to remove all causes of future difficulty, the United States have invited the Chippewa, Sac, and Fox, Menominie, Ioway, Sioux, Winnebago, and a portion of the Ottawa, Chippewa and Potawatomie Tribes of Indians living upon the Illinois, to assemble together, and in a spirit of mutual conciliation to accomplish these objects; and to aid therein, have appointed William Clark and Lewis Cass, Commissioners on their part, who have met the Chiefs, Warriors, and Representatives of the said tribes, and portion of tribes, at Prairie des Chiens, in the Territory of Michigan, and after full deliberation, the said tribes, and portions of tribes, have agreed with the United States, and with one another, upon the following articles.

Article 1

There shall be a firm and perpetual peace between the Sioux and Chippewas; between the Sioux and the confederated tribes of Sacs and Foxes; and between the Ioways and the Sioux.

Article 2

It is agreed between the confederated Tribes of the Sacs and Foxes, and the Sioux, that the Line between their respective countries shall be as follows: Commencing at the mouth of the Upper Ioway River, on the west bank of the Mississippi, and ascending the said Ioway river, to its left fork; thence up that fork to its source; thence crossing the fork of Red Cedar River, in a direct line to the second or upper fork of the Desmoines river; and thence in a direct line to the lower fork of the Calumet river; and down that river to its juncture with the Missouri river. But the Yancton band of the Sioux tribe, being principally interested in the establishment of the line from the Forks of the Desmoines to the Missouri, and not being sufficiently represented to render the definitive establishment of that line proper, it is expressly declared that the line from the forks of the Desmoines to the forks of the Calumet river, and down that river to the Missouri, is not to be considered as settled until the assent of the Yancton band shall be given thereto. And if the said band should refuse their assent, the arrangement of that portion of the boundary line shall be void, and the rights of the parties to the country bounded thereby, shall be the same as if no provision had been made for the extension of the line west of the forks of the Desmoines. And the Sacs and Foxes relinquish to the tribes interested therein, all their claim to land on the east side of the Mississippi river.

Article 3

The Ioways accede to the arrangement between the Sacs and Foxes, and the Sioux; but it is agreed between the Ioways and the confederated tribes of the Sacs and Foxes, that the Ioways have a just claim to a portion of the country between the boundary line described in the next preceding article, and the Missouri and Mississippi; and that the said Ioways, and Sacs and Foxes, shall peaceably occupy the same, until some satisfactory arrangement can be made between them for a division of their respective claims to country.

Article 4

The Ottoes not being represented at this Council, and the Commissioners for the United States being anxious that justice should be done to all parties, and having reason to believe that the Ottoes have a just claim to a portion of the country upon the Missouri, east and south of the boundary line dividing the Sacs and Foxes and the Ioways, from the Sioux, it is agreed between the parties interested therein, and the United States, that the claim of the Ottoes shall not be affected by any thing herein contained; but the same shall remain as valid as if this treaty had not been formed.

Article 5

It is agreed between the Sioux and the Chippewas, that the line dividing their respective countries shall commence at the Chippewa River, half a day's march below the falls; and from thence it shall run to Red Cedar River, immediately below the falls; from thence to the St. Croix River, which it strikes at a place called the standing cedar, about a day's paddle in a canoe, above the Lake at the mouth of that river; thence passing between two lakes called by the Chippewas "Green Lakes," and by the Sioux "the lakes they bury the Eagles in," and from thence to the standing cedar that "the Sioux Split;" thence to Rum River, crossing it at the mouth of a small creek called choking creek, a long day's march from the Mississippi; thence to a point of woods that projects into the prairie, half a day's march from the Mississippi; thence in a straight line to the mouth of the first river which enters the Mississippi on its west side above the mouth of Sac river; thence ascending the said river (above the mouth of Sac river) to a small lake at its source; thence in a direct line to a lake at the head of Prairie river, which is supposed to enter the Crow Wing river on its South side; thence to Otter-tail lake Portage; thence to said Ottertail lake, and down through the middle thereof, to its outlet; thence in a direct line, so as to strike Buffalo river, half way from its source to its mouth, and down the said river to Red River; thence descending Red river to the mouth of Outard or Goose creek: The eastern boundary of the Sioux commences opposite the mouth of Ioway river, on the Mississippi, runs back two or three miles to the bluffs, follows the bluffs, crossing Bad axe river, to the mouth of Black river, and from Black river to half a day's march below the Falls of the Chippewa River.

Article 6

It is agreed between the Chippewas and Winnebagoes, so far as they are mutually interested therein, that the southern boundary line of the Chippewa country shall commence on the Chippewa river aforesaid, half a day's march below the falls on that river, and run thence to the source of Clear Water river, a branch of the Chippewa; thence south to Black river; thence to a point where the woods project into the meadows, and thence to the Plover Portage of the Ouisconsin.

Article 7

It is agreed between the Winnebagoes and the Sioux, Sacs and Foxes, Chippewas and Ottawas, Chippewas and Potawatomies of the Illinois, that the Winnebago country shall be bounded as follows: south easterly by Rock River, from its source near the Winnebago lake, to the Winnebago village, about forty miles above its mouth; westerly by the east line of the tract, lying upon the Mississippi, herein secured to the Ottawa, Chippewa and Potawatomie Indians, of the Illinois; and also by the high bluff, described in the Sioux boundary, and running north to Black river: from this point the Winnebagoes claim up Black river, to a point due west from the source of the left fork of the Ouisconsin; thence to the source of the said fork, and down the same to the Ouisconsin; thence down the Ouisconsin to the portage, and across the portage to Fox river; thence down Fox river to the Winnebago lake, and to the grand Kan Kanlin, including in their claim the whole of Winnebago lake; but, for the causes stated in the next article, this line from Black river must for the present be left indeterminate.

Article 8

The representatives of the Menominies not being sufficiently acquainted with their proper boundaries, to settle the same definitively, and some uncertainty existing in consequence of the cession made by that tribe upon Fox River and Green Bay, to the New York Indians, it is agreed between the said Menominie tribe, and the Sioux, Chippewas, Winnebagoes, Ottawa, Chippewa and Potawatomie Indians of the Illinois, that the claim of the Menominies to any portion of the land within the boundaries allotted to either of the said tribes, shall not be barred by any stipulation herein; but the same shall remain as valid as if this treaty had not been concluded. It is, however, understood that the general claim of the Menominies is bounded on the north by the Chippewa country, on the east by Green Bay and lake Michigan extending as far south as Millawaukee river, and on the West they claim to Black River.

Article 9

The country secured to the Ottawa, Chippewa, and Potawatomie tribes of the Illinois, is bounded as follows: Beginning at the Winnebago village, on Rock river, forty miles from its mouth and running thence down the Rock river to a line which runs from Lake Michigan to the Mississippi, and with that line to the Mississippi, opposite to Rock Island; thence up that river to the United States reservation, at the mouth of the Ouisconsin; thence with the south and east lines of the said reservation to the Ouisconsin; thence, southerly, passing the heads of the small streams emptying into the Mississippi, to the Rock river at the Winnebago village. The Illinois Indians have also a just claim to a portion of the country bounded south by the Indian boundary line aforesaid, running from the southern extreme of lake Michigan, east by lake Michigan, north by the Menominie country, and north-west by Rock river. This claim is recognized in the treaty concluded with the said Illinois tribes at St. Louis, August 24, 1816, but as the Millewakee and Manetoowalk bands are not represented at this Council, it cannot be now definitively adjusted.

Article 10

All the tribes aforesaid acknowledge the general controlling power of the United States, and disclaim all dependence upon, and connection with, any other power. And the United States agree to, and recognize, the preceding boundaries, subject to the limitations and restrictions before provided. It being, however, well understood that the reservations at Fever River, at the Ouisconsin, and St. Peters, and the ancient settlements at Prairie des Chiens and Green Bay, and the land property thereto belonging, and the reservations made upon the Mississippi, for the use of the half breeds, in the treaty concluded with the Sacs and Foxes, August 24, 1824, are not claimed by either of the said tribes.

Article 11

The United States agree, whenever the President may think it necessary and proper, to convene such of the tribes, either separately or together, as are interested in the lines left unsettled herein, and to recommend to them an amicable and final adjustment of their respective claims, so that the work, now happily begun, may be consummated. It is agreed, however, that a Council shall be held with the Yancton band of the Sioux, during the year 1826, to explain to them the stipulations of this treaty, and to procure their assent thereto, should they be disposed to give it, and also with the Ottoes, to settle and adjust their title to any of the country claimed by the Sacs, Foxes, and Ioways.

Article 12

The Chippewa tribe being dispersed over a great extent of country, and the Chiefs of that tribe having requested, that such portion of them as may be thought proper, by the Government of the United States, may be assembled in 1826, upon some part of Lake Superior, that the objects and advantages of this treaty may be fully explained to them, so that the stipulations thereof may be observed by the warriors. The Commissioners of the United States assent thereto, and it is therefore agreed that a council shall accordingly be held for these purposes.

Article 13

It is understood by all the tribes, parties hereto, that no tribe shall hunt within the acknowledged limits of any other without their assent, but it being the sole object of this arrangement to perpetuate a peace among them, and amicable relations being now restored, the Chiefs of all the tribes have expressed a determination, cheerfully to allow a reciprocal right of hunting on the lands of one another, permission being first asked and obtained, as before provided for.

Article 14

Should any causes of difficulty hereafter unhappily arise between any of the tribes, parties hereunto, it is agreed that the other tribes shall interpose their good offices to remove such difficulties; and also that the government of the United States may take such measures as they may deem proper, to effect the same object.

Article 15

This treaty shall be obligatory on the tribes, parties hereto, from and after the date hereof, and on the United States, from and after its ratification by the government thereof.

Done, and signed, and sealed, at Prairie des Chiens, in the territory of Michigan, this nineteenth day of August, one thousand eight hundred and twenty-five, and of the independence of the United States the fiftieth.

William Clark, [L. S.]
Lewis Cass, [L. S.]
Sioux:
Wa-ba-sha, x or the leaf, [L. S.]
Pe-tet-te x Corbeau, little crow, [L. S.]

The Little x of the Wappitong tribe, [L. S.]
Tartunka-nasiah x Sussitong, [L. S.]
Sleepy Eyes, x Sossitong, [L. S.]
Two faces x do [L. S.]
French Crow x Wappacoota, [L. S.]
Kee-jee x do [L. S.]
Tar-se-ga x do [L. S.]
Wa-ma-de-tun-ka x black dog, [L. S.]
Wan-na-ta x Yancton, or he that charges on his enemies, [L. S.]
Red Wing x [L. S.]
Ko-ko-ma-ko x [L. S.]
Sha-co-pe x the Sixth, [L. S.]
Pe-ni-si-on x [L. S.]
Eta-see-pa x Wabasha's band, [L. S.]
Wa-ka-u-hee, x Sioux band, rising thunder, [L. S.]
The Little Crow, x Sussetong, [L. S.]
Po-e-ha-pa x Me-da-we-con-tong, or eagle head, [L. S.]
Ta-ke-wa-pa x Wappitong, or medicine blanket, [L. S.]
Tench-ze-part, x his bow, [L. S.]
Masc-pu-lo-chas-tosh, x the white man, [L. S.]
Te-te-kar-munch, x the buffaloman, [L. S.]
Wa-sa-o-ta x Sussetong, or a great of hail, [L. S.]
Oeyah-ko-ca, x the crackling tract, [L. S.]
Mak-to-wah-ke-ark, x the bear, [L. S.]
Winnebagoes:
Les quatres jambes, x [L. S.]
Carimine, x the turtle that walks, [L. S.]
De-ca-ri, x [L. S.]
Wan-ca-ha-ga, x or snake's skin, [L. S.]
Sa-sa-ma-ni, x [L. S.]
Wa-non-che-qua, x the merchant, [L. S.]
Chon-que-pa, x or dog's head, [L. S.]
Cha-rat-chon, x the smoker, [L. S.]
Ca-ri-ca-si-ca, x he that kills the crow, [L. S.]
Watch-kat-o-que, x the grand canoe, [L. S.]
Ho-wa-mick-a, x the little elk, [L. S.]
Menominees:
Ma-can-me-ta, x medicine bear, [L. S.]
Chau-wee-nou-mi-tai, x medicine south wind, [L. S.]
Char-o-nee, x [L. S.]

Ma-wesh-a, x the little wolf, [L. S.]
A-ya-pas-mis-ai, x the thunder that turns, [L. S.]
Cha-ne-pau, x the riband, [L. S.]
La-me-quon, x the spoon, [L. S.]
En-im-e-tas, x the barking wolf, [L. S.]
Pape-at, x the one just arrived, [L. S.]
O-que-men-ce, x the little chief, [L. S.]
Chippewas:
Shinguaba x W'Ossin, 1st chief of the Chippewa nation, Saulte St. Marie, [L. S.]
Gitspee x Jiauba, 2d chief, [L. S.]
Gitspee x Waskee, or le boeuf of la pointe lake Superior, [L. S.]
Nain-a-boozhu, x of la pointe lake Superior, [L. S.]
Monga, x Zid or loon's foot of Fond du Lac, [L. S.]
Weescoup, x or sucre of Fond du Lac, [L. S.]
Mush-Koas, x or the elk of Fond du Lac, [L. S.]
Nau-bun x Aqeezhik, of Fond du Lac, [L. S.]
Kau-ta-waubeta, x or broken tooth of Sandy lake, [L. S.]
Pugisaingegen, x or broken arm of Sandy lake, [L. S.]
Kwee-weezaishish, x or gross guelle of Sandy lake, [L. S.]
Ba-ba-see-kundade, x or curling hair of Sandy lake, [L. S.]
Paashineep, x or man shooting at the mark of Sandy lake, [L. S.]
Pu-ga-a-gik, x the little beef, Leech lake, [L. S.]
Pee-see-ker, x or buffalo, St. Croix band, [L. S.]
Nau-din, x or the wind, St. Croix band, [L. S.]
Nau-quan-a-bee, x of Mille lac, [L. S.]
Tu-kau-bis-hoo, x or crouching lynx of Lac Courte Oreille, [L. S.]
The Red Devil, x of Lac Courte Oreille, [L. S.]
The Track, x of Lac Courte Oreille, [L. S.]
Ne-bo-na-bee, x the mermaid Lac Courte Oreille, [L. S.]
Pi-a-gick, x the single man St. Croix, [L. S.]
Pu-in-a-ne-gi, x, or the hole in the day, Sandy lake, [L. S.]
Moose-o-mon-e, x plenty of elk, St. Croix band, [L. S.]
Nees-o-pe-na, x or two birds of Upper Red Cedar lake, [L. S.]
Shaata, x the pelican of Leech lake, [L. S.]
Che-on-o-quet, x the great cloud of Leech lake, [L. S.]
I-au-ben-see, x the little buck of Red lake, [L. S.]
Kia-wa-tas, x the tarrier of Leech lake, [L. S.]
Mau-ge-ga-bo, x the leader of Leech lake, [L. S.]
Nan-go-tuck, x the flame of Leech lake, [L. S.]
Nee-si-day-sish, x the sky of Red lake, [L. S.]

Pee-chan-a-nim, x striped feather of Sandy lake, [L. S.]
White Devil, x of Leech lake, [L. S.]
Ka-ha-ka, x the sparrow, Lac Courte Oreille, [L. S.]
I-au-be-ence, x little buck of Rice lake, Ca-ba-ma-bee, x the assembly of St. Croix, [L. S.]
Nau-gau-nosh, x the forward man lake Flambeau, [L. S.]
Caw-win-dow, x he that gathers berries of Sandy Lake, [L. S.]
On-que-ess, the mink, lake Superior, [L. S.]
Ke-we-ta-ke-pe, x all round the sky, [L. S.]
The-sees, x [L. S.]
Ottawas:
Chaboner, x or Chambly, [L. S.]
Shaw-fau-wick, x the mink, [L. S.]
Potawatomies:
Ignace, x [L. S.]
Ke-o-kuk, x [L. S.]
Che-chan-quose, x the little crane, [L. S.]
Taw-wa-na-nee, x the trader, [L. S.]
Sacs:
Na-o-tuk, x the stabbing chief, [L. S.]
Pish-ken-au-nee, x all fish, [L. S.]
Po-ko-nau-qua, x or broken arm, [L. S.]
Wau-kau-che, x eagle nose, [L. S.]
Quash-kaume, x jumping fish, [L. S.]
Ochaach, x the fisher, [L. S.]
Ke-o-kuck, x the watchful fox, [L. S.]
Skin-gwin-ee-see, the x ratler, [L. S.]
Was-ar-wis-ke-no, x the yellow bird, [L. S.]
Pau-ko-tuk, x the open sky, [L. S.]
Au-kaak-wan-e-suk, x he that vaults on the earth, [L. S.]
Mu-ku-taak-wan-wet, x [L. S.]
Mis-ke-bee, x the standing hair, [L. S.]
Foxes:
Wan-ba-law, x the playing fox, [L. S.]
Ti-a-mah, x the bear that makes the rocks shake, [L. S.]
Pee-ar-maski, x the jumping sturgeon, [L. S.]
Shagwa-na-tekwishu, x the thunder that is heard all over the world, [L. S.]
Mis-o-win, x moose deer horn, [L. S.]
No-ko-wot, x the down of the fur, [L. S.]
Nau-sa-wa-quot, x the bear that sleeps on the forks, [L. S.]

Shin-quin-is, x the ratler, [L. S.]
O-lo-pee-aau, x or Mache-paho-ta, the bear, [L. S.]
Keesis, x the sun, [L. S.]
No-wank, x he that gives too little, [L. S.]
Kan-ka-mote, x [L. S.]
Neek-waa, x [L. S.]
Ka-tuck-e-kan-ka, x the fox with a spotted breast, [L. S.]
Mock-to-back-sa-gum, x black tobacco, [L. S.]
Wes-kesa, x the bear family, [L. S.]
Ioways:
Ma-hos-ka, x the white cloud, [L. S.]
Pumpkin, x [L. S.]
Wa-ca-nee, x the painted medicine, [L. S.]
Tar-no-mun, x a great many deer, [L. S.]
Wa-hoo-ga, x the owl, [L. S.]
Ta-ca-mo-nee, x the lightning, [L. S.]
Wa-push-a, x the man killer, [L. S.]
To-nup-he-non-e, x the flea, [L. S.]
Mon-da-tonga, x [L. S.]
Cho-wa-row-a, x [L. S.]
Witnesses:
Thomas Biddle, secretary,
R. A. McCabe, Captain Fifth Infantry,
R. A. Forsyth,
N. Boilvin, United States Indian agent,
C. C. Trowbridge, sub Indian agent,
Henry R. Schoolcraft, United States Indian agent,
B. F. Harney, Surgeon U. S. Army,
W. B. Alexander, sub Indian agent,
Thomas Forsyth, agent Indian affairs,
Marvien Blondau,
David Bailey,
James M'Ilvaine, lieutenant U. S. Army,
Law. Taliaferro, Indian agent for Upper Mississippi,
John Holiday,
William Dickson,
S. Campbell, United States interpreter,
J. A. Lewis,
William Holiday,
Dunable Denejlevy,
Bela Chapman.

Treaties during Indian Removal, 1830–1849

Treaty of Dancing Rabbit Creek (1830)

The Treaty of Dancing Rabbit Creek (1830), signed on September 27, 1830, was the first removal treaty negotiated after the passage of the Indian Removal Act of 1830. By the terms of the treaty, the Choctaw Nation signed away all its land holdings east of the Mississippi River for land in Indian Territory. In exchange for their land, the Choctaws received a 20-year annuity of $20,000 as well as other monetary allowances to build schools, churches, and a tribal council house in Indian Territory.

The federal government had begun pressuring the Choctaws to relocate in 1820, when Andrew Jackson was commissioned to meet with three Choctaw district chiefs and other lesser Choctaw officials at Doak's Stand to discuss removal. All three chiefs opposed removal, but Jackson presented to them a bill, proposed by a Mississippi representative to Congress, that would prevent the Choctaws from using or settling on land west of the Mississippi. Although this sounds contrary to government policy, the federal officials thought that, as long as the Choctaws had free access to their western hunting grounds, they would never cede their Mississippi land. They reasoned that, if the Choctaws believed that the United States already owned the western land, the Natives might be willing to cede part of their eastern land in order to keep their western hunting grounds. The treaty did not require any Choctaws to leave their homes; those wishing to stay on the ceded land would receive a one-square-mile tract of land, to include their improvements.

The Choctaws' new territory had not yet been surveyed when the Treaty of Doak's Stand was ratified. When the land was surveyed, it was discovered that white settlements already existed on the land. The federal government believed it would be almost impossible to remove the white settlers, so government officials requested that a Choctaw delegation come to Washington in the fall of 1824 to negotiate a new boundary line for the Choctaws' western land.

After the treaty of 1825 was negotiated, the United States expected the Choctaws to leave for their new land in Indian Territory. However, the majority of the

Choctaws did not move. Consequently, the federal government and the state of Mississippi increased pressure on the Choctaws to remove. In 1829, the Mississippi legislature took strong action against the Choctaw people and extended Mississippi state laws over the Natives. In January 1830, the Choctaws became citizens of Mississippi; their tribal government was abolished, and any Native exercising the office of chief or headman became subject to fines and imprisonment. The federal government passed the Indian Removal Act and informed the Choctaw Nation that they would not be protected from hostile Mississippi State laws.

After Mississippi extended its laws over the Choctaws, the Natives were constantly harassed by white settlers. To obtain relief, the Choctaw leadership requested a meeting with federal officials at the Dancing Rabbit Creek campgrounds. The negotiations dragged on for about two weeks. When the negotiations began to fail, the government purchased the signatures of the leaders with valuable land grants, lifelong salaries, and other presents. In the end, the government secured the leadership's cooperation by playing to the Choctaw leadership's lust for money and power.

As soon as the Treaty of Dancing Rabbit Creek was signed, the Choctaw people let it be known that they were outraged by the actions of their chiefs. Different factions elected different chiefs, and anarchy prevailed in the Choctaw Nation. However, little could be done. A few Choctaws left immediately for Indian Territory in order to claim the best land, but most waited to be moved by the U.S. government in one of three planned moves in 1831, 1832, or 1833. Removal proved to be an extremely difficult experience for the Choctaws. Out of 14,000 tribal members and 512 slaves who left Mississippi during these years, at least 2,500 died during the travel west. More died after reaching Indian Territory due to inadequate food supplies and severe weather.

Around 6,000 Choctaws decided to take advantage of Article 14 of the treaty, which provided an opportunity for the Choctaws to remain in Mississippi; any head of household could apply for and receive U.S. citizenship, along with 640 acres of land. These people did not fare well, either. The Choctaw agency refused to let most of the Natives register for land allotments, and the paperwork for most of the remaining people who did register was lost. In the end, only 69 heads of household were officially registered. The vast majority of the Choctaws remaining in Mississippi became squatters living in isolated areas on poor farmland. They lost all access to schools and public services and survived as best they could by gathering nuts and wild berries and by growing corn, pumpkins, and potatoes. Some worked for white farmers picking cotton, hoeing the fields, and doing other menial tasks. Many of these people eventually went to Indian Territory during the 1840s.

Joyce Ann Kievit

Further Reading

Baird, W. David. *The Choctaw People*. Phoenix, AZ: Indian Tribal Series, 1973.

Debo, Angie. *The Rise and Fall of the Choctaw Republic*. Norman: University of Oklahoma Press, 1967.

Kidwell, Clara Sue. *Choctaws and Missionaries in Mississippi, 1818–1918*. Norman: University of Oklahoma Press, 1995.

McKee, Jesse O., and Jon A. Schlenker. *The Choctaws: Cultural Evolution of a Native American Tribe*. Jackson: University Press of Mississippi, 1980.

Document: Treaty of Dancing Rabbit Creek

The Treaty of Dancing Rabbit Creek, an agreement between the U.S. government and the Choctaws signed on September 27, 1830, was the first removal treaty negotiated after the passage of the Indian Removal Act of 1830.

A treaty of perpetual friendship, cession and limits, entered into by John H. Eaton and John Coffee, for and in behalf of the Government of the United States, and the Mingoes, Chiefs, Captains and Warriors of the Choctaw Nation, begun and held at Dancing Rabbit Creek, on the fifteenth of September, in the year eighteen hundred and thirty.

WHEREAS the General Assembly of the State of Mississippi has extended the laws of said State to persons and property within the chartered limits of the same, and the President of the United States has said that he cannot protect the Choctaw people from the operation of these laws; Now therefore that the Choctaw may live under their own laws in peace with the United States and the State of Mississippi they have determined to sell their lands east of the Mississippi and have accordingly agreed to the following articles of treaty:

Article 1

Perpetual peace and friendship is pledged and agreed upon by and between the United States and the Mingoes, Chiefs, and Warriors of the Choctaw Nation of Red People; and that this may be considered the Treaty existing between the parties all other Treaties heretofore existing and inconsistent with the provisions of this are hereby declared null and void.

Article 2

The United States under a grant specially to be made by the President of the U.S. shall cause to be conveyed to the Choctaw Nation a tract of country west of the Mississippi River, in fee simple to them and their descendants, to inure to them while they shall exist as a nation and live on it, beginning near Fort Smith where the Arkansas boundary crosses the Arkansas River, running thence to the source of the Canadian fork; if in the limits of the United States, or to those limits; thence due south to Red River, and down Red River to the west boundary of the Territory of Arkansas; thence north along that line to the beginning. The boundary of the same to be agreeably to the Treaty made and concluded at Washington City in the year 1825. The grant to be executed so soon as the present Treaty shall be ratified.

Article 3

In consideration of the provisions contained in the several articles of this Treaty, the Choctaw nation of Indians consent and hereby cede to the United States, the entire country they own and possess, east of the Mississippi River; and they agree to move beyond the Mississippi River, early as practicable, and will so arrange their removal, that as many as possible of their people not exceeding one half of the whole number, shall depart during the falls of 1831 and 1832; the residue to follow during the succeeding fall of 1833, a better opportunity in this manner will be afforded the Government, to extend to them the facilities and comforts which it is desirable should be extended in conveying them to their new homes.

Article 4

The Government and people of the United States are hereby obliged to secure to the said Choctaw Nation of Red People the jurisdiction and government of all the persons and property that may be within their limits west, so that no Territory or state shall ever have a right to pass laws for the government of the Choctaw Nation of Red People and their descendants; and that no part of the land granted them shall ever be embraced in any Territory or State; but the F. S. shall forever secure said Choctaw Nation from, and against, all laws except such as from time to time may be enacted in their own National Councils, not inconsistent with the Constitution, Treaties, and Laws of the United States; and except such as may, and which have been enacted by Congress, to the extent that Congress under the Constitution are required to exercise a legislation over Indian affairs. But the Choctaws, should this treaty be ratified, express a wish that Congress may grant to the Choctaws the right of punishing by their own laws any white man who shall come into their nation and infringe any of their national regulations.

Article 5

The United States are obliged to protect the Choctaws from domestic strife and from foreign enemies on the same principles that the citizens of the United States are protected, so that whatever would be a legal demand upon the U.S. for defense or for wrongs committed by an enemy, on a citizen of the U.S. shall be equally binding in favor of the Choctaws, and in all cases where the Choctaws shall be called upon by a legally authorized officer of the U.S. to fight an enemy, such Choctaw shall receive the pay and other emoluments, which citizens of the U.S. receive in such cases, provided, no war shall be undertaken or prosecuted by said Choctaw Nation but by declaration made in full Council, and to be approved by the U.S. unless it be in self defense against an open rebellion or against an enemy marching into their country, in which cases they shall defend, until the U.S. are advised thereof.

Article 6

Should a Choctaw or any party of Choctaws commit acts of violence upon the person or property of a citizen of the U.S. or join any war party against any neighbouring tribe of Indians, without the authority in the preceding article; and except to oppose an actual or threatened invasion or rebellion, such person so offending shall be delivered up to an officer of the U.S. if in the power of the Choctaw Nation, that such offender may be punished as may be provided in such cases, by the laws of the U.S.; but if such offender is not within the control of the Choctaw Nation, then said Choctaw Nation shall not be held responsible for the injury done by said offender.

Article 7

All acts of violence committed upon persons and property of the people of the Choctaw Nation either by citizens of the U.S. or neighbouring Tribes of Red People, shall be referred to some authorized Agent by him to be referred to the President of the U.S. who shall examine into such cases and see that every possible degree of justice is done to said Indian party of the Choctaw Nation.

Article 8

Offenders against the laws of the U.S. or any individual State shall be apprehended and delivered to any duly authorized person where such offender may be found in the Choctaw country, having fled from any part of U.S. but in all such cases application must be made to the Agent or Chiefs and the expense of his apprehension and delivery provided for and paid by the U. States.

Article 9

Any citizen of the U.S. who may be ordered from the Nation by the Agent and constituted authorities of the Nation and refusing to obey or return into the Nation without the consent of the aforesaid persons, shall be subject to such pains and penalties as may be provided by the laws of the U.S. in such cases. Citizens of the U.S. traveling peaceably under the authority of the laws of the U.S. shall be under the care and protection of the nation.

Article 10

No person shall expose goods or other article for sale as a trader, without a written permit from the constituted authorities of the Nation, or authority of the laws of the Congress of the U.S. under penalty of forfeiting the Articles, and the constituted authorities of the Nation shall grant no license except to such persons as reside in the Nation and are answerable to the laws of the Nation. The U.S. shall be particularly obliged to assist to prevent ardent spirits from being introduced into the Nation.

Article 11

Navigable streams shall be free to the Choctaws who shall pay no higher toll or duty than citizens of the U.S. It is agreed further that the U.S. shall establish one or more Post Offices in said Nation, and may establish such military post roads, and posts, as they may consider necessary.

Article 12

All intruders shall be removed from the Choctaw Nation and kept without it. Private property to be always respected and on no occasion taken for public purposes without just compensation being made therefor to the rightful owner. If an Indian unlawfully take or steal any property from a white man a citizen of the U.S. the offender shall be punished. And if a white man unlawfully take or steal any thing from an Indian, the property shall be restored and the offender punished. It is further agreed that when a Choctaw shall be given up to be tried for any offense against the laws of the U.S. if unable to employ counsel to defend him, the U.S. will do it, that his trial may be fair and impartial.

Article 13

It is consented that a qualified Agent shall be appointed for the Choctaws every four years, unless sooner removed by the President; and he shall be removed on petition of the constituted authorities of the Nation, the President being satisfied there is sufficient cause shown. The Agent shall fix his residence convenient to the great body of the people; and in the selection of an Agent immediately after the ratification of this Treaty, the wishes of the Choctaw Nation on the subject shall be entitled to great respect.

Article 14

Each Choctaw head of a family being desirous to remain and become a citizen of the States, shall be permitted to do so, by signifying his intention to the Agent within six months from the ratification of this Treaty, and he or she shall thereupon be entitled to a reservation of one section of six hundred and forty acres of land, to be bounded by sectional lines of survey; in like manner shall be entitled to one half that quantity for each unmarried child which is living with him over ten years of age; and a quarter section to such child as may be under 10 years of age, to adjoin the location of the parent. If they reside upon said lands intending to become citizens of the States for five years after the ratification of this Treaty, in that case a grant in fee simple shall issue; said reservation shall include the present improvement of the head of the family, or a portion of it. Persons who claim under this article shall not lose the privilege of a Choctaw citizen, but if they ever remove are not to be entitled to any portion of the Choctaw annuity.

Article 15

To each of the Chiefs in the Choctaw Nation (to wit) Greenwood Laflore, Nutackachie, and Mushulatubbe there is granted a reservation of four sections of land, two of which shall include and adjoin their present improvement, and the other two located where they please but on unoccupied unimproved lands, such sections shall be bounded by sectional lines, and with the consent of the President they may sell the same. Also to the three principal Chiefs and to their successors in office there shall be paid two hundred and fifty dollars annually while they shall continue in their respective offices, except to Mushulatubbe, who as he has an annuity of one hundred and fifty dollars for life under a former treaty, shall receive only the additional sum of one hundred dollars, while he shall continue in office as Chief; and if in addition to this the Nation shall think proper to elect an additional principal Chief of the whole to superintend and govern upon republican principles he shall receive annually for his services five hundred dollars, which allowance to the Chiefs and their successors in office, shall continue for twenty years. At any time when in military service, and while in service by authority of the U.S. the district Chiefs under and by selection of the President shall be entitled to the pay of Majors; the other Chief under the same circumstances shall have the pay of a Lieutenant Colonel. The Speakers of the three districts, shall receive twenty-five dollars a year for four years each; and the three secretaries one to each of the Chiefs, fifty dollars each for four years. Each Captain of the Nation, the number not to exceed ninety-nine, thirty-three from each district, shall be furnished upon removing to the West, with each a good suit of clothes and a broad sword as an outfit, and for four years commencing with the first of their removal shall each receive fifty dollars a year, for the trouble of keeping their people at order in settling; and whenever they shall be in military service by authority of the U.S. shall receive the pay of a captain.

Article 16

In wagons; and with steam boats as may be found necessary—the U.S. agree to remove the Indians to their new homes at their expense and under the care of discreet and careful persons, who will be kind and brotherly to them. They agree to furnish them with ample corn and beef, or pork for themselves and families for twelve months after reaching their new homes. It is agreed further that the U.S. will take all their cattle, at the valuation of some discreet person to be appointed by the President, and the same shall be paid for in money after their arrival at their new homes; or other cattle such as may be desired shall be furnished them, notice being given through their Agent of their wishes upon this subject before their removal that time to supply the demand may be afforded.

Article 17

The several annuities and sums secured under former Treaties to the Choctaw nation and people shall continue as though this Treaty had never been made.

And it is further agreed that the U.S. in addition will pay the sum of twenty thousand dollars for twenty years, commencing after their removal to the west, of which, in the first year after their removal, ten thousand dollars shall be divided and arranged to such as may not receive reservations under this Treaty.

Article 18

The U.S. shall cause the lands hereby ceded to be surveyed; and surveyors may enter the Choctaw Country for that purpose, conducting themselves properly and disturbing or interrupting none of the Choctaw people. But no person is to be permitted to settle within the nation, or the lands to be sold before the Choctaws shall remove. And for the payment of the several amounts secured in this Treaty, the lands hereby ceded are to remain a fund pledged to that purpose, until the debt shall be provided for and arranged. And further it is agreed, that in the construction of this Treaty wherever well founded doubt shall arise, it shall be construed most favorably towards the Choctaws.

Article 19

The following reservations of land are hereby admitted. To Colonel David Fulsom four sections of which two shall include his present improvement, and two may be located elsewhere, on unoccupied, unimproved land.

To I. Garland, Colonel Robert Cole, Tuppanahomer, John Pytchlynn, Charles Juzan, Johokebetubbe, Eaychahobia, Ofehoma, two sections, each to include their improvements, and to be bounded by sectional lines, and the same may be disposed of and sold with the consent of the President. And that others not provided for, may be provided for, there shall be reserved as follows:

First. One section to each head of a family not exceeding Forty in number, who during the present year, may have had in actual cultivation, with a dwelling house thereon fifty acres or more. Secondly, three quarter sections after the manner aforesaid to each head of a family not exceeding four hundred and sixty, as shall have cultivated thirty acres and less than fifty, to be bounded by quarter section lines of survey, and to be contiguous and adjoining.

Third; One half section as aforesaid to those who shall have cultivated from twenty to thirty acres the number not to exceed four hundred. Fourth; a quarter section as aforesaid to such as shall have cultivated from twelve to twenty acres, the number not to exceed three hundred and fifty, and one half that quantity to such as shall have cultivated from two to twelve acres, the number also not to exceed three hundred and fifty persons. Each of said class of cases shall be subject to the limitations contained in the first class, and shall be so located as to include that part of the improvement which contains the dwelling house. If a greater number shall be found to be entitled to reservations under the several classes of this article, than is stipulated for under the limitation prescribed, then and in that case the Chiefs separately or together shall determine the persons who shall be excluded in the respective districts.

Fifth; Any Captain the number not exceeding ninety persons, who under the provisions of this article shall receive less than a section, he shall be entitled, to an additional quantity of half a section adjoining to his other reservation. The several reservations secured under this article, may be sold with the consent of the President of the U.S. but should any prefer it or omit to take a reservation for the quantity he may be entitled to, the U.S. will on his removing pay fifty cents an acre, after reaching their new homes, provided that before the first of January next they shall adduce to the Agent, or some other authorized person to be appointed, proof of his claim and the quantity of it. Sixth; likewise children of the Choctaw Nation residing in the Nation, who have neither father nor mother a list of which, with satisfactory proof of Parentage and orphanage being filed with Agent in six months to be forwarded to the War Department, shall be entitled to a quarter section of Land, to be located under the direction of the President, and with his consent the same may be sold and the proceeds applied to some beneficial purpose for the benefit of said orphans.

Article 20

The U.S. agree and stipulate as follows, that for the benefit and advantage of the Choctaw people, and to improve their condition, their shall be educated under the direction of the President and at the expense of the U.S. forty Choctaw youths for twenty years. This number shall be kept at school, and as they finish their education others, to supply their places shall be received for the period stated. The U.S. agree also to erect a Council House for the nation at some convenient central point, after their people shall be settled; and a House for each Chief, also a Church for each of the three Districts, to be used also as school houses, until the Nation may conclude to build others; and for these purposes ten thousand dollars shall be appropriated; also fifty thousand dollars (viz.) twenty-five hundred dollars annually shall be given for the support of three teachers of schools for twenty years. Likewise there shall be furnished to the Nation, three Blacksmiths one for each district for sixteen years, and a qualified Mill Wright for five years; Also there shall be furnished the following articles, twenty-one hundred blankets, to each warrior who emigrates a rifle, moulds, wipers and ammunition. One thousand axes, ploughs, hoes, wheels and cards each; and four hundred looms. There shall also be furnished, one ton of iron and two hundred weight of steel annually to each District for sixteen years.

Article 21

A few Choctaw Warriors yet survive who marched and fought in the army with General Wayne, the whole number stated not to exceed twenty. These it is agreed shall hereafter while they live, receive twenty-five dollars a year; a list of them to be early as practicable, and within six months, made out, and presented to the Agent, to be forwarded to the War Department.

Article 22

The Chiefs of the Choctaws who have suggested that their people are in a state of rapid advancement in education and refinement, and have expressed a solicitude that they might have the privilege of a Delegate on the floor of the House of Representatives extended to them. The Commissioners do not feel that they can under a treaty stipulation accede to the request, but at their desire, present it in the Treaty, that Congress may consider of, and decide the application.

Done, and signed, and executed by the commissioners of the United States, and the chiefs, captains, and head men of the Choctaw nation, at Dancing Rabbit creek, this 27th day of September, eighteen and thirty.

> Jno. H. Eaton, [L. S.]
> Jno. Coffee, [L. S.]
> Greenwood Leflore, [L. S.]
> Musholatubbee, his x mark, [L. S.]
> Nittucachee, his x mark, [L. S.]
> Holarterhoomah, his x mark, [L. S.]
> Hopiaunchabubbee, his x mark, [L. S.]
> Zishomingo, his x mark, [L. S.]
> Captainthalke, his x mark, [L. S.]
> James Shield, his x mark, [L. S.]
> Pistiyubbee, his x mark, [L. S.]
> Yobalarunehabubbee, his x mark, [L. S.]
> Holubbee, his x mark, [L. S.]
> Robert Cole, his x mark, [L. S.]
> Mokelareharhopin, his x mark, [L. S.]
> Lewis Perry, his x mark, [L. S.]
> Artonamarstubbe, his x mark, [L. S.]
> Hopeatubbee, his x mark, [L. S.]
> Hoshahoomah, his x mark, [L. S.]
> Chuallahoomah, his x mark, [L. S.]
> Joseph Kincaide, his x mark, [L. S.]
> Eyarhocuttubbee, his x mark, [L. S.]
> Iyacherhopia, his x mark, [L. S.]

Offahoomah, his x mark, [L. S.]
Archalater, his x mark, [L. S.]
Onnahubbee, his x mark, [L. S.]
Pisinhocuttubbee, his x mark, [L. S.]
Tullarhacher, his x mark, [L. S.]
Little leader, his x mark, [L. S.]
Maanhutter, his x mark, [L. S.]
Cowehoomah, his x mark, [L. S.]
Tillamoer, his x mark, [L. S.]
Imnullacha, his x mark, [L. S.]
Artopilachubbee, his x mark, [L. S.]
Shupherunchahubbee, his x mark, [L. S.]
Nitterhoomah, his x mark, [L. S.]
Oaklaryubbee, his x mark, [L. S.]
Pukumna, his x mark, [L. S.]
Arpalar, his x mark, [L. S.]
Holber, his x mark, [L. S.]
Hoparmingo, his x mark, [L. S.]
Isparhoomah, his x mark, [L. S.]
Tieberhoomah, his x mark, [L. S.]
Tishoholarter, his x mark, [L. S.]
Mahayarchubbee, his x mark, [L. S.]
Artooklubbetushpar, his x mark, [L. S.]
Metubbee, his x mark, [L. S.]
Arsarkatubbee, his x mark, [L. S.]
Issaterhoomah, his x mark, [L. S.]
Chohtahmatahah, his x mark, [L. S.]
Tunnuppashubbee, his x mark, [L. S.]
Okocharyer, his x mark, [L. S.]
Hoshhopia, his x mark, [L. S.]
Warsharshahopia, his x mark, [L. S.]
Maarshunchahubbee, his x mark, [L. S.]
Misharyubbee, his x mark, [L. S.]
Daniel McCurtain, his x mark, [L. S.]
Tushkerharcho, his x mark, [L. S.]
Hoktoontubbee, his x mark, [L. S.]
Nuknacrahookmarhee, his x mark, [L. S.]
Mingo hoomah, his x mark, [L. S.]
James Karnes, his x mark, [L. S.]
Tishohakubbee, his x mark, [L. S.]
Narlanalar, his x mark, [L. S.]

Pennasha, his x mark, [L. S.]
Inharyarker, his x mark, [L. S.]
Mottubbee, his x mark, [L. S.]
Narharyubbee, his x mark, [L. S.]
Ishmaryubbee, his x mark, [L. S.]
James McKing, [L. S.]
Lewis Wilson, his x mark, [L. S.]
Istonarkerharcho, his x mark, [L. S.]
Hohinshamartarher, his x mark, [L. S.]
Kinsulachubbee, his x mark, [L. S.]
Emarhinstubbee, his x mark, [L. S.]
Gysalndalra, bm, his x mark, [L. S.]
Thomas Wall, [L. S.]
Sam. S. Worcester, [L. S.]
Arlartar, his x mark, [L. S.]
Nittahubbee, his x mark, [L. S.]
Tishonouan, his x mark, [L. S.]
Warsharchahoomah, his x mark, [L. S.]
Isaac James, his x mark, [L. S.]
Hopiaintushker, his x mark, [L. S.]
Aryoshkermer, his x mark, [L. S.]
Shemotar, his x mark, [L. S.]
Hopiaisketina, his x mark, [L. S.]
Thomas Leflore, his x mark, [L. S.]
Arnokechatubbee, his x mark, [L. S.]
Shokoperlukna, his x mark, [L. S.]
Posherhoomah, his x mark, [L. S.]
Robert Folsom, his x mark, [L. S.]
Arharyotubbee, his x mark, [L. S.]
Kushonolarter, his x mark, [L. S.]
James Vaughan, his x mark, [L. S.]
Phiplip, his x mark, [L. S.]
Meshameye, his x mark, [L. S.]
Ishteheka, his x mark, [L. S.]
Heshohomme, his x mark, [L. S.]
John McKolbery, his x mark, [L. S.]
Benjm. James, his x mark, [L. S.]
Tikbachahambe, his x mark, [L. S.]
Aholiktube, his x mark, [L. S.]
Walking Wolf, his x mark, [L. S.]

John Waide, his x mark, [L. S.]
Big Axe, his x mark, [L. S.]
Bob, his x mark, [L. S.]
Tushkochaubbee, his x mark, [L. S.]
Ittabe, his x mark, [L. S.]
Tishowakayo, his x mark, [L. S.]
Folehommo, his x mark, [L. S.]
John Garland, his x mark, [L. S.]
Koshona, his x mark, [L. S.]
Ishleyohamobe, his x mark, [L. S.]
Jacob Folsom, [L. S.]
William Foster, [L. S.]
Ontioerharcho, his x mark, [L. S.]
Hugh A. Foster, [L. S.]
Pierre Juzan, [L. S.]
Jno. Pitchlynn, jr., [L. S.]
David Folsom, [L. S.]
Sholohommastube, his x mark, [L. S.]
Tesho, his x mark, [L. S.]
Lauwechubee, his x mark, [L. S.]
Hoshehammo, his x mark, [L. S.]
Ofenowo, his x mark, [L. S.]
Ahekoche, his x mark, [L. S.]
Kaloshoube, his x mark, [L. S.]
Atoko, his x mark, [L. S.]
Ishtemeleche, his x mark, [L. S.]
Emthtohabe, his x mark, [L. S.]
Silas D. Fisher, his x mark, [L. S.]
Isaac Folsom, his x mark, [L. S.]
Hekatube, his x mark, [L. S.]
Hakseche, his x mark, [L. S.]
Jerry Carney, his x mark, [L. S.]
John Washington. his x mark, [L. S.]
Panshastubbee, his x mark, [L. S.]
P. P. Pitchlynn, his x mark, [L. S.]
Joel H. Nail, his x mark, [L. S.]
Hopia Stonakey, his x mark, [L. S.]
Kocohomma, his x mark, [L. S.]
William Wade, his x mark, [L. S.]
Panshstickubbee, his x mark, [L. S.]

Holittankchahubbee, his x mark, [L. S.]
Oklanowa, his x mark, [L. S.]
Neto, his x mark, [L. S.]
James Fletcher, his x mark, [L. S.]
Silas D. Pitchlynn, [L. S.]
William Trahorn, his x mark, [L. S.]
Toshkahemmitto, his x mark, [L. S.]
Tethetayo, his x mark, [L. S.]
Emokloshahopie, his x mark, [L. S.]
Tishoimita, his x mark, [L. S.]
Thomas W. Foster, his x mark, [L. S.]
Zadoc Brashears, his x mark, [L. S.]
Levi Perkins, his x mark, [L. S.]
Isaac Perry, his x mark, [L. S.]
Ishlonocka Hoomah, his x mark, [L. S.]
Hiram King, his x mark, [L. S.]
Ogla Enlah, his x mark, [L. S.]
Nultlahtubbee, his x mark, [L. S.]
Tuska Hollattuh, his x mark, [L. S.]
Kothoantchahubbee, his x mark, [L. S.]
Eyarpulubbee, his x mark, [L. S.]
Okentahubbe, his x mark, [L. S.]
Living War Club, his x mark, [L. S.]
John Jones, his x mark, [L. S.]
Charles Jones, his x mark, [L. S.]
Isaac Jones, his x mark, [L. S.]
Hocklucha, his x mark, [L. S.]
Muscogee, his x mark., [L. S.]
Eden Nelson, his x mark, [L. S.]
In presence of—
E. Breathitt secretary to the Commission,
William Ward, agent for Choctaws,
John Pitchlyn, United States interpreter,
M. Mackey, United States interpreter,
Geo. S. Gaines, of Alabama, R. P. Currin,
Luke Howard,
Sam. S. Worcester,
Jno. N. Byrn,
John Bell,
Jno. Bond.

SUPPLEMENTARY ARTICLES TO THE PRECEDING TREATY.
Sept. 28, 1830. 7 Stat., 340

Various Choctaw persons have been presented by the Chiefs of the nation, with a desire that they might be provided for. Being particularly deserving, an earnestness has been manifested that provision might be made for them. It is therefore by the undersigned commissioners here assented to, with the understanding that they are to have no interest in the reservations which are directed and provided for under the general Treaty to which this is a supplement.

As evidence of the liberal and kind feelings of the President and Government of the United States the Commissioners agree to the request as follows, (to wit) Pierre Juzan, Peter Pitchlynn, G. W. Harkins, Jack Pitchlynn, Israel Fulsom, Louis Laflore, Benjamin James, Joel H. Nail, Hopoynjahubbee, Onorkubbee, Benjamin Laflore, Michael Laflore and Allen Yates and wife shall be entitled to a reservation of two sections of land each to include their improvement where they at present reside, with the exception of the three first named persons and Benjamin Laflore, who are authorized to locate one of their sections on any other unimproved and unoccupied land, within their respective districts.

Article 2

And to each of the following persons there is allowed a reservation of a section and a half of land, (to wit) James L. McDonald, Robert Jones, Noah Wall, James Campbell, G. Nelson, Vaughn Brashears, R. Harris, Little Leader, S. Foster, J. Vaughn, L. Durans, Samuel Long, T. Magagha, Thos. Everge, Giles Thompson, Tomas Garland, John Bond, William Laflore, and Turner Brashears, the two first named persons, may locate one section each, and one section jointly on any unimproved and unoccupied land, these not residing in the Nation; The others are to include their present residence and improvement.

Also one section is allowed to the following persons (to wit) Middleton Mackey, Wesley Train, Choclehomo, Moses Foster, D. W. Wall, Charles Scott, Molly Nail, Susan Colbert, who was formerly Susan James, Samuel Garland, Silas Fisher, D. McCurtain, Oaklahoma, and Polly Fillecuthey, to be located in entire sections to include their present residence and improvement, with the exception of Molly Nail and Susan Colbert, who are authorized to locate theirs, on any unimproved unoccupied land.

John Pitchlynn has long and faithfully served the nation in character of U. States Interpreter, he has acted as such for forty years, in consideration it is agreed, in addition to what has been done for him there shall be granted to two of his children, (to wit) Silas Pitchlynn, and Thomas Pitchlynn one section of land each, to adjoin the location of their father; likewise to James Madison and Peter sons of Mushulatubbee one section of land each to include the old house and improvement where their father formerly lived on the old military road adjoining a large Prairie.

And to Henry Groves son of the Chief Natticache there is one section of land given to adjoin his father's land.

And to each of the following persons half a section of land is granted on any unoccupied and unimproved lands in the Districts where they respectively live (to wit) Willis Harkins, James D. Hamilton, William Juzan, Tobias Laflore, Jo Doke, Jacob Fulsom, P. Hays, Samuel Worcester, George Hunter, William Train, Robert Nail and Alexander McKee.

And there is given a quarter section of land each to Delila and her five fatherless children, she being a Choctaw woman residing out of the nation; also the same quantity to Peggy Trihan, another Indian woman residing out of the nation and her two fatherless children; and to the widows of Pushmilaha, and Pucktshenubbee, who were formerly distinguished Chiefs of the nation and for their children four quarter sections of land, each in trust for themselves and their children.

All of said last mentioned reservations are to be located under and by direction of the President of the U. States.

Article 3

The Choctaw people now that they have ceded their lands are solicitous to get to their new homes early as possible and accordingly they wish that a party may be permitted to proceed this fall to ascertain whereabouts will be most advantageous for their people to be located.

It is therefore agreed that three or four persons (from each of the three districts) under the guidance of some discreet and well qualified person or persons may proceed during this fall to the West upon an examination of the country.

For their time and expenses the U. States agree to allow the said twelve persons two dollars a day each, not to exceed one hundred days, which is deemed to be ample time to make an examination.

If necessary, pilots acquainted with the country will be furnished when they arrive in the West.

Article 4

John Donly of Alabama who has several Choctaw grand children and who for twenty years has carried the mail through the Choctaw Nation, a desire by the Chiefs is expressed that he may have a section of land, it is accordingly granted, to be located in one entire section, on any unimproved and unoccupied land.

Allen Glover and George S. Gaines licensed Traders in the Choctaw Nation, have accounts amounting to upwards of nine thousand dollars against the Indians who are unable to pay their said debts without distressing their families; a desire is expressed by the chiefs that two sections of land be set apart to be sold and the proceeds thereof to be applied toward the payment of the aforesaid debts. It is agreed that two sections of any unimproved and unoccupied land be granted to George S. Gaines who will sell the same for the best price he can obtain and apply the proceeds thereof to the credit of the Indians on their accounts due to the before mentioned Glover and Gaines; and shall make the application to the poorest Indian first.

At the earnest and particular request of the Chief Greenwood Laflore there is granted to David Haley one half section of land to be located in a half section on any unoccupied and unimproved land as a compensation, for a journey to Washington City with dispatches to the Government and returning others to the Choctaw Nation.

The foregoing is entered into, as supplemental to the treaty concluded yesterday. Done at Dancing Rabbit creek the 28th day of September, 1830.

Jno. H. Eaton, [L. S.]
Jno. Coffee, [L. S.]
Greenwood Leflore, [L. S.]
Nittucachee, his x mark, [L. S.]
Mushulatubbee, his x mark, [L. S.]
Offahoomah, his x mark, [L. S.]
Eyarhoeuttubbee, his x mark, [L. S.]
Iyaeherhopia, his x mark, [L. S.]
Holubbee, his x mark, [L. S.]
Onarhubbee, his x mark, [L. S.]
Robert Cole, his x mark, [L. S.]
Hopiaunchahubbee, his x mark, [L. S.]
David Folsom, [L. S.]
John Garland, his x mark, [L. S.]
Hopiahoomah, his x mark, [L. S.]
Captain Thalko, his x mark, [L. S.]
Pierre Juzan, [L. S.]
Immarstarher, his x mark, [L. S.]
Hoshimhamartar, his x mark, [L. S.]
In presence of—
E. Breathitt, Secretary to Commissioners,
W. Ward, Agent for Choctaws,
M. Mackey, United States Interpreter,
John Pitchlynn, United States Interpreter,
R. P. Currin,
Jno. W. Byrn,
Geo. S. Gaines.

Treaty of Cusseta (1832)

Signed on March 24, 1832, the Treaty of Cusseta (1832) was a land cession treaty that ceded all remaining Creek lands east of the Mississippi and resulted in Creek removal. Muscogee Creek leaders responded to Alabama's extension of jurisdiction over their lands by proposing that they cede lands but retain blocks of private reserves within Alabama under the control of individual families. They took these proposals to Washington, D.C., in March 1832. Secretary of War Lewis Cass disagreed with the size and number of the reserves, but he reached a compromise with the eight Muscogee Creek leaders on March 24.

The resulting treaty was not specifically a removal treaty, for even though the Creeks agreed to cede all their lands east of the Mississippi River, they were to receive allotments in Alabama that could be sold or retained under Creek ownership. By April 2, the U.S. Senate had unanimously ratified the treaty. Although the treaty called on the U.S. government both to assist those Creeks who wished to emigrate west and to guarantee Creek title to allotted lands in Alabama, the federal government refused to assist Creeks in Alabama when whites seized their lands anyway. Land speculators took advantage of the remaining Muscogee Creeks and perpetrated frauds resulting in utter turmoil and loss of the Creeks' homes.

The Creeks wandered around Alabama seeking food and shelter, eventually attacking white settlers and seizing crops and livestock in revenge. In 1836, Cass finally intervened, not as guarantor of Creek rights but instead to forcibly remove the remaining Creeks west of the Mississippi. The U.S. military accomplished what diplomacy could not, and by 1837, almost all of the 15,000 or so Muscogee Creeks had emigrated to the West.

Dewi I. Ball

Further Reading

Remini, Robert V. *The Legacy of Andrew Jackson: Essays on Democracy, Indian Removal and Slavery*. Baton Rouge: Louisiana State University Press, 1990.

Satz, Ronald N. *American Indian Policy in the Jacksonian Era*. Norman: University of Oklahoma Press, 2002.

Wallace, Anthony F. C. *The Long, Bitter Trail: Andrew Jackson and the Indians*. New York: Hill and Wang, 1993.

Document: Treaty of Cusseta

Articles of a treaty made at the City of Washington between Lewis Cass, thereto specially authorized by the President of the United States, and the Creek tribe of Indians.

Article 1

The Creek tribe of Indians cede to the United States all their land, East of the Mississippi river.

Article 2

The United States engage to survey the said land as soon as the same can be conveniently done, after the ratification of this treaty, and when the same is surveyed to allow ninety principal Chiefs of the Creek tribe to select one section each, and every other head of a Creek family to select one half section each, which tracts shall be reserved from sale for their use for the term of five years, unless sooner disposed of by them. A census of these persons shall be taken under the direction of the President and the selections shall be made so as to include the improvements of each person within his selection, if the same can be so made, and if not, then all the persons belonging to the same town, entitled to selections, and who cannot make the same, so as to include their improvements, shall take them in one body in a proper form. And twenty sections shall be selected, under the direction of the President for the orphan children of the Creeks, and divided and retained or sold for their benefit as the President may direct. Provided however that no selections or locations under this treaty shall be so made as to include the agency reserve.

Article 3

These tracts may be conveyed by the persons selecting the same, to any other persons for a fair consideration, in such manner as the President may direct. The contract shall be certified by some person appointed for that purpose by the President but shall not be valid 'till the President approves the same. A title shall be given by the United States on the completion of the payment.

Article 4

At the end of five years, all the Creeks entitled to these selections, and desirous of remaining, shall receive patents therefor in fee simple, from the United States.

Article 5

All intruders upon the country hereby ceded shall be removed therefrom in the same manner as intruders may be removed by law from other public land until the country is surveyed, and the selections made; excepting however from this provision those white persons who have made their own improvements, and not expelled the Creeks from theirs. Such persons may remain 'till their crops are gathered. After the country is surveyed and the selections made, this article shall not operate upon that part of it not included in such selections. But intruders shall, to whom the same may be assigned by the Creek tribe. But whenever the grantees of these tracts possess improvements, such tracts shall be so located as to include the improvements, and as near as may be in the centre. And there shall also be granted by patent to Benjamin Marshall one section of land, to include his improvements on the Chatahoochee River, to be bounded for one mile in a direct line along the said river, and to run back for quantity. There shall also be granted to Joseph Bruner a coloured man, one half section of land, for his services as an Interpreter.

Art. 7. All the locations authorized by this treaty, with the exception of that to Benjamin Marshall shall be made in conformity with the lines of the surveys; and the Creeks relinquish all claim for improvements.

Art. 8. An additional annuity of twelve thousand dollars shall be paid to the Creeks for the term of five years, and thereafter the said annuity shall be reduced to ten thousand dollars, and shall be paid for the term of fifteen years. All the annuities due to the Creeks shall be paid in such manner as the tribe may direct.

Art. 9. For the purpose of paying certain debts due by the Creeks, and to relieve them in their present distressed condition, the sum of one hundred thousand dollars, shall be paid to the Creek tribe, as soon as may be after the ratification hereof, to be applied to the payment of their just debts, and then to their own relief, and to be distributed as they may direct, and which shall be in full consideration of all improvements.

Art. 10. The sum of sixteen thousand dollars shall be allowed as a compensation to the delegation sent to this place, and for the payment of their expenses, and of the claims against them.

Art. 11 The following claims shall be paid by the United States.
For ferries, bridges and causeways, three thousand dollars, provided that the same shall become the property of the United States
For the payment of certain judgments obtained against the chiefs eight thousand five hundred and seventy dollars.
For losses for which they suppose the United States responsible seven thousand seven hundred and ten dollars.
For the payment of improvements under the treaty of 1826 one thousand dollars.
The three following annuities shall be paid for life
To Tuskehenhaw Cusetau. two hundred dollars.
To the Blind Usher King one hundred dollars.
To Noah Miko one hundred dollars.
There shall be paid the sum of fifteen dollars for each person who has emigrated without expense to the United States but the whole sum allowed under this provision shall not exceed fourteen hundred dollars.
There shall be divided among the persons who suffered in consequence of being prevented from emigrating, three thousand dollars.

(The)

in the manner before described, be removed from these selections for the term of five years from the ratification of this treaty or until the same are conveyed to white persons.

Article 6

Twenty-nine sections in addition to the foregoing may be located, and patents for the same shall then issue to those persons, being Creeks, to whom the same may be assigned by the Creek tribe. But whenever the grantees of these tracts possess improvements, such tracts shall be so located as to include the improvements, and as near as may be in the centre. And there shall also be granted by patent to Benjamin Marshall, one section of land, to include his improvements on the Chatahoochee river, to be bounded for one mile in a direct line along the said river, and to run back for quantity. There shall also be granted to Joseph Bruner a colored man, one half section of land, for his services as an interpreter.

Article 7

All the locations authorized by this treaty, with the exception of that of Benjamin Marshall shall be made in conformity with the lines of the surveys; and the Creeks relinquish all claim for improvements.

Article 8

An additional annuity of twelve thousand dollars shall be paid to the Creeks for the term of five years, and thereafter the said annuity shall be reduced to ten thousand dollars, and shall be paid for the term of fifteen years. All the annuities due to the Creeks shall be paid in such manner as the tribe may direct.

Article 9

For the purpose of paying certain debts due by the Creeks, and to relieve them in their present distressed condition, the sum of one hundred thousand dollars, shall be paid to the Creek tribe as soon as may be after the ratification hereof, to be applied to the payment of their just debts, and then to their own relief, and to be distributed as they may direct, and which shall be in full consideration of all improvements.

Article 10

The sum of sixteen thousand dollars shall be allowed as a compensation to the delegation sent to this place, and for the payment of their expenses, and of the claims against them.

Article 11

The following claims shall be paid by the United States.

For ferries, bridges and causeways, three thousand dollars, provided that the same shall become the property of the United States.

For the payment of certain judgments obtained against the chiefs eight thousand five hundred and seventy dollars.

For losses for which they suppose the United States responsible, seven thousand seven hundred and ten dollars.

For the payment of improvements under the treaty of 1826 one thousand dollars.

The three following annuities shall be paid for life.
To Tuske-hew-haw-Cusetaw two hundred dollars.
To the Blind Uchu King one hundred dollars.
To Neah Mico one hundred dollars.

There shall be paid the sum of fifteen dollars, for each person who has emigrated without expense to the United States, but the whole sum allowed under this provision shall not exceed fourteen hundred dollars.

There shall be divided among the persons, who suffered in consequence of being prevented from emigrating, three thousand dollars.

The land hereby ceded shall remain as a fund from which all the foregoing payments except those in the ninth and tenth articles shall be paid.

Article 12

The United States are desirous that the Creeks should remove to the country west of the Mississippi, and join their countrymen there; and for this purpose it is agreed, that as fast as the Creeks are prepared to emigrate, they shall be removed at the expense of the United States, and shall receive subsistence while upon the journey, and for one year after their arrival at their new homes—Provided however, that this article shall not be construed so as to compel any Creek Indian to emigrate, but they shall be free to go or stay, as they please.

Article 13

There shall also be given to each emigrating warrior a rifle, moulds, wiper and ammunition and to each family one blanket. Three thousand dollars, to be expended as the President may direct, shall be allowed for the term of twenty years for teaching their children. As soon as half their people emigrate, one blacksmith shall be allowed them, and another when two-thirds emigrate, together with one ton of iron and two hundred weight of steel annually for each blacksmith.—These blacksmiths shall be supported for twenty years.

Article 14

The Creek country west of the Mississippi shall be solemnly guarantied to the Creek Indians, nor shall any State or Territory ever have a right to pass laws for the government of such Indians, but they shall be allowed to govern themselves, so far as may be compatible with the general jurisdiction which Congress may think proper to exercise over them. And the United States will also defend them from the unjust hostilities of other Indians, and will also as soon as the boundaries of the Creek country West of the Mississippi are ascertained, cause a patent or grant to be executed to the Creek tribe; agreeably to the 3d section of the act of Congress of May 2d, [28,] 1830, entitled "An act to provide for an exchange of lands with the Indians residing in any of the States, or Territories, and for their removal West of the Mississippi."

Article 15

This treaty shall be obligatory on the contracting parties, as soon as the same shall be ratified by the United States. In testimony whereof, the said Lewis Cass, and the undersigned chiefs of the said tribe, have hereunto set their hands at the city of Washington, this 24th day of March, A. D. 1832.

> Lewis Cass,
> Opothleholo, his x mark,
> Tuchebatcheehadgo, his x mark,
> Efiematla, his x mark,
> Tuchebatche Micco, his x mark,
> Tomack Micco, his x mark,
> William McGilvery, his x mark,
> Benjamin Marshall.
> In the presence of—
> Samuel Bell,
> William R. King,
> John Tipton,
> William Wilkins,
> C. C. Clay,
> J. Speight,
> Samuel W. Mardis,
> J. C. Isacks,
> John Crowell, I. A.,
> Benjamin Marshall,
> Thomas Carr,
> John H. Brodnax,
> Interpreters.

Treaty of Payne's Landing (1832)

Signed on May 9, 1832, by James Gadsden for the United States and by 15 Seminole leaders, the Treaty of Payne's Landing (1832) arranged for the cession of Seminole lands in Florida and for their removal to Creek lands west of the Mississippi.

Florida settlers had long complained about "Indian depredations" committed by the Seminoles, and Georgia, Alabama, and Mississippi plantation owners protested that runaway slaves found refuge among these Florida Natives. Border disputes between Americans and the Seminoles had exploded into full-scale war in 1818, when forces led by Andrew Jackson invaded Florida to punish Seminoles and capture African Americans who lived among them.

In 1823, after Spain transferred control of Florida to the United States, the Seminoles signed a treaty with the United States, the Moultrie Creek Treaty (1823), that ceded the bulk of the Florida Peninsula to U.S. control. Discord between the Seminoles and Americans continued, however, as the Seminoles found living difficult on their reduced acreage. Fulfilling his charge under the new Indian Removal Act (1830), Colonel James Gadsden negotiated the Treaty of Payne's Landing, a removal treaty, with the Seminoles at Payne's Landing in northeastern Florida on May 9, 1832. This treaty stipulated that removal was conditioned on the Seminoles agreeing to settle in the western territory that the War Department had chosen for them. Under duress, the seven Seminoles who journeyed west to inspect their new land signed a new removal treaty with American agents at Fort Gibson on March 28, 1833 in Indian Territory. The treaty declared that the Seminoles agreed with the location of their new lands, accepted political unification with the Creeks, and assented to immediate emigration. Upon their return to Florida, the Seminole leaders renounced the Fort Gibson treaty as coerced, and the Seminoles refused to abide by the stipulations of either treaty.

Meanwhile, a Seminole band that lived along the Apalachicola River signed a separate removal treaty with Gadsden in October 1832, and they migrated to Texas in 1834. The confusion over which Seminoles had authority to accept removal for other Seminoles created an impasse that resulted in a bitter, drawn-out war between the Seminoles and the United States that began in 1835 and was often referred to as the Second Seminole War. That war did not end until 1842, when all but a fragment of the Seminoles had been killed or forcibly removed; it cost the United States $30 million to $40 million and 1,500 dead soldiers. Pockets of Seminoles and their African American brethren remained in Florida, however, and their descendants are still there.

Dewi I. Ball

Further Reading

Remini, Robert V. *The Legacy of Andrew Jackson: Essays on Democracy, Indian Removal and Slavery*. Baton Rouge: Louisiana State University Press, 1990.

Satz, Ronald N. *American Indian Policy in the Jacksonian Era*. Norman: University of Oklahoma Press, 2002.

Wallace, Anthony F.C. *The Long, Bitter Trail: Andrew Jackson and the Indians*. New York: Hill and Wang, 1993.

Document: Treaty of Payne's Landing

The Seminole Indians, regarding with just respect, the solicitude manifested by the President of the United States or the improvement of their condition, by recommending a removal to a country more suitable to their habits and wants than the one they at present occupy in the Territory of Florida, are willing that their confidential chiefs, Jumper, Fuch-a-lus-ti-had-jo, Charley Emartla, Coi-had-jo, Holati Emartla Ya-hadjo; Sam Jones, accompanied by their agent Major Phagan, and their faithful interpreter Abraham, should be sent at the expense of the United States as early as convenient to examine the country assigned to the Creeks west of the Mississippi river, and should they be satisfied with the character of that country, and of the favorable disposition of the Creeks to reunite with the Seminoles as one people; the articles of the compact and agreement, herein stipulated at Payne's landing on one Ocklewaha river, this ninth day of May, one thousand eight hundred and thirty-two, between James Gadsden, for and in behalf of the Government of the United States, and the undersigned chiefs and head-men for and in behalf of the Seminole Indians, shall be binding on the respective parties.

Article 1

The Seminole Indians relinquish to the United States, all claim to the lands they at present occupy in the Territory of Florida, and agree to emigrate to the country assigned to the Creeks, west of the Mississippi river; it being understood that an additional extent of territory, proportioned to their numbers, will be added to the Creek country, and that the Seminoles will be received as a constituent part of the Creek nation and be re-admitted to all the privileges as members of the same.

Article 2

For and in consideration of the relinquishment of claim in the first article of this agreement, and in full compensation for all the improvements, which may have been made on the lands thereby ceded; the United States stipulate to pay to the Seminole Indians, fifteen thousand, four hundred (15,400) dollars, to be divided among the chiefs and warriors of the several towns, in a ratio proportioned to their population, the respective proportions of each to be paid on their arrival in the country they consent to remove to; it being understood that their faithful interpreters Abraham and Cudjo shall receive two hundred dollars each of the above sum, in full remuneration for the improvements to be abandoned on the lands now cultivated by them.

Article 3

The United States agree to distribute as they arrive at their new homes in the Creek Territory, west of the Mississippi river, a blanket and a homespun frock, to each of the warriors, women and children of the Seminole tribe of Indians.

Article 4

The United States agree to extend the annuity for the support of a blacksmith, provided for in the sixth article of the treaty at Camp Moultrie for ten (10) years beyond the period therein stipulated, and in addition to the other annuities secured under that treaty: the United States agree to pay the sum of three thousand (3,000) dollars a year for fifteen (15) years, commencing after the removal of the whole tribe; these sums to be added to the Creek annuities, and the whole amount to be so divided, that the chiefs and warriors of the Seminole Indians may receive their equitable proportion of the same as members of the Creek confederation—

Article 5

The United States will take the cattle belonging to the Seminoles at the valuation of some discreet person to be appointed by the President, and the same shall be paid for in money to the respective owners, after their arrival at their new homes; or other cattle such as may be desired will be furnished them, notice being given through their agent of their wishes upon this subject, before their removal, that time may be afforded to supply the demand.

Article 6

The Seminoles being anxious to be relieved from repeated vexatious demands for slaves and other property, alleged to have been stolen and destroyed by them, so that they may remove unembarrassed to their new homes; the United States stipulate to have the same property investigated, and to liquidate such as may be satisfactorily established, provided the amount does not exceed seven thousand (7,000) dollars.—

Article 7

The Seminole Indians will remove within three (3) years after the ratification of this agreement, and the expenses of their removal shall be defrayed by the United States, and such subsistence shall also be furnished them for a term not exceeding twelve (12) months, after their arrival at their new residence; as in the opinion of the President, their numbers and circumstances may require, the emigration to commence as early as practicable in the year eighteen hundred and thirty-three (1833), and with those Indians at present occupying the Big Swamp, and other parts of the country beyond the limits as defined in the second article of the treaty concluded at Camp Moultrie creek, so that the whole of that proportion of the Seminoles may be removed within the year aforesaid, and the remainder of the tribe, in about equal proportions, during the subsequent years of eighteen hundred and thirty-four and five (1834 and 1835).

In testimony whereof, the commissioner, James Gadsden, and the undersigned chiefs and head men of the Seminole Indians, have hereunto subscribed their names and affixed their seals. Done at camp at Payne's landing, on the Ocklawaha river in the territory of Florida, on this ninth day of May, one thousand eight hundred and thirty-two, and of the independence of the United States of America the fifty-sixth.

>James Gadsden, [L. S.],
>Holati Emartla, his x mark, [L. S.],
>Jumper, his x mark, [L. S.],
>Fuch-ta-lus-ta-Hadjo, his x mark, [L. S.],
>Charley Emartla, his x mark, [L. S.],
>Coa Hadjo, his x mark, [L. S.],
>Ar-pi-uck-i, or Sam Jones, his x mark, [L. S.],
>Ya-ha Hadjo, his x mark, [L. S.],
>Mico-Noha, his x mark, [L. S.],
>Tokose-Emartla, or Jno. Hicks. his x mark, [L. S.],
>Cat-sha-Tusta-nuck-i, his x mark, [L. S.],
>Hola-at-a-Mico, his x mark, [L. S.],
>Hitch-it-i-Mico, his x mark, [L. S.],
>E-ne-hah, his x mark, [L. S.],
>Ya-ha-emartla Chup-ko, his mark, [L. S.],
>Moke-his-she-lar-ni, his x mark, [L. S.].
>Witnesses:
>Douglas Vass, Secretary to Commissioner,
>John Phagan, Agent,
>Stephen Richards, Interpreter,
>Abraham, Interpreter, his x mark,
>Cudjo, Interpreter, his x mark,
>Erastus Rogers,
>B. Joscan.

Treaty of Pontotoc Creek (1832)

The Treaty of Pontotoc Creek (October 20, 1832) was an Indian removal treaty that ceded Chickasaw lands east of the Mississippi in exchange for land west of the

Mississippi. The treaty was concluded in the Chickasaw Nation and signed by John Coffee for the United States and by 65 Chickasaw representatives.

Chickasaw leaders sought to acquire the best terms possible after the passage of the Indian Removal Act (1830). In the summer of 1830, Chickasaw representatives met with U.S. delegates, including President Andrew Jackson, at Franklin, Tennessee, and a treaty was signed on August 31. The Chickasaws agreed to cede their lands east of the Mississippi River in exchange for an equal amount of land in the West, but when a suitable area could not be found, this treaty became void. New negotiations for removal were undertaken in 1832 in Chickasaw Territory at Pontotoc Creek.

On October 20, the treaty was signed that ceded Chickasaw lands to the U.S. government; the lands were to be surveyed and sold immediately, and each adult Chickasaw was to receive a temporary allotment, which would also be sold and all monies therefrom placed in a fund to cover the costs of removal. Whites quickly settled on the Chickasaw lands beginning in 1832, despite a provision of the treaty promising that the U.S. government would prevent white intrusion until the Chickasaws had actually left Mississippi.

A suitable new homeland in the West was not found until January 1837, when the Chickasaws and Choctaws met at Doaksville, Choctaw Nation, in Indian Territory, and the Choctaws sold the western part of their new territory to the Chickasaws. Although this agreement between the two tribes was not a treaty with the United States, Jackson submitted the Treaty of Doaksville (1837) to the Senate for approval anyway, which was accomplished in February 1837. Further details about the exact extent of territory and rights granted the Chickasaws were decided in two additional agreements between the two Native American nations in 1854 and 1855.

Dewi I. Ball

Further Reading

Remini, Robert V. *The Legacy of Andrew Jackson: Essays on Democracy, Indian Removal and Slavery*. Baton Rouge: Louisiana State University Press, 1990.

Satz, Ronald N. *American Indian Policy in the Jacksonian Era*. Norman: University of Oklahoma Press, 2002.

Wallace, Anthony F. C. *The Long, Bitter Trail: Andrew Jackson and the Indians*. New York: Hill and Wang, 1993.

Document: Treaty of Pontotoc Creek

Articles of a treaty made and entered into between Genl. John Coffee, being duly authorized thereto, by the President of the United States, and the whole Chickasaw Nation, in General Council assembled, at the council House, on Pontitock Creek on the twentieth day of October, 1832.

THE Chickasaw Nation find themselves oppressed in their present situation; by being made subject to the laws of the States in which they reside. Being ignorant of the language and laws of the white man, they cannot understand or obey them. Rather than submit to this great evil, they prefer to seek a home in the west, where they may live and be governed by their own laws. And believing that they can procure for themselves a home, in a country suited to their wants and condition, provided they had the means to contract and pay for the same, they have determined to sell their country and hunt a new home. The President has heard the complaints of the Chickasaws, and like them believes they cannot be happy, and prosper as a nation, in their present situation and condition, and being desirous to relieve them from the great calamity that seems to await them, if they remain as they are—He has sent his Commissioner Genl. John Coffee, who has met the whole Chickasaw nation in Council, and after mature deliberation, they have entered into the following articles, which shall be binding on both parties, when the same shall be ratified by the President of the United States by and with the advice and consent of the Senate.

Article 1

For the consideration hereinafter expressed, the Chickasaw nation do hereby cede, to the United States, all the land which they own on the east side of the Mississippi river, including all the country where they at present live and occupy.

Article 2

The United States agree to have the whole country thus ceded, surveyed, as soon as it can be conveniently done, in the same manner that the public lands of the United States are surveyed in the States of Mississippi and Alabama, and as soon thereafter as may be practicable, to have the same prepared for sale. The President of the United States will then offer the land for sale at public auction, in the same manner and on the same terms and conditions as the other public lands, and such of the land as may not sell at the public sales shall be offered at private sale, in the same manner that other private sales are made of the United States lands.

Article 3

As a full compensation to the Chickasaw nation, for the country thus ceded, the United States agree to pay over to the Chickasaw nation, all the money arising from the sale of the land which may be received from time to time, after deducting therefrom the whole cost and expenses of surveying and selling the land, including every expense attending the same.

Article 4

The President being determined that the Chickasaw people shall not deprive themselves of a comfortable home, in the country where they now are, until they shall have provided a country in the west to remove to, and settle on, with fair prospects of future comfort and happiness—It is therefore agreed to, by the Chickasaw nation, that they will endeavor as soon as it may be in their power, after the ratification of this treaty, to hunt out and procure a home for their people, west of the Mississippi river, suited to their wants and condition; and they will continue to do so during the progress of the survey of their present country, as is provided for in the second article of this treaty. But should they fail to procure such a country to remove to and settle on, previous to the first public sale of their country here then and in that event, they are to select out of the surveys, a comfortable settlement for every family in the Chickasaw nation, to include their present improvements, if the land is good for cultivation, and if not they may take it in any other place in the nation, which is unoccupied by any other person. Such settlement must be taken by sections. And there shall be allotted to each family as follows (to wit): To a single man who is twenty-one years of age, one section—to each family of five and under that number two sections—to each family of six and not exceeding ten, three sections, and to each family over ten in number, four sections—and to families who own slaves, there shall be allowed, one section to those who own ten or upwards and such as own under ten, there shall be allowed half a section. If any person shall now occupy two places and wish to retain both, they may do so, by taking a part at one place, and a part at the other, and where two or more persons are now living on the same section, the oldest occupant will be entitled to remain, and the others must move off to some other place if so required by the oldest occupant. All of which tracts of land, so selected and retained, shall be held, and occupied by the Chickasaw people, uninterrupted until they shall find and obtain a country suited to their wants and condition. And the United States will guaranty to the Chickasaw nation, the quiet possession and uninterrupted use of the said reserved tracts of land, so long as they may live on and occupy the same. And when they shall determine to remove from said tracts of land, the Chickasaw nation will notify the President of the United States of their determination to remove, and thereupon as soon as the Chickasaw people shall remove, the President will proclaim the said reserved tracts of land for sale at public auction and at private sale, on the same terms and conditions, as is provided for in the second article of this treaty, to sell the same, and the net proceeds thereof, to be paid to the Chickasaw nation, as is provided for in the third article of this treaty.

Article 5

If any of the Chickasaw families shall have made valuable improvements on the places where they lived and removed from, on the reservation tracts, the same shall be valued by some discreet person to be appointed by the President, who shall assess the real cash value of all such improvements, and also the real cash value of all the land within their improvements, which they may have cleared and actually cultivated, at least one year in good farming order and condition. And such valuation of the improvements and the value of the cultivated lands as before mentioned, shall be paid to the person who shall have made the same. To be paid out of the proceeds of the sales of the ceded lands. The person who shall value such land and improvements, shall give to the owner thereof, a certificate of the valuation, which shall be a good voucher for them to draw the money on, from the proper person, who shall be appointed to pay the same, and the money shall be paid, as soon as may be convenient, after the valuation, to enable the owner thereof to provide for their families on their journey to their new homes. The provisions of this article are intended to encourage industry and to enable the Chickasaws to move comfortably. But least the good intended may be abused, by designing persons, by hiring hands and clearing more land, than they otherwise would do for the benefit of their families—It is determined that no payment shall be made for improved lands, over and above one-eighth part of the tract allowed and reserved for such person to live on and occupy.

Article 6

The Chickasaw nation cannot receive any part of the payment for their land until it shall be surveyed and sold; therefore, in order to the greater facilitate, in surveying and preparing the land for sale, and for keeping the business of the nation separate and apart from the business and accounts of the United States, it is proposed by the Chickasaws, and agreed to, that a Surveyor General be appointed by the President, by and with the advice and consent of the Senate, to superintend alone the surveying of this ceded country or so much thereof as the President may direct, who shall appoint a sufficient number of deputy surveyors, as may be necessary to complete the survey, in as short a time as may be reasonable and expedient. That the said Surveyor General be allowed one good clerk, and one good draftsman to aid and assist him in the business of his office, in preparing the lands for sale. It is also agreed that one land office be established for the sale of the lands, to have one Register and one Receiver of monies, to be appointed by the President, by and with the advice and consent of the senate, and each Register and Receiver to have one good clerk to aid and assist them in the duties of their office. The Surveyor's office, and the office of the Register and Receiver of money, shall be kept somewhere central in the nation, at such place as the President of the United States may direct. As the before mentioned officers, and clerks, are to be employed entirely in business of the nation, appertaining to preparing and selling the land, they will of course be paid out of the proceeds of the sales of the ceded lands. That the Chickasaws, may now understand as near as may be, the expenses that will be incurred in the transacting of this business—It is proposed and agreed to, that the salary of the Surveyor General be fifteen hundred dollars a year, and that the Register and Receiver of monies, be allowed twelve hundred dollars a year each, as a full compensation for their services, and all expenses, except stationary and postages on their official business, and that each of the clerks and draftsman be allowed seven hundred and fifty dollars a year, for their services and all expenses.

Article 7

It is expressly agreed that the United States shall not grant any right of preference, to any person, or right of occupancy in any manner whatsoever, but in all cases, of either public or private sale, they are to sell the land to the highest bidder, and also that none of the lands be sold in smaller tracts than quarter sections or fractional sections of the same size as near as may be, until the Chickasaw nation may require the President to sell in smaller tracts. The Chiefs of the nation have heard that at some of the sales of the United States lands, the people there present, entered into combinations, and united in purchasing much of the land, at reduced prices, for their own benefit, to the great prejudice of the Government, and they express fears, that attempts will be made to cheat them, in the same manner when their lands shall be offered at public auction. It is therefore agreed that the President will use his best endeavors to prevent such combinations, or any other plan or state of things which may tend to prevent the land selling for its full value.

Article 8

As the Chickasaws have determined to sell their country, it is desirable that the nation realize the greatest possible sum for their lands, which can be obtained. It is therefore proposed and agreed to that after the President shall have offered their lands for sale and shall have sold all that will sell for the Government price, then the price shall be reduced, so as to induce purchasers to buy, who would not take the land at the Government minimum price;—and it is believed, that five years from and after the date of the first sale, will dispose of all the lands, that will sell at the Government price. If then at the expiration of five years, as before mentioned, the Chickasaw nation may request the President to sell at such reduced price as the nation may then propose, it shall be the duty of the President to comply with their request, by first offering it at public and afterwards at private sale, as in all other cases of selling public lands.

Article 9

The Chickasaw nation express their ignorance, and incapacity to live, and be happy under the State laws, they cannot read and understand them, and therefore they will always need a friend to advise and direct them. And fearing at some day the Government of the United States may withdraw from them, the agent under whose instructions they have lived so long and happy—They therefore request that the agent may be continued with them, while here, and wherever they may remove to and settle. It is the earnest wish of the United States Government to see the Chickasaw nation prosper and be happy, and so far as is consistent they will contribute all in their power to render them so—therefore their request is granted. There shall be an agent kept with the Chickasaws as heretofore, so long as they live within the jurisdiction of the United States as a nation, either within the limits of the States where they now reside, or at any other place. And whenever the office of agent shall be vacant, and an agent to be appointed, the President will pay due respect to the wishes of the nation in selecting a man in all respects qualified to discharge the responsible duties of that office.

Article 10

Whenever the Chickasaw nation shall determine to remove from, and leave their present country, they will give the President of the United States timely notice of such intention, and the President will furnish them the necessary funds, and means for their transportation and journey, and for one years provisions, after they reach their new homes, in such quantity as the nation may require, and the full amount of such funds, transportation and provisions, is to be paid for, out of the proceeds of the sales of the ceded lands. And should the Chickasaw nation remove, from their present country, before they receive money, from the sale of the lands, hereby ceded; then and in that case, the United States shall furnish them any reasonable sum of money for national purposes, which may be deemed proper by the President of the United States, which sum shall also be refunded out of the sales of the ceded lands.

Article 11

The Chickasaw nation have determined to create a perpetual fund, for the use of the nation forever, out of the proceeds of the country now ceded away. And for that purpose they propose to invest a large proportion of the money arising from the sale of the land, in some safe and valuable stocks which will bring them in an annual interest or dividend, to be used for all national purposes, leaving the principal untouched, intending to use the interest alone. It is therefore proposed by the Chickasaws, and agreed to, that the sum to be laid out in stocks as above mentioned, shall be left with the government of the United States, until it can be laid out under the direction of the President of the United States, by and with the advice and consent of the Senate, in such safe and valuable stock as he may approve of, for the use and benefit of the Chickasaw nation. The sum thus to be invested, shall be equal to, at least three-fourths of the whole net proceeds of the sales of the lands; and as much more, as the nation may determine, if there shall be a surplus after supplying all the national wants. But it is hereby provided, that if the reasonable wants of the nation shall require more than one fourth of the proceeds of the sales of the land, then they may, by the consent of the President and Senate, draw from the government such sum as may be thought reasonable, for valuable national purposes, out of the three-fourths reserved to be laid out in stocks. But if any of the monies shall be thus drawn out of the sum first proposed, to be laid out on interest, the sum shall be replaced, out of the first monies of the nation, which may come into the possession of the United States government, from the sale of the ceded lands, over and above the reasonable wants of the nation. At the expiration of fifty years from this date, if the Chickasaw nation shall have improved in education and civilization, and become so enlightened, as to be capable of managing so large a sum of money to advantage, and with safety, for the benefit of the nation, and the President of the United States, with the Senate, shall be satisfied thereof, at that time, and shall give their consent thereto, the Chickasaw nation may then withdraw the whole, or any part of the fund now set apart, to be laid out in stocks, or at interest, and dispose of the same, in any manner that they may think proper at that time, for the use and benefit of the whole nation; but no part of said fund shall ever be used for any other purpose, than the benefit of the whole Chickasaw nation. In order to facilitate the survey and sale of the lands now ceded, and to raise the money therefrom as soon as possible, for the foregoing purpose, the President of the United States is authorized to commence the survey of the land as soon as may be practicable, after the ratification of this treaty.

Article 12

The Chickasaws feel grateful to their old chiefs for their long and faithful services, in attending to the business of the nation. They believe it a duty, to keep them from want in their old and declining age—with those feelings, they have looked upon their old and beloved chief Tish-o-mingo, who is now grown old, and is poor and not able to live, in that comfort, which his valuable life and great merit deserve. It is therefore determined to give him out of the national funds, one hundred dollars a year during the balance of his life, and the nation request him to receive it, as a token of their kind feelings for him, on account of his long and valuable services. Our old and beloved Queen Puc-caun-la, is now very old and very poor. Justice says the nation ought not to let her suffer in her old age; it is therefore determined to give her out of the national funds, fifty dollars a year during her life, the money to be put in the hands of the agent to be laid out for her support, under his direction, with the advice of the chiefs.

Article 13

The boundary line between the lands of the Chickasaws and Choctaws, has never been run, or properly defined, and as the Choctaws have sold their country to the United States, they now have no interest in the decision of that question. It is therefore agreed to call on the old Choctaw chiefs, to determine the line to be run, between the Chickasaws and their former country. The Chickasaws, by a treaty made with the United States at Franklin in Tennessee, in Aug. 31, 1830, (a) declared their line to run as follows, to wit: Beginning at the mouth of Oak tibby-haw and running up said stream to a point, being a marked tree, on the old Natches road, one mile southwardly from Wall's old place. Thence with the Choctaw boundary, and along it, westwardly through the Tunicha old fields, to a point on the Mississippi river, about twenty-eight miles by water below where the St. Francis river enter said stream on the west side. It is now agreed, that the surveys of the Choctaw country which are now in progress, shall not cross the line until the true line shall be decided and determined; which shall be done as follows, the agent of the Choctaws on the west side of the Mississippi shall call on the old and intelligent chiefs of that nation, and lay before them the line as claimed by the Chickasaws at the Franklin treaty, and if the Choctaws shall determine that line to be correct, then it shall be established and made the permanent line, but if the Choctaws say the line strikes the Mississippi river higher up said stream, then the best evidence which can be had from both nations, shall be taken by the agents of both nations, and submitted to the President of the United States for his decision, and on such evidence, the President will determine the true line on principles of strict justice.

Article 14

As soon as the surveys are made, it shall be the duty of the chiefs, with the advice and assistance of the agent to cause a correct list to be made out of all and every tract of land, which shall be reserved, for the use and benefit of the Chickasaw people, for their residence, as is provided for in the fourth article of this treaty, which list, will designate the sections of land, which are set apart for each family or individual in the nation, shewing the precise tracts which shall belong to each and every one of them, which list shall be returned to the register of the land office, and he shall make a record of the same, in his office, to prevent him from offering any of said tracts of land for sale, and also as evidence of each person's lands. All the residue of the lands will be offered by the President for sale.

Article 15

The Chickasaws request that no persons be permitted to move in and settle on their country before the land is sold. It is therefore agreed, that no person, whatsoever, who is not Chickasaw or connected with the Chickasaws by marriage, shall be permitted to come into the country and settle on any part of the ceded lands until they shall be offered for sale, and then there shall not be any person permitted to settle on any of the land, which has not been sold, at the time of such settlement, and in all cases of a person settling on any of the ceded lands contrary to this express understanding, they will be intruders, and must be treated as such, and put off of the lands of the nation.

In witness of all and every thing herein determined, between the United States and the whole Chickasaw nation in general council assembled, the parties have hereunto set their hands and seals, at the council-house, on Pontitock creek, in the Chickasaw nation, on the twentieth day of October, one thousand eight hundred and thirty-two.

John Coffee, [L. S.]
Ish-te-ho-to-pa, [king,] his x mark, [L. S.]
Tish-o-min-go, his x mark, [L. S.]
Levi Colbert, his x mark, [L. S.]
George Colbert, his x mark, [L. S.]
William M'Gilvery, his x mark, [L. S.]
Samuel Sely, his x mark, [L. S.]
To-pul-kah, his x mark, [L. S.]
Isaac Albertson, his x mark, [L. S.]
Em-ub-by, his x mark, [L. S.]
Pis-tah-lah-tubbe, his x mark, [L. S.]
Ish-tim-o-lut-ka, his x mark, [L. S.]
James Brown, his x mark, [L. S.]
Im-mah-hoo-lo-tubbe, his x mark, [L. S.]
Ish-ta-ha-chah, his x mark,[L. S.]
Lah-fin-hubbe, his x mark, [L. S.]
Shop-pow-me, his x mark, [L. S.]
Nin-uck-ah-umba, his x mark, [L. S.]
Im-mah-hoo-la-tubbe, his x mark, [L. S.]
Illup-pah-umba, his x mark, [L. S.]
Pitman Colbert, [L. S.]
Con-mush-ka-ish-kah, his x mark, [L. S.]
James Wolfe, [L. S.]
Bah-ha-kah-tubbe, his x mark, [L. S.]
E. Bah-kah-tubbe, his x mark, [L. S.]
Captain Thompson, his x mark, [L. S.]
New-berry, his x mark, [L. S.]
Bah-ma-hah-tubbe, his x mark, [L. S.]
John Lewis, his x mark, [L. S.]
I-yah-hou-tubbe, his x mark, [L. S.]
Tok-holth-la-chah, his x mark, [L. S.]
Oke-lah-nah-nubbe, his x mark, [L. S.]
Im-me-tubbe, his x mark, [L. S.]
In-kah-yea, his x mark, [L. S.]
Ah-sha-cubbe, his x mark, [L. S.]
Im-moh-ho-bah, his x mark, [L. S.]
Fit-chah-pla, his x mark, [L. S.]

Unte-mi-ah-tubbe, his x mark, [L. S.]
Oke-lah-hin-lubbe, his x mark, [L. S.]
John Glover, his x mark, [L. S.]
Bah-me-hubbe, his x mark, [L. S.]
Hush-tah-tah-ubbe, his x mark, [L. S.]
Un-ti-ha-kah-tubbe, his x mark, [L. S.]
Yum-mo-tubbe, his x mark, [L. S.]
Oh-ha-cubbe, his x mark, [L. S.]
Ah-fah-mah, his x mark, [L. S.]
Ah-ta-kin-tubbe, his x mark, [L. S.]
Ah-to-ko-wah, his x mark, [L. S.]
Tah-ha-cubbe, his x mark, [L. S.]
Kin-hoi-cha, his x mark, [L. S.]
Ish-te-ah-tubbe, his x mark, [L. S.]
Chick-ah-shah-nan-ubbe, his x mark, [L. S.]
Che-wut-ta-ha, his x mark, [L. S.]
Fo-lut-ta-chah, his x mark, [L. S.]
No-wo-ko, his x mark, [L. S.]
Win-in-a-pa, his x mark, [L. S.]
Oke-lah-shah-cubbe, his x mark, [L. S.]
Ish-ta-ki-yu-ka-tabbe, his x mark, [L. S.]
Mah-te-ko-shubbe, his x mark, [L. S.]
Tom-chick-ah, his x mark, [L. S.]
Ei-o-che-tubbe, his x mark, [L. S.]
Nuck-sho-pubbe, his x mark, [L. S.]
Fah-lah-mo-tubbe, his x mark, [L. S.]
Co-chub-be, his x mark, [L. S.]
Thomas Sely, his x mark, [L. S.]
Oke-lah-sha-pi-a, his x mark, [L. S.]
Signed and sealed in the presence of—
Ben. Reynolds, Indian agent,
John L. Allen, subagent,
Nath. Anderson, secretary to the commissioner,
Benj. Love, United States interpreter,
Robert Gordon, Mississippi,
George Wightman, of Mississippi,
John Donley, Tennessee,
D. S. Parrish, Tennessee,
S. Daggett, Mississippi,
Wm. A. Clurm,
G. W. Long.

Treaty of Chicago (1833)

The Treaty of Chicago (1833) was negotiated in September 26, 1833, in Chicago and it arranged for the cession of lands in northeastern Illinois, southeastern Wisconsin, and southern Michigan. It also provided for the removal of the United Band of Ottawas, Chippewas, and Potawatomis from the region. As a result of both the rapid expansion in settlement in the western Great Lakes region and the military might displayed by federal and local governments in the Black Hawk War a year earlier, representatives of the United Band and other Potawatomi groups agreed to meet with U.S. commissioners. At the end of the negotiations, the Natives had ceded approximately 5 million acres, and most had agreed to relocate to new homes west of the Mississippi River.

By the early 1830s, the advancement of American settlement and the opening of the Erie Canal had tremendously increased the scale of American migration into the western Great Lakes region. The non-Native population of Illinois alone had tripled in the period from statehood in 1818 to 1830. Although initial settlement had focused on the lead mining region in the northwestern part of the state, the scope had begun to change. This encroachment, combined with the passage of the Indian Removal Act (1830), increased the pressure on resident tribal groups to move to lands west of the Mississippi. In the fall of 1833, three government-designated treaty commissioners met in Chicago with the representatives of some of the largest Native landholders remaining in the region. More than 8,000 Native Americans and whites gathered by the shores of Lake Michigan to participate in the negotiations, which lasted for more than two weeks.

The treaty can be separated into two parts. The first and largest portion of the treaty addressed the negotiations made with the representatives of the United Band of Ottawa, Chippewa, and Potawatomi Indians. In this section, the United Band ceded claims to all of its lands in northeastern Illinois and southeastern Wisconsin, which consisted of approximately 5 million acres. In return, the United States granted an equal amount of land located just north of the state of Missouri, to which the Indians were required to remove within three years from the date of ratification of the treaty. Additional articles provided money for education, agriculture, debt payments, and expenses related to the future removal. The second part of the treaty encompassed several supplementary agreements and addressed separate negotiations with the Potawatomi residents of southern Michigan. These bands and their main spokesperson, Pokagun, represented the strongest opposition to removal among the participating American Indian groups. As a result of this resistance to relocation, the treaty commissioners negotiated a separate accord with these American Indians. Although the primary supplement did arrange for the cession of all their lands in southern Michigan, an addendum allowed for some of these Michigan Potawatomis to move onto lands in northern Michigan, as opposed to lands west of the Mississippi.

Assessment of this treaty's impact must take into account a number of issues. In the first place, the treaty arranged the removal of a significant population of Native Americans from the western Great Lakes region and opened up 5 million acres to American settlers. But the treaty's influence went beyond this cession of Native-owned lands. Significantly, the treaty and its addenda illustrated some of the ways in which populations of Native peoples avoided removal. In particular, Pokagun's stance against the land cession led to the treaty addendum that provided an exemption for his band in southern Michigan. This community of Potawatomis maintained a presence in the region long after the United Band had moved to the Council Bluffs area in Iowa Territory. Finally, the negotiations in 1833 illustrated the growing influence of individuals of mixed descent within the United Band in particular. Two of the men designated as chiefs who signed the treaty, Billy Caldwell and Alexander Robinson, were not men born into the United Band. Caldwell, or Saukenuk, came from a Mohawk-Irish lineage; Robinson, or Cheecheebinquay, from an Ottawa-British one. Both men received lifetime annuities through the treaty as well as $5,000 each to pay debts incurred through trading with the United Bands.

John P. Bowes

Further Reading

Clifton, James A. *The Prairie People: Continuity and Change in Potawatomi Indian Culture 1665–1965*. Lawrence: The Regents Press of Kansas, 1977.

Edmunds, R. David. *The Potawatomis, Keepers of the Fire*. Norman: University of Oklahoma Press, 1978.

Tanner, Helen Hornbeck, ed. *Atlas of Great Lakes Indian History*. Norman: University of Oklahoma Press, 1987.

Document: Treaty of Chicago

Articles of a treaty made at Chicago, in the State of Illinois, on the twenty-sixth day of September, in the year of our Lord one thousand eight hundred and thirty-three, between George B. Porter, Thomas J. V. Owen and William Weatherford, Commissioners on the part of the United States of the one part, and the United Nation of Chippewa, Ottowa and Potawatamie Indians of the other part, being fully represented by the Chiefs and Head-men whose names are hereunto subscribed—which Treaty is in the following words, to wit:

Article 1

The said United Nation of Chippewa, Ottowa, and Potawatamie Indians, cede to the United States all their land, along the western shore of Lake Michigan, and between this Lake and the land ceded to the United States by the Winnebago nation, at the

Chipley

Schedule "A"

(referred to in the Treaty, containing the sums payable to Individuals in lieu of Reservations.)

	Dollars
Jesse Walker	1500.
Henry Cleveland	800.
Rachel Hall	600.
Sylvia Hall	600.
Joseph Laframboise & Children	1000.
Victoire Sorthier & her children	700.
Jean Bt. Miranda	300
Jane Miranda — For each of whom John H. Kinzie	200.
Rosetta Miranda — is Trustee	300.
Thomas Miranda	400.
Alexander Muller (Gholson Kercheval Trustee)	800.
Paschal Muller, Do. Do.	800.
Margaret Muller	200.
Socra Muller	200.
Angelique Chevalier	200.
Josette Chevallier	200
Joseph Chevalier	400.
Fanny Leclerc (Captain David Hunter, Trustee.)	400.
Daniel Bourassa's children	600.
Nancy Contraman	
Sally Contraman — For each of whom J. B. Campbell is Trustee	600
Betsey Contraman	
Alexis Laframboise	800.
Alexis Laframbois' children	1200.
Mrs. Mann's children	600.
Mrs. Mann (daughter of Antoine Ouilmet)	400.
Carried over $	13800

treaty of Fort Armstrong made on the 15th September 1832—bounded on the north by the country lately ceded by the Menominees, and on the south by the country ceded at the treaty of Prairie du Chien made on the 29th July 1829—supposed to contain about five millions of acres.

Article 2

In part consideration of the above cession it is hereby agreed, that the United States shall grant to the said United Nation of Indians to be held as other Indian lands are held which have lately been assigned to emigrating Indians, a tract of country west of the Mississippi river, to be assigned to them by the President of the United States—to be not less in quantity than five millions of acres, and to be located as follows: beginning at the mouth of Boyer's river on the east side of the Missouri river, thence down the said river to the mouth of Naudoway river, thence due east to the west line of the State of Missouri, thence along the said State line to the northwest corner of the State, thence east along the said State line to the point where it is intersected by the western boundary line of the Sacs and Foxes—thence north along the said line of the Sacs and Foxes, so far as that when a straight line shall be run therefrom to the mouth of Boyer's river (the place of beginning) it shall include five millions of acres. And as it is the wish of the Government of the United States that the said nation of Indians should remove to the country thus assigned to them as soon as conveniently can be done; and it is deemed advisable on the part of their Chiefs and Headmen that a deputation should visit the said country west of the Mississippi and thus be assured that full justice has been done, it is hereby stipulated that the United States will defray the expenses of such deputation, to consist of not more than fifty persons, to be accompanied by not more than five individuals to be nominated by themselves, and the whole to be under the general direction of such officer of the United States Government as has been or shall be designated for the purpose.—And it is further agreed that as fast as the said Indians shall be prepared to emigrate, they shall be removed at the expense of the United States, and shall receive subsistence while upon the journey, and for one year after their arrival at their new homes.—It being understood, that the said Indians are to remove from all that part of the land now ceded, which is within the State of Illinois, immediately on the ratification of this treaty, but to be permitted to retain possession of the country north of the boundary line of the said State, for the term of three years, without molestation or interruption and under the protection of the laws of the United States.

Article 3

And in further consideration of the above cession, it is agreed, that there shall be paid by the United States the sums of money hereinafter mentioned: to wit.

One hundred thousand dollars to satisfy sundry individuals, in behalf of whom reservations were asked, which the Commissioners refused to grant: and also to indemnify the Chippewa tribe who are parties to this treaty for certain lands along the shore of Lake Michigan, to which they make claim, which have been ceded to the United States by the Menominee Indians—the manner in which the same is to be paid is set forth in Schedule "A" hereunto annexed.

One hundred and fifty thousand dollars to satisfy the claims made against the said United Nation which they have here admitted to be justly due, and directed to be paid, according to Schedule "B" hereunto annexed.

One hundred thousand dollars to be paid in goods and provisions, a part to be delivered on the signing of this treaty and the residue during the ensuing year.

Two hundred and eighty thousand dollars to be paid in annuities of fourteen thousand dollars a year, for twenty years.

One hundred and fifty thousand dollars to be applied to the erection of mills, farm houses, Indian houses and blacksmith shops, to agricultural improvements, to the purchase of agricultural implements and stock, and for the support of such physicians, millers, farmers, blacksmiths and other mechanics, as the President of the United States shall think proper to appoint.

Seventy thousand dollars for purposes of education and the encouragement of the domestic arts, to be applied in such manner, as the President of the United States may direct.—[The wish of the Indians being expressed to the Commissioners as follows: The united nation of Chippewa, Ottowa and Potawatamie Indians being desirous to create a perpetual fund for the purposes of education and the encouragement of the domestic arts, wish to invest the sum of seventy thousand dollars in some safe stock, the interest of which only is to be applied as may be necessary for the above purposes. They therefore request the President of the United States, to make such investment for the nation as he may think best. If however, at any time hereafter, the said nation shall have made such advancement in civilization and have become so enlightened as in the opinion of the President and Senate of the United States they shall be capable of managing so large a fund with safety they may withdraw the whole or any part of it.]

Four hundred dollars a year to be paid to Billy Caldwell, and three hundred dollars a year, to be paid to Alexander Robinson, for life, in addition to the annuities already granted them—Two hundred dollars a year to be paid to Joseph Lafromboise and two hundred dollars a year to be paid to Shabehnay, for life.

Two thousand dollars to be paid to Wau-pon-eh-see and his band, and fifteen hundred dollars to Awn-kote and his band, as the consideration for nine sections of land, granted to them by the 3d Article of the Treaty of Prairie du Chien of the 29th of July 1829 which are hereby assigned and surrendered to the United States.

Article 4

A just proportion of the annuity money, secured as well by former treaties as the present, shall be paid west of the Mississippi to such portion of the nation as shall have removed thither during the ensuing three years.—After which time, the whole amount of the annuities shall be paid at their location west of the Mississippi.

Article 5

[Stricken out.]

This treaty after the same shall have been ratified by the President and Senate of the United States, shall be binding on the contracting parties.

In testimony whereof, the said George B. Porter, Thomas J. V. Owen, and William Weatherford, and the undersigned chiefs and head men of the said nation of Indians, have hereunto set their hands at Chicago, the said day and year.

> G. B. Porter,
> Th. J. V. Owen,
> William Weatherford,
> To-pen-e-bee, his x mark,
> Sau-ko-noek,
> Che-che-bin-quay, his x mark,
> Joseph, his x mark,
> Wah-mix-i-co, his x mark,
> Ob-wa-qua-unk, his x mark,
> N-saw-way-quet, his x mark,
> Puk-quech-a-min-nee, his x mark,
> Nah-che-wine, his x mark,
> Ke-wase, his x mark,
> Wah-bou-seh, his x mark,
> Mang-e-sett, his x mark,
> Caw-we-saut, his x mark,
> Ah-be-te-ke-zhic, his x mark,
> Pat-e-go-shuc, his x mark,
> E-to-wow-cote, his x mark,
> Shim-e-nah, his x mark,
> O-chee-pwaise, his x mark,
> Ce-nah-ge-win, his x mark,
> Shaw-waw-nas-see, his x mark,
> Shab-eh-nay, his x mark,
> Mac-a-ta-o-shic, his x mark,
> Squah-ke-zic, his x mark,
> Mah-che-o-tah-way, his x mark,
> Cha-ke-te-ah, his x mark,
> Me-am-ese, his x mark,
> Shay-tee, his x mark,

Kee-new, his x mark,
Ne-bay-noc-scum, his x mark,
Naw-bay-caw, his x mark,
O'Kee-mase, his x mark,
Saw-o-tup, his x mark,
Me-tai-way, his x mark,
Na-ma-ta-way-shuc, his x mark,
Shaw-waw-nuk-wuk, his x mark,
Nah-che-wah, his x mark,
Sho-bon-nier, his x mark,
Me-nuk-quet, his x mark,
Chis-in-ke-bah, his x mark,
Mix-e-maung, his x mark,
Nah-bwait, his x mark,
Sen-e-bau-um, his x mark,
Puk-won, his x mark,
Wa-be-no-say, his x mark,
Mon-tou-ish, his x mark,
No-nee, his x mark,
Mas-quat, his x mark,
Sho-min, his x mark,
Ah-take, his x mark,
He-me-nah-wah, his x mark,
Che-pec-co-quah, his x mark,
Mis-quab-o-no-quah, his x mark,
Wah-be-Kai, his x mark,
Ma-ca-ta-ke-shic, his x mark,
Sho-min, (2d.) his x mark,
She-mah-gah, his x mark,
O'ke-mah-wah-ba-see, his x mark,
Na-mash, his x mark,
Shab-y-a-tuk, his x mark,
Ah-cah-o-mah, his x mark,
Quah-quah, tah, his x mark,
Ah-sag-a-mish-cum, his x mark,
Pa-mob-a-mee, his x mark,
Nay-o-say, his x mark,
Ce-tah-quah, his x mark,
Ce-ku-tay, his x mark,
Sauk-ee, his x mark,
Ah-quee-wee, his x mark,

Ta-cau-ko, his x mark,
Me-shim-e-nah, his x mark,
Wah-sus-kuk, his x mark,
Pe-nay-o-cat, his x mark,
Pay-maw-suc, his x mark,
Pe-she-ka, his x mark,
Shaw-we-mon-e-tay, his x mark,
Ah-be-nab, his x mark,
Sau-sau-quas-see, his x mark,
In presence of—
Wm. Lee D. Ewing, secretary to commission,
E. A. Brush,
Luther Rice, interpreter,
James Conner, interpreter,
John T. Schermerhorn, commissioner, etc. west,
A. C. Pepper, S. A. R. P.
Gho. Kercheval, sub-agent,
Geo. Bender, major, Fifth Regiment Infantry,
D. Wilcox, captain, Fifth Regiment,
J. M. Baxley, captain, Fifth Infantry,
R. A. Forsyth, U. S. Army,
L. T. Jamison, lieutenant, U. S. Army,
E. K. Smith, lieutenant, Fifth Infantry,
P. Maxwell, assistant surgeon,
J. Allen, lieutenant, Fifth Infantry,
I. P. Simonton, lieutenant, U. S. Army,
George F. Turner, assistant surgeon, U. S. Army,
Richd. J. Hamilton,
Robert Stuart,
Jona. McCarty,
Daniel Jackson, of New York,
Jno. H. Kinzie,
Robt. A. Kinzie,
G. S. Hubbard,
J. C. Schwarz, adjutant general M. M.
Jn. B. Beaubrier,
James Kinzie,
Jacob Beeson,
Saml. Humes Porter,
Andw. Porter,
Gabriel Godfroy,

A. H. Arndt,
Laurie Marsh,
Joseph Chaunier,
John Watkins,
B. B. Kercheval,
Jas. W. Berry,
Wm. French,
Thomas Forsyth,
Pierre Menard, Fils,
Edmd. Roberts,
Geo. Hunt,
Isaac Nash.

SCHEDULE "A."

(Referred to in the Treaty, containing the sums payable to Individuals in lieu of Reservations.)

Dollars.
Jesse Walker 1500
Henry Cleveland 800
Rachel Hall 600
Sylvia Hall 600
Joseph Laframboise and children 1000
Victoire Porthier and her children 700
Jean Bt. Miranda
Jane Miranda
Rosetta Miranda
Thomas Miranda} For each of whom John H. Kinzie is Trustee 300
200
300
400
Alexander Muller, Gholson Kercheval, trustee 800
Paschal Muller, Gholson Kercheval, trustee 800
Margaret Muller 200
Socra Muller 200
Angelique Chevalier 200
Josette Chevallier 200
Joseph Chevalier 400
Fanny Leclare (Captain David Hunter, Trustee) 400
Daniel Bourassa's children 600
Nancy Contraman
Sally Contraman
Betsey Contraman} For each of whom J. B Campbell is Trustee 600

Alexis Laframboise 800
Alexis Laframbois' children 1200
Mrs. Mann's children 600
Mrs. Mann (daughter of Antoine Ouilmet) 400
Geo. Turkey's children (Fourtier) Th. J. V. Owen Trustee 500
Jacques Chapeau's children, Th. J. V. Owen Trustee 600
Antonie Roscum's children 750
Francois Burbonnais' Senrs. children 400
Francis Burbonnais'Jnr. children 300
John Bt. Cloutier's children, (Robert A. Kinsie Trustee) 600
Claude Lafromboise's children 300
Antoine Ouilmet's children 200
Josette Ouilmot (John H. Kinzie, Trustee) 200
Mrs. Welsh (daughter of Antoine Ouilmet) 200
Alexander Robinson's children 400
Billy Caldwell's children 600
Mo-ah-way 200
Medare B. Beaubien 300
Charles H. Beaubien 300
John K. Clark's Indian children, (Richard J. Hamilton, Trustee) 400
Josette Juno and her children 1000
Angelique Juno 300
Josette Beaubien's children 1000
Mah-go-que's child (James Kinzie, Trustee) 300
Esther, Rosene and Eleanor Bailly 500
Sophia, Hortense and Therese Bailly 1000
Rosa and Mary children of Hoo-mo-ni-gah wife of Stephen Mack 600
Jean Bt. Rabbu's children 400
Francis Chevallier's children 800
Mrs. Nancy Jamison and child 800
Co-pah, son of Archange 250
Martha Burnett (R. A. Forsyth, Trustee) 1000
Isadore Chabert's child (G. S. Hubbard Trustee) 400
Chee-bee-quai or Mrs. Allen 500
Luther Rice and children 2500
John Jones 1000
Pierre Corbonno's Children 800
Pierre Chalipeaux's children 1000
Phoebe Treat and children 1000
Robert Forsyth of St. Louis Mo 500
Alexander Robinson 5000

Billy Caldwell 5000
Joseph Laframboise 3000
Nis noan see (B. B. Kercheval Trustee) 200
Margaret Hall 1000
James, William, David and Sarah children of Margaret Hall 3200
Margaret Ellen Miller, Montgomery Miller and Finly Miller, grandchildren of Margaret Hall, for each of whom Richard J. Hamilton of Chicago is Trustee 800
Jean Letendre's children 200
Bernard Grignon 100
Josette Polier 100
Joseph Vieux, Jacques Vieux, Louis Vieux, and Josette Vieux each $100 400
Angelique Hardwick's children 1800
Joseph Bourassa and Mark Bourassa 200
Jude Bourassa and Therese Bourassa 200
Dollars.
Stephen Bourassa and Gabriel Bourassa 200
Alexander Bourassa and James Bourassa 200
Elai Bourassa and Jerome Bourassa 200
M. D. Bourassa 100
Ann Rice and her Son William M. Rice and Nephew John Leib 1000
Agate Biddle and her children 900
Magdaline Laframboise and her son 400
Therese Schandler 200
Joseph Daily's son and daughter Robert and Therese 500
Therese Lawe and George Lawe 200
David Lawe and Rachel Lawe 200
Rebecca Lawe and Maria Lawe 200
Polly Lawe and Jane Lawe 200
Appotone Lawe 100
Angelique Vieux and Amable Vieux 200
Andre Vieux and Nicholas Vieux 200
Pierre Vieux and Maria Vieux 200
Madaline Thibeault 100
Paul Vieux and Joseph Vieux 200
Susanne Vieux 100
Louis Grignon and his son Paul 200
Paul Grignon Sen'r. and Amable Grignon 200
Perish and Robert Grignon 200
Catist Grignon and Elizabeth Grignon 200
Ursal Grignon and Charlotte Grignon 200
Louise Grignon and Rachel Grignon 200

Agate Porlier and George Grignon 200
Amable Grignon and Emily Grignon 200
Therese Grignon and Simon Grignon 200
William Burnett (B. B. Kercheval Trustee) 1000
Shan-na-nees 400
Josette Beaubien 500
For the Chippewa, Ottawa, and Potawatamie Students at the Choctaw Academy. The Hon. R. M. Johnson to be the Trustee. 5000
James and Richard J. Connor 700
Pierre Duverney and Children 300
Joshua Boyd's Children (Geo. Boyd Esq to be the Trustee.) 500
Joseph Bailly 4000
R. A. Forsyth 3000
Gabriel Godfroy 2420
Thomas R. Covill 1300
George Hunt 750
James Kinzie 5000
Joseph Chaunier 550
John and Mark Noble 180
Alexis Provansalle 100
One hundred thousand dollars $100,000
SCHEDULE "B."
(Referred to in the treaty containing the sums payable to individuals, on claims admitted to be justly due, and directed to be paid.) [See Second Amendment, at end of this treaty.]
Dollars.
Brewster Hogan & Co. 343
John S. C. Hogan 50
Frederick H. Contraman 200
Brookfield & Bertrand 100
R. E. Heacock 100
George W. McClure, U. S. A. 125
David McKee 180
Oliver Emmell 300
George Hollenbeck 100
Martha Gray 78
Charles Taylor 187
Joseph Naper 71
John Mann 200
James Walker 200
Dollars.

John Blackstone 100
Harris & McCord 175
George W. Dole 133
George Haverhill 60
William Whistler, U. S. A. 1000
Squire Thompson 100
C. C. Trowbridge 2000
Louis Druillard 350
Abraham Francis 25
D. R. Bearss & Co 250
Dr. E. Winslow 150
Nicholas Klinger 77
Joseph Porthier 200
Clark Hollenbeck 50
Henry Enslen 75
Robert A. Kinzie 1216
Joseph Ogie 200
Thomas Hartzell 400
Calvin Britain 46
Benjamin Fry 400
Pierre F. Navarre 100
C. H. Chapman 30
James Kinzie 300
G. S. Hubbard 125
Jacque Jenveaux 150
John B. Du Charme 55
John Wright 15
James Galloway 200
William Marquis 150
Louis Chevalier, Adm'r of J. B. Chevalier dec'd 112
Solomon McCullough 100
Joseph Curtis 50
Edward E. Hunter 90
Rachel Legg 25
Peter Lamseet 100
Robert Beresford 200
G. W. & W. Laird 150
M. B. Beaubien 440
Jeduthan Smith 60
Edmund Weed 100
Philip Maxwell, U. S. A. 35

Henry Gratiot 116
Tyler K. Blodgett 50
Nehemiah King 125
S. P. Brady 188
James Harrington 68
Samuel Ellice 50
Peter Menard, Maumee 500
John W. Anderson 350
David Bailey 50
Wm. G. Knaggs 100
John Hively 150
John B. Bertrand, Sen'r 50
Robert A. Forsyth 3000
Maria Kercheval 3000
Alice Hunt 3000
Jane C. Forsyth 3000
John H. Kinzie 5000
Ellen M. Wolcott 5000
Maria Hunter 5000
Robert A. Kinzie 5000
Samuel Godfroy 120
John E. Schwarz 4800
Joseph Loranger 5000
H. B. and G. W. Hoffman 358
Phelps & Wendell 660
Henry Johns 270
Benjamin C. Hoyt 20
John H. Kinzie, in trust for the heirs of Jos. Miranda, dec'd 250
Francis Burbonnais, Senr 500
Francis Burbonnais, junr 200
R. A. Forsyth, in trust for Catherine McKenzie 1000
James Laird 50
Montgomery Evans 250
Joseph Bertrand, jr 300
Dollars.
George Hunt 900
Benjamin Sherman 150
W. and F. Brewster, Assignees of Joseph Bertrand, Senr 700
John Forsyth, in trust for the heirs of Charles Peltier, dec'd 900
William Hazard 30
James Shirley 125

Jacob Platter 25
John B. Bourie 2500
B. B. Kercheval 1500
Charles Lucier 75
Mark Beaubien 500
Catharine Stewart 82
Francis Mouton 200
Dr. William Brown 40
R. A. Forsyth, in trust for heirs of Charles Guion 200
Joseph Bertrand, Senr 652
Moses Rice 800
James Connor 2250
John B. Du Charme 250
Coquillard & Comparet 5000
Richard J. Hamilton 500
Adolphus Chapin 80
John Dixon 140
Wm. Huff 81
Stephen Mack, in trust for the heirs of Stephen Mack, dec'd 500
Thomas Forsyth 1500
Felix Fontaine 200
Jacque Mette 200
Francis Boucher 250
Margaret Helm 2000
O. P. Lacy 1000
Henry and Richard J. Connor 1500
James W. Craig 50
R. A. Forsyth (Maumee) 1300
Antoine Peltier do. 200
R. A. Forsyth, in trust for Wau-se-on-o-quet 300
John E. Hunt 1450
Payne C. Parker 70
Isaac Hull 1000
Foreman Evans 32
Horatio N. Curtis 300
Ica Rice 250
Thomas P. Quick 35
George B. Woodcox 60
John Woodcox 40
George B. Knaggs 1400
Ebenezer Read 100

George Pomeroy 150
Thomas K. Green 70
William Mieure, in trust for Willis Fellows 500
Z. Cicott 1800
John Johnson 100
Antoine Antilla 100
John Baldwin 500
Isaac G. Bailey 100
James Cowen 35
Joseph D. Lane 50
T. E. Phelps 250
Edmund Roberts 50
Augustus Bona 60
E. C. Winter & Co 1850
Charles W. Ewing 200
Antoine Ouilmett 800
John Bt. Chandonai, ($1000 of this sum to be paid to Robert Stuart, agent of American Fur Company, by the particular request of Jno. B. Chandonai,) 2500
Lowrin Marsh 3290
P. & J. J. Godfroy 2000
David Hull 500
Andrew Drouillard 500
Jacob Beeson & Co 220
Jacob Beeson 900
John Anderson 600
John Green 100
James B. Campbell 600
Dollars.
Pierre Menard, Jun. in right of G. W. Campbell 250
George E. Walker 1000
Joseph Thebault 50
Gideon Lowe, U. S. A. 160
Pierre Menard, Jun 2000
John Tharp 45
Pierre Menard, Junr. in trust for Marie Tremblê 500
Henry B. Stillman 300
John Hamblin 500
Francois Pagê 100
George Brooks 20
Franklin McMillan 100
Lorance Shellhouse 30

Martin G. Shellhouse 35
Peter Bellair 150
Joseph Morass 200
John I. Wendell 2000
A. T. Hatch 300
Stephen Downing 100
Samuel Miller 100
Moses Hardwick 75
Margaret May 400
Frances Felix 1100
John B. Bourie 500
Harriet Ewing 500
Nancy Hedges 500
David Bourie 500
Caroline Ferry 500
Bowrie & Minie 500
Charles Minie 600
Francis Minie 700
David Bourie 150
Henry Ossum Reed 200
Françoise Bezion 2500
Dominique Rousseau 500
Hanna & Taylor 1570
John P. Hedges 1000
Francoise Chobare 1000
Isadore Chobare 600
Jacob Leephart 700
Amos Amsden 400
Nicholas Boilvin 350
Archibald Clyburn 200
William Conner (Michigan) 70
Tunis S. Wendall 500
Noel Vasseur 800
James Abbott, agent of the American Fur Company 2300
Robert Stewart, agent of the American Fur Company 17000
Solomon Jeauneau 2100
John Bt. Beaubien 250
Stephen Mack, Jnr 350
John Lawe 3000
Alexis Larose 1000
Daniel Whitney 1350

P. & A. Grignon 650
Louis Grignon 2000
Jacques Vieux 2000
Laframboise & Bourassa 1300
Heirs of N. Boilvin, deceased 1000
John K. Clark 400
William G. & G. W. Ewing 5000
Rufus Hitchcock 400
Reed and Coons 200
B. H. Laughton 1000
Rufus Downing 500
Charles Reed
200
One hundred and seventy-five thousand dollars $175,000
The above claims have been admitted and directed to be paid, only in case they be accepted in full of all claims and demands up to the present date.

Th. J. V. Owen,
William Weatherford.

Agreeably to the stipulations contained in the 3d Article of the Treaty, there have been purchased and delivered at the request of the Indians, goods, provisions and horses to the amount of sixty-five thousand dollars (leaving the balance to be supplied in the year one thousand eight hundred and thirty-four, thirty-five thousand dollars.)

As evidence of the purchase and delivery as aforesaid under the direction of the said Commissioners, and that the whole of the same have been received by the said Indians, the said George B. Porter, Thomas J. V. Owen and William Weatherford, and the undersigned Chiefs and Head-men on behalf of the said United Nation of Indians have hereunto set their hands the twenty-seventh day of September in the year of our Lord one thousand eight hundred and thirty-three.

G. B. Porter,
Th. J. V. Owen,
William Weatherford,
Jo-pen-e-bee, his x mark,
We-saw, his x mark,
Ne-kaw-nosh-kee, his x mark,
Wai-saw-o-ke-ne-aw, his x mark,
Ne-see-waw-bee-tuck, his x mark,
Kai-kaw-tai-mon, his x mark,

Saw-ko-nosh,
Tshee-Tshee-chin-be-quay, his x mark,
Joseph, his x mark,
Shab-e-nai, his x mark,
Ah-be-te-ke-zhic, his x mark,
E-to-won-cote, his x mark,
Shab-y-a-tuk, his x mark,
Me-am-ese, his x mark,
Wah-be-me-mee, his mark,
Shim-e-nah, his x mark,
We-in-co, his x mark,
In presence of—
Wm. Lee D. Ewing, secretary to the commission,
R. A. Forsyth, U. S. Army,
Madn. F. Abbott,
Saml. Humes Porter,
Andw. Porter,
Joseph Bertrand, junr.
Jno. H. Kinzie,
James Conner, interpreter,
J. E. Schwarz, adjutant-general, M. M.
Sept. 27, 1833. | 7 Stat., 442.

Articles supplementary, to the treaty made at Chicago, in the State of Illinois, on the 26th day of September, one thousand eight hundred and thirty-three, between George B. Porter, Thomas J. V. Owen and William Weatherford, Commissioners on the part of the United States, of the one part, and the United Nation of Chippewa, Ottowa, and Potawatamie Indians, of the other part, concluded at the same place on the twenty-seventh day of September, one thousand eight hundred and thirty-three, between the said Commissioners on the part of the United States of the one part, and the Chiefs and Head-men of the said United Nation of Indians, residing upon the reservations of land situated in the Territory of Michigan, south of Grand river, of the other part.

Article 1

The said chiefs and head-men cede to the United States, all their land situate in the Territory of Michigan south of Grand river being the reservation at Notawasepe of 4 miles square contained in the 3d clause of the 2d article of the treaty made at Chicago, on the 29th day of August 1821, and the ninety-nine sections of land contained in the treaty made at St. Joseph on the 19th day of Sept. 1827;—and also the tract of land on St. Joseph river opposite the town of Niles, and extending to the line of the State of Indiana, on which the villages of To-pe-ne-bee and Pokagon are situated, supposed to contain about 49 sections.

Article 2

In consideration of the above cession, it is hereby agreed that the said chiefs and head-men and their immediate tribes shall be considered as parties to the said treaty to which this is supplementary, and be entitled to participate in all the provisions therein contained, as a part of the United Nation; and further, that there shall be paid by the United States, the sum of one hundred thousand dollars: to be applied as follows.

Ten thousand dollars in addition to the general fund of one hundred thousand dollars, contained in the said treaty to satisfy sundry individuals in behalf of whom reservations were asked which the Commissioners refused to grant;—the manner in which the same is to be paid being set forth in the schedule "A," hereunto annexed.

Twenty-five thousand dollars in addition to the sum of one hundred and fifty thousand dollars contained in the said Treaty, to satisfy the claims made against all composing the United Nation of Indians, which they have admitted to be justly due, and directed to be paid according to Schedule "B," to the Treaty annexed.

Twenty-five thousand dollars, to be paid in goods, provisions and horses, in addition to the one hundred thousand dollars contained in the Treaty.

And forty thousand dollars to be paid in annuities of two thousand dollars a year for twenty years, in addition to the two hundred and eighty thousand dollars inserted in the Treaty, and divided into payments of fourteen thousand dollars a year.

Article 3

All the Indians residing on the said reservations in Michigan shall remove therefrom within three years from this date, during which time they shall not be disturbed in their possession, nor in hunting upon the lands as heretofore. In the mean time no interruption shall be offered to the survey and sale of the same by the United States. In case, however, the said Indians shall sooner remove the Government may take immediate possession thereof.

Article 4

[Stricken out. See 4th Amendment at end of treaty.]
These supplementary articles after the same shall have been ratified by the President and Senate of the United States shall be binding on the contracting parties.

In testimony whereof, the said George B. Porter, Thomas J. V. Owen, and William Weatherford, and the undersigned chiefs and head men of the said United Nation of Indians, have hereunto set their hands at Chicago, the said day and year.

G. B. Porter,
Th. J. V. Owen,

William Weatherford,
To-pen-e-bee, his x mark,
We-saw, his x mark,
Ne-kaw-nosh-kee, his x mark,
Wai-saw-o-ko-ne-aw, his x mark,
Po-ka-gon, his x mark,
Kai-kaw-tai-mon, his x mark,
Pe-pe-ah, his x mark,
Ne-see-waw-bee-tuck, his x mark,
Kitchee-bau, his x mark,
Pee-chee-ko, his x mark,
Nai-gaw-geucke, his x mark,
Wag-maw-kan-so, his x mark,
Mai-go-sai, his x mark,
Nai-chee-wai, his x mark,
Aks-puck-sick, his x mark,
Kaw-kai-mai, his x mark,
Mans-kai-sick, his x mark,
Pam-ko-wuck, his x mark,
No-taw-gai, his x mark,
Kauk-muck-kisin, his x mark,
Wee-see-mon, his x mark,
Mo-so-ben-net, his x mark,
Kee-o-kum, his x mark,
Maatch-kee, his x mark,
Kaw-bai-me-sai, his x mark,
Wees-ke-qua-tap, his x mark,
Ship-she-wuh-no, his x mark,
Wah-co-mah-o-pe-tuk, his x mark,
Ne-so-wah-quet, his x mark,
Shay-o-no, his x mark,
Ash-o-nees, his x mark,
Mix-i-nee, his x mark,
Ne-wah-ox-sec, his x mark,
Sauk-e-mau, his x mark,
Shaw-waw-nuk-wuk, his x mark,
Mo-rah, his x mark,
Suk-see, his x mark,
Quesh-a-wase, his x mark,
Pat-e-go-to, his x mark,
Mash-ke-oh-see, his x mark,

Mo-nase, his x mark,
Wab-e-kaie, his x mark,
Shay-oh-new, his x mark,
Mo-gua-go, his x mark,
Pe-qua-shuc, his x mark,
A-muwa-noc-sey, his x mark,
Kau-ke-che-ke-to, his x mark,
Shaw-waw-nuk-wuk, his x mark,
In presence of—
Wm. Lee D. Ewing, secretary to the commission,
E. A. Brush,
Luther Rice, interpreter,
James Conner, interpreter,
Joseph Bertrand, jr., interpreter,
Geo. Kercheval, sub Indian agent,
J. L. Thompson, lieutenant Fifth Infantry,
J. Allen, lieutenant Fifth Infantry.
P. Maxwell, assistant surgeon U. S. Army,
Geo. F. Turner, assistant surgeon U. S. Army,
B. B. Kercheval,
Thomas Forsyth,
Daniel Jackson, of New York,
J. E. Schwarz, adjutant-general M. M.
Robt. A. Kinzie,
G. S. Hubbard,
Geo. Bender, major Fifth Regiment Infantry,
D. Wilcox, captain Fifth Regiment,
J. M. Baxley, captain Fifth Infantry,
R. A. Forsyth, U. S. Army,
L. T. Jamison, lieutenant U. S. Army,
O. K. Smith, lieutenant Fifth Infantry,
L. M. Taylor,
Pierre Menard, fils,
Jacob Beeson.
Samuel Humes Porter,
Edmd. Roberts,
Jno. H. Kinzie,
Jas. W. Berry,
Gabriel Godfroy, jr.
Geo. Hunt,
A. H. Arndt,

Andw. Porter,

Isaac Nash,

Richard J. Hamilton.

SCHEDULE "A",

Referred to in the Article supplementary to the Treaty, containing the sums payable to Individuals, in lieu of Reservations of Land.

Dollars.

Po-ka-gon 2000

Rebecca Burnett

Mary Burnett} Edward Brooks Trustee for each 500

250

Martha Burnett (R. A. Forsyth Trustee) 250

Madaline Bertrand 200

Joseph Bertrand Junr 200

Luke Bertrand Junr 200

Benjamin Bertrand 200

Lawrence Bertrand 200

Theresa Bertrand 200

Amable Bertrand 200

Julianne Bertrand 200

Joseph H. Bertrand 100

Mary M. Bertrand 100

M. L. Bertrand 100

John B. Du Charme 200

Elizabeth Du Charme (R. A. Forsyth Trustee) 800

George Henderson 400

Mary Nado and children 400

John Bt. Chandonai 1000

Charles Chandonai

Mary Chandonai (For each of whom R. A. Forsyth is Trustee) 400

Mary St. Comb and children 300

Sa-gen-nais' daughter 200

Me-chain, daughter of Pe-che-co 200

Alexis Rolan 200

Polly Neighbush 200

Francois Page's wife and children 200

Pierre F. Navarre's children 100

Jarmont (half breed) 100

Ten thousand dollars $10,000

Sept. 27, 1833.

Agreeably to the stipulations contained in the Articles supplementary to the Treaty, there have been purchased and delivered at the request of the Indians, Goods, Provisions and Horses to the amount of fifteen thousand dollars (leaving the balance to be supplied hereafter ten thousand dollars.)

As evidence of the purchase and delivery as aforesaid, under the direction of the said commissioners, and that the whole of the same been received by the said Indians, and the said George B. Porter, Thomas J. V. Owen, and William Weatherford, and the undersigned chiefs and head men on behalf of the said United Nation of Indians, have hereunto set their hands the twenty-seventh day of September, in the year of our Lord one thousand eight hundred and thirty-three.

G. B. Porter,
Th. J. V. Owen,
William Weatherford,
To-pen-e-bee, his x mark,
Wee-saw, his x mark,
Ne-kaw-nosh-kee, his x mark,
Wai-saw-o-ko-ne-aw, his x mark,
Ne-see-waw-be-tuk, his x mark,
Kai-kaw-tai-mon, his x mark,
Saw-Ka-Nosh, his x mark,
Tshee-tshee-chin-ke-bequay, his x mark,
Joseph, his x mark,
Shab-e-nai, his x mark,
Ah-be-to-ke-Zhic, his x mark,
E-to-wau-coto, his x mark,
Shab-y-a-tuk, his x mark,
Me-am-ese, his x mark,
Wah-be-me-mee, his x mark,
Shim-e-nah, his x mark,
We-in-co, his x mark,
In presence of—
Wm. Lee D. Ewing, secretary to the commission,
R. A. Forsyth, U. S. Army,
John H. Kinzie,
Madn. F. Abbott,
Saml. Humes Porter,

Joseph Bertrand, junr.
Andw. Porter,
J. E. Schwarz, adjutant-general M. M.
James Conner, interpreter.

On behalf of the Chiefs and Head men of the United Nation of Indians who signed the treaty to which these articles are supplementary we hereby, in evidence of our concurrence therein, become parties thereto.

And, as since the signing of the treaty a part of the band residing on the reservations in the Territory of Michigan, have requested, on account of their religious creed, permission to remove to the northern part of the peninsula of Michigan, it is agreed that in case of such removal the just proportion of all annuities payable to them under former treaties and that arising from the sale of the reservation on which they now reside shall be paid to them at, L'arbre, Croche

Witness our hands, the said day and year.
Saw-ka-nosh, his x mark,
Che-ohe-bin-quay, his x mark,
Ah-be-te-ke-zhic, his x mark,
Shab-e-nay, his x mark,
O-cheep-pwaise, his x mark,
Maug-e-sett, his x mark,
Shim-e-nah, his x mark,
Ke-me-nah-wah, his x mark,
In the presence of—
Wm. Lee D. Ewing, secretary to the commission,
Jno. H. Kinzie,
Richd. J. Hamilton,
Robert Stuart,
R. A. Forsyth, U. S. Army,
Saml. Humes Porter,
J. E. Schwarz, adjutant-genera. M. M.
James Conner, interpreter.

The Commissioners certify that when these supplementary articles were ready for signature, the original paper of which the annexed is a copy was presented by Messrs. Peter and James J. Godfroy, and the due execution of it was made satisfactorily appear to the Commissioners, the subscribing witnesses R A Forsyth and Robert A Kinzie being present.—The Chiefs and Head men present recognizing this as a reservation, it was agreed that it shall be considered in the same light as though the purport of the instrument had been inserted in the body of the treaty;—with the understanding that the rejection of it by the President and Senate of the United States shall not affect the validity of the treaty.

G. B. PORTER,
TH. J. V. OWEN,
WILLIAM WEATHERFORD.
(Copy of the instrument referred to in the above certificate.—)

May 18, 1830.

Know all men by these presents that we the undersigned Chiefs and Young men of the Potawatamie tribe of Indians living at Na-to-wa-se-pe in the territory of Michigan, for and in consideration of the friendship and sundry services rendered to us by Peter and James J. Godfroy we do hereby by these presents give, grant, alien, transfer and convey unto the said Godfroys their heirs and assigns forever one entire section of land situate lying and being on our reserve of Na-to-wa-se-pe, in the Territory aforesaid to be located by said Godfroys wherever on said reserve they shall think it more to their advantage and benefit.

It is moreover the wishes of the undersigned Chiefs and Young men as aforesaid, that so soon as there shall be a treaty held between the United States and our said tribe of Pottawatamies, that our great father the President confirm and make good this our grant unto them, the said Godfroys by issuing a patent therefor to them and to their heirs forever.—In so doing our great father will accomplish the wishes of his children.

Done at Detroit, this eighteenth day of May, A. D. one thousand eight hundred and thirty.

In witness whereof, we have hereunto signed, sealed, and set our hands and seals, the day and year last above written.

Penenchese, his x mark, [L. S.]
Pit-goit-ke-se, his x mark, [L. S.]
Nah-o-te-nan, his x mark, [L. S.]
Ke-a-sac-wa, his x mark, [L. S.]
Sko-paw-ka, his x mark, [L. S.]
Ce-ce-baw, his x mark, [L. S.]
Na-wa-po-to, his x mark, [L. S.]
To-ta-gas, his x mark, [L. S.]
Pierre Morin, alias Perish, his x mark, [L. S.]
We-say-gah, his x mark, [L. S.]
Signed, sealed, and delivered in the presence of us—
R. A. Forsyth,
Robt. A. Kinzie,

G. Godfroy,
Witnesses to the signature of Pierre Morin, alias Perish, and Wa-say-gah.
Richard Godfroy,
Francis Mouton.
Chicago, Illinois, Oct. 1, 1834.
THO. J. V. OWEN, Esqr.
U. S. Indian Agent.
Oct. 1, 1834.

FATHER: Feeling a disposition to comply with the resolution of Senate of the United States, and the views of the Government in relation to an alteration in the boundaries of the country ceded to the United nation of Chippewa, Ottawa, and Potawatamie Indians at the treaty at Chicago in the State of Illinois, concluded on the 26th and 27th days of September 1833:—we therefore propose as the chiefs of the said united nation, and for and on their behalf that we will accept of the following alteration in the boundaries of the said tract of country viz:—Beginning at the mouth of Boyer's river; thence down the Missouri river, to a point thereon; from which a due east line would strike the northwest corner of the State of Missouri; thence along the said east line, to the northwest corner of said State; then along the northern boundary line of the said State of Missouri, till it strikes the line of the lands of the Sac and Fox Indians; thence northwardly along said line to a point from which a west line would strike the sources of the Little Sioux river; thence along said west line, till it strikes the said sources of said river; then down said river to its mouth; thence down the Missouri river to the place of beginning: Provided the said boundary shall contain five million of acres; but should it contain more, then said boundaries are to be reduced so as to contain the said five millions of acres.

And, in consideration of the alteration of said boundary we ask that ten thousand dollars should be paid to such commissioner, as shall be designated by us to receive the same west of the Mississippi river, at such place on the tract of country ceded to the said united nation as we may designate, and to be applied, as we may direct for the use and benefit of the said nation. And the further sum of two thousand dollars to be paid to Gholson Kercheval, of Chicago, Ill.: for services rendered the said united nation of Indians during the late war, between the U. S. Government and the Sacs and Foxes; and the further sum of one thousand dollars to George E. Walker for services rendered the said United nation, in bringing Indian prisoners, from west of the Mississippi river to Ottawa, Lasalle county, Ill. for whose appearance at the circuit court of said county, the said nation was bound.

The foregoing propositions are made with the expectation, that with the exception of the alteration in the proposed boundary, and the indemnity herein demanded as an equivalent for said exchange, the whole of the treaty made and concluded at this place on the 26th and 27th days of September 1833, be ratified as made and concluded at that time, within the space of five months from the present date; otherwise it is our wish that the whole of the said treaty should be considered as cancelled.

In witness whereof, we, the undersigned chiefs of the said United Nation of Chippewa, Ottowa, and Pattawatamie Indians, being specially delegated with power and authority to effect this negotiation, have hereto set our hands and seals, at Chicago, in the State of Illinois, on the first day of October, A. D. 1834.

R. Caldwell, [L. S.]
Kee-tshee-zhing-ee-beh, his x mark, [L. S.]
Tshee-tshee-beeng-guay, his x mark, [L. S.]
Joseph, his x mark, [L. S.]
Ob-ee-tah-kee-zhik, his x mark, [L. S.]
Wau-bon-see, his x mark, [L. S.]
Kay-kot-ee-mo, his x mark, [L. S.]
In presence of—
Richd. J. Hamilton,
Jno. H. Kenzie,
Dr. P. Maxwell, U. S. Army,
J. Grant, jr.,
E. M. Owen,
J. M. Baxley, captain Fifth Infantry.

Treaty of New Echota (1835)

The Treaty of New Echota (1835) was a removal agreement between the federal government and a minority faction of the Cherokee Nation signed on December 29, 1835, in the town of New Echota, Georgia. According to the terms of the treaty, the Cherokee Nation exchanged all their land east of Mississippi for a large tract of land in Indian Territory and $5 million.

In 1830, Congress passed the Indian Removal Act, which provided funds for the president to conduct land-exchange treaties with Natives living east of the Mississippi. Initially, federal negotiators tried to coerce principal chief John Ross and members of the Cherokee National Council to remove to the West. When federal negotiators were unable to convince the elected Cherokee leadership to sign a removal treaty, President Andrew Jackson sent General William Carroll and Reverend John Schermerhorn to draw up a treaty with a few prominent Cherokees who favored removal. Members of this faction, later called the Treaty Party, included Major Ridge, John Ridge, Stand Watie, and Elias Boudinot.

Major Ridge was a former acting chief of the Cherokee Nation and a wealthy, slave-owning planter. He was familiar with the laws of the Nation and knew he was in violation of the Blood Law, which made the sale or cession of Cherokee land a crime punishable by death. However, he and other members of the faction were greatly disturbed by the constant harassment they and other Natives received from white settlers. In 1829 and 1830, the Georgia legislature passed a series of laws that outlawed the Cherokee government and authorized a survey of Cherokee land and a lottery to distribute the land to the white residents of Georgia. The legislature also passed the Indian Code, which prohibited Cherokees from testifying in court against white persons, mining gold on their own land, speaking against removal, and meeting in council.

After several trips to Washington to talk to federal officials and a survey of the countryside, Ridge believed that it was in the best interest of the Cherokee Nation as a whole to relocate in the West. He thought that further resistance to federal removal demands would be futile, that the Cherokees should get the best terms possible from the government and depart before there was more bloodshed.

Immediately after signing the document and receiving their payment from the government, the members of the Treaty Party moved west. They selected the best land in the new Cherokee Nation and made alliances with the three thousand "Old Settler" Cherokees, who had left the main body of the Cherokee Nation in the late 18th and early 19th centuries for various reasons. While the Treaty Party adjusted to their homes in the West, principal chief John Ross, members of the Cherokee National Council, and the vast majority of the Cherokees living in the East repudiated the treaty and refused to move.

They vigorously protested the treaty and made their cause known to the American people. Regardless of the protests, the Senate ratified the treaty by one vote in May 1836. Undaunted, the Cherokee Nation continued to lobby against the treaty and to postpone the removal process. In April 1838, approximately 15,600 of the 16,000 members of the Cherokee Nation signed and presented a petition to Congress requesting that the treaty be voided. Congress ignored the petition.

In May 1838, federal officials became frustrated with the Cherokee resistance. President Martin Van Buren ordered General Winfield Scott and 7,000 soldiers to round up all Cherokees living in Georgia, Alabama, and Tennessee, and place them into camps to prepare for removal. To discourage the people from running away and returning to their homes, Scott had all Cherokee property burned and all crops destroyed. The forced march to the West began during the summer of 1838 and continued through the harsh winter of 1839. Of 16,543 Cherokees and 1,592 slaves removed, one quarter of the people died. The Cherokees call their trek west *Nunna daul Tsuny*—"the trail where they cried."

Once the majority of the Cherokees arrived in the West, the three distinct groups of Cherokee people—the Old Settlers, the Treaty Party, and the Ross Party—were expected to merge into one single nation. Unfortunately, the transition was not easy. Many of the new arrivals were furious with the members of the Treaty Party and wanted to avenge the loss of their relatives and the loss of their homeland. However, Chief John Ross would not authorize the execution of the Treaty Party members.

On the night of June 21, 150 to 200 people gathered at Takatoka Camp Ground to discuss recent events. Angry about removal and holding the Treaty Party responsible for their losses, they decided that now was the right time to enforce the Blood Law on the signers of the Treaty of New Echota. They drew lots to select the assassins. Early in the morning of June 22, the assassins left the campgrounds in search of Major Ridge, John Ridge, Elias Boudinot, and Stand Watie. Both of the Ridges and Boudinot were executed; Stand Watie was able to escape. The executions intensified the preexisting tribal divisions and caused an intermittent civil war to rage through the Cherokee Nation for the next 40 years.

Joyce Ann Kievit

Further Reading

Foreman, Grant. *Indian Removal: The Emigration of the Five Civilized Tribes of Indians*. Norman: University of Oklahoma Press, 1953.

Moulton, Gary E., ed. *The Papers of Chief John Ross*, 2 vols. Norman: University of Oklahoma Press, 1985.

Treaty Site—New Echota, Georgia

Today, New Echota is a historic park located in Calhoun, Georgia. Several timber buildings located at the junction of the Coosawatee and Conasauga Rivers are the only remaining relics of the capital established by the Cherokee Nation in 1825. The story of New Echota begins with change and the hopes of the Cherokees (Ani'-Yun' wiya, or "The People") and ends tragically with the death of a group of important leaders and the forced removal of the majority of the nation's citizens to present-day Oklahoma.

The name New Echota was derived from Chota, an important historic Cherokee city located in present-day Tennessee. Chota describes the center and heart of the Ani'-Yun' wiya.

The Cherokee capital included the print shop of the *Cherokee Phoenix and Indian Advocate*, a bilingual newspaper written and edited by Elias Boudinot (Buck Oowaite) using the Cherokee alphabet invented by Sequoyah in 1821. The printing house was constructed late in 1827. The Vann Tavern, home of missionary Samuel Worcester, one of the major supporters of the Cherokees in Georgia, was also located in the capital. Cherokee surveyors planned the town with a central square and wide main streets. More than 50 people made their homes in the new capital, and many more came to shop, to do business at the government offices, and to attend meetings at the Council House. The Council House in New Echota, along with the Supreme Court building, was the heart of the new government. New Echota was the capital of the eight districts of the Cherokee Nation, which included Hickory Log, Chickmaugee, Chattoogee, Amoah, Etowah, Tahquohee, Awuohee, and Coosewatee. Each district sent four delegates to the National Council, the lower house; in turn, these members elected 12 individuals to the National Committee, an upper house. The National Committee was responsible for electing the main chief, the assistant chief, and the Cherokee Nation's treasurer. This governmental design changed the traditional Cherokee clan organization and instead used the model of the U.S. government: an upper and lower legislature, a high court, and an executive branch. The Council House and the Supreme Court building in New Echota were visible symbols of the new Cherokee Nation. Political treaties changing the course of the nation were debated and signed at the new capital. The Treaty of New Echota (1835) was instrumental in the downfall and eventual assassination of three important Cherokee leaders. Elias Boudinot, John Ridge, and Major Ridge signed a treaty to sell eastern lands, including the area of New Echota, in exchange for land in present-day Oklahoma. The choice to sign and depart for land in Indian Territory or to stay and fight what seemed to be an unstoppable government from taking Cherokee lands in Georgia was a controversial and detailed decision. Not all Cherokees thought that leaving was the only option. Many of the tribe had left for new lands before the treaty in 1835. The Cherokee Nation presented a challenge, asking the U.S. high court to block the removal of the Cherokees from their lands in Georgia as required by the Cherokee Removal Act (1830). The Supreme Court of the United States sided with the Cherokee Nation, but U.S. president Andrew Jackson would not recognize the court decision and ordered removal. The group was forcibly taken from the capital in 1838. This forced removal was known as the Trail of Tears.

After the Cherokees were removed or moved away from the capital, the buildings fell into disrepair. The newspaper offices had been burned to the ground in a raid by the Georgia Guard in 1834. The once-proud capital was a ghost town by 1838. Town structures were torn down for wood or simply lifted from their foundations and relocated to other areas. Today, visitors to New Echota can see recreations of buildings that made up the Cherokee Nation in

1830. In the mid-1950s, Lewis Larsen, Joe Caldwell, and a group of archaeologists began research and restoration work. The Supreme Court and print shop have been reconstructed, and the Vann Tavern has been restored. New Echota is listed on the United States National Register of Historic Places and began operation as a state park in 1962. The buildings are open to the public and host educational events to celebrate Cherokee history and heritage throughout the year.

Pamela Lee Gray

Further Reading

Bays, Brad A. *Townsite Settlement and Dispossession in the Cherokee Nation, 1866–1907.* New York and London: Garland, 1998.

Conley, Robert J. *The Cherokee Nation: A History.* Albuquerque: University of New Mexico Press, 2005.

Finger, John R. *The Eastern Band of Cherokees: 1819–1900.* Knoxville: University of Tennessee Press, 1984.

Document: Treaty of New Echota

Articles of a treaty, concluded at New Echota in the State of Georgia on the 29th day of Decr. 1835 by General William Carroll and John F. Schermerhorn commissioners on the part of the United States and the Chiefs Head Men and People of the Cherokee tribe of Indians.

WHEREAS the Cherokees are anxious to make some arrangements with the Government of the United States whereby the difficulties they have experienced by a residence within the settled parts of the United States under the jurisdiction and laws of the State Governments may be terminated and adjusted; and with a view to reuniting their people in one body and securing a permanent home for themselves and their posterity in the country selected by their forefathers without the territorial limits of the State sovereignties, and where they can establish and enjoy a government of their choice and perpetuate such a state of society as may be most consonant with their views, habits and condition; and as may tend to their individual comfort and their advancement in civilization.

And whereas a delegation of the Cherokee nation composed of Messrs. John Ross. Richard Taylor Danl. McCoy Samuel Gunter and William Rogers with full power and authority to conclude a treaty with the United States did on the 28th day of February 1835 stipulate and agree with the Government of the United States to

Schedule

Schedule and estimated value of the Osage half breed Reservations within the Territory ceded to the Cherokees West of the Mississippi (, referred to in Article 5 on the foregoing treaty) viz:

Augustus Clamont one Section	$6000.
James " " "	1000.
Paul " " "	1300.
Henry " " "	800.
Anthony " " "	1800.
Rosalie " " "	1800.
Emilia D. of Mihanga	1000.
Emilia D. of Shemianga	1300.
	$15,000.

I hereby certify that the above Schedule is the estimated value of the Osage Reservations; as made out and agreed upon with Col. A. P. Chouteau who represented himself as the Agent or Guardian of the above Reservees.

March 14th 1835.

J. F. Schermerhorn

submit to the Senate to fix the amount which should be allowed the Cherokees for their claims and for a cession of their lands east of the Mississippi river, and did agree to abide by the award of the Senate of the United States themselves and to recommend the same to their people for their final determination.

And whereas on such submission the Senate advised "that a sum not exceeding five millions of dollars be paid to the Cherokee Indians for all their lands and possessions east of the Mississippi river."

And whereas this delegation after said award of the Senate had been made, were called upon to submit propositions as to its disposition to be arranged in a treaty which they refused to do, but insisted that the same "should be referred to their nation and there in general council to deliberate and determine on the subject in order to ensure harmony and good feeling among themselves."

And whereas a certain other delegation composed of John Ridge, Elias Boudinot, Archilla Smith S. W. Bell John West Wm. A. Davis and Ezekiel West, who represented that portion of the nation in favor of emigration to the Cherokee country west of the Mississippi entered into propositions for a treaty with John F. Schermerhorn commissioner on the part of the United States which were to be submitted to their nation for their final action and determination:

And whereas the Cherokee people at their last October council at Red Clay, fully authorized and empowered a delegation or committee of twenty persons of their nation to enter into and conclude a treaty with the United States commissioner then present, at that place or elsewhere and as the people had good reason to believe that a treaty would then and there be made or at a subsequent council at New Echota which the commissioners it was well known and understood, were authorized and instructed to convene for said purpose; and since the said delegation have gone on to Washington city, with a view to close negotiations there, as stated by them notwithstanding they were officially informed by the United States commissioner that they would not be received by the President of the United States; and that the Government would transact no business of this nature with them, and that if a treaty was made it must be done here in the nation, where the delegation at Washington last winter urged that it should be done for the purpose of promoting peace and harmony among the people; and since these facts have also been corroborated to us by a communication recently received by the commissioner from the Government of the United States and read and explained to the people in open council and therefore believing said delegation can effect nothing and since our difficulties are daily increasing and our situation is rendered more and more precarious uncertain and insecure in consequence of the legislation of the States; and seeing no effectual way of relief, but in accepting the liberal overtures of the United States.

And whereas Genl William Carroll and John F. Schermerhorn were appointed commissioners on the part of the United States, with full power and authority to conclude a treaty with the Cherokees east and were directed by the President to convene the people of the nation in general council at New Echota and to submit said propositions to them with power and authority to vary the same so as to meet the views of the Cherokees in reference to its details.

And whereas the said commissioners did appoint and notify a general council of the nation to convene at New Echota on the 21st day of December 1835; and informed them that the commissioners would be prepared to make a treaty with the Cherokee people who should assemble there and those who did not come they should conclude gave their assent and sanction to whatever should be transacted at this council and the people having met in council according to said notice.

Therefore the following articles of a treaty are agreed upon and concluded between William Carroll and John F. Schermerhorn commissioners on the part of the United States and the chiefs and head men and people of the Cherokee nation in general council assembled this 29th day of Decr 1835.

Article 1

The Cherokee nation hereby cede relinquish and convey to the United States all the lands owned claimed or possessed by them east of the Mississippi river, and hereby release all their claims upon the United States for spoliations of every kind for and in consideration of the sum of five millions of dollars to be expended paid and invested in the manner stipulated and agreed upon in the following articles But as a question has arisen between the commissioners and the Cherokees whether the Senate in their resolution by which they advised "that a sum not exceeding five millions of dollars be paid to the Cherokee Indians for all their lands and possessions east of the Mississippi river" have included and made any allowance or consideration for claims for spoliations it is therefore agreed on the part of the United States that this question shall be again submitted to the Senate for their consideration and decision and if no allowance was made for spoliations that then an additional sum of three hundred thousand dollars be allowed for the same.

Article 2

Whereas by the treaty of May 6th 1828 and the supplementary treaty thereto of Feb. 14th 1833 with the Cherokees west of the Mississippi the United States guarantied and secured to be conveyed by patent, to the Cherokee nation of Indians the following tract of country "Beginning at a point on the old western territorial line of Arkansas Territory being twenty-five miles north from the point where the territorial line crosses Arkansas river, thence running from said north point south on the said territorial line where the said territorial line crosses Verdigris river; thence down said Verdigris river to the Arkansas river; thence down said Arkansas to a point where a stone is placed opposite the east or lower bank of Grand river at its junction with the Arkansas; thence running south forty-four degrees west one mile; thence in a straight line to a point four miles northerly, from the mouth of the north fork of the Canadian; thence along the said four mile line to the Canadian; thence down the Canadian to the Arkansas; thence down the Arkansas to that point on the Arkansas where the eastern Choctaw boundary strikes said river and running thence with the western line of Arkansas Territory as now defined, to the southwest corner of Missouri; thence along the western Missouri line to the land assigned the Senecas; thence on the south line of the Senecas to Grand river; thence up said Grand river as far as the south line of the Osage reservation, extended if necessary; thence up and between said south Osage line extended west if necessary, and a line drawn due west from the point of beginning to a certain distance west, at which a line running north and south from said Osage line to said due west line will make seven millions of acres within the whole described boundaries. In addition to the seven millions of acres of land thus provided for and bounded, the United States further guaranty to the Cherokee nation a perpetual outlet west, and a free and unmolested use of all the country west of the western boundary of said seven millions of acres, as far west as the sovereignty of the United States and their right of soil extend:

Provided however That if the saline or salt plain on the western prairie shall fall within said limits prescribed for said outlet, the right is reserved to the United States to permit other tribes of red men to get salt on said plain in common with the Cherokees; And letters patent shall be issued by the United States as soon as practicable for the land hereby guaranteed."

And whereas it is apprehended by the Cherokees that in the above cession there is not contained a sufficient quantity of land for the accommodation of the whole nation on their removal west of the Mississippi the United States in consideration of the sum of five hundred thousand dollars therefore hereby covenant and agree to convey to the said Indians, and their descendants by patent, in fee simple the following additional tract of land situated between the west line of the State of Missouri and the Osage reservation beginning at the southeast corner of the same and runs north along the east line of the Osage lands fifty miles to the northeast corner thereof; and thence east to the west line of the State of Missouri; thence with said line south fifty miles; thence west to the place of beginning; estimated to contain eight hundred thousand acres of land; but it is expressly understood that if any of the lands assigned the Quapaws shall fall within the aforesaid bounds the same shall be reserved and excepted out of the lands above granted and a pro rata reduction shall be made in the price to be allowed to the United States for the same by the Cherokees.

Article 3

The United States also agree that the lands above ceded by the treaty of Feb. 14 1833, including the outlet, and those ceded by this treaty shall all be included in one patent executed to the Cherokee nation of Indians by the President of the United States according to the provisions of the act of May 28 1830. It is, however, agreed that the military reservation at Fort Gibson shall be held by the United States. But should the United States abandon said post and have no further use for the same it shall revert to the Cherokee nation. The United States shall always have the right to make and establish such post and military roads and forts in any part of the Cherokee country, as they may deem proper for the interest and protection of the same and the free use of as much land, timber, fuel and materials of all kinds for the construction and support of the same as may be necessary; provided that if the private rights of individuals are interfered with, a just compensation therefor shall be made.

Article 4

The United States also stipulate and agree to extinguish for the benefit of the Cherokees the titles to the reservations within their country made in the Osage treaty of 1825 to certain half-breeds and for this purpose they hereby agree to pay to the persons to whom the same belong or have been assigned or to their agents or guardians whenever they shall execute after the ratification of this treaty a satisfactory conveyance for the same, to the United States, the sum of fifteen thousand dollars according to a schedule accompanying this treaty of the relative value of the several reservations.

And whereas by the several treaties between the United States and the Osage Indians the Union and Harmony Missionary reservations which were established for their benefit are now situated within the country ceded by them to the United States; the former being situated in the Cherokee country and the latter in the State of Missouri. It is therefore agreed that the United States shall pay the American Board of Commissioners for Foreign Missions for the improvements on the same what they shall be appraised at by Capt. Geo. Vashon Cherokee sub-agent Abraham Redfield and A. P. Chouteau or such persons as the President of the United States shall appoint and the money allowed for the same shall be expended in schools among the Osages and improving their condition. It is understood that the United States are to pay the amount allowed for the reservations in this article and not the Cherokees.

Article 5

The United States hereby covenant and agree that the lands ceded to the Cherokee nation in the forgoing article shall, in no future time without their consent, be included within the territorial limits or jurisdiction of any State or Territory. But they shall secure to the Cherokee nation the right by their national councils to make and carry into effect all such laws as they may deem necessary for the government and protection of the persons and property within their own country belonging to their people or such persons as have connected themselves with them: provided always that they shall not be inconsistent with the constitution of the United States and such acts of Congress as have been or may be passed regulating trade and intercourse with the Indians; and also, that they shall not be considered as extending to such citizens and army of the United States as may travel or reside in the Indian country by permission according to the laws and regulations established by the Government of the same.

Article 6

Perpetual peace and friendship shall exist between the citizens of the United States and the Cherokee Indians. The United States agree to protect the Cherokee nation from domestic strife and foreign enemies and against intestine wars between the several tribes. The Cherokees shall endeavor to preserve and maintain the peace of the country and not make war upon their neighbors they shall also be protected against interruption and intrusion from citizens of the United States, who may attempt to settle in the country without their consent; and all such persons shall be removed from the same by order of the President of the United States. But this is not intended to prevent the residence among them of useful farmers mechanics and teachers for the instruction of Indians according to treaty stipulations.

Article 7

The Cherokee nation having already made great progress in civilization and deeming it important that every proper and laudable inducement should be offered to their people to improve their condition as well as to guard and secure in the most effectual manner the rights guaranteed to them in this treaty, and with a view to illustrate the liberal and enlarged policy of the Government of the United States towards the Indians in their removal beyond the territorial limits of the States, it is stipulated that they shall be entitled to a delegate in the House of Representatives of the United States whenever Congress shall make provision for the same.

Article 8

The United States also agree and stipulate to remove the Cherokees to their new homes and to subsist them one year after their arrival there and that a sufficient number of steamboats and baggage-wagons shall be furnished to remove them comfortably, and so as not to endanger their health, and that a physician well supplied with medicines shall accompany each detachment of emigrants removed by the Government. Such persons and families as in the opinion of the emigrating agent are capable of subsisting and removing themselves shall be permitted to do so; and they shall be allowed in full for all claims for the same twenty dollars for each member of their family; and in lieu of their one year's rations they shall be paid the sum of thirty-three dollars and thirty-three cents if they prefer it.

Such Cherokees also as reside at present out of the nation and shall remove with them in two years west of the Mississippi shall be entitled to allowance for removal and subsistence as above provided.

Article 9

The United States agree to appoint suitable agents who shall make a just and fair valuation of all such improvements now in the possession of the Cherokees as add any value to the lands; and also of the ferries owned by them, according to their net income; and such improvements and ferries from which they have been dispossessed in a lawless manner or under any existing laws of the State where the same may be situated.

The just debts of the Indians shall be paid out of any monies due them for their improvements and claims; and they shall also be furnished at the discretion of the President of the United States with a sufficient sum to enable them to obtain the necessary means to remove themselves to their new homes, and the balance of their dues shall be paid them at the Cherokee agency west of the Mississippi. The missionary establishments shall also be valued and appraised in a like manner and the amount of them paid over by the United States to the treasurers of the respective missionary societies by whom they have been established and improved in order to enable them to erect such buildings and make such improvements among the Cherokees west of the Mississippi as they may deem necessary for their benefit. Such teachers at present among the Cherokees as this council shall select and designate shall be removed west of the Mississippi with the Cherokee nation and on the same terms allowed to them.

Article 10

The President of the United States shall invest in some safe and most productive public stocks of the country for the benefit of the whole Cherokee nation who have removed or shall remove to the lands assigned by this treaty to the Cherokee nation west of the Mississippi the following sums as a permanent fund for the purposes hereinafter specified and pay over the net income of the same annually to such person or persons as shall be authorized or appointed by the Cherokee nation to receive the same and their receipt shall be a full discharge for the amount paid to them viz: the sum of two hundred thousand dollars in addition to the present annuities of the nation to constitute a general fund the interest of which shall be applied annually by the council of the nation to such purposes as they may deem best for the general interest of their people. The sum of fifty thousand dollars to constitute an orphans' fund the annual income of which shall be expended towards the support and education of such orphan children as are destitute of the means of subsistence. The sum of one hundred and fifty thousand dollars in addition to the present school fund of the nation shall constitute a permanent school fund, the interest of which shall be applied annually by the council of the nation for the support of common schools and such a literary institution of a higher order as may be established in the Indian country. And in order to secure as far as possible the true and beneficial application of the orphans' and school fund the council of the Cherokee nation when required by the President of the United States shall make a report of the application of those funds and he shall at all times have the right if the funds have been misapplied to correct any abuses of them and direct the manner of their application for the purposes for which they were intended. The council of the nation may by giving two years' notice of their intention withdraw their funds by and with the consent of the President and Senate of the United States, and invest them in such manner as they may deem most proper for their interest. The United States also agree and stipulate to pay the just debts and claims against the Cherokee nation held by the citizens of the same and also the just claims of citizens of the United States for services rendered to the nation and the sum of sixty thousand dollars is appropriated for this purpose but no claims against individual persons of the nation shall be allowed and paid by the nation. The sum of three hundred thousand dollars is hereby set apart to pay and liquidate the just claims of the Cherokees upon the United States for spoliations of every kind, that have not been already satisfied under former treaties.

Article 11

The Cherokee nation of Indians believing it will be for the interest of their people to have all their funds and annuities under their own direction and future disposition hereby agree to commute their permanent annuity of ten thousand dollars for the sum of two hundred and fourteen thousand dollars, the same to be invested by the President of the United States as a part of the general fund of the nation: and their present school fund amounting to about fifty thousand dollars shall constitute a part of the permanent school fund of the nation.

Article 12

Those individuals and families of the Cherokee nation that are averse to a removal to the Cherokee country west of the Mississippi and are desirous to become citizens of the States where they reside and such as are qualified to take care of themselves and their property shall be entitled to receive their due portion of all the personal benefits accruing under this treaty for their claims, improvements and per capita; as soon as an appropriation is made for this treaty.

Such heads of Cherokee families as are desirous to reside within the States of No. Carolina, Tennessee, and Alabama subject to the laws of the same; and who are qualified or calculated to become useful citizens shall be entitled, on the certificate of the commissioners to a preemption right to one hundred and sixty acres of land or one quarter section at the minimum Congress price; so as to include the present buildings or improvements of those who now reside there and such as do not live there at present shall be permitted to locate within two years any lands not already occupied by persons entitled to pre-emption privilege under this treaty and if two or more families live on the same quarter section and they desire to continue their residence in these States and are qualified as above specified they shall, on receiving their pre-emption certificate be entitled to the right of pre-emption to such lands as they may select not already taken by any person entitled to them under this treaty.

It is stipulated and agreed between the United States and the Cherokee people that John Ross, James Starr, George Hicks, John Gunter, George Chambers, John Ridge, Elias Boudinot, George Sanders, John Martin, William Rogers, Roman Nose Situwake, and John Timpson shall be a committee on the part of the Cherokees to recommend such persons for the privilege of pre-emption rights as may be deemed entitled to the same under the above articles and to select the missionaries who shall be removed with the nation; and that they be hereby fully empowered and authorized to transact all business on the part of the Indians which may arise in carrying into effect the provisions of this treaty and settling the same with the United States. If any of the persons above mentioned should decline acting or be removed by death; the vacancies shall be filled by the committee themselves.

It is also understood and agreed that the sum of one hundred thousand dollars shall be expended by the commissioners in such manner as the committee deem best for the benefit of the poorer class of Cherokees as shall remove west or have removed west and are entitled to the benefits of this treaty. The same to be delivered at the Cherokee agency west as soon after the removal of the nation as possible.

Article 13

In order to make a final settlement of all the claims of the Cherokees for reservations granted under former treaties to any individuals belonging to the nation by the United States it is therefore hereby stipulated and agreed and expressly understood by the parties to this treaty—that all the Cherokees and their heirs and descendants to whom any reservations have been made under any former treaties with the United States, and who have not sold or conveyed the same by deed or otherwise and who in the opinion of the commissioners have complied with the terms on which the reservations were granted as far as practicable in the several cases; and which reservations have since been sold by the United States shall constitute a just claim against the United States and the original reservee or their heirs or descendants shall be entitled to receive the present value thereof from the United States as unimproved lands. And all such reservations as have not been sold by the United States and where the terms on which the reservations were made in the opinion of the commissioners have been complied with as far as practicable, they or their heirs or descendants shall be entitled to the same. They are hereby granted and confirmed to them—and also all persons who were entitled to reservations under the treaty of 1817 and who as far as practicable in the opinion of the commissioners, have complied with the stipulations of said treaty, although by the treaty of 1819 such reservations were included in the unceded lands belonging to the Cherokee nation are hereby confirmed to them and they shall be entitled to receive a grant for the same. And all such reservees as were obliged by the laws of the States in which their reservations were situated, to abandon the same or purchase them from the States shall be deemed to have a just claim against the United States for the amount by them paid to the States with interest thereon for such reservations and if obliged to abandon the same, to the present value of such reservations as unimproved lands but in all cases where the reservees have sold their reservations or any part thereof and conveyed the same by deed or otherwise and have been paid for the same, they their heirs or descendants or their assigns shall not be considered as having any claims upon the United States under this article of the treaty nor be entitled to receive any compensation for the lands thus disposed of. It is expressly understood by the parties to this treaty that the amount to be allowed for reservations under this article shall not be deducted out of the consideration money allowed to the Cherokees for their claims for spoilations and the cession of their lands; but the same is to be paid for independently by the United States as it is only a just fulfillment of former treaty stipulations.

Article 14

It is also agreed on the part of the United States that such warriors of the Cherokee nation as were engaged on the side of the United States in the late war with Great Britain and the southern tribes of Indians, and who were wounded in such service shall be entitled to such pensions as shall be allowed them by the Congress of the United States to commence from the period of their disability.

Article 15

It is expressly understood and agreed between the parties to this treaty that after deducting the amount which shall be actually expended for the payment for improvements, ferries, claims, for spoilations, removal subsistence and debts and claims upon the Cherokee nation and for the additional quantity of lands and goods for the poorer class of Cherokees and the several sums to be invested for the general national funds; provided for in the several articles of this treaty the balance whatever the same may be shall be equally divided between all the people belonging to the Cherokee nation east according to the census just completed; and such Cherokees as have removed west since June 1833 who are entitled by the terms of their enrollment and removal to all the benefits resulting from the final treaty between the United States and the Cherokees east they shall also be paid for their improvements according to their approved value before their removal where fraud has not already been shown in their valuation.

Article 16

It is hereby stipulated and agreed by the Cherokees that they shall remove to their new homes within two years from the ratification of this treaty and that during such time the United States shall protect and defend them in their possessions and property and free use and occupation of the same and such persons as have been dispossessed of their improvements and houses; and for which no grant has actually issued previously to the enactment of the law of the State of Georgia, of December 1835 to regulate Indian occupancy shall be again put in possession and placed in the same situation and condition, in reference to the laws of the State of Georgia, as the Indians that have not been dispossessed; and if this is not done, and the people are left unprotected, then the United States shall pay the several Cherokees for their losses and damages sustained by them in consequence thereof. And it is also stipulated and agreed that the public buildings and improvements on which they are situated at New Echota for which no grant has been actually made previous to the passage of the above recited act if not occupied by the Cherokee people shall be reserved for the public and free use of the United States and the Cherokee Indians for the purpose of settling and closing all the Indian business arising under this treaty between the commissioners of claims and the Indians.

The United States, and the several States interested in the Cherokee lands, shall immediately proceed to survey the lands ceded by this treaty; but it is expressly agreed and understood between the parties that the agency buildings and that tract of land surveyed and laid off for the use of Colonel R. J. Meigs Indian agent or heretofore enjoyed and occupied by his successors in office shall continue subject to the use and occupancy of the United States, or such agent as may be engaged specially superintending the removal of the tribe.

Article 17

All the claims arising under or provided for in the several articles of this treaty, shall be examined and adjudicated by such commissioners as shall be appointed by the President of the United States by and with the advice and consent of the Senate of the United States for that purpose and their decision shall be final and on their certificate of the amount due the several claimants they shall be paid by the United States. All stipulations in former treaties which have not been superseded or annulled by this shall continue in full force and virtue.

Article 18

Whereas in consequence of the unsettled affairs of the Cherokee people and the early frosts, their crops are insufficient to support their families and great distress is likely to ensue and whereas the nation will not, until after their removal be able advantageously to expend the income of the permanent funds of the nation it is therefore agreed that the annuities of the nation which may accrue under this treaty for two years, the time fixed for their removal shall be expended in provision and clothing for the benefit of the poorer class of the nation and the United States hereby agree to advance the same for that purpose as soon after the ratification of this treaty as an appropriation for the same shall be made. It is however not intended in this article to interfere with that part of the annuities due the Cherokees west by the treaty of 1819.

Article 19

This treaty after the same shall be ratified by the President and Senate of the United States shall be obligatory on the contracting parties.

Article 20

[Supplemental article. Stricken out by Senate.]

In testimony whereof, the commissioners and the chiefs, head men, and people whose names are hereunto annexed, being duly authorized by the people in general council assembled, have affixed their hands and seals for themselves, and in behalf of the Cherokee nation.

I have examined the foregoing treaty, and although not present when it was made, I approve its provisions generally, and therefore sign it.

Wm. Carroll,
J. F. Schermerhorn.
Major Ridge, his x mark, [L. S.]
James Foster, his x mark, [L. S.]
Tesa-ta-esky, his x mark, [L. S.]
Charles Moore, his x mark, [L. S.]
George Chambers, his x mark, [L. S.]
Tah-yeske, his x mark, [L. S.]
Archilla Smith, his x mark, [L. S.]
Andrew Ross, [L. S.]
William Lassley, [L. S.]
Cae-te-hee, his x mark, [L. S.]
Te-gah-e-ske, his x mark, [L. S.]Robert Rogers, [L. S.]
John Gunter, [L. S.]
John A. Bell, [L. S.]
Charles F. Foreman, [L. S.]
William Rogers, [L. S.]
George W. Adair, [L. S.]
Elias Boudinot, [L. S.]
James Starr, his x mark, [L. S.]
Jesse Half-breed, his x mark, [L. S.]
Signed and sealed in presence of—
Western B. Thomas, secretary.
Ben. F. Currey, special agent.

M. Wolfe Batman, first lieutenant, sixth U. S. infantry, disbursing agent.
Jon. L. Hooper, lieutenant, fourth Infantry.
C. M Hitchcock, M. D., assistant surgeon, U.S.A.
G. W. Currey,
Wm. H. Underwood,
Cornelius D. Terhune,
John W. H. Underwood.
In compliance with instructions of the council at New Echota, we sign this treaty.
Stand Watie,
John Ridge.
March 1, 1836.
Witnesses:
Elbert Herring,
Alexander H. Everett,
John Robb,
D. Kurtz,
Wm.Y. Hansell,
Samuel J. Potts,
Jno. Litle,
S. Rockwell.
Dec. 31, 1835 | 7 Stat., 487.

Whereas the western Cherokees have appointed a delegation to visit the eastern Cherokees to assure them of the friendly disposition of their people and their desire that the nation should again be united as one people and to urge upon them the expediency of accepting the overtures of the Government; and that, on their removal they may be assured of a hearty welcome and an equal participation with them in all the benefits and privileges of the Cherokee country west and the undersigned two of said delegation being the only delegates in the eastern nation from the west at the signing and sealing of the treaty lately concluded at New Echota between their eastern brethren and the United States; and having fully understood the provisions of the same they agree to it in behalf of the western Cherokees. But it is expressly understood that nothing in this treaty shall affect any claims of the western Cherokees on the United States.

In testimony whereof, we have, this 31st day of December, 1835, hereunto set our hands and seals.

James Rogers,
John Smith.
Delegates from the western Cherokees.
Test:

Ben. F. Currey, special agent.
M. W. Batman, first lieutenant, Sixth Infantry,
Jno. L. Hooper, lieutenant, Fourth Infantry, Elias Boudinot.

Treaty with the Chippewa (1837)

The Treaty with the Chippewa (January 14, 1837) was between the United States and three groups of the Ojibwes across Minnesota, Wisconsin, and Michigan. After extensive negotiations between the parties near present-day Minneapolis and St. Paul, the United States agreed to provide the Ojibwes with cash annuities, blankets, rifles, cooking utensils, and other provisions in exchange for the cession of the timber-rich lands in northern Wisconsin and eastern Minnesota. Of more value to the Ojibwes was the agreement of the United States to refrain from seeking to remove the Native Americans from the lands they ceded and to provide payments to traders to whom the Ojibwes were heavily in debt. In an era in which the United States was actively engaged in removing the Native Americans from the eastern portion of the country, the treaty of 1837 with the Ojibwes was unique because it contained no removal clause. With the Ojibwes able to hunt, fish, and gather on the lands they ceded to the United States in the treaty of 1837 (and in subsequent treaties in 1842 and 1854), they had legal footing to challenge the U.S. government, in the late 1900s, to retain the right to hunt and fish that had been increasingly disputed throughout the late 19th and 20th centuries.

The primary circumstance that led to the treaty of 1837 was the interest of the United States in the bounty of timber resources located in northern Wisconsin. The Ojibwes, who had established a reliance on—and had sunk into debt to—traders who had provided them with guns, blankets, and other necessary equipment during the fur trading era, were willing to negotiate with the United States to alleviate their economic difficulties. Commissioner Henry Dodge, the Wisconsin territorial governor acting on behalf of the United States, called together more than a 1,000 Ojibwes from various locations in Wisconsin, Minnesota, and Michigan to negotiate the sale of the timber-rich lands. The three major groups represented were the Ojibwes of the Mississippi, the Ojibwes of Lake Superior, and the Pillager Ojibwes. Dodge stressed to these groups that the United States desired the land in northern Wisconsin specifically for its timber resources. As the forests were a renewable resource, the Ojibwes agreed to cede the land under the important stipulation that they could continue to hunt, fish, and gather on it, provided they did so peacefully and did not interfere with logging operations. In exchange for the land, Dodge was authorized to pay $9,500 in currency, $19,000 in goods, $3,000 to support three blacksmiths, $1,000 for agricultural pursuits, $2,000 in provisions, $500 for tobacco, and money to settle debts between the Ojibwes and their traders.

The land the United States acquired from the treaty of 1837 was for logging operations and not initially intended for white settlement; thus, there was no massive influx of settlers who sought to displace the Ojibwes in the years following the treaty. It was not until the reservation system was created in 1854 that the Ojibwe way of life became radically altered; even then, they retained the right to hunt and fish on the land they ceded. The treaty of 1837 set in motion the tradition of a non-removal policy by the United States that appeared again in the 1842 and 1854 treaties with the Ojibwes. The Ojibwes have not forgotten this important aspect of the treaties, and in the late 1900s many groups asserted in court the right to hunt and fish on ceded land, for the growing inclination of the United States in the late 19th and 20th centuries was to restrict those rights. The lasting impact of these cases has yet to be determined.

Troy Henderson

Further Reading

McClurken, James M., ed. *Fish in the Lakes, Wild Rice, and Game in Abundance: Testimony on Behalf of Mille Lacs Ojibwe Hunting and Fishing Rights.* East Lansing: Michigan State University Press, 2000.

Satz, Ronald. *Chippewa Treaty Rights: The Reserve Rights of Wisconsin's Chippewa Indians in Historical Perspective.* Madison: Wisconsin Academy of Sciences, Arts and Letters, 1991.

Document: Treaty with the Chippewa

The Treaty with the Chippewa—leading to the cession of lands in northern Wisconsin and eastern Minnesota—was established between the Chippewas (Ojibwe) and the federal government on January 14, 1837.

Articles of a treaty made and concluded at Detroit, in the State of Michigan, on the fourteenth day of January, in the year of our Lord eighteen hundred and thirty-seven, between the United States of America by their commissioner, Henry R. Schoolcraft, and the Saganaw tribe of the Chippewa nation, by their chiefs and delegates, assembled in council.

Article 1

The said tribe cede to the United States the following tracts of land, lying within the boundaries of Michigan; namely; One tract of eight thousand acres, on the river Au Sable. One tract of two thousand acres, on the Misho-wusk or Rifle river. One tract of six thousand acres, on the north side of the river Kawkawling. One tract of five thousand seven hundred and sixty acres upon Flint river, including the site of Reaums village, and a place called Kishkawbawee. One tract of eight thousand acres on the head of the Cass (formerly Huron) river, at the village of Otusson. One island in the Saganaw bay, estimated at one thousand acres, being the island called Shaingwaukokaug, on which Mukokoosh formerly lived. One tract of two thousand acres at Nababish, on the Saganaw river. One tract of one thousand acres, on the east side of the Saganaw river. One tract of six hundred and forty acres, at Great Bend, on Cass river. One tract of two thousand acres at the mouth of Point Augrais river. One tract of one thousand acres, on the Cass river at Menoquet's village. One tract of ten thousand acres on the Shiawassee river at Ketchewaundauguminik or Big Lick. One tract of six thousand acres at the Little Forks, on the Tetabwasing river. One tract of six thousand acres at the Black-Birds' town, on the Tetabwasing river. One tract of forty thousand acres, on the west side of the Saganaw river. The whole containing one hundred and two thousand four hundred acres, be the same more or less.

Article 2

The said Indians shall have the right of living upon the tracts at the river Augrais, and Mushowusk or Rifle rivers, on the west side of Saganaw bay, for the term of five years, during which time no white man shall be allowed to settle on said tracts, under a penalty of five hundred dollars, to be recovered, at the suit of the informer; one half to the benefit of said informer, the other half to the benefit of the Indians.

Article 3

The United States agree to pay to the said Indians, in consideration of the lands above ceded, the net proceeds of the sales thereof, after deducting the expense of survey and sale, together with the incidental expenses of this treaty. The lands shall be surveyed in the usual manner, and offered for sale, as other public lands, at the land offices of the proper districts, as soon as practicable after the ratification of this treaty. A special account of the sales shall be kept at the Treasury, indicating the receipts from this source, and after deducting therefrom the sums hereinafter set apart, for specified objects, together with all other sums, justly chargeable to this fund, the balance shall be invested, under the direction of the President, in some public stock, and the interest thereof shall be annually paid to the said tribe, in the same manner, and with the same precautions, that annuities are paid. Provided, That, if the said Indians shall, at the expiration of twenty years, or at any time thereafter, require the said stock to be sold, and the proceeds thereof distributed among the whole tribe, or applied to the advancement of agriculture, education, or any other useful object, the same may be done, with the consent of the President and Senate.

Article 4

The said Indians hereby set apart, out of the fund, created by the sale of their lands, the following sums, namely;

For the purchase of goods and provisions, to be delivered to them, as soon as practicable after the ratification of this treaty, forty thousand dollars.

For distribution among the heads of families, to be paid to them, as an annuity in 1837, ten thousand dollars.

For a special payment to each of the principal chiefs, agreeably to a schedule annexed, five thousand dollars.

For the support of schools, among their children, ten thousand dollars. For the payment of their just debts, accruing since the treaty of Ghent, and before the signing of this treaty, forty thousand dollars.

For compensating American citizens, upon whose property this tribe committed depredations after the surrender of Detroit in 1812, ten thousand dollars.

For meeting the payment of claims which have been considered and allowed by the chiefs and delegates in council, as per schedule B hereunto annexed, twelve thousand two hundred and forty-three dollars, and seventy-five cents.

For vaccine matter, and the services of a physician, one hundred dollars per annum for five years.

For the purchase of tobacco to be delivered to them, two hundred dollars per annum for five years.

The whole of these sums shall be expended under the direction of the President, and the following principles shall govern the application. The goods and provisions shall be purchased by an agent, or officer of the Government, on contract, and delivered to them, at their expense, as early as practicable, after the ratification of the treaty. The annuity of ten thousand dollars shall be divided among the heads of families, agreeably to a census, to be taken for the purpose. The school fund shall be put at interest, by investment in stocks, and the interest applied annually to the object, commencing in the year 1840, but the principal shall constitute a permanent fund for twenty years, nor shall the stock be sold, nor the proceeds diverted, at that period, without the consent of the President and Senate.

The monies set apart for the liquidation of their debts, and for depredations, committed by them, shall be paid, under such precautions for ascertaining the justice of the indebtedness or claim, as the President may direct, but no payment shall be made, under either head, which is not supported by satisfactory proof, and sanctioned by the Indians: and if any balance of either sum remains, it shall be immediately divided by the disbursing officer, among the Indians. The other items of expenditure, mentioned in this article, shall be disbursed, under the usual regulations of the Indian Department, for insuring faithfulness and accountability in the application of the money.

Article 5

The United States will advance the amount set apart in the preceding article for the purchase of goods and provisions, and the payment of debts, and depredations by the Indians, also the several sums stipulated to be paid to the chiefs, and distributed to the Indians as an annuity in 1837, and the amount set apart for claims allowed by the Indians, together with the expense of this negotiation.

Article 6

The said tribe agrees to remove from the State of Michigan, as soon as a proper location can be obtained. For this purpose, a deputation shall be sent, to view the country, occupied by their kindred tribes, west of the most westerly point of Lake Superior, and if an arrangement for their future and permanent residence can be made in that quarter, which shall be satisfactory to them, and to the Government, they shall be permitted to form a reunion, with such tribes, and remove thereto. If such arrangement cannot be effected, the United States will afford its influence in obtaining a location for them at such place, west of the Mississippi, and southwest of the Missouri, as the legislation of Congress may indicate. The agency of the exploration, purchase, and removal will be performed by the United States, but the expenses attending the same shall be chargeable to said Indians at the Treasury, to be refunded out of the proceeds of their lands, at such time and in such manner as the Secretary of the Treasury shall deem proper.

Article 7

It is agreed, that the smith's shop shall be continued among the Saganaws, together with the aid in agriculture, farming utensils, and cattle, secured to them under the treaty of September 24th 1819, as fixed, in amount, by the act of Congress of May 15th 1820. But the President is authorized to direct the discontinuance of the stated farmers should he deem proper, and the employment of a supervisor or overseer, to be paid out of this fund, who shall procure the services, and make the purchases required, under such instructions as may be issued by the proper department. And the services shall be rendered, and the shop kept, at such place or places, as may be most beneficial to the Indians. It shall be competent for the Government, at the request of the Indians, seasonably made, to furnish them agricultural products, or horses and saddlery, in lieu of said services, whenever the fund will justify it. Provided, That the whole annual expense, including the pay of the supervisor, shall not exceed the sum of two thousand dollars, fixed by the act herein above referred to.

Article 8

The United States, agree to pay to the said tribe, as one of the parties to the treaty, concluded at Detroit, on the 17th of November 1807, the sum of one thousand dollars, to quiet their claim, to two reservations of land, of two sections each, lying in Oakland county, in the State of Michigan, which were ceded to the Government by the Pottowatomies of St. Joseph's, on the nineteenth of September 1827. This sum will be paid to the chiefs, who are designated in the schedule referred to, in the fourth article, at the same time and place, that the annuities for the present year are paid to the tribe. And the said tribe hereby relinquish, and acknowledge full satisfaction, for any claim they now have, or have ever possessed, to the reservations aforesaid.

Article 9

Nothing in this treaty shall be construed to affect the payment of any annuity, due to the said tribe, by any prior treaty. But the same shall be paid as heretofore.

Article 10

Should not the lands herein ceded, be sold, and the avails thereof, vested for said tribe, as provided in the third article, before the thirtieth day of September of the present year, so that the annual interest of such investment may be relied on, to constitute an annuity for said tribe in the year eighteen hundred and thirty-eight, the United States will, during the said year 1838, advance the same amount which is provided for that object in the fourth article of this treaty, which sum shall be refunded to the Treasury by said tribe with interest, out of any fund standing to their credit, at the discretion of the Secretary of the Treasury.

Article 11

The usual expenses, attending the formation of this treaty, will be paid by the United States, provided, that the Government may, in the discretion of the President, direct the one moiety thereof to be charged to the Indian fund, created by the third article of this treaty.

In testimony whereof, the said Henry R. Schoolcraft, commissioner on the part of the United States, and the chiefs and delegates of the said tribe, have hereunto set their hands, and affixed their marks, at the city of Detroit in Michigan, the day and year above written.

    Henry R. Schoolcraft, Commissioner.
    Ogima Keegido,
    Naum Gitchigomee,
    Osau Wauban,
    Penayseewubee,
    Washwa,
    Peenaysee Weegezhig,
    Mauk Esaut,
    Peetwayweetum,
    Tontagonee,
    Kaitchenoding,
    Maishkoodagwana,
    Naishkayshig,
    Wasso,
    Pabaumosh,
    Monetogaubwee,
    Aindunossega,

Ugahbakwum,
Shawun Epenaysee,
Waubredoaince,
Sheegunageezhig,
Etowanaquot,
Mukuday Ghenien,
Mukuckoosh,
Penayshee Weegezhig, the 2d,
Mazinos,
Pondiac,
Nawa Geezhig.
Francis Willett Shearman, secretary.
Henry Whiting, major, U. S. Army
J. P. Simonton, captain, U. S. Army.
Z. Pitcher, surgeon, U. S. Army.
Henry Connor, subagent.
Robert Stuart.
Jno. Hulbert.
Douglass Houghton.
G. D. Williams.
William Johnston.
Joseph F. Menoy, interpreter.
John A. Drew.
Darius Lawson.
Charles H. Rodd.
(To the Indian names are subjoined marks.)

Schedule of the names of chiefs entitled to payments under the fourth and eighth articles of the foregoing treaty:

The following chiefs, representing the several bands of the tribe of the Saganaws, are entitled to receive the several sums of five hundred and one hundred dollars each, to wit:

1. Ogima Kegido
2. Shawun, Epenaysse
3. Naum Gitchegomee
4. Mauk Esaub
5. Muckuk, Kosh
6. Peteway, Weetum
7. Paypah, Monshee

8. Tontagonee

9. Wasse

10. Wahputo-ains

HENRY R. SCHOOLCRAFT,
Commissioner.

Treaty of La Pointe (1842)

The Treaty of La Pointe with the Ojibwes (or Chippewas) took place at La Pointe, Wisconsin, between the United States and 23 distinct bands of the Ojibwes, which represented two major groups called the Ojibwes of Lake Superior and the Ojibwes of the Mississippi. Like the 1837 treaty with the Ojibwes, the 1842 treaty involved the cession of lands to the United States in exchange for annuity payments, provisions, an agricultural fund, and, most important for the Ojibwes, the right to hunt, fish, and gather on the land they ceded. The land ceded in the treaty of 1842 included the western portion of the Upper Peninsula of Michigan and the last of the Ojibwe lands in northern Wisconsin. Although the U.S. government had a growing inclination to displace the Ojibwes from their homelands in the 1840s and early 1850s, the 1842 treaty continued the unique tradition of nonremoval established by the United States and the Ojibwes in the treaty of 1837.

Pressured by the profitability of the mineral deposits on the southern shore of Lake Superior, the United States commissioned Robert Stuart, former chief factor of the American Fur Company, to acquire the land that contained the valuable resources. Stuart was given instructions by the commissioner of Indian affairs to attempt to include a stipulation in the treaty that would remove the Lake Superior Ojibwes westward to lands held by the Ojibwes of the Mississippi, to form a common territory for both groups. This act of combining Native American groups into political entities that did not exist naturally was characteristic of U.S. policy of that time. The Ojibwes of Lake Superior and the Ojibwes of the Mississippi balked at the idea of being categorized together as well as at the notion of removal.

Recognizing the Ojibwe concern over the removal clause, Stuart did not force the issue, and the content of the treaty of 1842 was very similar to the treaty of 1837. The Ojibwes retained the right to hunt, fish, and gather on the land they ceded to the United States, but Stuart made it clear that future removal was a possibility. The discretion to remove the Ojibwes at a future date was given to the president of the United States. In exchange for the land in the western Upper Peninsula of Michigan and a portion of northern Wisconsin, the Ojibwes were given annual payments of

$12,500 in currency, $10,500 in goods, $2,000 to support two blacksmiths, $1,000 to support two farmers, $1,200 to support two carpenters, $2,000 to support schools, $2,000 for tobacco, and money to settle debts with traders to whom the Ojibwes were in debt.

By supporting schools, carpenters, farmers, and blacksmiths, the United States was clearly attempting to inject elements of white society into the Ojibwe culture. Like the missionaries who had established themselves among the Ojibwes, the United States embarked on "civilizing" the Ojibwes by encouraging the Native Americans to adopt a lifestyle similar to that of white society. Paradoxically, the policy of the United States was also to threaten the removal of the Ojibwes, which did nothing to help incorporate them into "civilized" society. After the treaty of 1842 was signed, confusion over which Ojibwes would receive the annuity payments, as well as a growing threat by the United States to remove the Ojibwes, led to another treaty negotiation in 1854.

Troy Henderson

Further Reading

Cleland, Charles E. *Rites of Conquest: The History and Culture of Michigan's Native Americans*. Ann Arbor: University of Michigan Press, 1992.

Danziger, Edmund Jefferson, Jr. *The Chippewas of Lake Superior*. Norman: University of Oklahoma Press, 1978.

McClurken, James M., ed. *Fish in the Lakes, Wild Rice, and Game in Abundance: Testimony on Behalf of Mille Lacs Ojibwe Hunting and Fishing Rights*. East Lansing: Michigan State University Press, 2000.

Document: Treaty of La Pointe

Articles of a treaty made and concluded at La Pointe of Lake Superior, in the Territory of Wisconsin, between Robert Stuart commissioner on the part of the United States, and the Chippewa Indians of the Mississippi, and Lake Superior, by their chiefs and headmen.

Article 1

THE Chippewa Indians of the Mississippi and Lake Superior, cede to the United States all the country within the following bounderies; viz: beginning at the mouth of Chocolate river of Lake Superior; thence northwardly across said lake to intersect the boundery line between the United States and the Province of Canada; thence up said Lake Superior, to the mouth of the St. Louis, or Fond du Lac river (including all the islands in said lake); thence up said river to the American Fur Company's trading post, at the southwardly bend thereof, about 22 miles from its mouth; thence south to intersect the line of the treaty of 29th July 1837, with the Chippewas of the Mississippi; thence along said line to its southeastwardly extremity, near the Plover portage on the Wisconsin river; thence northeastwardly, along the boundery line, between the Chippewas and Menomonees, to its eastern termination, (established by the treaty held with the Chippewas, Menomonees, and Winnebagoes, at Butte des Morts, August 11th 1827) on the Skonawby river of Green Bay; thence northwardly to the source of Chocolate river; thence down said river to its mouth, the place of beginning; it being the intention of the parties to this treaty, to include in this cession, all the Chippewa lands eastwardly of the aforesaid line running from the American Fur Company's trading post on the Fond du Lac river to the intersection of the line of the treaty made with the Chippewas of the Mississippi July 29th 1837.

Article 2

The Indians stipulate for the right of hunting on the ceded territory, with the other usual privileges of occupancy, until required to remove by the President of the United States, and that the laws of the United States shall be continued in force, in respect to their trade and inter course with the whites, until otherwise ordered by Congress.

Article 3

It is agreed by the parties to this treaty, that whenever the Indians shall be required to remove from the ceded district, all the unceded lands belonging to the Indians of Fond du Lac, Sandy Lake, and Mississippi bands, shall be the common property and home of all the Indians, party to this treaty.

Article 4

In consideration of the foregoing cession, the United States, engage to pay to the Chippewa Indians of the Mississippi, and Lake Superior, annually, for twenty-five years, twelve thousand five hundred (12,500) dollars, in specie, ten thousand five hundred (10,500) dollars in goods, two thousand (2,000) dollars in provisions and tobacco, two thousand (2,000) dollars for the support of two blacksmiths shops, (including pay of smiths and assistants, and iron steel &c.) one thousand (1,000) dollars for pay of two farmers, twelve hundred (1,200) for pay of two carpenters, and two thousand (2,000) dollars for the support of schools for the Indians party to this treaty; and further the United States engage to pay the sum of five thousand (5,000) dollars as an agricultural fund, to be expended under the direction of the Secretary of War. And also the sum of seventy-five thousand (75,000) dollars, shall be allowed for the full satisfaction of their debts within the ceded district, which shall be examined by the commissioner to this treaty, and the amount to be allowed decided upon by him, which shall appear in a schedule hereunto annexed. The United States shall pay the amount so allowed within three years.

Whereas the Indians have expressed a strong desire to have some provision made for their half breed relatives, therefore it is agreed, that fifteen thousand (15,000) dollars shall be paid to said Indians, next year, as a present, to be disposed of as they, together with their agent, shall determine in council.

Article 5

Whereas the whole country between Lake Superior and the Mississippi, has always been understood as belonging in common to the Chippewas, party to this treaty; and whereas the bands bordering on Lake Superior, have not been allowed to participate in the annuity payments of the treaty made with the Chippewas of the Mississippi, at St. Peters July 29th 1837, and whereas all the unceded lands belonging to the aforesaid Indians, are hereafter to be held in common, therefore, to remove all occasion for jealousy and discontent, it is agreed that all the annuity due by the said treaty, as also the annuity due by the present treaty, shall henceforth be equally divided among the Chippewas of the Mississippi and Lake Superior, party to this treaty, so that every person shall receive an equal share.

Article 6

The Indians residing on the Mineral district, shall be subject to removal therefrom at the pleasure of the President of the United States.

Article 7

This treaty shall be obligatory upon the contracting parties when ratified by the President and Senate of the United States.

In testimony whereof the said Robert Stuart commissioner, on the part of the United States, and the chiefs and headmen of the Chippewa Indians of the Mississippi and Lake Superior, have hereunto set their hands, at La Pointe of Lake Superior, Wisconsin Territory this fourth day of October in the year of our Lord one thousand eight hundred and forty-two.

Robert Stuart, Commissioner.
Jno. Hulbert, Secretary.

Crow wing River,	Po go ne gi shik,	1st	chief.
Do.	Son go com ick,	2d	do.
Sandy Lake,	Ka non do ur uin zo,	1st	do.
Do.	Na tum e gaw bon,	2d	do.
Gull Lake,	Ua bo jig,	1st	do.
Do.	Pay pe si gon de bay,	2d	do.
Red Ceder Lake,	Kui ui sen shis,	1st	do.
Do.	Ott taw wance,	2d	do.
Po ke gom maw,	Bai ie jig,	1st	do.
Do.	Show ne aw,	2d	do.
Wisconsin River,	Ki uen zi,	1st	do.

Do.	Wi aw bis ke kut te way,	2d	do.
Lac de Flambeau,	A pish ka go gi,	1st	do.
Do.	May tock cus e quay,	2d	do.
Do.	She maw gon e,	2d	do.
Lake Bands,	Ki ji ua be she shi,	1st	do.
Do.	Ke kon o tum,	2d	do.
Fon du Lac,	Shin goob,	1st	do.
Do.	Na gan nab,	2d	do.
Do.	Mong o zet,	2d	do.
La Pointe,	Gitchi waisky,	1st	do.
Do.	Mi zi,	2d	do.
Do.	Ta qua gone e,	2d	do.
Onlonagan,	O kon di kan,	1st	do.
Do.	Kis ke taw wac,	2d	do.
Ance,	Pe na shi,	1st	do.
Do.	Guck we san sish,	2d	do.
Vieux Desert,	Ka she osh e,	1st	do.
Do.	Medge waw gwaw wot,	2d	do.
Mille Lac,	Ne qua ne be,	1st	do.
Do.	Ua shash ko kum,	2d	do.
Do.	No din,	2d	do.
St. Croix,	Be zhi ki,	1st	do.
Do.	Ka bi na be,	2d	do.
Do. SnakeRiver,	Ai aw bens,	2d	do.
Chippewa River,	Sha go bi,	1st	do.
Lac Courtulle,	Ua be she shi,	1st	do.
Do.	Que way zhan sis,	2d	do.
Do.	Ne na nang eb,	1st	do.
	Be bo kon uen,	2d	do.
	Ki uen zi.	2d	do.

In presence of—
Henry Blanchford, interpreter.
Samuel Ashmun, interpreter.
Justin Rice.
Charles H. Oakes.
William A. Aitkin.
William Brewster.
Charles M. Borup.
Z. Platt.
C. H. Beaulieau.
L. T. Jamison.
James P. Scott.
Cyrus Mendenhall.
L. M. Warren.

Schedule of claims examined and allowed by Robert Stuart, commissioner, under the treaty with the Chippewa Indians of the Mississippi and Lake Superior, concluded at La Pointe, October 4th 1842, setting forth the names of claimants, and their proportion of allowance of the seventy-five thousand dollars provided in the fourth article of the aforesaid treaty, for the full satisfaction of their debts, as follows:

No. of claim.	Name of claimant.	Proportion of $75,000. set apart in 4th article of treaty.
1	Edward F. Ely	$50 80
2	Z. Platt, esq., attorney for George Berkett	484 67
3	Cleveland North Lake Co	1,485 67
4	Abraham W. Williams	75 03
5	William Brewster	2,052 67
	This claim to be paid as follows, viz:	
6	William Brewster, or order $1,929 77	61 67
7	Charles W. Borup, or order 122 90	57 55
8	———	28 58
9	$2,052 67	186 16
10	———	6 46
11	George Copway	182 42
12	John Kahbege	301 48
13	Alixes Carpantier	1,101 00
14	John W. Bell	325 46
15	Antoine Picard	69 00
16	Michael Brisette	234 92
17	Francois Dejaddon	596 84
18	Pierre C. Duvernay	366 84
19	Jean Bts. Bazinet	322 52
20	John Hotley	499 27
21	Francois Charette	516 82
22	Clement H. Beaulieu, agent for the estate of Bazil Beaulieu, dec'd	169 05
23	Francois St. Jean and George Bonga	13,365 30
24	Louis Ladebauche	
25	Peter Crebassa	935 67
26	B. T. Kavanaugh	73 41
27	Augustin Goslin	192 35
28	American Fur Company	12 57
29	This claim to be paid as follows, viz:	596 03
30	American Fur Company 12,565 10	35 24
31	Charles W. Borup	1,771 63
32	800 20	390 27
33	———	1,991 62
34	$13,365 30	1,566 65
35	———	959 13
36	William A. Aitken	144 32
37	James P. Scott	170 35
38	Augustin Bellanger	205 60
39	Louis Corbin	167 05
40	Alexes Corbin	614 30
41	George Johnston	64 78
42	Z. Platt, esq., attorney for Sam'l Ashman	531 50
43	Z. Platt, esq., attorney for Wm. Johnson	209 18

44	Z. Platt, esq., attorney for estate of Dan'l Dingley		18 80
45	Lyman M. Warren		732 50
46	Estate of Michael Cadotte, disallowed.		3,157 10
47	Z. Platt. esq., attorney for estate of E. Roussain		37,994 98
48	Joseph Dufault		1,118 60
49	Z. Platt, esq., attorney for Antoine Mace		4,309 21
50	Michael Cadotte		1,074 70
51	Z. Platt, esq., att'y for Francois Gauthier		1,275 56
52	Z. Platt, esq., att'y for Joseph Gauthier		62 00
53	Z. Platt, esq., attorney for J. B. Uoulle		2,067 10
54	Jean Bts. Corbin		
	John Hulbert		17 62
55	Jean Bts. Couvellion		
	Nicholas Da Couteau, withdrawn.		$75,000 00
	Pierre Cotte		
	W. H. Brockway and Henry Holt, executors to the estate of John Holliday, dec'd. John Jacob Astor		
	This claim to be paid as follows, viz:		
	Charles W. Borup	1,676 90	
	Z. Platt, esq	2,621 80	
	John Jacob Astor	23,696 28	
	$27,994 98		
	Z. Platt. esq., attorney for Thos. Connor		
	Charles H. Oakes		
	Z. Platt, esq., attorney for Wm. Morrison		
	Z. Platt, esq., att'y for Isaac Butterfield		
	J. B. Van Rensselaer		
	William Brewster and James W. Abbot		
	The parties to this claim request no payment be made to either without their joint consent, or until a decision of the case be had, in a court of justice.		
	William Bell		

Robert Stuart, Commissioner.
Jno. Hulbert, Secretary.

Confederate, Reconstruction, and Unratified Treaties, 1850–1871

Treaty of Fort Laramie (1851)

The first Treaty of Fort Laramie, signed at Fort Laramie in southeastern Wyoming on September 17, 1851, established formal relations between the U.S. government and the northern plains American Indian nations. The purpose of the treaty was to ensure the safety of the increasing number of overland travelers crossing the plains. The encroaching European American population was competing with American Indians for available resources, and the number of reprisals conducted by both sides was mounting at that time.

The treaty was signed on behalf of the United States by D. D. Mitchell, superintendent of Indian affairs, and Thomas Fitzpatrick, Indian agent. Both commissioners were appointed and authorized for this special occasion by the president. The present American Indian leaders represented nations residing south of the Missouri River, east of the Rocky Mountains, and north of Texas, namely the Sioux (referring to Lakotas, Dakotas, and Nakotas), Cheyennes, Arapahos, Crows, Assiniboines, Mandans, and Arikaras.

The treaty contains eight articles, which bound the Native American nations to make peace with one another, to recognize the right of the United States to establish roads and posts within their respective territories, and to make restitution for any wrongs committed by their people against the citizens of the United States. The Native American nations were further supposed to acknowledge the prescribed boundaries of their respective territories and to select head chiefs, through whom all national business would be conducted. The United States bound itself to protect the Natives against U.S. citizens and to deliver certain annuities. If any Native nation violated a single provision of the treaty, the annuities could be withheld.

The Senate ratified the first Treaty of Fort Laramie on May 24, 1852; however, an amendment changing the annuities from 50 to 10 years, with an additional five years at the discretion of the president, was subject to acceptance by the Native nations. Assent of all the nations was procured; the last were the Crows who assented on September 18, 1854. The treaty was never published as ratified in the

U.S. Statutes at Large; consequently, there has been some discussion concerning its validity. The Department of the Interior inadvertently failed to certify the ratification of the treaty by the Native nations to the State Department; therefore, the treaty was not promulgated by the president of the United States. However, in subsequent agreements and by decisions of the court of claims (*Moore v. the United States* and *Roy v. the United States*), the treaty was recognized as in force.

Due to the lack of good interpreters, the terms of the treaty were not fully explained to most of the Native leaders present at the council grounds. The 10,000 Natives gathered at their camps near Fort Laramie paid more attention to the fact that many nations that had previously fought each other were engaging in diverse ways of peacemaking there, and that celebrations, dancing, hand games, and various kinds of races were continuing for several days.

The Lakotas, dominating the treaty negotiations on the Native side, had significant influence on the demarcation of the territorial boundaries. Although most of the Native nations retained their usual territory, the Northern Cheyennes were not given title to their land, which adjoined the Lakota land. Instead, they were assigned a territory, together with the Southern Cheyennes and Arapahos, between the North Fork of the Platte River and the Arkansas River in the south. This treaty gave the Lakota rights to the Black Hills and other land that was inhabited by the Northern Cheyennes, thus provoking the dispute over the Black Hills between these nations.

Drawing the boundaries of territories assigned to the Native nations made it possible for the United States to negotiate with specific nations to secure land cessions from them. In the long run, the treaty contributed to the ultimate loss of almost all Native land involved, which was eventually opened up for settlement by European Americans. Temporary peace, secured by the Treaty of Fort Laramie of 1851, enabled many settlers to cross the plains and populate what are today the states of Oregon and California. The fact that, in an effort to secure better control over Native nations, they were made responsible for any crimes committed within their territories led to many accusations, although not always correct ones. A treaty originally written to ensure peace and to serve as a cost-effective alternative to war fueled disputes, leading ultimately to the Indian Wars and the subsequent decimation of Native populations.

Antonie Dvorakova

Further Reading

Berthrong, Donald J. *The Southern Cheyennes*. Norman: University of Oklahoma Press, 1963.

Kappler, Charles Joseph, ed. *Indian Treaties, 1778–1883*. New York: Interland, 1972.

Stands In Timber, John, and Margot Liberty. *Cheyenne Memories*, 2nd ed. New Haven, CT, and London: Yale University Press, 1998.

Treaty Site—Fort Laramie, Wyoming

Fort Laramie, located in eastern Wyoming, served first as a major trading post and after 1849 as a U.S. Army post. The post played a significant role in the region by protecting overland travelers and as a major juncture, first for the fur trade and later for the Plains Indian campaigns. In 1851 and in 1868, important treaties were signed at the fort with northern plains tribes. The fort was abandoned by the military in 1890 and serves today as a National Historic Site.

Aspiring to take advantage of the lucrative fur trade in the region, William Sublette and Robert Campbell, two experienced traders, established Fort Laramie in 1834. The fort is located on the left bank of the Laramie River about a mile above its junction with the North Platte River. At the time of its establishment, Fort Laramie was the first permanent settlement of white men in the heart of the buffalo country. The name of the fort changed over time. In 1834, it was named Fort William; and in 1841, when the second fort was built, its name was changed to Fort John. All along, Fort Laramie was the most popular name for the place. After the military took over in 1849, this popular name was retained and made official. The name comes from the nearby river, which was named after French trapper Jacques Laramie.

On June 26, 1849, the U.S. Army purchased the post for $4,000 from the American Fur Company, which had acquired it in 1836. The site was ideal for a military post. It was located on the Platte River line of overland march and was widely influential in the fur trade of the region. In addition, the fort was outside the buffalo ranges of the plains tribes and therefore did not interfere with their major commissary. As overland travel increased rapidly, the U.S. Army recognized the growing importance of the region. The need to protect travelers from Native Americans was a major concern for the military. Following the purchase, the army embarked on a major transformation of the post. At first, old buildings were occupied by the military units, but gradually they were torn down; by 1862, they had been replaced completely with new structures.

The U.S. Army used the fort mainly to aid overland travelers and to control Natives. For travelers, the fort provided supplies, medical care, communication facilities, and other services. The army also improved the trails. Fort Laramie was in many ways an isolated community in the middle of the plains, but for many travelers it functioned as an important landmark of civilization amid wilderness.

The fort had a significant role in the Indian wars. Many small skirmishes were fought in the vicinity, but Fort Laramie's main function was as a supply station for the soldiers during the northern Plains Indian campaigns. In 1851 and 1868, two major treaties with the northern plains tribes were signed at the fort. With these treaties, the Natives surrendered most of their claims to the region. The Sioux and Cheyenne campaigns of 1876 and 1877 saw the last major military confrontations with Native Americans in the region.

With the coming of the railroads and increasing settlement, the role of the fort changed. The Union Pacific railway ran 70 miles to the south, and the Chicago Northwestern ran 50 miles to the north; no longer on the main routes of travel, the fort began to decline in importance. In the late 1870s, ranchers and homesteaders moved into the region. At first, the fort served as a supply center and offered protection for many of these settlers; but in 1890, four years after recommendations were made for its abandonment and one year after the decision was reached, the troops marched away from Fort Laramie for the last time.

For nearly 50 years, the fort was allowed to decay. In 1937, Wyoming appropriated funds for the purchase of the former military site and its donation to the federal government. In 1938, the Fort Laramie Historic Site became a unit in the National Park System. The fort has been restored to its 1876 appearance.

Janne Lahti

Further Reading

Hafen, Le Roy R., and Francis Marion Young. *Fort Laramie and the Pageant of the West, 1834–1890*. Lincoln: University of Nebraska Press, 1984.

Hedren, Paul L. *Fort Laramie and the Great Sioux War*. Norman: University of Oklahoma Press, 1988.

Nadeau, Remi. *Fort Laramie and the Sioux*. Santa Barbara, CA: Crest, 1997.

Document: Treaty of Fort Laramie

Articles of a treaty made and concluded at Fort Laramie, in the Indian Territory, between D. D. Mitchell, superintendent of Indian affairs, and Thomas Fitzpatrick, Indian agent, commissioners specially appointed and authorized by the President of the United States, of the first part, and the chiefs, headmen, and braves of the following Indian nations, residing south of the Missouri River, east of the Rocky Mountains, and north of the lines of Texas and New Mexico, viz, the Sioux or Dahcotahs, Cheyennes, Arrapahoes, Crows. Assinaboines, Gros-Ventre Mandans, and Arrickaras, parties of the second part, on the seventeenth day of September, A. D. one thousand eight hundred and fifty-one.

Article 1

The aforesaid nations, parties to this treaty, having assembled for the purpose of establishing and confirming peaceful relations amongst themselves, do hereby covenant and agree to abstain in future from all hostilities whatever against each other, to maintain good faith and friendship in all their mutual intercourse, and to make an effective and lasting peace.

Article 2

The aforesaid nations do hereby recognize the right of the United States Government to establish roads, military and other posts, within their respective territories.

Article 3

In consideration of the rights and privileges acknowledged in the preceding article, the United States bind themselves to protect the aforesaid Indian nations against the commission of all depredations by the people of the said United States, after the ratification of this treaty.

Article 4

The aforesaid Indian nations do hereby agree and bind themselves to make restitution or satisfaction for any wrongs committed, after the ratification of this treaty, by any band or individual of their people, on the people of the United States, whilst lawfully residing in or passing through their respective territories.

Article 5

The aforesaid Indian nations do hereby recognize and acknowledge the following tracts of country, included within the metes and boundaries hereinafter designated, as their respective territories, viz:

The territory of the Sioux or Dahcotah Nation, commencing the mouth of the White Earth River, on the Missouri River: thence in a southwesterly direction to the forks of the Platte River: thence up the north fork of the Platte River to a point known as the Red Bute, or where the road leaves the river; thence along the range of mountains known as the Black Hills, to the head-waters of Heart River; thence down Heart River to its mouth; and thence down the Missouri River to the place of beginning.

The territory of the Gros Ventre, Mandans, and Arrickaras Nations, commencing at the mouth of Heart River; thence up the Missouri River to the mouth of the Yellowstone River; thence up the Yellowstone River to the mouth of Powder River in a southeasterly direction, to the head-waters of the Little Missouri River; thence along the Black Hills to the head of Heart River, and thence down Heart River to the place of beginning.

The territory of the Assinaboin Nation, commencing at the mouth of Yellowstone River; thence up the Missouri River to the mouth of the Muscle-shell River; thence from the mouth of the Muscle-shell River in a southeasterly direction until it strikes the head-waters of Big Dry Creek; thence down that creek to where it empties into the Yellowstone River, nearly opposite the mouth of Powder River, and thence down the Yellowstone River to the place of beginning.

The territory of the Blackfoot Nation, commencing at the mouth of Muscle-shell River; thence up the Missouri River to its source; thence along the main range of the Rocky Mountains, in a southerly direction, to the head-waters of the northern source of the Yellowstone River; thence down the Yellowstone River to the mouth of Twenty-five Yard Creek; thence across to the head-waters of the Muscle-shell River, and thence down the Muscle-shell River to the place of beginning.

The territory of the Crow Nation, commencing at the mouth of Powder River on the Yellowstone; thence up Powder River to its source; thence along the main range of the Black Hills and Wind River Mountains to the head-waters of the Yellowstone River; thence down the Yellowstone River to the mouth of Twenty-five Yard Creek; thence to the head waters of the Muscle-shell River; thence down the Muscle-shell River to its mouth; thence to the head-waters of Big Dry Creek, and thence to its mouth.

The territory of the Cheyennes and Arrapahoes, commencing at the Red Bute, or the place where the road leaves the north fork of the Platte River; thence up the north fork of the Platte River to its source; thence along the main range of the Rocky Mountains to the head-waters of the Arkansas River; thence down the Arkansas River to the crossing of the Santa Fé road; thence in a northwesterly direction to the forks of the Platte River, and thence up the Platte River to the place of beginning.

It is, however, understood that, in making this recognition and acknowledgement, the aforesaid Indian nations do not hereby abandon or prejudice any rights or claims they may have to other lands; and further, that they do not surrender the privilege of hunting, fishing, or passing over any of the tracts of country heretofore described.

Article 6

The parties to the second part of this treaty having selected principals or head-chiefs for their respective nations, through whom all national business will hereafter be conducted, do hereby bind themselves to sustain said chiefs and their successors during good behavior.

Article 7

In consideration of the treaty stipulations, and for the damages which have or may occur by reason thereof to the Indian nations, parties hereto, and for their maintenance and the improvement of their moral and social customs, the United States bind themselves to deliver to the said Indian nations the sum of fifty thousand dollars per annum for the term of ten years, with the right to continue the same at the discretion of the President of the United States for a period not exceeding five years thereafter, in provisions, merchandise, domestic animals, and agricultural implements, in such proportions as may be deemed best adapted to their condition by the President of the United States, to be distributed in proportion to the population of the aforesaid Indian nations.

Article 8

It is understood and agreed that should any of the Indian nations, parties to this treaty, violate any of the provisions thereof, the United States may withhold the whole or aportion of the annuities mentioned in the preceding article from the nation so offending, until, in the opinion of the President of the United States, proper satisfaction shall have been made.

In testimony whereof the said D. D. Mitchell and Thomas Fitzpatrick commissioners as aforesaid, and the chiefs, headmen, and braves, parties hereto, have set their hands and affixed their marks, on the day and at the place first above written.

D. D. Mitchell
Thomas Fitzpatrick
Commissioners.
Sioux:
Mah-toe-wha-you-whey, his x mark.
Mah-kah-toe-zah-zah, his x mark.
Bel-o-ton-kah-tan-ga, his x mark.
Nah-ka-pah-gi-gi, his x mark.
Mak-toe-sah-bi-chis, his x mark.
Meh-wha-tah-ni-hans-kah, his x mark.
Cheyennes:
Wah-ha-nis-satta, his x mark.
Voist-ti-toe-vetz, his x mark.
Nahk-ko-me-ien, his x mark.
Koh-kah-y-wh-cum-est, his x mark.
Arrapahoes:
Bè-ah-té-a-qui-sah, his x mark.
Neb-ni-bah-seh-it, his x mark.
Beh-kah-jay-beth-sah-es, his x mark.
Crows:
Arra-tu-ri-sash, his x mark.
Doh-chepit-seh-chi-es, his x mark.
Assinaboines:
Mah-toe-wit-ko, his x mark.
Toe-tah-ki-eh-nan, his x mark.
Mandans and Gros Ventres:
Nochk-pit-shi-toe-pish, his x mark.

She-oh-mant-ho, his x mark.
Arickarees:
Koun-hei-ti-shan, his x mark.
Bi-atch-tah-wetch, his x mark.
In the presence of—
A. B. Chambers, secretary.
S. Cooper, colonel, U. S. Army.
R. H. Chilton, captain, First Drags.
Thomas Duncan, captain, Mounted Riflemen.
Thos. G. Rhett, brevet captain R. M. R.
W. L. Elliott, first lieutenant R. M. R.
C. Campbell, interpreter for Sioux.
John S. Smith, interpreter for Cheyennes.
Robert Meldrum, interpreter for the Crows.
H. Culbertson, interpreter for Assiniboines and Gros Ventres.
Francois L'Etalie, interpreter for Arick arees.
John Pizelle, interpreter for the Arrapahoes.
B. Gratz Brown.
Robert Campbell.
Edmond F. Chouteau.

Treaty with the Chippewa (1854)

Negotiations for the Treaty with the Chippewa (1854) took place at La Pointe, Wisconsin, between the United States and two groups of the Ojibwes (or Chippewas): the Ojibwes Lake Superior and the Ojibwes of the Mississippi. In the 1854 treaty, the Ojibwes ceded their lands in northeastern Minnesota to the United States in exchange for annuity payments over 20 years and the creation of a patchwork of reservations within the land ceded by the Ojibwes in the treaties of 1837, 1842, and 1854. In something of a compromise between the U.S. government, which had unsuccessfully attempted to remove the Ojibwes from their lands in the late 1840s and early 1850s, and the Ojibwes, who had strongly asserted their desire to remain on their homelands, the 1854 treaty created a reservation system, and the Ojibwes retained their rights to hunt, fish, and gather on all of the lands they ceded. Yet, because of the growing presence of white settlers in the late 1800s and 1900s on the land the Ojibwes had once occupied, the opportunity for the Ojibwes to continue to live in a traditional lifestyle dwindled after 1854.

The principal issue that led to the treaty of 1854 with the Ojibwes centered on removal. In 1850, President Zachary Taylor issued an order that revoked the privileges of the Ojibwes under the treaties of 1837 and 1842 and called for the removal of the Ojibwes to the lands they had not yet ceded. This decision sparked numerous petitions from missionaries, American citizens, and Ojibwe leaders who stood staunchly against the removal of the Ojibwes. In 1852, Ojibwe leaders Pishake, Kisketuhug, and Oshaga traveled from La Pointe to Washington to argue their case to President Millard Fillmore. Eventually, the United States relented, and Commissioner of Indian Affairs George Manypenny sent agents David Herriman and Henry Gilbert to La Pointe in 1854 to negotiate a treaty with the Ojibwes that would purchase for the United States the mineral-rich district in northeastern Minnesota and set up reservations for the Ojibwes on the land they ceded. The Ojibwes, who preferred the creation of reservations to removal, agreed to meet at La Pointe for treaty negotiations.

More than 4,000 Ojibwes met at La Pointe in 1854 to take part in or witness the treaty negotiations. Instead of combining the Ojibwes of the Mississippi and the Ojibwes of Lake Superior into a single entity to represent the Ojibwes, as previous treaty negotiators had done, Henry Gilbert recognized the resentment between the two groups and separated them during the negotiations. Treaty negotiations concluded with the Ojibwes of Lake Superior receiving two-thirds of the annuity benefits and the Ojibwes of the Mississippi receiving the remaining one-third. The Ojibwes ceded the land in northeastern Minnesota for 20-year annuities in the form of money, cattle, cooking utensils, building materials, funds for education, money for the settlement of debts with traders, and various other funds and supplies designed to assist assimilation into white society. Of more importance, the 1854 treaty also set up a group of small reservations for the Ojibwes dispersed across the lands they ceded in northeastern Minnesota, northern Wisconsin, and the Upper Peninsula of Michigan. Reservations were established for the following Ojibwe bands in 1854: L'Anse and Vieux De Sert, La Pointe, Lac De Flambeau, Lac Court Orielles, Fond du Lac, Grand Portage, and Ontonagon.

The Ojibwes retained their rights to hunt and fish on the lands they ceded under the treaties of 1837, 1842, and 1854, yet the growing presence of white settlers throughout the late 1800s and 1900s led to the depletion of resources and the impracticability of maintaining a traditional lifestyle. Thus, the treaty of 1854 and the creation of the reservation system was a watershed in Ojibwe history that significantly altered the Ojibwe lifestyle.

Troy Henderson

Further Reading

Cleland, Charles E. *Rites of Conquest: The History and Culture of Michigan's Native Americans*. Ann Arbor: University of Michigan Press, 1992.

Danziger, Edmund Jefferson, Jr. *The Chippewas of Lake Superior*. Norman: University of Oklahoma Press, 1978.

McClurken, James M., ed. *Fish in the Lakes, Wild Rice, and Game in Abundance: Testimony on Behalf of Mille Lacs Ojibwe Hunting and Fishing Rights*. East Lansing: Michigan State University Press, 2000.

Document: Treaty with the Chippewa

Articles of a treaty made and concluded at La Pointe, in the State of Wisconsin, between Henry C. Gilbert and David B. Herriman, commissioners on the part of the United States, and the Chippewa Indians of Lake Superior and the Mississippi, by their chiefs and head-men.

Article 1

The Chippewas of Lake Superior hereby cede to the United States all the lands heretofore owned by them in common with the Chippewas of the Mississippi, lying east of the following boundary-line, to wit: Beginning at a point, where the east branch of Snake River crosses the southern boundary-line of the Chippewa country, running thence up the said branch to its source, thence nearly north, in a straight line, to the mouth of East Savannah River, thence up the St. Louis River to the mouth of East Swan River, thence up the East Swan River to its source, thence in a straight line to the most westerly bend of Vermillion River, and thence down the Vermillion River to its mouth.

The Chippewas of the Mississippi hereby assent and agree to the foregoing cession, and consent that the whole amount of the consideration money for the country ceded above, shall be paid to the Chippewas of Lake Superior, and in consideration thereof the Chippewas of Lake Superior hereby relinquish to the Chippewas of the Mississippi, all their interest in and claim to the lands heretofore owned by them in common, lying west of the above boundry-line.

Article 2

The United States agree to set apart and withhold from sale, for the use of the Chippewas of Lake Superior, the following-described tracts of land, viz:

1st. For the L'Anse and Vieux De Sert bands, all the unsold lands in the following townships in the State of Michigan: Township fifty-one north range thirty-three west; township fifty-one north range thirty-two west; the east half of township fifty north range thirty-three west; the west half of township fifty north range thirty-two west, and all of township fifty-one north range thirty-one west, lying west of Huron Bay.

2d. For the La Pointe band, and such other Indians as may see fit to settle with them, a tract of land bounded as follows: Beginning on the south shore of Lake Superior, a few miles west of Montreal River, at the mouth of a creek called by the Indians Ke-che-se-be-we-she, running thence south to a line drawn east and west through the centre of township forty-seven north, thence west to the west line of said township, thence south to the southeast corner of township forty-six north,

Grand Portage Band.

Shaw gaw naw sheence
  or The Little Englishman 1st Chief his X Mark

May mosh caw wosh
  Headman — his X Mark

Aw de Konse
  or The Little Rein Deer 2nd Chief his X Mark

Way we ge wom
  Headman — his X Mark

Fond Du Lac Band.

Shing goope
  or The Balsom 1st Chief his X Mark

Mawn go sit.
  or The Loons Foot 2nd Chief his X Mark

May quaw me we ge zhick
  Headman — his X Mark

Keesh kewk
  Headman — his X Mark

Caw taw waw be day
  Headman — his X Mark

O daw gee —
  Headman — his X Mark

Ke che aw ke wain ze
  Headman — his X Mark

Naw gaw nub
  or The foremost Sitter 2nd Chief his X Mark

Ain ne maw sung
  2nd Chief his X Mark

Naw aw bun way
  Headman his X Mark

Wain ge maw tub
  Headman — his X Mark

Aw ke wain zeence
  Headman his X Mark

Shay way be nay se
  Headman his X Mark

Paw pa oh.
  Headman — his X Mark

Lac Court Oreille Band.

Aw ke wain ze.
  or The old Man 1st Chief his X Mark

Key no zhance
  or The Little Stock Fish 2nd Chief his X Mark

Ke che pe nay se
  or The Big Bird 2nd Chief his X Mark

Ke che waw be shay she

Nay naw ong gay be
  or The Dressing Bird 1st Chief his X Mark

Ozhaw waw sco ge zhick
  or The Blue Sky 2nd Chief his X Mark

I yaw banse —
  or The Little Buck 2nd Chief his X Mark

Ke che e nin ne

range thirty-two west, thence west the width of two townships, thence north the width of two townships, thence west one mile, thence north to the lake shore, and thence along the lake shore, crossing Shag-waw-me-quon Point, to the place of beginning. Also two hundred acres on the northern extremity of Madeline Island, for a fishing ground.

3d. For the other Wisconsin bands, a tract of land lying about Lac De Flambeau, and another tract on Lac Court Orielles, each equal in extent to three townships, the boundaries of which shall be hereafter agreed upon or fixed under the direction of the President.

4th. For the Fond Du Lac bands, a tract of land bounded as follows: Beginning at an island in the St. Louis River, above Knife Portage, called by the Indians Paw-paw-sco-me-me-tig, running thence west to the boundary-line heretofore described, thence north along said boundary-line to the mouth of Savannah River, thence down the St. Louis River to the place of beginning. And if said tract shall contain less than one hundred thousand acres, a strip of land shall be added on the south side thereof, large enough to equal such deficiency.

5th. For the Grand Portage band, a tract of land bounded as follows: Beginning at a rock a little east of the eastern extremity of Grand Portage Bay, running thence along the lake shore to the mouth of a small stream called by the Indians Maw-ske-gwaw-caw-maw-se-be, or Cranberry Marsh River, thence up said stream, across the point to Pigeon River, thence down Pigeon River to a point opposite the starting-point, and thence across to the place of beginning.

6th. The Ontonagon band and that subdivision of the La Pointe band of which Buffalo is chief, may each select, on or near the lake shore, four sections of land, under the direction of the President, the boundaries of which shall be defined hereafter. And being desirous to provide for some of his connections who have rendered his people important services, it is agreed that the chief Buffalo may select one section of land, at such place in the ceded territory as he may see fit, which shall be reserved for that purpose, and conveyed by the United States to such person or persons as he may direct.

7th. Each head of a family, or single person over twenty-one years of age at the present time of the mixed bloods, belonging to the Chippewas of Lake Superior, shall be entitled to eighty acres of land, to be selected by them under the direction of the President, and which shall be secured to them by patent in the usual form.

Article 3

The United States will define the boundaries of the reserved tracts, whenever it may be necessary, by actual survey, and the President may, from time to time, at his discretion, cause the whole to be surveyed, and may assign to each head of a family or single person over twenty-one years of age, eighty acres of land for his or their separate use; and he may, at his discretion, as fast as the occupants become capable of transacting their own affairs, issue patents therefor to such occupants, with such restrictions of the power of alienation as he may see fit to impose. And he may also, at his discretion, make rules and regulations, respecting the disposition of the lands in case of the death of the head of a family, or single person occupying the same, or in case of its abandonment by them. And he may also assign other lands in exchange for mineral lands, if any such are found in the tracts herein set apart. And he may also make such changes in the boundaries of such reserved tracts or otherwise, as shall be necessary to prevent interference with any vested rights. All necessary roads, highways, and railroads, the lines of which may run through any of the reserved tracts, shall have the right of way through the same, compensation being made therefor as in other cases.

Article 4

In consideration of and payment for the country hereby ceded, the United States agree to pay to the Chippewas of Lake Superior, annually, for the term of twenty years, the following sums, to wit: five thousand dollars in coin; eight thousand dollars in goods, household furniture and cooking utensils; three thousand dollars in agricultural implements and cattle, carpenter's and other tools and building materials, and three thousand dollars for moral and educational purposes, of which last sum, three hundred dollars per annum shall be paid to the Grand Portage band to enable them to maintain a school at their village. The United States will also pay the further sum of ninety thousand dollars, as the chiefs in open council may direct, to enable them to meet their present just engagements. Also the further sum of six thousand dollars, in agricultural implements, household furniture, and cooking utensils, to be distributed at the next annuity payment, among the mixed bloods of said nation. The United States will also furnish two hundred guns, one hundred rifles, five hundred beaver-traps, three hundred dollars' worth of ammunition, and one thousand dollars' worth of ready-made clothing, to be distributed among the young men of the nation, at the next annuity payment.

Article 5

The United States will also furnish a blacksmith and assistant, with the usual amount of stock, during the continuance of the annuity payments, and as much longer as the President may think proper, at each of the points herein set apart for the residence of the Indians, the same to be in lieu of all the employees to which the Chippewas of Lake Superior may be entitled under previous existing treaties.

Article 6

The annuities of the Indians shall not be taken to pay the debts of individuals but satisfaction for depredations committed by them shall be made by them in such manner as the President may direct.

Article 7

No spirituous liquors shall be made, sold, or used on any of the lands herein set apart for the residence of the Indians, and the sale of the same shall be prohibited in the Territory hereby ceded, until otherwise ordered by the President.

Article 8

It is agreed, between the Chippewas of Lake Superior and the Chippewas of the Mississippi, that the former shall be entitled to two-thirds, and the latter to one-third, of all benefits to be derived from former treaties existing prior to the year 1847.

Article 9

The United States agree that an examination shall be made, and all sums that may be found equitably due to the Indians, for arrearages of annuity or other thing, under the provisions of former treaties, shall be paid as the chiefs may direct.

Article 10

All missionaries, and teachers, and other persons of full age, residing in the territory hereby ceded, or upon any of the reservations hereby made by authority of law, shall be allowed to enter the land occupied by them at the minimum price whenever the surveys shall be completed to the amount of one quarter-section each.

Article 11

All annuity payments to the Chippewas of Lake Superior, shall hereafter be made at L'Anse, La Pointe, Grand Portage, and on the St. Louis River; and the Indians shall not be required to remove from the homes hereby set apart for them. And such of them as reside in the territory hereby ceded, shall have the right to hunt and fish therein, until otherwise ordered by the President.

Article 12

In consideration of the poverty of the Bois Forte Indians who are parties to this treaty, they having never received any annuity payments, and of the great extent of that part of the ceded country owned exclusively by them, the following additional stipulations are made for their benefit. The United States will pay the sum of ten thousand dollars, as their chiefs in open council may direct, to enable them to meet their present just engagements. Also the further sum of ten thousand dollars, in five equal annual payments, in blankets, cloth, nets, guns, ammunitions, and such other articles of necessity as they may require.

They shall have the right to select their reservation at any time hereafter, under the direction of the President; and the same may be equal in extent, in proportion to their numbers, to those allowed the other bands, and be subject to the same provisions.

They shall be allowed a blacksmith, and the usual smithshop supplies, and also two persons to instruct them in farming, whenever in the opinion of the President it shall be proper, and for such length of time as he shall direct.

It is understood that all Indians who are parties to this treaty, except the Chippewas of the Mississippi, shall hereafter be known as the Chippewas of Lake Superior. Provided, That the stipulation by which the Chippewas of Lake Superior relinquishing their right to land west of the boundary-line shall not apply to the Bois Forte band who are parties to this treaty.

Article 13

This treaty shall be obligatory on the contracting parties, as soon as the same shall be ratified by the President and Senate of the United States.

In testimony whereof, the said Henry C. Gilbert, and the said David B. Herriman, commissioners as aforesaid, and the undersigned chiefs and headmen of the Chippewas of Lake Superior and the Mississippi, have hereunto set their hands and seals, at the place aforesaid, this thirtieth day of September, one thousand eight hundred and fifty-four.

Henry C. Gilbert,
David B. Herriman,
Commissioners.
Richard M. Smith, Secretary.
La Pointe Band:
Ke-che-waish-ke, or the Buffalo, 1st chief, his x mark. [L. S.]
Chay-che-que-oh, 2d chief, his x mark. [L. S.]
A-daw-we-ge-zhick, or Each Side of the sky, 2d chief, his x mark. [L. S.]
O-ske-naw-way, or the Youth, 2d chief, his x mark. [L. S.]
Maw-caw-day-pe-nay-se, or the Black Bird, 2d chief, his x mark. [L. S.]
Naw-waw-naw-quot, headman, his x mark. [L. S.]
Ke-wain-zeence, headman, his x mark. [L. S.]
Waw-baw-ne-me-ke, or the White Thunder, 2d chief, his x mark. [L. S.]
Pay-baw-me-say, or the Soarer, 2d chief, his x mark. [L. S.]
Naw-waw-ge-waw-nose, or the Little Current, 2d chief, his x mark. [L. S.]
Maw-caw-day-waw-quot, or the Black Cloud, 2d chief, his x mark. [L. S.]
Me-she-naw-way, or the Disciple, 2d chief, his x mark. [L. S.]
Key-me-waw-naw-um, headman, his x mark. [L. S.]
She-gog headman, his x mark. [L. S.]
Ontonagon Band:
O-cun-de-cun, or the Buoy 1st chief, his x mark. [L. S.]
Waw-say-ge-zhick, or the Clear Sky, 2d chief, his x mark. [L. S.]
Keesh-ke-taw-wug, headman, his x mark. [L. S.]

L'Anse Band:
David King, 1st chief, his x mark. [L. S.]
John Southwind, headman, his x mark. [L. S.]
Peter Marksman, headman, his x mark. [L. S.]
Naw-taw-me-ge-zhick, or the First Sky, 2d chief, his x mark. [L. S.]
Aw-se-neece, headman, his x mark. [L. S.]
Vieux De Sert Band:
May-dway-aw-she, 1st chief, his x mark. [L. S.]
Posh-quay-gin, or the Leather, 2d chief, his x mark. [L. S.]
Grand Portage Band:
Shaw-gaw-naw-sheence, or the Little Englishman, 1st chief, his x mark. [L. S.]
May-mosh-caw-wosh, headman, his x mark. [L. S.]
Aw-de-konse, or the Little Reindeer, 2d chief, his x mark. [L. S.]
Way-we-ge-wam, headman, his x mark. [L. S.]
Fond Du Lac Band:
Shing-goope, or the Balsom, 1st chief, his x mark. [L. S.]
Mawn-go-sit, or the Loon's Foot, 2d chief, his x mark. [L. S.]
May-quaw-me-we-ge-zhick, headman, his x mark. [L. S.]
Keesh-kawk, headman, his x mark. [L. S.]
Caw-taw-waw-be-day, headman, his x mark. [L. S.]
O-saw-gee, headman, his x mark. [L. S.]
Ke-che-aw-ke-wain-ze, headman, his x mark. [L. S.]
Naw-gaw-nub, or the Foremost Sitter, 2d chief, his x mark. [L. S.]
Ain-ne-maw-sung, 2d chief, his x mark. [L. S.]
Naw-aw-bun-way, headman, his x mark. [L. S.]
Wain-ge-maw-tub, headman, his x mark. [L. S.]
Aw-ke-wain-zeence, headman, his x mark. [L. S.]
Shay-way-be-nay-se, headman, his x mark. [L. S.]
Paw-pe-oh, headman, his x mark. [L. S.]
Lac Court Oreille Band:
Aw-ke-wain-ze, or the Old Man, 1st chief, his x mark. [L. S.]
Key-no-zhance, or the Little Jack Fish, 1st chief, his x mark. [L. S.]
Key-che-pe-nay-se, or the Big Bird, 2d chief, his x mark. [L. S.]
Ke-che-waw-be-shay-she, or the Big Martin, 2d chief, his x mark. [L. S.]
Waw-be-shay-sheence, headman, his x mark. [L. S.]
Quay-quay-cub, headman, his x mark. [L. S.]
Shaw-waw-no-me-tay, headman, his x mark. [L. S.]
Nay-naw-ong-gay-be, or the Dressing Bird, 1st chief, his x mark. [L. S.]
O-zhaw-waw-sco-ge-zhick, or the Blue Sky, 2d chief, his x mark. [L. S.]
I-yaw-banse, or the Little Buck, 2d chief, his x mark. [L. S.]

Ke-che-e-nin-ne, headman, his x mark. [L. S.]
Haw-daw-gaw-me, headman, his x mark. [L. S.]
Way-me-te-go-she, headman, his x mark. [L. S.]
Pay-me-ge-wung, headman, his x mark. [L. S.]
Lac Du Flambeau Band:
Aw-mo-se, or the Wasp, 1st chief, his x mark. [L. S.]
Ke-nish-te-no, 2d chief, his x mark. [L. S.]
Me-gee-see, or the Eagle, 2d chief, his x mark. [L. S.]
Kay-kay-co-gwaw-nay-aw-she, headman, his x mark. [L. S.]
O-che-chog, headman, his x mark. [L. S.]
Nay-she-kay-gwaw-nay-be, headman, his x mark. [L. S.]
O-scaw-bay-wis, or the Waiter, 1st chief, his x mark. [L. S.]
Que-we-zance, or the White Fish, 2d chief, his x mark. [L. S.]
Ne-gig, or the Otter, 2d chief, his x mark. [L. S.]
Nay-waw-che-ge-ghick-may-be, headman, his x mark. [L. S.]
Quay-quay-ke-cah, headman, his x mark. [L. S.]
Bois Forte Band:
Kay-baish-caw-daw-way, or Clear Round the Prairie, 1st chief, his x mark. [L. S.]
Way-zaw-we-ge-zhick-way-sking, headman, his x mark. [L. S.]
O-saw-we-pe-nay-she, headman, his x mark. [L. S.]
The Mississippi Bands:
Que-we-san-se, or Hole in the Day, head chief, his x mark. [L. S.]
Caw-nawn-daw-waw-win-zo, or the Berry Hunter, 1st chief, his x mark. [L. S.]
Waw-bow-jieg, or the White Fisher, 2d chief, his x mark. [L. S.]
Ot-taw-waw, 2d chief, his x mark. [L. S.]
Que-we-zhan-cis, or the Bad Boy, 2d chief, his x mark. [L. S.]
Bye-a-jick, or the Lone Man, 2d chief, his x mark. [L. S.]
I-yaw-shaw-way-ge-zhick, or the Crossing Sky, 2d chief, his x mark. [L. S.]
Maw-caw-day, or the Bear's Heart, 2d chief, his x mark. [L. S.]
Ke-way-de-no-go-nay-be, or the Northern Feather, 2d chief, his x mark. [L. S.]
Me-squaw-dace, headman, his x mark. [L. S.]
Naw-gaw-ne-gaw-bo, headman, his x mark. [L. S.]
Wawm-be-de-yea, headman, his x mark. [L. S.]
Waish-key, headman, his x mark. [L. S.]
Caw-way-caw-me-ge-skung, headman, his x mark. [L. S.]
My-yaw-ge-way-we-dunk, or the One who carries the Voice, 2d chief, his x mark. [L. S.]
John F. Godfroy, Interpreters.
Geo. Johnston, Interpreters.
S. A. Marvin, Interpreters.

Louis Codot, Interpreters.
Paul H. Beaulieu, Interpreters.
Henry Blatchford, Interpreters.
Peter Floy, Interpreters.
Executed in the presence of—
Henry M. Rice,
J. W. Lynde,
G. D. Williams,
B. H. Connor,
E. W. Muldough,
Richard Godfroy,
D. S. Cash,
H. H. McCullough,
E. Smith Lee,
Wm. E. Vantassel,
L. H. Wheeler.

Menominee Treaty (1856)

The Menominee Treaty of 1856 required the Menominee Indians in Wisconsin to cede portions of reservation land to the federal government, in order to relocate Munsee-Stockbridge Indians. Since the 1820s, the Menominee Indians had a unique relationship with Christianized New York Indians, including the Oneidas, Stockbridges, Munsees, and Brothertowns. These groups negotiated with the Menominees of Wisconsin as early as 1821 to live on their tribal lands. Because some of the tribal members of the Native Americans from New York had learned about property rights, many Menominees opted to protest such interactions. The federal government, however, achieved some resolution at the Treaty of Prairie du Chien in 1825 wherein the tribes involved agreed under the auspices of "peace and friendship."

Over the next three decades, the Menominees experienced increasing shrinkage of their native homelands. By 1848, the Menominees signed a treaty ceding the western portion of their territory in exchange for 600,000 acres in Minnesota territory. However, Menominee tribal leaders led by Osh Koshm determined the land to be substandard. The Menominees retained 276,000 acres of their Wisconsin tribal land in heavily forested regions along the Oconto and Wolf Rivers under a treaty in 1854. Finally, the Menominee Treaty of 1856 required the Menominees to cede two townships of approximately 44,000 acres of the southwestern corner of their reservation to the Stockbridge and Munsee Indians.

Donald L. Fixico

Further Reading

Beck, David R. M. *The Struggle for Self-Determination: The History of the Menominee Indians since 1854*. Lincoln: University of Nebraska, 2005.

Herzberg, Stephen J. "The Menominee Indians: From Treaty to Termination." *The Wisconsin Magazine of History* 60, no. 4 (Summer 1977), 266–329.

Loew, Patty. *Indian Nations of Wisconsin: Histories of Endurance and Renewal*. Madison: Wisconsin Historical Society Press, 2013.

Document: Treaty with the Menominee

Whereas a treaty was entered into at Stockbridge, in the State of Wisconsin, on the fifth of the present month, between the United States of America on the one part, and the Stockbridge and Munsee tribes of Indians on the other, stipulating that a new home shall be furnished to the said Stockbridge and Munsee Indians, near the south line of the Menomonee reservation; and

Whereas the United States desire to locate said Stockbridges and Munsees near the said line in the western part of the said reservation, on lands on which no permanent settlements have been made by the Menomonees; and

Whereas there is no objection on the part of the Menomonees to the location of the Stockbridges and Munsees in their neighborhood, therefore this agreement and convention has been entered into.

Articles of agreement made and concluded at Keshena, State of Wisconsin, on the eleventh day of February, in the year of our Lord eighteen hundred and fifty-six, between Francis Huebschmann, commissioner on the part of the United States, and the Menomonee tribe of Indians, assembled in general council.

Article 1

The Menomonee tribe of Indians cede to the United States a tract of land, not to exceed two townships in extent, to be selected in the western part of their present reservation on its south line, and not containing any permanent settlements made by any of their number, for the purpose of locating thereon the Stockbridge and Munsee Indians, and such others of the New York Indians as the United States may desire to remove to the said location within two years from the ratification hereof.

Article 2

The United States agree to pay for the said cession, in case the said New York Indians will be located on the said lands, at the rate of sixty cents per acre; and it is hereby stipulated, that the monies so to be paid shall be expended in a like manner, to promote the improvement of the Menomonees, as is stipulated by the third article of the treaty of May twelfth, eighteen hundred and fifty-four, for the expenditure of the forty thousand dollars which had been set aside for their removal and subsistence, west of the Mississippi, by the treaty of October eighteenth, eighteen hundred and forty-eight.

Article 3

To promote the welfare and the improvement of the said Menomonees, and friendly relations between them and the citizens of the United States, it is further stipulated—

1. That in case this agreement and the treaties made previously with the Menomonees should prove insufficient, from causes which cannot now been [be] foreseen, to effect the said objects, the President of the United States may, by and with the advice and consent of the Senate, adopt such policy in the management of the affairs of the Menomonees as in his judgment may be most beneficial to them; or Congress may, hereafter, make such provision by law as experience shall prove to be necessary.
2. That the Menomonees will suppress the use of ardent spirits among their people, and resist, by all prudent means, its introduction in their settlements.
3. That the President of the United States, if deemed by him conducive to the welfare of the Menomonees, may cause their annuity monies to be paid to them in semi-annual or quarterly instalments.
4. That all roads and highways, laid out by authority of law, shall have right of way through the lands of the said Indians on the same terms as are provided by law for their location through lands of citizens of the United States.

Article 4

This instrument shall be binding upon the contracting parties whenever the same shall be ratified by the President and Senate of the United States.

In testimony whereof, the said Francis Huebschmann, commissioner as aforesaid, and the chiefs and headmen of the said Menomonee tribe, in presence and with the consent of the warriors and young men of the said tribe, assembled in general council, have hereunto set their hands and seals at the place and on the day and year hereinbefore written.

    Francis Huebschmann. [L. S.]
    Commissioner on the part of the United States.
    Osh-kosh, his x mark. [L. S.]
    Sho-ne-niew, his x mark. [L. S.]
    Ke-she-na, his x mark. [L. S.]
    La-motte, his x mark. [L. S.]
    Pe-quah-kaw-nah, his x mark. [L. S.]
    Car-ron, his x mark. [L. S.]

Wau-ke-chon, his x mark. [L. S.]
Ah-kamote, his x mark. [L. S.]
Ah-yah-metah, his x mark. [L. S.]
Osh-ke-he-na-niew, his x mark. [L. S.]
Kotch-kaw-no-naew, his x mark. [L. S.]
Sho-ne-on, his x mark. [L. S.]
Wa-pa-massaew, his x mark. [L. S.]
Naw-no-ha-toke, his x mark. [L. S.]
Match-a-kin-naew, his x mark. [L. S.]
Mah-mah-ke-wet, his x mark. [L. S.]
Ko-man-e-kim, his x mark. [L. S.]
Shaw-puy-tuck, his x mark. [L. S.]
Oken-a-po-wet, his x mark. [L. S.]
Way-taw-say, his x mark. [L. S.]
Naw-kaw-chis-ka, his x mark. [L. S.]
Wa-ta-push, his x mark. [L. S.]
Py-aw-wah-say, his x mark. [L. S.]
Way-aich-kiew, his x mark. [L. S.]
Ay-oh-sha, his x mark. [L. S.]
Mo-sha-hart, his x mark. [L. S.]
Signed and sealed in presence of—
Benja Hunkins, Indian agent.
Talbot Pricket, United States interpreter.
Theodore Koven, secretary to commissioner.
John Wiley.
R. Otto Skolla.
H. L. Murny.
Benjamin Rice.
John Werdchaff.
Stephen Canfield.
Thomas Heaton.

Reconstruction Treaties with the Cherokee, Choctaw, Chickasaw, Creeks, and Seminole (1866)

These agreements were made between the United States and the Seminole, Choctaw, Chickasaw, Creek, and Cherokee Nations between February and August 1866. All five Native groups had signed treaties of alliance with the Confederacy in 1861; as a result, the federal government declared that the tribes had lost all rights to annuities and land promised in former treaties.

The negotiations with the five nations began in September 1865 with a 12-day meeting at Fort Smith, Arkansas. During the conference, the federal government stated the seven basic stipulations required in each treaty. First, each nation had to enter into a treaty of peace and friendship with the United States, with other Native American nations, and between tribal factions. Second, they were to assist the federal government in pacifying the western Native peoples. Third, slavery had to be abolished, all slaves were to be unconditionally emancipated, and the freed slaves had to be incorporated into the tribes or other suitable provisions made for former slaves. Fourth, involuntary servitude could be tolerated only as punishment for a crime. Fifth, each nation holding land in Indian Territory had to set aside land for the settlement of Kansas Natives. Sixth, all tribes of Indian Territory were expected to prepare for the eventual consolidation of all Natives under one government. Finally, no white persons, except those connected with the military or assigned as Indian agents and employees of the government and of internal improvement agencies, were to be permitted to reside in Indian Territory unless they had been formally incorporated into the tribe. The Natives would have some ability to negotiate how much land each nation forfeited, the size of rights-of-way for railroads, and the status of former slaves.

The Seminole delegation was the first to arrive in Washington. The inexperienced and impoverished representatives were war-weary and just wanted to go home; consequently, they put up little resistance to the demands of federal negotiators. In the Treaty with the Seminole (1866), they agreed to all the demands of the Fort Smith meeting, ceding their entire homeland for 15 cents an acre, and they agreed to purchase 200,000 acres from the Creek Nation at 50 cents an acre. Their treaty established rights-of-way for railroads, abolished slavery, and stated that all Seminoles, freedmen, and adopted white people would have equal rights within the nation.

The harsh treaty with the Seminole was followed a few weeks later by the far more benevolent Treaty with the Choctaw and Chickasaw (1866). The two nations hired an attorney and worked closely together. Overall, the Choctaws, the Chickasaws, and their attorneys proved to be very able negotiators, and the Choctaws and Chickasaws did not incur any liability or forfeiture of land as a result of their alignment with the Confederacy. They were not forced to grant citizenship to their former slaves. If the two nations did not pass legislation providing for the civil rights of their former slaves, the United States would use $300,000 of Choctaw and Chickasaw money to relocate the people of African descent elsewhere. Rights-of-way were established for railroads, and the Choctaws and Chickasaws made provisions to purchase stock in the company that built through their nation. They were to pay for the stock by selling to the railroad sections of land six miles wide on each side of the track.

The Creek Nation's negotiations in many ways mirrored the Seminole negotiations. The delegates did not resist federal demands, and they accepted all the Fort Smith demands. In the Treaty with the Creek (1866), they ceded the west half of the Creek domain, estimated to contain 3,250,560 acres; they adopted their freedmen, established rights-of-way for the railroads, and accepted provisions for the eventual consolidation of all Natives under one government.

The most contentious negations were with the Cherokees, who sent both Southern and Union representatives; federal officials played the two factions against each other. After months of bitter debate, federal negotiators dismissed the Loyal Cherokee delegation and concluded a treaty with the minority southern representatives. This treaty was never recognized, and a few weeks later, the Loyal delegation was invited back. In the end, the Cherokees agreed to most of the Fort Smith provisions with the Treaty with the Cherokee (1866). Former slaves were granted citizenship and were to have equal rights with other Cherokee citizens. The nation was also forced to sell the Neutral Lands, but they refused to sell the Cherokee Strip. Fortunately, on the issue of land cession, the Loyal faction negotiated better terms than the other four nations did. The land was to be appraised by two disinterested parties and then to be sold to the highest bidder, and the Cherokee Nation was guaranteed at least $1.25 per acre.

The unique sovereign status of the five nations allowed Indian commissioners to make demands of the slave-owning Native Americans that were not made of former Confederate states. No former Confederate State was required to give up territory as war reparations, yet all five nations were required to cede or lease land so the federal government could concentrate all unwanted indigenous people in Indian Territory. Furthermore, although Southern slaveowners simply had to free their slaves, Natives were required to give their freedmen land and, in some cases, tribal membership and a share of tribal funds. In effect, three nations lost the right to determine their own tribal membership.

Joyce Ann Kievit

Further Reading

Abel, Annie Heloise. *The American Indian under Reconstruction*. Cleveland: Arthur H. Clark. Reprint, St. Clair Shores, MI: Scholarly Press, 1972.

Foreman, Grant. *The Five Civilized Tribes: Cherokee, Chickasaw, Choctaw, Creek, Seminole*. Norman: University of Oklahoma Press, 1934.

Foreman, Grant. *Indian Removal: The Emigration of the Five Civilized Tribes of Indians*. Norman: University of Oklahoma Press, 1932.

Kappler, Charles J., ed. *Indian Affairs: Laws and Treaties*, vol. 2. New York: AMS Press, 1971.

Document: Treaty with the Seminole

Articles of a treaty made and concluded at Washington, D.C., March 21, A.D., 1866, between the United States Government, by its commissioners, D.N. Cooley,

Commissioner of Indian Affairs, Elijah Sells, superintendent of Indian affairs, and Ely S. Parker, and the Seminole Indians, by their chiefs, John Chup-co, or Long John, Cho-cote-harjo, Fos-ha[r]-jo, John F. Brown.

Whereas existing, treaties between the United States and the Seminole Nation are insufficient to meet their mutual necessities; and

Whereas the Seminole Nation made a treaty with the so-called Confederate States, August 1st, 1861, whereby they threw off their allegiance to the United States, and unsettled their treaty relations with the United States, and thereby incurred the liability of forfeiture of all lands and other property held by grant or gift of the United States; and whereas a treaty of peace and amity was entered into between the United States and the Seminole and other tribes at Fort Smith, September 13 [10,] 1865, whereby the Seminoles revoked, canceled. and repudiated the said treaty with the so-called Confederate States; and whereas the United States, through its commissioners, in said treaty of peace promised to enter into treaty with the Seminole Nation to arrange and settle all questions relating to and growing out of said treaty with the so-called Confederate States; and whereas the United States, in view of said treaty of the Seminole Nation with the enemies of the Government of the United States, and the consequent liabilities of said Seminole Nation, and in view of its urgent necessities for more lands in the Indian Territory, requires a cession by said Seminole Nation of part of its present reservation, and is willing to pay therefor a reasonable price, while at the same time providing new and adequate land for them:

Now, therefore, the United States, by its commissioners aforesaid, and the above-named delegates of the Seminole Nation, the day and year above written, mutually stipulate and agree, on behalf of the respective parties, as follows, to wit;

Article 1

There shall be perpetual peace between the United States and the Seminole Nation, and the Seminoles agree to be and remain firm allies of the United States, and always faithfully aid the Government thereof to suppress insurrection and put down its enemies.

The Seminoles also agree to remain at peace with all other Indian tribes and with themselves. In return for these pledges of peace and friendship, the United States guarantee them quiet possession of their country, and protection against hostilities on the part of other tribes; and, in the event of such hostilities, that the tribe commencing and prosecuting the same shall make just reparation therefor. Therefore the Seminoles agree to a military occupation of their country at the option and expense of the United States.

A general amnesty of all past offences against the laws of the United States, committed by any member of the Seminole Nation, is hereby declared; and the

14

leased or rented to, or occupied by any one or the Chiefs of the Seminole Nation according to its laws and regulations: *Provided Also*, That Officers, Servants and Employees of said rail road necessary to its construction and management, shall not be excluded from such necessary occupancy, they being subject to the provisions of the Indian Intercourse Law, and such rules and regulations as may be established by the Secretary of the Interior; nor shall any conveyance of said lands be made to the party building and managing said road until its Completion as a first class rail road and its acceptance as such by the Secretary of the Interior.

Article 6. Inasmuch as there are no Agency buildings upon the new Seminole Reservation. It is therefore further agreed that the United States have caused to be constructed at an Expense not exceeding ten thousand ($10,000.00) dollars suitable Agency buildings the site whereof shall be selected by the Agent of said tribe under the direction of the Superintendent of Indian Affairs, in Consideration whereof the Seminole Nation hereby relinquish and Cede forever to the United States, the residue of those lands upon which said Agency buildings shall be elected which land shall revert to said nation when no longer used by the United States, upon said nation paying a fair value for said buildings at the time vacated.

Article 7. The Seminole Nation agrees to such legislation as Congress and the President may deem necessary for the better administration of the rights of Person and Property

Seminoles, anxious for the restoration of kind and friendly feelings among themselves, do hereby declare an amnesty for all past offenses against their government, and no Indian or Indians shall be proscribed or any act of forfeiture or confiscation passed against those who have remained friendly to or taken up arms against the United States, but they shall enjoy equal privileges with other members of said tribe, and all laws heretofore passed inconsistent herewith are hereby declared inoperative.

Article 2

The Seminole Nation covenant that henceforth in said nation slavery shall not exist, nor involuntary servitude, except for and in punishment of crime, whereof the offending party shall first have been duly convicted in accordance with law, applicable to all the members of said nation. And inasmuch as there are among the Seminoles many persons of African descent and blood, who have no interest or property in the soil, and no recognized civil rights it is stipulated that hereafter these persons and their descendants, and such other of the same race as shall be permitted by said nation to settle there, shall have and enjoy all the rights of native citizens, and the laws of said nation shall be equally binding upon all persons of whatever race or color, who may be adopted as citizens or members of said tribe.

Article 3

In compliance with the desire of the United States to locate other Indians and freedmen thereon, the Seminoles cede and convey to the United States their entire domain, being the tract of land ceded to the Seminole Indians by the Creek Nation under the provisions of article first, (1st,) treaty of the United States with the Creeks and Seminoles, made and concluded at Washington, D. C., August 7, 1856. In consideration of said grant and cession of their lands, estimated at two million one hundred and sixty-nine thousand and eighty (2,169,080) acres, the United States agree to pay said Seminole Nation the sum of three hundred and twenty-five thousand three hundred and sixty-two ($325,362) dollars, said purchase being at the rate of fifteen cents per acre. The United States having obtained by grant of the Creek Nation the westerly half of their lands, hereby grant to the Seminole Nation the portion thereof hereafter described, which shall constitute the national domain of the Seminole Indians. Said lands so granted by the United States to the Seminole Nation are bounded and described as follows, to wit: Beginning on the Canadian River where the line dividing the Creek lands according to the terms of their sale to the United States by their treaty of February 6, 1866, following said line due north to where said line crosses the north fork of the Canadian River; thence up said north fork of the Canadian River a distance sufficient to make two hundred thousand acres by running due south to the Canadian River; thence down said Canadian River to the place of beginning. In consideration of said cession of two hundred thousand acres of land described above, the Seminole Nation agrees to pay therefor the price of fifty cents per acre, amounting to the sum of one hundred thousand dollars, which amount shall be deducted from the sum paid by the United States for Seminole lands under the stipulations above written. The balance due the Seminole Nation after making said deduction, amounting to one hundred thousand dollars, the United States agree to pay in the following manner, to wit: Thirty thousand dollars shall be paid to enable the Seminoles to occupy, restore, and improve their farms, and to make their nation independent and self-sustaining, and shall be distributed for that purpose under the direction of the Secretary of the Interior; twenty thousand dollars shall be paid in like manner for the purpose of purchasing agricultural implements, seeds, cows, and other stock; fifteen thousand dollars shall be paid for the erection of a mill suitable to accommodate said nation of Indians; seventy thousand dollars to remain in the United States Treasury, upon which the United States shall pay an annual interest of five per cent.; fifty thousand of said sum of seventy thousand dollars shall be a permanent school-fund, the interest of which shall be paid annually and appropriated to the support of schools; the remainder of the seventy thousand dollars, being twenty thousand dollars, shall remain a permanent fund, the interest of which shall be paid annually for the support of the Seminole government; forty thousand three hundred and sixty-two dollars shall be appropriated and expended for subsisting said Indians, discriminating in favor of the destitute; all of which amounts, excepting the seventy thousand dollars to remain in the Treasury as a permanent fund, shall be paid upon the ratification of said treaty, and disbursed in such manner as the Secretary of the Interior may direct. The balance, fifty thousand dollars, or so much thereof as may be necessary to pay the losses ascertained and awarded as hereinafter provided, shall be paid when said awards shall have been duly made and approved by the Secretary of the Interior. And in case said fifty thousand dollars shall be insufficient to pay all said awards, it shall be distributed pro rata to those whose claims are so allowed; and until said awards shall be thus paid, the United States agree to pay to said Indians, in such manner and for such purposes as the Secretary of the Interior may direct, interest at the rate of five per cent. per annum from the date of the ratification of this treaty.

Article 4

To reimburse such members of the Seminole Nation as shall be duly adjudged to have remained loyal and faithful to their treaty relations to the United States, during the recent rebellion of the so-called Confederate States for the losses actually sustained by them thereby, after the ratification of this treaty, or so soon thereafter as the Secretary of the Interior shall direct, he shall appoint a board of commissioners, not to exceed three in number, who shall proceed to the Seminole country and investigate and determine said losses. Previous to said investigation the agent of the Seminole Nation shall prepare a census or enumeration of said tribe, and make a roll of all Seminoles who did in no manner aid or abet the enemies of the Government, but remained loyal during said rebellion; and no award shall be made by said commissioners for such losses unless the name of the claimant appear on said roll, and no compensation shall be allowed any person for such losses whose name does not appear on said roll, unless said claimant, within six months from the date of the completion of said roll, furnishes proof satisfactory to said board, or to the Commissioner of Indian Affairs, that he has at all times remained loyal to the United States, according to his treaty obligations. All evidence touching said claims shall be taken by said commissioners, or any of them, under oath, and their awards made, together with the evidence, shall be transmitted to the Commissioner of Indian Affairs, for his approval, and that of the Secretary of the Interior. Said commissioners shall be paid by the United States such compensation as the Secretary of the Interior may direct. The provisions of this article shall extend to and embrace the claims for losses sustained by loyal members of said tribe, irrespective of race or color, whether at the time of said losses the claimants shall have been in servitude or not; provided said claimants are made members of said tribe by the stipulations of this treaty.

Article 5

The Seminole Nation hereby grant a right of way through their lands to any company which shall be duly authorized by Congress, and shall, with the express consent and approbation of the Secretary of the Interior, undertake to construct a railroad from any point on their eastern to their western or southern boundary; but said railroad company, together with all its agents and employees, shall be subject to the laws of the United States relating to the intercourse with Indian tribes, and also to such rules and regulations as may be prescribed by the Secretary of the Interior for that purpose. And the Seminoles agree to sell to the United States, or any company duly authorized as aforesaid, such lands, not legally owned or occupied by a member or members of the Seminole Nation lying along the line of said contemplated railroad, not exceeding on each side thereof a belt or strip of land three miles in width, at such price per acre as may be eventually agreed upon between said Seminole Nation and the party or parties building said road—subject to the approval of the President of the United States: Provided, however, That said land thus sold shall not be reconveyed, leased, or rented to, or be occupied by, any one not a citizen of the Seminole Nation, according to its laws and recognized usages: Provided also, That officers, servants, and employées of said railroad necessary to its construction and management shall not be excluded from such necessary occupancy, they being subject to the provisions of the Indian-intercourse laws, and such rules and regulations as may be established by the Secretary of the Interior; nor shall any conveyance of said lands be made to the party building and managing said road, until its completion as a first-class railroad and its acceptance as such by the Secretary of the Interior.

Article 6

Inasmuch as there are no agency buildings upon the new Seminole reservation, it is therefore further agreed that the United States shall cause to be constructed, at an expense not exceeding ten thousand (10,000) dollars, suitable agency buildings, the site whereof shall be selected by the agent of said tribe, under the direction of the superintendent of Indian affairs; in consideration whereof, the Seminole Nation hereby relinquish and cede forever to the United States one section of their lands upon which said agency buildings shall be directed, [erected,] which land shall revert to said nation when no longer used by the United States, upon said nation paying a fair value for said buildings at the time vacated.

Article 7

The Seminole Nation agrees to such legislation as Congress and the President may deem necessary for the better administration of the rights of person and property within the Indian Territory: Provided, however, [That] said legislation shall not in any manner interfere with or annul their present tribal organization, rights, laws, privileges, and customs.

The Seminole Nation also agree that a general council, consisting of delegates elected by each nation, a tribe lawfully resident within the Indian Territory, may be annually convened in said Territory which council shall be organized in such manner and possess such powers as are hereinafter described:

1st. After the ratification of this treaty, and as soon as may be deemed practicable by the Secretary of the Interior, and prior to the first session of said council, a census or enumeration of each tribe lawfully resident in said Territory shall be taken, under the direction of the superintendent of Indian affairs, who, for that purpose, is hereby authorized to designate and appoint competent persons, whose compensation shall be fixed by the Secretary of the Interior and paid by the United States.

2d. The first general council shall consist of one member from each tribe, and an additional member for each one thousand Indians, or each fraction of a thousand greater than five hundred, being members of any tribe lawfully resident in said Territory, and shall be elected by said tribes, respectively, who may assent to the establishment of said general council; and if none should be thus formally selected by any nation or tribe, the said nation or tribe shall be represented in said general council by the chiefs and head-men of said tribes, to be taken in the order of their rank, in the same number and proportion as above indicated. After the said census shall have been taken and completed, the superintendent of Indian affairs shall publish and declare to each tribe the number of members of said council to which they shall be entitled under the provisions of this article; and the persons so entitled to represent said tribe shall meet at such time and place as he shall appoint; but thereafter the time and place of the sessions of said council shall be determined by its action: Provided, That no session in any one year shall exceed the term of thirty days, And provided That special sessions of said council may be called by said superintendent whenever, in his judgment, or that of the Secretary of the Interior, the interest of said tribes shall require.

3d. Said general council shall have power to legislate upon all rightful subjects and matters pertaining to the intercourse and relations of the Indian tribes and nations resident in said Territory; the arrest and extradition of criminals and offenders escaping from one tribe to another; the administration of justice between members of the several tribes of said Territory, and persons other than Indians and members of said tribes or nations; the construction of works of internal improvement and the common defence and safety of the nation of said Territory. All laws enacted by said council shall take effect at such time as may therein be provided, unless suspended by direction of the Secretary of the Interior or the President of the United States. No law shall be enacted inconsistent with the Constitution of the United States, or the laws of Congress, or existing treaty stipulations with the United States; nor shall said council legislate upon matters pertaining to the organization, laws, or customs of the several tribes except as herein provided for.

4th. Said council shall be presided over by the superintendent of Indian affairs, or, in case of his absence for any cause, the duties of said superintendent enumerated in this article shall be performed by such person as the Secretary of the Interior may direct.

5th. The Secretary of the Interior shall appoint a secretary of said council, whose duty it shall be to keep an accurate record of all the proceedings of said council, and who shall transmit a true copy of all such proceedings, duly certified by the superintendent of Indian affairs, to the Secretary of the Interior immediately after the session of said council. He shall be paid out of the Treasury of the United States an annual salary of five hundred dollars.

6th. The members of said council shall be paid by the United States the sum of four dollars per diem during the time actually in attendance upon the sessions of said council, and at the rate of four dollars for every twenty miles necessarily traveled by them in going to said council and returning to their homes, respectively, to be certified by the secretary of the said council and the sup[erintenden]t of Indian affairs.

7th. The Seminoles also agree that a court or courts may be established in said Territory, with such jurisdiction and organized in such manner as Congress may by law provide.

Article 8

The stipulations of this treaty are to be a full settlement of all claims of said Seminole Nation for damages and losses of every kind growing out of the late rebellion, and all expenditures by the United States of annuities in clothing and feeding refugee and destitute Indians since the diversion of annuities for that purpose, consequent upon the late war with the so-called Confederate States. And the Seminoles hereby ratify and confirm all such diversions of annuities heretofore made from the funds of the Seminole Nation by the United States. And the United States agree that no annuities shall be diverted from the object for which they were originally devoted by treaty stipulations, with the Seminoles, to the use of refugee and destitute Indians, other than the Seminoles or members of the Seminole Nation, after the close of the present fiscal year, June thirtieth, eighteen hundred and sixty-six.

Article 9

The United States re-affirms and reassumes all obligations of treaty stipulations entered into before the treaty of said Seminole Nation with the so-called Confederate States, August first, eighteen hundred and sixty-one, not inconsistent herewith; and further agree to renew all payments of annuities accruing by force of said treaty stipulations, from and after the close of the present fiscal year, June thirtieth, in the year of our Lord one thousand eight hundred and sixty-six, except as is provided in article eight, (viii.)

Article 10

A quantity of land not exceeding six hundred and forty acres, to be selected according to legal subdivisions, in one body, and which shall include their improvements, is hereby granted to every religious society or denomination which has erected, or which, with the consent of the Indians, may hereafter erect, buildings within the Seminole country for missionary or educational purposes; but no land thus granted, nor the buildings which have been or may be erected thereon, shall ever be sold or otherwise disposed of except with the consent and approval of the Secretary of the Interior. And whenever any such land or buildings shall be so sold or disposed of, the proceeds thereof shall be applied, under the direction of the Secretary of the Interior, to the support and maintenance of other similar establishments for the benefit of the Seminoles and such other persons as may be, or may hereafter become, members of the tribe according to its laws, customs, and usages.

Article 11

It is further agreed that all treaties heretofore entered into between the United States and the Seminole Nation which are inconsistent with any of the articles or provisions of this treaty shall be, and are hereby, rescinded and annulled.

In testimony whereof, the said Dennis N. Cooley, Commissioner of Indian affairs, Elijah Sells, superintendent of Indian affairs, and Col. Ely S. Parker, as aforesaid, and the undersigned, persons representing the Seminole nation, have hereunto set their hands and seals the day and year first above written.

Dennis N. Cooley, [SEAL.]
Commissioner of Indian Affairs.
Elijah Sells, [SEAL.]
Superintendent Indian Affairs.
Col. Ely S. Parker [SEAL.]
Special commissioner.
John Chup-co, his x mark. [SEAL.]
King or head chief.
Cho-cote-harjo, his x mark, [SEAL.]
Counselor.
Fos-harjo, his x mark, chief. [SEAL.]
John F. Brown, [SEAL.]
Special delegate for Southern Seminoles.
In presence of—
Robert Johnson, his x mark.
United States interpreter for Seminole Indians.
Geo. A. Reynolds, United States Indian agent for Seminoles.
Ok-tus-sus-har-jo, his x mark, or Sands.
Cow-e-to-me-ko, his x mark.
Che-chu-chee, his x mark.
Harry Island, his x mark.
United States interpreter for Creek Indians.
J. W. Dunn, United States Indian agent for the Creek Nation.
Perry Fuller.
Signed by John F. Brown, special delegate for the Southern Seminoles, in presence of, this June thirtieth, eighteen hundred and sixty-six—
W. R. Irwin.
J. M. Tebbetts.
Geo. A. Reynolds, United States Indian agent.
Robert Johnson, his x mark, United States interpreter.

Medicine Lodge Treaty (1867)

The Medicine Lodge Treaty was negotiated in three sessions with the largest American Indian nations of the southern plains—the Cheyennes, Arapahos, Comanches, Kiowas, and Kiowa-Apaches—between October 21 and October 28, 1867. This treaty represented the last effort by the United States to solve its conflict with these nations in a diplomatic way. Extensive European American intrusion into the central and southern plains had culminated during the Colorado gold rush of 1859;

the resulting uneasiness was expressed in reprisals on both sides during the 1860s. After the Sand Creek Massacre in 1864 and the burning of another Cheyenne village at Pawnee Fork in 1867, Cheyenne war parties retaliated with raids. The treaty aimed not only at securing peace but also at confining the American Indians to reservations, where they would be assimilated. The treaty thus marked the beginning of the reservation period.

Indian agent Colonel Jesse Leavenworth met with the pertinent Native leaders to negotiate a place for the signing of the treaty. The Medicine Lodge Creek site in Southern Kansas, 70 miles west-southwest of Wichita, was chosen as a compromise, allowing easy transportation of gifts from Fort Larned. The Native nations were hesitant to go farther north, where they risked attack or exposure to the outbreak of cholera along the Arkansas River.

The members of the U.S. Peace Commission were Generals Alfred Terry, William Harney, John Sanborn, and Christopher Augur; Senator John B. Henderson; Commissioner N. G. Taylor; and Colonel Samuel Tappan. A number of newspaper correspondents were present. One of them, H.M. Stanley, reported that there were 150 lodges of the Kiowas, with their representatives Sitting Bear (Satank) and White Bear (Satanta); 100 lodges of the Comanches, with Ten Bears and Silver Brooch; 171 lodges of the Arapahos, with Little Raven and Yellow Bear; 85 lodges of the Kiowa-Apaches, with Poor Bear; and 250 lodges of the peaceful fraction of the Cheyennes, with Black Kettle and Little Robe. The chiefs of the militant Cheyenne band Dog Soldiers, such as Tall Bull and Bull Bear, did not agree with the treaty at first. The Cheyennes came and signed only after they finished their ceremonies of Sacred Arrows Renewal, when Black Kettle persuaded them to do so.

The negotiations were conducted in three sessions; the result of each was a treaty between the Peace Commission and the Native American nations represented at each session. The Kiowas and Comanches signed on October 21, the Kiowa-Apaches on the same day, and the Cheyennes and Arapahos on October 28, 1867. Because the terms of the treaties were nearly identical, and the three documents were a result of a single peace effort, the treaty is usually referred to as one single treaty.

The peace agreement guaranteed the right of European Americans to travel over emigrant roads through the southern and central plains, the safety of the railroads and their construction, and cession of the American Indian land. The Comanches, Kiowas, and Kiowa-Apaches were assigned a reservation in southwestern Indian Territory between the Red River and the Washita River. The Cheyennes and Arapahos were granted a reservation in northeastern Indian Territory between the Arkansas River and the Cimarron River. All these nations were expected to adopt the European American pattern of civilization on their reservations. The Medicine Lodge treaty provided for the compulsory education of children between ages six and sixteen, a resident Indian agent, a physician, a farmer, and other permanent agency personnel. Any head of a family could select 320 acres of land within the reservation for private farming, whereas single adults would receive eight acres. Compensating for previous treaty agreements, the U.S. government bound itself to deliver clothing and to provide funds for the benefit of the Native American nations for a period of 30 years.

The treaty was successful in setting an example for a new period in the plains conflict, but it did not stop the frontier wars. Detainment of promised provisions, the activities of liquor peddlers, continuing intertribal warfare, and the impending breakdown of the buffalo economy—related to European American encroachment—created a dismal situation that led to more killing on both sides. Eventually, nearly two years after concluding the treaty, all the tribal nations settled down on their reservations. The treaty was a clear declaration of the further intentions of the United States. Up to this time, the Native nations had been just pushed aside from the settlement areas of the European Americans and allowed to live in their own ways. Now they would be forced to assimilate.

Antonie Dvorakova

Further Reading

Berthrong, Donald, J. *The Southern Cheyennes*. Norman: University of Oklahoma Press, 1963.

Grinnell, George Bird. *The Fighting Cheyennes*. Norman: University of Oklahoma Press, 1956.

Jones, Douglas C. *The Treaty of Medicine Lodge: The Story of the Great Council as Told by Eyewitnesses*. Norman: University of Oklahoma Press, 1966.

Kappler, Charles Joseph, ed. *Indian Treaties, 1778–1883*. New York: Interland, 1972.

Document: Medicine Lodge Treaty

Articles of a treaty and agreement made and entered into at the Council Camp on Medicine Lodge Creek, seventy miles south of Fort Larned, in the State of Kansas, on the twenty-eighth day of October, eighteen hundred and sixty-seven, by and between the United States of America, represented by its commissioners duly appointed thereto, to wit: Nathaniel G. Taylor, William S. Harney, C. C. Augur, Alfred H. Terry, John B. Sanborn, Samuel F. Tappan and John B. Henderson, of the one part, and the Cheyenne and Arapahoe tribes of Indians, represented by their chiefs and head-men duly authorized and empowered to act for the body of the people of said tribes—the names of said chiefs and head-men being hereto subscribed—of the other part, witness:

Article 1

From this day forward all war between the parties to this agreement shall forever cease. The Government of the United States desires peace, and its honor is here

On the part of the Cheyennes

O-to-ah-nac-co.	Bull Bear	his ● mark	seal
Mokie-tav-a-to.	Black Kettle	his + mark	seal
Nac-co-hah-ket.	Little Bear	his + mark	seal
Mo-a-vo-va-ast	Spotted Elk	his + mark	seal
Is-se-von-ne-be	Buffalo Chief	his + mark	seal
Vip-po-nah	Slim Face	his + mark	seal
Wo-pah-ah	Grey Head	his + mark	seal
O-ni-hah-Ket	Little Rock	his ● mark	seal
Mu-mo-Ki, or	Curly Hair	his + mark	seal
O-to-ah-hais-tu.	Tall Bull	his + mark	seal
Wo-po-ham, or	White Horse	his + mark	seal
Itah-Kel-home-mah,	Little Robe	his + mark	seal
Min-nin-ne-wah	Whirlwind	his + mark	seal
Mo-yan-histe-histonge	Heap of Birds	his + mark	seal

On the part of the Arapahoes

Little Raven	his + mark	(seal)
Yellow Bear	his + mark	(seal)
Storm	his + mark	(seal)
White Rabbit	his + mark	(seal)
Spotted Wolf	his + mark	(seal)
Little Big Mouth	his + mark	(seal)
Young Colt	his + mark	(seal)
Tall Bear	his + mark	(seal)

pledged to keep it. The Indians desire peace, and they now pledge their honor to maintain it.

If bad men among the whites, or among other people subject to the authority of the United States, shall commit any wrong upon the person or property of the Indians, the United States will, upon proof made to the agent and forwarded to the Commissioner of Indian Affairs at Washington City, proceed at once to cause the offender to be arrested and punished according to the laws of the United States, and also reimburse the injured person for the loss sustained.

If bad men among the Indians shall commit a wrong or depredation upon the person or property of any one, white, black, or Indian, subject to the authority of the United States and at peace therewith, the tribes herein named solemnly agree that they will, on proof made to their agent, and notice by him, deliver up the wrongdoer to the United States, to be tried and punished according to its laws; and in case they wilfully refuse so to do, the person injured shall be re-imbursed for his loss from the annuities or other moneys due or to become due to them under this or other treaties made with the United States. And the President, on advising with the Commissioner of Indian Affairs, shall prescribe such rules and regulations for ascertaining damages, under the provisions of this article, as in his judgment may be proper. But no such damages shall be adjusted and paid until thoroughly examined and passed upon by the Commissioner of Indian Affairs and the Secretary of the Interior, and no one sustaining loss, while violating, or because of his violating, the provisions of this treaty or the laws of the United States, shall be re-imbursed therefor.

Article 2

The United States agrees that the following district of country, to wit: commencing at the point where the Arkansas River crosses the 37th parallel of north latitude, thence west on said parallel—the said line being the southern boundary of the State of Kansas—to the Cimarone River, (sometimes called the Red Fork of the Arkansas River), thence down said Cimarone River, in the middle of the main channel thereof, to the Arkansas River; thence up the Arkansas River, in the middle of the main channel thereof, to the place of beginning, shall be and the same is hereby set apart for the absolute and undisturbed use and occupation of the Indians herein named, and for such other friendly tribes or individual Indians, as from time to time they may be willing, with the consent of the United States, to admit among them; and the United States now solemnly agrees that no persons except those herein authorized so to do, and except such officers, agents, and employés of the Government as may be authorized to enter upon Indian reservations in discharge of duties enjoined by law, shall ever be permitted to pass over, settle upon, or reside in the territory described in this article, or in such territory as may be added to this reservation for the use of said Indians.

Article 3

If it should appear from actual survey or other examination of said tract of land, that it contains less than one hundred and sixty acres of tillable land for each person who at the time may be authorized to reside on it, under the provisions of this treaty, and a very considerable number of such persons shall be disposed to commence cultivating the soil as farmers, the United States agrees to set apart for the use of said Indians as herein provided, such additional quantity of arable land adjoining to said reservation, or as near the same as it can be obtained, as may be required to provide the necessary amount.

Article 4

The United States agrees at its own proper expense to construct at some place near the center of said reservation, where timber and water may be convenient, the following buildings, to wit: a warehouse or store-room for the use of the agent in storing goods belonging to the Indians, to cost not exceeding fifteen hundred dollars; an agency-building for the residence of the agent, to cost not exceeding three thousand dollars; a residence for the physician, to cost not more than three thousand dollars; and five other buildings, for a carpenter, farmer, blacksmith, miller, and engineer, each to cost not exceeding two thousand dollars; also a school-house or mission-building, so soon as a sufficient number of children can be induced by the agent to attend school, which shall not cost exceeding five thousand dollars. The United States agrees, further, to cause to be erected on said reservation, near the other buildings herein authorized, a good steam circular saw-mill, with a grist-mill and shingle machine attached; the same to cost not exceeding eight thousand dollars.

Article 5

The United States agrees that the agent for said Indians in the future shall make his home at the agency building; that he shall reside among them, and keep an office open at all times for the purpose of prompt and diligent inquiry into such matters of complaint by and against the Indians as may be presented for investigation, under the provisions of their treaty stipulations, as also for the faithful discharge of other duties enjoined on him by law. In all cases of depredation on person or property, he shall cause the evidence to be taken in writing and forwarded, together with his finding, to the Commissioner of Indian Affairs, whose decision, subject to the revision of the Secretary of the Interior, shall be binding on the parties to this treaty.

Article 6

If any individual, belonging to said tribes of Indians, or legally incorporated with them, being the head of a family, shall desire to commence farming, he shall have the privilege to select, in the presence and with the assistance of the agent then in charge, a tract of land within said reservation not exceeding three hundred and twenty acres in extent, which tract when so selected, certified, and recorded in the land-book as herein directed, shall cease to be held in common, but the same may be occupied and held in the exclusive possession of the person selecting it, and of his family, so long as he or they may continue to cultivate it. Any person over eighteen years of age, not being the head of a family, may in like manner select and cause to be certified to him, or her, for purposes of cultivation, a quantity of land not exceeding eighty acres in extent, and thereupon be entitled to the exclusive possession of the same as above directed.

For each tract of land so selected, a certificate containing a description thereof, and the name of the person selecting it, with a certificate indorsed thereon, that the same has been recorded, shall be delivered to the party entitled to it by the agent, after the same shall have been recorded by him in a book to be kept in his office, subject to inspection, which said book shall be known as the "Cheyenne and Arapahoe Land Book." The President may at any time order a survey of the reservation, and, when so surveyed, Congress shall provide for protecting the rights of settlers in their improvements, and may fix the character of the title held by each.

The United States may pass such laws on the subject of alienation and descent of property, and on all subjects connected with the government of the Indians on said reservations, and the internal police thereof as may be thought proper.

Article 7

In order to insure the civilization of the tribes entering into this treaty, the necessity of education is admitted, especially by such of them as are or may be settled on said agricultural reservation, and they therefore pledge themselves to compel their children, male and female, between the ages of six and sixteen years, to attend school; and it is hereby made the duty of the agent for said Indians to see that this stipulation is strictly complied with; and the United States agrees that for every thirty children between said ages, who can be induced or compelled to attend school, a house shall be provided, and a teacher competent to teach the elementary branches of an English education shall be furnished, who will reside among said Indians, and faithfully discharge his or her duties as a teacher. The provisions of this article to continue for not less than twenty years.

Article 8

When the head of a family or lodge shall have selected lands and received his certificate as above directed, and the agent shall be satisfied that he intends in good faith to commence cultivating the soil for a living, he shall be entitled to receive seeds and agricultural implements for the first year, not exceeding in value one hundred dollars; and for each succeeding year he shall continue to farm for a period of three years more, he shall be entitled to receive seeds and implements as aforesaid, not exceeding in value twenty-five dollars.

And it is further stipulated that such persons as commence farming shall receive instruction from the farmer herein provided for; and whenever more than one hundred persons shall enter upon the cultivation of the soil, a second blacksmith shall be provided, with such iron, steel, and other material as may be needed.

Article 9

At any time after ten years from the making of this treaty the United States shall have the privilege of withdrawing the physician, farmer, blacksmith, carpenter, engineer, and miller, herein provided for, but in case of such withdrawal, an additional sum, thereafter, of ten thousand dollars per annum shall be devoted to the education of said Indians, and the Commissioner of Indian Affairs shall upon careful inquiry into their condition make such rules and regulations for the expenditure of said sum as will best promote the educational and moral improvement of said tribes.

Article 10

In lieu of all sums of money or other annuities provided to be paid to the Indians herein named, under the treaty of October fourteenth, eighteen hundred and sixty-five, made at the mouth of Little Arkansas, and under all treaties made previous thereto, the United States agrees to deliver at the agency house on the reservation herein named, on the fifteenth day of October, of each year, for thirty years, the following articles, to wit:

For each male person over fourteen years of age, a suit of good, substantial woolen clothing, consisting of coat, pantaloons, flannel shirt, hat, and a pair of home-made socks.

For each female over twelve years of age, a flannel skirt, or the goods necessary to make it, a pair of woolen hose, twelve yards of calico and twelve yards of cotton domestics.

For the boys and girls under the ages named, such flannel and cotton goods as may be needed to make each a suit as aforesaid, together with a pair of woolen hose for each.

And in order that the Commissioner of Indian Affairs may be able to estimate properly for the articles herein named, it shall be the duty of the agent each year to forward to him a full and exact census of the Indians on which the estimate from year to year can be based.

And, in addition to the clothing herein named, the sum of twenty thousand dollars shall be annually appropriated for a period of thirty years, to be used by the Secretary of the Interior in the purchase of such articles as, from time to time, the condition and necessities of the Indians may indicate to be proper. And if at any time, within the thirty years, it shall appear that the amount of money needed for clothing, under this article, can be appropriated to better uses for the tribe herein named, Congress may, by law, change the appropriation to other purposes; but in no event, shall the amount of this appropriation be withdrawn or discontinued for the period named. And the President shall, annually, detail an officer of the Army to be present, and attest the delivery of all the goods herein named to the Indians, and he shall inspect and report on the quantity and quality of the goods and the manner of their delivery.

Article 11

In consideration of the advantages and benefits conferred by this treaty, and the many pledges of friendship by the United States, the tribes who are parties to this agreement hereby stipulate that they will relinquish all right to occupy permanently the territory outside of their reservation as herein defined, but they yet reserve the right to hunt on any lands south of the Arkansas so long as the buffalo may range thereon in such numbers as to justify the chase; and no white settlements shall be permitted on any part of the lands contained in the old reservation as defined by the treaty made between the United States and the Cheyenne, Arapahoe, and Apache tribes of Indians, at the mouth of the Little Arkansas, under date of October fourteenth, eighteen hundred and sixty-five, within three years from this date, and they, the said tribes, further expressly agree:

1st. That they will withdraw all opposition to the construction of the railroad now being built on the Smoky Hill River, whether it be built to Colorado or New Mexico.

2d. That they will permit the peaceable construction of any railroad not passing over their reservation, as herein defined.

3d. That they will not attack any persons at home or travelling, nor molest or disturb any wagon-trains, coaches, mules, or cattle belonging to the people of the United States or to persons friendly therewith.

4th. They will never capture or carry off from the settlements white women or children.

5th. They will never kill or scalp white men, nor attempt to do them harm.

6th. They withdraw all pretense of opposition to the construction of the railroad now being built along the Platte River, and westward to the Pacific Ocean; and they will not in future object to the construction of railroads, wagon-roads, mail-stations, or other works of utility or necessity, which may be ordered or permitted by the laws of the United States. But should such roads or other works be constructed on the lands of their reservation, the Government will pay the tribe whatever amount of damage may be assessed by three disinterested commissioners to be appointed by the President for that purpose, one of said commissioners to be a chief or head-man of the tribe.

7th. They agree to withdraw all opposition to the military posts or roads now established, or that may be established, not in violation of treaties heretofore made or hereafter to be made with any of the Indian tribes.

Article 12

No treaty for the cession of any portion or part of the reservation herein described, which may be held in common, shall be of any validity or force as against the said Indians unless executed and signed by at least three-fourths of all the adult male Indians occupying or interested in the same; and no cession by the tribe shall be understood or construed in such manner as to deprive without his consent any individual member of the tribe of his rights to any tract of land selected by him as provided in Article 6 of this treaty.

Article 13

The United States hereby agree to furnish annually to the Indians the physician, teachers, carpenter, miller, engineer, farmer, and blacksmiths, as herein contemplated, and that such appropriations shall be made from time to time, on the estimates of the Secretary of the Interior, as will be sufficient to employ such persons.

Article 14

It is agreed that the sum of five hundred dollars, annually, for three years from date, shall be expended in presents to the ten persons of said tribe who, in the judgment of the agent, may grow the most valuable crops for the respective year.

Article 15

The tribes herein named agree that when the agency-house and other buildings shall be constructed on the reservation named, they will regard and make said reservation their permanent home, and they will make no permanent settlement elsewhere, but they shall have the right, subject to the conditions and modifications of this treaty, to hunt on the lands south of the Arkansas River, formerly called theirs, in the same manner as agreed on by the treaty of the "Little Arkansas," concluded the fourteenth day of October, eighteen hundred and sixty-five.

In testimony of which, we have hereunto set our hands and seals, on the day and year aforesaid.

N. G. Taylor, [SEAL.]
President of Indn. Commission.
Wm. S. Harney, [SEAL.]
Major-General, Brevet, &c.

C. C. Augur, [SEAL.]
Brevet Major-General.
Alfred H. Terry, [SEAL.]
Brevet Major-General.
John B. Sanborn, [SEAL.]
Commissioner.
Samuel F. Tappan. [SEAL.]
J. B. Henderson. [SEAL.]
Attest:
Ashton S. H. White, secretary.
Geo. B. Willis, phonographer.
On the part of the Cheyennes:
O-to-ah-nac-co, Bull Bear, his x mark, [SEAL.]
Moke-tav-a-to, Black Kettle, his x mark, [SEAL.]
Nac-co-hah-ket, Little Bear, his x mark, [SEAL.]
Mo-a-vo-va-ast, Spotted Elk, his x mark, [SEAL.]
Is-se-von-ne-ve, Buffalo Chief, his x mark, [SEAL.]
Vip-po-nah, Slim Face, his x mark, [SEAL.]
Wo-pah-ah, Gray Head, his x mark, [SEAL.]
O-ni-hah-ket, Little Rock, his x mark, [SEAL.]
Ma-mo-ki, or Curly Hair, his x mark, [SEAL.]
O-to-ah-has-tis, Tall Bull, his x mark, [SEAL.]
Wo-po-ham, or White Horse, his x mark, [SEAL.]
Hah-ket-home-mah, Little Robe, his x mark, [SEAL.]
Min-nin-ne-wah, Whirlwind, his x mark, [SEAL.]
Mo-yan-histe-histow, Heap of Birds, his x mark, [SEAL.]
On the part of the Arapahoes:
Little Raven, his x mark, [SEAL.]
Yellow Bear, his x mark, [SEAL.]
Storm, his x mark, [SEAL.]
White Rabbit, his x mark, [SEAL.]
Spotted Wolf, his x mark, [SEAL.]
Little Big Mouth, his x mark, [SEAL.]
Young Colt, his x mark, [SEAL.]
Tall Bear, his x mark, [SEAL.]
Attest:
C. W. Whitaker, interpreter.
H. Douglas, major, Third Infantry.
Jno. D. Howland, clerk Indian Commission.
Sam'l. S. Smoot, United States surveyor.

A. A. Taylor.
Henry Stanley, correspondent.
John S. Smith, United States interpreter.
George Bent, interpreter.
Thos. Murphy, superintendent Indian affairs.

Treaty of Fort Bridger (1868)

The official title of the Treaty of Fort Bridger (1868) is "Treaty between the United States of America and the Eastern Band of Shoshones and the Bannack Tribe of Indians." Concluded on July 3, 1868, at Fort Bridger, Wyoming (then Utah Territory), and proclaimed on February 24, 1869, this treaty remains the basis for the sovereign relations between the United States and both the Eastern Shoshone Tribe of the Wind River Reservation (Wyoming) and the Shoshone-Bannock Tribes of the Fort Hall Reservation (Idaho). The treaty declared continued peaceful relations between the parties, established the Wind River Reservation, provided for a Bannock Reservation in Idaho, provided for extensive off-reservation resource rights, allowed individual Natives to take up tracts of land in severalty, and included assistance for agricultural development and education.

The various bands of Shoshones and Bannocks had maintained generally peaceful relations with the United States during the overland migration and had been parties to previous treaties both ratified and unratified. Washakie, the principal chief of the Eastern Shoshones, was renowned for his friendship with the United States as well as his influence among his own people. He was a signatory of the ratified Treaty of Fort Bridger (1863). The most influential Bannock leader, Taghee, had approved the Soda Springs treaty of October 1863 (part of the same series of treaties negotiated by James Duane Doty), but a legal technicality prevented its ratification. The treaties in 1863 included no land cessions, nor did they designate reservations.

The Fort Bridger treaty of 1868 was the final treaty negotiated by the Indian Peace Commission of 1867–1868. Conceived of as an all-encompassing solution to the "Indian problem" in the American West, the peace commission negotiated treaties with the tribes of the northern and southern plains and the Navajos (Dinés) as well as the Shoshones and Bannocks. The commission consisted of four civilians and four generals, including General William T. Sherman and Commissioner of Indian Affairs Nathaniel G. Taylor. General Christopher C. Augur was the sole member of the commission present at Fort Bridger. Washakie spoke for the Eastern Shoshones, while Taghee represented the Bannocks (in fact, his followers were a mixed band of Shoshones and Bannocks).

Article II of the treaty established the boundaries of the Wind River Reservation and provided for the creation of a "Bannack Reservation." Washakie claimed "all the country lying between the meridian of Salt Lake City and the line of the North Platte River to the mouth of the Sweetwater," and wanted "the valley of the Wind River and lands on its tributaries as far east as the Popo-agie" for his reservation. The original dimensions of the Wind River Reservation were reduced by agreements in 1872 and 1898.

General Augur sought to consolidate all the bands on a single reservation, but Taghee refused and demanded a separate reservation that would include the Fort Hall area and the Great Camas Prairie of south central Idaho. Augur relented, but as he was "not sufficiently acquainted" with Idaho's geography, he did not specify the reservation's exact boundaries. Augur was also apparently unaware that the Fort Hall Reservation had already been created by executive order in June 1867. Instead, Article II provided that, at a future date, the president might set apart the reservation which was to include "reasonable portions of the 'Port neuf' [Fort Hall] and 'Kansas [sic] Prairie' countries." The clerk's obvious misspelling of *Kamas* gave later interlopers a specious claim to that area. The federal government never fulfilled its promise to reserve a portion of the Great Camas Prairie. A subsequent executive order designated the Fort Hall Reservation as the Bannock Reservation under the terms of the Fort Bridger treaty. The original dimensions of the reservation were reduced by agreements in 1880, 1881, 1887, and 1900.

The off-reservation provisions of the Fort Bridger treaty are especially noteworthy. Article IV of the treaty reserved to the Shoshones and Bannocks "the right to hunt on the unoccupied lands of the United States so long as game be found thereon, and so long as peace subsists among the whites and Indians on the borders of the hunting districts."

Gregory E. Smoak

Further Reading

Augur, C.C. "C. C. Augur to President of the Indian Peace Commission, Omaha, Nebraska, 4 October 1868." *Bureau of Indian Affairs, Irregular Sized Papers*. Washington, DC: Record Group 75, U.S. National Archives, 1868.

Deloria, Vine, Jr., and Raymond J. DeMallie. "Introduction," in *Proceedings of the Great Peace Commission of 1867–1869*, 1–30. Washington, DC: The Institute for the Development of Indian Law, 1975.

Prucha, Francis Paul. *American Indian Treaties: The History of a Political Anomaly*. Berkeley and Los Angeles: University of California Press, 1994.

St. Germain, Jill. *Indian Treaty Making Policy in the United States and Canada, 1867–1877*. Lincoln: University of Nebraska Press, 2001.

Document: Treaty of Fort Bridger

Articles of a treaty made and concluded at Fort Bridger, Utah Territory, on the third day of July, in the year of our Lord one thousand eight hundred and sixty-eight, by and between the undersigned commissioners on the part of the United States, and the undersigned chiefs and head-men of and representing the Shoshonee (eastern band) and Bannack tribes of Indians, they being duly authorized to act in the premises:

Article 1

From this day forward peace between the parties to this treaty shall forever continue. The Government of the United States desires peace, and its honor is hereby pledged to keep it. The Indians desire peace, and they hereby pledge their honor to maintain it. If bad men among the whites, or among other people subject to the authority of the United States, shall commit any wrong upon the person or property of the Indians, the United States will, upon proof made to the agent and forwarded to the Commissioner of Indian Affairs, at Washington City, proceed at once to cause the offender to be arrested and punished according to the laws of the United States, and also re-imburse the injured person for the loss sustained. If bad men among the Indians shall commit a wrong or depredation upon the person or property of any one, white, black, or Indian, subject to the authority of the United States, and at peace therewith, the Indians herein named solemnly agree that they will, on proof made to their agent and notice by him, deliver up the wrong-doer to the United States, to be tried and punished according to the laws; and in case they wilfully refuse so to do, the person injured shall be re-imbursed for his loss from the annuities or other moneys due or to become due to them under this or other treaties made with the United States. And the President, on advising with the Commissioner of Indian Affairs, shall prescribe such rules and regulations for ascertaining damages under the provisions of this article as in his judgment may be proper. But no such damages shall be adjusted and paid until thoroughly examined and passed upon by the Commissioner of Indian Affairs, and no one sustaining loss while violating or because of his violating the provisions of this treaty or the laws of the United States, shall be reimbursed therefor.

Article 2

It is agreed that whenever the Bannacks desire a reservation to be set apart for their use, or whenever the President of the United States shall deem it advisable for them to be put upon a reservation, he shall cause a suitable one to be selected for them in their present country, which shall embrace reasonable portions of the "Port Neuf" and "Kansas Prairie" countries, and that, when this reservation is declared, the United States will secure to the Bannacks the same rights and privileges therein, and make the same and like expenditures therein for their benefit, except the agency-house and residence of agent, in proportion to their numbers, as herein provided for the Shoshonee reservation. The United States further agrees that the following district of country, to wit: Commencing at the mouth of Owl Creek and running due south to the crest of the divide between the Sweet-water and Papo Agie Rivers; thence along the crest of said divide and the summit of Wind River Mountains to the longitude of North Fork of Wind River; thence due north to mouth of said North Fork and up its channel to a point twenty miles above its mouth; thence in a straight line to head-waters of Owl Creek and along middle of channel of Owl Creek to place of beginning, shall be and the same is set apart for the absolute and undisturbed use and occupation of the Shoshonee Indians herein named, and for such other friendly tribes or individual Indians as from time to time they may be willing, with the consent of the United States, to admit amongst them; and the United States now solemnly agrees that no persons except those herein designated and authorized so to do, and except such officers, agents, and employés of the Government as may be authorized to enter upon Indian reservations in discharge of duties enjoined by law, shall ever be permitted to pass over, settle upon, or reside in the territory described in this article for the use of said Indians, and henceforth they will and do hereby relinquish all title, claims, or rights in and to any portion of the territory of the United States, except such as is embraced within the limits aforesaid.

Article 3

The United States agrees, at its own proper expense, to construct at a suitable point of the Shoshonee reservation a warehouse or store-room for the use of the agent in storing goods belonging to the Indians, to cost not exceeding two thousand dollars; an agency building for the residence of the agent, to cost not exceeding three thousand; a residence for the physician, to cost not more than two thousand dollars; and five other buildings, for a carpenter, farmer, blacksmith, miller, and engineer, each to cost not exceeding two thousand dollars; also a school-house or mission building so soon as a sufficient number of children can be induced by the agent to attend school, which shall not cost exceeding twenty-five hundred dollars. The United States agrees further to cause to be erected on said Shoshonee reservation, near the other buildings herein authorized, a good steam circular-saw mill, with a grist-mill and shingle-machine attached, the same to cost not more than eight thousand dollars.

Article 4

The Indians herein named agree, when the agency house and other buildings shall be constructed on their reservations named, they will make said reservations their permanent home, and they will make no permanent settlement elsewhere; but they shall have the right to hunt on the unoccupied lands of the United States so long as game may be found thereon, and so long as peace subsists among the whites and Indians on the borders of the hunting districts.

Article 5

The United States agrees that the agent for said Indians shall in the future make his home at the agency building on the Shoshonee reservation, but shall direct and supervise affairs on the Bannack reservation; and shall keep an office open at all times for the purpose of prompt and diligent inquiry into such matters of complaint by and against the Indians as may be presented for investigation under the provisions of their treaty stipulations, as also for the faithful discharge of other duties enjoined by law. In all cases of depredation on person or property he shall cause the evidence to be taken in writing and forwarded, together with his finding, to the Commissioner of Indian Affairs, whose decision shall be binding on the parties to this treaty.

Article 6

If any individual belonging to said tribes of Indians, or legally incorporated with them, being the head of a family, shall desire to commence farming, he shall have the privilege to select, in the presence and with the assistance of the agent then in charge, a tract of land within the reservation of his tribe, not exceeding three hundred and twenty acres in extent, which tract so selected, certified, and recorded in the "land-book," as herein directed, shall cease to be held in common, but the same may be occupied and held in the exclusive possession of the person selecting it, and of his family, so long as he or they may continue to cultivate it. Any person over eighteen years of age, not being the head of a family, may in like manner select and cause to be certified to him or her, for purposes of cultivation, a quantity of land not exceeding eighty acres in extent, and thereupon be entitled to the exclusive possession of the same as above described. For each tract of land so selected a certificate, containing a description thereof, and the name of the person selecting it, with a certificate indorsed thereon that the same has been recorded, shall be delivered to the party entitled to it by the agent, after the same shall have been recorded by him in a book to be kept in his office subject to inspection, which said book shall be known as the "Shoshone (eastern band) and Bannack land-book." The President may at any time order a survey of these reservations, and when so surveyed Congress shall provide for protecting the rights of the Indian settlers in these improvements, and may fix the character of the title held by each. The United States may pass such laws on the subject of alienation and descent of property as between Indians, and on all subjects connected with the government of the Indians on said reservations, and the internal police thereof, as may be thought proper.

Article 7

In order to insure the civilization of the tribes entering into this treaty, the necessity of education is admitted, especially of such of them as are or may be settled on said agricultural reservations, and they therefore pledge themselves to compel their children, male and female, between the ages of six and sixteen years, to attend school; and it is hereby made the duty of the agent for said Indians to see that this stipulation is strictly complied with; and the United States agrees that for every thirty children between said ages who can be induced or compelled to attend school, a house shall be provided and a teacher competent to teach the elementary branches of an English education shall be furnished, who will reside among said Indians and faithfully discharge his or her duties as a teacher. The provisions as this article to continue for twenty years.

Article 8
When the head of a family or lodge shall have selected lands and received his certificate as above directed, and the agent shall be satisfied that he intends in good faith to commence cultivating the soil for a living, he shall be entitled to receive seeds and agricultural implements for the first year, in value one hundred dollars, and for each succeeding year he shall continue to farm, for a period of three years more, he shall be entitled to receive seeds and implements as aforesaid in value twenty-five dollars per annum. And it is further stipulated that such persons as commence farming shall receive instructions from the farmers herein provided for, and whenever more than one hundred persons on either reservation shall enter upon the cultivation of the soil, a second blacksmith shall be provided, with such iron, steel, and other material as may be required.

Article 9
In lieu of all sums of money or other annuities provided to be paid to the Indians herein named, under any and all treaties heretofore made with them, the United States agrees to deliver at the agency-house on the reservation here in provided for, on the first day of September of each year, for thirty years, the following articles, to wit:

For each male person over fourteen years of age, a suit of good substantial woollen clothing, consisting of coat, hat, pantaloons, flannel shirt, and a pair of woollen socks; for each female over twelve years of age, a flannel skirt, or the goods necessary to make it, a pair of woollen hose, twelve yards of calico; and twelve yards of cotton domestics.

For the boys and girls under the ages named, such flannel and cotton goods as may be needed to make each a suit as aforesaid, together with a pair of woollen hose for each. And in order that the Commissioner of Indian Affairs may be able to estimate properly for the articles herein named, it shall be the duty of the agent each year to forward to him a full and exact census of the Indians, on which the estimate from year to year can be based; and in addition to the clothing herein named, the sum of ten dollars shall be annually appropriated for each Indian roaming and twenty dollars for each Indian engaged in agriculture, for a period of ten years, to be used by the Secretary of the Interior in the purchase of such articles as from time to time the condition and necessities of the Indians may indicate to be proper. And if at any time within the ten years it shall appear that the amount of money needed for clothing under this article can be appropriated to better uses for the tribes herein named, Congress may by law change the appropriation to other purposes; but in no event shall the amount of this appropriation be withdrawn or discontinued for the period named. And the President shall annually detail an officer of the Army to be present and attest the delivery of all the goods herein named to the Indians, and he shall inspect and report on the quantity and quality of the goods and the manner of their delivery.

Article 10

The United States hereby agrees to furnish annually to the Indians the physician, teachers, carpenter, miller, engineer, farmer, and blacksmith, as herein contemplated, and that such appropriations shall be made from time to time, on the estimates of the Secretary of the Interior, as will be sufficient to employ such persons.

Article 11

No treaty for the cession of any portion of the reservations herein described which may be held in common shall be of any force or validity as against the said Indians, unless executed and signed by at least a majority of all the adult male Indians occupying or interested in the same; and no cession by the tribe shall be understood or construed in such manner as to deprive without his consent, any individual member of the tribe of his right to any tract of land selected by him, as provided in Article 6 of this treaty.

Article 12

It is agreed that the sum of five hundred dollars annually, for three years from the date when they commence to cultivate a farm, shall be expended in presents to the ten persons of said tribe who, in the judgment of the agent, may grow the most valuable crops for the respective year.

Article 13

It is further agreed that until such time as the agency-buildings are established on the Shoshonee reservation, their agent shall reside at Fort Bridger, U. T., and their annuities shall be delivered to them at the same place in June of each year.

   N. G. Taylor, [SEAL.],
   W. T. Sherman, [SEAL.]
   Lieutenant-General.Wm. S. Harney, [SEAL.],

John B. Sanborn, [SEAL.],
S. F. Tappan, [SEAL.],
C. C. Augur, [SEAL.],
Brevet Major-General, U. S. Army, Commissioners.,
Alfred H. Terry, [SEAL.],
Brigadier-General and Brevet Major-General, U. S. Army
Attest:
A. S. H. White, Secretary
Shoshones:
Wash-a-kie, his x mark,
Wau-ny-pitz, his x mark,
Toop-se-po-wot, his x mark,
Nar-kok, his x mark,
Taboonshe-ya, his x mark,
Bazeel, his x mark,
Pan-to-she-ga, his x mark,
Ninny-Bitse, his x mark.
Bannacks:
Taggee, his x mark.
Tay-to-ba, his x mark.
We-rat-ze-won-a-gen, his x mark.
Coo-sha-gan, his x mark.
Pan-sook-a-motse, his x mark.
A-wite-etse, his x mark.
Witnesses:
Henry A. Morrow,
Lieutenant-Colonel Thirty-sixth Infantry and, Brevet Colonel U. S. Army. Commanding Fort Bridger,
Luther Manpa, United States Indian agent,
W. A. Carter,
J. Van Allen Carter, interpreter.

Treaty of Fort Laramie (1868)

In the spring of 1868, a conference was held at Fort Laramie, in present day Wyoming, that resulted in the Treaty of Fort Laramie (1868). Concluded on April 29, 1868, this treaty was to bring peace between the whites and the Sioux who agreed to settle within the Black Hills reservation in the Dakota Territory.

The United States Indian Peace Commission, comprising military officers, ministers, and civilian reformers, formed in 1867 to end hostilities and accelerate the "concentration" and "domestication" of Native Americans on reservations through a reborn civilization program. The Peace Commission first negotiated treaties with Native American nations of the southern plains before turning its attention to those of the northern plains, in particular the Sioux, who remained intent on defending their territory against settlers on the Bozeman Trail and against hordes of white hunters who slaughtered buffalo herds from railroad cars. In late April 1868, after agreeing to the demands of the great Sioux leader Red Cloud that the United States abandon its forts on the Bozeman Trail, the Peace Commission gathered with Red Cloud and other Sioux chiefs to negotiate a major treaty at Fort Laramie in an effort to end the so-called Red Cloud War.

Under the terms of this treaty, war was to cease, peace was to be kept, and offenders against the tribe or against whites were to be arrested and punished. Damages were to be decided by the commissioner of Indian affairs. Other concerns of the treaty were reservation boundaries, persons allowed to enter or reside thereon, land selection, additional land for farming, surveys, patents and citizenship, and certificates issued and recorded in the Sioux Land-Book. Additionally, right-of-way was granted for the building of roads, railroads, and military posts. The United States was to supply an agent's residence and office, a schoolhouse, teachers, seeds, agricultural implements, farming instruction, a second blacksmith, a physician, and a farmer. Delivery of goods in lieu of money or other annuities was allowed. An annual census was to be taken each year, and appropriations were to continue for 30 years. An army officer was to attest to all delivery of goods. The reservation was to be a permanent home of the tribes, and no treaty for cession of reservation land would be valid unless three-fourths of all adult males of the tribe agreed. The United States agreed that the country north of the North Platte River and east of the summits of the Bighorn Mountains would be unceded Indian Territory and agreed that no white person or persons would be allowed to settle upon or occupy any portion of that land without permission of the tribes. This treaty released the United States from obligations made in previous treaties to furnish money, goods, or land.

The most important of these provisions confirmed that the United States would abandon its forts in Sioux Territory, granted to the Sioux the "Great Sioux Reservation" in present-day South Dakota, and guaranteed access to and hunting rights in "unceded Indian territory" adjacent to the reservation, which included the Black Hills. In addition, the annuities to the Sioux were for the purpose of expanding the civilization program and remaking the Sioux in the image of the Christian yeoman farmer. For example, Article 7 read as follows: "In order to insure the civilization of the Indians. . ., the necessity of education is admitted. . ., and [the Sioux] therefore pledge themselves to compel their children, male and female . . . to attend school." Thus, the treaty laid the foundation of a program of coercive assimilation that would cause great social and cultural trauma for the Sioux, even as it sowed the seeds of future military conflict over the status of the Black Hills, considered sacred ground to the Sioux. The treaty, in short, failed to produce peace. And the United States failed to uphold its honor to maintain it.

The treaty was signed by Commissioners William T. Sherman, William S. Harney, Alfred H. Terry, C. C. Augur, J. B. Henderson, Nathaniel G. Taylor, John B. Sanborn, and Samuel F. Tappan for the United States; by 25 chiefs and headmen of the Brule, Oglala, Miniconjou, Yanktonai, Hunkpapa, Blackfeet, Cuthead, Two-Kettle, Sans Arcs, and Santee bands of the Sioux Nation; and by 26 representatives of the Arapaho Nation.

John P. Bowes

Further Reading

Nadeau, Remi. *Fort Laramie and the Sioux*. Santa Barbara, CA: Crest, 1997.

Ostler, Jeffrey. *The Plains Sioux and U.S. Colonialism from Lewis and Clark to Wounded Knee*. Cambridge, UK: Cambridge University Press, 2004.

Robinson, W. Stitt. *Early American Indian Documents: Treaties and Laws, 1607–1789*, Vol. 5: *Virginia Treaties, 1723–1775*. Frederick, MD: University Publications of America, 1987.

Document: Treaty of Fort Laramie

Articles of a treaty made and concluded by and between Lieutenant-General William T. Sherman, General William S. Harney, General Alfred H. Terry, General C. C. Augur, J. B. Henderson, Nathaniel G. Taylor, John B. Sanborn, and Samuel F. Tappan, duly appointed commissioners on the part of the United States, and the different bands of the Sioux Nation of Indians, by their chiefs and head-men, whose names are hereto subscribed, they being duly authorized to act in the premises.

Article 1

From this day forward all war between the parties to this agreement shall forever cease. The Government of the United States desires peace, and its honor is hereby pledged to keep it. The Indians desire peace, and they now pledge their honor to maintain it.

If bad men among the whites, or among other people subject to the authority of the United States, shall commit any wrong upon the person or property of the Indians, the United States will, upon proof made to the agent and forwarded to the Commissioner of Indian Affairs at Washington City, proceed at once to cause the offender to be arrested and punished according to the laws of the United States, and also re-imburse the injured person for the loss sustained.

If bad men among the Indians shall commit a wrong or depredation upon the person or property of any one, white, black, or Indians, subject to the authority of the United States, and at peace therewith, the Indians herein named solemnly agree that they will, upon proof made to their agent and notice by him, deliver up the wrong-doer to the United States, to be tried and punished according to its laws; and in case they wilfully refuse so to do, the person injured shall be re-imbursed for his loss from the annuities or other moneys due or to become due to them under this or other treaties made with the United States. And the President, on advising with the Commissioner of Indian Affairs, shall prescribe such rules and regulations for ascertaining damages under the provisions of this article as in his judgment may be proper. But no one sustaining loss while violating the provisions of this treaty or the laws of the United States shall be re-imbursed therefor.

Article 2

The United States agrees that the following district of country, to wit, viz: commencing on the east bank of the Missouri River where the forty-sixth parallel of north latitude crosses the same, thence along low-water mark down said east bank to a point opposite where the northern line of the State of Nebraska strikes the river, thence west across said river, and along the northern line of Nebraska to the one hundred and fourth degree of longitude west from Greenwich, thence north on said meridian to a point where the forty-sixth parallel of north latitude intercepts the same, thence due east along said parallel to the place of beginning; and in addition thereto, all existing reservations on the east bank of said river shall be, and the same is, set apart for the absolute and undisturbed use and occupation of the Indians herein named, and for such other friendly tribes or individual Indians as from time to time they may be willing, with the consent of the United States, to admit amongst them; and the United States now solemnly agrees that no persons except those herein designated and authorized so to do, and except such officers, agents, and employés of the Government as may be authorized to enter upon Indian reservations in discharge of duties enjoined by law, shall ever be permitted to pass over, settle upon, or reside in the territory described in this article, or in such territory as may be added to this reservation for the use of said Indians, and henceforth they will and do hereby relinquish all claims or right in and to any portion of the United States or Territories, except such as is embraced within the limits aforesaid, and except as hereinafter provided.

Article 3

If it should appear from actual survey or other satisfactory examination of said tract of land that it contains less than one hundred and sixty acres of tillable land for each person who, at the time, may be authorized to reside on it under the provisions of this treaty, and a very considerable number of such persons shall be disposed to commence cultivating the soil as farmers, the United States agrees to set apart, for the use of said Indians, as herein provided, such additional quantity of arable land, adjoining to said reservation, or as near to the same as it can be obtained, as may be required to provide the necessary amount.

Article 4

The United States agrees, at its own proper expense, to construct at some place on the Missouri River, near the center of said reservation, where timber and water may be convenient, the following buildings, to wit: a warehouse, a store-room for the use of the agent in storing goods belonging to the Indians, to cost not less than twenty-five hundred dollars; an agency-building for the residence of the agent, to cost not exceeding three thousand dollars; a residence for the physician, to cost not more than three thousand dollars; and five other buildings, for a carpenter, farmer, blacksmith, miller, and engineer, each to cost not exceeding two thousand dollars; also a school-house or mission-building, so soon as a sufficient number of children can be induced by the agent to attend school, which shall not cost exceeding five thousand dollars.

The United States agrees further to cause to be erected on said reservation, near the other buildings herein authorized, a good steam circular-saw mill, with a grist-mill and shingle-machine attached to the same, to cost not exceeding eight thousand dollars.

Article 5

The United States agrees that the agent for said Indians shall in the future make his home at the agency-building; that he shall reside among them, and keep an office open at all times for the purpose of prompt and diligent inquiry into such matters of complaint by and against the Indians as may be presented for investigation under the provisions of their treaty stipulations, as also for the faithful discharge of other duties enjoined on him by law. In all cases of depredation on person or property he shall cause the evidence to be taken in writing and forwarded, together with his findings, to the Commissioner of Indian Affairs, whose decision, subject to the revision of the Secretary of the Interior, shall be binding on the parties to this treaty.

Article 6

If any individual belonging to said tribes of Indians, or legally incorporated with them, being the head of a family, shall desire to commence farming, he shall have the privilege to select, in the presence and with the assistance of the agent then in charge, a tract of land within said reservation, not exceeding three hundred and twenty acres in extent, which tract, when so selected, certified, and recorded in the "land-book," as herein directed, shall cease to be held in common, but the same may be occupied and held in the exclusive possession of the person selecting it, and of his family, so long as he or they may continue to cultivate it.

Any person over eighteen years of age, not being the head of a family, may in like manner select and cause to be certified to him or her, for purposes of cultivation, a quantity of land not exceeding eighty acres in extent, and thereupon be entitled to the exclusive possession of the same as above directed.

For each tract of land so selected a certificate, containing a description thereof and the name of the person selecting it, with a certificate endorsed thereon that the same has been recorded, shall be delivered to the party entitled to it, by the agent, after the same shall have been recorded by him in a book to be kept in his office, subject to inspection, which said book shall be known as the "Sioux Land-Book."

The President may, at any time, order a survey of the reservation, and, when so surveyed, Congress shall provide for protecting the rights of said settlers in their improvements, and may fix the character of the title held by each. The United States may pass such laws on the subject of alienation and descent of property between the Indians and their descendants as may be thought proper. And it is further stipulated that any male Indians, over eighteen years of age, of any band or tribe that is or shall hereafter become a party to this treaty, who now is or who shall hereafter become a resident or occupant of any reservation or Territory not included in the tract of country designated and described in this treaty for the permanent home of the Indians, which is not mineral land, nor reserved by the United States for special purposes other than Indian occupation, and who shall have made improvements thereon of the value of two hundred dollars or more, and continuously occupied the same as a homestead for the term of three years, shall be entitled to receive from the United States a patent for one hundred and sixty acres of land including his said improvements, the same to be in the form of the legal subdivisions of the surveys of the public lands. Upon application in writing, sustained by the proof of two disinterested witnesses, made to the register of the local land-office when the land sought to be entered is within a land district, and when the tract sought to be entered is not in any land district, then upon said application and proof being made to the Commissioner of the General Land-Office, and the right of such Indian or Indians to enter such tract or tracts of land shall accrue and be perfect from the date of his first improvements thereon, and shall continue as long as he continues his residence and improvements, and no longer. And any Indian or Indians receiving a patent for land under the foregoing provisions, shall thereby and from thenceforth become and be a citizen of the United States, and be entitled to all the privileges and immunities of such citizens, and shall, at the same time, retain all his rights to benefits accruing to Indians under this treaty.

Article 7

In order to insure the civilization of the Indians entering into this treaty, the necessity of education is admitted, especially of such of them as are or may be settled on said agricultural reservations, and they therefore pledge themselves to compel their children, male and female, between the ages of six and sixteen years, to attend school; and it is hereby made the duty of the agent for said Indians to see that this stipulation is strictly complied with; and the United States agrees that for every thirty children between said ages who can be induced or compelled to attend school, a house shall be provided and a teacher competent to teach the elementary branches of an English education shall be furnished, who will reside among said Indians, and faithfully discharge his or her duties as a teacher. The provisions of this article to continue for not less than twenty years.

Article 8

When the head of a family or lodge shall have selected lands and received his certificate as above directed, and the agent shall be satisfied that he intends in good faith to commence cultivating the soil for a living, he shall be entitled to receive seeds and agricultural implements for the first year, not exceeding in value one hundred dollars, and for each succeeding year he shall continue to farm, for a period of three years more, he shall be entitled to receive seeds and implements as aforesaid, not exceeding in value twenty-five dollars.

And it is further stipulated that such persons as commence farming shall receive instruction from the farmer herein provided for, and whenever more than one hundred persons shall enter upon the cultivation of the soil, a second blacksmith shall be provided, with such iron, steel, and other material as may be needed.

Article 9

At any time after ten years from the making of this treaty, the United States shall have the privilege of withdrawing the physician, farmer, blacksmith, carpenter, engineer, and miller herein provided for, but in case of such withdrawal, an additional sum thereafter of ten thousand dollars per annum shall be devoted to the education of said Indians, and the Commissioner of Indian Affairs shall, upon careful inquiry into their condition, make such rules and regulations for the expenditure of said sum as will best promote the educational and moral improvement of said tribes.

Article 10

In lieu of all sums of money or other annuities provided to be paid to the Indians herein named, under any treaty or treaties heretofore made, the United States agrees to deliver at the agency-house on the reservation herein named, on or before the first day of August of each year, for thirty years, the following articles, to wit:

> For each male person over fourteen years of age, a suit of good substantial woolen clothing, consisting of coat, pantaloons, flannel shirt, hat, and a pair of home-made socks.

> For each female over twelve years of age, a flannel skirt, or the goods necessary to make it, a pair of woolen hose, twelve yards of calico, and twelve yards of cotton domestics.
> For the boys and girls under the ages named, such flannel and cotton goods as may be needed to make each a suit as aforesaid, together with a pair of woolen hose for each.

And in order that the Commissioner of Indian Affairs may be able to estimate properly for the articles herein named, it shall be the duty of the agent each year to forward to him a full and exact census of the Indians, on which the estimate from year to year can be based.

And in addition to the clothing herein named, the sum of ten dollars for each person entitled to the beneficial effects of this treaty shall be annually appropriated for a period of thirty years, while such persons roam and hunt, and twenty dollars for each person who engages in farming, to be used by the Secretary of the Interior in the purchase of such articles as from time to time the condition and necessities of the Indians may indicate to be proper. And if within the thirty years, at any time, it shall appear that the amount of money needed for clothing under this article can be appropriated to better uses for the Indians named herein, Congress may, by law, change the appropriation to other purposes; but in no event shall the amount of this appropriation be withdrawn or discontinued for the period named. And the President shall annually detail an officer of the Army to be present and attest the delivery of all the goods herein named to the Indians, and he shall inspect and report on the quantity and quality of the goods and the manner of their delivery. And it is hereby expressly stipulated that each Indian over the age of four years, who shall have removed to and settled permanently upon said reservation and complied with the stipulations of this treaty, shall be entitled to receive from the United States, for the period of four years after he shall have settled upon said reservation, one pound of meat and one pound of flour per day, provided the Indians cannot furnish their own subsistence at an earlier date. And it is further stipulated that the United States will furnish and deliver to each lodge of Indians or family of persons legally incorporated with them, who shall remove to the reservation herein described and commence farming, one good American cow, and one good well-broken pair of American oxen within sixty days after such lodge or family shall have so settled upon said reservation.

Article 11

In consideration of the advantages and benefits conferred by this treaty, and the many pledges of friendship by the United States, the tribes who are parties to this agreement hereby stipulate that they will relinquish all right to occupy permanently the territory outside their reservation as herein defined, but yet reserve the right to hunt on any lands north of North Platte, and on the Republican Fork of the Smoky

Hill River, so long as the buffalo may range thereon in such numbers as to justify the chase. And they, the said Indians, further expressly agree:

1st. That they will withdraw all opposition to the construction of the railroads now being built on the plains.

2d. That they will permit the peaceful construction of any railroad not passing over their reservation as herein defined.

3d. That they will not attack any persons at home, or travelling, nor molest or disturb any wagon-trains, coaches, mules, or cattle belonging to the people of the United States, or to persons friendly therewith.

4th. They will never capture, or carry off from the settlements, white women or children.

5th. They will never kill or scalp white men, nor attempt to do them harm.

6th. They withdraw all pretence of opposition to the construction of the railroad now being built along the Platte River and westward to the Pacific Ocean, and they will not in future object to the construction of railroads, wagon-roads, mail-stations, or other works of utility or necessity, which may be ordered or permitted by the laws of the United States. But should such roads or other works be constructed on the lands of their reservation, the Government will pay the tribe whatever amount of damage may be assessed by three disinterested commissioners to be appointed by the President for that purpose, one of said commissioners to be a chief or head-man of the tribe.

7th. They agree to withdraw all opposition to the military posts or roads now established south of the North Platte River, or that may be established, not in violation of treaties heretofore made or hereafter to be made with any of the Indian tribes.

Article 12

No treaty for the cession of any portion or part of the reservation herein described which may be held in common shall be of any validity or force as against the said Indians, unless executed and signed by at least three-fourths of all the adult male Indians, occupying or interested in the same; and no cession by the tribe shall be understood or construed in such manner as to deprive, without his consent, any individual member of the tribe of his rights to any tract of land selected by him, as provided in article 6 of this treaty.

Article 13

The United States hereby agrees to furnish annually to the Indians the physician, teacher, carpenter, miller, engineer, farmer, and blacksmiths as herein contemplated, and that such appropriations shall be made from time to time, on the estimates of the Secretary of the Interior, as will be sufficient to employ such persons.

Article 14

It is agreed that the sum of five hundred dollars annually, for three years from date, shall be expended in presents to the ten persons of said tribe who in the judgment of the agent may grow the most valuable crops for the respective year.

Article 15

The Indians herein named agree that when the agency-house or other buildings shall be constructed on the reservation named, they will regard said reservation their permanent home, and they will make no permanent settlement elsewhere; but they shall have the right, subject to the conditions and modifications of this treaty, to hunt, as stipulated in Article 11 hereof.

Article 16

The United States hereby agrees and stipulates that the country north of the North Platte River and east of the summits of the Big Horn Mountains shall be held and considered to be unceded Indian territory, and also stipulates and agrees that no white person or persons shall be permitted to settle upon or occupy any portion of the same; or without the consent of the Indians first had and obtained, to pass through the same; and it is further agreed by the United States that within ninety days after the conclusion of peace with all the bands of the Sioux Nation, the military posts now established in the territory in this article named shall be abandoned, and that the road leading to them and by them to the settlements in the Territory of Montana shall be closed.

Article 17

It is hereby expressly understood and agreed by and between the respective parties to this treaty that the execution of this treaty and its ratification by the United States Senate shall have the effect, and shall be construed as abrogating and annulling all treaties and agreements heretofore entered into between the respective parties hereto, so far as such treaties and agreements obligate the United States to furnish and provide money, clothing, or other articles of property to such Indians and bands of Indians as become parties to this treaty, but no further.

In testimony of all which, we, the said commissioners, and we, the chiefs and headmen of the Brulé band of the Sioux nation, have hereunto set our hands and seals at Fort Laramie, Dakota Territory, this twenty-ninth day of April, in the year one thousand eight hundred and sixty-eight.

N. G. Taylor, [SEAL.]
W. T. Sherman, [SEAL.]

Lieutenant-General.
Wm. S. Harney, [SEAL.]
Brevet Major-General U. S. Army.
John B. Sanborn, [SEAL.]
S. F. Tappan, [SEAL.]
C. C. Augur, [SEAL.]
Brevet Major-General.
Alfred H. Terry, [SEAL.]
Brevet Major-General U. S. Army.
Attest:
A. S. H. White, Secretary.

Executed on the part of the Brulé band of Sioux by the chiefs and headmen whose names are hereto annexed, they being thereunto duly authorized, at Fort Laramie, D. T., the twenty-ninth day of April, in the year A. D. 1868.

Ma-za-pon-kaska, his x mark, Iron Shell. [SEAL.]
Wah-pat-shah, his x mark, Red Leaf. [SEAL.]
Hah-sah-pah, his x mark, Black Horn. [SEAL.]
Zin-tah-gah-lat-skah, his x mark, Spotted Tail [SEAL.]
Zin-tah-skah, his x mark, White Tail. [SEAL.]
Me-wah-tah-ne-ho-skah, his x mark, Tall Mandas. [SEAL.]
She-cha-chat-kah, his x mark, Bad Left Hand. [SEAL.]
No-mah-no-pah, his x mark, Two and Two. [SEAL.]
Tah-tonka-skah, his x mark, White Bull. [SEAL.]
Con-ra-washta, his x mark, Pretty Coon. [SEAL.]
Ha-cah-cah-she-chah, his x mark, Bad Elk. [SEAL.]
Wa-ha-ka-zah-ish-tah, his x mark, Eye Lance. [SEAL.]
Ma-to-ha-ke-tah, his x mark, Bear that looks behind. [SEAL.]
Bella-tonka-tonka, his x mark, Big Partisan. [SEAL.]
Mah-to-ho-honka, his x mark, Swift Bear. [SEAL.]
To-wis-ne, his x mark, Cold Place. [SEAL.]
Ish-tah-skah, his x mark, White Eyes. [SEAL.]
Ma-ta-loo-zah, his x mark, Fast Bear. [SEAL.]
As-hah-kah-nah-zhe, his x mark, Standing Elk. [SEAL.]
Can-te-te-ki-ya, his x mark, The Brave Heart. [SEAL.]
Shunka-shaton, his x mark, Day Hawk. [SEAL.]
Tatanka-wakon, his x mark, Sacred Bull. [SEAL.]
Mapia shaton, his x mark, Hawk Cloud. [SEAL.]
Ma-sha-a-ow, his x mark, Stands and Comes. [SEAL.]
Shon-ka-ton-ka, his x mark, Big Dog. [SEAL.]

Confederate, Reconstruction, and Unratified Treaties, 1850–1871 | 357

Attest:
Ashton S. H. White, secretary of commission.
George B. Withs, phonographer to commission.
Geo. H. Holtzman.
John D. Howlano.
James C. O'Connor.
Chas. E. Guern, interpreter.
Leon F. Pallardy, interpreter.
Nicholas Janis, interpreter.

Executed on the part of the Ogallalah band of Sioux by the chiefs and headmen whose names are hereto subscribed, they being thereunto duly authorized, at Fort Laramie, the twenty-fifth day of May, in the year A. D. 1868.

Tah-shun-ka-co-qui-pah, his x mark, Man-afraid-of-his-horses. [SEAL.]
Sha-ton-skah, his x mark, White Hawk. [SEAL.]
Sha-ton-sapah, his x mark, Black Hawk. [SEAL.]
E-ga-mon-ton-ka-sapah, his x mark, Black Tiger. [SEAL.]
Oh-wah-she-cha, his x mark, Bad Wound. [SEAL.]
Pah-gee, his x mark, Grass. [SEAL.] Wah-non-reh-che-geh, his x mark, Ghost Heart. [SEAL.] Con-reeh, his x mark, Crow [SEAL.]
Oh-he-te-kah, his x mark, The Brave. [SEAL.]
Tah-ton-kah-he-yo-ta-kah, his x mark, Sitting Bull. [SEAL.]
Shon-ka-oh-wah-mon-ye, his x mark, Whirlwind Dog. [SEAL.]
Ha-hah-kah-tah-miech, his x mark, Poor Elk. [SEAL.]
Wam-bu-lee-wah-kon, his x mark, Medicine Eagle. [SEAL.]
Chon-gah-ma-he-to-hans-ka, his x mark, High Wolf. [SEAL.]
Wah-se-chun-ta-shun-kah, his x mark, American Horse. [SEAL.]
Mah-hah-mah-ha-mak-near, his x mark, Man that walks under the ground. [SEAL.]
Mah-to-tow-pah, his x mark, Four Bears. [SEAL.]
Ma-to-wee-sha-kta, his x mark, One that kills the bear. [SEAL.]
Oh-tah-kee-toka-wee-chakta, his x mark, One that kills in a hard place. [SEAL.]
Tah-ton-kah-ta-miech, his x mark, The poor Bull. [SEAL.]
Oh-huns-ee-ga-non-sken, his x mark, Mad Shade. [SEAL.]
Shah-ton-oh-nah-om-minne-ne-oh-minne, his x mark, Whirling Hawk. [SEAL.]
Mah-to-chun-ka-oh, his x mark, Bear's Back. [SEAL.]
Che-ton-wee-koh, his x mark, Fool Hawk. [SEAL.]
Wah-hoh-ke-za-ah-hah, his x mark, One that has the lance. [SEAL.]
Shon-gah-manni-toh-tan-ka-seh, his x mark, Big Wolf Foot. [SEAL.]
Eh-ton-kah, his x mark, Big Mouth. [SEAL.]

Ma-pah-che-tah, his x mark, Bad Hand. [SEAL.]
Wah-ke-yun-shah, his x mark, Red Thunder. [SEAL.]
Wak-sah, his x mark, One that Cuts Off. [SEAL.]
Cham-nom-qui-yah, his x mark, One that Presents the Pipe. [SEAL.]
Wah-ke-ke-yan-puh-tah, his x mark, Fire Thunder. [SEAL.]
Mah-to-nonk-pah-ze, his x mark, Bear with Yellow Ears. [SEAL.]
Con-ree-teh-ka, his x mark, The Little Crow. [SEAL.]
He-hup-pah-toh, his x mark, The Blue War Club. [SEAL.]
Shon-kee-toh, his x mark, The Blue Horse. [SEAL.]
Wam-Balla-oh-con-quo, his x mark, Quick Eagle. [SEAL.]
Ta-tonka-suppa, his x mark, Black Bull. [SEAL.]
Moh-to-ha-she-na, his x mark, The Bear Hide. [SEAL.]
Attest:
S. E. Ward.
Jas. C. O'Connor.
J. M. Sherwood.
W. C. Slicer.
Sam Deon.
H. M. Matthews.
Joseph Bissonette, interpreter.
Nicholas Janis, interpreter.
Lefroy Jott, interpreter.
Antoine Janis, interpreter.

Executed on the part of the Minneconjon band of Sioux by the chiefs and headmen whose names are hereto subscribed, they being thereunto duly authorized.

At Fort Laramie, D. T., May 26, '68, 13 names.
Heh-won-ge-chat, his x mark, One Horn. [SEAL.]
Oh-pon-ah-tah-e-manne, his x mark, The Elk that bellows Walking. [SEAL.]
At Fort Laramie, D. T., May 25, '68, 2 names.
Heh-ho-lah-reh-cha-skah, his x mark, Young White Bull. [SEAL.]
Wah-chah-chum-kah-coh-kee-pah, his x mark, One that is afraid of Shield. [SEAL.]
He-hon-ne-shakta, his x mark, The Old Owl. [SEAL.]
Moc-pe-a-toh, his x mark, Blue Cloud. [SEAL.]
Oh-pong-ge-le-skah, his x mark, Spotted Elk. [SEAL.]
Tah-tonk-ka-hon-ke-schne, his x mark, Slow Bull. [SEAL.]
Shonk-a-nee-shah-shah-a-tah-pe, his x mark, The Dog Chief. [SEAL.]
Ma-to-tah-ta-tonk-ka, his x mark, Bull Bear. [SEAL.]
Wom-beh-le-ton-kah, his x mark, The Big Eagle. [SEAL.]

Ma-toh-eh-schne-lah, his x mark, The Lone Bear. [SEAL.]
Mah-toh-ke-su-yah, his x mark, The One who Remembers the Bear. [SEAL.]
Ma-toh-oh-he-to-keh, his x mark, The Brave Bear. [SEAL.]
Eh-che-ma-heh, his x mark, The Runner. [SEAL.]
Ti-ki-ya, his x mark, The Hard. [SEAL.]
He-ma-za, his x mark, Iron Horn. [SEAL.]
Attest:
Jas. C. O'Connor.
Wm. H. Brown.
Nicholas Janis, interpreter.
Antoine Janis, interpreter.

Executed on the part of the Yanctonais band of Sioux by the chiefs and headmen whose names are hereto subscribed, they being thereunto duly authorized.

Mah-to-non-pah, his x mark, Two Bears. [SEAL.]
Ma-to-hna-skin-ya, his x mark, Mad Bear. [SEAL.]
He-o-pu-za, his x mark, Louzy. [SEAL.]
Ah-ke-che-tah-che-ca-dan, his x mark, Little Soldier. [SEAL.]
Mah-to-e-tan-chan, his x mark, Chief Bear. [SEAL.]
Cu-wi-h-win, his x mark, Rotten Stomach. [SEAL.]
Skun-ka-we-tko, his x mark, Fool Dog. [SEAL.]
Ish-ta-sap-pah, his x mark, Black Eye. [SEAL.]
Ih-tan-chan, his x mark, The Chief. [SEAL.]
I-a-wi-ca-ka, his x mark, The one who Tells the Truth. [SEAL.]
Ah-ke-che-tah, his x mark, The Soldier. [SEAL.]
Ta-shi-na-gi, his x mark, Yellow Robe. [SEAL.]
Nah-pe-ton-ka, his x mark, Big Hand. [SEAL.]
Chan-tee-we-kto, his x mark, Fool Heart. [SEAL.]
Hoh-gan-sah-pa, his x mark, Black Catfish. [SEAL.]
Mah-to-wah-kan, his x mark, Medicine Bear. [SEAL.]
Shun-ka-kan-sha, his x mark, Red Horse. [SEAL.]
Wan-rode, his x mark, The Eagle. [SEAL.]
Can-hpi-sa-pa, his x mark, Black Tomahawk. [SEAL.]
War-he-le-re, his x mark, Yellow Eagle. [SEAL.]
Cha-ton-che-ca, his x mark, Small Hawk, or Long Fare. [SEAL.]
Shu-ger-mon-e-too-ha-ska, his x mark, Tall Wolf. [SEAL.]
Ma-to-u-tah-kah, his x mark, Sitting Bear. [SEAL.]
Hi-ha-cah-ge-na-skene, his x mark, Mad Elk. [SEAL.]
Arapahoes:
Little Chief, his x mark. [SEAL.]

Tall Bear, his x mark. [SEAL.]
Top Man, his x mark. [SEAL.]
Neva, his x mark. [SEAL.]
The Wounded Bear, his x mark. [SEAL.]
Thirlwind, his x mark. [SEAL.]
The Fox, his x mark. [SEAL.]
The Dog Big Mouth, his x mark. [SEAL.]
Spotted Wolf, his x mark. [SEAL.]
Sorrel Horse, his x mark. [SEAL.]
Black Coal, his x mark. [SEAL.]
Big Wolf, his x mark. [SEAL.]
Knock-knee, his x mark. [SEAL.]
Black Crow, his x mark. [SEAL.]
The Lone Old Man, his x mark. [SEAL.]
Paul, his x mark. [SEAL.]
Black Bull, his x mark. [SEAL.]
Big Track, his x mark. [SEAL.]
The Foot, his x mark. [SEAL.]
Black White, his x mark. [SEAL.]
Yellow Hair, his x mark. [SEAL.]
Little Shield, his x mark. [SEAL.]
Black Bear, his x mark. [SEAL.]
Wolf Mocassin, his x mark. [SEAL.]
Big Robe, his x mark. [SEAL.]
Wolf Chief, his x mark. [SEAL.]
Witnesses:
Robt. P. McKibbin, captain, Fourth Infantry, brevet lieutenant-colonel, U. S. Army, commanding Fort Laramie.
Wm. H. Powell, brevet major, captain, Fourth Infantry.
Henry W. Patterson, captain, Fourth Infantry.
Theo. E. True, second lieutenant, Fourth Infantry.
W. G. Bullock.
Chas. E. Guern, special Indian interpreter for the peace commission.
Makh-pi-ah-lu-tah, his x mark, Red Cloud. [SEAL.]
Wa-ki-ah-we-cha-shah, his x mark, Thunder Man. [SEAL.]
Ma-zah-zah-geh, his x mark, Iron Cane. [SEAL.]
FORT LARAMIE, WG. T.,
Nov. 6, 1868.
Wa-umble-why-wa-ka-tuyah, his x mark, High Eagle. [SEAL.]
Ko-ke-pah, his x mark, Man Afraid. [SEAL.]
Wa-ki-ah-wa-kou-ah, his x mark, Thunder Flying Running. [SEAL.]
Witnesses:

W. McE. Dye, brevet colonel, U. S. Army, commanding.
A. B. Cain, captain, Fourth Infantry, brevet major, U. S. Army.
Robt. P. McKibbin, captain, Fourth Infantry, brevet lieutenant-colonel, U. S. Army.
Jno. Miller, captain, Fourth Infantry.
G. L. Luhn, first lieutenant, Fourth Infantry, brevet captain, U. S. Army.
H. C. Sloan, second lieutenant, Fourth Infantry.
Whittingham Cox, first lieutenant, Fourth Infantry.
A. W. Vogdes, first lieutenant, Fourth Infantry.
Butler D. Price, second lieutenant, Fourth Infantry.
HEADQRS., FORT LARAMIE,
Novr. 6, '68.
Executed by the above on this date.
All of the Indians are Ogallalahs excepting Thunder Man and Thunder Flying Running, who are Brulés.
Wm. McE. Dye,
Major Fourth Infantry, and Brevet-Colonel U. S. Army, Commanding.
Attest:
Jas. C. O'Connor.
Nicholas Janis, interpreter.
Franc. La Framboise, interpreter.
P. J. De Smet, S. J., missionary among the Indians.
Saml. D. Hinman, B. D., missionary.

Executed on the part of the Uncpapa band of Sioux, by the chiefs and headmen whose names are hereto subscribed, they being thereunto duly authorized.

Co-kam-i-ya-ya, his x mark, The Man that Goes in the Middle. [SEAL.]
Ma-to-ca-wa-weksa, his x mark, Bear Rib. [SEAL.]
Ta-to-ka-in-yan-ke, his x mark, Running Antelope. [SEAL.]
Kan-gi-wa-ki-ta, his x mark, Looking Crow. [SEAL.]
A-ki-ci-ta-han-ska, his x mark, Long Soldier. [SEAL.]
Wa-ku-te-ma-ni, his x mark, The One who Shoots Walking. [SEAL.]
Un-kca-ki-ka, his x mark, The Magpie. [SEAL.]
Kan-gi-o-ta, his x mark, Plenty Crow. [SEAL.]
He-ma-za, his x mark, Iron Horn. [SEAL.]
Shun-ka-i-na-pin, his x mark, Wolf Necklace. [SEAL.]
I-we-hi-yu, his x mark, The Man who Bleeds from the Mouth. [SEAL.]
He-ha-ka-pa, his x mark, Elk Head. [SEAL.]
I-zu-za, his x mark, Grind Stone. [SEAL.]
Shun-ka-wi-tko, his x mark, Fool Dog. [SEAL.]
Ma-kpi-ya-po, his x mark, Blue Cloud. [SEAL.]
Wa-mln-pi-lu-ta, his x mark, Red Eagle. [SEAL.]

Ma-to-can-te, his x mark, Bear's Heart. [SEAL.]
A-ki-ci-ta-i-tau-can, his x mark, Chief Soldier. [SEAL.]
Attest:
Jas. C. O'Connor.
Nicholas Janis, interpreter.
Franc. La Frambois[e], interpreter.
P. J. De Smet, S. J., missionary among the Indians.
Saml. D. Hinman, missionary.

Executed on the part of the Blackfeet band of Sioux by the chiefs and headmen whose names are hereto subscribed, they being thereunto duly authorized.

Can-te-pe-ta, his x mark, Fire Heart. [SEAL.]
Wan-mdi-kte, his x mark, The One who kills Eagle. [SEAL.]
Sho-ta, his x mark, Smoke. [SEAL.]
Wan-mdi-ma-ni, his x mark, Walking Eagle. [SEAL.]
Wa-shi-cun-ya-ta-pi, his x mark, Chief White Man. [SEAL.]
Kan-gi-i-yo-tan-ke, his x mark, Sitting Crow. [SEAL.]
Pe-ji, his x mark, The Grass. [SEAL.]
Kda-ma-ni, his x mark, The One that Rattles as he Walks. [SEAL.]
Wah-han-ka-sa-pa, his x mark, Black Shield. [SEAL.]
Can-te-non-pa, his x mark, Two Hearts. [SEAL.]
Attest:
Jas. C. O'Connor.
Nicholas Janis, interpreter.
Franc. La Framboise, interpreter.
P. J. De Smet, S. J., missionary among the Indians.
Saml. D. Hinman, missionary.

Executed on the part of the Cutheads band of Sioux by the chiefs and headmen whose names are hereto subscribed, they being thereunto duly authorized.

To-ka-in-yan-ka, his x mark, The One who Goes Ahead Running. [SEAL.]
Ta-tan-ka-wa-kin-yan, his x mark, Thunder Bull. [SEAL.]
Sin-to-min-sa-pa, his x mark, All over Black. [SEAL.]
Can-i-ca, his x mark, The One who Took the Stick. [SEAL.]
Pa-tan-ka, his x mark, Big Head. [SEAL.]
Attest:
Jas. C. O'Connor.
Nicholas Janis, interpreter.
Franc. La Frambois[e], interpreter.

P. J. De Smet, S. J., missionary among the Indians.
Saml. D. Hinman, missionary.

Executed on the part of the Two Kettle band of Sioux by the chiefs and headmen whose names are hereto subscribed, they being thereunto duly authorized.

Ma-wa-tan-ni-han-ska, his x mark, Long Mandan. [SEAL.]
Can-kpe-du-ta, his x mark, Red War Club. [SEAL.]
Can-ka-ga, his x mark, The Log. [SEAL.]
Attest:
Jas. C. O'Connor.
Nicholas Janis, interpreter.
Franc. La Framboise, interpreter.
P. J. De Smet, S. J., missionary among the Indians.
Saml. D. Hinman, missionary to the Dakotas.

Executed on the part of the Sans Arch band of Sioux by the chiefs and headmen whose names are hereto annexed, they being thereunto duly authorized.

He-na-pin-wa-ni-ca, his x mark, The One that has Neither Horn. [SEAL.]
Wa-inlu-pi-lu-ta, his x mark, Red Plume. [SEAL.]
Ci-tan-gi, his x mark, Yellow Hawk. [SEAL.]
He-na-pin-wa-ni-ca, his x mark, No Horn. [SEAL.]
Attest:
Jas. C. O'Connor.
Nicholas Janis, interpreter.
Franc. La Frambois[e], interpreter.
P. J. De Smet, S. J., missionary among the Indians.
Saml. D. Hinman, missionary.

Executed on the part of the Santee band of Sioux by the chiefs and headmen whose names are hereto subscribed, they being thereunto duly authorized.

Wa-pah-shaw, his x mark, Red Ensign. [SEAL.]
Wah-koo-tay, his x mark, Shooter. [SEAL.]
Hoo-sha-sha, his x mark, Red Legs. [SEAL.]
O-wan-cha-du-ta, his x mark, Scarlet all over. [SEAL.]
Wau-mace-tan-ka, his x mark, Big Eagle. [SEAL.]
Cho-tan-ka-e-na-pe, his x mark, Flute-player. [SEAL.]
Ta-shun-ke-mo-za, his x mark, His Iron Dog. [SEAL.]
Attest:

Saml. D. Hinman, B. D., missionary.

J. N. Chickering,

Second lieutenant, Twenty-second Infantry, brevet captain, U. S. Army.

P. J. De Smet, S. J.

Nicholas Janis, interpreter.

Franc. La Framboise, interpreter.

Treaty with the Navajo (1868)

On June 1, 1868, after four years in an American internment camp, Navajo leaders, including Barboncito and Manuelito, signed what would be the Navajo people's last treaty with the United States. The Treaty with the Navajos (1868) is a symbol of the Navajo Nation's sovereign status, although, like other indigenous nations, it is still dependent upon the United States. Importantly, the treaty allowed the Dinés ("the People") to return to their beloved homeland after four years in an internment camp at Fort Sumner, New Mexico. The Navajos commemorated the signing of the 1868 treaty in 1968 and 1999.

The colonial Southwest was a place where indigenous peoples successively encountered three different foreign cultures: the Spaniards, the Mexicans, and finally the Americans, each of which sought to impose their ways of life on the indigenous peoples. Pueblo peoples like the Santo Domingo, the Acoma, and the San Juan, among others, appeared to accept imposed values and policies of the colonizers; however, they practiced their own way of life, including their religion, in secret. The Dinés, who were different from their Pueblo neighbors in lifeways, openly thwarted colonial expansion, including that of the Americans, beginning in 1846.

One of the most enduring legacies that shaped southwestern cultures was the slave trade, which intensified with the Spanish and then peaked in the 1860s under American rule. Slave traders targeted Navajo women and children; as a result, cycles of peace and conflict characterized Navajo relationships with colonizers. By the 1860s, Navajos could no longer resist American westward expansion and were subjected to an all-out war, in which they were defeated. In 1864, more than 10,000 Navajos were sent to an internment camp near Fort Sumner, New Mexico.

Following the U.S. federal policy of forcing indigenous peoples to relocate to reservations and exterminating them if they resisted, General James Carleton conceived an assimilation plan for the Navajos. They would be removed to an internment camp at Bosque Redondo, near Fort Sumner in northeastern New Mexico. There, they would become farmers, would live in villages, and would be instructed in Christianity and other American practices. To force Navajo surrender, Carleton enlisted the Indian fighter Kit Carson, who literally scorched Dinétah (the Navajo homeland). In 1863, Carson and his men traveled through Navajo country destroying cornfields, slaughtering livestock, burning hogans, and cutting down peach orchards. By 1864, the Navajos were rendered destitute, and they turned themselves in at the American forts. Thousands of Navajos made the journey, the Long Walk, to Carleton's prison.

The Navajos suffered immensely on the Long Walk, for slave raiders waited to steal unsuspecting women and children, and soldiers shot the elderly and pregnant women who could not keep up with the rest. As they crossed the Rio Grande River, many were swept away by the rapids and drowned. The journey ended at the prison camp, where they endured starvation, poverty, sickness, and cold for four long years. Manuelito remained free until 1866 when, ill and starving, he and his band turned themselves in and also made the journey to the prison. The Dinés were unsuccessful at farming because of the poor soil and water. Outside the fort's perimeters, Comanches and New Mexicans waited to steal women and children for the slave trade.

Finally, in 1868, the United States admitted that the assimilation plan was a failure. They were also no longer willing to pay the cost of keeping the Dinés at the internment camp. At first, it seemed a possibility that the Navajos could be sent to Indian Territory, where many other indigenous peoples had been sent. Barboncito, a respected peace chief, spoke on behalf of his people: "I hope to God you will not ask me to go to any other country than my own." Eventually, Navajo leaders persuaded the military officers to allow them to return to their homeland.

On June 1, 1868, Navajo leaders signed a treaty with the United States. Navajo leaders agreed to peace between their people and the Americans. Most important to the Navajos was that they would return to their homeland. Other stipulations included the restoration of property seized in times of conflict, trade provisions, and 160-acre land allotments for Navajo families. Navajo leaders promised not to obstruct the building of a railroad that would slice through their best pasturing lands. They promised that their children would go to American schools.

The United States promised to keep the peace as well. They also promised annuities as compensation for lands taken and agreed to provide sheep, goats, and horses so that Navajos could reestablish their pastoral economy. The treaty of 1868 is the last one the Navajos signed with the U.S. government, although a number of executive orders increased the size of the Navajo Reservation up to the early 20th century.

On June 18, the People formed a column that stretched at least 10 miles long. They were going home. The old people wept in relief. Back home in Dinétah, Navajo families returned to their former homes and reestablished their lives. Their prayers to the Holy People had been answered. The Dinés prospered. Their livestock increased. They continued to follow the teachings of their ancestors. They have not forgotten the Long Walk and the prison camp at Bosque Redondo. They also remember the courage and bravery of their leaders during those dark times. Today, the Navajo Nation government continues to remind the U.S. government of the treaty of 1868 and its agreement to recognize and uphold Navajo sovereignty.

Jennifer Nez Denetdale

Further Reading

Bighorse, Tiana. *Bighorse the Warrior*, edited by Noel Bennet. Tucson: University of Arizona Press, 1990.

Iverson, Peter. *Diné: A History of the Navajos*. Albuquerque: University of New Mexico Press, 2002.

Roessel, Ruth. *Navajo Stories of the Long Walk Period*. Tsaile, AZ: Navajo Community College Press, 1973.

Tapahonso, Luci. *Sáanii Dahataal: The Women Are Singing*. Tucson: University of Arizona Press, 1993.

Document: Treaty with the Navajo

Articles of a treaty and agreement made and entered into at Fort Sumner, New Mexico, on the first day of June, one thousand eight hundred and sixty-eight, by and between the United States, represented by its commissioners, Lieutenant-General W. T. Sherman and Colonel Samuel F. Tappan, of the one part, and the Navajo Nation or tribe of Indians, represented by their chiefs and head-men, duly authorized and empowered to act for the whole people of said nation or tribe, (the names of said chiefs and head-men being hereto subscribed,) of the other part, witness:

Article 1

From this day forward all war between the parties to this agreement shall forever cease. The Government of the United States desires peace, and its honor is hereby pledged to keep it. The Indians desire peace, and they now pledge their honor to keep it. If bad men among the whites, or among other people subject to the authority of the United States, shall commit any wrong upon the person or property of the Indians, the United States will, upon proof made to the agent and forwarded to the Commissioner of Indian Affairs at Washington City, proceed at once to cause the offender to be arrested and punished according to the laws of the United States, and also to reimburse the injured persons for the loss sustained. If the bad men among the Indians shall commit a wrong or depredation upon the person or property of any one, white, black, or Indian, subject to the authority of the United States and at peace therewith, the Navajo tribe agree that they will, on proof made to their agent, and on notice by him, deliver up the wrongdoer to the United States, to be tried and punished according to its laws; and in case they wilfully refuse so to do, the person injured shall be reimbursed for his loss from the annuities or other moneys due or to become due to them under this treaty, or any others that may be made with the United States. And the President may prescribe such rules and regulations for ascertaining damages under this article as in his judgment may be proper; but no such damage shall be adjusted and paid until examined and passed upon by the Commissioner of Indian Affairs, and no one sustaining loss whilst violating, or because of his violating, the provisions of this treaty or the laws of the United States, shall be reimbursed therefor.

Article 2

The United States agrees that the following district of country, to wit: bounded on the north by the 37th degree of north latitude, south by an east and west line passing through the site of old Fort Defiance, in Cañon Bonito, east by the parallel of longitude which, if prolonged south, would pass through old Fort Lyon, or the Ojo-de-oso, Bear Spring, and west by a parallel of longitude about 109° 30° west of Greenwich, provided it embraces the outlet of the Cañon-de-Chilly, which cañon is to be all included in this reservation, shall be, and the same is hereby, set apart for the use and occupation of the Navajo tribe of Indians, and for such other friendly tribes or individual Indians as from time to time they may be willing, with the consent of the United States, to admit among them; and the United States agrees that no persons except those herein so authorized to do, and except such officers, soldiers, agents, and employées of the Government, or of the Indians, as may be authorized to enter upon Indian reservations in discharge of duties imposed by law, or the orders of the President, shall ever be permitted to pass over, settle upon, or reside in, the territory described in this article.

Article 3

The United States agrees to cause to be built, at some point within said reservation, where timber and water may be convenient, the following buildings: a warehouse, to cost not exceeding twenty-five hundred dollars; an agency building for the residence of the agent, not to cost exceeding three thousand dollars; a carpenter-shop and blacksmith-shop, not to cost exceeding one thousand dollars each; and a schoolhouse and chapel, so soon as a sufficient number of children can be induced to attend school, which shall not cost to exceed five thousand dollars.

Article 4

The United States agrees that the agent for the Navajos shall make his home at the agency building; that he shall reside among them, and shall keep an office open at all times for the purpose of prompt and diligent inquiry into such matters of complaint by or against the Indians as may be presented for investigation, as also for the faithful discharge of other duties enjoined by law. In all cases of depredation on person or property he shall cause the evidence to be taken in writing and forwarded, together with his finding, to the Commissioner of Indian Affairs, whose decision shall be binding on the parties to this treaty.

Article 5

If any individual belonging to said tribe, or legally incorporated with it, being the head of a family, shall desire to commence farming, he shall have the privilege to select, in the presence and with the assistance of the agent then in charge, a tract of land within said reservation, not exceeding one hundred and sixty acres in extent, which tract, when so selected, certified, and recorded in the "land-book" as herein described, shall cease to be held in common, but the same may be occupied and held in the exclusive possession of the person selecting it, and of his family, so long as he or they may continue to cultivate it. Any person over eighteen years of age, not being the head of a family, may in like manner select, and cause to be certified to him or her for purposes of cultivation, a quantity of land, not exceeding eighty acres in extent, and thereupon be entitled to the exclusive possession of the same as above directed. For each tract of land so selected a certificate containing a description thereof, and the name of the person selecting it, with a certificate endorsed thereon, that the same has been recorded, shall be delivered to the party entitled to it by the agent, after the same shall have been recorded by him in a book to be kept in his office, subject to inspection, which said book shall be known as the "Navajo land-book." The President may at any time order a survey of the reservation, and when so surveyed, Congress shall provide for protecting the rights of said settlers in their improvements, and may fix the character of the title held by each.

The United States may pass such laws on the subject of alienation and descent of property between the Indians and their descendants as may be thought proper.

Article 6

In order to insure the civilization of the Indians entering into this treaty, the necessity of education is admitted, especially of such of them as may be settled on said agricultural parts of this reservation, and they therefore pledge themselves to compel their children, male and female, between the ages of six and sixteen years, to attend school; and it is hereby made the duty of the agent for said Indians to see that this stipulation is strictly complied with; and the United States agrees that, for every thirty children between said ages who can be induced or compelled to attend school, a house shall be provided, and a teacher competent to teach the elementary branches of an English education shall be furnished, who will reside among said Indians, and faithfully discharge his or her duties as a teacher. The provisions of this article to continue for not less than ten years.

Article 7

When the head of a family shall have selected lands and received his certificate as above directed, and the agent shall be satisfied that he intends in good faith to commence cultivating the soil for a living, he shall be entitled to receive seeds and agricultural implements for the first year, not exceeding in value one hundred dollars, and for each succeeding year he shall continue to farm, for a period of two years, he shall be entitled to receive seeds and implements to the value of twenty-five dollars.

Article 8

In lieu of all sums of money or other annuities provided to be paid to the Indians herein named under any treaty or treaties heretofore made, the United States agrees to deliver at the agency-house on the reservation herein named, on the first day of September of each year for ten years, the following articles, to wit: Such articles of clothing, goods, or raw materials in lieu thereof, as the agent may make his estimate for, not exceeding in value five dollars per Indian—each Indian being encouraged to manufacture their own clothing, blankets, &c.; to be furnished with no article which they can manufacture themselves. And, in order that the Commissioner of Indian Affairs may be able to estimate properly for the articles herein named, it shall be the duty of the agent each year to forward to him a full and exact census of the Indians, on which the estimate from year to year can be based. And in addition to the articles herein named, the sum of ten dollars for each person entitled to the beneficial effects of this treaty shall be annually appropriated for a period of ten years, for each person who engages in farming or mechanical pursuits, to be used by the Commissioner of Indian Affairs in the purchase of such articles as from time to time the condition and necessities of the Indians may indicate to be proper; and if within the ten years at any time it shall appear that the amount of money needed for clothing, under the article, can be appropriated to better uses for the Indians named herein, the Commissioner of Indian Affairs may change the appropriation to other purposes, but in no event shall the amount of this appropriation be withdrawn or discontinued for the period named, provided they remain at peace. And the President shall annually detail an officer of the Army to be present and attest the delivery of all the goods herein named to the Indians, and he shall inspect and report on the quantity and quality of the goods and the manner of their delivery.

Article 9

In consideration of the advantages and benefits conferred by this treaty, and the many pledges of friendship by the United States, the tribes who are parties to this agreement hereby stipulate that they will relinquish all right to occupy any territory outside their reservation, as herein defined, but retain the right to hunt on any unoccupied lands contiguous to their reservation, so long as the large game may range thereon in such numbers as to justify the chase; and they, the said Indians, further expressly agree:

1st. That they will make no opposition to the construction of railroads now being built or hereafter to be built across the continent.
2d. That they will not interfere with the peaceful construction of any railroad not passing over their reservation as herein defined.
3d. That they will not attack any persons at home or travelling, nor molest or disturb any wagon-trains, coaches, mules, or cattle belonging to the people of the United States, or to persons friendly therewith.
4th. That they will never capture or carry off from the settlements women or children.
5th. They will never kill or scalp white men, nor attempt to do them harm.
6th. They will not in future oppose the construction of railroads, wagon-roads, mail stations, or other works of utility or necessity which may be ordered or permitted by the laws of the United States; but should such roads or other works be constructed on the lands of their reservation, the Government will pay the tribe whatever amount of damage may be assessed by three disinterested commissioners to be appointed by the President for that purpose, one of said commissioners to be a chief or head-men of the tribe.
7th. They will make no opposition to the military posts or roads now established, or that may be established, not in violation of treaties heretofore made or hereafter to be made with any of the Indian tribes.

Article 10

No future treaty for the cession of any portion or part of the reservation herein described, which may be held in common, shall be of any validity or force against said Indians unless agreed to and executed by at least three-fourths of all the adult male Indians occupying or interested in the same; and no cession by the tribe shall be understood or construed in such manner as to deprive, without his consent, any individual member of the tribe of his rights to any tract of land selected by him as provided in article [5] of this treaty.

Article 11

The Navajos also hereby agree that at any time after the signing of these presents they will proceed in such manner as may be required of them by the agent, or by the officer charged with their removal, to the reservation herein provided for, the United

States paying for their subsistence en route, and providing a reasonable amount of transportation for the sick and feeble.

Article 12

It is further agreed by and between the parties to this agreement that the sum of one hundred and fifty thousand dollars appropriated or to be appropriated shall be disbursed as follows, subject to any condition provided in the law, to wit:

1st. The actual cost of the removal of the tribe from the Bosque Redondo reservation to the reservation, say fifty thousand dollars.
2d. The purchase of fifteen thousand sheep and goats, at a cost not to exceed thirty thousand dollars.
3d. The purchase of five hundred beef cattle and a million pounds of corn, to be collected and held at the military post nearest the reservation, subject to the orders of the agent, for the relief of the needy during the coming winter.
4th. The balance, if any, of the appropriation to be invested for the maintenance of the Indians pending their removal, in such manner as the agent who is with them may determine.
5th. The removal of this tribe to be made under the supreme control and direction of the military commander of the Territory of New Mexico, and when completed, the management of the tribe to revert to the proper agent.

Article 13

The tribe herein named, by their representatives, parties to this treaty, agree to make the reservation herein described their permanent home, and they will not as a tribe make any permanent settlement elsewhere, reserving the right to hunt on the lands adjoining the said reservation formerly called theirs, subject to the modifications named in this treaty and the orders of the commander of the department in which said reservation may be for the time being; and it is further agreed and understood by the parties to this treaty, that if any Navajo Indian or Indians shall leave the reservation herein described to settle elsewhere, he or they shall forfeit all the rights, privileges, and annuities conferred by the terms of this treaty; and it is further agreed by the parties to this treaty, that they will do all they can to induce Indians now away from reservations set apart for the exclusive use and occupation of the Indians, leading a nomadic life, or engaged in war against the people of the United States, to abandon such a life and settle permanently in one of the territorial reservations set apart for the exclusive use and occupation of the Indians. In testimony of all which the said parties have hereunto, on this the first day of June, one thousand eight hundred and sixty-eight, at Fort Sumner, in the Territory of New Mexico, set their hands and seals.

W. T. Sherman, Lieutenant-General, Indian Peace Commissioner.
S. F. Tappan, Indian Peace Commissioner.
Barboncito chief, his x mark,
Armijo, his x mark,
Delgado, his mark,
Manuelito, his x mark,
Largo, his x mark,
Herrero, his x mark,
Chiqueto, his x mark,
Muerto de Hombre, his x mark,
Hombro, his x mark,
Narbono, his x mark,
Narbono Segundo, his x mark,
Gañado Mucho, his x mark
Council:
Riquo, his x mark,
Juan Martin, his x mark,
Serginto, his x mark,
Grande, his x mark,
Inoetenito, his x mark,
Muchachos Mucho, his x mark,
Chiqueto Segundo, his x mark,
Cabello Amarillo, his x mark,
Francisco, his x mark,
Torivio, his x mark,
Desdendado, his x mark,
Juan, his x mark,
Guero, his x mark,
Gugadore, his x mark,
Cabason, his x mark,
Barbon Segundo, his x mark,
Cabares Colorados, his x mark
Attest:
Geo. W. G. Getty, colonel Thirty-seventh Infantry, brevet major-general U. S. Army,
B. S. Roberts, brevet brigadier-general U. S. Army, lieutenant-colonel Third Cavalry,

J. Cooper McKee, brevet lieutenant-colonel, surgeon U. S. Army,
Theo. H. Dodd, United States Indian agent for Navajos,
Chas. McClure, brevet major and commissary of subsistence, U. S. Army,
James F. Weeds, brevet major and assistant surgeon, U. S. Army,
J. C. Sutherland, interpreter,
William Vaux, chaplain U. S. Army

Appendix A: Treaties by Tribe

Tribe	Treaty Name
Aionai	Treaty with the Comanche, Aionai, Anadarko, Caddo, Etc., 1846
Anadarko	Treaty with the Comanche, Aionai, Anadarko, Caddo, Etc., 1846
Apache	Treaty with the Apache, 1852
	Treaty with the Apache, Cheyenne, and Arapaho, 1865
	Treaty with the Cheyenne and Arapaho, 1865
	Treaty with the Comanche, Kiowa, and Apache, 1853
	Treaty with the Kiowa, Comanche, and Apache, 1867
Appalachicola	Treaty with the Appalachicola Band, 1832
	Treaty with the Appalachicola Band, 1833
Arapaho	Treaty with the Apache, Cheyenne, and Arapaho, 1865
	Treaty with the Arapaho and Cheyenne, 1861
	Treaty with the Cheyenne and Arapaho, 1865
	Treaty with the Cheyenne and Arapaho, 1867
	Treaty with the Northern Cheyenne and Northern Arapaho, 1868
	Treaty of Fort Laramie with Sioux, Etc., 1851
	Treaty with the Sioux—Brulé, Oglala, Miniconjou, Yanktonai, Hunkpapa, Blackfeet, Cuthead, Two Kettle, Sans Arcs, and Santee—and Arapaho
Arikara	Treaty with the Arikara Tribe, 1825
	Agreement at Fort Berthold, 1866
	Treaty of Fort Laramie with Sioux, Etc., 1851
Assinaboine	Treaty of Fort Laramie with Sioux, Etc., 1851
Bannock	Treaty with the Eastern Band Shoshoni and Bannock, 1868
Belantse-Etoa or Minitaree	Treaty with the Belantse-Etoa or Minitaree Tribe, 1825
Blackfeet	Treaty with the Blackfeet, 1855
	Treaty with the Blackfeet Sioux, 1865
Blood	Treaty with the Blackfeet, 1855

Appendix A: Treaties by Tribe

Tribe	Treaty Name
Brothertown	Treaty with the New York Indians, 1838
Caddo	Treaty with the Caddo, 1835
	Treaty with the Comanche, Aionai, Anadarko, Caddo, Etc., 1846
Cahokia	Treaty with the Peoria, Etc., 1818
Cayuga	Agreement with the Five Nations of Indians, 1792
	Treaty with the Six Nations, 1784
	Treaty with the New York Indians, 1838
	Treaty with the Six Nations, 1789
	Treaty with the Six Nations, 1794
Cayuse	Treaty with the Walla-Walla, Cayuse, Etc., 1855
Chasta	Treaty with the Chasta, Etc., 1854
Cherokee	Treaty with the Cherokee, 1785
	Treaty with the Cherokee, 1791
	Treaty with the Cherokee, 1794
	Treaty with the Cherokee, 1798
	Treaty with the Cherokee, 1804
	Treaty with the Cherokee, 1805, October 25
	Treaty with the Cherokee, 1805, October 27
	Treaty with the Cherokee, 1806
	Treaty with the Cherokee, 1816, March 22 (two treaties on the same day)
	Treaty with the Cherokee, 1816, September 14
	Treaty with the Cherokee, 1817
	Treaty with the Cherokee, 1819
	Treaty with the Western Cherokee, 1828
	Treaty with the Western Cherokee, 1833
	Treaty with the Cherokee, 1835
	Treaty with the Cherokee, 1846 [Western Cherokee]
	Treaty with the Cherokee, 1866
	Treaty with the Cherokee, 1868
	Agreement with the Cherokee, 1835 (Unratified)
	Agreement with the Cherokee and Other Tribes in the Indian Territory, 1865
	Treaty with the Comanche, Etc., 1835
Cheyenne	Treaty with the Apache, Cheyenne, and Arapaho, 1865
	Treaty with the Arapaho and Cheyenne, 1861
	Treaty with the Cheyenne Tribe, 1825
	Treaty with the Cheyenne and Arapaho, 1865
	Treaty with the Cheyenne and Arapaho, 1867

Tribe	Treaty Name
	Treaty with the Northern Cheyenne and Northern Arapaho, 1868
	Treaty of Fort Laramie with Sioux, Etc., 1851
Chickasaw	Agreement with the Cherokee and Other Tribes in the Indian Territory, 1865
	Treaty with the Chickasaw, 1786
	Treaty with the Chickasaw, 1801
	Treaty with the Chickasaw, 1805
	Treaty with the Chickasaw, 1816
	Treaty with the Chickasaw, 1818
	Treaty with the Chickasaw, 1832, October 20
	Treaty with the Chickasaw, 1832, October 22
	Treaty with the Chickasaw, 1830
	Treaty with the Chickasaw, 1834
	Treaty with the Choctaw and Chickasaw, 1837
	Treaty with the Chickasaw, 1852
	Treaty with the Choctaw and Chickasaw, 1854
	Treaty with the Choctaw and Chickasaw, 1855
	Treaty with the Choctaw and Chickasaw, 1866
Chippewa	Treaty with the Chippewa, Etc., 1808
	Treaty with the Chippewa, 1819
	Treaty with the Chippewa, 1820
	Treaty with the Ottawa and Chippewa, 1820
	Treaty with the Chippewa, 1826
	Treaty with the Chippewa, Etc., 1827
	Treaty with the Chippewa, Etc., 1829
	Treaty with the Chippewa, Etc., 1833
	Treaty with the Chippewa, 1836
	Treaty with the Chippewa, 1837, January 14
	Treaty with the Chippewa, 1837, July 29
	Treaty with the Chippewa, 1837, December 20
	Treaty with the Chippewa, 1838
	Treaty with the Chippewa, 1839
	Treaty with the Chippewa, 1842
	Treaty with the Chippewa of the Mississippi and Lake Superior, 1847
	Treaty with the Chippewa, 1854
	Treaty with the Chippewa, 1855
	Treaty with the Chippewa of Saginaw, Etc., 1855
	Treaty with the Chippewa, Etc., 1859

Tribe	Treaty Name
	Treaty with the Chippewa of the Mississippi and the Pillager and Lake Winnibigoshish Bands, 1863
	Treaty with the Chippewa—Red Lake and Pembina Bands, 1863
	Treaty with the Chippewa—Red Lake and Pembina Bands, 1864
	Treaty with the Chippewa, Mississippi, and Pillager and Lake Winnibigoshish Bands, 1864
	Treaty with the Chippewa of Saginaw, Swan Creek, and Black River, 1864
	Treaty with the Chippewa—Bois Forte Band, 1866
	Treaty with the Chippewa of the Mississippi, 1867
	Treaty with the Ottawa, Etc., 1807
	Treaty with the Ottawa, Etc., 1816
	Treaty with the Ottawa, Etc., 1821
	Treaty with the Ottawa, Etc., 1836
	Treaty with the Ottawa and Chippewa, 1855
	Treaty with the Pillager Band of Chippewa Indians, 1847
	Treaty with the Potawatomi Nation, 1846
	Treaty with the Chippewa of Sault Ste. Marie, 1855
	Treaty with the Sioux, Etc., 1825
	Treaty with the Winnebago, Etc., 1828
	Chippewa (cont.) Treaty with the Wyandot, Etc., 1785
	Treaty with the Wyandot, Etc., 1789
	Treaty with the Wyandot, Etc., 1795
	Treaty with the Wyandot, Etc., 1805
	Treaty with the Wyandot, Etc., 1815
	Treaty with the Wyandot, Etc., 1817
	Treaty with the Wyandot, Etc., 1818
Choctaw	Agreement with the Cherokee and Other Tribes in the Indian Territory, 1865
	Treaty with the Choctaw and Chickasaw, 1837
	Treaty with the Choctaw, 1786
	Treaty with the Choctaw, 1801
	Treaty with the Choctaw, 1802
	Treaty with the Choctaw, 1803
	Treaty with the Choctaw, 1805
	Treaty with the Choctaw, 1816
	Treaty with the Choctaw, 1820
	Treaty with the Choctaw, 1825
	Treaty with the Choctaw, 1830

Tribe	Treaty Name
	Treaty with the Choctaw and Chickasaw, 1854
	Treaty with the Choctaw and Chickasaw, 1855
	Treaty with the Choctaw and Chickasaw, 1866
	Treaty with the Comanche, Etc., 1835
	Treaty with the Comanche and Kiowa, 1865
Clack-A-Mas	Treaty with the Kalapuya, Etc., 1855
Columbia	Agreement with the Columbia and Colville, 1883
Colville	Agreement with the Columbia and Colville, 1883
Comanche	Treaty with the Comanche, Etc., 1835
	Treaty with the Comanche, Aionai, Anadarko, Caddo, Etc., 1846
	Treaty with the Comanche, Kiowa, and Apache, 1853
	Treaty with the Kiowa and Comanche, 1867
	Treaty with the Kiowa, Comanche, and Apache, 1867
	Agreement with the Cherokee and Other Tribes in the Indian Territory, 1865
Creeks	Treaty with the Creeks, 1790
	Treaty with the Creeks, 1796
	Treaty with the Creeks, 1802
	Treaty with the Creeks, 1805
	Treaty with the Creeks, 1814
	Treaty with the Creeks, 1818
	Treaty with the Creeks, 1821, January 8 (two treaties on the same day, same place)
	Treaty with the Creeks, 1825
	Treaty with the Creeks, 1826
	Creeks (cont.) Treaty with the Creeks, 1827
	Treaty with the Creeks, 1832
	Treaty with the Creeks, 1833
	Treaty with the Creeks, 1838
	Treaty with the Creeks and Seminole, 1845
	Treaty with the Creeks, 1854
	Treaty with the Creeks, Etc., 1856
	Treaty with the Creeks, 1866
	Agreement with the Creeks, 1825 (Unratified)
Crow	Treaty with the Crow Tribe, 1825
	Treaty with the Crows, 1868
	Agreement with the Crows, 1880 (Unratified)
	Treaty of Fort Laramie with Sioux, Etc., 1851

Tribe	Treaty Name
Dakota	Treaty with the Blackfeet Sioux, 1865
	Treaty of Fort Laramie with Sioux, Etc., 1851
De Chutes	Treaty with the Middle Oregon Tribes, 1865
	Treaty with the Tribes of Middle Oregon, 1855
Delaware	Treaty with the Delawares, 1778
	Treaty with the Delawares, Etc., 1803
	Treaty with the Delawares, 1804
	Treaty with the Delawares, Etc., 1805
	Treaty with the Delawares, Etc., 1809
	Treaty with the Delawares, 1818
	Treaty with the Delawares, 1829, August 3
	Treaty with the Delawares, 1829, September 24
	Treaty with the Delawares, 1854
	Treaty with the Delawares, 1860
	Treaty with the Delawares, 1861
	Treaty with the Delawares, 1866
	Agreement with the Delawares and Wyandot, 1843
	Supplementary Treaty with the Miami, Etc., 1809
	Treaty with the Shawnee, Etc., 1832
	Treaty with the Wyandot, Etc., 1785
	Treaty with the Wyandot, Etc., 1789
	Treaty with the Wyandot, Etc., 1795
	Treaty with the Wyandot, Etc., 1805
	Treaty with the Wyandot, Etc., 1814
	Treaty with the Wyandot, Etc., 1815
	Treaty with the Wyandot, Etc., 1817
	Treaty with the Wyandot, Etc., 1818
Dwamish	Treaty with the Dwamish, Suquamish, Etc., 1855
Eel River	Treaty with the Delawares, Etc., 1803
	Treaty with the Delawares, Etc., 1805
	Treaty with the Delawares, Etc., 1809
	Treaty with the Eel River, Etc., 1803
	Eel River (cont.) Supplementary Treaty with the Miami, Etc., 1809
	Treaty with the Miami, 1828
	Treaty with the Wyandot, Etc., 1795
Five Nations	Agreement with the Five Nations of Indians, 1792
Flathead	Treaty with the Blackfeet, 1855

Tribe	Treaty Name
	Treaty with the Flatheads, Etc., 1855
Fox	Treaty with the Foxes, 1815
Gros Ventres	Treaty with the Blackfeet, 1855
	Agreement at Fort Berthold, 1866
	Treaty of Fort Laramie with Sioux, Etc., 1851
Illinois	Treaty with the Kaskaskia, Etc., 1832
	Treaty with the Peoria, Etc., 1818
Iowa	Treaty with the Iowa, 1815
	Treaty with the Iowa, 1824.
	Treaty with the Iowa, Etc., 1836.
	Treaty with the Iowa, 1837
	Treaty with the Iowa, 1838
	Treaty with the Iowa, 1854
	Treaty with the Sauk and Fox, Etc., 1830
	Treaty with the Sauk and Fox, Etc., 1861
	Treaty with the Sioux, Etc., 1825
Kalapuya	Treaty with the Kalapuya, Etc., 1855
	Treaty with the Umpqua and Kalapuya, 1854
Kansa	Treaty with the Kansa, 1815
	Treaty with the Kansa, 1825
	Treaty with the Kansa, 1825
	Treaty with Kansa Tribe, 1846
	Treaty with the Kansa Tribe, 1859
	Treaty with the Kansa Indians, 1862
Kaskaskia	Treaty with the Delawares, Etc., 1803
	Treaty with the Eel River, Etc., 1803
	Treaty with the Kaskaskia, 1803
	Treaty with the Kaskaskia, Etc., 1832
	Treaty with the Kaskaskia, Peoria, Etc., 1854
	Treaty with the Peoria, Etc., 1818
	Treaty with the Seneca, Mixed Seneca and Shawnee, Quapaw, Etc., 1867
	Treaty with the Wyandot, Etc., 1795
Ka-Ta-Ka	Treaty with the Kiowa, Etc., 1837
Keechy	Treaty with the Comanche, Aionai, Anadarko, Caddo, Etc., 1846
Kickapoo	Treaty with the Delawares, Etc., 1803
	Treaty with the Eel River, Etc., 1803

Tribe	Treaty Name
	Treaty with the Kickapoo, 1809
	Treaty with the Kickapoo, 1815
	Treaty with the Wea and Kickapoo, 1816
	Treaty with the Kickapoo, 1819, July 30
	Treaty with the Kickapoo, 1819, August 30
	Treaty with the Kickapoo, 1820
	Treaty with the Kickapoo of the Vermilion 1820
	Treaty with the Kickapoo, 1832
	Treaty with the Kickapoo, 1854
	Treaty with the Kickapoo, 1862
	Treaty with the Wyandot, Etc., 1795
Kik-Ial-Lus	Treaty with the Dwamish, Suquamish, Etc., 1855
Kiowa	Treaty with the Comanche, Kiowa, and Apache, 1853
	Treaty with the Comanche and Kiowa, 1865
	Treaty with the Kiowa, Etc., 1837
	Treaty with the Kiowa and Comanche, 1867
	Treaty with the Kiowa, Comanche, and Apache, 1867
Klamath	Treaty with the Klamath, Etc., 1864
Kootenay	Treaty with the Blackfeet, 1855
	Treaty with the Flatheads, Etc., 1855
Lepan	Treaty with the Comanche, Aionai, Anadarko, Caddo, Etc., 1846
Long-Wha	Treaty with the Comanche, Aionai, Anadarko, Caddo, Etc., 1846
Lummi	Treaty with the Dwamish, Suquamish, Etc., 1855
Makah	Treaty with the Makah, 1815
	Treaty with the Makah Tribe, 1825
	Treaty with the Makah, 1855
Mandan	Agreement at Fort Berthold, 1866
	Treaty with the Mandan Tribe, 1825
	Treaty of Fort Laramie with Sioux, Etc., 1851
Me-Sek-Wi-Guilse	Treaty with the Dwamish, Suquamish, Etc., 1855
Menominee	Treaty with the Chippewa, Etc., 1827
	Treaty with the Menominee, 1817
	Treaty with the Menominee, 1831, February 8
	Treaty with the Menominee, 1831, February 17
	Treaty with the Menominee, 1832
	Treaty with the Menominee, 1836
	Treaty with the Menominee, 1848

Tribe	Treaty Name
	Treaty with the Menominee, 1854
	Treaty with the Menominee, 1856
	Treaty with the Sioux, Etc., 1825
Miami	Treaty with the Delawares, Etc., 1803
	Treaty with the Delawares, Etc., 1805
	Treaty with the Delawares, Etc., 1809
	Supplementary Treaty with the Miami, Etc., 1809
	Treaty with the Miami, 1818
	Treaty with the Miami, 1826
	Treaty with the Miami, 1828
	Treaty with the Miami, 1834
	Treaty with the Miami, 1838
	Treaty with the Miami, 1840
	Treaty with the Miami, 1854
	Treaty with the Seneca, Mixed Seneca and Shawnee, Quapaw, Etc., 1867
	Treaty with the Wyandot, Etc., 1795
	Treaty with the Wyandot, Etc., 1814
	Treaty with the Wyandot, Etc., 1815
	Middle Oregon Tribes Treaty with the Middle Oregon Tribes, 1865
	Treaty with the Tribes of Middle Oregon, 1855
	Minitaree or Belantse-Etoa Treaty with the Belantse-Etoa or Minitaree Tribe, 1825
Mitchigamia	Treaty with the Peoria, Etc., 1818
Modoc	Treaty with the Klamath, Etc., 1864
Mohawk	Treaty with the Mohawk, 1797
	Treaty with the Six Nations, 1784
	Treaty with the Six Nations, 1789
	Treaty with the Six Nations, 1794
Molala	Treaty with the Kalapuya, Etc., 1855
	Treaty with the Molala, 1855
Muscogee	Treaty with the Comanche, Etc., 1835
Munsee	Treaty with the Chippewa, Etc., 1859
	Treaty with the New York Indians, 1838
	Treaty with the Stockbridge and Munsee, 1839
	Treaty with the Stockbridge and Munsee, 1856
	Treaty with the Wyandot, Etc., 1805

Tribe	Treaty Name
Navajo	Treaty with the Navaho, 1849
	Treaty with the Navaho, 1868
New York Indians	Treaty with the New York Indians, 1838
Nez Percé	Treaty with the Blackfeet, 1855
	Treaty with the Nez Percé, 1855
	Treaty with the Nez Percé, 1863
	Treaty with the Nez Percé, 1868
Nisqually	Treaty with the Nisqualli, Puyallup, Etc., 1854
Noo-Wha-Ha	Treaty with the Dwamish, Suquamish, Etc., 1855
Omaha	Treaty with the Omaha, 1854
	Treaty with the Omaha, 1865
	Treaty with the Oto, Etc., 1836
	Treaty with the Sauk and Fox, Etc., 1830
Oneida	Agreement with the Five Nations of Indians, 1792
	Treaty with the Six Nations, 1784
	Treaty with the New York Indians, 1838
	Treaty with the Oneida, Etc., 1794
	Treaty with the Oneida, 1838
	Treaty with the Six Nations, 1789
	Treaty with the Six Nations, 1794
Onondaga	Agreement with the Five Nations of Indians, 1792
	Treaty with the Six Nations, 1784
	Treaty with the Six Nations, 1789
	Treaty with the Six Nations, 1794
	Treaty with the New York Indians, 1838
Osage	Agreement with the Cherokee and Other Tribes in the Indian Territory, 1865
	Treaty with the Comanche, Etc., 1835
	Treaty with the Osage, 1808
	Treaty with the Osage, 1815
	Treaty with the Osage, 1818
	Treaty with the Osage, 1822
	Treaty with the Osage, 1825
	Treaty with the Great and Little Osage, 1825
	Treaty with the Osage, 1839
	Treaty with the Osage, 1865
Oto	Treaty with the Oto, 1817
Oto and Missouri	Treaty with the Confederated Oto and Missouri, 1854

Tribe	Treaty Name
	Treaty with the Oto and Missouri Tribe, 1825
	Treaty with the Oto and Missouri, 1833
	Treaty with the Oto, Etc., 1836
	Treaty with the Oto and Missouri, 1854
	Treaty with the Sauk and Fox, Etc., 1830
Ottawa	Treaty with the Chippewa, Etc., 1808
	Treaty with the Ottawa and Chippewa, 1820
	Treaty with the Chippewa, Etc., 1829
	Treaty with the Chippewa, Etc., 1833
	Treaty with the Ottawa, Etc., 1807
	Treaty with the Ottawa, Etc., 1816
	Treaty with the Ottawa, Etc., 1821
	Treaty with the Ottawa, 1831
	Treaty with the Ottawa, 1833
	Treaty with the Ottawa, Etc., 1836
	Treaty with the Ottawa and Chippewa, 1855
	Treaty with the Ottawa of Blanchard's Fork and Roche De Boeuf, 1862
	Treaty with the Potawatomi Nation, 1846
	Treaty with the Seneca, Mixed Seneca and Shawnee, Quapaw, Etc., 1867
	Treaty with the Sioux, Etc., 1825
	Treaty with the Winnebago, Etc., 1828
	Treaty with the Wyandot, Etc., 1785
	Treaty with the Wyandot, Etc., 1789
	Treaty with the Wyandot, Etc., 1795
	Treaty with the Wyandot, Etc., 1805
	Treaty with the Wyandot, Etc., 1815
	Treaty with the Wyandot, Etc., 1817
	Treaty with the Wyandot, Etc., 1818
Pawnee	Treaty with the Grand Pawnee, 1818
	Treaty with the Noisy Pawnee, 1818
	Treaty with the Pawnee Republic, 1818
	Treaty with the Pawnee Marhar, 1818
	Treaty with the Pawnee Tribe, 1825
	Treaty with the Pawnee, 1833
	Treaty with the Pawnee—Grand, Loups, Republicans, Etc., 1848
	Treaty with the Pawnee, 1857
Peoria	Treaty with the Kaskaskia, Etc., 1832

Tribe	Treaty Name
	Treaty with the Kaskaskia, Peoria, Etc., 1854
	Treaty with the Peoria, Etc., 1818
	Treaty with the Seneca, Mixed Seneca and Shawnee, Quapaw, Etc., 1867
Piankeshaw	Treaty with the Delawares, Etc., 1803
	Treaty with the Eel River, Etc., 1803
	Treaty with the Kaskaskia, Peoria, Etc., 1854
	Treaty with the Piankeshaw, 1804
	Treaty with the Piankashaw, 1805
	Treaty with the Piankashaw, 1815
	Treaty with the Piankashaw and Wea, 1832
	Agreement with the Piankeshaw, 1818 (Unratified)
	Treaty with the Seneca, Mixed Seneca and Shawnee, Quapaw, Etc., 1867
	Treaty with the Wyandot, Etc., 1795
Piegan	Treaty with the Blackfeet, 1855
Ponca	Treaty with the Ponca, 1817
	Treaty with the Ponca, 1825
	Treaty with the Ponca, 1858
	Treaty with the Ponca, 1865
Potawatomi	Treaty with the Chippewa, Etc., 1808
	Treaty with the Chippewa, Etc., 1829
	Treaty with the Chippewa, Etc., 1833
	Treaty with the Delawares, Etc., 1803
	Treaty with the Delawares, Etc., 1805
	Treaty with the Delawares, Etc., 1809
	Supplementary Treaty with the Miami, Etc., 1809
	Treaty with the Ottawa, Etc., 1807
	Treaty with the Ottawa, Etc., 1816
	Treaty with the Ottawa, Etc., 1821
	Treaty with the Potawatomi, 1815
	Treaty with the Potawatomi, 1818
	Treaty with the Potawatomi, 1826
	Treaty with the Potawatomi, 1827
	Treaty with the Potawatomi, 1828
	Treaty with the Potawatomi, 1832, October 20
	Treaty with the Potawatomi, 1832, October 26
	Treaty with the Potawatomi, 1832, October 27
	Treaty with the Potawatomi, 1834, December 4
	Treaty with the Potawatomi, 1834, December 10

Tribe	Treaty Name
	Treaty with the Potawatomi, 1834, December 16
	Treaty with the Potawatomi, 1834, December 17
	Treaty with the Potawatomi, 1836, March 26
	Treaty with the Potawatomi, 1836, March 29
	Treaty with the Potawatomi, 1836, April 11
	Treaty with the Potawatomi, 1836, April 22 (two treaties on the same day)
	Treaty with the Potawatomi, 1836, August 5
	Treaty with the Potawatomi, 1836, September 20
	Treaty with the Potawatomi, 1836, September 22
	Treaty with the Potawatomi, 1836, September 23
	Treaty with the Potawatomi, 1837
	Treaty with the Potawatomi Nation, 1846
	Treaty with the Potawatomi, 1861
	Treaty with the Potawatomi, 1866
	Treaty with the Potawatomi, 1867
	Treaty with the Sioux, Etc., 1825
	Treaty with the Winnebago, Etc, 1828
	Treaty with the Wyandot, Etc., 1789
	Treaty with the Wyandot, Etc., 1795
	Treaty with the Wyandot, Etc., 1805
	Treaty with the Wyandot, Etc., 1815
	Treaty with the Wyandot, Etc., 1817
	Treaty with the Wyandot, Etc., 1818
Puyallup	Treaty with the Nisqualli, Puyallup, Etc., 1854
Quapaw	Agreement with the Cherokee and Other Tribes in the Indian Territory, 1865
	Treaty with the Comanche, Etc., 1835
	Treaty with the Quapaw, 1818
	Treaty with the Quapaw, 1824
	Treaty with the Quapaw, 1833
	Treaty with the Seneca, Mixed Seneca and Shawnee, Quapaw, Etc., 1867
Qui-Nai-Elt	Treaty with the Quinaielt, Etc., 1855
Quil-Leh-Ute	Treaty with the Quinaielt, Etc., 1855
Ricara	Treaty with the Arikara Tribe, 1825
	Agreement at Fort Berthold, 1866
	Treaty of Fort Laramie with Sioux, Etc., 1851
Rogue River	Treaty with the Rogue River, 1853
	Treaty with the Rogue River, 1854

Tribe	Treaty Name
	Agreement with the Rogue River, 1853 (Unratified)
Sac and Fox	Treaty with the Fox, 1815
	Treaty with the Iowa, Etc., 1836.
	Treaty with the Sauk and Fox, 1804
	Treaty with the Sauk, 1815
	Treaty with the Sauk, 1816
	Treaty with the Sauk and Fox, 1822
	Treaty with the Sauk and Fox, 1824
	Treaty with the Sauk and Fox, Etc., 1830
	Treaty with the Sauk and Fox, 1832
	Treaty with the Sauk and Fox Tribe, 1836, September 27
	Treaty with the Sauk and Fox, 1836, September 28 (two treaties on the same day, same place)
	Treaty with the Sauk and Fox, 1837, October 21
	Treaty with the (Missouri) Sauk and Fox, 1837, October 21
	Treaty with the Sauk and Fox, 1842
	Treaty with the Sauk and Fox of Missouri, 1854
	Treaty with the Sauk and Fox, 1859
	Treaty with the Sauk and Fox, Etc., 1861
	Treaty with the Sauk and Fox, 1867
	Treaty with the Sioux, Etc., 1825
	Treaty with the Wyandot, Etc., 1789
Sa-Heh-Wamish	Treaty with the Nisqualli, Puyallup, Etc., 1854
Sah-Ku-Meh-Hu	Treaty with the Dwamish, Suquamish, Etc., 1855
Scotons	Treaty with the Chasta, Etc., 1854
Seminole	Agreement with the Cherokee and Other Tribes in the Indian Territory, 1865
	Treaty with the Creeks and Seminole, 1845
	Treaty with the Creeks, Etc., 1856
	Treaty with the Florida Tribes of Indians, 1823
	Treaty with the Seminole, 1832
	Treaty with the Seminole, 1833
	Treaty with the Seminole, 1866
Seneca	Agreement with the Cherokee and Other Tribes in the Indian Territory, 1865
	Treaty with the Comanche, Etc., 1835

Tribe	Treaty Name
	Agreement with the Five Nations of Indians, 1792
	Treaty with the Six Nations, 1784
	Treaty with the New York Indians, 1838
	Treaty with the Seneca, 1802
	Treaty with the Seneca, 1802
	Treaty with the Seneca, 1831
	Treaty with the Seneca, Etc., 1831
	Treaty with the Seneca and Shawnee, 1832
	Treaty with the Seneca, 1842
	Treaty with the Seneca, Tonawanda Band, 1857
	Treaty with the Seneca, Mixed Seneca and Shawnee, Quapaw, Etc., 1867
	Agreement with the Seneca, 1797
	Agreement with the Seneca, 1823 (Unratified)
	Treaty with the Six Nations, 1789
	Treaty with the Six Nations, 1794
	Treaty with the Wyandot, Etc., 1814
	Treaty with the Wyandot, Etc., 1815
	Treaty with the Wyandot, Etc., 1817
	Treaty with the Wyandot, Etc., 1818
	Seven Nations of Canada Treaty with the Seven Nations of Canada, 1796
Shawnee	Agreement with the Cherokee and Other Tribes in the Indian Territory, 1865
	Treaty with the Chippewa, Etc., 1808
	Treaty with the Delawares, Etc., 1803
	Treaty with the Seneca, Etc., 1831
	Treaty with the Seneca and Shawnee, 1832
	Treaty with the Seneca, Mixed Seneca and Shawnee, Quapaw, Etc., 1867
	Treaty with the Shawnee, 1786
	Treaty with the Shawnee, 1825
	Treaty with the Shawnee, 1831
	Treaty with the Shawnee, Etc., 1832
	Treaty with the Shawnee, 1854
	Treaty with the Wyandot, Etc., 1795
	Treaty with the Wyandot, Etc., 1805
	Treaty with the Wyandot, Etc., 1814
	Treaty with the Wyandot, Etc., 1815

Tribe	Treaty Name
	Treaty with the Wyandot, Etc., 1817
	Treaty with the Wyandot, Etc., 1818
S'homamish	Treaty with the Nisqualli, Puyallup, Etc., 1854
Shoshoni	Treaty with the Eastern Shoshoni, 1863
	Treaty with the Shoshoni—Northwestern Bands, 1863
	Treaty with the Western Shoshoni, 1863
	Treaty with the Eastern Band Shoshoni and Bannock, 1868
Shoshoni-Goship	Treaty with the Shoshoni-Goship, 1863
Sioux	Treaty with the Blackfeet Sioux, 1865
	Treaty with the Hunkpapa Band of the Sioux Tribe, 1825
	Treaty with the Sioune and Oglala Tribes, 1825 (Also Ogallala)
	Treaty with the Oto, Etc., 1836—Yankton and Santee Bands
	Treaty with the Sauk and Fox, Etc., 1830—Medawah-Kanton, Wahpacoota, Wahpeton, Sissetong [Sisseton], Yanckton [Yancton] and Santie Bands
	Treaty with the Sioux of the Lakes, 1815
	Treaty with the Sioux of St. Peter's River, 1815
	Treaty with the Sioux, 1816
	Treaty with the Teton, Etc., Sioux, 1825—Teton, Yancton and Yanctonies Bands
	Treaty with the Sioux, Etc., 1825
	Treaty with the Sioux, 1836, September 10
	Treaty with the Sioux, 1836, November 30
	Treaty with the Sioux, 1837
	Treaty with the Sioux—Sisseton and Wahpeton Bands, 1851
	Treaty with the Sioux—Mdewakanton and Wahpakoota Bands, 1851
	Treaty of Fort Laramie with Sioux, Etc., 1851
	Treaty with the Sioux, 1858—Mendawakanton and Wahpahoota Bands
	Treaty with the Sioux, 1858—Sisseeton and Wahpaton Bands
	Treaty with the Sioux—Miniconjou Band, 1865 (Also Minneconjon)
	Treaty with the Sioux—Lower Brulé Band, 1865
	Treaty with the Sioux—Two-Kettle Band, 1865
	Treaty with the Sioux—Sans Arcs Band, 1865
	Treaty with the Sioux—Hunkpapa Band, 1865 (Also Onkpahpah)

Tribe	Treaty Name
	Treaty with the Sioux—Yanktonai Band, 1865
	Treaty with the Sioux—Upper Yanktonai Band, 1865
	Treaty with the Sioux—Oglala Band, 1865 (Also Ogallala; O'Galla)
	Treaty with the Sioux—Sisseton and Wahpeton Bands, 1867 (Also Sissiton)
	Treaty with the Sioux—Brulé, Oglala, Miniconjou, Yanktonai, Hunkpapa, Blackfeet, Cuthead, Two Kettle, Sans Arcs, and Santee—and Arapaho
	Treaty with the Sioux, 1805
	Agreement with the Sisseton and Wahpeton Bands of Sioux Indians, 1872 (Unratified)
	Amended Agreement with Certain Sioux Indians, 1873—Sisseton and Wahpeton Bands
	Agreement with the Sioux of Various Tribes, 1882–83 (Unratified)—Pine Ridge, Rosebud, Standing Rock, Cheyenne River, and Lower Brulé Agencies
	Treaty with the Yankton Sioux, 1815
	Treaty with the Yankton Sioux, 1837
	Treaty with the Yankton Sioux, 1858
Six Nations	Treaty with the Six Nations, 1784
	Treaty with the Six Nations, 1789
	Treaty with the Six Nations, 1794
Skai-Wha-Mish	Treaty with the Dwamish, Suquamish, Etc., 1855
Skagit	Treaty with the Dwamish, Suquamish, Etc., 1855
S'klallam	Treaty with the S'Klallam, 1855
Sk-Tah-Le-Jum	Treaty with the Dwamish, Suquamish, Etc., 1855
Snake	Treaty with the Klamath, Etc., 1864
	Treaty with the Snake, 1865
Snohomish	Treaty with the Dwamish, Suquamish, Etc., 1855
Snoqualmoo	Treaty with the Dwamish, Suquamish, Etc., 1855
Squawskin	Treaty with the Nisqualli, Puyallup, Etc., 1854
Squi-Aitl	Treaty with the Nisqualli, Puyallup, Etc., 1854
Squin-Ah-Nush	Treaty with the Dwamish, Suquamish, Etc., 1855
St. Regis	Treaty with the New York Indians, 1838
	Treaty with the Seven Nations of Canada, 1796
Stehchass	Treaty with the Nisqualli, Puyallup, Etc., 1854

Tribe	Treaty Name
Steilacoom	Treaty with the Nisqualli, Puyallup, Etc., 1854
Stockbridge	Agreement with the Five Nations of Indians, 1792
	Treaty with the New York Indians, 1838
	Treaty with the Oneida, Etc., 1794
	Treaty with the Stockbridge and Munsee, 1839
	Treaty with the Stockbridge Tribe, 1848
	Treaty with the Stockbridge and Munsee, 1856
Suquamish	Treaty with the Dwamish, Suquamish, Etc., 1855
Tah-Wa-Carro	Treaty with the Comanche, Aionai, Anadarko, Caddo, Etc., 1846
	Treaty with the Kiowa, Etc., 1837
Tamarois	Treaty with the Peoria, Etc., 1818
Tenino	Treaty with the Middle Oregon Tribes, 1865
	Treaty with the Tribes of Middle Oregon, 1855
Teton	Treaty with the Teton, 1815
Tonkawa	Treaty with the Comanche, Aionai, Anadarko, Caddo, Etc., 1846
T'peek-Sin	Treaty with the Nisqualli, Puyallup, Etc., 1854
Tum-Waters	Treaty with the Kalapuya, Etc., 1855
Tuscarora	Agreement with the Five Nations of Indians, 1792
	Treaty with the New York Indians, 1838
	Treaty with the Oneida, Etc., 1794
	Treaty with the Six Nations, 1784
	Treaty with the Six Nations, 1789
	Treaty with the Six Nations, 1794
Umatilla	Treaty with the Walla-Walla, Cayuse, Etc., 1855
Umpqua	Treaty with the Chasta, Etc., 1854
	Treaty with the Umpqua—Cow Creek Band, 1853
	Treaty with the Umpqua and Kalapuya, 1854
Upper Pend D'oreille	Treaty with the Blackfeet, 1855
	Treaty with the Flatheads, Etc., 1855
Utah	Treaty with the Utah, 1849
	Treaty with the Utah—Tabeguache Band, 1863
Ute	Treaty with the Ute, 1868
Waco	Treaty with the Comanche, Aionai, Anadarko, Caddo, Etc., 1846
Walla-Walla	Treaty with the Middle Oregon Tribes, 1865
	Treaty with the Tribes of Middle Oregon, 1855
	Treaty with the Walla-Walla, Cayuse, Etc., 1855
Wasco	Treaty with the Middle Oregon Tribes, 1865
	Treaty with the Tribes of Middle Oregon, 1855

Appendix A: Treaties by Tribe | 393

Tribe	Treaty Name
Wea	Treaty with the Delawares, Etc., 1803
	Treaty with the Delawares, Etc., 1805
	Treaty with the Kaskaskia, Peoria, Etc., 1854
	Treaty with the Wea and Kickapoo, 1816
	Supplementary Treaty with the Miami, Etc., 1809
	Treaty with the Piankashaw and Wea, 1832
	Treaty with the Seneca, Mixed Seneca and Shawnee, Quapaw, Etc., 1867
	Treaty with the Wea, 1809
	Treaty with the Wea, 1818
	Treaty with the Wea, 1820
	Treaty with the Wyandot, Etc., 1795
Winnebago	Treaty with the Chippewa, Etc., 1827
	Treaty with the Sioux, Etc., 1825
	Treaty with the Winnebago, 1816
	Treaty with the Winnebago, Etc., 1828
	Treaty with the Winnebago, 1829
	Treaty with the Winnebago, 1832
	Treaty with the Winnebago, 1837
	Treaty with the Winnebago, 1846
	Treaty with the Winnebago, 1855
	Treaty with the Winnebago, 1859
	Treaty with the Winnebago, 1865
Witchetaw	Treaty with the Comanche, Etc., 1835
	Treaty with the Comanche, Aionai, Anadarko, Caddo, Etc., 1846
Wyandot	Treaty with the Chippewa, Etc., 1808
	Agreement with the Delawares and Wyandot, 1843
	Treaty with the Eel River, Etc., 1803
	Treaty with the Ottawa, Etc., 1807
	Treaty with the Seneca, Mixed Seneca and Shawnee, Quapaw, Etc., 1867
	Treaty with the Wyandot, Etc., 1785
	Treaty with the Wyandot, Etc., 1789
	Treaty with the Wyandot, Etc., 1795
	Treaty with the Wyandot, Etc., 1805
	Treaty with the Wyandot, Etc., 1814
	Treaty with the Wyandot, Etc., 1815
	Treaty with the Wyandot, Etc., 1817
	Treaty with the Wyandot, Etc., 1818

Tribe	Treaty Name
	Treaty with the Wyandot, 1818
	Treaty with the Wyandot, 1832
	Treaty with the Wyandot, 1836
	Treaty with the Wyandot, 1842
	Treaty with the Wyandot, 1850
	Treaty with the Wyandot, 1855
Yakima	Treaty with the Yakima, 1855

Source: Charles J. Kappler. *Indian Affairs: Laws and Treaties*. Washington DC: Government Printing Office, 1904.

Appendix B:
Canadian First Nations Treaties

Peace and Friendship Treaties
Peace Treaty (1725)

Peace and Friendship Treaty (1752)

Huron–British Treaty (1760)

Peace and Friendship Treaty (1760)

Peace and Friendship Treaty (1761)

Treaty of Amity, Commerce and Navigation (Jay) Treaty (1794)

Upper Canada
Michillimackinac Island, No. 1 (1781)

Niagara Purchase Treaty No. 381 (1781)

Treaty No. 116 (1786)

McKee Treaty, No. 2 (1790)

Between the Lakes Purchase and Collins Purchase, No. 3 (1792)

Brant Tract, No. 3 ¾ (1795)

London Township Treaty No. 6 (1796)

Sombra Township Treaty No. 7 (1796)

Treaty No. 8 (1797)

Penetanguishene Treaty No. 5 (1798)

St. Joseph's Island Treaty No. 11 (1798)

Treaty No. 12 (1800)

Toronto Purchase, No. 13 (1805)

Head of the Lake Treaty No. 14 (1806)

Lake Simcoe Treaty No. 16 (1815)

Lake Simcoe–Nottawasaga Treaty No. 18 (1818)

Ajetance Treaty No. 19 (1818)

Rice Lake Treaty No. 20 (1818)

Long Woods Treaty No. 25 (1820)

Rideau Purchase, No. 27 ¼ (1822)

Huron Tract, no. 29 (1827)

Manitoulin Island Treaty No. 45 (1836)

Saugeen Treaty No. 45 ½ (1836)

Saugeen Peninsula Treaty No. 72 (1854)

Manitoulin Island Treaty No. 94 (1862)

Douglas Treaties

Teechamitsa Tribe—Country lying between Esquimait and Point Albert (1850)

Kosampson Tribe—Esquimalt Peninsula and Colquite Valley (1850)

Swengwhung Tribe—Victoria Peninsula, South of Colitz (1850)

Chilcowitch Tribe—Point Gonzales (1850)

Whyomilth Tribe—North-West of Esquimalt Harbour (1850)

Che-konein Tribe—Point Gonzales to Cedar Hill (1850)

Ka-kyaakan Tribe—Metchosin (1850)

Chewhaytsum Tribe—Sooke (1850)

Sooke Tribe—North-West of Sooke Inlet (1850)

Queackar Tribe—Fort Rupert (1851)

Quakeolth Tribe—Fort Rupert (1851)

Saanich Tribe—South Saanich (1852)

Saanich Tribe—North Saanich (1852)

Saalequunn Tribe—Nanaimo (1854)

Robinson Treaties

Ojibwa Indians of Lake Superior (1850)

Ojibwa Indians of Lake Huron (1850)

Appendix B: Canadian First Nations Treaties | 397

The Numbered Treaties

No. 1 (1871)
No. 2 (1871)
No. 3 (1873)
No. 4 (1874)
No. 5 (1875)
No. 6 (1876)
No. 7 (1877)
No. 8 (1808)
No. 9 (1905)
No. 10 (1906)
No. 11 (1921)

Williams Treaties

Chippewa Indians of Christian Island, Georgina Island and Rama (1923)
Mississauga Indians of Rice Lake, Mud Lake, Scugog Lake and Alderville (1923)

Modern Treaties

James Bay and Northern Quebec Agreement (1975)
Northeastern Quebec Agreement (1978)
Inuvialuit Final Agreements (1984)
Gwich'in Comprehensive Land Agreement (1992)
Land Claim Agreement (1993)
Nunavut Land Claims Agreement (1993)
Nacho Nyak Dun Final Agreement (1993)
Vuntut Gwitchinn Final Agreement (1993)
Sahtu Dene and Metis Comprehensive Land Agreement Claim (1993)
Nisga'a Final Agreement (1999)
The Labrador Inuit Land Claims Agreement (2003)
The Tlicho (Dogrib) Land Claims and Self-Government Agreement (2003)

Index

Note: Page numbers in *italics* refer to illustrations.

Abenaki tribe, 93
Acoma peoples, 364
Act of 1871, xv
Adams, John, 30
Adams, John Quincy, 100, 111–112
addenda treaties, 142–144
African Americans
 in Indian Territory, 147–148
 as runaway slaves, 115, 224
Alabama Coushattas, 104
Alaska Native villages, 3
Alexander VI (pope), 22
Algonquin tribe, 93
Alibamon Nation, 29
American Revolution, 60
 Battle of Lexington, *61*
Anadarko tribe, 145
Anishinabe Confederacy, 191. *See also*
 Ojibwes
annuities, 97–98, 140, 145, 239. *See also*
 Treaty topics, payment and annuities
Apache (Plains)
 alliance with Kiowas and
  Comanches, 153
 during the Civil War, 146
 at the Medicine Lodge Council, xvi–xvii
 treaties with, 139, *140*
 treaty with Texas, 39
 war in Arizona and the southern
  Plains, 149
 See also Plains Indians
Apalachicola band, 145

Arapaho Nation
 boundaries of, 302
 at the Fort Laramie agreement, xix
 land cession by, 144
 land rights of, 141
 at the Medicine Lodge council, xvi
 northern branch, 153
 reservation for, 153, 329
 treaties with, 149, *150*, 153, 297–298,
  300, 328–329, 348
 warfare conducted by, 149
Arikara Nation
 boundaries of, 301
 at the Fort Laramie agreement, xix
 land rights of, 141
 treaties with, 103, 149, 297–298, 300
Arkansas Territory, 99
Armstrong, John, 159
Articles of Confederation, 29, 32
 and the Continental Congress, 84–88
assimilation, 42, 45, 64, 330
 of the Navajo Nation, 364–365
Assiniboine Nation
 boundaries of, 301–302
 land rights of, 141
 treaties with, 141, 142, 149,
  297–298, 300
Association of Indians, *69*
Atcheson, Nathaniel, 35
Atoka Agreement, 12
Augur, Christopher C., 329, 330, 339,
 340, 348

Bannock Reservation, 339, 340
Bannock tribe, 149, 339. *See also* Shoshone-Bannock tribes; Treaty of Fort Bridger
Barbeyrac, Jean, 23
Barboncito (Navajo leader), 364, 365
Battle of Fallen Timbers, *13*, *90*, 91, 92, 175
Battle of Horseshoe Bend, 109
Battle of Lexington, *61*
Battle of the Thames, 102
Becancours Indians, 93
Bell, S.W., 271
Black, Hugo, 48
Black Hawk War, 110, 122
Black Hills reservation, 346
Black Kettle (Cheyenne leader), 329
Blackfeet agreement, 141
Blackfeet Nation
    boundaries of, 302
    at the Fort Laramie agreement, xix
    land rights of, 141
    treaties with, 141, 142, 348, 362
blacksmiths, xix, 130, 133, 145, 150, 209, 222, 226, 242, 283, 291, 292, 309, 311, 333, 335, 337, 342, 344, 345, 347, 350, 352, 354, 367
Blood tribe, 141, 142
Blue Jacket (Shawnee leader), 94
Bodin, Jean, 23
Bois Forte Indians, 310
Boldt decision, *131*
Boudinot, Elias (Buck Oowaite), 118–119, 265, 267, 271
boundaries, xix, 33. *See also* Treaty topics, boundaries
Bouquet, Henry, 159
Brandt (Brant), Joseph (Mohawk sachem) (Thayendanega), 33, *34*, 88, 93
British North America. *See* Canada
Brotherton (Brothertown) Indians, 120, 191, 314
Brown, John F. (Seminole leader), 320
Brule Lakota
    treaties with, 149, 348, 355–357
    See also Lakota Nation
Bryan v. Itasca County, Minnesota, 46

Buffalo Creek treaty, xvi
buffalo hunting, 142, 151, 347
Bull Bear (Cheyenne leader), 329
Bureau of Indian Affairs (BIA), xviii, xx, 37, 47, 64, 129
    Federal Acknowledgment Process, 104
Burke Act, 64
Butler, Elizur, 38, 118
Butler, Richard, 86

Caddo tribe, 145
Cahokia tribe, 101
Calder v. Attorney General of British Columbia, 67
Caldwell, Billy (Saukenuk; United Band representative), 239
Caldwell, Joe, 269
California gold rush, 39, 41, 130
California Indians, 3, 41, 130
Camp Stevens treaty, 138
Campbell, Robert, 299
Canada
    colonization in, 53
    status of aboriginal people in, 71–73
Canadian treaties, xv, 14, 27, 53–54, 56–57, 76–77
    American Independence to Canadian Independence, 59–63, 64–66
    authority to negotiate, 27
    and the Canadian Constitution, 53
    and the doctrine of discovery, 54–56
    Douglas Treaties, xv
    and guardianship/wardship, 63–64
    history of, 53–54, 56–57, 76–77
    with Indian tribes, xv, xxi, 14, 27
    legal interpretation principles, 73–76
    modern legal status of, 73
    Modern Treaties, xv, 67–71
    numbered treaties, 66
    Peace and Friendship treaties, 57–59
    and the position of Aboriginal peoples, 71–73
    Robinson and Williams treaties, xv
    treaties from 1867 to 1930, 66–67
    Upper Canada, xv
Carimine (Ho-Chunk leader), 191
Carleton, James, 364–365

Carlisle Indian School, 42
Carpenter v. Shaw, 46
carpenters, 291, 333, 335, 337, 342, 345, 350, 352, 354
Carroll, William, 265, 269, 271–272
Carson, Kit, 146, 365
Cartwright, George, 59
Cass, Lewis, 110, 114, 121, 177, 191, 218
Casserly, Eugene, 42
Catholic Church, 21–23, 54, 121, 262. *See also* Christianity
Cattaraugus Reservation, 93
Caughnawagas Indians, 93
Cayuga Nation
  boundaries of, 170–171
  in the Six Nations, 168
  treaties with, 58, 83, 85–86, 87, 92, 93, 120
  See also Iroquois Confederacy; Six Nations
Cayuse people, 138
Chambly (Odawa chief), 191
Chapin, Israel, 168, 169
Chasta (Shasta) tribe, 133, 137
Cheecheebinquay (Alexander Robinson; United Band representative), 239
Chemakum tribe, 137
Cherokee Nation
  boundaries of, 165, 272–273
  during the Civil War, 40, 267
  Confederate treaties, 14, 146
  court battles, 118
  court system, 148
  eight districts of, 268
  land cessions, 123
  lawsuit against Georgia, 36, 37, 39, 46, 63, 65, 116, 117
  loss of tribal land, 100
  in New Echota, 267–269
  of North Carolina, 103
  "Old Settlers," 266
  pressure to remove, 109
  purchase of land from, 96
  reconstruction treaties, 147, 148
  removal of, 116, 118–119, 128, 266–267
  Ross Party, 266
  sovereignty of, 36, 39, 110, 116, 163–164
  state jurisdiction over lands of, 112
  suing the state of Georgia, 116
  treaties with, xxi, 9–10, 12, 14, 29, 61, 83, 85–86, 87, 89, 91, 92, 96, 98–100, 107, 153, 162–164, 265–267
  treaties with Great Britain, 12, 14
  treaties with other tribes, 14
  Treaty Party, 118–119, 265–266
  treaty with Confederate states, 14
  as U.S. allies, 109
  See also Treaty of New Echota (1835)
Cherokee Nation v. Georgia, 36, 37, 39, 46, 63, 65, 116, 117
Cherokee National Council, 265, 266
Cherokee of North Carolina, 103
Cherokee treaty of 1817, 99, 100
Cherokee treaty of 1828, 98, 99
Cheyenne-Arapaho Reservation, 153
Cheyenne Dog Soldiers, 149, 329
Cheyenne Nation
  boundaries of, 302
  dog soldiers, 149, 329
  at the Fort Laramie agreement, xix
  land cession, 144
  land rights of, 141
  at the Medicine Lodge council, xvi, 150
  northern branch, 153
  removal of, 153
  reservation for, 329
  Sand Creek massacre, 146, 149, 329
  treaties with, 103, 153, 297–298, 300, 328–329
  warfare conducted by, 149
Cheyenne River Sioux, xxi
Chickasaw Nation
  boundaries of, 234–235
  boundary disputes, 143
  Confederate treaties, 144, 145
  delegates to Washington, 15
  during the Civil War, 40
  hostilities with, 91
  land cessions, 123
  loss of tribal land, 100
  pressure to remove, 109
  purchase of land from, 96

reconstruction treaties, 147, 148
removal of, 114–115, 128, 142, 143, 227–228
state jurisdiction over lands of, 112
treaties with, xxi, 12, 61, 86, 89, 92, 96, 107, 114–115, 142, 227–228
treaty with Spain, 29
Chinook tribe, 132
Chippewa (Ojibway) Nation
boundaries of, 178–180, 193–194, 195, 196, 264
hostilities with, 89
land cessions, 140
opposition to U.S. policies, 101
removal of, 123, 238–239
treaties with, xix, xx, 17, 33, 85–86, 87, 94, 102, 123, 146, 174–175, 283–289, 306–311
treaty with England, 27
See also Ojibwes; Treaty of Prairie du Chien
Chitto Harjo (Crazy Snake), *4*
Cho-cote-harjo (Seminole leader), 320
Choctaw Nation
boundaries of, 203–204, 234–235
boundary disputes, 143
during the Civil War, 40
Confederate treaties, 144, 145
hostilities with, 91
land cessions, 123
loss of tribal land, 100
Mississippi tribe, 114
MOWA (Mobile-Washington), 104
payments to, 98
pressure to remove, 109
purchase of land from, 96
reconstruction treaties, 147, 148
removal of, 113–114, 128, 142–143, 201–202
state jurisdiction over lands of, 112
treaties with, xxi, 12, 14, 61, 85–86, 92, 96, 99, 107, 113–114, 142, 201–202
treaties with other tribes, 9–10
treaty with Spain, 29
as U.S. allies, 109
See also Treaty of Dancing Rabbit Creek
Choctaw Nation v. Oklahoma, 46

Chouteau, A. P., 274
Christianity, 42, 55, 129. *See also* Catholic Church
Chup-co, John ("Long John" Seminole leader), 320
Civil War, 39–40, 144–147
Clallam tribe, 137
Clark, George Rogers, 83, 87
Clark, William, 120, 191
Clatsop tribe, 132
Clay, Henry, 110
Clear Sky (Onondaga leader), 168
Clinton, George, 92–93
Coalition of Eastern Native Americans, 104
Coffee, John, 113, 228
colonialism, 127, 129
Colorado gold rush, 39, 328
Columbus, Christopher, 22, *24*
Comanche-Kiowa-Apache treaty (1854), 139
Comanche tribe
alliance with Kiowas and Plains Apaches, 153
Confederate treaties, 145, 146
Medicine Lodge treaty, xvi, 44, 150
reservation for, 329
and the slave trade, 365
treaties with, 16, 139, 328–329
treaty with Texas, 39
warfare conducted by, 149
Comanches of the Staked Plains, 145
compacts, 7
Confederate Cherokee Convention, 145
Confederate states
treaties with Native Americans, xv, 10, 14, 18, 40, 144–147
See also Civil War
Congressional ratification, xxi, 4–5, 14, 30–31, 41–42, 88, 120–121, 122, 141, 228, 266
Connecticut colony, 27–28
Conoy Indians, 83
Continental Congress
under the Articles of Confederation, 84–88
treaties with Indian tribes, 83

Cooley, D.N., 319, 327
Copper Treaty, 123
Cornplanter (Seneca sachem), 90, 92, 94, 168
council, xvi
County of Oneida v. Oneida Indian Nation, 46
Coushatta Indians, 104
Covenant Chain, 58
Crazy Snake Rebellion, *4*
Cree Indians, 68, 73, 103, 141
Creek Nation
   boundary disputes, 143–144
   during the Civil War, 40, 146
   Confederate treaties, 144–145
   land cessions, 123
   loss of tribal land, 100
   Lower Town band, 98, 100
   National Council of, 100
   pressure to remove, 109
   purchase of land from, 96
   reconstruction treaties, 148
   Red Stick tribe, 109, 111
   removal of, 114
   Seminole unification with, 115
   treaties with, 38–39, 31–32, 89, 91, 92, 96, 98, 109, 114
   treaty with Georgia, 87
   Upper Town band, 98, 100
   as U.S. allies, 109
   See also Muscogee Creek tribe
Creek Treaty (1856), 144
Creek Treaty (1861), 144–145
Creek war (1813–1814), 98, 100
Crow Nation
   boundaries of, 302
   and the Fort Laramie agreement, xix, 49
   land rights of, 141
   treaties with, 141, 149, 153, 297–298, 300
cultural issues, xvii–xviii, 105
Cuthead tribe, 348, 362–363

Dakota Nation
   boundaries of, 301
   treaties with, 190–191, 297–298, 300
   See also Sioux Nation

Dart, Anson, 131–132
Davis, William A., 271
Dawes Act (Dawes Allotment Act), *4*, *11*, 42, 43, 64, 116
Declaration of Independence (U.S.), 82
DeCoteau v. District Court for the Tenth Judicial District, 46, 48
Delaware (Lenápe) Nation
   boundaries of, 178–180
   Confederate treaties, 145
   Fort Pitt treaty, xv, *8*, 29–30, 39, *61*, 84
   land cessions, 140
   removal of, 9–10
   treaties with, xix, 33, 83, 85–86, 87, 94, 97, 100, 101, 102, 120, 157–158
   treaties with American colonies, 28
   treaties with other tribes, 9–10, 14
   as U.S. allies, 101
   See also Treaty of Fort Pitt (1778)
Deline First Nation, 71
Department of Indian and Northern Affairs (Canada), 72
Department of the Interior, xviii, 31, 37, 129, 135, 136, 298
Deserontyon, John, 93
Dias, Bartolomeu, 22
Diné Nation. *See* Navajo (Diné) Nation
doctrine of aboriginal title, 67–70, 76
doctrine of discovery, 54–56
Dodge, Henry, 122, 283
Dog Soldiers, 149, 329
Domestic dependent nation status, 36–38, 63–64, 105, 116–117, 134
Doty, James Duane, 339
Douglas Treaties, xv
Duane, James, 85
Dutch. *See* Netherlands, treaties with Indian tribes
Duwamish tribe, 137

Eastern Abenakis, 93
eastern sioux, 123. *See also* Sioux Nation
Eaton, John, 113, 118
education
   boarding schools, 42, 67, 147
   in Canada, 73

specified in treaties, xvi, 40, 96, 209, 276–277, 329, 334, 343–344, 351–352, 368
Eel River Miamis
  boundaries of, 178–180
  treaties with, 94, 100, 101, 174–175
  See also Miami Nation
Egyptian-Hittite peace treaty, 22
engineers, 333, 335, 337, 342, 350, 352, 354
England. See Great Britain
Equal Employment Opportunity Act of 1964, 47
Eskimos. See Inuit Nation
Euchee people, 148
Explanatory Note of 1796, 34

Fallen Timbers, Battle of, *13*, *90*, 91, 92, 175
farmers, 275, 291, 329, 333, 335, 337, 342, 345, 347, 350, 352, 354
Farmer's Brother (Seneca leader), 92, 94, 168
Federal Power Commission v. Tuscarora Indian Nation, 48
Fifth Amendment (U.S. Constitution), 44
Fillmore, Millard, 305
First Nations Peoples
  land claims of, 68–70
  and self-determination, 70–71
  treaties with, xv, xxi, 53
  and treaty interpretation, 73–77
  See also Canadian treaties
First Seminole War, 100, 115, 143. See also Seminole Wars
Fish Carrier (Cayuga leader), 168
Fitzpatrick, Thomas, 297, 300, 303
Five Civilized Tribes
  Confederate treaties, 145
  reconstruction treaties, 147
  removal of, 128
  treaties with, 40
  See also Cherokee Nation; Chickasaw Nation; Choctaw Nation; Creek Nation; Seminole Nation
Flathead Nation, 138, 141
Florida tribes

  and the gaming industry, xxi
  loss of tribal land, 100
  treaties with, 96, 100
  See also Seminole Nation
Fond du Lac band of Ojibwe, 305, 308. See also Ojibwes
Forbes, John, 159
Fort Duquesne, 158–159
Fort Hall Reservation, 339, 340
Fort Harmar treaties, 30, 87–88, 89
Fort Laramie, Wyoming, 299–300
Fort Laramie Historic Site, 300
Fort Laramie peace conference, 153
Fort Laramie treaty. See Treaty of Fort Laramie (1851); Treaty of Fort Laramie (1868)
Fort Pitt, 158–159
Fort Pitt Treaty. See Treaty of Fort Pitt (1778)
Fos-ha(r)-jo (Seminole leader), 320
Fox, Joel, 48
Fox tribe
  boundaries of, 192–193, 194
  as British allies, 101
  hostilities with, 110
  land cessions, 140, 144
  removal of, 191
  treaties with, 83, 103, 191
  See also Sac (Sauk) tribe; Treaty of Prairie du Chien
France
  acquisition of Louisiana Territory, 95
  exploration by, 22–23
  Indians as allies of, 174
  treaties with Canadian Indian Nations, 54
  treaties with Indian tribes, xv, 26, 58–59
  treaty with Huron Nation, 26
  treaty with Onondaga, 26
  treaty with Six Nations, 26
  treaty with United States (Louisiana Cession), 33
French and Indian War, 82, *82*
French Revolution, 61
Freylinghuysen, Theodore, 112
Frontier Wars, 176

Gadsden, James, 115–116, 224
Gadsden Purchase, 39
gaming, xxi, 13, 104, 136
Gardiner, James B., 120
General Allotment Act, 10, 134
George III (king of England), 60
Georgia treaties with Indian tribes, 87
Geronimo (Apache leader), *140*
ghost dancers, *128*
gift giving, xvii, xix, 25, 58. *See also* treaty topics, gifts, goods, or presents
Gilbert, Henry, 305
Gill, Aurilien, *69*
Gordon, Harry, 159
Grand Council of the Cree, 68. *See also* Cree Indians
Grand Portage band of Ojibwe, 305, 308. *See also* Ojibwes
Grant, Ulysses S., 41
Great Britain
    exploration by, 22–23
    Indian alliances with, 168, 174–175
    treaties with Canadian Indian Nations, 54
    treaties with Indian tribes, xv, 7, 14, 18, 26–27, 30, 35, 58, 59–60, 83
    U.S. treaties with, 38
Great Council at Prairie du Chien. *See* Treaty of Prairie du Chien
Great Lakes Indians, 6, 12, 17, 25, 66, 191, 238–239
Great Peace Commission. *See* United States Indian Peace Commission
Great Plains Indians, 3, 146, 149
Great Sioux Nation, 144, 153. *See also* Sioux Nation
Great Sioux Reservation, 347
Great-Tree (Seneca sachem), 90
Greene, Nathaniel, 176
Greenville, Ohio, 176–177
Gros Ventre tribe, xix, 140, 141, 142, 300, 301. *See also* Mandan Nation
guardianship, 63–64
Guess, George (Sequoyah), 98
Gunter, Samuel, 269
Gutenberg, Johannes, 21
Gwich'in Final Agreement, 68

Half-Town (Seneca sachem), 90
Handsome Lake (Seneca prophet), 92, 94
Harmar, Josiah, 89, *90*
Harmony Missionary reservation, 274
Harney, William S., 329, 330, 348
Harrison, William Henry, *13*, 101, 176
Haudenosaunee, 168–169. *See also* Iroquois League; Iroquois Nation; Six Nations
Hawkins, Benjamin, 164
Henderson, John B., 329, 330, 348
Hendrick Aupaumut (Stockbridge chief), 92
Henry the Navigator (prince of Portugal), 22
Herriman, David, 305
Hidatsa tribe, 149
Ho-Chunks. *See* Winnebago (Ho-Chunk) tribe
Hoh people, 137
Homestead Act, 42
Hopson, Peregrine Thomas, 27
Horseshoe Bend, Battle of, 109
Houmas, 104, 105
House Concurrent Resolution 108, 64
Hudson's Bay Company, 66
Huebschmann, Francis, 316
Hunkpapa tribe, 348
Huron Nation, 26, 58, 93
Hydro-Quebec, 68

Illinois Nation, 31
Indian Act (Canada), 71
Indian Appropriations Act, 154
Indian Code, 266
Indian Health Service, 104
Indian Nations (Canada), 69
Indian Office, 31. *See also* Bureau of Indian Affairs
Indian Peace Commission (United States Indian Peace Commission), 41, 149–150, 153, 329, 339, 346–347
"Indian Problem," 129, 339
Indian removal
    after the Civil War, 9–10
    "civilization" plan, 108, 110
    Jackson's support for, 35–36

origins of the policy, 107–113
in the South, 113–116
voluntary, 111–112
Indian Removal Act of 1830, *111*, 112–113, 116, 191, 201–202, 228, 265
Indian Removal treaties
racist moral justification for, 110
Treaties with the Chickasaw (1830 and 1832), 114–115
treaties with the Miami, 122
treaties with the New York Indians, 120–121
treaties with the Ohio Valley Indians, 119–120
treaties with the Potawatomi, 121–122
treaties with the Winnebago, Chippewa (Ojobway), Eastern Sioux, and Menominee, 122–124
Treaty with the Cherokee at New Echota (1835), 116, 118–119
Treaty with the Choctaw at Dancing Rabbit Creek (1830), 113–114
Treaty with the Creek (1832), 114
Treaty with the Seminole (1832 and 1833), 115–116
Indian Reorganization Act, 64, 134–135
Indian Specific Claims Commission (Canada), 70
Indian Territory, 128, 140, 142, 144, 153
during the Civil War, 146
Indian Trade and Intercourse Acts, 89–90, 92–93, 95, 98
Indian tribes. *See* Native Americans; *specific tribes or Nations by name*
International law, 23, 31, 39, 45, 54, 81
interpreters, xv, xvii, 298
Inuit Nation, 53–54, 68, 69, 71–73, 76
Inuvialuit (or Western Arctic) Final Agreement, 68
Iowa Nation, 101, 103, 140, 144, 193. *See also* Treaty of Prairie du Chien
Iroquois Confederacy, 30, 33, *34*, 58, *58*, 168. *See also* Cayuga Nation; Mohawk Nation; Oneida Nation; Onondaga Nation; Seneca (Seneka) Nation; Six Nations; Tuscarora Nation
Iroquois tribes, 26, 93, 120, 157, 174
Isabella (queen of Spain), 22

Jackson, Andrew, 35–36, 65, 100, 108, 109, 111–112, *111*, 115, 120, 121, 122, 191, 201–202, 224, 228, 265
James Bay and Northern Quebec Agreement, 68, *69*
James Bay Development Corporation, 68
Jay, John, 93
Jay Treaty, 32, 33, 34
Jefferson, Thomas, 93, 95, 99, 108, 176
Jena Choctaws, 104
John II (king of Portugal), 22
John Kill Buck (Delaware leader), 159–160
Johnson, Richard, 121
Johnson, William, 82
Johnson v. M'Intosh, 55–56, 117, 130, 134
Johnston, Joseph, 148
Jones v. Meehan, 46

Kalapuya Nation, 131, 133, 137
Kansa tribe
as British allies, 101
treaties with, xx, 103, 146
Kappler, Charles J., 141
Kashaya Pomo tribe, 14
Kaskaskia tribe
boundaries of, 178–180
land cessions, 140
treaties with, 94, 100, 101, 102, 120, 174–175
Kickapoo tribe
boundaries of, 178–180
hostilities with, 87, 89
land cessions, 140
opposition to U.S. policies, 101
treaties with, xvi, 94, 100, 101, 102–103, 120, 174–175
Kieft, Willem, *27*
Kieft War, *27*
kinship relations, xvii, xix–xx
Kiowa-Apaches
reservation for, 329
treaties with, *150*, 328–329
Kiowa-Comanche Reservation, 151
Kiowa-Comanche-Apache Reservations, 153
Kiowa tribe

alliance with Comanches and Plains
    Apaches, 153
Confederate treaties, 145
Medicine Lodge treaty, xvi, 44, 150
reservation for, 329
treaties with, 16, 139, 149, 328–329
warfare conducted by, 149
Kisketuhug (Ojibwe leader), 305
Klamath tribe, xx, 146
Knox, Henry, 30, 88–89, 107
Kutenai Nation, 138, 141

La Pointe band of Ojibwe, 305, 306, 308.
    See also Ojibwes
Labrador Inuit Land Claims Agreement, 69
Labrador Métis, 70. *See also* Métis peoples
Lac Court Orielles band of Ojibwe, 305,
    308. *See also* Ojibwes
Lac De Flambeau band of Ojibwe, 305.
    See also Ojibwes
LaFlore, Greenwood (Choctaw leader), 207
Lake of Two Mountains Indians, 93
Lakota Nation
    Brule tribe, 149, 348, 355–357
    desiring return of their land, 15
    Miniconjou tribe, *128*, 348, 358–359
    treaties with, 141, 153, 297–298
    See also Oglala Lakota; Sioux Nation
Lakota Reservation, 153
land cessions, 133–134. *See also* Treaty
    topics, land cessions
Land in Severalty Act, 43. *See also* Dawes
    Act (Dawes Allotment Act)
Land Ordinance of 1785, 87
land payments, 141–142. *See also* Treaty
    topics, payments and annuities
Langtree, Samuel, 32
language issues, xv, xvii, 8–9, 298
L'Anse band of Ojibwe, 305, 306. *See also*
    Ojibwes
Larsen, Lewis, 269
law enforcement authority, 7, 13. *See
    also* Treaty topics, law enforcement
    authority
Law of Nationa (Vattel), 23, 25
Le Flore, Greenwood (Choctaw leader),
    14, 113
Leavenworth, Jesse, 329

Lee, Robert E., 148
Lenápes. *See* Delaware (Lenápe) Nation
Lewis, Andrew, 159–160
Lewis, Thomas, 159–160
Lexington, Battle of, *61*
Little Beard, 93
Little Billy (Seneca leader), 168
Little Raven (Arapaho leader), 329
Little Robe (Cheyenne leader), 329
Little Turtle (Miami leader), *13*, 89, 94
Lone Wolf (Kiowa leader), 151
Lone Wolf v. Hitchcock, 16, 44, 46,
    151–152
Long Walk, 365
Lord Dunsmore's War, 175
Lorettes, 93
Louis, Max, *69*
Louisiana Cession, 33
Louisiana Purchase, 95, 108
Louisiana Territory, 95, 99, 100–103,
    108, 177
Lumbees, 104

Madison, James, 102
Major Crimes Act, 43, 44, 116
Makah tribe, 137
Makivik Corporation, 68
Malecite Nation, 70, 83
Maliseet Nation, 59
Mandan Nation
    at the Fort Laramie agreement, xix
    land rights of, 140
    treaties with, 103, 149, 297–298
    See also Gros Ventre tribe
manifest destiny, 110, 129
Manuel, George, *69*
Manuelito (Navajo leader), 364, 365
Manypenny, George, 305
Market Revolution, 109
Marshall, John, 17, 36, 37, 38–39, 44,
    55–56, 62–63, 65, 67, 105, 116,
    117, 118
Marshall fishing decision, 70
Marshall Trilogy, 117
Martin, Joseph, 164
Mashantucket Pequot, 103
Massachusetts (colony), treaties with
    Indian tribes, 27–28

Massachusetts (state), treaties with Indian tribes, 87
Mather, Thomas, 187, 189
McClanahan v. Arizona State Tax Commission, 47
McCoy, Daniel, 269
McGillivray, Alexander (Muscogee Creek leader), 28
McIntosh, William, 100
McLachlin, Beverley, 73
Mdewakanton tribe, 140
Meadow Lake Tribal Council, 71
mechanics, 242, 275
Medicine Creek convention, 137
Medicine Lodge Council, xvi, 150, *150*
Medicine Lodge Treaty (1867)
    articles, 329, 331–337
    background, 149, 328–329
    facsimile, *330*
    signatories, 337–339
    violations of, 44
Medicine Lodge Treaty (second), 153
Medicine Lodge treaty (third), 153
Meigs, R. J., 280
Menominee Reservation, 135
Menominee Treaty (1856)
    articles, 315–316
    background, 314
    signatories, 316–317
Menominee tribe
    boundaries of, 194–195
    as British allies, 101
    friction with other tribes, 191
    removal of, 123, 191
    termination of trust status, xxi
    treaties with, 120, 123, 314
    See also Treaty of Prairie du Chien
Menominee Tribe of Indians v. United States, 48
Métis peoples
    dealings with Canadian government, 53–54, 67, 69–70, 73, 75
    Labrador tribe, 70
    and self-determination, 70–71
    and treaty interpretation, 73–76
Mexican War, 39
Mexico, treaties with Indian tribes, 14, 29

Miami Nation
    boundaries of, 178–180
    hostilities with, 87, 89, 175
    land cessions, 140
    removal of, 122
    treaties with, 33, 94, 100, 101, 102, 122, 174–175
    Treaty of Greenville, *13*, 175
    See also Eel River Miamis; Treaty of Greenville
Micmac tribe, 27
Mikasuki Seminoles, 143, 144. *See also* Seminole Nation
Mi'kmaq Nation, 59, 70
Miller, Samuel F., 44
millers, 209, 242, 333, 335, 337, 342, 345, 350, 352, 354
Mingo tribe, 175, 203
Miniconjou Lakota
    on reservation, *128*
    treaties with, 348, 358–359
Minisink Indians, 28
Ministaree tribe, 103
Minnesota Territory, 123
Minnesota v. Mille Lacs Band of Chippewa Indians, 17, 46, 48
M'Intosh, Lachlan, 164
missionaries, 38, 110, 118, 278, 291, 305, 310
Mississippi Choctaws, 114
Mississippi Territory, 109
Missouri tribe, 140
Mitchell, D.D., 297, 300, 303
Mitchigamia tribe, 101
Modoc tribe, xx, 146
Mohawk Nation
    and the Jay Treaty, 33
    in the Six Nations, 168
    treaties with, 85–86, 93
    treaty with Netherlands, 26, *58*
    See also Brandt (Brant), Joseph; Iroquois Confederacy; Six Nations
Mohawks of Kahnawake, 71
Mohican Nation Stockbridge-Munsee bands, 191
Molala Nation, 131, 137
Monroe, James, 111

Montana v. United States, 49
Moore v. the United States, 298
Morris, Robert, 93
Morton v. Mancari, 47
Moultrie Creek Treaty, 224
MOWA (Mobile-Washington) Choctaws, 104
Munsee Indians, 120, 314
Muscogee Creek Confederacy, 35
Muscogee Creek tribe
   Crazy Snake rebellion, *4*
   reconstruction treaties, 147
   removal of, 114, 128, 142
   treaties with, xxi, 28–29, 107, 142, 144, 218
   treaties with Confederate states, 10
   tribal government, xviii
   See also Creek Nation
Mushulatubbe (Choctaw leader), 113, 207

Nakota Nation
   treaties with, 297–298
   See also Sioux Nation
Nanticoke Indians, 83
National Council of the Creek, 100. *See also* Creek Nation
National Environmental Protection Act (1969), 135
National Indian Brotherhood, *69*
Native American children
   care and custody of, 13, 72
   education of, 40, 42, 67, 96, 98, 222, 285, 329, 333, 334, 342, 344, 347, 350, 352, 365, 367, 368
   as victims of slave traders, 364, 365
Native American Rights fund, 104
Native Americans
   and Christopher Columbus, *24*
   Spanish laws and policies toward, 24–25
   state-recognized tribes, 103–105
   U.S. negotiations with, 42
   See also Native American children
natural laws, 25, 26
Navajo (Diné) Nation
   during the Civil War, 146
   legal jurisdiction of, 47
   negotiation with states, 12
   treaties with, 138–139, 153, 339
   See also Treaty with the Navajo (1868)
Navajo (Navaho) treaty of 1849, xix, 138. *See also* Treaty with the Navajo (1868)
Navajo Reservation, xxi, 365, 367
Neah Bay treaty, 137
Netherlands, treaties with Indian tribes, 26, 27, 58
Nevada v. Hicks, 117
New Echota, Georgia, 267–269. *See also* Treaty of New Echota (1835)
New Jersey colony, treaties with Indian tribes, 28
New Mexico Territory, 138–139, 144
New York, treaty with Six Nations, 32
New York Indians
   Christianized, 314
   removal of, 120–121
   treaties with, xvi, 120–121
Nez Perce Nation
   treaties with, xx, 138, 141, 146, 153
Nippising tribe, 93
Nisga'a Final Agreement, 69, 71
Nisga'a Nation, 67
Nisqually tribe, 48, 137
Nitakechi (Choctaw leader), 113
Non-Intercourse Act, 61
Northeastern Quebec Agreement, 68
Northern Quebec Inuit Association, 68. *See also* Inuit Nation
Northwest Indians, 3
Northwest Ordinance, 87
Northwest Territory, 87, 88, 91, 100–103
Nunavut Land Claims Agreement, 68
Nutackachie (Choctaw leader), 207

O'Connor, Sandra Day, 117
Odawas. *See* Ottawa tribe
Oglala Lakota
   treaties with, 149, 348, 357–358
   See also Lakota Nation
Ohio tribes, 174
Ohio Valley Indians, removal of, 119–120
Ojibwes (Anishinabes)
   in the Anishinabe Confederacy, 191
   fishing rights of, xxi

Grand Portage band, 305, 308
Fond du Lac band, 305, 308
La Pointe band, 305, 306, 308
Lac Court Orielles band, 305, 308
Lac De Flambeau band, 305
of Lake Superior, 283, 290, 305, 310
L'Anse band, 305, 306
of the Mississippi, 283, 290, 305, 310
Ontonagon band, 305, 308
Pillager band, 283
removal of, 191, 304–305
treaties with, 17, 190–191, 283–284, 290–291
tribal government, xviii
Vieux De Sert band, 305, 306
See also Chippewa (Ojibway) Nation
Oliphant v. Suquamish Indian Tribe, 48, 117
Omaha tribe
land cessions, 140
treaties with, xx, 103, 146
Oneida Nation
boundaries of, 170–171
relocation of, 191
in the Six Nations, 168
treaties with, 86, 87, 92, 93, 120, 314
treaty with Netherlands, *58*
as U.S. allies, 30, 83, 86
See also Iroquois Confederacy; Six Nations
Onondaga Nation
boundaries of, 170–171
in the Six Nations, 168
treaties with, 85–86, 87, 92, 93, 120
treaty with France, 26
treaty with Netherlands, *58*
See also Iroquois Confederacy; Six Nations
Ontonagon band of Ojibwe, 305, 308. See also Ojibwes
Oregon Donation Act, 131
Oregon Territory, 39, 130–132, 133, 137
treaties with Indians in, *131*
Osage Nation
Confederate treaties, 10, 145, 146
oil rights of, xxi

reconstruction treaties, 148
treaties with, 103, 147, 187–190
Osceola (Seminole leader), xvii
Oshaga (Ojibwe leader), 305
O'Sullivan, John Louis, 32
Oswegatchies, 93
Oto tribe, 140
Ottawa tribe
in the Anishinabe Confederacy, 191
boundaries of, 178–180, 193, 195, 264
land cessions, 140
opposition to U.S. policies, 101
removal of, 238–239
treaties with, xx, 85, 85–86, 87, 94, 102, 120, 146, 174–175, 238–239
treaty with England, 27
See also Treaty of Prairie du Chien

Pacific Northwest Indians, 5–6
Paiute tribe, 149
Papal authority, 21–23
Parker, Ely S., 41, 320, 327
Passamaquoddy Nation, 59, 83
Pawnee Indians, 103, 148
Peace Commission (United States Indian Peace Commission), 41, 149–150, 153, 329, 339, 346–347
Peace Establishment Army, 176
Pennsylvania, treaty with Six Nations, 32
Pennsylvania colony, treaties with Indian tribes, 26–28
Penobscot Nation, 59, 83
Pensacola treaty, 28
Peoria tribe
land cessions, 140
treaties with, 102, 120
Pequot (Mashantucket tribe), 103
physicians, 150, 242, 275, 286, 329, 333, 335, 337, 342, 345, 347, 350, 352, 354
Piankashaw tribe
boundaries of, 87, 178–180
opposition to U.S. policies, 101
treaties with, 94, 100, 120, 174–175
Pickens, Andrew, 164
Pickering, Timothy, 90, 92–93, 168, 170
Piegan tribe, 141, 142
Pike, Albert, 144

Pillager Ojibwes, 283. *See also* Ojibwes
Pine Ridge Reservation, *128*
Pine Tree Treaty, 123
Pipe, the (Delaware leader), 159–160
Pishake (Ojibwe leader), 305
Pitchlynn, Peter (Choctaw leader), 148
Plains Apaches. *See* Apache (Plains); Plains Indians
Plains Indians
    treaties with, xvi, 41, 297–298, 328–329
    See also Apache (Plains)
plenary power, 151–153
Poarch Creek of Alabama, 103, 104
Point Elliott treaty, 137
Point No Point treaty, 137
Pokagun (Potawatomi leader), 238
Pomo Indians
    Koshaya tribe, 14
    treaty with Russia, 29
Ponca Nation
    relocation of, 148
    treaties with, xx, 103, 146
Pontiac (Ottawa leader), *82*
Pontiac's War (Pontiac's Revolt), *82*, 175
Poor Bear (Kiowa-Apache leader), 329
Portugal, exploration by, 21–22
Potawatomi tribe
    in the Anishinabe Confederacy, 191
    boundaries of, 178–180, 195, 264
    Catholic members, 121, 262
    removal of, 191, 238–239
    treaties with, xvi, xix, 87, 100, 101, 102, 121–122, 174–175
    treaties with England, 27
    See also Treaty of Chicago (1833); Treaty of Prairie du Chien
Prairie du Chien meeting, xvi, xviii
property law, 15
protocol, xvii
Public Health Service, 64
Public Law 280, 116
Pueblo Indians, 3, 105, 364
Puget Sound tribes, 12
Puyallup tribe, 48, 137

Quapaw Nation, 103, 145, 148
Queets people, 137
Quileute people, 137
Quinault people, 137

R v. Powley, 70
reconstruction treaties, 147–151, 153–154
Red Cloud (Oglala Sioux leader), 153, 347
Red Cloud War, 347
Red Jacket (Seneca leader), 92, 94, 168, 169
Red Stick Creeks, 109, 111. *See also* Creek Nation
Redfield, Abraham, 274
Reeves, Benjamin, 187, 189
Regina v. Bernard, 75
Regina v. Marshall, 73, 75
Regina v. White and Bob, 73
Reign of Terror, xxi
reservations
    Apache, *140*
    Arapaho, 153, 329
    Bannock, 149, 339
    Black Hills, 346
    Cattaraugus, 93
    Cherokee, 274
    Cheyenne, 329
    Cheyenne-Arapaho, 153
    Comanche, 329
    Fort Hall, 339, 340
    Harmony Missionary, 274
    Kiowa, 329
    Kiowa-Apache, 329
    Kiowa-Comanche, 150, 151
    Kiowa-Comanche-Apache, 153
    Lakota, 153
    location and oversight of, 127–129, *140*
    Menominee, 135
    Navajo, xxi, 365, 367
    Ojibwe, 305
    Osage, 147
    Pine Ridge, *128*
    Shoshone, 153
    Sioux, 347
    St. Regis, 93
    Union Missionary, 274
    Warm Springs, 135
    Wind River, 339, 340
reserved rights doctrine, 5–6
revenue-sharing agreements, 7

Ridge, John, 118–119, 265, 267, 271
Ridge, Major, 118–119, 265–266, 267
Robinson, Alexander (Cheecheebinquay; United Band representative), 239
Robinson and Williams treaties, xv
Robinson-Huron Treaty, 66
Robinson-Superior Treaty, 66
Robinson Treaties, 66
Roger, Robert, *82*
Rogers, William, 269
Roger's Rangers, *82*
Rogue River peoples, 133, 137
Rogue River treaty of 1854, 133
Ross, John, 118–119, 265, 266–267, 269
Royal Proclamation of 1763, 60, 61, 65, 82
Russia, treaty with Pomo Indians, 29

Sac (Sauk) tribe
    boundaries of, 192–193, 194
    hostilities with, 110
    land cessions, 140, 144
    removal of, 191
    treaties with, 87, 102–103, 191
    as U.S. allies, 101
    See also Fox tribe; Treaty of Prairie du Chien
Sahewamish tribe, 137
Sahtu Dene and Métis Comprehensive Land Claim Agreement, 68–69
San Juan peoples, 364
Sanborn, John B., 329, 330, 348
Sand Creek massacre, 146, 149, 329
Sandusky tribe, 101
Sans Arc Sioux, 348, 363. *See also* Sioux Nation
Santa Fe trail, 187
Santee Sioux
    hostilities with, 146, 153
    peace treaties with, 153
    treaties with, 348, 363–364
    See also Sioux Nation
Santo Domingo peoples, 364
Sauk Nation. *See* Sac (Sauk) tribe
Saukenuk (Billy Caldwell), 239
Schermerhorn, John, 265, 269, 271–272
Scoton tribe, 133, 137
Scott, Winfield, 119, 266

Second Seminole War, 116, 143, 224. *See also* Seminole Wars
self-determination policy, 64
Sells, Elijah, 320, 327
Seminole Nation
    boundary disputes, 143–144
    during the Civil War, 40, 146
    Confederate treaties, 10, 145
    and the gaming industry, xxi
    hostilities against, 111
    Mikasuki tribe, 143, 144
    reconstruction treaties, 147, 148
    removal of, 115–116, 128, 142, 143, 143–144
    treaties with, 107, 115–116, 142, 145, 224
    unification with Creeks, 115
    See also Treaty with the Seminole (1866)
Seminole Nation West, 144
Seminole treaty (1861), 145
Seminole Wars
    First (1818), 100, 115, 143
    Second (1835), 116, 143, 224
Seneca (Seneka) Nation
    boundaries of, 170–171
    land cessions, 140
    purchase of land from, 93–94
    reconstruction treaties, 148
    relations with, 87
    return of land to, 92
    in the Six Nations, 168
    treaties with, 83, 85–86, 93, 102, 120–121
    treaty with the Netherlands, *58*
    as U.S. allies, 101
    Washington's assurance to, 90
    See also Iroquois Confederacy; Six Nations
Sequoyah (George Guess), 98
Seven Nations of Canada, 93
Seven Years' War, 60, 175
Shasta (Chasta) tribe, 133, 137
Shawnee Nation
    boundaries of, 178–180
    Confederate treaties, 145
    hostilities with, 87

included in the Cherokee Nation, 10
land cessions, 140
opposition to U.S. policies, 101
reconstruction treaties, 148
treaties with, 33, 83, 86, 94, 100, 102–103, 120, 174–175
treaties with other tribes, 14
treaties with Texas, 39
as U.S. allies, 101
Western tribe, 145
See also Tecumseh (Shawnee chief)
Sherman, William Tecumseh, 149, 339, 348
Shoshone-Bannock tribes, 153, 339–340
Shoshone tribe
Eastern band, 339–340
reservation, 153
treaties with, xx, 146, 149
Sibley, George, 187, 189
Silver Brooch (Comanche leader), 329
Sioux Nation
boundaries of, 192–193, 193–194, 194, 301
as British allies, 101
Cheyenne River tribe, xxi
eastern, 123
at the Fort Laramie agreement, xix
land rights of, 140
sacred pipe ceremony, 25
Sans Arc tribe, 348, 363
Santee tribe, 146, 153, 348, 363–364
Sisseton tribe, xix, 140, 142
Standing Rock tribe, xxi
treaties with, 103, 191, 297–298, 300, 346–348
Two Kettle tribe, 348, 363
Uncpapa tribe, 361–362
Wahpeton tribe, xix, 140, 142
Yanktonai (Yankton) tribe, 149, 153, 148, 159–361, 192–193, 195
See also Dakota Nation; Great Sioux Nation; Lakota Nation; Nakota Nation; Treaty of Fort Laramie; Treaty of Prairie du Chien
Sioux Valley First Nation, 71
Sisseton Sioux, xix, 140, 142. *See also* Sioux Nation

Sitting Bear (Satank; Kiowa leader), 329
Six Nations
boundaries of, 170–171
Delawares dependent on, 157
Massachusetts' negotiation with, 87
treaties with, 83, 87–88, 168–174
treaties with American colonies, 27–28
treaty with France, 26
treaty with New York and Pennsylvania, 32
U.S. government dealing with, 89, 91, 92
Washington's assurances to, 90
See also Cayuga Nation; Iroquois Confederacy; Mohawk Nation; Oneida Nation; Onondaga Nation; Seneca (Seneka) Nation; Tuscarora Nation
slavery
abolition of, 147, 318, 319
runaway slaves, 115, 224
southwest slave trade, 364, 365
Smith, Archilla, 271
Smith, Edmund Kirby, 148
Smith, Edward P., 97
smoking the pipe, xvii, 25
Snake (Shoshone) tribe, 141. *See also* Shoshone tribe
Soda Springs treaty, 339
Sokoki Abenaki tribe, 93
South Slave Métis Tribal Council, 70
Southwest Indians, 41
sovereignty
of the Cherokee Nation, 36, 39, 110, 116, 163–164
concept of, 23
of the Delawares, 9, 158
Native American, 116–118, 134, 138
of the Navajo Nation, 47, 364, 366
in the North, 119–124
and the reserved rights doctrine, 5–6
of the Seminoles, 144
of the Six Nations, 168, 169
in the South, 118–119
termination of, 152
territorial, 15–16
in treaty agreements, 3–4, 7, 9, 13, 14, 21, 25, 31, 49, 58

of the tribes, xvi, xviii, xxi, 3–4, 9, 10, 12, 18, 37, 43, 47–48, 50, 54, 62–63, 65, 76, 104, 151
of the U.S., xvi, 37, 49, 130
See also Domestic dependent nation status
Spain
  exploration by, 21, 22
  negotiations with Native Americans, 23–25
  transfer of Louisiana Territory to France, 95
  treaties with Indian tribes, 7, 28
Squaxin S'Homamish tribe, 137
Squiaitl tribe, 137
St. Clair, Arthur, 88, 89
St. Francis Indians, treaties with, 93
St. Regis Indians, 93, 120
St. Regis Reservation, treaties with, 93
Standing Rock Sioux, xxi. See also Sioux Nation
Stanley, H.M., 329
Stanwix, John, 159
state-recognized tribes, 103–105
Statute of Westminster, 27
Stehchass tribe, 137
Steilacoom tribe, 137
Stevens, Isaac, *131*
Stockbridge Indians, 120, 314
Stuart, John, 82
Stuart, Robert, 290, 293, 294
Sublette, William, 299
Sun Dance, xvi
Supreme Court decisions (U.S.), 62–63
  Bryan v. Itasca County, Minnesota, 46
  Carpenter v. Shaw, 46
  Cherokee Nation v. Georgia, 36, 37, 39, 46, 63, 65, 117
  Choctaw Nation v. Oklahoma, 46
  County of Oneida v. Oneida Indian Nation, 46
  DeCoteau v. District Court for the Tenth Judicial District, 46, 48
  Federal Power Commission v. Tuscarora Indian Nation, 48
  Johnson v. M'Intosh, 55–56, 117, 130, 134

Jones v. Meehan, 46
Lone Wolf v. Hitchcock, 16, 44, 46, 151–152
Marshall Trilogy, 117
McClanahan v. Arizona State Tax Commission, 47
Menominee Tribe of Indians v. United States, 48
Minnesota v. Mille Lacs Band of Chippewa Indians, 17, 46, 48
Montana v. United States, 49
Moore v. the United States, 298
Morton v. Mancari, 47
Nevada v. Hicks, 117
Oliphant v. Suquamish Indian Tribe, 48, 117
Tulee v. Washington, 46
United States v. Michigan, 48
United States v. Sioux Nation of Indians, 152
United States v. Wheeler, 47, 48
United States v. Winans, 5
U.S. v. Kagama, 43–44, 46
U.S. v. Shoshone Tribe, 46
Warren Trading Post v. Arizona Tax Commission, 47
Washington v. Washington State Commercial Passenger Fishing Vessel Ass'n., 46, 48
Williams v. Lee, 37, 47
Winters v. United States, 6
Worcester v. Georgia, 37, 39, 44, 55–56, 63–64, 65, 117, 118
Supreme Court of Canada decisions
  Calder v. Attorney General of British Columbia, 67
  R v. Powley, 70
  Regina v. Bernard, 75
  Regina v. Marshall, 73, 75
Suquamish tribe, 48–49, 137
surplus lands, 129–132, 151

Taghee (Bannock leader), 339, 340
Talapuche Nation, 29
Tall Bull (Cheyenne leader), 329
Tamaroi tribe, 101
Tapeeksin tribe, 137

Tappan, Samuel F., 329, 330, 348
Tawakoni tribe, 145
taxation jurisdiction, 7
Taylor, Nathaniel G., 149, 329, 330, 339, 348
Taylor, Richard, 269
Taylor, Zachary, 123
teachers, xix, 130, 145, 209, 275, 276, 310, 334, 337, 344, 345, 347, 352, 354, 368
Tecumseh (Shawnee chief), 35, 101, 102, 109, 175, 177
Ten Bears (Comanche leader), 329
Tenskwatawa (Shawnee prophet), 101–102, 109, 175, 177
Tenth Amendment, 6
Terry, Alfred H., 149, 329, 330, 348
Texas
  treaties with Indian tribes, 39
  U.S. purchase of, 39
Texas Indian Commission, 104
Thames, Battle of the, 102
Thayendanega (Joseph Brandt/Brant), 33, 34, 88, 93
Thompson, Smith, 38
Tigua tribe, 104, 105
Tillamook tribe, 132
timber resources, 283
Tlicho (Dogrib) Land Claims and Self-Government Agreement, 69
Tonkawa tribe, 39, 145
Touching the pen, xviii
trading posts, 94, 95–96
Trail of Tears, 164, 268
treaties
  in the 20th century, 45–50
  addenda, 142–144
  canons of Indian treaty construction, 16–17
  with the Confederate states, xv, 10, 14, 18, 40, 144–147
  defined, 23
  early American, 29–36, 38–41
  end of treaty making, xv, 4, 10, 41–45, 154
  with European governments, xv, 7, 12, 14, 18, 23–29, 33, 174–175
  force and effect of, 17–18
  with Great Britain, xv, 7, 14, 18, 26–27, 30, 35, 38, 58, 59–60, 83
  international (history of), 21–23
  with Mexico, 14, 29
  native perspectives, 13–16
  negotiations, 7–9, 14, 16–17, 25–26, 56–57
  oral vs. written, xviii, 8, 16
  with other tribes, xv, 7, 14, 56, 115, 145
  post-Civil War, 10
  pre-Revolutionary War, 7, 26, 26–27
  Reconstruction, 147–151, 153–154
  with states, 12–13, 32, 87
  unratified, 132–134, 137–141
  See also Canadian treaties; Congressional ratification; Indian Removal treaties; Treaty topics
treaties of Fort Harmar, 30, 87–88, 89
Treaties with the Chickasaw (1830 and 1832), 114–115
Treaties with the Seminole, 115–116
Treaty at Fort Finney with the Shawnee, 86
Treaty at Fort McIntosh with the Wyandot, Delaware, Chippewa, and Ottawa, 85–86
Treaty at Fort Stanwix with the Seneca, Mohawk, Onondaga, and Cayuga, 85–86
Treaty at Hopewell, South Carolina, 61
  with the Cherokee, 85–86
  with the Chickasaw, 86
  with the Choctaw, 85–86
Treaty between the Cherokee and Delaware, 9–10
Treaty between the United States of America and the Eastern Band of Shoshones and the Bannack Tribe of Indians. See Treaty of Fort Bridger
Treaty Commission, 41
Treaty of Albany, 58, 58–59
Treaty of Amity, Commerce, and Navigation. See Jay Treaty
Treaty of August 7, 1790, 32
Treaty of August 19, 1825, 32
Treaty of August 24, 1835, 32
Treaty of Big Tree, 93

Treaty of Chicago (1833)
  articles, 239, 241–243
  background, 238–239
  boundaries, 264–265
  facsimile, *240*
  gifts, goods, or presents, 255, 261
  land allotments, 263
  payments to individuals, 264
  permission for Catholics to remain in Michigan, 262
  Schedule A, sums payable, 246–249
  Schedule B, sums payable, 249–255
  signatories, 243–246, 255–256, 257–260, 261–262, 263–264, 265
  supplementary articles, 256–257
  supplementary articles, Schedule A, sums payable, 260
Treaty of Cusseta
  articles, 218–219, 221–223
  background, 218
  facsimile, *220*
  signatories, 223
Treaty of Dancing Rabbit Creek (Treaty with the Choctaw) (1830), 14, 17, 113–114
  articles, 203–210
  background, 201–202
  signatories, 210–214, 217
  supplementary articles, 215–217
Treaty of Doaks' Stand, 201
Treaty of Doaksville, 228
Treaty of Fort Bridger
  articles, 341–345
  background, 339–340
  signatories, 345–346
Treaty of Fort Finney, 87
Treaty of Fort Gibson, xvii
Treaty of Fort Jackson, 109
Treaty of Fort Laramie (1851), xix, xxi, 49, 140–141
  articles, 300–303
  background, 297–298
  signatories, 303–304
  treaty site, 299–300
Treaty of Fort Laramie (1868), 149
  articles, 348–355
  background, 346–348
  signatories, 355–364

Treaty of Fort McIntosh (Treaty with the Wyandot, etc.), 87
Treaty of Fort Pitt (1778), *8*, 9
  articles, 160–162
  background, 157–158
  location of signing, 158–159
  signatories, 162
Treaty of Fort Stanwix (Treaty with the Six Nations), 87, 89, 92, 169
Treaty of Ghent, 35, 99, 102
Treaty of Greenville (1795) (Treaty with the Wyandot, etc.), *13*, *90*, 94, 100, 176
  articles, 178–183
  background, 174–175
  signatories, 183–186
  treaty site, 176–177
Treaty of Greenville (1814) (second treaty), 176
Treaty of Guadalupe Hidalgo, 130, 138
Treaty of Holston (1791), 164
Treaty of Hopewell (1785), 38
  articles, 164–167
  background, 162–164
  signatories, 167–168
Treaty of January 9, 1789, 32
Treaty of January 21, 1785, 32
Treaty of July 2, 1791, 32
Treaty of July 22, 1814, 32
Treaty of June 16, 1802, 32
Treaty of June 19, 1859, 32
Treaty of La Pointe (1842)
  articles, 291–293
  background, 290–291
  schedule of claims, 294–296
  signatories, 293–294
Treaty of March 6, 1861, 32
Treaty of March 12, 1858, 32
Treaty of May 24, 1835, 32
Treaty of May 26, 1837, 32
Treaty of Medicine Creek, 48
Treaty of Medicine Lodge. *See* Medicine Lodge Treaty
Treaty of New Echota (1835), 116, 118–119
  articles, 269, 271–281
  background, 265–267
  facsimile, *270*
  signatories, 281–283

treaty site, 267–269
Treaty of New York, 28, 29
Treaty of November 10, 1808, 32
Treaty of November 28, 1785, 32
Treaty of October 22, 1784, 32
Treaty of Paris, 84, 85, 175
Treaty of Payne's Landing (1812)
   articles, 225–227
   background, 224
   signatories, 227
Treaty of Peace (American war of independence), 32, 34
Treaty of Pontotoc Creek (1832)
   articles, 228–236
   background, 227–228
   signatories, 236–237
Treaty of Prairie du Chien, 314
   articles, 192–196
   background, 190–191
   signatories, 196–200
Treaty of the Dalles, 137
Treaty of Tordesillas (1494), 22
Treaty of Versailles, 60
Treaty of Westphalia, 23
Treaty Party, 265–266
Treaty topics
   agents for tribes, xvi, 206, 232–233, 276, 333, 343, 345, 350, 367–368
   alliances, 40
   assurance of good faith, 161–162
   blacksmiths, xix, 130, 145, 150, 209, 222, 226, 242, 283, 291, 309, 310, 333, 335, 337, 342, 345, 347, 350, 352, 354
   boundaries, xvi, 32, 35, 143, 165, 170–171, 178–180, 192–196, 234–235, 264, 298, 301–302, 308–309
   carpenters, 291, 333, 335, 337, 342, 345, 350, 352, 354
   civilization and agriculture, xvi, 94, 95–96, 129, 133–134, 290, 333–335, 343, 350–351, 368
   construction of agency buildings, 325, 333, 342, 350, 367
   control of tribal movements, xx
   education, xvi, 40, 96, 209, 276–277, 329, 334, 343–344, 351–352, 368
   engineers, 333, 335, 337, 342, 350, 352, 354
   farmers, 275, 291, 329, 333, 335, 337, 342, 345, 347, 350, 352, 354
   forbidding non-Indians from settling on Indian lands, xvi, 32, 165, 181–182, 219, 221
   forbidding revenge or retaliation, 172, 182–183
   forgiveness of hostilities, 160
   former treaties null and void, 147, 183
   forts and military posts, xvi, 9, 32, 139, 141, 301, 337, 354
   gifts, goods, or presents, xvi, xvii, 171–172, 222, 226, 255, 261, 334–336, 344–345, 352–353, 369
   hunting, fishing, and gathering rights, xvi, xix, 47–48, 49, 65, 66, 70, 75, 137, 138, 141–142, 150, 181, 182, 196, 284, 290, 292, 305, 340, 342–343, 353–354, 369–370
   investments, 233–234, 276–277
   land acquisition, xx–xxi, 15, 32, 86, 94, 96, 102–103, 105, 142
   land allotments, xvi, xix, 5, 10–12, 40, 133–134, 203–204, 208–209, 215–217, 219, 349–350
   land cessions, xvi, 40, 41, 66, 100–101, 102–103, 107, 109, 113–114, 114, 115–116, 120, 121–122, 122–124, 130, 137, 138, 139–140, 143, 144, 147, 171, 176–177, 208, 216, 218–219, 225, 229, 238–239, 239, 241, 256–257, 272, 273–274, 283–285, 290, 291, 304, 306, 315, 322–323, 353
   land claim settlements, 68–69, 70
   land exchange, 99
   land for church buildings, 327
   land granted to leaders, 207
   land rights, 69–70, 140, 170, 180–181 272–273, 278–279, 292–293, 370
   law enforcement authority, 7, 13, 161, 204, 205, 206, 223, 274–275, 325–326
   mail routes, xvi
   mechanics, 242, 275

military alliances, 7, 28–29, 32, 56–57, 160–161
military pensions, 210, 279
millers, 209, 242, 333, 335, 337, 342, 345, 350, 352, 354
missions, xvi
passports, 32
payments and annuities, xvi, 65–66, 66, 189, 208, 221–222, 225, 226, 229, 234, 241–243, 257, 274, 277, 279, 283, 285–286, 287–288, 290–291, 293, 302–303, 309, 310, 315–316, 323, 327, 337, 371
payments to individuals, 230–231, 263, 289
peace among tribes, 196
peace and friendship, xvi, xvii, 28, 30, 40, 57–60, 83–84, 86, 94, 95, 102–103, 127, 137, 138, 140, 141, 146, 160, 166–167, 168, 170, 178, 192, 203, 275, 300–301, 320, 322, 330, 332, 341, 348–349, 366–367
permission for Catholics to remain in Michigan, 262
physicians, 150, 242, 275, 286, 329, 333, 335, 337, 342, 345, 347, 350, 352, 354
property liquidation, 226
protection for travelers, 188–189, 204–205, 297–298, 301
provision for remaining as a citizen, 206–207, 277–278
railroads, xvi, 130, 143, 144, 147, 309, 318–319, 324, 329, 336, 347, 354, 365, 369–370
refraining from violence, 336, 354, 370
removal to new lands, 207–208, 216, 222, 226–227, 229–230, 233, 241, 257, 275, 279–281, 286–288, 292–293, 304–305, 342–343
reservations, xvi, 306, 308, 332–333, 337, 341–342, 349, 355, 367, 370–372
restitution for wrongs, 301
returning criminals, xvi, 32, 38, 43, 86, 139, 165–166, 205
returning prisoners or hostages, xvi, 32, 86, 102, 163, 164, 178

revenue-sharing agreements, 7
right to declare war and conclude treaties with third powers, 32
right to send deputy to Congress, 166, 210, 275
roads and free passage, xvi, 139, 188, 189, 316, 324, 336
sale of alcohol, xvi, 310, 316
scalping, xvi, 336, 354, 370
settlement of claims, 326–327
slavery, xvi, 147, 318, 319, 322
sovereignty, xvi, xviii, 3, 47
stolen horses, xvi
survey and sale of land, 231–232, 235–236
taxation jurisdiction, 47
teachers, xix, 130, 145, 209, 275, 276, 310, 334, 337, 344, 345, 347, 352, 354, 368
trade, xvi, 33, 44, 86, 94, 103, 161, 166, 182, 205–206, 274–275
use of navigable streams, 206
Treaty with the Cherokee at New Echota (1835). *See* Treaty of New Echota (1835)
Treaty with the Chippewa (1837)
  articles, 284–288
  background, 283–284
  signatories, 288–289
Treaty with the Chippewa (1842), 17
Treaty with the Chippewa (1847), 17
Treaty with the Chippewa (1854), 17
  articles, 306, 308–311
  background, 304–305
  facsimile, *307*
  signatories, 311–314
Treaty with the Choctaw. *See* Treaty of Dancing Rabbit Creek (Treaty with the Choctaw) (1830)
Treaty with the Creek (1832), 114
Treaty with the Delaware. *See* Treaty of Fort Pitt (1778)
Treaty with the Great and Little Osage, 187
  articles, 187–189
  signatories, 189–190
Treaty with the Kiowa and Comanche of 1867, 16
Treaty with the Navajo (1868)

articles, 366–372
background, 364–366
signatories, 372–373
Treaty with the Nisqually, Puyallup, etc. (Treaty of Medicine Creek), 48
Treaty with the Seminole (1866)
articles, 320, 322–327
background, 319–320
facsimile, *321*
signatories, 328
See also Seminole Treaty (1861)
Treaty with the Sioux, etc. *See* Treaty of Fort Laramie
Treaty with the Sioux and Chippewa, Sacs and Fox, Menominie, Ioway, Sioux, Winnebago and a portion of the Ottawa, Chippewa, Potawattomie Tribes. *See* Treaty of Prairie du Chien
Treaty with the Six Nations (1789), 87–88
Treaty with the Six Nations (1794)
articles, 170–172
background, 168–169
signatories, 172–174
Treaty with the Six Nations, Delaware, Shawnee, and Ottawa (1775), 83
Treaty with the Wyandotte. *See* Treaty of Greenville (1795)
tribal governments, xx, 3–5, 7, 10, 12, 13, 15, 18, 40, 43, 47, 100, 117, 134–135, 151, 152, 202
trust, xviii, xxi, 37, 63–64, 103, 117, 134–135
Trust land, 134–136
Tulee v. Washington, 46
Tuscarora Nation
in the Six Nations, 58, 168
treaties with, 86, 120
as U.S. allies, 30, 83, 86
See also Iroquois Confederacy; Six Nations
Twana tribe, 137
Two Kettle Sioux, 348, 363
Two Row Wampum Treaty. *See* Treaty of Albany

Umatilla people, 138
Umpqua tribe, 133, 137

Uncpapa Sioux, 361–362. *See also* Sioux Nation
Union Missionary reservation, 274
United Anishnabeg Council, 71
United Band of Ottowas, Chippewas, and Potawatomis, 238–239
United Empire Loyalists (UELs), 60
United States Indian Peace Commission, 41, 149–150, 153, 329, 339, 346–347
United States v. Michigan, 48
United States v. Sioux Nation of Indians, 152
United States v. Wheeler, 47, 48
United States v. Winans, 5
Upper Pend d'Oreilles tribe, 141
U.S. Constitution
Fifth Amendment, 44
Indian treaties under, 88–94
ratification of, 30
Tenth Amendment, 6
U.S. v. Kagama, 43–44, 46
U.S. v. Shoshone Tribe, 46
Ute tribe, xx, 146, 153

Van Buren, Martin, 120–121, 122, 266
Vashon, George, 274
Vattel, Emmerich de, 23, 25
Vieux De Sert band of Ojibwe, 305, 306. *See also* Ojibwes
Vitoria, Francisco de, 24–25, 54

Wabanaki Confederacy, 59. *See also* Maliseet Nation; Mi'kmaq Nation; Passamaquoddy Nation; Penobscot Nation
Wabash Nation, 31
Waco tribe, 145
Wahpakoota tribe, 140
Wahpeton Sioux, xix, 140, 142. *See also* Sioux Nation
Walker, John, 83
Walla Walla Indians, 137, 138
War Department, 31
War of 1812, 34–35, 98–99, 109, 176
Ward, William, 114
wardship, 63–64
Warm Springs Reservation, 135
Warren Trading Post v. Arizona Tax Commission, 47

Wasco Nation, 137
Washakie (Eastern Shoshone leader), 339
Washington, George, 30–31, 60, 85, 88, 90, 107, 129, 159, 163, 168
Washington Territory, 130–132
Washington Territory treaties, 137–138
Washington v. Washington State Commercial Passenger Fishing Vessel Ass'n., 46, 48
water rights, 5–6
Watie, Stand, 118–119, 148, 265, 267
Wayne, Anthony, *13*, 89, 91, 94, 176
Wea tribe
  boundaries of, 87, 178–180
  treaties with, 94, 100, 101, 102, 120, 174–175
Wells, William, *13*
West, Ezekiel, 271
West, John, 271
Western Arctic final agreement, 68
White Bear (Satanta; Kiowa leader), 329
White Eyes (Delaware leader), 159–160
Wichita tribe
  Confederate treaties, 145, 146
  treaty with Texas, 39
Willamette valley treaties, 132
Williams treaties, xv
Williams v. Lee, 37, 47
Wind River Reservation, 339, 340
Winnebago (Ho-Chunk) tribe
  boundaries of, 194
  as British allies, 101
  friction with miners, 191
  land cessions, 140
  removal of, 122–123
  treaties with, xx, 83, 102, 122–123, 146
  See also Treaty of Prairie du Chien
Winters v. United States, 6
Wirt, William, 36, 38
Wisconsin Death March, 123
Woodlands Indians, 3
Worcester, Samuel, 38, 118, 267
Worcester v. Georgia, 37, 39, 44, 55–56, 63–64, 65, 117, 118
Wounded Knee massacre, *128*
Wyandot Nation
  boundaries of, 178–180
  hostilities with, 89
  land cessions, 140
  treaties with, 30, 33, 85–86, 87, 94, 102, 120, 174–176
  as U.S. allies, 101
  See also Treaty of Greenville (1795)

Yakama/Yakima Nation, 5, 138
Yanktonai (Yancton) Sioux
  Treaty of Fort Laramie, 149, 153, 346–348, 359–361
  Treaty of Prairie du Chien, 192–196
Yellow Bear (Arapaho leader), 329
Yukon First Nation Final Agreements, 69, 71
Yukon Indians-Canada-Yukon Umbrella Final Agreement, 69

About the Editor

DONALD L. FIXICO (Shawnee, Sac and Fox, Muscogee Creek, and Seminole) is distinguished foundation professor of history, distinguished scholar of sustainability in the Wrigley Global Institute of Sustainability, and affiliate faculty in American Indian studies at Arizona State University. He has worked on more than 20 documentaries about American Indians and is the author or editor of 14 books on American Indians, including *Call for Change: The Medicine Way of American Indian History, Ethos, and Reality*.

www.ingramcontent.com/pod-product-compliance
Lightning Source LLC
Chambersburg PA
CBHW060504300426
44112CB00017B/2547